HANDBOOK OF FINANCIAL INTERMEDIATION AND BANKING

HANDBOOKS
IN
FINANCE

Series Editor

WILLIAM T. ZIEMBA

Advisory Editors

KENNETH J. ARROW
GEORGE C. CONSTANTINIDES
B. ESPEN ECKBO
HARRY M. MARKOWITZ
ROBERT C. MERTON
STEWART C. MYERS
PAUL A. SAMUELSON
WILLIAM F. SHARPE

ELSEVIER

AMSTERDAM • BOSTON • HEIDELBERG • LONDON
NEW YORK • OXFORD • PARIS • SAN DIEGO
SAN FRANCISCO • SINGAPORE • SYDNEY • TOKYO
North-Holland is an imprint of Elsevier

N·H

HANDBOOK OF FINANCIAL INTERMEDIATION AND BANKING

Edited by

Anjan V. Thakor
Arnoud W. A. Boot

ELSEVIER

AMSTERDAM • BOSTON • HEIDELBERG • LONDON
NEW YORK • OXFORD • PARIS • SAN DIEGO
SAN FRANCISCO • SINGAPORE • SYDNEY • TOKYO
North-Holland is an imprint of Elsevier

N·H

North-Holland is an imprint of Elsevier

Radarweg 29, PO Box 211, 1000 AE Amsterdam, The Netherlands
Linacre House, Jordan Hill, Oxford OX2 8DP, UK
30 Corporate Drive, Suite 400, Burlington, MA 01803, USA
525 B Street, Suite 1900, San Diego, California 92101-4495, USA

British Library Cataloguing in Publication Data
A catalogue record for this book is available from the British Library.

Library of Congress Cataloging-in-Publication Data
Handbook of financial intermediation & banking / edited by Anjan V. Thakor, Arnoud Boot.
p. cm. – (Handbooks in finance)
Includes bibliographical references and index.
ISBN 978-0-444-51558-2 (hbk.)
1. Intermediation (Finance) 2. Banks and banking. I. Thakor, Anjan V. II. Boot, Arnoud W. A. (Willem Alexander), 1960- III. Title: Handbook of financial intermediation and banking.
HG3891.5.H36 2008
332.1–dc22

2008012456

For information on all Elsevier publications visit our website at *www.books.elsevier.com*

Printed in the United States of America
08 09 10 11 12 13 9 8 7 6 5 4 3 2 1

Contents

List of Contributors

Franklin Allen, University of Pennsylvania, Philadelphia, PA, USA

Xudong An, Department of Finance, College of Business Administration, San Diego State University, San Diego, CA, USA

Mitchell Berlin, Research Department, Federal Reserve Bank of Philadelphia, Philadelphia, PA, USA

Sudipto Bhattacharya, London School of Economics, London, UK

Arnoud W. A. Boot, University of Amsterdam, Amsterdam, The Netherlands

Elena Carletti, Center for Financial Studies, University of Frankfurt, Frankfurt, Germany

Tim Critchfield, Federal Deposit Insurance Corporation, Division of Insurance and Research, Washington, DC, USA

Amil Dasgupta, Department of Finance, London School of Economics, London, UK

Hans Degryse, Faculty of Economics and Applied Economics, Hogenheuvel College, Leuven, Belgium

Yonghen Deng, Lusk Center for Real Estate, School of Policy, Planning and Development, University of Southern California, Los Angeles, CA, USA

Robert DeYoung, University of Kansas, School of Business, Lawrence, KS, USA

Mark J. Flannery, Department of Finance, Graduate School of Business Administration, University of Florida, Gainesville, FL, USA

Paolo Fulghieri, Kenan-Flagler Business School, University of North Carolina, Chapel Hill, NC, USA

Amar Gande, Edwin L. Cox School of Business, Southern Methodist University, Dallas, TX, USA

Eitan Goldman, Indiana University, Bloomington, Indiana, USA

Alexander Guembel, Lincoln College, Oxford University, Oxford, UK

Kenneth D. Jones, Federal Deposit Insurance Corporation, Division of Insurance and Research, Washington, DC, USA

Paul H. Kupiec, Federal Deposit Insurance Corporation, Center for Financial Research, Washington, DC, USA

Bruce N. Lehmann, University of California, San Diego, La Jolla, CA, USA

Loretta J. Mester, Federal Reserve Bank of Philadelphia and the Wharton School, University of Pennsylvania, Philadelphia, PA, USA

Steven Ongena, CentER, Tilburg University, Department of Finance, Tilburg, The Netherlands

Christine A. Parlour, Haas School of Business, University of California, Berkeley, CA, USA

Andrea Prat, London School of Economics and Political Science, London, UK

Kasturi P. Rangan, Booz Allen Hamilton, McLean, VA, USA

Anthony B. Sanders, W. P. Carey College of Business, Arizona State University, Tempe, AZ, USA

Duane J. Seppi, Department of Financial Economics, Tepper School of Business, Carnegie Mellon University, Pittsburgh, PA, USA

Philip E. Strahan, Carroll School of Management, Boston College, Chestnut Hill, MA, USA

Anjan V. Thakor, Olin School of Business, Washington University, St. Louis, MO, USA

Allan Timmermann, Department of Economics, University of California, San Diego, La Jolla, CA, USA

Xavier Vives, IESE Business School, Barcelona, Spain

Lu Zheng, University of California, Irvine, CA, USA

Preface

At one time, perhaps before the emergence of market microstructure as a rich field for research, financial intermediation was viewed by many as a distinct subfield of finance, along with corporate finance and asset pricing/investments. Although dominated by banking, financial intermediation also includes studies of nondepository institutions such as insurance companies, mutual funds, credit rating agencies, and the like. Some would even include market microstructure. The distinctiveness of financial intermediation as a research area stemmed in part from the fact that it was a highly specialized area, replete with institutional detail, banking practices, and descriptions of regulations, and was somewhat disconnected from the mainstream paradigm shifts that were occurring in corporate finance and asset pricing.

There has been a sea change in this landscape in the past 30 years or so, a period that has, not coincidentally, also seen a meteoric rise in the popularity of asymmetric information and agency theory as legitimate approaches to research in economics and finance. In the absence of an explicit recognition and modeling of these frictions, the fundamental Modigliani–Miller irrelevance theorems relating to capital structure and dividend policy, as well as the separation theorems relating to investment and financing policy, made it difficult even to visualize what economic functions financial intermediaries really served, let alone develop theories that could explain *how* banks and other financial intermediaries were intimately connected with the financial policy choices of firms and thereby highlight the joining at the hip of financial intermediation and corporate finance research.

Agency theory and asymmetric information kept opening a variety of new doors for research in corporate finance, thereby transforming the field. Almost concurrently, asymmetric information and agency theory had an even more profound transformational effect on financial intermediation research, seemingly paradoxically engendering two diametrically opposed phenomena. On the one hand, financial intermediation research in the past 20–30 years has allowed the field to develop a somewhat distinct research identity in terms of issues, questions, and paradigms. Examples of this abound. Financial intermediary existence, credit rationing, collateral, relationship banking, various forms of bank regulation, and deposit insurance are just a few examples. On the other hand, financial intermediation research has moved so close to corporate finance research that research in these two subfields of finance is virtually indistinguishable in terms of tools and research methodologies. Consequently, one could legitimately view financial intermediation research as a subset of corporate finance research. As far as analytical approaches go, examining bank-borrower or bank-regulator moral hazard in financial intermediation is really no different from examining firm-bondholder moral hazard in corporate finance. Empirically examining whether bank lending has information content by measuring cumulative abnormal returns (CARs) associated with the stock price dynamics of firms around bank loan announcement dates is not that different from exploring the signaling content of dividend changes. Extracting the implications of viewing equity as a call option on total assets is conceptually the same as extracting the implications of viewing deposit insurance as a put option for the bank. The list goes on and on.

The vanishing of the lines of distinction between corporate finance research and financial intermediation research is a natural outcome of the fact that the contemporary research efforts in both subfields have been drawing their intellectual inspiration from the same wells: asymmetric information and agency theory. It is partly for this reason that this book is dedicated to issues that straddle the (vanishing) boundary, if one even exists, between financial intermediation research and corporate finance research. Apart from the fact that the various strands of the research surveyed and synthesized in this book are connected by the commonality of the information-theoretic tools on which they rely, another common element is that "design" issues are prominent in much of the discussion: security and contract design, institutional design, the design of optimal regulation, and the design of trading mechanisms and markets. In this sense, the book's focus is akin to that in Tirole's book, where design issues are discussed using the tools of information economics and contract theory (see Tirole 2006).

Six topics are covered in this book: design of securities and contracts; market microstructure; credit market implications of bank size, scope, and structure; mutual funds; bank regulation; and finally the interaction between interbank competition, regulation, and banking stability. We invited leading researchers in these areas to act as section editors for these six topics. Each section editor was asked to perform two tasks: select specific issues to be explored within that topic and invite prominent and active researchers on those issues to produce articles that reviewed and synthesized the research done on those issues thus far, with indications for future research. We are very pleased with the outcome. We have 15 outstanding chapters in this book besides this preface, each representing an original contribution that achieves the twin goals of research review and synthesis of an important topic.

Why should you read this book? There are two simple reasons. First, good reviews are rare. This book has not one but numerous excellent reviews that provide valuable perspectives on a host of issues that are well represented in the research published in the top journals today. Second, on each topic, the section editors have provided not only an overview of the chapters in their sections, but also a succinct description of the important research questions that should be addressed in future research. Thus, there is a wealth of potentially interesting new research ideas here.

Section 1, edited by Franklin Allen, is concerned with security design. Rather than taking observed financial securities as given, this literature goes back to first principles and endogenizes these securities as optimal financial contracts under specific circumstances. This is an exciting field of study that has relied heavily on the creative use of agency and asymmetric information to generate striking new insights about why financial securities take the form they do and how the endogenously-arising rationale for the existence of these securities can help us understand the security issuance timing and capital structure decisions of firms. A significant advantage of endogenizing security design using only primitives is that it allows us to comprehend more clearly why these securities are deployed even when they generate distortions of various sorts. For example, it is well known that the credit rationing in Stiglitz and Weiss (1981) or the asset-substitution moral hazard in Jensen and Meckling (1976) could be avoided if borrowers were not using debt contracts to raise financing, which raises the obvious question of why firms don't use alternative contracts. The chapters in the section on security design confront the following questions: (1) When is a debt contract optimal? (2) What role does asymmetric information play in explaining certain features of debt contracts? (3) How is securitization—which involves pooling together and then the tranching of debt securities—structured?

Chapter 1, by Fulghieri and Goldman, provides an insightful synthesis of the literature that seeks to address the first question and explain why debt contracts arise and the circumstances in which it is efficient to use them. Moreover, they also address the second question by pointing out that, once the debt contract is endogenized, the addition of various sorts of asymmetric information paves the way for the emergence of subordination and maturity structures, collateral requirements, and so on as important endogenous elements of debt contract design.

These issues of debt contract design and innovations in debt contracting are addressed in Chapter 2, by An, Deng, and Sanders, who take up the third question and explain how securitization helps ameliorate asymmetric information problems and also provide an empirical analysis of securitization structures using data on commercial mortgage-backed securities. The evidence here provides a plethora of insights into the mechanics of securitization and the economic functions it serves.

As Allen points out, these two chapters reflect what has been the predominant focus in the security design literature, namely, explaining debt contracts. But numerous other issues related to security design that are not covered in these papers have begun to attract research attention. These include endogenous justifications for the emergence of equity securities, the interaction between security design and corporate governance, the design of corporate charters, security design in an international context, security design as a component of auction design, and security design with heterogeneous beliefs and learning. We would like to add two more to this list. One is the interaction between security design and corporate information disclosure, which is as yet underexplored (see Boot and Thakor 2001). In particular, the question of how security design affects information acquisition incentives in financial markets is interesting and relevant. The other is the role of heterogeneous beliefs in determining the design of securities as well as firms' security issuance and capital structure decisions, which is an area loaded with potential. These are all exciting topics that should be studied more in future research. There is a significant chance that future research in this area will move the frontiers of financial intermediation and corporate finance.

As many researchers have explored the design of securities, others have focused on the design of trading mechanisms and markets. A special case is limit order markets, which is the topic of Section 2 in the book. This section consists of an excellent survey by Parlour and Seppi, Chapter 3. The topic of limit orders is especially important because most equity and derivative exchanges in the world today are either pure electronic limit order markets or permit limit orders in addition to on-exchange market making. Given two decades of theoretical and empirical research on market microstructure issues, it is an opportune time for Parlour and Seppi to pose this question: What has been accomplished theoretically in studies of limit order markets?

In addressing this question, the authors survey a vast literature on the subject and cover both the significant new insights this literature has generated as well as the questions that remain to be addressed. The authors address five main issues in their survey: price formation in dynamic limit order markets, issues of liquidity supply and demand in limit order markets, the dynamics of the limit order book, the process of information aggregation, and intermarket competition involving limit order markets competing with hybrid markets that have both dealers and limit orders.

The key messages that emerge are the following. First, unlike Walrasian markets, there is *no* unique market-clearing price in dynamic limit order markets. Rather, a sequence of prices is associated with bilateral trades. Second, because of the blurred distinction between liquidity supply and demand in limit order markets, it is *not* possible to extract unambiguously the compensation for liquidity provision that is embedded in limit order quotes. Third, the dynamics of the limit order book are such that trades and prices may exhibit path dependence. Fourth, since limit order books contain prospective information about future price volatility and order flow, they can be a source of information for those who seek to engage in informed trading. Finally, if the only friction in the market is asymmetric information, then limit order markets can provide the most liquidity and hence implement price schedules that are immune to competition from other trading mechanisms. However, if noninformational frictions exist, then pure limit order markets may be driven out by other market forms, including markets that combine dealers and limit orders.

Despite these impressive insights, Parlour and Seppi note that much remains to be done. They note that the following research questions may hold the most promise: (1) What individual investor order submission strategies aggregate into the observed aggregate order flow? (2) How does the fact that investors trade groups of stocks affect their order submission decisions compared to the situation in which investors trade just one stock? (3) What is the interaction between the characteristics of the limit order book and asset pricing? (4) What are the social welfare implications of limit order markets in a variety of situations? (5) What guidance can limit order theory provide about how observations should be aggregated in empirical research (to deal with the problem of very large order flow data sets) and which exogenous instruments should be used to deal with the thorny endogeneity problem arising from the fact that many observable variables from limit order markets are endogenously determined?

Although the issues of how securities are designed and how trading mechanisms are designed are conceptually related, the extent of overlap between these two streams of research has been quite limited thus far. While the potential connections between market microstructure and asset pricing have already begun to be explored, the linkages between security design and the design of trading mechanisms in markets are also worth thinking about. For example, security design is often predicated on the recognition of certain informational frictions and is aimed at designing specific features of the security to optimize an objective function in light of the assumed informational frictions. But the impact of the design of the security on the issuer of the security often depends on the market mechanism used for trading that security. Hence, the choice of the trading mechanism can impinge on optimal security design.

In designing a financial *system*, there are three main pillars one has to design: the securities/contracts that are used for financial transactions, the market structures and trading mechanisms that are used to execute these transactions, and the financial institutions that enable the execution of *nonmarket* transactions as well as market transactions (e.g., the role of banks in securitization). Section 3 of the book, edited by Mitchell Berlin, comprises three chapters that address the design of financial institutions from an industrial organization (IO) perspective. The big question addressed collectively by these contributions is: What factors determine the boundaries, size, and internal structure of financial intermediaries?

In the first chapter in this section, Chapter 4, Strahan poses three questions that his contribution seeks to address: (1) What implications do bank size and structure have for lending behavior? (2) Is relationship banking feasible in a deregulated market? (3) Why are deposit taking and lending combined within a single institution, the bank? Strahan's overall conclusion from surveying the empirical literature is that larger banks are more efficient and lend more on average, so credit availability is augmented by bank size. The evidence regarding the relationship between bank size and the availability of relationship loans is mixed, but there is no compelling evidence that points to the demise of relationship banking in a deregulated market. On the issue of the jointedness of deposit taking and lending, Strahan concludes that little is known that truly establishes the synergies between these activities. Berlin observes that this question can be dealt with merely as a special case of the issue of vertical integration in IO and that the banking literature could fruitfully "borrow" more from the well-established IO literature on this topic.

In the second chapter in this section, Chapter 5, Mester examines economies of scale and scope in banking. One of the conundrums in this literature is that a vast body of empirical research in this area had established that scale economies in banking were fully exhausted at a relatively small size—as little as $500 million in assets—and yet the existence of many very large banks seemed to offer evidence to the contrary. Mester asks: At what size are scale economies in banking truly exhausted? Mester observes that more recent work in this area has helped dramatically to revise upward these optimal size estimates, primarily by being explicitly cognizant of the intermediary functions of banks as reflected in risk taking and financial capital.

In the final chapter in this section, Chapter 6, Gande turns to the *scope* of banking, which essentially deals with another kind of joining of activities within a bank: lending and underwriting. Since the dismantling of the Glass–Steagall restrictions on U.S. banks in 1999, commercial and investment banking activities can be conducted under the same corporate roof. Gande surveys the empirical literature on this topic to address this question: What are the efficiency gains, if any, from permitting banks to offer both lending and securities underwriting services? Gande's conclusion is that significant efficiency gains might be realized when lending and underwriting are joined, but definitive answers are elusive since competition effects could also explain the lower spreads post-1999.

In his overview of this section, Berlin notes that many interesting research questions remain unanswered or only partially answered. In particular, what is the optimal internal organization of financial intermediaries? Should banks combine transaction and relationship lending (see Boot and Thakor 2000)? What is the role of loan syndication, and when is it optimal? What role will credit bureaus play in affecting the informational rents of banks? As is apparent, some of these questions are at the interface between the design of securities and the design of institutions, so "hitchhiking" on the insights of the security design literature may prove to be of some value in future attempts to address these questions.

In Section 4, edited by Sudipto Bhattacharya, issues related to mutual funds are taken up. A mutual fund is merely a special kind of financial intermediary, and it is important to place mutual funds in the broader framework of financial intermediaries by carefully delineating the economic functions they serve, which in turn requires good measures of mutual fund performance to assess whether they deliver a risk–return package that dominates what investors can do on their own. The three chapters in this section collectively deal with the following questions: (1) How do we measure mutual fund performance? (2) How do investors choose between mutual funds, given the issues in alignment of interests between fund managers and investors and the difficulties in measuring fund performance accurately? (3) What incentives do mutual fund managers have, and how can they be aligned with those of investors?

The first issue is taken up in Chapter 7, by Lehmann and Timmermann, who highlight the econometric challenges in assessing mutual fund performance. They conclude that it is exceedingly difficult to get much power to detect abnormal skills among fund managers using conventional econometric tests on performance evaluation. This exacerbates the principal agent issues associated with fund delegation and worsens the problem of asymmetric information between fund managers and investors. Thus, one of the central messages of this chapter is closely aligned with the information-theoretic themes of this book.

The second question is the focus of Chapter 8, by Zheng. While emphasizing that the overarching conclusion emerging from the empirical research on mutual funds is that investors are better off with low-cost index funds than with actively managed funds,

Zheng finds a strong interaction between investor behavior and the strategies of mutual funds, which could either help or hurt investors. And, as suggested by the conclusion of Lehmann and Timmermann, investor behavior may itself be constrained by their inability to infer fund manager skill reliably.

The third question is addressed in Chapter 9, by Bhattacharya, Dasgupta, Guembel, and Prat, who focus on the potential divergence of interests and the consequent incentives for fund managers to adopt herding strategies. In a sense, the Lehmann and Timmermann chapter and the one by Bhattacharya, Dasgupta, Guembel, and Prat are related. While Lehmann and Timmermann point out how difficult it is to use fund performance to extract reliable inferences about (abnormal) skills in fund managers, Bhattacharya, Dasgupta, Guembel, and Prat examine the consequences of this for fund manager behavior.

An interesting question that remains to be addressed is the extent to which the existence of mutual funds affects the kinds of securities and contacts that are designed. For example, would a firm design its securities differently when a wide range of mutual fund alternatives are available to investors? Perhaps not. But the potential interplay between mutual funds and security/contract design is worth contemplating.

Section 5 of this book, edited by Mark Flannery, deals with bank regulation, including capital requirements and scope and entry restrictions, and how this has influenced the size, scope, and design of banks. Some of the questions posed in this section are: (1) Why did banking consolidation occur when it did in the United States, and what can we say about the future? (2) How did the structure and operations of banks evolve in the future, and how are banks likely to position themselves in the future? (3) Why has there been so much excess capital in banking? (4) How will the Basel II capital regulation be implemented, and what will be its likely effect?

The first question is addressed in Chapter 10, by Jones and Critchfield. They conclude that the structure of the U.S. banking industry has been significantly restricted by regulation, and yet they note that by the 1990s most regulatory restrictions had been dismantled. Jones and Critchfield offer this changed regulatory landscape along with numerous other reasons to explain the dynamics of the consolidation in the banking industry that has been under way for some time. They predict that the consolidation trend will continue in the United States.

In Chapter 11, DeYoung examines the second question. He studies the evolution of banking over the past two decades and observes, like Jones and Critchfield, that bank specialization has been limited by government regulatory restrictions. He concludes that in the future, large banks are likely to offer customized "hard information" products, whereas small banks are likely to specialize in dealing with "soft information" transactions (see Stein 2002).

Flannery and Rangan take up the third question in Chapter 12. They document that bank capital in the United States has been rising steadily all through the 1990s and in the new century. The average bank holding company had 400 basis points more equity capital in 2001 than required under Basel I. They explain this excess capital on the grounds that it is evidence that market discipline (one of the pillars of the Basel II capital accord) is working, as banks are voluntarily choosing to keep capital beyond that required by regulation in response to market signals about the optimal level of capital to absorb asset risk.

In Chapter 13, Kupiec addresses the fourth question. Flannery notes in his section review that the U.S. implementation of Basel II will involve an additional "leverage standard," essentially mandating a minimum level of equity capital as a fraction of on-balance-sheet total assets. For several banks, this may supersede the Basel II standard, that is, be more binding. Under Basel II, many large banks will be able to determine their own capital levels based on guidelines related to a fairly comprehensive assessment of various risks. Kupiec develops a simulation model to assess the effects of Basel II, including procyclicality in capital standards. Based on his simulation analysis, Kupiec is skeptical about the economic justification for Basel II, and he even wonders if Basel II could be considered a minimum global capital standard, given the wide latitude it will provide national regulators. Kupiec's conclusions complement the finding of the many interesting papers on this topic in a special issue of the *Journal of Financial Intermediation* 13(2), 2004, Special Issue on Bank Capital Adequacy Regulation Under the New Basel Accord (see von Thadden 2004).

Although not covered by the chapters in this section, bank regulation is intricately connected with the topics covered earlier in the book, for at least three reasons. First, regulation inspires innovations in the designs of banks as well as the securities with which they raise capital; for example, if it is not privately optimal to raise equity capital to meet regulatory capital requirements, banks may choose other types of securities that may qualify—such as perpetual preferred stock—or come up with other innovations, such as Euro deposits, to circumvent reserve requirements. Second, regulations such as capital requirements can also induce banks to introduce new products for their *customers*. Witness the emergence of "debt consolidation" products offered by banks that provide additional mortgage financing to borrowers to help them pay off credit card debt, given the higher bank capital requirements against credit cards than against mortgages under Basel I. Third, several innovations, such as developments in securitization, help banks to manage their balance sheets optimally in light of the capital requirements they face.

Section 6, the final section of the book, edited by Xavier Vives, extends the regulation perspective of the previous section to include interbank competition. This is an important issue because regulators worldwide have been relaxing barriers to entry into banking and encouraging competition. These initiatives have not been without controversy, however, since there are many who believe that (excessive) competition can diminish banking stability. The big-picture questions addressed in this section are: (1) How does interbank competition affect banking stability and the efficacy of regulation? (2) What are the sources of bank rents, and how does interbank competition affect these rents?

The first question is addressed in Chapter 14, by Carletti, within the context of the theoretical literature. She notes that the standard view is that competition reduces banks' rents, thereby reducing their charter values and inviting greater recklessness in risk choices, which contributes to diminished bank stability. However, she concludes that the standard competitive paradigm is inappropriate for banking because asymmetric information, switching costs, and network externalities create entry barriers of their own and facilitate the differentiation that counteracts to some extent the rent-sapping effect of competition (see Boot and Thakor 2000). Indeed, it is possible to reach exactly the opposite conclusion from what is commonly believed, namely, that competition can actually enhance bank stability (see Boyd and De Nicoló 2006). It is therefore not even clear whether there is a tradeoff between competition and stability. Carletti notes that this remains an unsettled issue, particularly on the question of how regulation should be designed in the face of a potentially complex interplay between competition and banking stability (see Carletti, Cerasi, and Daltung 2007, Degryse and Ongena 2007).

The second question is examined in Chapter 15, by Degryse and Ongena, within the context of the empirical literature. They conclude that an increase in interbank competition causes banks to rely more on fee income from stable relationships with customers (consistent with the theoretical prediction in Boot and Thakor 2000), and that switching costs (see Kim, Kliger, and Vale 2003) as well as regulatory protection are important sources of rents for banks.

The messages that emerge from this section suggest that much work remains to be done on the issue of how bank competition affects bank stability. A largely unexplored issue is the effect of interbank competition on the types of securities banks will be induced to design. How will bank competition, financial innovation incentives (security design), and banking stability interact?

To summarize, the six topics covered in this book touch on a wide range of issues pertaining to the design of securities, institutions, trading mechanisms and markets, industry structure, and regulation. The dazzling array of insights emerging from these different yet connected strands of the literature have been nicely summarized by the section editors, and a host of unanswered questions for future research have been cataloged. We hope this encourages bold new initiatives to tackle these important and exciting research questions.

Arnoud W. A. Boot
University of Amsterdam

Anjan V. Thakor
Washington University at St. Louis

References

Boot, A. W. A., and A. V. Thakor. 2000. Can Relationship Banking Survive Competition? *Journal of Finance* 55(2) (April), 679–714.

Boot, A. W. A., and A. V. Thakor. 2001. The Many Faces of Information Disclosure, *Review of Financial Studies* 14(4), 1021–1058.

Boyd, J., and G. De Nicoló. 2006. The Theory of Bank Risk Taking and Competition Revisited, *Journal of Finance* 60(3), 1329–1343.

Carletti, E., V. Cerasi, and S. Daltung. 2007. Multiple-Bank Lending, Diversification, and Free-Riding in Monitoring, *Journal of Financial Intermediation* 16(3), 425–451.

Degryse, H., and S. Ongena. 2007. The Impact of Competition on Bank Orientation, *Journal of Financial Intermediation* 16(3), 399–424.

Jensen, M., and W. H. Meckling. 1976. Theory of the Firm: Managerial Behavior, Agency Costs and Ownership Structure, *Journal of Financial Economics* 3, 305–360.

Kim, M., D. Kliger, and B. Vale. 2003. Estimating Switching Costs: The Case of Banking, *Journal of Financial Intermediation* 12(1), 25–56.

Stein, J. 2002. Information Production and Capital Allocation: Decentralized Versus Hierarchical Firms, *Journal of Finance* 57, 1891–1922.

Stiglitz, J., and A. Weiss. 1981. Credit Rationing in Markets with Imperfect Information, *American Economic Review* 71(3) (June), 393–410.

Tirole, J. 2006. *The Theory of Corporate Finance.* Princeton University Press, Princeton, NJ.

von Thadden, E. 2004. Bank Capital Adequacy Regulation Under the New Basel Accord, *Journal of Financial Intermediation* 13(2), 90–95.

Introduction to the Series

The Handbooks in Finance are intended to be a definitive source for comprehensive and accessible information. Each volume in the series presents an accurate, self-contained survey of a subfield of finance, suitable for use by finance and economics professors and lecturers, professional researchers, and graduate students and as a teaching supplement. The goal is to have a broad group of outstanding volumes in various areas of finance.

William T. Ziemba
University of British Columbia

SECTION 1

Design of Contracts and Securities

Overview by Franklin Allen
University of Pennsylvania

Financial intermediaries use contracts with their customers and sell securities in financial markets. The design of the contracts they use and the securities they issue is thus of fundamental importance. The first chapter in this section, Chapter 1, by Paolo Fulghieri and Eitan Goldman, considers the design of debt contracts. The second chapter, Chapter 2, by Xudong An, Yongheng Deng, and Anthony B. Sanders, is concerned with the design of securities. In particular, it focuses on structured financing and the determination of subordination levels.

Chapter 1, Fulghieri and Goldman's chapter, provides a nice synthesis of the literature on the design of debt contracts. The basic question in much of this literature is to determine situations where debt contracts are optimal. The authors start by considering a static one-period framework. They consider the papers that show that debt contracts are optimal if it is costly to check whether the borrower is able to make the contractual payment or not. They then go on to consider the multiperiod case and the situation where the checking can be random rather than deterministic. While the costly state verification literature focuses on the allocation of cash flows, there is also a significant literature on the allocation of control rights. Here, if the borrower cannot make the payment, the penalty is that it is no longer possible to use the assets. A third strand of the literature considers the role of debt in providing incentives for entrepreneurs to work hard and take appropriate risks. All the literature considered up to this point in the chapter assumes that the borrower has the same information as the lender. The next section focuses on what happens if the borrower has superior information. Finally, the rationale for the structure of debt contracts in terms of maturity structure, collateral, and covenants is considered.

Chapter 2, An, Deng, and Sanders' chapter is concerned with securitization. They consider how pools of loans can be sold in tranches to help overcome the asymmetric-information problem between issuer and investor. They start with a survey of the theoretical literature on this topic. These papers are concerned with explaining why there are different levels of subordination, with senior tranches having very low levels of risk and junior tranches much higher levels. The remainder of the chapter contains an empirical analysis of the structuring of securitizations using data from commercial mortgage-backed securities (CMBS). It is found that the deal cutoff debt service coverage ratio (DSCR) and loan-to-value (LTV) ratio, the composition of property types, and the prepayment protection explain most of the cross-sectional variation in subordination levels.

A number of factors concerning the design of contracts and securities are omitted in these two chapters. The focus is almost entirely on debt. There is also a literature analyzing the rationale for equity. For example, Fluck (1998, 1999) and Myers (2000) consider why corporations should use outside equity rather than other types of security. More recently, Dittmar and Thakor (2007) provide a theory of equity issuance based on differences in beliefs. Boot, Radhakrishnan, and Thakor (2006) consider the choice between public and private equity, given a tradeoff between managerial autonomy and the cost of capital.

A significant part of the literature on equity is concerned with corporate governance issues. Grossman and Hart (1988) and Harris and Raviv (1988, 1989) were early papers considering the allocation of voting rights to shares. They were concerned with identifying circumstances where one-share–one-vote is optimal. Full accounts of this literature are given in Harris and Raviv (1991, 1992), Allen and Gale (1994), and Allen and Winton (1995).

More recent literature has focused on the optimal design of corporate charters. Bebchuk (2002) shows how the existence of asymmetric information at the time a corporate charter is structured can explain many empirical observations that are difficult to understand in standard settings with symmetric information. For example, one puzzle has been why companies going public in the United States usually include antitakeover provisions. In an asymmetric-information context, such provisions can provide a signal. Remmers (2004) shows how mutual find shares can be designed to ensure good governance of these institutions. It is somewhat surprising that there is not more literature on corporate governance and security design. It is a rich area for future research.

Another area not covered in this section is the role of security design in an international context. Shiller (1993) suggests a wide range of markets to improve risk sharing in a variety of contexts, including between countries. Geanakoplos and Kubler (2003) use a security design approach to consider whether a country's debt should be denominated in domestic currency or U.S. dollars. Bisin and Acharya (2005) consider the role of security design in ensuring optimal risk sharing when markets are incomplete. This is also an important area for future research.

In addition to these areas of research, there are a number of interesting contributions to the security and contract design literature that take off in new directions. Garmaise (2001) considers firms that raise money in markets where investors have diverse beliefs but are rational, in the sense that they condition on available data. It is shown that in this situation the optimal design of securities is quite different from the case where there are rational expectations and differences in beliefs are due to differences in information. In particular, under rational beliefs, optimal securities maximize differences in opinion, whereas under rational expectations, they minimize them.

Noe, Rebello, and Wang (2006) consider markets where agents initially have different beliefs and then learn adaptively. In particular, agents learn optimally using genetic algorithms. It is shown that the securities that are issued in the long run in this environment have stable payoffs in most states but involve large losses in some states. This is again very different from the standard rational expectations paradigm, where optimal securities involve payoffs in a single state.

DeMarzo, Kremer, and Skryzpacz (2005) contrast informal and formal mechanisms for selling items when the means of payment is securities rather than cash. With an informal mechanism, the bidders design the securities to offer and sellers choose the most attractive. In this case, the structure of the securities can convey information and there is effectively a signaling game. In a formal mechanism, the seller commits to consider a limited menu of offers. Among other things it is shown that informal mechanisms are the lowest generators of revenue across a wide set of possible mechanisms.

In conclusion, the two chapters in this section provide an introduction to some of the issues concerned with the design of contracts and securities. Many other issues remain, and there is much research to be done in this area.

References

Allen, F., and D. Gale. 1994. *Financial Innovation and Risk Sharing*. MIT Press, Cambridge, MA.

Allen, F., and A. Winton. 1995. Corporate Finance Structure, Incentives, and Optimal Contracting, in R. Jarrow, V. Maksimovic, and W. Ziemba (eds.), *Finance*. North-Holland, Amsterdam, pp. 693–717.

Bebchuk, L. 2002. Asymmetric Information and the Choice of Corporate Governance Arrangements, *Harvard Law and Economics Discussion Paper No. 398*.

Bisin, A., and V. Acharya. 2005. Optimal Financial-Market Integration and Security Design, *Journal of Business* 78, 2397–2433.

Boot, A., G. Radhakrishnan, and A. Thakor 2006. The Entrepreneur's Choice Between Private and Public Ownership, *Journal of Finance* 61, 803–836.

DeMarzo, P., I. Kremer, and A. Skryzpacz. 2005. Bidding with Securities: Auctions and Security Design, *American Economic Review* 95, 936–959.

Dittmar, A., and A. Thakor. 2007. Why Do Firms Issue Equity? *Journal of Finance*, February 2007, Vol. 62-1, pp. 1–54.

Fluck, Z. 1998. Optimal Financial Contracting: Debt Versus Outside Equity, *Review of Financial Studies* 11, 383–419.

Fluck, Z. 1999. The Dynamics of the Management–Shareholder Conflict, *Review of Financial Studies* 12, 379–404.

Garmaise, M. 2001. Rational Beliefs and Security Design, *Review of Financial Studies* 14, 1183–1213.

Geanakoplos, J., and F. Kubler. 2003. Dollar-Denominated Debt and Optimal Security Design, *Cowles Foundation Discussion Paper No. 1449*.

Grossman, S., and O. Hart. 1988. One Share–One Vote and the Market for Corporate Control, *Journal of Financial Economics* 20, 175–202.

Harris, M., and A. Raviv. 1988. Corporate Governance: Voting Rights and Majority Rule, *Journal of Financial Economics* 20, 55–86.

Harris, M., and A. Raviv. 1989. The Design of Securities, *Journal of Financial Economics* 24, 255–287.

Harris, M., and A. Raviv. 1991. The Theory of Capital Structure, *Journal of Finance* 46, 297–355.

Harris, M., and A. Raviv. 1992. Financial Contracting Theory, in J. J. Laffont (ed.), *Advances in Economic Theory*, Vol. 1. Cambridge University Press, Cambridge, pp. 64–150.

Myers, S. 2000. Outside Equity, *Journal of Finance* 55, 1005–1037.

Noe, T., M. Rebello, and J. Wang. 2006. The Evolution of Security Designs, *Journal of Finance* 61, 2103–2105.

Remmers, B. 2004. Strengthening Mutual Fund Corporate Governance: A Security Design Approach. Working paper, Virginia Tech.

Shiller, R. 1993. *Macro Markets: Creating Institutions for Managing Society's Largest Economic Risks*, Oxford University Press, Oxford.

CHAPTER 1

The Design of Debt Contracts

Paolo Fulghieri
University of North Carolina, Chapel Hill

Eitan Goldman
Indiana University, Bloomington

We would like to thank Franklin Allen and Merih Sevilir for very helpful comments, and Hung-Chia (Scott) Hsu for excellent research assistance.

HANDBOOK OF FINANCIAL INTERMEDIATION AND BANKING

1. INTRODUCTION

From the seminal work of Modigliani and Miller (1958) we know that in perfect capital markets the value of a firm is not affected by its choice of financial structure. This implies that the design of the contractual features of the specific securities the firm issues to raise capital is irrelevant. More generally, it also implies that the identity of the counterpart to the transaction, whether it be a financial institution or anonymous traders in the financial markets, is irrelevant.

This picture changes dramatically when the firm and investors operate under conditions of asymmetric information. The presence of informational asymmetries impairs a firm's ability to raise capital because it makes it more difficult to design financial contracts that protect both firms and investors from opportunistic behavior.

Asymmetric information can originate in several different circumstances. To fix ideas, we start by developing a simple framework that will be useful for organizing in a systematic way the models discussed in this chapter. We consider the problem faced by an entrepreneur wishing to raise capital to undertake an investment project. The investment project requires a certain investment I (the size of the investment either may be fixed or may be chosen optimally by the entrepreneur) and at a later date generates output x. The output level depends on both the selection of an action $a \varepsilon A$ taken by the entrepreneur, and the realization of the future state of the world $\omega \varepsilon \Omega$. The action, a, is a complete description of how the entrepreneur will manage the firm, including the use of the capital raised from investors. The selected action, a, and the state of the world, ω, jointly determine output according to the production function $X(a, \omega)$. Entrepreneurs and investors may be either risk averse or risk neutral, and they all have access to a risk-free technology yielding a rate of return $r \geq 0$.

In our most basic setting, entrepreneurs and investors interact over a single time period (see the timeline in Figure 1). This basic setting can easily be extended into a dynamic framework in which the one-period model is repeated over time. At the beginning of the period, $t = 0$, the entrepreneur, who may have an initial wealth W_0, seeks financing from a number $n \geq 1$ of investors. Funds are raised via a contractual agreement that will specify the conditions under which financing takes place, including the amount of capital contributed by investors, the rules for sharing future payoffs, and, possibly, restrictions on the entrepreneur's behavior during the period spanned by the contractual agreement. Before the contract is negotiated (and finalized), the

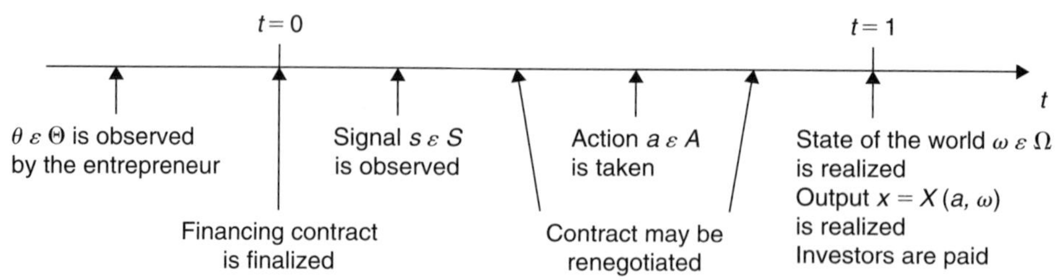

FIGURE 1 The basic model.

entrepreneur may have access to information that is relevant for the determination of the value of the securities issued by him and therefore for their fair pricing. We model this precontractual information by assuming that the entrepreneur observes the realization of a random variable $\theta \varepsilon \Theta$, which we can interpret as a "signal" on the future state of the world ω. The parameter θ identifies the entrepreneur's "type." The entrepreneur's ability to obtain this precontractual private information places investors at an information disadvantage and exposes them to adverse selection.

After the entrepreneur and investors finalize the contract (that is, after the securities are "sold" to the investors) and before the action $a \varepsilon A$ is taken, the entrepreneur may observe a second signal, $s \varepsilon S$. This signal s may be publicly observable, or it may be observed privately by the entrepreneur. Following the observation of the signal, the entrepreneur and investors may wish to renegotiate their original contract.

Once renegotiation is completed, the entrepreneur chooses the action $a \varepsilon A$ that will contribute to the determination of the final output x. The choice of the action a may include the determination of the amount of capital that is invested in the technology, I, as well as any other action that is relevant for the entrepreneur and investors. Either this action may be observable by everyone or it may be carried out privately by the entrepreneur, exposing the investors to moral hazard.

After the action a is chosen, a second round of contract renegotiations may take place. Finally, the state of the world $\omega \varepsilon \Omega$ is realized, and output x is determined according to the production function $X(a, \omega)$. At this point, the entrepreneur must allocate a part, y, of the output to investors as a reward for their investment. The distribution of output to investors will be determined on the basis of the contractual agreement established at the outset and possibly modified at the interim renegotiation stages. This distribution may be impaired by the fact that outside investors may observe the realization of output x only after paying a certain verification cost, k_1. After the verification cost is paid, output may be publicly observed, or it may be observed privately only by the investor who paid it. We characterize these situations as those of costly state verification, CSV.

The entrepreneur's problem at the outset of the game is to design contracts that allow him to pursue efficiently all profitable investment opportunities. If capital markets are perfect, and thus no information problem exists, entrepreneurs and investors are always able to write optimal contracts that lead to efficient outcomes. In this case, assuming that financial markets are perfectly competitive, the entrepreneur will offer a contract that maximizes his own expected utility, $\mathrm{EU}(\theta, a, \omega, \ldots)$, subject to appropriate individual rationality constraints for investors. The presence of information asymmetries may impair optimal contracting either because of the possibility of precontractual information (adverse selection) or because the entrepreneur can privately take payoff-relevant actions (moral hazard) or because the final output may be observed by outsiders only at a cost (CSV). Thus, the presence of these informational asymmetries impairs the entrepreneur's ability to write contracts with investors and may result in inefficient outcomes.

Note that the entrepreneur's ability to enter into contracts with investors is also impaired in situations in which relevant variables (such as the intermediate signal s, the entrepreneurial action a, and the final output x, among others) are observable by both the entrepreneur and investors but not by third parties in charge of enforcing contracts. In this case, contracts contingent on such variables are not enforceable in a court of law. We will refer to these situations as those of observability but noncontractibility.

In the situation just described, the entrepreneur may want to write contracts that reduce the adverse impact of information asymmetries, improving his payoff. In this chapter we discuss the circumstances in which debt contracts emerge endogenously as optimal contracts. We also discuss how the inclusion of additional contractual features, such as seniority, maturity, and collateral, may be used by the entrepreneur and investors to mitigate the adverse impact of information asymmetries.

In this chapter we take a relatively narrow approach and focus explicitly on debt contracts as optimal securities. Thus, we have only an incidental discussion of the instances in which other securities may emerge from an optimal security design problem. Notably, we do not discuss the case of equity contracts as optimal securities (see, for example, Myers 2000 and Fluck 1998 and 1999, among many others) or the optimal security design problem in the context of incomplete markets and symmetric information (see, for example, Allen and Gale 1988). We also do not discuss the optimal combination of debt with other securities, such as equity, to determine the optimal financial structure of the entrepreneur's venture. For excellent reviews of optimal financial contracting, see Allen and Winton (1995) and Harris and Raviv (1991, 1992).

2. DEBT CONTRACTS AND COSTLY STATE VERIFICATION

The primary aim of this chapter is to determine under what circumstances a security having the characteristics of the standard debt contract emerges, in equilibrium, as an optimal security. One of the first papers addressing this issue was Townsend (1979). In this paper, a risk-averse entrepreneur endowed with a risky technology seeks financing from a single investor. The entrepreneur and the investor care only about end-of-period wealth. Information is asymmetric, in that the output of the technology, x, may be observed at no cost only by the entrepreneur, while it can be observed by the investor only after paying a state-dependent verification cost, $k_1(x)$. Thus, the model is of the CSV type.

In this setting, a contract is a pair of functions $\{y(x), v(x)\}$ specifying the state-dependent payment $y(x)$ made by the entrepreneur to the investor, and the state-dependent verification policy $v(x)$, with $v(x) = 1$ if verification occurs and $v(x) = 0$ if no verification occurs. Townsend (1979) shows that if the investor is risk neutral and the verification costs are constant, $k_1(x) = k_1$ for all x, the optimal contract is such that

1. Verification occurs only in the "bad" states, that is, $v(x) = 1$ for $x < \underline{x}$, for a certain threshold level $\underline{x}$;
2. In the states without verification, $v(x) = 0$, the entrepreneur pays the investor a predetermined fixed amount F.

3. In the states with verification, $v(x) = 1$, the predetermined state-dependent amount $y(x)$ paid by the entrepreneur to the investor has the property that $y(x) + k_1 < F$.

Thus, optimal contracts have the debtlike features that no verification occurs when the entrepreneur makes a certain fixed prespecified payment, and state verification occurs only in the "bad states," that is, when the entrepreneur's output x is below a certain predetermined threshold $\underline{x}$. The intuition is as follows. First, incentive compatibility requires that if no verification occurs, the entrepreneur makes a constant payment, F. In addition, if verification occurs, incentive compatibility requires that the payment $y(x)$ must be smaller than in the nonverification states, $y(x) \leq F$. Finally, because of entrepreneurial risk aversion, the optimal contract calls for some risk sharing and, thus, allows the entrepreneur to make the smaller payments in states in which output is lower. This implies that in the states of the world in which verification occurs, which we can interpret as "bankruptcy" states, the optimal sharing rule between entrepreneurs and investors will typically allow the entrepreneur to keep some of the firm's output for personal consumption. Therefore, the optimal contract has the property that the investor will not recover all possible output under bankruptcy and, rather, allows for some debt forgiveness.

Gale and Hellwig (1985) consider a risk-neutral entrepreneur seeking financing from a single investor. The assumption that the entrepreneur is risk neutral allows for the derivation of the standard debt contract as the outcome of an explicit optimal security design problem. The paper also adopts a CSV framework and assumes that while the entrepreneur observes output x at no cost, the investor can observe output only at a cost, $k_1(\omega, I)$, which may depend on both the state of the world ω and the investment level, I. In addition, if verification occurs, the entrepreneur will suffer a certain nonpecuniary (fixed) cost k_0.

In this setting a contract is a 4-tuple $\{I, K, y(\omega), v(\omega)\}$ specifying the investment made in the technology, I, the amount contributed by the investor, K, the repayment schedule (net of verification costs) to the investor, $y(\omega)$, and the verification schedule, $v(\omega)$, contingent on the realization of the state of the world $\omega \,\varepsilon\, \Omega$. By using the revelation principle (see Myerson 1979 and Harris and Townsend 1981), the optimal contract is determined by the program

$$
\begin{aligned}
&\max && E[X(\omega, I) + (1+r)(W_0 + K - I) - y(\omega) - (k_0 + k_1)v(\omega)] \\
&\text{subject to} && \text{i. } Ey(\omega) \geq (1+r)K \\
& && \text{ii. } y(\omega) \leq X(\omega, I) - k_1 v(\omega) + (1+r)(W_0 + K - I) \qquad (1) \\
& && \text{iii. } \omega \in \operatorname{argmax}_\sigma X(\omega, I) + (1+r)(W_0 + K - I) - y(\sigma) - k_1 v(\sigma) \\
& && \text{iv. } I \geq 0, \quad K \leq I \leq K + W_0.
\end{aligned}
$$

The optimal contract solving Problem (1) maximizes the entrepreneur's expected utility subject to the investor's individual rationality constraint (i), the end-of-period feasibility constraint (ii), the incentive compatibility constraint (that is, the "truth-telling" constraint) (iii), and the nonnegativity and investment feasibility constraints (iv). The optimal contract solving Problem (1) has the following properties:

1. *Maximum equity participation* It requires the entrepreneur to contribute all his wealth, $I = K + W_0$.
2. *Fixed repayment* $y(\omega) = F$, for some $F > 0$ whenever the state of the world is not verified, $v(\omega) = 0$.
3. *Bankruptcy decision* The state of the world is verified whenever $x < F$.
4. *Maximum recovery* If verification occurs, $v(\omega) = 1$, investors recover all that is left after the verification costs are paid: $y(\omega) = X(\omega, I) - k_1$.

Thus, the optimal security is a *standard debt contract with maximum equity participation*.

It is interesting to compare the level of investment characterized in Problem (1) with the first-best investment that is obtained in absence of verification costs (that is, when $k_1 = k_0 = 0$). Gale and Hellwig (1985) show that, if the state of the world is verified with a positive probability when the firm invests at the first-best level and if verification costs are strictly positive in those states, then the level of investment specified in the optimal contract that solves Problem (1) is strictly lower than the first-best level. This means that the presence of bankruptcy costs leads to *underinvestment*.

A feature of the Gale and Hellwig model is that verification (bankruptcy) costs paid by the entrepreneur, k_0, are exogenously given. Diamond (1984) considers a model similar to the one in Gale and Hellwig (1985) but in which the bankruptcy costs are derived endogenously as part of the optimal contract. In this model, risk-neutral entrepreneurs seek financing from investors for an investment project. Each project now requires a unit investment, $K = I = 1$, which is provided by the participation of n different investors. The project's output, $x = \omega$, can be observed only by the entrepreneur, and no verification technology is available to outside investors. Thus, strictly speaking, the model is again cast in a CSV setting, with "prohibitively large" investors' verification costs, k_1. The absence of a (viable) verification technology implies that investors receive a payment only if the entrepreneur has the incentive to do so. The entrepreneur's incentive to reward investors for their investment depends on a nonpecuniary penalty k_0 that may be imposed on him. In contrast to Gale and Hellwig's model, here the penalty k_0 is chosen endogenously as an integral part of the optimal contract.

In Diamond's setting an optimal contract is a pair $\{y(x), k_0(y)\}$ specifying the payment $y(x)$ that the entrepreneur makes to the investors, given the realized output, x, and the nonpecuniary penalty, $k_0(y)$, imposed on the entrepreneur as a function of the payment he makes to investors. The optimal contract $\{y(x), k_0(y)\}$ satisfies

$$\begin{aligned} \max_{k_0, y} \quad & E_x\{\max_{y \in [0, x]} x - y - k_0(y)\} \\ \text{subject to} \quad & \text{i. } y \in \arg\max_{y \in [0, x]} x - y - k_0(y), \\ & \text{ii. } E_x\{\arg\max_{y \in [0, x]} x - y - k_0(y)\} \geq 1 + r, \end{aligned} \tag{2}$$

where (i) is the incentive compatibility constraint and (ii) is the investor's individual rationality constraint. The optimal contract has the properties that

1. $y(x) = \min\{x, F\}$, where F is the smallest solution to

$$\Pr\{x < F\} \times E_x\{x \mid x < F\} + F \times \Pr\{x \geq F\} = 1 + r; \qquad (3)$$

2. $k_0(y) = \min\{F - y, 0\}$.

Thus, the optimal contract is a standard debt contract with maximum recovery. Note that the optimal contract requires that the entrepreneur not suffer any penalty if he pays investors the fixed payment F. The contractual penalty $k_0(y)$ is optimally set to give the entrepreneur the incentives to pay all the output to the investors, to minimize the penalty. Note also that, under the optimal contract, the entrepreneur will be in default in the states in which $x < F$, and he will suffer the nonpecuniary costs $F - x$. Thus, the optimal contract is costly.

2.1. Multiperiod Contracts

The previous models explain debtlike features of optimal contracts in a static one-period framework. Chang (1990) examines a two-period extension of the basic Townsend model. In Chang's model the entrepreneur makes the initial investment I in a technology, which now generates an output both at $t = 1$, denoted x_1, and at a later date $t = 2$, denoted x_2. Output at each date is observable by the outside investor only after paying a verification cost $k_t(x_t)$, $t = 1, 2$. Both the entrepreneur and the investor are risk neutral. Chang shows that the optimal contract involves the entrepreneur making a payment to the investor at both dates, with verification occurring at each date $t = 1, 2$ only if output level, x_t, falls below a certain critical level $\overline{x}_t$. Furthermore, the optimal contract gives the entrepreneur the option to make a larger payment at the first date (if the first-period output is high) in order to reduce the residual payment at the second date. In addition, it is optimal to restrict the entrepreneur's ability at the first date either to make payments to himself or to borrow additional funds. These properties imply that the optimal contract is again a debt contract requiring interim payments (which can be interpreted as coupons or a sinking fund provision), with features like call (prepayment) provisions and covenants restricting the borrower's ability to pay interim dividends and to incur additional debt.

In a similar spirit, Chang (2005) examines the infinite-horizon version of the basic Townsend (1979) model, in which the entrepreneur is risk averse and the investor is risk neutral. If output is not storable and if the entrepreneur has no other access to credit markets, the contract with the investor is the only vehicle available to the entrepreneur for intertemporal consumption smoothing. This implies that the intertemporal dimension weakens the entrepreneur's incentive compatibility condition and, thus, makes it easier for the investor to extract payments from the entrepreneur, reducing the need for monitoring.

2.2. Stochastic Monitoring

The original Townsend (1979) paper suggests that optimal contracts may also include stochastic verification policies (rather than the simple deterministic ones discussed earlier) whereby the threat of verification is sufficient to induce honesty from the entrepreneur, thus reducing the expected verification costs. This possibility is further explored by Border and Sobel (1987). Their study shows that if both the entrepreneur and the investor are risk neutral, in the case of stochastic monitoring, payments by the entrepreneur to the investor, $y(x)$, are monotonically increasing in output x, while the verification probability, $p(x)$, is a decreasing function of output x. Thus, with stochastic monitoring, payments and verification probability have the same "flavor" as the standard debt contract obtained in a deterministic verification setting, in that entrepreneurs pay more to the investor in the "better" states, and investors increase the monitoring probability in the "worse" states.

A critical assumption of Border and Sobel's is that investor and entrepreneur are both risk neutral. Risk aversion complicates optimal contracts for two reasons: First, it invites risk sharing among agents (creating essential interdependencies among agents); second, it makes verification costly because, as discussed earlier, the probability of monitoring is greater in the "bad states," in which output is lower, that is, in the states that are of greatest concern to risk-averse agents. These observations open the question of whether the monotonicity properties of Border and Sobel survive under risk aversion.

The role of risk aversion in optimal contracts is explored by Mookherjee and Png (1989). Their paper shows that deterministic verification policies are in general not optimal even under risk aversion and that entrepreneurial risk aversion may lead to optimal contracts in which the entrepreneur's consumption is not necessarily a monotonic function of the firm's output. Krasa and Villamil (1994) and Winton (1995) extend Townsend's and Border and Sobel's results to the case in which both the entrepreneur and the investor are risk averse. These studies show that optimal contracts have the properties that the payments from the entrepreneur to the investor (weakly) increase with the firm's output x, that is, $y'(x) \geq 0$, and the monitoring probability $p(x)$ decreases with the realization of output, x.

Furthermore, Boyd and Smith (1994) show that, in a risk-neutral setting, with stochastic monitoring, the optimal contract does not look like a standard debt contract anymore because it involves defaults and debt forgiveness also in states in which the entrepreneur is fully able to pay the investor. After calibrating the model, they also argue that with plausible assumptions on key parameters the welfare losses from using standard debt contracts are minimal. They conclude that this small welfare loss helps to explain the wide use of standard debt contracts even in the presence of bankruptcy costs.

Finally, Boyd and Smith (1999) show that if the entrepreneur has access to two (risky) technologies, one (superior) technology that generates unverifiable returns, and another (inferior) that generates verifiable returns, the optimal contract is characterized by a mixture of debt and outside equity. In this setting, investment in the inferior technology with verifiable returns is financed by equity and allows the entrepreneur to smooth the future income stream. In the optimal contract, equity holders receive low payments in the bad states and are compensated by greater payments in the good states. In the bad states, the technology with verifiable output can generate some liquidity that the entrepreneur can apply to repay the debt used to finance the superior technology with nonverifiable output, reducing the expected verification costs.

3. DEBT CONTRACTS AND THE ALLOCATION OF CONTROL RIGHTS

In the CSV models discussed in the previous section, the entrepreneur is induced to repay investors either because investors can pay a verification cost and observe output directly or because the entrepreneur is penalized if the payment to investors falls short of a certain predetermined amount. In Hart and Moore (1989, 1998) and Bolton and Scharfstein (1990), the penalty suffered by the entrepreneur in case of default is modeled explicitly in the form of the loss of control over the use of assets. The loss of control gives the entrepreneur the incentive to pay back investors, if he has sufficient wealth to do so. Thus, these models are essentially dynamic, in that the entrepreneur makes the required payments to investors in order to enjoy future rents that he can obtain only by maintaining control of the assets. Giving investors the control rights over a firm's assets on default (with the possible outcome of inefficient liquidation) allows investors sufficient power to extract payments from the entrepreneur. Hence, control rights become a critical feature of the debt contract.

In Bolton and Scharfstein (1990) the entrepreneur has no wealth and is endowed with a technology lasting for two periods. In each period, the technology requires a fixed investment I and generates a level of output $x_t \in \{\underline{x}, \overline{x}\}$, with $\underline{x} < \overline{x}$. The smaller output, $\underline{x}$, is contractible and is obtained with probability π; the larger output, $\overline{x}$, is observable but noncontractible and is obtained with probability $1 - \pi$. It is assumed that $\underline{x} < I$, that $\overline{\overline{x}} = \pi\underline{x} + (1 - \pi)\overline{x} > I$, and that assets have no liquidation value. This implies that in a single-period horizon the investor has no means to extract sufficient payments from the entrepreneur (he can extract at most the verifiable cash flow $\underline{x}$) and, thus, that the entrepreneur cannot raise sufficient funds to implement the project. In contrast, in a repeated setting the investor can make the availability of financing at $t = 1$ contingent on payments made in earlier periods. This allows her to extract greater payments from the entrepreneur.

The optimal contract $\{y_1(x), y_2(x)\}$ is one in which the entrepreneur pays in the second period the contractible output, $\underline{x}$, that is, $y_2(x) = \underline{x}$. In the first period, the entrepreneur pays the investor the lower contractible cash flow $\underline{x}$ when this output level is realized, and the output level expected for the second period, $\overline{\overline{x}}$, when the noncontractible output $\overline{x}$ is realized. Thus, $y_1(\underline{x}) = \underline{x}$, and $y_1(\overline{x}) = \overline{\overline{x}}$, that is, $y_1(x) = \min(x, F)$, where $F = \overline{\overline{x}}$. Furthermore, if the entrepreneur makes the contractual payment for the first period, F, the investor refinances the entrepreneur by providing sufficient funds for the second-period investment, I; the investor does not refinance the entrepreneur if the low payment $\underline{x}$ is realized (in which case the project is terminated). Given this continuation/termination policy, the payment schedule is incentive compatible. This can be seen by noting that if in the first period the larger output $\overline{x}$ is realized, the entrepreneur is indifferent between (1) paying the investor the lower contractible amount $\underline{x}$ and having a payoff equal to $\overline{x} - \underline{x}$ and (2) paying the investors the contractual amount of $\overline{\overline{x}}$ and earning a payoff equal to $\overline{x} - \overline{\overline{x}}$ for the first period plus the expected payoff of $\overline{\overline{x}} - \underline{x}$ for the second period. Thus, the optimal contract is a debt contract that requires a fixed payment F, together with a commitment to refinance the entrepreneur if the payment is made and liquidation otherwise.

In Hart and Moore (1989, 1998), a risk-neutral entrepreneur is endowed with a production technology that requires a single fixed investment I at $t = 0$ and generates a cash flow x_t at dates $t = 1, 2$. After the realization of x_1, the firm's assets can be liquidated at $t = 1$ for a liquidation value $L \leq x_2$; thereafter, the assets liquidation value goes to zero. Funds not returned to investors can be reinvested by the entrepreneur at the rate ρ, with $1 \leq \rho \leq x_2/L$. The quadruple $\{x_1, x_2, L, \rho\}$ is a random variable realized at $t = 1$, and it is observable by both the entrepreneur and the investors but is not contractible. Hence, contracts directly contingent on the realization of these variables are not enforceable.

Because cash flows are not contractible, investors can hope to extract a payment from the entrepreneur only by threatening to liquidate the assets at $t = 1$. Thus, investors can extract a payment from the entrepreneur only at $t = 1$ (since after that the asset's liquidation value is zero). Hart and Moore consider a contract in which at $t = 0$ investors provide the entrepreneur with financing in the amount of $K = I - W_0 + T$, where $T \geq 0$ represents a transfer over and above what is needed for the project. The amount T is invested by the entrepreneur in a private savings account that cannot be seized by investors. In return, the entrepreneur promises to pay investors F and, if in default, to give investors the right to seize the assets and possibly liquidate the firm. Note that the entrepreneur can, at his discretion, use funds from the savings account (funded by the transfer T) to repay investors, thus reducing the need for asset liquidation.

Without the right to seize the firm's assets, investors will never be able to extract any payment from the entrepreneur. The maximum payment investors can extract from the entrepreneur, given their right to seize the firm's assets, is determined as follows. At $t = 2$, investors cannot extract any payment because the assets have no liquidation value. By making the payment F at $t = 1$, the entrepreneur maintains control of the firm's assets and secures for himself the right to enjoy the assets' cash flow at $t = 2$. If no payment is made at $t = 1$, investors obtain control of the assets, but since liquidation is inefficient, they have an incentive to renegotiate the contract with the entrepreneur. Renegotiation is modeled as follows. With probability α, the entrepreneur makes a "take-it-or-leave-it" offer to investors, where α represents the entrepreneur's bargaining power. Investors have the option to liquidate the asset at a value L, and, therefore, the entrepreneur must give them at least L. Note that some inefficient liquidations must occur if $T + x_1 < L$. With probability $1 - \alpha$, investors make a take-it-or-leave-it offer to the entrepreneur. Since the entrepreneur can always keep $T + x_1$, which represents his "status quo" point, investors will be able to extract a payment of $T + x_1 - (T + x_1 - x_2)/\rho$ if the entrepreneur is not cash constrained (i.e., if $T + x_1 \geq x_2$) and to extract a payment of $T + x_1 + [1 - (T + x_1)/x_2]L$ if the entrepreneur is cash constrained (i.e., if $T + x_1 < x_2$), in which case some liquidation occurs inefficiently. Thus, in state (x_1, x_2, L, ρ), investors can receive at most

$$\overline{F}(x_1, x_2, L, T, \rho) = \alpha L + (1 - \alpha) \min \left\{ T + x_1 + \left[1 - \frac{T + x_1}{x_2}\right] L; \; T + x_1 - \frac{T + x_1 - x_2}{\rho} \right\} \tag{4}$$

and the creditor will receive at most

$$\widehat{F} = \min\{\overline{F}; F\}. \tag{5}$$

Given Problems (4) and (5), the payoff to the entrepreneur will be $(x_1 + T - \widehat{F})\rho + x_2$ if $x_1 + T > \widehat{F}$, since in this case the entrepreneur is sufficiently liquid to pay investors, and it will be $[1 - (\widehat{F} - x_1 - T)/L]x_2$ if $x_1 + T \leq \widehat{F}$, since in this case the entrepreneur will have to liquidate a fraction of the assets $[1 - (\widehat{F} - x_1 - T)/L]$ to make the payment $\widehat{F}$. Thus, the entrepreneur's payoff is

$$\Pi(x_1, x_2, L, T, \rho) = \min \left\{ \left[1 - \frac{\widehat{F} - T - x_1}{L}\right] x_2; (x_2 + T - \widehat{F})\rho \right\}. \tag{6}$$

The entrepreneur's problem is then to solve

$$\begin{aligned} \max_{F,T} \quad & E\Pi(x_1, x_2, L, T, \rho) \\ \text{subject to} \quad & E\widehat{F}(x_1, x_2, L, T, \rho) \geq I + T - W_0. \end{aligned} \tag{7}$$

Examination of Problems (5) and (6) reveals the distinct roles of F and T in the maximization Problem (7). An increase in F decreases the entrepreneur's payoff in the nondefault states and makes default more likely, while an increase in T increases his payoff in all states. However, an increase in T must be offset by a more-than-proportional increase in F to satisfy the investors' individual rationality constraint (since, in the default states, investors receive less than F as the outcome of debt renegotiation). Thus, a rise in both T and F that satisfies the investors' individual rationality constraint helps the entrepreneur in the default states and hurts him in the nondefault states. The payment T therefore allows the entrepreneur to shift resources from the "good," nondefault, states into the "bad," default, states. The transfer is helpful because it allows the entrepreneur to limit inefficient liquidations in the bad states, but it comes at the cost of a reduction in the reinvestment at rate r in the good states. The optimal contract (T, F) will trade off the costs and benefits of cross-subsidization between states. These considerations suggest that contracts will tend to have low T and F values ("fast contracts") when the reinvestment opportunities ρ are expected to be high and that they will have high T and F values ("slow contracts") when expected liquidation losses are very costly.

In Zender (1991), the allocation of the control rights is used to improve investment decisions. In this study, both the entrepreneur and the investor are risk neutral and output is verifiable. However, the realization of the second cash flow, x_2, requires at $t = 1$ (after the realization of a public signal s_1 on the future cash flow x_2) a second investment I_1, which affects the probability distribution of x_2. The party in control at that time (i.e., the entrepreneur or the investor) makes the investment I_1 by using first-period cash flow x_1, and he or she retains the residual $x_1 - I_1$. The level of investment I_1 is observable only by the agent who makes the investment, introducing moral hazard. Zender shows that the optimal security jointly determines the allocation of the cash-flow rights at $t = 2$ and of the control rights at $t = 1$, which is made contingent on the observation of the signal s_1.

The joint determination of the cash-flow and control rights in the security design problem allows the entrepreneur (and the investor) to improve the efficiency of the investment decision. Zender (1991) shows that, depending on the properties of the conditional distribution $f(x_2 \mid s_1)$, it is possible to implement the first-best investment decision by writing a set of contracts that give the control rights, at $t = 1$, to the agent who is the residual claimant at $t = 2$. Thus, the optimal contract is a combination of debt and equity, where in the good states (high realization of the signal s_1) control rights rest with equity holders, and in the bad states (low realization of the signal s_1) control is allocated to the creditor, who now makes the investment decision. Note that the allocation of the control rights to the investor in the bad state may not be the only case in which the transfer of control is optimal. In other cases, the optimal contract may specify the transfer of control to the investor in certain good states. Kalay and Zender (1997) show that the state-contingent transfer of control may be achieved through the inclusion of warrants in the financing contract, improving incentives. Thus, the use of convertible securities (such as convertible debt or convertible preferred stock) complements bankruptcy as a mechanism for transferring control from the entrepreneur to outside investors.

Finally, Harris and Raviv (1995) consider the optimal security design problem in a setting similar to that of Hart and Moore (1989). This paper analyzes, in addition to the optimal design of the security, the optimal design of the negotiation game between the entrepreneur and investors. In particular, Harris and Raviv allow for a negotiation game at $t = 1$ in which both players simultaneously make a verifiable announcement of the state of nature; after that, payments and liquidation are determined as a function of these announced reports. The key result of this paper is that this *universal game* can achieve a more efficient outcome than the one proposed by Hart and Moore (1989). The reason is that making payments and liquidation decisions contingent on these reports indirectly allows for contracts to become state contingent and therefore to further reduce inefficient liquidations.

4. DEBT CONTRACTS AND THE PROVISION OF INCENTIVES

In the models discussed so far no consideration is given to the importance of giving the entrepreneur sufficient incentives to take the appropriate action $a \varepsilon A$. The problem of providing appropriate incentives to the entrepreneur is, however, a critical issue because debt contracts in which default risk is a distinct possibility distort the entrepreneur's incentives and may lead him either to exert too little effort (i.e., see the underinvestment problem of Myers 1977) or to take too many risks (i.e., see the risk-shifting problem of Jensen and Meckling 1976 and Galai and Masulis 1976).

When the entrepreneur's choice of the action $a \varepsilon A$ is not contractible while output is observable, investors are exposed to moral hazard, and the design of optimal-incentive contracts becomes critical. For a risk neutral entrepreneur, the optimal-incentive contract prescribes that the entrepreneur pay the investors a fixed flat payment (see Shavell 1979 and Harris and Raviv 1979), thus leading to risk-free debt. In many cases, and arguably the most common ones, limited liability makes these contracts infeasible. The effect of limited liability on the choice of optimal-incentive contracts is examined in Innes (1990). In that paper, both the entrepreneur and investors are risk neutral, avoiding risk-sharing considerations, and the entrepreneur's action $a \varepsilon A$ increases expected output, in the sense of the monotone likelihood ratio property (MLRP) of Milgrom (1981). Informally, this means that a high-output realization is more likely to be the result of a high level of the action a rather than a low one. In this case, the optimal incentive contract has a "live-or-die" feature, whereby the entrepreneur pays the investor a constant share of output when output is below a certain critical level and retains all the output otherwise. In this case, the entrepreneur captures all the benefits of effort in the better states, maximizing his incentives to exert effort. If the optimal-incentive contract must also satisfy the condition of being monotonic in output (to eliminate the entrepreneur's incentive to manipulate the firm's profits, for example, by borrowing funds and artificially inflating output to reduce the payment to the investor), the optimal contract is again a standard debt contract: The entrepreneur's effort is maximized by a contract that gives the entrepreneur maximal payoff in the high-output states and minimal payoff in the low-output states—that is, by a standard debt contract.

Entrepreneurial risk neutrality is critical in Innes (1990) to obtain that the optimal contract is a standard debt contract. In general, if the entrepreneur is risk averse, optimal contracts require some risk sharing between the (possibly risk-neutral) investor and the entrepreneur, making standard debt contracts suboptimal. Thus, the desire to provide appropriate incentives to the entrepreneur comes at a cost of inefficient risk sharing. This implies that the entrepreneur and the investor will find it optimal to renegotiate the initial contract once it is known to both parties that the entrepreneur has taken the action $a \varepsilon A$ and therefore that the incentive provision is no longer necessary. Contract renegotiation will also be beneficial because it allows the entrepreneur and investors to achieve optimal risk sharing by using relatively simple contracts (see Gale 1991). The possibility of renegotiation, optimal ex post, is, however, problematic ex ante because it is anticipated by the entrepreneur and this undermines his incentives. Matthews (2001) examines the problem of the optimal ex ante contract design when renegotiation is possible and finds that standard debt contracts are again (approximately) optimal in the class of monotonic contracts with limited liability.

Chiesa (1992) shows that if the interim signal $s \varepsilon S$ is observable to both the entrepreneur and the investor but is not verifiable, the optimal contract is again a debt contract, in which the investor now holds a warrant on entrepreneur's equity and the entrepreneur has the option, if the warrant is exercised, to settle with a (delayed) cash payment to the investor. In this setting, the investor observes the realization of the interim signal s and decides whether or not to exercise the warrant. The entrepreneur, rather than diluting his equity, prefers to settle with a cash payment at the maturity of the debt, effectively increasing the payment to the investor. In this way, the investor's decision to exercise the warrant (contingent on the observation of the signal) and accept the cash settlement option results in a state-contingent payment to the investor that shifts payments from bad states into good states. This strategy reduces the debt-overhang problem, improves the entrepreneur's incentives, and alleviates the moral hazard problem.

In a similar vein, Povel and Raith (2004) consider a version of Hart and Moore's (1998) model in which the level of investment I and the entrepreneurial action a may not be observable (and thus contractible) by the investor. The unobservable action a may be interpreted either as entrepreneurial effort or as the choice of a risky project (generating risk shifting). Povel and Raith show that the optimal contract is again a debt contract, in which the probability of liquidating the project is chosen optimally to induce the entrepreneur either to invest in the project or to exert effort or to choose a project with a desirable risk profile.

5. DEBT CONTRACTS UNDER ASYMMETRIC INFORMATION

The common feature of the models discussed in the previous sections is that the entrepreneur and investors have access, at the time they negotiate the financing terms, to the same information. The availability to the entrepreneur of precontractual payoff-relevant information exposes investors to adverse selection and impairs the entrepreneur's ability to raise capital.

Assume now that at the outset of the game the entrepreneur privately observes the realization of the variable $\theta \varepsilon \Theta$. The parameter θ induces a conditional probability distribution function (PDF) over output $P(x \mid \theta)$ and identifies an entrepreneur's "type." Investors respond to the potential "lemon problem" (see Akerlof 1970) by financing entrepreneurs at terms that reflect the average quality of the pool of entrepreneurs seeking financing. In this way, the presence of asymmetric information causes a wealth transfer from better-quality entrepreneurs to lower-quality ones, increasing the financing cost of better-than-average entrepreneurs. Two influential papers, Myers and Majluf

(1984) and Myers (1984), suggest that, under these circumstances entrepreneurs with better information can reduce the "lemon discount" they face by adopting a financing strategy that follows a well-defined "pecking order": They should satisfy their financing needs first by using securities that are less sensitive to information asymmetries, such as safer debt, and then by progressively using securities that have increasing information sensitivity, such as riskier debt and finally equity.

Whether the presence of asymmetric information necessarily leads to a preference for securities with low information sensitivity over information-sensitive ones (and, thus, to a preference for debt over equity) has been investigated by several papers in the subsequent literature.

The ability of the entrepreneur to commit his own wealth to the project may be useful in discouraging lower-quality entrepreneurs from seeking financing, improving the average quality of the pool of entrepreneurs facing investors. Narayanan (1988) assumes that the parameter $\theta \varepsilon \Theta$ orders the PDF of output, $P(x \mid \theta)$, by "first-order stochastic dominance" (FOSD) (that is, $P(x \mid \theta_1) < P(x \mid \theta_0)$ for any $\theta_0 < \theta_1$); that entrepreneurs may have projects with negative net present value (NPV); and that the choice of financing is exogenously restricted to either risky debt or equity. By using risky debt rather than equity, entrepreneurs with better information reduce the wealth transfer to the lower-quality entrepreneurs (that is, those with negative-NPV projects) and discourage them from investing in the project, leading them to drop out of the market. Thus, the use of debt improves the average quality of the pool of entrepreneurs who seek financing and reduces adverse selection costs.

Noe (1988) shows that if entrepreneurs have no initial wealth and their precontractual private information, θ, does not resolve all the residual uncertainty (that is, it does not fully reveal the realization of the final output x), the preference for debt over equity is not a generic implication of asymmetric information, even when the private information θ orders the PDF of output $P(x \mid \theta)$ by FOSD. Specifically, the paper offers an example in which the entrepreneur may be one of three possible types, $\Theta = \{\theta_1; \theta_2; \theta_3\}$, where θ_i is a "better" type than θ_j if and only if $i > j$. Entrepreneurs of the better type, θ_3, pool with the lower type, θ_1, and both issue risky debt, while entrepreneurs of intermediate value, θ_2, separate and issue (fairly priced) equity. This happens because the lower type prefers to pool with the better type and to issue overvalued debt rather than mimicking the middle type and issue overvalued equity. The better type prefers to pool with the lower type and issue undervalued debt rather than mimicking the middle type and issue undervalued equity. The intermediate type prefers to issue equity and separate, rather than issuing undervalued debt.

The specific properties that the probability distribution of the project's output, $P(x \mid \theta)$, must satisfy to ensure that a firm's insiders prefer debt over equity are identified by Nachman and Noe (1994). This study assumes that entrepreneurs have access only to positive-NPV projects and imposes minimal restrictions on the set of admissible securities, $y(x)$, by assuming that entrepreneurs can issue any security that satisfies limited liability, $0 \leq y(x) \leq x$, and monotonicity, $0 \leq y'(x) \leq 1$. The paper shows that the predictions of the pecking order theory hold if and only if the parameter θ orders the

PDF of output, $P(x \mid \theta)$, by *conditional* stochastic dominance, that is, if the conditional probability

$$P(y \mid x, \theta) = \frac{P(x + y \mid \theta) - P(x \mid \theta)}{1 - P(x \mid \theta)} \tag{8}$$

is ordered by FOSD by θ for all x. Conditional stochastic dominance, in turn, implies that

$$R(\theta_1, \theta_2) = \frac{1 - P(x \mid \theta_2)}{1 - P(x \mid \theta_1)}, \quad \text{for any } \theta_1 < \theta_2 \tag{9}$$

is nondecreasing in x (note that FOSD implies only that $R(\theta_1, \theta_2) \geq 1$). Ratio in Problem (9) has the interesting interpretation of representing the marginal cost of increasing the payout for type θ_2 relative to type θ_1. For debt to be optimal, it is necessary (and sufficient) that the relative incremental cost of increasing a payout for a better type of entrepreneur is nondecreasing in the output level x. In this case, better types are better off increasing the payout to investors in the low-output states and reducing the payout to investors in the high-payout states. These considerations, together with the requirement that the security be monotonic in output, lead to the optimality of debt contracts.

The importance of the assumption that the entrepreneur has access only to positive-NPV projects is highlighted by Ravid and Spiegel (1997). In their model, entrepreneurs have access to a limited number of positive-NPV projects, but they can freely create projects with any arbitrary output distributions $P(x)$ as long as these projects have a negative NPV. In this case, only contracts that are linear in output x, namely, equity contracts, are immune to manipulation. This happens because linear contracts are the only ones that align the entrepreneur's interest with the investors'.

In the real world, debt contracts often come in simple form, that is, payments from the entrepreneur to the investor are not made contingent on information that is publicly available. For example, in standard debt contracts the entrepreneur makes noncontingent payments, whereas in income bonds interest payments are made contingent on certain accounting measures of profits. If the entrepreneur is risk averse, such noncontingent contracts are in general suboptimal because they forego some risk-sharing opportunities that are offered by the linking of payments to (noisy) signals of the true state of the world (see, in the context of moral hazard, Holmstrom 1979 and Shavell 1979). This raises the question of why noncontingent debt contracts are so pervasive. In an adverse selection context, Allen and Gale (1992) show that if the signals to be included in the debt contract (for example, accounting measures) can be manipulated by the entrepreneur, the proposal by the entrepreneur to include contingencies in the financing contract may be interpreted by the investor as a bad signal on the entrepreneur's private information. This happens when entrepreneurs of the "good" type have lower incentives to manipulate the signal than do those of the "bad" type and, therefore, can separate by offering noncontingent contracts. In this setting, equilibrium entrepreneurs of different types pool and offer noncontingent contracts, which are the only contracts in which entrepreneurs have no incentive to manipulate the signal.

An important assumption of Nachman and Noe (1994) is that outside investors are endowed with an exogenous amount of information and that information acquisition plays no role in the entrepreneur's security design problem. Boot and Thakor (1993) examine the case in which some investors can, by paying a certain cost, learn the realization of θ, reducing the extent of the asymmetric information. Informed investors, however, have limited wealth and can purchase only a small number of shares, determined endogenously. Securities are sold by the entrepreneur in an anonymous market, in which prices are set competitively by risk-neutral market makers. The ability of equilibrium security prices to reflect the information produced by the informed investors is reduced by the presence of noisy (uninformed) investors. Entrepreneurs are one of two possible types, "good" and "bad," sell their firm in its entirety, and are willing to accept any price determined in equilibrium by the market makers (that is, they have no reservation price for their firm). Boot and Thakor show that the entrepreneur's revenue-maximizing strategy is to split the claims on the firm's output into one information-sensitive security, such as equity, and a second less information-sensitive security, such as debt. The intuition is that by creating an information-sensitive security, entrepreneurs reward information acquisition and induce more investors to become informed. Entrepreneurs with more valuable firms benefit because greater information production moves the (expected) equilibrium prices closer to the greater intrinsic value of the securities they sell.

Note that in Boot and Thakor (1993) the value to investors of becoming informed derives from their ability to trade against liquidity traders. Thus, the increase in information production from the creation of these two securities relies critically on how the liquidity traders split their trading between the two securities. For example, if most of the liquidity traders choose to trade in the security that is less information sensitive, then information production will actually decrease following the creation of the two securities. Goldman (2005) shows explicitly that the aggregate level of information production can either increase or decrease following a spin-off of an all-equity firm (i.e., a firm that switches from having one information-sensitive security to having two). His analysis allows for any possible split of the initial liquidity traders between the two newly created securities.

One implication of Boot and Thakor's model is that entrepreneurs should always prefer to use an information-sensitive security, such as equity, to an information-insensitive one, such as debt; this reaches the opposite conclusion of the pecking order theory. Fulghieri and Lukin (2001) reconcile the findings of Boot and Thakor with those of Myers and Majluf (1984) as follows. In a setting similar to that of Boot and Thakor, they assume that entrepreneurs seek financing only to the extent necessary to fund the investment, I, thus requiring entrepreneurs to maintain a residual interest in their firms. Entrepreneurs have either "good' or "bad" projects, where bad projects are those that have a negative NPV. Securities are sold by the entrepreneur in an anonymous market, in which prices are set competitively by risk-neutral market makers who observe aggregate order flow. This differs from Boot and Thakor (1993) in that now a low realization of uninformed investors' demand can decrease aggregate order flow to the point that the equilibrium price set by the market makers is too low to enable the entrepreneur to raise the desired amount I, leading to a failure of the security issuance.

Fulghieri and Lukin (2001) show that the promotion of informed trading by the issuance of equity rather than risky debt is beneficial to good-quality entrepreneurs only if the equilibrium amount of informed trading is sufficiently large and, thus, the cost of acquiring information is low. This can be seen as follows. With no informed trading, both good and bad projects are successfully financed for any realization of the order flow (because, on average, they have a positive NPV), and entrepreneurs issue a security with low information sensitivity for precisely the same reasons as the one discussed in Myers and Majluf (1984). With informed trading, order flow is informative on project quality, and, thus, it affects the price of the securities issued by the entrepreneur. When information production costs are high (and, thus, the equilibrium amount of informed trading is low), the use of an information-sensitive security such as equity promotes informed trading only moderately. When, instead, information production costs are low (and therefore the equilibrium amount of informed trading is high), the promotion of informed trading by the issuance of an information-sensitive security increases the probability that securities are issued and that the project is implemented. Thus, when the information production costs are relatively high, the entrepreneur follows optimally the prescriptions of the pecking order theory and prefers debt to equity; when, instead, the information production costs are relatively low, the entrepreneur prefers to use equity rather than debt, counter to the pecking order theory. Moreover, Fulghieri and Lukin show that the benefits of promoting information acquisition through equity financing are greater when it is needed most, that is, in cases in which the entrepreneur faces greater information asymmetry. Finally, the paper solves the optimal security design problem, showing that when information production costs are large, the entrepreneur will issue risky debt, and that when information production costs are low, the entrepreneur will issue a security with a convex payoff, such as equity plus warrants.

A key assumption of the previous papers is that entrepreneurs optimally design the security they offer for sale in the interim (in the sense of Holmstrom and Myerson 1983), that is, *after* they have observed their private information. However, it is interesting to examine the entrepreneurs' security design problem *before* they learn their private information, that is, before the realization of $\theta \varepsilon \Theta$. The difference between the ex ante and the interim security design problems is critical since, ex ante, entrepreneurs face uncertainty on the private information that they will receive, that is, on their own type. Entrepreneurs solve the ex ante security design problem by anticipating that because of the private information they will receive, they will not face a perfectly elastic demand function for their securities, even in competitive capital markets. Rather, as discussed in Leland and Pyle (1977), rational investors anticipate that entrepreneurs will be willing to sell a greater amount of securities (relative to what they maintain in their portfolio) when these have lower value according to their private information. Thus, the presence of private information leads quite naturally to downward-sloping demand functions for securities and, therefore, to illiquid securities markets.

The ex ante optimal security design problem is tackled by DeMarzo and Duffie (1999). Risk-neutral entrepreneurs choose the design of the security put up for sale, that is, its payoff y, before they observe their private information, $\theta \, \varepsilon \, \Theta$. The security payoff y is restricted to be a monotonic increasing function of the firm's output x and, possibly, of an additional public signal, $s \, \varepsilon \, S$; that is, $y(x, s) \, \varepsilon \, [0, x]$. Entrepreneurs design the security payoff $y(x, s)$ anticipating that investors will be willing to pay a price, V, which depends (endogenously) on the choice of the payoff structure $y(x, s)$ of the security put up for sale (that is, on the specific security design) and on the fraction q of the security that is held by the entrepreneur in his portfolio. Thus, $V = V(y(x, s), q)$. An entrepreneur anticipates that she will in general obtain a better price if she retains a greater fraction q, but at the expense of suffering a cost per unit of retained output. The sale of the security occurs only after the entrepreneur observes the private information. Demarzo and Duffie show that if the private information θ has a "uniform worse case" (a property that is shown to be weaker than MLRP), then the solution to the ex ante optimal security design problem is again a standard debt contract. This happens because the severity of the illiquidity faced in the interim by the entrepreneur depends on the sensitivity of the security offered for sale to the entrepreneur's private information. Thus, by issuing a security with low information sensitivity, the entrepreneur reduces the future illiquidity, which enables her to reduce costly retention.

In a subsequent paper, DeMarzo (2005) shows that if the entrepreneur designs the security payoff *after* he learns the private information θ, the optimal contract is still a standard debt contract, in which now the face value is a decreasing function of θ. Thus, a larger debt issue is interpreted by investors as negative signal about the valuation of the firm. More generally, DeMarzo considers an entrepreneur endowed with multiple assets and examines the problem of whether or not he should pool his assets in a single firm ("pooling") and the subsequent priority structure of the securities issued ("tranching"). Pooling assets in the same firms has an information-destruction effect. This is beneficial to the entrepreneur if he is uninformed at the time of the securities' issuance, since it reduces the underpricing due to the "winner's curse" problem (see Rock 1986). Pooling is detrimental if the entrepreneur is informed when the securities are issued, since it reduces his flexibility to sell selectively each security depending on the private information he has obtained. Furthermore, DeMarzo shows that pooling and tranching are beneficial when the residual risks of assets are not too highly correlated, since this strategy allows the entrepreneur to create a low-risk, highly liquid security which he would be able to sell for a better value.

Biais and Mariotti (2005) extend DeMarzo and Duffie's analysis and assume that the entrepreneur does not face fully competitive investors (as in DeMarzo and Duffie 1999) but, rather, liquidity suppliers with a certain market power. The entrepreneur again designs the security before becoming informed, that is, before observing θ. The optimal security design problem results again in a standard debt contract, that is, a security with low information sensitivity, in which the choice of the face value of the debt allows the entrepreneur to reduce the rents extracted by the liquidity provider.

In DeMarzo and Duffie (1999), security design is made by the entrepreneur before becoming informed. Inderst and Mueller (2006a), conversely, examine the security design problem faced by a risk-neutral, uninformed investor in the case in which the investor (rather than the entrepreneur) becomes informed before deciding whether or not to provide financing to the entrepreneur. Specifically, the investor privately observes the realization of the signal θ and, given the contract design chosen in advance, must then decide whether or not to finance the risk-neutral entrepreneur. The signal θ is informative on output level; that is, $F(x, \theta)$ again satisfies MLRP. The entrepreneur has no wealth, so the investor must provide full financing. Under the first-best case, the project is undertaken if and only if the observed signal θ is greater than a certain critical level θ_c, which depends on the investment I and on the entrepreneur's reservation utility. The security design problem is made interesting by the fact that the investor's decision to finance the entrepreneur is subject to two kinds of biases (with respect to the first-best decision rule). The first bias is that the investor does not internalize the entrepreneur's reservation utility, leading to more frequent acceptances of the project than under the first-best case (i.e., the investor is too aggressive). The second bias is that the investor must surrender surplus to the entrepreneur, leading to less frequent acceptances of the project than under the first-best case (i.e., the investor is too conservative). Inderst and Mueller show that when the second effect prevails, that is, when the investor is too conservative, the solution to the optimal security design problem is a standard debt contract: $y(x) = \min\{x; F\}$, where $F > I$. The intuition is as follows: By giving the investor the entire payoff in the low states, the contract brings the critical threshold, θ_c, closer to the first-best case. Conversely, when the investor is too aggressive, the optimal contract is levered equity: $y(x) = \max\{x - F; 0\}$, with $F > 0$. This implies that the standard debt contract emerges again as the outcome of an optimal security design problem in cases in which investors are by their nature too conservative. In addition, Inderst and Mueller (2006b) show that adding collateral may also reduce the inefficient lender's acceptance decision by improving the investor's payoff for low- but still positive-NPV projects that would otherwise be rejected.

6. THE STRUCTURE OF DEBT CONTRACTS

Debt contracts rarely come in the "plain vanilla" form discussed in the previous sections. More realistically, debt contracts include specific provisions designed to mitigate further the effect of asymmetric information and, thus, to facilitate the effective financing of the entrepreneur's project. In this section, we discuss the role of specific characteristics of debt contracts, such as seniority, maturity structure, collateral, and covenants. Note that while these contractual features are very often bundled together in the same debt contract, for expositional purposes we discuss them individually in separate subsections.

6.1. Seniority

Debt seniority is defined as the priority that a claim holder has over other claim holders when the firm's cash flow is insufficient to pay all obligations. Seniority can matter in the case of liquidation or bankruptcy, but it is also relevant for the case in which debt restructuring takes place, because it defines the payoffs in the state of no agreement. Note that debt maturity implies some form of seniority. This is because short-tem debt, by virtue of the fact that it is paid earlier, is essentially senior to long-term debt. In this section, we discuss seniority in the strict sense, that is, the priority structure of claims maturing at any given date. We defer to Section 6.2, on maturity structure, the discussion of the more general issue of combining seniority and maturity structure.

In the basic CSV setting discussed in Section 2, the optimality of the debt contract is established under the assumption that either the entrepreneur receives financing from a single investor or he borrows from multiple investors who observe the outcome of the state verification simultaneously. If the entrepreneur needs to raise capital from more than one investor and the outcome of the state verification is now privately observed by the investor who performed the verification, the standard debt contract is no longer optimal. Winton (1995) shows that in this case symmetric debt contracts are suboptimal because (1) they entail duplication of verification cost, and (2) they involve suboptimal risk sharing. Assuming investors are risk neutral, the optimal contracts are debtlike contracts with absolute priority among investors holding claims with different seniority. The entrepreneur issues separate "tranches" of debt, where investor i has debt with a face value of F_i and where seniority is defined as the region over which an investor chooses to monitor. For two investors i and j, if i monitors for all reported output $x < F_i$ and j monitors for all reported output $x < F_j$, then i is said to be senior to j if $F_j > F_i$. Furthermore, Winton shows that if all investors are identical, that is, if they have the same risk preferences and endowments, debtlike contracts of varying seniority still dominate symmetric contracts with identical seniority. While seniority reduces the value of junior debt (making it more risky), in most cases the benefit of reducing verification costs outweighs the reduction in risk sharing among investors.

Seniority of claims also matters because it affects investors' incentives. Park (2000) considers a situation in which the entrepreneur may engage in asset substitution by taking on a risky (rather than a riskless) project. In this setting, monitoring by investors can deter the entrepreneur from this opportunistic behavior. Park endogenizes the incentive to monitor and argues that in order to minimize the contracting costs, the entrepreneur must maximize the investors' incentive to monitor. This can be achieved with an optimal debt structure in which the investor with the smallest monitoring cost receives senior debt and the investor(s) with the highest monitoring cost receive(s) junior debt. The reason is as follows. The incentives to monitor are greater when the benefits from the monitoring activity are greater. Because senior debt holders do not get paid in full upon liquidation, they will have an incentive to monitor the entrepreneur and thus prevent asset substitution. Hence, investors with lower monitoring costs should hold a claim senior to all other investors in liquidation. Junior debt holders, however, will not receive much in liquidation and therefore have little incentive to monitor. Thus, junior claims should be held by investors with the highest cost of monitoring.

In addition to affecting investors' incentives, seniority structure can also influence the entrepreneur's incentives to fight off investors in the case of financial distress, for example, through costly litigation. Litigation under financial distress is inefficient because it has the sole effect of redistributing wealth across agents and therefore represents a pure deadweight cost. Welch (1997) considers a case in which the entrepreneur has (exogenously) issued debt to two investor types: a large investor (say, a bank) and a group of small investors. Welch's model analyzes the entrepreneur's ex ante decision regarding which of the two types of investors should hold a senior claim. Welch shows that, all else held equal, if the firm wants to minimize the costs of wasteful lobbying during the bankruptcy process, then it should award seniority to the investor with the lowest lobbying cost (i.e., the bank). With no lobbying, the court (by assumption) is more likely to rule in favor of the absolute priority rule. Hence, the junior debt holder will have the weakest incentive to engage in lobbying activities. Thus, to minimize lobbying costs, the entrepreneur should give the junior claims to the investor with the highest lobbying cost and the senior claim to the bank that has the lowest lobbying cost.

6.2. Maturity Structure

Closely related to the issue of seniority is the choice of debt maturity structure. Debt seniority and maturity are closely related features of debt contracts because debt with a short maturity is in a way senior to debt with a longer maturity. Stewart Myers was the first to recognize the importance of the maturity date of debt relative to the timing of the entrepreneur's investment opportunities. In Myers (1977), the entrepreneur is endowed with the option to invest (say, at $t = 1$ in our setting) in a new positive-NPV project. The paper shows that if the entrepreneur has outstanding debt (issued, for example, at the beginning date $t = 0$) and maturing at a later date (say, at $t = 2$), he may prefer to forego the new project rather than committing additional capital. This happens whenever the NPV of the new project is smaller than the total wealth that is transferred to the existing debt holders as a result of the acceptance of the new project. Thus, issuing debt at $t = 0$ reduces the entrepreneur's incentives to undertake profitable projects in the future, generating an underinvestment (or, debt-overhang) problem.

The foregoing underinvestment problem is caused by the presence of existing debt that matures after the expiration of the new investment opportunity. This implies that, by careful choice of the debt maturity structure, the entrepreneur may alleviate the adverse-incentive effect of debt. This is shown in the study by Barnea, Haugen, and Senbet (1980), who argue that the combined issuance of short-term debt, maturing before the expiration of the new investment opportunity, along with long-term debt with a call provision, restores investment incentives and eliminates the underinvestment problem.

The fact that the presence of long-term debt leads to underinvestment is not always detrimental but may in fact be desirable in situations in which the entrepreneur has an incentive to overinvest. Berkovitch and Kim (1990) consider the problem faced by the entrepreneur at $t = 1$, when the firm already has debt outstanding (issued, say, at $t = 0$ to acquire assets) and needs to finance an additional project whose returns are his private information. The choice of seniority between the existing long-term debt and the new short-term debt issued at $t = 1$ affects the entrepreneur's incentives to over- and underinvest in the new project. Their paper shows that if the likelihood of overinvestment is high (i.e., when the new project is more likely to have a negative NPV), then new debt issued at $t = 1$ should be junior to the existing long-term debt. This is because junior debt limits the additional amount that the entrepreneur can borrow and hence discourages investment. Conversely, when the new project is more likely to have a positive NPV, it is optimal to reduce the possibility of underinvestment by allowing the entrepreneur to issue new debt senior to existing long-term debt. Finally, the authors show that when the future investment is known to all, then the optimal new debt is one that is fully collateralized by the new project, with no recourse to existing assets. Thus, with no information asymmetry, the best outcome is achieved by separating the projects from existing assets-in-place.

Houston and Venkataraman (1994) also focus on the costs and benefits of the underinvestment problem caused by debt and on the beneficial impact of debt on the forcing of liquidation in cases in which the entrepreneur has the incentive to invest in projects with negative NPV. They show that the entrepreneur can commit at $t = 0$ to an optimal liquidation policy at $t = 1$ with an appropriate mix of short- and long-term debt. In particular, short-term debt is higher the higher the expected liquidation value.

In a similar vein, in Hart and Moore (1995) the entrepreneur is assumed to have private benefits of control, which implies that he always wishes to invest in new projects (provided that he has access to capital), even when these projects are inefficient. In Hart and Moore's setting, overinvestment may occur at the interim, $t = 1$, when the entrepreneur can invest in a new project that requires a new investment in the amount of I_1 and generates at $t = 2$ an (additional) cash flow equal to Δx_2. The entrepreneur's ability to invest in new projects at $t = 1$ is constrained in two ways. First, the presence of short-term debt, with face value F_1 and maturing at $t = 1$, forces the entrepreneur to disburse cash flows from assets-in-place, x_1, to investors, thereby limiting his ability to invest in the new project. The use of short-term debt, however, may come at the cost of potential inefficient liquidation at $t = 1$ of assets-in-place to repay maturing short-term debt. Second, the presence of *senior* long-term debt, with face value F_2 and maturing at $t = 2$, limits the entrepreneur's ability to raise additional capital at $t = 1$ by borrowing against future earnings. Hart and Moore (1995) argue that the long-term debt (issued at $t = 0$) should be senior to any short-term debt that the entrepreneur would issue at $t = 1$. Specifically, if long-term debt is senior, the entrepreneur can raise enough capital and invest in the new project at $t = 1$ if and only if $x_1 + x_2 + \Delta x_2 - F_2 \geq I_1 + F_1$ (assuming risk neutrality and no discounting). If, instead, long-term debt is junior, the entrepreneur is able to raise money and invest in the new project only if $x_1 + x_2 + \Delta x_2 \geq I_1 + F_1$. Thus, if existing long-term debt is junior, the entrepreneur can raise more capital, exacerbating the overinvestment problem. Seniority of long-term debt tightens the entrepreneur's budget constraint at $t = 1$ and limits his ability to raise capital and invest in negative-NPV projects. The benefit of the seniority of long-term debt, however, comes at the cost of foregoing some positive-NPV projects at $t = 1$, when the (expected) value of future cash flow, x_2, is low and the entrepreneur cannot raise sufficient funds to invest in profitable new projects.

The optimal choice of debt maturity structure must be made in harmony with the time profile of the payoff of firm assets. The issue of the appropriate matching between the maturity structure of assets and liabilities is examined by Hart and Moore (1994), which is a dynamic extension of Hart and Moore (1989, 1998), discussed in Section 3. In

Hart and Moore (1994), project cash flows, x_t, and debt payments accrue continuously over a finite horizon, $t \varepsilon [0, T]$. The debt maturity structure is modeled as the rate at which debt payments are made. Debt contracts with slower debt payments imply longer maturity. The main problem faced by the entrepreneur is that he cannot commit not to withdraw his human capital from the project. This means that under any debt contract and at any given point in time, the investor cannot receive more than $\max(0.5x_t, L_t)$, where the first term is the present value of what the investor can get in renegotiation with the entrepreneur following a default (under the assumption that entrepreneur and investor split the continuation payoff) and the second term is what the investor can get if he chooses to liquidate. Liquidation, however, is inefficient, due to the loss of the entrepreneur's human capital.

Under these circumstances, the authors show that the amount of long-term debt the entrepreneur can issue is constrained by the investor's understanding that debt value will be renegotiated down to $\max(0.5x_t, L_t)$. In turn, short-term debt maturing at τ cannot be greater than what can be repaid with existing cash flows and cash flows retained from excess profits saved from $t < \tau$. Although the model yields a multiplicity of debt maturities for the contracts that achieve first-best outcome, the authors show that the intertemporal profile of project returns affects the maturity structure of the slowest and fastest possible debt contracts. For example, when more of the project returns arrive early (or are front-loaded), the debt payments become faster (i.e., have lower maturity). This is because the investor has less to bargain over in the future, and hence he requires more payments up front. Furthermore, if the entrepreneur has a greater discount rate than the investor (which can happen if the entrepreneur has profitable investment opportunities), the optimal contract is unique and is the slowest possible debt contract (i.e., has the longer maturity).

Using a framework similar to that of Hart and Moore, Berglof and Von Thadden (1994) show the importance of maturity when the entrepreneur is again able to default strategically and threaten to withdraw his human capital. In this model, the entrepreneur has assets in place that generate cash flows, x_t, over two periods, $t = 1, 2$. While assets, with a liquidation value L_t, can be pledged to investors, cash flows cannot. The problem arises when asset value L_t is not large enough to induce investors to provide sufficient capital for investment. In this case, the only way to raise the necessary capital is to write a contract that induces the entrepreneur to give some of the noncontractible cash flow at the first date, x_1, to the investor. The entrepreneur has an incentive to do so because the investor can liquidate the project if not paid at the interim date, $t = 1$. This would result in a loss to the entrepreneur of the $t = 2$ cash flow, x_2. The main tradeoff is as follows. A higher debt payment at $t = 1$ (that is, a short maturity) results in more inefficient liquidation, but too small of a payment at $t = 1$ will not allow investors to recoup their initial expenditure, hindering investment. The ability to raise capital is further complicated by the fact that even when the $t = 1$ cash flows are high, the entrepreneur may still threaten to withdraw his human capital. Debt maturity then plays an additional role in the renegotiation game between the entrepreneur and the investor. Berglof and Von Thadden show that in order to minimize the amount of inefficient liquidation, the optimal contract needs to minimize the ex post surplus that the entrepreneur is able to extract from the investor via strategic default at $t = 1$ when cash flows are high. This can be achieved by maximizing the investors' bargaining power, or, rather, by minimizing their loss from liquidation. Because liquidation is harmful to long-term investors, the optimal contract separates investors into senior short-term lenders, who negotiate with the borrower at $t = 1$, and junior long-term lenders, who do not force liquidation. This choice of debt structure strengthens the short-term investor's position and, thus, minimizes the entrepreneur's incentive to default strategically on the loan in the hopes of renegotiating and getting better terms.

More recently, DeMarzo and Fishman (2006) have offered a theory of optimal long-term debt and outside equity in combination with a credit facility that allows the entrepreneur to smooth out temporary shocks to cash flow. They reconsider the Hart and Moore (1994) model, in which a risk-neutral entrepreneur is endowed with a project that requires an investment I and generates a stochastic cash flow x_t and a liquidation payoff of L_t for $t \varepsilon [0, T]$. Cash flows, x_t, are identically and independently distributed (so there is no "learning") and can be diverted by the entrepreneur at a cost (making concealing cash flows inefficient). The paper solves for the optimal security design problem, showing that the optimal contract can be implemented by means of simple securities, whereby the investor holds a combination of long-term debt and equity and then provides the entrepreneur with a credit line. The entrepreneur, who holds the residual equity, must make a periodic payment on the long-term debt, and this payment is made either out of the periodic cash flow, x_t, or by drawing on the credit line. If the entrepreneur cannot meet the periodic payment on the long-term debt, the project may be liquidated (with a certain probability). In equilibrium, the entrepreneur uses all excess cash to pay down the credit line and then makes a dividend payment to equity rather than concealing cash flows. Thus, he finances consumption from the dividends received on his equity position.

DeMarzo and Sannikov (2006) reformulate the DeMarzo and Fishman (2006) model within a continuous-time framework. Their paper shows that, in addition to debt, equity, and a credit line, the firm will optimally hold cash as a requirement for obtaining the credit line. This cash holding allows the entrepreneur to obtain a greater credit line and provides an infusion of cash (the return on the cash holdings), which may be valuable when the risk of loss is high. Furthermore, termination of the project is deterministic (no randomization is necessary, as in DeMarzo and Fishman 2006). Sannikov (2006) extends the model further by assuming that at the outset of the project, the entrepreneur has private information on the mean of the future cash flow distribution. Sannikov shows that in this case the optimal contract is a credit line with a growing credit limit, with the requirement that the entrepreneur contribute at the outset a certain minimum amount of initial capital. The minimum equity participation by the entrepreneur is needed to discourage entrepreneurs with unworthy projects from mimicking the behavior of entrepreneurs with positive-NPV projects and having access to the credit line offered by investors. Furthermore, the increasing-credit-limit feature is due to adverse selection, which limits the amount that investors can give to the entrepreneur; over time, investors are willing to increase the credit limit as the entrepreneur signals to investors his type by making the accrued contractual payments on existing debt.

Debt maturity structure also affects the entrepreneur's exposure to adverse changes in credit quality and, therefore, to liquidity risk. This problem was first examined in Flannery (1986), which shows how the choice of debt maturity can be used by good entrepreneurs (i.e., those with good information at $t = 0$ about future cash flow), to signal their type and thus separate from bad entrepreneurs. In Flannery's model, entrepreneurs need to raise debt to finance a two-period project. The assumed cash flow distribution implies that short-term debt, maturing at $t = 1$, is riskless but that long-term debt, maturing at $t = 2$, is not. Good entrepreneurs have a higher probability of high cash flow, and this information is updated in the first period. Thus, short-term debt is preferred by good entrepreneurs because it allows for more information-sensitive securities, while bad entrepreneurs prefer long-term debt. However, since the choice of debt reveals information, bad entrepreneurs mimic good ones, and hence all entrepreneurs pool at $t = 0$ and issue short-term debt (which is priced based on the average entrepreneur type). Flannery further shows that, if refinancing is costly (for example, if it requires a fixed transaction cost), then good entrepreneurs can separate themselves by issuing short-term debt, incurring the fixed cost of refinancing at $t = 1$ but also obtaining a lower refinancing rate due to the separation from bad types, which now issue long-term debt.

In Flannery (1986), entrepreneurs issuing short-term debt do not face the risk of liquidation, that is, the risk of not being able to refinance their debt at $t = 1$. The effect of liquidation risk on debt maturity and seniority is examined in Diamond (1991, 1993). In these papers, the entrepreneur is again endowed with a technology lasting for two periods, but output is generated only in the second period, $t = 2$. The technology can either be "good" ($\theta = G$) or "bad" ($\theta = B$), and it is private information to the entrepreneur at $t = 0$. Good technologies are viable, while bad technologies have a negative NPV (in terms of cash flows). This implies that type B entrepreneurs must always pool with type G ones. The $t = 0$ probability that $\theta = G$ represents the entrepreneur's initial credit rating. The tension in the model comes from the fact that the entrepreneur has private benefits of control, which implies that he never wants voluntarily to liquidate the project at $t = 1$. Investors, who do not know the entrepreneur's type, receive at $t = 1$ a signal on entrepreneur type, which can either be good or bad. A bad signal induces the investor to reduce the probability that the entrepreneur is of good quality and thus represents a "downgrade" of credit rating; similarly, a good signal represents an "upgrade." After observing this signal, lenders have the option to liquidate the firm, unless the borrower is able to raise additional debt and pay off the initial short-term debt. The basic inefficiency is that lenders want to liquidate the firm at $t = 1$ too often because they do not internalize the borrower's private benefits of control.

When capital is raised at $t = 0$, the entrepreneur's project type is unknown, and hence debt is priced based on the average quality. The optimal financing mix is determined by type G entrepreneurs, since type B entrepreneurs always mimic type G ones. For type G entrepreneurs, the benefit of short-term debt, maturing at $t = 1$ when new information becomes available, is that it allows them to refinance debt at a better rate (with some probability) if they receive an upgrade. However, this comes at the risk of receiving a downgrade, forcing them to refinance at a worse rate or possibly to be liquidated. The benefit of long-term debt is that it allows the entrepreneur to lock in the interest rate at the current credit rating. The implications of the model are that issuers with either a very high or a very low initial credit rating will prefer to issue short-term debt. This is because borrowers with very low credit ratings will not be able to raise long-term debt (the promised face value is too high), while borrowers with very high credit ratings are less likely to receive a credit downgrade and therefore will want to capitalize on the arrival of new information and, thus, the possibility of a credit upgrade. When the average issuer quality is not too extreme, the optimal debt structure is to issue either long-term debt or a mix of long- and short-term debt. The optimal mix of debt maturity attempts to minimize the likelihood of early liquidation and loss of private benefits while maximizing the sensitivity of debt to the arrival of new information (via increasing short-term debt, which may be refinanced at the intermediate date).

The role of seniority is further discussed in Diamond (1993), which uses a setting similar to that of Diamond (1991). Here, the choice of seniority between long-term debt issued at $t = 0$ and short-term debt issued at $t = 1$ (after the new information becomes available) is modeled explicitly. Diamond shows that seniority can be used to increase efficiency by maximizing the sensitivity of contracts to the release of interim information while keeping the probability of liquidation at a fixed level. Debt seniority is modeled as the amount of $t = 2$ cash flow, x_2, that investors who provide long-term debt at $t = 0$ allow the entrepreneur to pledge at $t = 1$ to new investors, who provide new short-term debt. If at $t = 0$ the entrepreneur has issued long-term debt maturing at $t = 2$ with face value F_2, and if $F_{1,2}$ is the maximum face value of new short-term debt that the entrepreneur is allowed to issue at $t = 1$, then $F_{1,2} > x_2 - F_2$ means that long-term debt is junior to the new short-term debt, and $F_{1,2} < x_2 - F_2$ means that long-term debt is senior to the new short-term debt. The paper shows that the entrepreneur should be allowed to issue at $t = 1$ as much senior short-term debt as possible, that is, to set $F_{1,2} = x_2$. The intuition can be seen as follows. First, the liquidation decision at $t = 1$ is constant for any given ratio between $F_{1,2}$ and the amount of short-term debt maturing at $t = 1$, F_1. This happens because if F_1 and $F_{1,2}$ both increase by, say, a dollar, then the entrepreneur can raise an additional dollar at $t = 1$ by issuing an additional dollar of face value of new debt maturing at $t = 2$, thus not affecting the liquidation probability at $t = 1$. Second, since type B entrepreneurs offer the same contract as the type G ones, a type G entrepreneur will choose the contract that, for a given level of liquidation, maximizes the information sensitivity of the contract. This is because additional information sensitivity reduces his expected cost of financing. Maximum information sensitivity can be achieved by setting $F_{1,2}$ to its maximum value of x_2.

While Diamond (1991) shows that asymmetric information favors issuance of short-term debt, Goswani, Noe, and Rebello (1995, 1997) argue that the temporal distribution of asymmetric information may lead to a preference for long-term debt as well. In their model, entrepreneurs can be either of a good type ($\theta = G$) or a bad type ($\theta = B$), and they invest in a project with cash flows, x_t, that accrue in both $t = 1$ and $t = 2$. The type G entrepreneur has a higher probability of obtaining higher cash flows than a type B. Here again, only pooling equilibria obtain, in which the optimal debt structure is determined by the type G entrepreneurs. Unlike Diamond (1991), who shows that with no liquidation costs (i.e., loss of managerial private benefits) short-term debt is always optimal, Goswani, Noe, and Rebello demonstrate that the optimal debt maturity structure depends on the temporal pattern of information asymmetry. Specifically, when the information asymmetry regards primarily the short-term cash flow, x_1, an entrepreneur's preference for short-term or long-term debt depends on the default risk at $t=1$. In the absence of interim default risk (that is, if the short-term debt maturing at $t=1$ is fully repaid), the type G entrepreneur prefers to issue short-term debt to take advantage of the favorable reduction of information asymmetry that will result at $t=1$. If, on the contrary, the interim default risk is sufficiently large, then when there is sufficiently large asymmetry information on the short-term cash flow, x_1, the information advantage of short-term debt vanishes and the type G entrepreneur prefers to issue long-term debt. When, instead, the information asymmetry concerns primarily long-term cash flows, that is, x_2, and the degree of information symmetry increases over time, the entrepreneur prefers to issue long-term debt, maturing at $t=2$, with covenants that restrict interim dividends. In this case, the entrepreneur does not benefit from issuing short-term debt, because of the small information advantage offered when refinancing at $t=1$. Dividend constraints allow the entrepreneur to commit interim cash flow, on which there is relatively less information asymmetry, to secure the repayment of the long-term debt.

Finally, Rajan (1992) analyzes the choice of maturity structure in the context of debt that is privately placed with informed investors (such as banks). In his model, the entrepreneur exerts a noncontractible effort, after which the investor and the entrepreneur privately observe the same signal on the final payoff. Signals can be either "good," in which case the project should be continued, or "bad," in which case the project should be liquidated. Entrepreneurs benefit from project continuation and always prefer that the project be completed. If short-term debt is used, then the investor, after observing a good signal, can extract surplus from the entrepreneur by threatening not to refinance the project. Thus, short-term debt allows the investor to hold up the entrepreneur at future refinancing dates, with a negative effect on the incentives to exert effort. If long-term debt is used, then the entrepreneur, after observing a bad signal, can extract surplus from the investor by threatening to continue the project, even if it is unprofitable for the investor. Thus, long-term debt allows the entrepreneur to hold up the investor at future dates when liquidation is efficient. In anticipation of the future surplus loss to the entrepreneur, the investor will require ex ante a greater contractual interest rate, with a negative impact on the entrepreneur's incentives. Thus, the entrepreneur will choose ex ante the maturity structure of debt that gives better effort incentives.

6.3. Collateral

In many cases, the debt contract requires the entrepreneur to pledge specific assets to a specific (class of) investor(s) as collateral for the loan. The wide use of collateral in debt contracts cannot be explained if collateral simply results in a change in default risk and therefore in a reallocation of risk between the borrower and the existing lender. The main insight of the research that analyzes the costs and benefits of collateral is to show how collateral can affect either the moral-hazard and adverse-selection problem faced by the investor who lends to the entrepreneur or the moral-hazard problem faced by the entrepreneur when dealing with his investors.

One of the first papers showing the beneficial role of collateral was Stulz and Johnson (1985). This paper argues that issuing collateralized (or secured) debt can reduce the Myers (1977) underinvestment problem. As discussed in the previous section, the presence of existing debt reduces the entrepreneur's incentives to contribute further capital to the undertaking of a new investment project, because it will result in a wealth transfer to the lender. Stulz and Johnson show that the entrepreneur can reduce this wealth transfer by financing (part of) the new investment by issuing new debt collateralized by the new project's assets. Thus, the use of collateralized debt helps restore the entrepreneur's investment incentives.

Collateral is also a common feature of bank loans. Several papers show that collateral plays a key role in reducing the extent of credit rationing. Credit rationing arises in situations in which the adverse-selection or moral-hazard problem faced by investors is worsened by an increase of the loan's interest rate. This may happen, for example, because a higher interest rate induces high-quality entrepreneurs to drop from the market, leaving only the low-quality ones as potential borrowers and thereby worsening the pool of loan applicants (see Stiglitz and Weiss 1981). In these cases, investors may prefer to keep the lending interest rate to a level below the one necessary to clear markets.

Bester (1985), Besanko and Thakor (1987), and Chan and Thakor (1987) show that credit rationing may no longer occur in equilibrium when banks are allowed to compete by choosing both collateral and interest rates. These authors find that collateral can be used to separate good entrepreneurs from bad ones, thus eliminating the need to ration credit. The key argument is that when bank loan contracts can vary both the size of the collateral and the interest rate charged, then good entrepreneurs will self-select by choosing contracts with low interest rates but high collateral, while bad entrepreneurs will choose the contracts with high rates but low collateral. This happens because collateral is paid in the state in which the project fails, while interest payments are made in the state in which the project succeeds. Thus, better borrowers will prefer to post collateral in return for lower interest as a way to signal their type. This in turn improves credit allocation and market efficiency. Interestingly, Chan and Thakor (1987) show that this result depends on the type of equilibrium studied. In particular, in a competitive equilibrium in which banks earn zero profits, if all rents accrue to entrepreneurs, then the use of collateral will eliminate credit rationing. However, if all the rents accrue to depositors, then the use of collateral will still result in some rationing in equilibrium.

Collateral may also be beneficial in avoiding inefficient liquidation. Bester (1994) shows that when project returns are observed only by the entrepreneur, the threat of liquidation provides the entrepreneur with the incentive to pay the lender. If the entrepreneur does not repay the loan, the lender can either liquidate the project or renegotiate down the debt contract. This possibility, however, gives the entrepreneur the incentive to default strategically even when returns are high enough to repay the loan. Bester shows that collateral lowers the surplus the entrepreneur obtains in the renegotiation that follows a strategic default. In the mixed strategy equilibrium, collateral is used to make these strategic defaults less likely and hence to minimize the expected deadweight costs of liquidation.

The presence of collateral also has an impact on the investors' incentives. Rajan and Winton (1995) study the impact of collateral on the incentive of lenders to monitor and liquidate (if necessary) the entrepreneur's project. They show that by giving one investor (specifically, a bank) the ability to request additional collateral upon obtaining negative information, the firm can increase the bank's incentive to monitor. This feature is beneficial because other investors free-ride on banks' monitoring efforts, leading to underinvestment in monitoring. The bank's ability to request more collateral (and therefore to obtain more senior claims) increases the bank's expected returns from monitoring and therefore its incentives to monitor.

The use of collateral, however, is not always beneficial. Manove, Padilla, and Pagano (2001) analyze the effect of collateral on a bank's incentives to conduct the initial screening of potential borrowers. They argue that screening and collateral are substitutes, because higher collateral reduces a bank's exposure to default risk and thus reduces its incentives to screen. Furthermore, if screening is a value-enhancing activity, then too much collateral may have a negative impact on efficiency; hence, limitations on the use of collateral may improve credit markets' efficiency. Note that in this model, competitive banks charge the correct (fair) interest rate on average, and so they do not have an incentive to screen at the socially efficient level. However, in monopolistic credit markets, the bank is able to extract the entire surplus from the entrepreneur, and therefore it internalizes all efficiency gains from monitoring. Thus, in this case the monopolistic bank would require lower levels of collateral and engage in the socially optimal level of screening. Collateral restrictions, then, only matter for sufficiently competitive credit markets.

Finally, Habib and Johnsen (1999) take the view, as in Aghion and Bolton (1992) and Zender (1991), that debt can be used as a mechanism to redeploy assets. They model a situation in which an asset can have two uses whose value depends on the state of nature. In the good state the assets' best use is at the hands of the entrepreneur, while in the bad state the assets' best use is at the hands of the lender. When both parties need to make asset-specific investments, ex ante contracting via a secured debt solves the investment distortion problem. If debt is not secured, then ex post bargaining in the bad state leads to lower incentives for the lender to invest ex ante in identifying better redeployment opportunities. Thus, the use of collateral allows the lender to capture the entire surplus from his actions in the bad state. This arrangement, by avoiding bargaining in the state in which the lender has the best alternative use for the asset, improves the lender's incentives ex ante, thereby improving efficiency.

6.4. The Number of Creditors

In the standard static CSV framework, minimization of the verification costs implies that the entrepreneur should seek financing from the smallest possible number of investors. Increasing the number of creditors may be beneficial in the dynamic setting of Bolton and Scharfstein (1990) and Hart and Moore (1989, 1998) because it can induce the entrepreneur to make greater payment to investors. The presence of multiple investors can, in this way, effectively impose greater discipline on the entrepreneur, and it allows him to obtain financing for projects that would not be financed otherwise (thus increasing efficiency).

This possibility is examined in Bolton and Scharfstein (1996). Consider again the basic Bolton and Scharfstein (1990) setting, in which the entrepreneur's assets may be partitioned into two distinct classes (for example, two separate production facilities) and each class is pledged to a distinct investor. Assets have a greater value if employed together and if employed by the entrepreneur rather than by an external buyer. If the entrepreneur at $t = 1$ is in a liquidity default (that is, the low state is realized), he does not have the resources to pay the contractual payment to investors. In this case, investors liquidate the assets and sell them to a potential buyer. The buyer will have to pay more for the assets when they are dispersed among separate investors than when assets are concentrated in the hands of a single investor (this happens because the buyer's Shapley value is lower when he bargains with two investors). Similarly, if the entrepreneur at $t = 1$ is not liquidity constrained (that is, the high state is realized) but strategically defaults, investors will be able to extract a greater payment from the entrepreneur when assets are dispersed among several investors rather than concentrated.

Dispersing assets among several investors, therefore, has the effect of enabling investors to extract greater payments from either the entrepreneur (in the good states) or outside buyers (in the bad states). The latter possibility, however, may backfire if it reduces the likelihood that a buyer emerges (for example, because the buyer must pay some up-front costs to acquire the necessary skills to manage the assets). This implies that low-quality entrepreneurs (with a high probability of default) should seek financing from a single source (say, a bank), while high-quality entrepreneurs (with a low probability of default) should seek financing from a large number of creditors.

The benefits of obtaining financing from a large number of investors is stressed also by Dewatripont and Maskin (1995). In this case, entrepreneurs have private information on their project's quality: Good projects are completed at $t = 1$; bad projects give no payoff at $t = 1$ and are completed only at $t = 2$. The bad project's payoff may be increased by having the investor exert some effort at $t = 1$. If the entrepreneur seeks financing from only one source, the investor will exert more effort toward making the continuation of a bad project profitable. If the entrepreneur seeks financing from multiple sources, investors will be less willing to exert effort, making the continuation of a bad project unprofitable. Thus, financing from multiple investors leads to the termination of bad projects and, thus, "hardens" the entrepreneur's budget constraint and makes the entrepreneur unwilling to initiate them at $t = 0$. This implies that if bad projects are socially wasteful (that is, if they generate a negative social surplus), financing from multiple sources increases efficiency because it deters entrepreneurs endowed with bad projects from seeking financing. It also implies that a decentralized financial system, in which entrepreneurs must seek financing from several decentralized investors, may be preferable to a centralized financial system dominated by few large investors.

Seeking financing from a large number of investors does not always allow entrepreneurs to obtain a larger amount of funds. Bris and Welch (2005) argue that having a large number of investors creates a free-rider problem among them, and the ensuing moral hazard in teams (see Holmstrom 1982) reduces the investors' ability to recover a payment from entrepreneurs who are in financial distress. However, recovery requires investors to sustain dissipative collection costs and has a purely redistributive effect. Thus, seeking financing from a large number of investors is ex ante desirable, since it reduces the dissipative costs of recovery. Costly concentration of financing from a small number of investors, however, can be used by good entrepreneurs to signal their value to investors, if some precontractual asymmetric information exists.

The number of creditors is also important when financial intermediaries, such as banks, act as relationship lenders who monitor borrowers and collect private information that can be used strategically to hold up the entrepreneur (see Rajan 1992). Von Thadden (1994) shows that the presence of multiple banks can reduce their ex post ability to extract rents, thereby restoring incentives. Similarly, in Holmstrom and Tirole (1997), simultaneous financing by uninformed and informed investors (i.e., banks) reduces the surplus allocated to informed investors, allowing entrepreneurs to reduce their cost of financing. Carletti (2004) shows that the presence of multiple banks reduces their incentives to overmonitor entrepreneurs. In Detragiache, Garella, and Guiso (2000), financing through multiple banks reduces the chances that entrepreneurial projects are liquidated due to a bank's liquidity crunch. In Carletti, Cerasi, and Daltung (2006), multiple-bank lending allows banks to finance more independent projects, increasing diversification and, thus, monitoring incentives. Further discussion of the specific role of banks as investors is beyond the scope of this chapter.

7. CONCLUDING REMARKS

In this chapter we have considered the problem faced by an entrepreneur seeking to raise capital in competitive markets to finance a project. We have taken a very narrow view, examining the circumstances in which the optimal security issued by the entrepreneur has the structure of a debt contract. Our main focus has been on the role of certain specific contractual features that usually characterize debt contracts, such as seniority, maturity, and the use of collateral. While discussing the choice of seeking financing from a single investor as compared to a larger number of investors, we have deliberately ignored other important issues, such as the role of bank debt versus publicly traded debt; financial distress and the role of debt renegotiation before and during bankruptcy; the role of other contractual features, such as call and conversion options; and more complex security design issues.

References

Aghion, P., and P. Bolton. 1992. An Incomplete Contracts Approach to Financial Contracting, *Review of Economic Studies* 59(3), 473–494.

Akerlof, G. 1970. The Market for "Lemons": Quality Uncertainty and the Market Mechanism, *Quarterly Journal of Economics* 84(3), 488–500.

Allen, F., and D. Gale. 1988. Optimal Security Design, *Review of Financial Studies* 1, 229–263.

Allen, F., and D. Gale. 1992. Measurement Distortion and Missing Contingencies in Optimal Contracts, *Economic Theory* 2, 1–26.

Allen, F., and A. Winton. 1995. Corporate Finance Structure, Incentives, and Optimal Contracting, in R. Jarrow, V. Maksimovic, and W. Ziemba (eds.), *Finance*, North-Holland, Amsterdam, pp. 693–717.

Barnea, A., R. A. Haugen, and L. W. Senbet. 1980. A Rationale for Debt Maturity Structure and Call Provisions in the Agency Theoretic Framework, *Journal of Finance* 35, 1223–1234.

Berglof, E., and L. Von Thadden. 1994. Short-Term versus Long-Term Interests: A Model of Capital Structure with Multiple Investors, *Quarterly Journal of Economics* 109, 1055–1084.

Berkovitch, E., and H. Kim. 1990. Financial Contracting and Leverage-Induced Over- and Underinvestment Incentives, *Journal of Finance* 45(3), 765–794.

Besanko, D., and A. Thakor. 1987. Collateral and Rationing: Sorting Equilibria in Monopolistic and Competitive Credit Markets, *International Economic Review* 28(3), 671–689.

Bester, H. 1985. Screening versus Rationing in Credit Markets with Imperfect Information, *American Economic Review* 75(4), 850–855.

Bester, H. 1994. The Role of Collateral in a Model of Debt Renegotiation, *Journal of Money, Credit & Banking* 26, 72–86.

Biais, B., and T. Mariotti. 2005. Strategic Liquidity Supply and Security Design, *Review of Economic Studies* 72(3), 615–649.

Bolton, P., and D. S. Scharfstein. 1990. A Theory of Predation Based on Agency Problems in Financial Contracting, *American Economic Review* 80(1), 93–106.

Bolton, P., and D. S. Scharfstein. 1996. Optimal Debt Structure and the Number of Creditors, *Journal of Political Economy* 104, 1–25.

Boot, A. W. A., and A. V. Thakor. 1993. Security Design, *Journal of Finance* 48(4), 1349–1378.

Border, K. C., and J. Sobel. 1987. Samurai Accountant—A Theory of Auditing and Plunder, *Review of Economic Studies* 54(4), 525–540.

Boyd, J. H., and B. D. Smith. 1994. How Good Are Standard Debt Contracts? Stochastic versus Nonstochastic Monitoring in a Costly State Verification Environment, *Journal of Business* 67(4), 539–561.

Boyd, J. H., and B. D. Smith. 1999. The Use of Debt and Equity in Optimal Financial Contracts, *Journal of Financial Intermediation* 8(4), 270–316.

Bris, A., and I. Welch. 2005. The Optimal Concentration of Creditors (April 2004), *Yale ICF Working Paper No. 00-65; Cowles Foundation Discussion Paper No. 1338*.

Carletti, E. 2004. The Structure of Relationship Lending, Endogenous Monitoring and Loan Rates, *Journal of Financial Intermediation* 13, 58–86.

Carletti, E., V. Cerasi, and S. Daltung. 2006. Multiple-Bank Lending: Diversification and Free-Riding Monitoring. Working paper, CFS, University of Frankfurt.

Chan, Y. S., and A. Thakor. 1987. Collateral and Competitive Equilibria with Moral Hazard and Private Information, *Journal of Finance* 42, 345–364.

Chang, C. 1990. The Dynamic Structure of Optimal Debt Contracts, *Journal of Economic Theory* 52(1), 68–86.

Chang, C. 2005. Dynamic Costly State Verification, *Economic Theory* 25, 887–916.

Chiesa, G. 1992. Debt and Warrants: Agency Problems and Mechanism Design, *Journal of Financial Intermediation* 2, 237–254.

DeMarzo, P. 2005. The Pooling and Tranching of Securities: A Model of Informed Intermediation, *Review of Financial Studies* 18(1), 1–35.

DeMarzo, P., and D. Duffie. 1999. A Liquidity-Based Model of Security Design, *Econometrica* 67(1), 65–99.

DeMarzo, P., and M. Fishman. 2006. Optimal Long-Term Financial Contracting, Forthcoming, *Review of Financial Studies*.

DeMarzo, P., and Y. Sannikov. 2006. Optimal Security Design and Dynamic Capital Structure in a Continuous-Time Agency Model, *Journal of Finance* 61(6), 2681–2724.

Detragiache, E., P. Garella, and L. Guiso. 2000. Multiple versus Single Banking Relationships: Theory and Evidence, *Journal of Finance* 55, 1133–1161.

Dewatripont, M., and E. Maskin. 1995. Credit and Efficiency in Centralized and Decentralized Economies, *Review of Economic Studies* 62, 541–555.

Diamond, D. 1984. Financial Intermediation and Delegated Monitoring, *Review of Economic Studies* 51(3), 393–414.

Diamond, D. 1991. Debt Maturity Structure and Liquidity Risk, *Quarterly Journal of Economics* 106(3), 709–737.

Diamond, D. 1993. Seniority and Maturity of Debt Contracts, *Journal of Financial Economics* 33(3), 341–368.

Flannery, M. 1986. Asymmetric Information and Risky Debt Maturity Choice, *Journal of Finance* 41(1), 19–37.

Fluck, Z. 1998. Optimal Financial Contracting: Debt versus Outside Equity, *Review of Financial Studies* 11(2), 383–419.

Fluck, Z. 1999. The Dynamics of the Management–Shareholder Conflict, *Review of Financial Studies* 12, 379–404.

Fulghieri, P., and D. Lukin. 2001. Information Production, Dilution Costs, and Optimal Security Design, *Journal of Financial Economics* 61(1), 3–42.

Galai, D., and R. Masulis. 1976. The Option Pricing Model and the Risk Factor of Stock, *Journal of Financial Economics* 3(1), 53–81.

Gale, D. 1991. Optimal Risk Sharing through Renegotiation of Simple Contracts, *Journal of Financial Intermediation* 1(4), 283–306.

Gale, D., and M. Hellwig. 1985. Incentive-Compatible Debt Contracts—The One-Period Problem, *Review of Economic Studies* 52(4), 647–663.

Goldman, E. 2005. Organizational Form, Information Collection, and the Value of the Firm, *Journal of Business* 78(3), 817–840.

Goswami, G., T. Noe, and M. Rebello. 1995. Debt Financing under Asymmetric Information, *Journal of Finance* 50, 633–659.

Goswami, G., T. Noe, and M. Rebello. 1997. Cash Flows and Debt Maturity, *Economica* 64, 303–316.

Habib, M., and B. Johnsen. 1999. The Financing and Redeployment of Specific Assets, *Journal of Finance* 54(2), 693–720.

Harris, M., and A. Raviv. 1979. Optimal Incentive Contracts with Imperfect Information, *Journal of Economic Theory* 20, 231–259.

Harris, M., and A. Raviv. 1991. The Theory of Capital Structure, *Journal of Finance* 46, 297–355.

Harris, M., and A. Raviv. 1992. Financial Contracting Theory, in J. J. Laffont (ed.), *Advances in Economic Theory*, Vol. 1, Cambridge University Press, Cambridge.

Harris, M., and A. Raviv. 1995. The Role of Games in Security Design, *Review of Financial Studies* 8(2), 327–367.

Harris, M., and R. M. Townsend. 1981. Resource Allocation under Asymmetric Information, *Econometrica* 49(1), 33–64.

Hart, O., and J. Moore. 1989. Default and Renegotiation: A Dynamic Model of Debt, *MIT working paper No. 520*; revised as University of Edinburgh Discussion paper, August 1989.

Hart, O., and J. Moore. 1994. A Theory of Debt Based on the Inalienability of Human Capital, *Quarterly Journal of Economics* 109(4), 841–879.

Hart, O., and J. Moore. 1995. Debt and Seniority: An Analysis of the Role of Hard Claims in Constraining Management, *American Economic Review* 85(3), 567–585.

Hart, O., and J. Moore. 1998. Default and Renegotiation: A Dynamic Model of Debt, *Quarterly Journal of Economics* 113(1), 1–41.

Holmstrom, B. 1979. Moral Hazard and Observability, *Bell Journal of Economics* 10, 74–91.

Holmstrom, B. 1982. Moral Hazard in Teams, *Bell Journal of Economics* 13, 324–340.

Holmstrom, B., and R. B. Myerson. 1983. Efficient and Durable Decision Rules with Incomplete Information, *Econometrica* 51(6), 1799–1819.

Holmstrom, B., and J. Tirole. 1997. Financial Intermediation, Loanable Funds, and the Real Sector, *Quarterly Journal of Economics* 112, 663–691.

Houston, J., and S. Venkataraman. 1994. Optimal Maturity Structure with Multiple Debt Claims, *Journal of Financial and Quantitative Analysis* 29, 179–197.

Inderst, R., and H. Mueller. 2006a. Informed Lending and Optimal Security Design, *Journal of Finance* 61, 2137–2162.

Inderst, R., and H. Mueller. 2006b. A Lender-Based Theory of Collateral, Forthcoming, *Journal of Financial Economics*.

Innes, R. D. 1990. Limited-Liability and Incentive Contracting with Ex-Ante Action Choices, *Journal of Economic Theory* 52(1), 45–67.

Jensen, M. C., and W. H. Meckling. 1976. Theory of the Firm: Managerial Behavior, Agency Costs and Ownership Structure, *Journal of Financial Economics* 3, 303–360.

Kalay, A., and J. Zender. 1997. Bankruptcy, Warrants, and State-Contingent Changes in the Ownership of Control, *Journal of Financial Intermediation* 6, 347–379.

Krasa, S., and A. Villamil. 1994. Optimal Multilateral Contracts, *Economic Theory* 4, 167–187.

Leland, H., and Pyle, D. 1977. Informational Asymmetries, Financial Structure, and Financial Intermediation, *Journal of Finance* 32(2), 371–387.

Manove, M., J. Padilla, and M. Pagano. 2001. Collateral versus Project Screening: A Model of Lazy Banks, *RAND Journal of Economics* 32(4), 726–744.

Matthews, S. 2001. Renegotiating Moral Hazard Contracts under Limited Liability and Monotonicity, *Journal of Economic Theory* 97, 1–29.

Milgrom, P. 1981. Good News and Bad News: Representation Theorems and Applications, *Bell Journal of Economics* 13, 380–391.

Modigliani, F., and M. Miller. 1958. The Cost of Capital, Corporate Finance, and the Theory of Investment, *American Economic Review* 48(3), 261–297.

Mookherjee, D., and I. Png. 1989. Optimal Auditing, Insurance, and Redistribution, *Quarterly Journal of Economics* 104(2), 399–415.

Myers, S. C. 1977. Determinants of Corporate Borrowing, *Journal of Financial Economics* 5, 147–176.

Myers, S. C. 1984. The Capital Structure Puzzle, *Journal of Finance* 39(3), 575–592.

Myers, S. C. 2000. Outside Equity, *Journal of Finance* 55(3), 1005–1037.

Myers, S. C., and N. S. Majluf. 1984. Corporate Financing and Investment Decisions When Firms Have Information That Investors Do Not Have, *Journal of Financial Economics* 13(2), 187–221.

Myerson, R. 1979. Incentive Compatibility and the Bargaining Problem, *Econometrica* 47, 61–73.

Nachman, D. C., and T. H. Noe. 1994. Optimal Design of Securities under Asymmetric Information, *Review of Financial Studies* 7(1), 1–44.

Narayanan, M. P. 1988. Debt versus Equity under Asymmetric Information, *Journal of Financial and Quantitative Analysis* 23(1), 39–51.

Noe, T. 1988. Capital Structure and Signaling Game Equilibria, *Review of Financial Studies* 1(4), 321–355.

Park, C. 2000. Monitoring and Structure of Debt Contracts, *Journal of Finance* 55(5), 2157–2195.

Povel, P., and M. Raith. 2004. Optimal Debt with Unobservable Investments, *RAND Journal of Economics* 35(3), 599–616.

Rajan, R. 1992. Insiders and Outsiders: The Choice between Informed and Arm's-Length Debt, *Journal of Finance* 47(4), 1367–1400.

Rajan, R., and A. Winton. 1995. Covenants and Collateral as Incentives to Monitor, *Journal of Finance* 50, 1113–1146.

Ravid, S. A., and M. Spiegel. 1997. Optimal Financial Contracts for a Start-up with Unlimited Operating Discretion, *Journal of Financial and Quantitative Analysis* 32(3), 269–286.

Rock, K. 1986. Why New Issues Are Underpriced, *Journal of Financial Economics* 15(1–2), 187–212.

Sannikov, Y. 2006. Agency Problems, Screening and Increasing Credit Lines. Working paper, University of California at Berkeley.

Shavell, S. 1979. Risk Sharing and Incentives in the Principal and Agent Relationship, *Bell Journal of Economics* 10(1), 55–73.

Stiglitz, J., and L. Weiss. 1981. Credit Rationing in Markets with Imperfect Information, *American Economic Review* 71, 393–410.

Stulz, R., and H. Johnson. 1985. An Analysis of Secured Debt, *Journal of Financial and Quantitative Analysis* 14, 501–521.

Townsend, R. M. 1979. Optimal Contracts and Competitive Markets with Costly State Verification, *Journal of Economic Theory* 21, 265–293.

Von Thadden, L. 1994. The Commitment of Finance, Duplicated Monitoring, and the Investment Horizon. Unpublished manuscript, University of Basel.

Welch, I. 1997. Why Is Bank Debt Senior? A Theory of Asymmetry and Claim Priority Based on Influence Costs, *Review of Financial Studies* 10(4), 1203–1236.

Winton, A. 1995. Costly State Verification and Multiple Investors: The Role of Seniority, *Review of Financial Studies* 8(1), 91–123.

Zender, J. 1991. Optimal Financial Instruments, *Journal of Finance* 46(5), 1645.

CHAPTER 2

Subordination Levels in Structured Financing

Xudong An
Department of Finance, College of Business Administration, San Diego State University.

Yongheng Deng
Lusk Center for Real Estate, School of Policy, Planning, and Development, University of Southern California.

Anthony B. Sanders
W.P. Carey College of Business, Arizona State University.

The authors are grateful for helpful comments from Franklin Allen, Mark Flannery, Dwight Jaffee, Tim Riddiough, and Sally Gordon.

Abstract

Duffie and DeMarzo (1999), DeMarzo (2005), and Riddiough (1997) discuss the design of asset-backed securities, particularly the senior-subordinated structure that is commonly used with mortgage-backed securities. The advantage for the creation of a low-risk security in a senior-subordinated structure is that it would help solve the asymmetric information problem between the financial intermediary and investors. However, these papers do not provide empirical support for the types and characteristics of assets (loans) that would help solve the asymmetric information problem.

The critical determinant for creating a low-risk security in a senior-subordinated structure is the subordination level. Subordination levels determine the amount of credit support that the senior bonds (or tranches) require from the subordinated bonds (or tranches) and are provided by the financial intermediaries and rating agencies. Thus, both the financial intermediaries and ratings agencies play an important role in the pricing and risk management of structured finance products.

In order to determine the nature of the assets that are required to create a low-risk security in a senior-subordinated structure, we perform a deal level analysis using commercial mortgage-backed securities (CMBS). We find that debt service coverage ratio (DSCR), a commonly used measure of default risk, is a very important variable in subordination design. In addition, measures of property type and prepayment protection are found to be important as well. Furthermore, we find that the property type and prepayment protection change in terms of importance over time.

1. INTRODUCTION

The structured finance market has grown rapidly during the past two decades.[1] An attractive feature of structured finance to investors is the senior-subordinated debt structure, where cash flows from the underlying loan pool are allocated to various tranches of securities (bonds) according to certain rules. Typically, prepayments of principal are often distributed first to the senior tranches, while losses due to default are allocated first to the subordinated tranches. Therefore, investors buying senior tranches expect to be well protected from credit risks, while those holding subordinated tranches will get higher expected returns. This senior-subordinated structure allows the financial intermediary to create a low-risk security that can potentially overcome the asymmetric information problem between the issuer and the investor.

In this senior-subordinated structure, bond subordination levels are key variables because they determine how much credit support senior tranches have from the subordinated tranches. Subordination levels are determined, in part, by critical ex ante measures of default. A stylized fact about subordination levels is that there exists a time series trend showing subordination levels declining systematically over time for one type of

[1]For example, CMBS annual issuance in the United States grew from less than $1 billion in 1985 to $169 billion in 2005. CMBS outstanding at the end of 2005 reached $550 billion, which accounts for about 21 percent of the $2.6 trillion commercial mortgages outstanding.

structured financing: commercial mortgage-backed securities (CMBS). While papers such as DeMarzo and Duffie (1999), DeMarzo (2005), and Riddiough (1997) discuss the advantages for the creation of a low-risk security in a senior-subordinated structure, they do not provide empirical support for the types and characteristics of assets (loans) that would help solve the asymmetric-information problem.

In this chapter, we provide empirical support for the types and characteristics of assets (loans) that allow the financial intermediary to create a low-risk security in a senior-subordinated structure. Using cross-sectional tests of subordination levels in CMBS deals, we examine how AAA (low-risk) and BBB (higher-risk) bond subordination levels can be explained by both credit and noncredit variables at the deal level. We pay special attention to the roles of the original LTV and the original DSCR, while existing literature suggests neither will be a good credit risk predictor for commercial mortgages. Second, we examine whether subordination levels change over time and identify the fundamental drivers of the changes in subordination.

In Section 2, we introduce structured finance and the pooling and tranching of assets. In Section 3, we briefly summarize the mechanism of CMBS structure and subordination. Section 4 explains our research questions and empirical approach. Sections 4 and 5 describe the data and model results. Concluding remarks are in the final section.

2. STRUCTURED FINANCING AND THE POOLING AND TRANCHING OF ASSETS

Structured financing has revolutionalized the debt and capital markets. By pooling and tranching financial promises, the structured financing process permits the separation of securities, with differing seniority corresponding to different risk and characteristics. Furthermore, it permits the delinking of the credit risk of the underlying assets from the credit risk of originators. Allen and Gale (1988), Boot and Thakor (1993), and DeMarzo and Duffie (1999) provide thorough analyses of these new innovations and develop theoretical models of optimal security design based on capital structure and a general equilibrium framework.

Consider a financial intermediary faced with the decision to sell individual assets or to pool the assets and sell the pool. The financial intermediary has an informational advantage over the investor purchasing the individual asset or pool. Since the financial intermediary has superior information about the asset, there exists a "lemons problem," where the investor has difficulty distinguishing the good assets from the bad assets for sale. In an attempt to solve this asymmetric-information problem, Leland and Pyle (1977) and DeMarzo and Duffie (1999) developed signaling models of the sale, where the financial intermediary (issuer) signals a high-value security retaining a portion of the issue. Winton (1995, 2003) extended DeMarzo and Duffie (1999) by allowing endogenous institutional liquidity needs and accounting for the effect of monitoring costs in the optimal security design. DeMarzo (2005) shows that pooling of the individual assets prior to sale is not advantageous to an informed intermediary because pooling of the assets can destroy the asset-specific information held by the intermediary. By eliminating the intermediary's potential to sell individual assets aggressively, this information-destruction effect reduces the payoff to the intermediary.

DeMarzo (2005) shows that, rather than simply pooling assets for sale, the optimal security to issue is a debt security backed by the asset pool. If there is a beneficial risk-diversification effect of pooling, the intermediary can issue a low-risk debt security from a large pool as well as a higher-risk debt security. The low-risk debt security is less sensitive to the intermediary's private information; hence, it is more liquid. DeMarzo (2005) also shows that as the size of the pool grows large, the risk-diversification effect dominates the information-destruction effect. The result is that pooling and tranching are optimal for the intermediary.[2]

Another strand of literature related to this topic focused on the structure and the effectiveness of the financial intermediaries (DeLong 1991) and the monitoring process in structured finance (Thakor 1982, Diamond 1984, Ramakrishnan and Thakor 1984). In the CMBS market (as well as in other credit derivative securities markets), rating agencies have played an important role in monitoring and certifying the credit risks associated with different tranches of the securities. It is worth noting that rating agencies provide credit rating matrices to reflect their opinion of the ability of a security issue to meet its financial commitments on a timely basis. However, credit rating does not measure other risks in the CMBS markets, such as market risk, the risk of loss in market value due to interest rates, as well as the security's potential for price appreciation. So the rating agencies' role in the structured finance market is not to provide credit risk management; rather, they function as financial monitors or certifiers. Weinstein (1977), Gorton and Pennacchi (1990), and Thompson and Vaz (1990) examine the function and effectiveness of intermediaries and rating agencies in structured finance.

3. CMBS STRUCTURE

Commercial mortgage-backed securities are an example of a structured finance product where assets are pooled and tranched. Commercial mortgages are pooled together by CMBS issuers, and several tranches of securities are created and sold to investors.[3] The actual CMBS market is more complex than typically portrayed in the aforementioned studies and includes entities with special expertise, such as lender/loan seller, loan underwriter, CMBS issuer, CMBS underwriter, master servicer, special servicer, and rating agency.[4] These additional entities serve to manage risk more effectively.

[2] Other papers that examine the securitization process include Glaeser and Kallal (1997) and Riddiough (1997).

[3] While DeMarzo (2005) and others discuss the inclusion of lenders in the process, this does not add anything to our discussion.

[4] In order to reduce problems related to fraud and negligence in underwriting, the deals contain representations and warranties protecting investors.

The average CMBS deal has over $1 billion in underlying assets (commercial mortgage loans), and the average number of commercial mortgage loans in a deal pool is 150. The average commercial mortgage loan size is $7.4 million. A typical CMBS is formed when an issuer deposits commercial mortgage loans into a trust.[5] The issuer then creates a series of tranches (bonds) backed by the loans and creates the senior-subordinated debt structure. The tranches have varying credit qualities, from AAA and AA (senior tranche) to BB and B (subordinated) and to unrated (first loss),[6] given that any return of principal generated by amortization, prepayment, and default is allocated to the highest-rated tranche first and then to the lower-rated tranches, while any losses that arise from a loan default is charged against the principal balance of the lowest-rated tranche outstanding (first loss piece).[7] Any interest received from outstanding principal is paid to all tranches.[8]

3.1. CMBS Subordination

For each CMBS tranche, the subordination level is defined as the proportion of principal outstanding of other tranches with lower rating. It reflects "credit support" of that tranche. Rating agencies play a key role in determining subordination levels at deal cut-off. Typically, the CMBS issuer proposes a debt structure, and the rating agencies work independently to examine whether the proposed structure can ensure that the tranches reach certain ratings, such as AAA, AA, A, and BBB. If not, rating agencies usually suggest that the issuer remove certain loans from the pool or change the amount of tranches in order to assign specific ratings to the tranches.[9] CMBS investors rely on the quality certification given by rating agencies and ascertain credit quality differences between different tranches based mainly on their ratings.[10]

Each rating agency has its own internal model for determining subordination levels. However, the general framework is approximately the same. Rating agencies perform three levels of analysis:

1. On the property level, based on the commercial mortgage loan underwriters' cash flow report, rating agencies adjust the property net operating income (NOI) based on their own judgments of whether the number in underwriting report is sustainable given current market conditions, and they deduct capital items such

[5] The loans could be bought from traditional lenders or portfolio holders or from conduit loan originators.

[6] Many CMBS deals also have an interest only (IO) tranche, which absorbs excess interest payment.

[7] This type of structure is often referred to as the *reverse waterfall* structure.

[8] It is noteworthy that many CMBS deals vary from this simple structure. For more information, see Sanders (1999) and Wheeler (2001). For other issues, such as commercial mortgage underwriting, form of the trust, servicing, and commercial loan evaluation, see Sanders (1999), Geltner and Miller (2001), and Wheeler (2001).

[9] Usually two or more rating agencies are invited to rate CMBS, and the proposing-revision process for subordination goes recursively. Moody's, Standard and Poor's, and Fitch are three current major CMBS rating agencies.

[10] Rating agencies also monitor each CMBS bond after its issuance; and as in the corporate bond market, they upgrade or downgrade bonds according to the change in the CMBS pool performance.

as capital reserves, tenant improvement, and leasing commissions to form the so called net cash flow (NCF). Rating agencies then calculate property values using their own capitalization rates, which could be different from the current market capitalization rate.[11] Rating agencies then calculate their "stressed" LTV and DSCR for each loan and feed their stressed LTVs and DSCRs into a loss matrix to form the basic credit support assessments.

2. On the loan level, rating agencies look at borrower quality, amortization, cash management, and cross- and overcollateralization to adjust their basic credit support assessments. After doing this, rating agencies aggregate their analysis into the pool level and assign subordination to each proposed CMBS tranches.[12]
3. Finally, rating agencies perform portfolio-level analysis, which examines pool diversity, information quality, and legal and structural issues and makes any final adjustments to the subordination levels for each CMBS bond.

It is noteworthy that there is no standard for subordination design. Each rating agency "learns by doing" as the industry develops (Riddiough 2004). An interesting fact about subordination is that subordination levels have declined systematically since 1997. Researchers argue that this decline is the result of rating agencies' being overly conservative at the beginning of the CMBS market development; and when the ratings agencies develop a greater familiarity with the product and the market, they apply less stringent subordination criteria (Sanders 1999, Geltner and Miller 2001, Wheeler 2001, and Downing and Wallace 2005).

4. RESEARCH QUESTION AND EMPIRICAL APPROACH

DeMarzo (2005) argues that if there is a beneficial risk-diversification effect of pooling, the intermediary can issue a low-risk debt security from a large pool as well as a higher-risk debt security. The low-risk debt security is less sensitive to the intermediary's private information and, as a result, is more liquid. But how does the financial intermediary (in conjunction with the ratings agencies) determine the subordination required to create a low-risk (AAA) security? Stated differently, what subordination level is sufficient to convince investors that the security is less sensitive to the intermediary's private information?

The first question we want to address is the characteristics the financial intermediary and rating agency find compelling to reduce investor losses on the low-risk security. A parallel question concerning CMBS subordination design is whether cross-sectional differentials in subordination reflect differences in credit risks of CMBS pools.

[11] For example, Moody's uses a stabilized cap rate to try to achieve a "through-the-cycle" property value.

[12] Although rating agencies perform property and loan analysis mainly on an individual basis, they sometimes review only a random sample (40–60 percent) of the loans when the number of mortgages in the pool is large, the pool was originated with uniform underwriting standards, and the distribution of the loan balance is not widely skewed.

CMBS bond subordination should reflect the bond lifetime CMBS pool expected loss. Although rating agencies try to incorporate the analysis of future market trends into the subordination design, predicting CMBS deals' potential loss over the long term precisely is a challenging task. For example, an increasing number of studies has shown that it is the contemporaneous loan-to-value ratio (LTV) and debt-service-coverage ratio (DSCR), rather than the original LTV and DSCR, that determines commercial mortgage default risk[13] (e.g., Archer et al. 2001, Ambrose and Sanders 2003, Ciochetti et al. 2002, and Deng, Quigley, and Sanders 2005). Although rating agencies have been trying other static variables very different from the original LTV and DSCR,[14] concerns have arisen about the accuracy of using some "one-shot" static control variables in the long-term prediction.

4.1. The Deal Subordination Regression

In order to address this concern, we propose an empirical test based on a deal level. In this deal-level analysis, we examine how AAA and BBB bond subordination levels are related to deal-level credit and noncredit variables. Following linear regression model is estimated based on observations measured at deal-cutoff point:

$$S_i = \alpha + X_i\beta + \varepsilon_i, \quad i = 1, \ldots, n, \tag{1}$$

where S_i is the AAA/BBB subordination level of deal i, X_i is a vector of deal credit and noncredit variables, including DSCR, overcollateralization, property type composition, prepayment constraints, and loan size concentration measures, and ε_i is the normally distributed disturbance.

We pay special attention to the roles of the original LTV and original DSCR. Due to the reasons discussed earlier, we expect these two factors to be insignificant on AAA and BBB subordination. We also include deal-cutoff dummies to measure how the subordination levels and their determinants vary over time. By estimating this model, we can infer what kind of factors explain the cross-sectional variations in subordination.

4.2. The Chow Test for Structural Change

To capture the potential shift in subordination levels in contracts over time due to the empirical observation that CMBS issuers and rating agencies tend to be conservative in the early stage of CMBS market development and are becoming less stringent with

[13]It is argued that the original LTV and DSCR might be endogenous to commercial mortgage default risk, e.g., because commercial mortgage loan origination is a negotiation process, when a lender/originator perceives that a commercial mortgage has higher risk than usual, one important instrument he would use is to adjust the amount of loan he issues, which results in a lower LTV and higher DSCR.

[14]Some rating agencies use their own stressed LTV and DSCR, which may be very different from the original LTV and DSCR used here.

subordination design,[15] we also run a model with time trend:

$$S_i = \alpha + X_i\beta + D_i\gamma + \varepsilon_i, \quad i = 1, \ldots, n, \tag{2}$$

where D_i is a set of dummy variables for the cutoff year.

However, model 2 implies a restriction that rating agencies will use constant weights in their credit rating matrices when the market is changing over time. Given the existing literature on credit rating agencies' "learning by doing" behavior (Sanders 1999, Geltner and Miller 2001, Riddiough 2004, and Downing and Wallace 2005), such a restriction is highly unrealistic. To test the "learning by doing" hypothesis, we follow the standard Chow test procedure to test potential structural change during our sampling period (Greene 2003). Basically we perform F-tests on the constraint model and the unconstraint model. The test statistics are:

$$F(J, n_1 + n_2 - 2k) = \frac{\left(e^{*\prime}e^* - e^{1\prime}e^1 - e^{2\prime}e^2\right)/J}{\left(e^{1\prime}e^1 + e^{2\prime}e^2\right)/(n_1 + n_2 - 2k)}, \tag{3}$$

where e^* is the residual vector from the constraint model, e^1 and e^2 are residual vectors from the unconstraint models based on the prestructural change and poststructural change subsamples, J is the number of constraints, n_1 and n_2 are the numbers of observations in the prestructural change and poststructural change subsamples, and k is the number of explanatory variables in the unconstraint models.

5. DATA

We construct a dataset on CMBS deals based on information collected from CMBS.com.[16] The raw database contains 718 CMBS deals, and it covers virtually all CMBS deals made in the United States during the period 1995 to early 2005. The data-collection point is April 1, 2005. For each deal, we have detailed information on deal characteristics, such as cutoff date, balance, LTV, DSCR, AAA and BBB subordinations, and property type composition. Current (data-collecting point) values of LTV, DSCR, balance, and AAA and BBB subordinations are also recorded.

We focus on conduit deals and those deals with all fixed-rate loans underlying the pools. Conduit deals are those deals with underlying commercial mortgage loans originated for the sole purpose of securitization.[17] Conduit deals usually have more uniform underwriting standards than other deals, such as portfolio deals and single-borrower deals. Our final sample contains 350 observations, which is 48.75 percent of the raw sample.

[15]See Sanders (1999), Geltner and Miller (2001), Riddiough (2004), and Downing and Wallace (2005) for a discussion.

[16]The company was sold to Standard & Poor's first and later to Backshop.

[17]In contrast, another important type of deal, the portfolio deal, has underlying loans originally held in whole-loan form by lenders or other investors and then sold to CMBS issuers.

TABLE 1 Cutoff Year Distribution of the CMBS Conduit Deals in Our Sample

Year	Frequency	Percentage	Percentage of all deals in the year
1995	2	0.57	6.67
1996	10	2.86	19.61
1997	24	6.86	41.38
1998	35	10.00	47.95
1999	37	10.57	44.58
2000	30	8.57	44.78
2001	40	11.43	66.67
2002	38	10.86	63.33
2003	56	16.00	62.92
2004	62	17.71	63.27
2005	16	4.57	76.19
Total	350	100	

All data are from CMBS.com. The data-collection date was April 1, 2005. The 350 deals are conduit deals with all fixed-rate loans underlying them.

Table 1 shows the cutoff year distribution of these 350 conduit deals. In 1995, only two deals are in our sample, while 2004 has 62 deals. Table 1 also shows the percentage of conduit deals of all deals in each year. It shows an increasing popularity of conduit deals over time.

Table 2 reports the descriptive statistics of the 350 deals. On average, 150 commercial mortgage loans underly each deal. The minimum number of loans underlying the deal is 28, and some deals have hundreds of loans underlying them. CMBS deals are huge, with an average cutoff balance of $1.110 billion. The largest deal has a cutoff of $3.723 billion. AAA subordination levels range from 9 percent to 37 percent, and BBB subordination levels range from 0 percent to 17 percent. The average AAA subordination level is 21 percent. The weighted-average LTVs at cutoff are between 43 percent and 77 percent, which reflects much lower LTVs of commercial mortgage loans than those of residential loans. The mean cutoff debt service coverage ratio is 1.57. CMBS.com also reports the estimated LTV at maturity of each deal, which is a proxy for balloon risk. The average estimated LTV at maturity is 57 percent. On average, about 2 percent of loans have overcollateralization. CMBS loans are of various property types. Usually a deal contains different property type loans. The property type composition is shown in Table 2. Most CMBS loans have prepayment constraints, such as yield maintenance, lockout, and defeasance. The coverage measures shown in Table 2 are calculated as the weighted-average mortgage term (in months) covered by lockout, yield maintenance, and defeasance. Early originated commercial mortgage loans

TABLE 2 Descriptive Statistics of Our Sample Deals

Variable	Mean	Std Dev.	Minimum	Maximum
Number of assets at cutoff	150	78	28	664
Deal cutoff balance (000s)	1,110,103	514,808	77,962	3,722,686
AAA subordination	0.21	0.06	0.09	0.37
BBB subordination	0.07	0.04	0.00	0.17
Cutoff LTV	0.68	0.04	0.43	0.77
Cutoff DSCR	1.57	0.25	0.92	3.13
Estimated LTV at maturity	0.57	0.08	0.22	1.54
Overcollateralization	0.02	0.08	0.00	0.83
Share of multifamily loans (in $)	0.21	0.12	0.00	1.00
Share of retail, anchored loans	0.26	0.13	0.00	0.64
Share of retail, unanchored loans	0.07	0.08	0.00	0.65
Share of office loans	0.24	0.12	0.00	0.59
Share of industrial loans	0.08	0.05	0.00	0.32
Share of health care loans	0.01	0.05	0.00	0.82
Share of full-service hotel loans	0.03	0.04	0.00	0.18
Share of limited-service hotel loans	0.03	0.05	0.00	0.39
Share of self-storage space loans	0.02	0.03	0.00	0.27
Share of mixed-use property loans	0.03	0.04	0.00	0.31
Share of mobile home loans	0.03	0.03	0.00	0.19
Share of warehouse loans	0.01	0.02	0.00	0.19
Share of other property loans	0.00	0.01	0.00	0.09
Share of amount of the largest loan	0.09	0.06	0.02	0.40
Share of amount of the five largest loans	0.27	0.10	0.09	0.66
Yield maintenance coverage	0.58	0.23	0.05	0.96
Lockout coverage	0.28	0.24	0.00	0.91
Defeasance coverage	0.51	0.26	0.00	0.94
Number of deals	350			

Cutoff LTV and cutoff DSCR are from the CMBS.com database, which are calculated as a weighted average of loan LTV and DSCR of all loans in each specific CMBS pool at cutoff. Estimated LTV at maturity, also from CMBS.com, is a proxy measure of balloon risk.

usually have lockout terms, which cover 28 percent of the sample months. Since 2003, defeasance has become a very popular form of prepayment constraint, which covers over 50 percent of our sample months. In fact, some investors regard defeasance as a way to get around prepayment constraint, since it allows the borrower to refinance the loan as long as Treasury securities are used to replace the underlying property as collateral.

6. RESULTS

6.1. Regression Results

Table 3 reports regression results of both AAA and BBB subordination levels. Since credit risk is the most important concern of CMBS investments, and rating agencies are reported to pay special attention to DSCR, we first run the simple models that include only DSCR and an intercept as explanatory variables (model 1).[18] The results show that DSCR is indeed a very important variable in subordination design. It is negatively related to both AAA and BBB subordination levels, and it has substantial explanatory power of subordination levels. Variation in DSCR explains about 30 percent of variations in both AAA and BBB subordination levels.

In the more complicated model, we add a number of variables. For example, we add estimated LTV at maturity as a measure of balloon risk; we add property composition variables; we also include prepayment constraint variables. Most of the relationships seen from the estimates conform to expectation; e.g., the higher the percentage of retail, anchored loans, the lower the subordination levels are (multifamily loan share is omitted as a reference), and the higher the percentage of self-storage loans, the higher the subordination levels are. In addition, yield maintenance coverage is negatively related to subordination levels, because it mitigates prepayment risk. In contrast, defeasance coverage is significant and positive, possibly because defeasance gives the borrower the option to refinance and thus introduces refinance risk to CMBS investors. There

TABLE 3 Estimates of the CMBS Deal Subordination Models[a]

	AAA subordination		BBB subordination	
	Model 1	Model 2	Model 1	Model 2
Intercept	0.436*** (0.018)	0.431*** (0.018)	0.198*** (0.011)	0.188*** (0.014)
Cutoff DSCR	−0.145*** (0.012)	−0.034*** (0.006)	−0.081*** (0.007)	−0.021*** (0.005)
Estimated LTV at Maturity		0.029 (0.018)		0.001 (0.014)
Overcollateralization		0.016 (0.02)		0.022 (0.016)
Share of retail, anchored loans		−0.072*** (0.016)		−0.009 (0.012)
Share of retail, unanchored loans		−0.028 (0.022)		−0.001 (0.017)

Continued

[18]We don't include the cutoff LTV in our model because it is highly correlated with DSCR.

TABLE 3 *Continued*

	AAA subordination		BBB subordination	
	Model 1	Model 2	Model 1	Model 2
Share of office loans		−0.051**		−0.020
		(0.016)		(0.012)
Share of industrial loans		−0.214***		−0.033
		(0.032)		(0.024)
Share of health care loans		0.012		0.045*
		(0.028)		(0.021)
Share of full-service hotel loans		0.022		0.000
		(0.037)		(0.028)
Share of limited-service hotel loans		0.034		0.105***
		(0.033)		(0.025)
Share of self-storage property loans		0.109*		0.051
		(0.054)		(0.042)
Share of mixed-use property loans		−0.028		−0.012
		(0.032)		(0.025)
Share of mobile home loans		0.000		−0.034
		(0.042)		(0.032)
Share of warehouse loans		−0.151*		−0.092
		(0.066)		(0.051)
Share of other loans		0.244*		0.004
		(0.11)		(0.085)
The largest loan weights over 15 percent		0.001		−0.004
		(0.005)		(0.004)
Share of top five loans		−0.074***		−0.064***
		(0.02)		(0.015)
Yield maintenance coverage		−0.279***		−0.160***
		(0.022)		(0.017)
Lockout coverage		−0.002		−0.003
		(0.006)		(0.005)
Defeasance coverage		0.085***		0.067***
		(0.02)		(0.015)
N	350	350	350	350
Adjusted *R*-square	0.3079	0.8707	0.2962	0.7622

[a]Dependent variable: AAA/BBB subordination at cutoff.
These are OLS estimates. Standard errors are in parentheses.
* $p < 0.05$; ** $p < 0.01$; *** $p < 0.001$.
We exclude from the regressions some deal-level information, such as cutoff LTV, number of loans, and cutoff balance, because of the multicollinearity problem.

are some surprises: Overcollateralization has no impact on CMBS subordination levels, although we know it reduced commercial mortgage credit risk. Share of office loans is negatively related to subordination levels, which contradicts the common wisdom that office loans are riskier than multifamily loans. The share of top five loans is negatively related to subordination levels, which is contrary to the notion that diversification helps reduce credit risk. However, one possible explanation for this surprise is that the share of top five loans is correlated with shares of loans in California, which are less risky. The BBB subordination model generally has the same results, although property types seem to be less important.

The overall fit of the models is quite strong. The simple linear regression models explain nearly 90 percent of the variations in AAA subordination levels and nearly 80 percent of the variations in BBB subordination levels.

The existing literature suggests that subordination levels contract over time because CMBS issuers and rating agencies tend to be conservative in the early stage of CMBS market development and become less stringent with subordination design (Sanders 1999, Geltner and Miller 2001, Riddiough 2004, and Downing and Wallace 2005). Therefore, we perform an additional analysis of subordination with time trend. The results are shown in Table 4. In the first set of models, including a simple time trend as an explanatory variable suggests that subordination levels contract 1.5 percent every year. In the second set of models, we use year dummies rather than a simple time trend. The results are consistent with the simple time trend model: We see monotonically decreasing subordination levels reflected in the dummy variable coefficients. Other results do not change in the time trend model as compared to the base model in Table 3.

6.2. Structural Change and Chow Tests

The debt market experienced important changes during our study period of 1995–2005. For example, the Russian bond default in 1998 caused "flight to quality" in the debt market (reflected by the widening of credit spread in late 1998 and early 1999, see Figure 1). During 2001 and 2002, the economy experienced a recession (reflected by the surge of credit spread in 2002, see Figure 1); the yield slope was very steep during that period (see Figure 2). Starting in 2003, the commercial mortgage market saw important changes, such as the rising popularity of defeasance. Therefore, we want to examine whether there are structural changes in subordination design.

We first stratify the sample into four subsamples and then run separate models with each subsample. The results are shown in Table 5. Generally, the models are stable over time. For example, DSCR is consistently significant in the AAA subordination level model, and the share of industrial loans is also negatively significant during all four subperiods. For AAA subordination, the only change comes from the prepayment constraint variables. Changing from the 1995–1998 period to the 1998–1999 period, yield maintenance becomes significant. Defeasance becomes a significant variable only starting in 2001. In the BBB subordination level models, DSCR seems not to be a significant factor during the periods of 1995–1998 and 2001–2002. The share of limited-service hotel loans had a significant positive impact during 1995–1998 but became insignificant

TABLE 4 Estimates of the CMBS Deal Subordination Models with Time Trend[a]

	AAA subordination		BBB subordination	
	Model 1	Model 2	Model 1	Model 2
Intercept	0.413*** (0.016)	0.403*** (0.017)	0.183*** (0.014)	0.180*** (0.015)
Cutoff DSCR	−0.031*** (0.006)	−0.038*** (0.006)	−0.020*** (0.005)	−0.017*** (0.005)
Estimated LTV at maturity	0.048** (0.016)	0.035* (0.015)	0.006 (0.013)	0.006 (0.014)
Overcollateralization	0.015 (0.018)	0.019 (0.017)	0.022 (0.015)	0.025 (0.015)
Share of retail, anchored loans	−0.064*** (0.014)	−0.065*** (0.014)	−0.007 (0.012)	−0.007 (0.012)
Share of retail, unanchored loans	−0.040* (0.02)	−0.048* (0.019)	−0.005 (0.017)	−0.004 (0.017)
Share of office loans	−0.035* (0.014)	−0.030* (0.014)	−0.016 (0.012)	−0.016 (0.012)
Share of industrial loans	−0.189*** (0.029)	−0.182*** (0.028)	−0.026 (0.024)	−0.037 (0.025)
Share of health care loans	0.021 (0.025)	0.015 (0.025)	0.048* (0.021)	0.064** (0.022)
Share of full-service hotel loans	−0.008 (0.034)	−0.010 (0.033)	−0.009 (0.028)	−0.002 (0.029)
Share of limited-service hotel loans	−0.052 (0.031)	−0.050 (0.03)	0.080** (0.026)	0.072** (0.026)
Share of self-storage property loans	0.113* (0.049)	0.119* (0.047)	0.052 (0.041)	0.071 (0.041)
Share of mixed-use property loans	0.003 (0.029)	0.012 (0.028)	−0.003 (0.025)	−0.003 (0.025)
Share of mobile home loans	−0.035 (0.038)	−0.030 (0.037)	−0.044 (0.032)	−0.046 (0.032)
Share of warehouse loans	−0.101 (0.06)	−0.032 (0.058)	−0.077 (0.05)	−0.086 (0.051)
Share of other loans	0.197* (0.1)	0.080 (0.095)	−0.010 (0.084)	−0.010 (0.084)
The largest loan weights over 15 percent	−0.003 (0.005)	−0.006 (0.005)	−0.005 (0.004)	−0.005 (0.004)

Continued

TABLE 4 *Continued*

	AAA subordination		BBB subordination	
	Model 1	Model 2	Model 1	Model 2
Share of top five loans	−0.058** (0.018)	−0.046* (0.018)	−0.059*** (0.015)	−0.061*** (0.016)
Yield maintenance coverage	−0.096** (0.029)	−0.117*** (0.03)	−0.108*** (0.024)	−0.092*** (0.027)
Lockout coverage	−0.002 (0.006)	0.003 (0.007)	−0.003 (0.005)	−0.010 (0.006)
Defeasance coverage	0.049** (0.018)	0.063*** (0.018)	0.056*** (0.015)	0.049** (0.016)
Time trend	−0.015*** (0.002)		−0.004** (0.001)	
YR 97		−0.004 (0.008)		−0.021** (0.007)
YR 98		−0.005 (0.008)		−0.013 (0.007)
YR 99		−0.028*** (0.008)		−0.017* (0.007)
YR 00		−0.063*** (0.01)		−0.022* (0.009)
YR 01		−0.075*** (0.011)		−0.028** (0.01)
YR 02		−0.073*** (0.012)		−0.028* (0.011)
YR 03		−0.089*** (0.013)		−0.044*** (0.012)
YR 04		−0.110*** (0.015)		−0.046*** (0.014)
YR 05		−0.122*** (0.017)		−0.050*** (0.015)
N	350	350	350	350
Adjusted *R*-square	0.8944	0.9073	0.7677	0.7731

[a]Dependent variable: AAA/BBB subordination at cutoff.
These are OLS estimates. Standard errors are in parentheses.
* $p < 0.05$; ** $p < 0.01$; *** $p < 0.001$.
We exclude from the regressions some deal-level information, such as cutoff LTV, number of loans, and cutoff balance, because of the multicollinearity problem.

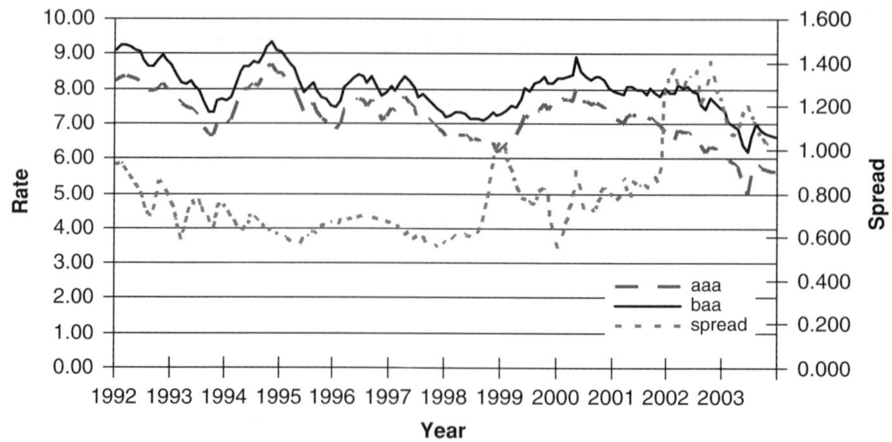

FIGURE 1 Bond rates and credit spread.

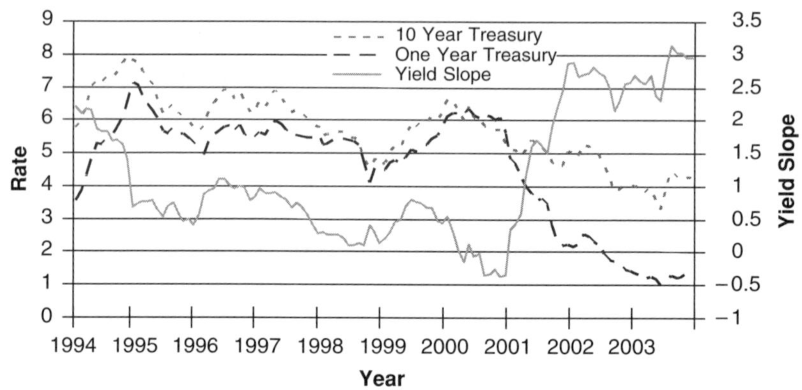

FIGURE 2 Interest rates and yield slope.

thereafter. The stratified-sample results suggest that the intercept changes substantially over time.

In addition to the stratified-sample regressions, we perform the Chow tests for structural changes. The results are summarized in Table 6. For AAA subordination, the first set of tests shows that the hypotheses of no parameter change at 1998, 2000, and 2002 are rejected. Further tests show that changing from the 2001–2002 period to the 2003–2005 period, the parameter change comes only from the intercept. At the break point at the end of 1998, only the intercept and the yield maintenance coefficient change; and at the break point of 2000, only the intercept and the defeasance coefficient change. These results are consistent with previous stratified-sample results, showing that rating agencies probably only shifted the overall subordination

TABLE 5 Estimates of the CMBS Deal Subordination Models Using Stratified Samples[a]

	AAA subordination				BBB subordination			
	1995–1998	1999–2000	2001–2002	2003–2005	1995–1998	1999–2000	2001–2002	2003–2005
Intercept	0.426***	0.590***	0.394***	0.332***	0.181***	0.247***	0.184***	0.115***
	(0.032)	(0.047)	(0.028)	(0.02)	(0.031)	(0.03)	(0.03)	(0.019)
Cutoff DSCR	−0.075**	−0.081**	−0.041***	−0.020**	−0.027	−0.055**	−0.014	−0.014*
	(0.024)	(0.025)	(0.01)	(0.006)	(0.023)	(0.016)	(0.011)	(0.006)
Share of retail, anchored loans	−0.040	−0.077*	−0.122***	−0.012	0.007	−0.001	−0.066	0.024
	(0.02)	(0.033)	(0.035)	(0.018)	(0.02)	(0.021)	(0.036)	(0.017)
Share of office loans	−0.003	−0.026	−0.065*	−0.004	−0.018	0.013	−0.083*	0.010
	(0.038)	(0.038)	(0.031)	(0.016)	(0.037)	(0.024)	(0.033)	(0.016)
Share of industrial loans	−0.132*	−0.279***	−0.225***	−0.114*	0.030	−0.042	−0.034	−0.052
	(0.064)	(0.071)	(0.051)	(0.048)	(0.063)	(0.046)	(0.053)	(0.047)
Share of health care loans	0.006	0.131	−0.158	0.174	0.038	0.102	−0.066	0.485
	(0.024)	(0.178)	(0.21)	(0.359)	(0.024)	(0.114)	(0.219)	(0.347)
Share of limited-service hotel loans	−0.001	−0.100	0.092	−0.118	0.110**	0.086	0.128	0.078
	(0.042)	(0.08)	(0.133)	(0.074)	(0.04)	(0.051)	(0.138)	(0.071)
Share of self-storage property loans	0.151	0.057	0.066	0.070	−0.011	0.004	0.118	0.002
	(0.084)	(0.144)	(0.104)	(0.074)	(0.082)	(0.092)	(0.108)	(0.072)
Share of warehouse loans	−0.205	−0.076	−0.020	−0.061	−0.545	−0.125	−0.063	−0.064
	(0.771)	(0.142)	(0.082)	(0.126)	(0.75)	(0.091)	(0.085)	(0.122)
Share of other loans	0.293	0.360	−0.030	0.170	−0.154	−0.019	0.023	0.145
	(0.17)	(0.234)	(0.231)	(0.139)	(0.166)	(0.149)	(0.24)	(0.135)
Share of top five loans	0.026	−0.093	−0.077*	−0.072***	−0.039	−0.083*	−0.043	−0.067***
	(0.031)	(0.049)	(0.037)	(0.018)	(0.03)	(0.031)	(0.038)	(0.018)
Yield maintenance coverage	−0.058	−0.436***	−0.221***	−0.312***	−0.130**	−0.191*	−0.138*	−0.100**
	(0.05)	(0.112)	(0.061)	(0.031)	(0.048)	(0.072)	(0.064)	(0.03)
Defeasance coverage	0.000	0.070	0.169***	0.188***	0.037	0.063	0.078	0.055*
	(0.029)	(0.065)	(0.038)	(0.023)	(0.029)	(0.041)	(0.04)	(0.023)
N	71	67	78	134	71	67	78	134
Adjusted *R*-square	0.3107	0.6694	0.5705	0.5359	0.2183	0.4320	0.2055	0.1956

[a]Dependent variable: AAA/BBB subordination at cutoff.
These are OLS estimates. Standard errors are in parentheses.
* $p < 0.05$; ** $p < 0.01$; *** $p < 0.001$.

levels over time rather than changing their models according to changes in the CMBS market.

The Chow tests on BBB subordination level models show that at the break points of 1998 and 2000, the models do not change at all. In addition, only the intercept changes from the 2001–2002 period to the 2003–2005 period.

TABLE 6 Chow Tests of Structural Change in Subordination Models

	Test statistics (critical value)		
	No change in parameter vector	Change in intercept only	Change in intercept and another coefficient only
Panel A: AAA subordination			
Break points			
1998	7.06 (1.8)	2.69 (1.8)	0.52 (1.85) (yield maintenance)
2000	7.05 (1.8)	2.14 (1.8)	0.16 (1.85) (defeasance)
2002	4.61 (1.8)	1.07 (1.8)	
Panel B: AAA subordination			
Break points			
1998	0.63 (1.8)		
2000	0.97 (1.8)		
2002	1.91 (1.8)	0.33 (1.8)	

The table shows the Chow test statistics together with critical values (in parenthes) at 95 percent significance level. From these results, we see there are structural changes of the relationship between AAA subordination levels and deal information in 1998, 2000, and 2002. The intercept and coefficient of the yield maintenance coverage variable change at the end of 1998; the intercept and coefficient of the defeasance coverage variable change at the end of 2000; however, only the intercept in the subordination model changes at the end of 2002. For BBB subordination, the tests reject the hypothesis that the relationships between BBB subordination and deal information change in 1998 and 2000. The only change is a simple shift in the constant term at the end of 2002.

7. CONCLUSION

Subordination plays an important role in the senior-subordinated structure of securitized transactions such as CMBS. Optimal subordination design is in the interests of CMBS investors, issuers, and rating agencies because subordination levels determine how investors buying senior CMBS bonds are protected from credit risk and how much an issuer can get out of a certain commercial mortgage pool. Rating agencies essentially decide subordination levels for each CMBS deal.

We performed cross-sectional tests of differentials in CMBS subordination levels. The results show that CMBS deal cutoff DSCR, property type composition, and prepayment protection are significant factors for CMBS bond subordination, and they explain about 90 percent of cross-sectional variations in AAA subordination levels and about 80 percent of variations in BBB subordination levels; surprisingly, cutoff LTV and DSCR themselves explain about 30 percent of the variations in subordination. In terms of the evolution of subordination levels, we observe that subordination levels have declined over time and that the primary drivers of subordination have changed as well. In particular, the growth of defeasance as a tool for prepayment protection has been observed.

References

Allen, Franklin, and Douglas Gale. 1988. Optimal Security Design, *Review of Financial Studies* 1, 229–263.

Ambrose, Brent W., and Anthony B. Sanders. 2003. Commercial Mortgage-Backed Securities: Prepayment and Default, *Journal of Real Estate Finance and Economics* 26(2–3), 179–196.

Archer, Wayne R., Peter J. Elmer, David M. Harrison, and David C. Ling. 2002. Determinants of Multifamily Mortgage Default, *Real Estate Economics* 30(3), 445–473.

Boot, Arnoud W. A., and Anjan V. Thakor. 1993. Security Design, *Journal of Finance* 48, 1349–1378.

Ciochetti, Brian A., Yongheng Deng, Bin Gao, and Rui Yao. 2002. The Termination of Commercial Mortgage Contracts Through Prepayment and Default: A Proportional Hazard Approach with Competing Risks, *Real Estate Economics* 30(4), 595–633.

DeLong, J. Bradford. 1991. Did J. P. Morgan's Men Add Value?: An Economist's Perspective on Financial Capitalism, in Peter Temin (ed.), *Inside the Business Enterprise: Historical Perspectives on the Use of Information*, University of Chicago Press, Chicago, pp. 205–236.

DeMarzo, Peter. 2005. The Pooling and Tranching of Securities: A Model of Informed Intermediation, *Review of Financial Studies* 18, 1–35.

DeMarzo, Peter, and Darrell Duffie. 1999. A Liquidity-Based Model of Security Design, *Econometrica* 67, 65–99.

Deng, Yongheng, John M. Quigley, and Robert Van Order. 2000. Mortgage Terminations, Heterogeneity and the Exercise of Mortgage Options, *Econometrica* 68(2), 275–307.

Deng, Yongheng, John M. Quigley, and Anthony B. Sanders. 2005. Commercial Mortgage Terminations: Evidence from CMBS, working paper presented at the 2005 Annual American Real Estate and Urban Economics Association (AREUEA) Meetings.

Diamond, Douglas. 1984. Financial Intermediation and Delegated Monitoring, *Review of Financial Studies* 51, 393–414.

Downing, Christopher, and Nancy Wallace. 2005. Commercial Mortgage-Backed Securities: How Much Subordination is Enough?, working paper, University of California at Berkeley.

Gaur, Vishal, Sridhar Seshadri, and Marti G. Subrahmanyam. 2005. Intermediation and Value Creation in an Incomplete Market, FMA European Conference 2005 working paper.

Geltner, David, and Norman G. Miller. 2001. *Commercial Real Estate Analysis and Investments*. South-Western College Publishing, Mason, Ohio.

Glaeser, Edward, and Hedi Kallal. 1997. Thin Markets, Asymmetric Information, and Mortgage-Backed Securities, *Journal of Financial Intermediation* 6, 64–86.

Gorton, Gary, and George Pennachi. 1990. Financial Intermediaries and Liquidity Creation, *Journal of Finance* 45, 49–71.

Greene, William H. 2003. *Econometric Analysis*, 5th ed. Prentice Hall, Upper Saddle River, NJ.

Leland, Hayne, and David Pyle. 1977. Information Asymmetries, Financial Structure and Financial Intermediaries, *Journal of Finance* 32, 371–387.

Ramakrishnan, Ram T. S., and Anjan V. Thakor. 1984. Information Reliability and a Theory of Financial Intermediation, *Review of Financial Studies* 51(3), 415–432.

Riddiough, Timothy J. 1997. Optimal Design and Governance of Asset-Backed Securities, *Journal of Financial Intermediation* 6, 121–152.

Riddiough, Timothy J. 2004. Commercial Mortgage-Backed Securities: An Exploration into Agency, Innovation, Information, and Learning in Financial Markets. Mimeo, University of Wisconsin, Madison.

Sanders, Anthony B. 1999. Commercial Mortgage-Backed Securities, in Frank J. Fabozzi (ed.), *The Handbook of Fixed-Income Securities*. McGraw-Hill, New York.

Thakor, Anjan V. 1982. An Exploration of Competitive Signaling Equilibria with "Third-Party" Information Production: The Case of Debt Insurance, *Journal of Finance* 37(3), 717–739.

Thompson, G. Rodney, and Peter Vaz. 1990. Dual Bond Ratings: A Test of the Certification Function of Rating Agencies, *Financial Review* 25(3), 457–471.

Weinstein, Mark L. 1977. The Effect of a Rating Change Announcement on Bond Price, *Journal of Financial Economics* 5, 329–350.

Wheeler, Darrell. 2001. A Guide to Commercial Mortgage-Backed Securities, in Lakhbir Hayre (ed.), *Guide to Mortgage-Backed and Asset-Backed Securities*. John Wiley & Sons, New York.

Winton, Andrew. 1995. Costly State Verification and Multiple Investors: The Role of Seniority, *Review of Financial Studies* 8(1), 91–123.

Winton, Andrew. 2003. Institutional Liquidity Needs and the Structure of Monitored Finance, *Review of Financial Studies* 16(4), 1273–1313.

SECTION 2

Market Structure and Structure of Financial Markets

CHAPTER 3

Limit Order Markets: A Survey

Christine A. Parlour
University of California Berkeley

Duane J. Seppi
Carnegie Mellon University

We thank the authors of the research reviewed here for their insights into the microstructure of limit order markets and apologize for any errors or misrepresentations in our discussion of their work. We thank Arnoud Boot for asking us to undertake this survey and Thierry Foucault, Gene Kandel, Ioanid Rosu, and Chester Spatt for helpful comments.

1. INTRODUCTION

When Walras sought inspiration in the nineteenth century for his eponymous model of markets, the Paris Bourse ran batch auctions. Periodically, an auctioneer aggregated orders and announced a market-clearing price. Later, in the 1980s, when Kyle (1985) and Glosten and Milgrom (1985) published their own eponymous theories of financial markets, the intermediation activities of NYSE specialists, the Tokyo Saitori, Nasdaq and London dealers, and floor traders in the Chicago futures pits were central to the trading process. As of 2008, most equity and derivative exchanges around the world are either pure electronic limit order markets or at least allow for customer limit orders in addition to on-exchange market making.[1] This is specifically true of Euronext Paris, the successor to the Paris Bourse. The NYSE has progressively expanded the role of customer limit orders in its own trading process and, in addition, has recently acquired two limit order markets, Archipelago and Euronext. Nasdaq has had to adapt to the growing market share of ECN limit order markets while the electronic futures market ICE has taken market share away from floor-based futures exchanges. Given the prevalence of limit order trading, this chapter assays what we know and don't know about the economics of limit order markets.

A limit order is an ex ante precommitment (t, j, x, p) made on date t to trade up to a given amount x of a security j at a prespecified limit price p. The order is in force until filled or cancelled. Unexecuted limit orders queue up in a limit order book. Limit orders are executed when other investors submit market orders or marketable limit orders. In particular, a market order is a request to trade immediately at the best price currently available in the market. Market clearing of limit orders is discriminatory: Each limit order executed in a transaction is filled at its respective limit price. It is this discriminatory execution property that distinguishes a limit order market from call markets with a uniform market-clearing price (e.g., as in Walras or Kyle 1989).

Markets typically impose price and time priority rules on limit order execution. *Price priority* means that limit orders offering better terms of trade—limit sells at lower prices and limit buys at higher prices—execute ahead of limit orders at worse prices. *Time priority* means that, at each price p, older limit orders are executed before more recent limit orders. The queuing discipline is thus "first in, first out," which rewards first-movers providing liquidity at a given price. Taken together, the price and time priority of a limit order translates directly into a probability distribution over execution timing.

Other market design issues also affect limit orders. Some exchanges restrict trading to limit orders and market orders exclusively. Others permit additional ex post liquidity provision by on-exchange market makers, who decide how much to trade after a market order arrives. The specialist on the NYSE behaves in this way. Exchanges also have a range of informational transparency. In an open book, all limit orders are observable to all investors; in a closed book, traders cannot see the book. Some exchanges only disclose limit orders at a restricted set of prices. Others allow "iceberg" orders, where

[1] See Jain (2005) and Swan and Westerholm (2006).

part of a limit order is hidden from other traders. In addition, the information disclosed about investor identity varies across exchanges.

The basic economics of the trading process with limit orders follows from limit orders being ex ante commitments to provide liquidity. Demsetz (1968) highlights the importance of inventory and waiting costs due to delays in limit order execution. Cohen et al. (1981) describe the tradeoff between execution probability and price improvement in the choice between limit orders and market orders, and show that the asynchronous arrival of investors and orders fundamentally changes the trading process relative to a Walrasian call. In particular, the uncertain arrival of future traders means that the probability of execution jumps discontinuously going from a very aggressive limit order to a market order. The resulting *gravitational pull* of trading at existing quotes leads directly to a noninfinitesimal bid-ask spread. Copeland and Galai (1983) point out that ex ante commitments to trade, such as limit orders and binding dealer quotes, give options to other traders to trade at the quoted prices. As such, limit orders are at an informational disadvantage, since they can be *picked off* by later investors who receive updated public information or who have private information.

The ongoing research challenge is, theoretically, to model and analyze these basic intuitions in a rigorous equilibrium framework and, empirically, to quantify the importance of the various causal relations and, operationally, to develop optimized algorithms for practical use. This is no easy task. Despite the simplicity of limit orders themselves, the economic interactions in limit order markets are complex because the associated state and action spaces are extremely large and because trading with limit orders is dynamic and generates nonlinear payoffs. A limit order executes against future market orders and competes against both existing limit orders and against limit orders that may be submitted in the future. Thus, when choosing limit prices and quantities for (potentially multiple) limit orders and choosing quantities for market orders, a trader needs to condition on everything that can affect the future evolution of the trading process. This potentially includes a complete description of the existing limit order book—namely, all quantities for multiple orders at multiple prices from multiple past investors at multiple points in time—as well as the histories of all past trades and orders. The high dimensionality of limit order markets is a challenge for theoretical modeling and empirical estimation as well as, more practically, for trading. Dynamic trading strategies also involve decisions about how frequently to monitor changing market conditions and when and how to modify or cancel unexecuted limit orders. Lastly, limit orders have nonlinear payoffs. In some future states they execute (and have linear payoffs in future cash flows), while in others they do not.

Research on limit orders is an area of intense activity. Over the last decade this effort has produced a number of significant new insights. Consequently, now is a good time to take stock of what has been accomplished and what is still left to be done. Our survey describes the main conceptual insights about limit orders and points out connections between theory and empirical evidence. We also highlight modeling obstacles and the devices used to surmount them. Some of the main themes follow.

Price formation The process of price formation in dynamic limit order markets differs fundamentally from sequential Walrasian markets and from dynamic dealer markets. The Walrasian "market-clearing" price reflects an aggregation of supply and demand throughout the entire economy. In contrast, investors arrive and trade asynchronously in a limit order market, so there is no unique marketwide "market-clearing" price. Rather, there is a sequence of bilateral transaction prices at which endogenously matched pairs of investors choose to trade over time. Similarly, the changing identity of limit order submitters is different from the Ptolemaic market makers in Kyle (1985) and Glosten and Milgrom (1985), who continuously set quotes at the informational and economic center of the market.

Liquidity The distinction between liquidity supply and demand can be blurred in limit order markets. Investors with active trading motives may post limit orders that are more aggressive than those a disinterested liquidity provider would use but less aggressive than market orders. Such limit orders are something in between pure liquidity supply and pure liquidity demand. In the extreme, limit buys (sells) can be posted above (below) the "efficient" price given public information.[2] Thus, quotes in limit order markets cannot always be decomposed into an efficient price plus a nonnegative compensation for liquidity provision.

Dynamics Limit order books change over time in response to parametric changes in the environment and because of random ebbs and flows in the realized supply and demand for liquidity. Trades and prices in limit order markets can also exhibit path dependencies given the sequence in which buyers and sellers arrive in the market.

Information aggregation Given the risk of being adversely picked off and of costly nonexecution, limit order books should impound forward-looking information about future price volatility, the intensity of future adverse selection, and future order flow. This has been confirmed empirically. A richer picture is also emerging about the interaction between information and the supply and demand for liquidity. Limit orders are not just susceptible to being picked off by informed trading; they are also potentially a vehicle for informed trading themselves.

Intermarket competition Glosten (1994) shows that competitive limit order markets can provide maximal liquidity in the face of adverse selection frictions. In such environments, limit order markets are "inevitable," in the sense that they can implement "competition-proof" price schedules. However, limit order markets are not inevitable given noninformational frictions. In particular, hybrid markets combining dealers and limit orders can coexist with, and even drive out, pure limit order markets when there are order submission costs.

Understanding the economics of trading processes generally and of limit orders specifically is important for at least three audiences. First and most practically, investors and trading desks want to reduce their trading costs. Limit orders are potentially executed at better prices than market orders, but they run the risk of nonexecution and are exposed to a winner's curse problem of being adversely picked off if the security's value moves past the limit price before the limit order can be cancelled. The

[2]The *efficient price* is a term of art used to describe a statistically derived component of asset prices that excludes high-frequency microstructure "noise" due to inventory effects and compensation for liquidity.

optimal choice depends on the dynamics of future order submission decisions of other investors.

Second, exchanges are businesses that face competitive pressures to make their product (the ability to trade) more attractive to their customers (investors). The fact that so many exchanges are now organized as limit order markets suggests that this market design attracts investors and, thus, business for exchanges. The reasons why and conditions under which limit order trading is attractive are, however, rooted in the economics of the interactions between investors that limit orders facilitate. Exchanges also grapple with how best to implement limit order trading in terms of market transparency and whether to have solely limit orders or whether to have a hybrid structure with both investor limit orders and market makers.

Third, economists outside of market microstructure are recognizing a deeper connection between trading, liquidity, and asset pricing. The fact that an asset can be traded makes asset valuation a social activity. Optimal risk sharing and consumption smoothing requires heterogeneous investors with higher valuations to buy securities from investors with lower valuations. In a market with low trading frictions, securities can be valued under the expectation that cash flows will be received over time by the investors who attach the highest valuations to them. As Harrison and Kreps (1978) show, the resale option associated with a tradable asset determines its value. Hence, trading is not just a mechanism for price discovery; trading also creates value by allowing investors to reshuffle security ownership over time as their personal valuations change.

Frictions that prevent investors from trading and realizing gains-from-trade actually lower the ex ante value of assets. The frictions of interest here are not, however, exogenous costs but, rather, coordination problems that arise when investors arrive to trade asynchronously with different information about asset cash flows and about the availability of potential counterparties. To the extent that the rules of trade affect which potential trades are actually consummated, the choice of the trading mechanism can affect allocations and, hence, social welfare. The growing literature on liquidity and asset pricing suggests, moreover, that the interaction between trading mechanisms and asset prices is significant.[3] A natural question, therefore, is whether society is better off because of the global adoption of limit order markets.

Our survey is preceded by several excellent earlier reviews. O'Hara (1995) is the first comprehensive overview of the microstructure literature. Madhavan (2000) and Biais, Glosten, and Spatt (2005) describe subsequent advances in microstructure theory, and Hasbrouck (2007) explains tests and methods used in empirical microstructure. Harris (2003) reviews lessons and insights of microstructure research for practitioners and policy makers. By contrast, our survey is focused specifically on limit order markets. This more narrow focus is justified because today limit order markets are the dominant institution for trading equities and other exchange-traded securities.

[3]See Amihud and Mendelson (1986), Brennan and Subrahmanyam (1996), Easley, Hvidkjaer, and O'Hara (2002), and Pastor and Stambaugh (2003).

2. MODELING LIMIT ORDERS

Microstructure questions of optimal trading and price discovery are usually considered separately from questions of portfolio choice and asset pricing, and vice versa. This is mathematically convenient but potentially misleading. Investor trading decisions should ultimately be understood in the context of investor portfolio choices.

In the canonical portfolio problem, an investor i chooses a portfolio strategy θ_i consisting of holdings $(\theta_{i1t}, \ldots, \theta_{iNt})$ in N securities at each date t to maximize her lifetime expected utility from consumption,

$$\max_{\theta_i} \; u_i(c_{it_0}) + E_{t_0}\left[\sum_{t=t_1}^{T} e^{-\rho_i(t-t_0)} u_i(c_{it})\right], \tag{1}$$

subject to a budget constraint on consumption $c_{it} = \sum_{j=1}^{N}(\theta_{ijt-1} - \theta_{ijt})P_{jt} + \theta_{ijt-1}D_{jt}$. Here, D_{jt} are cash distributions paid at date t by asset j. This standard formulation assumes a competitive Walrasian market. At each date t there is a market-clearing price P_{jt} for stock j at which the investor's trades $x_{ijt} = \theta_{ijt} - \theta_{ijt-1}$ are executed. Thus, the investor solves Eq. (1), taking market-clearing prices and the ability to trade at those prices as given. Indeed, the fact that the problem is formulated in terms of asset holdings θ_{ijt} rather than trades x_{ijt} implicitly presumes that trade execution is both certain and effortless. The corresponding asset pricing process is usually represented as a rational expectations equilibrium.

Definition 2.1. A rational expectations equilibrium in a Walrasian market is a set of asset prices and portfolio holding strategies such that at each date: (i) the supply and demand for each security are equated, (ii) each investor's portfolio strategy is optimal given the market-clearing prices, and (iii) investor beliefs are rational given the available information.

Market institutions have evolved since the batched call auctions of Walras' time to allow for continuous trading. The fact that investors trade asynchronously complicates both market-clearing (i.e., connecting buyers and sellers) and price discovery (i.e., aggregating information to value future cash flows). When the arrival asynchronicity is too severe, dealers intermediate trades between investors. In most high volume markets, however, early investors can use limit orders, effectively, to negotiate trades with later investors.

The individual investor portfolio optimization problem changes dramatically in limit order markets. Rather than submitting a single order x_{ijt} for an exact amount to be traded at a known market-clearing price at a precise date t, investors potentially submit vectors of market and limit orders so as to react to random fluctuations in buying and selling interest over time. Since limit order execution is uncertain, investors do not know with certainty how much they will actually trade at date t given their submitted orders. This leads to random slippage between the investor's ideal portfolio and her actual holdings depending on how many limit orders are executed. In other words, portfolio holdings are stochastic. Consequently, the order submission decision can be viewed as inducing an optimal probability distribution from which an investor's realized trades and trade prices will be drawn.

Given the priority rules of a limit order market, an investor i arrives at date t with current security holdings θ_{ijt-1} and possibly a set x_{ijt}^{O} of old orders still outstanding. She then submits instructions x_{ijt}^{I} consisting of new limit and market orders and any cancellations of old orders. Given her orders and the subsequent flow of orders $\boldsymbol{M}_{jt}$ from all other investors in the market, let $x_{ijt} = x(x_{ijt}^{O}, x_{ijt}^{I}, \boldsymbol{M}_{jt})$ denote the realized number of shares traded by investor i between date t and the next time, $t+1$, she enters the market. Let $\overline{P}_{ijt} = \overline{P}(x_{ijt}^{O}, x_{ijt}^{I}, \boldsymbol{M}_{jt})$ denote the average price for these trades. Investor i does not know the flow of future orders from other investors when she submits her instructions x_{ijt}^{I}. Thus, the investor's problem in a limit order market is to use a dynamic order submission strategy that maximizes lifetime expected utility from consumption:

$$\max_{x_i^I} E_{t_0}\left[u_i\left(\sum_{j=1}^{N}\theta_{ij0}D_{j0} - x_{ij0}\overline{P}_{ij0}\right) + \sum_{t=t_1}^{\infty} e^{-\rho_i(t-t_0)}u_i\left(\sum_{j=1}^{N}\left[\theta_{ij0} + \sum_{s=0}^{t-1} x_{ijs}\right]D_{jt} - x_{ijt}\overline{P}_{ijt}\right)\right], \tag{2}$$

given the uncertainty in consumption induced by randomness in the cash flow process $\boldsymbol{D}_{jt}$ and by randomness in the order flow process $\boldsymbol{M}_{jt}$.

The optimization problem in Eq. (2) is more complex than the standard problem in Eq. (1) for three reasons. First, the action space at each decision date t is larger. Rather than just submitting a single order x_{ijt}, the investor in (2) makes multidimensional decisions about order type (i.e., whether to submit market orders, limit orders, or some combination of the two), limit order aggressiveness (i.e., at what prices to post limit orders), and order quantities (i.e., how many shares for each order). Second, the state space is larger. Rather than just conditioning on cash flow information and the corresponding market-clearing prices P_{jt}, the investor in (2) also conditions on everything that can affect the aggregate order flow process $\boldsymbol{M}_{jt}$ since $\boldsymbol{M}_{jt}$ affects the probability distribution over which orders will execute, $x(x_{ijt}^{O}, x_{ijt}^{I}, \boldsymbol{M}_{jt})$, and over the prices, $\overline{P}(x_{ijt}^{O}, x_{ijt}^{I}, \boldsymbol{M}_{jt})$, at which they will execute. This includes the composition of the current book and the history of past order submissions. Third, the decision dates $t_0, t_1, \ldots$ themselves in (2) are chosen by investor i rather than being predetermined dates for aggregate market clearing. Continuously monitoring the market is costly, so investors do not trade continuously. Thus, the order submission dates for investor i can be modeled as Poisson events that occur with an intensity $\gamma(t, \mathcal{J}_{it})dt$ that depends on agent i's information $\mathcal{J}_{it}$ set at time t. The content and dynamics of $\mathcal{J}_{it}$ is agent-specific and can include private and public information about cash flows, common cross-investor trading motives, and investor-specific private value motives to trade.

The trading process in a limit order market is a continuous-time game in which a sequence of investors randomly enter (and reenter) the market to solve portfolio/trading problems as in (2). In particular, each investor has her own individual Poisson order submission dates t. When aggregated together, the actions of all of the investors collectively determine the dynamics of the marketwide order flows M_{jt}. The economics of market clearing in such an environment is dramatically different from a Walrasian market. In particular, the notion of aggregate supply and demand being equated at a market-clearing price is replaced with the weaker notion of a Nash equilibrium in investor trading strategies, where prices are simply the outcome of a series of bilateral transactions.

Definition 2.2. A rational expectations equilibrium in a dynamic limit order market is a set of prices and order submission strategies such that at each date: (i) trades occur when arriving investors prefer trading with existing limit orders via market orders rather than submitting new limit orders of their own, (ii) transaction prices satisfy the market's priority rules, (iii) each investor's order submission strategy is optimal given the order flows from the other investors, and (iv) investors' beliefs are rational given their available information about future cash flows and about the endogenous dynamics of the market-wide flow of orders M_{jt}.

No existing models, to our knowledge, formally embed dynamic limit order submission decisions in a dynamic portfolio choice problem as in (2) or integrate aggregate limit order flow dynamics with consumption-based equilibrium asset pricing. Instead, issues of "how" investors trade are decoupled from issues of "why" they trade.

Once the order submission problem is detached from the portfolio problem, it is necessary to specify reduced-form trading preferences. Clearly, investors want to execute at the most favorable prices possible. More fundamentally, however, a trading benefit is needed to proxy for the consumption utility derived from trading. Otherwise, there would be no trading at all. One approach is to penalize traders if they fail to achieve a trading target. Another is to assume investors have private values, due to tax or hedging considerations, for particular portfolio positions. These potential private payoffs depreciate over time until trades are completed. Yet another approach penalizes execution waiting time directly. An important point in Engle and Ferstenberg (2006), however, is that reduced-form trading preferences ultimately should be compatible with investors' consumption preferences. Extreme trading risk aversion, for example, is probably not consistent with low consumption risk aversion. Moreover, investors should be indifferent between trading strategies that achieve comparable consumption flows.

A variety of modeling assumptions reduce the dimensionality of the investor action and state spaces and simplify interactions between investors. Our taxonomy of models highlights assumptions about the order type decision, the timing of trades, the informational environment, and the extent of competition. Some models assume that the use of limit orders or market orders is exogenous; others explicitly model the choice between limit and market orders. The timing of trade can be static or dynamic. In static batch models, orders are aggregated across multiple investors and executed simultaneously in one round of trade. The trading uncertainty is about execution risk: Limit orders may or may not be executed. In sequential arrival models, traders arrive in the market and submit orders one at a time. Execution uncertainty is augmented with timing uncertainty about when limit orders will execute. The information environment in different models sometimes allows for adverse selection. When some investors have private information, limit orders are also exposed to valuation risk, since the value of the underlying asset may be correlated with the states in which limit orders execute. Models also differ in whether there is perfect or imperfect competition in liquidity provision and about the role of contemporaneous competition versus intertemporal competition via asynchronous limit order submissions at different dates.

Similar problems of dimensionality are encountered in empirical studies of limit order data. For tractability, empirical tests focus on a small set of economic actions—order type choices, order quantities, order aggressiveness, and order and transaction timing—and condition on a relatively small number of empirical summary statistics for the state of the market.

2.1. Static Equilibrium Models

The first equilibrium limit order models are static and have trading by investors with sharply differentiated demands for immediacy. Rock (1996) started this approach, followed by Glosten (1994) and Seppi (1997). At an initial date 1, passive *liquidity suppliers* submit limit orders into a limit order book. These investors have no intrinsic motive to trade. They only trade to be compensated for providing liquidity to other investors with a demand for immediacy. At a later date 2, an *active trader* arrives and demands immediacy via a market order for a random number of shares x, which is then crossed against the limit order book from date 1. This cross occurs with or without the ex post intermediation of a specialist. The goal is to describe the shape of the aggregate limit order book given perfect contemporaneous competition among liquidity providers.

Limit orders are exposed to a variety of costs and risks. For concreteness, we focus on limit sells and let Q_j denote the cumulative quantity of limit sells at or below a generic price p_j. First is the possibility of nonexecution. In particular, the trading rules of an exchange determine the set Γ_j of market orders that cause the marginal (i.e., last) limit order submitted at p_j to execute. For example, time priority in a pure limit order market implies that $x \in \Gamma_j$ if the market order is large enough, $x \geq Q_j$, to fill the entire queue up through p_j.[4] Second is valuation risk due to public and private information. The expected asset value conditional on the realized market order x is represented by a monotone function $v(x)$ that reflects "picking off" risk, as in Copeland and Galai (1983), when subsequent markets are conditioned on future public information, and the possibility of active traders' trading on private information. This leads to the *upper tail*

[4]Pro rata allocation and randomization are other possible order allocation rules for pure limit order markets. Seppi (1997) characterizes the executable sets Γ_j in a hybrid market with a specialist in terms of thresholds that depend on the specialist's profit from undercutting or not undercutting limit orders at price p_j. A similar intuition is implicit in Ready (1999) when specialists have the option to "stop" execution of a market order and then condition their undercutting decision on subsequent information. Internalization of customer order flow can also give broker-dealers a similar "last mover" advantage in their decision of how much liquidity to provide. See Kavajecz (1999) and Harris and Panchapagesan (2005) for empirical evidence of strategic specialist behavior vis-à-vis the limit order book.

expectation property, whereby liquidity providers recognize that the value of the asset is conditional on the information content of the market orders that trigger execution of different limit orders. Third, there may be up-front order submission costs c_j, as in Seppi (1997), and ex post order execution costs g_j, as in Sandås (2001) and Foucault and Menkveld (2008).

The shape of the aggregate book is determined by the ex ante profitability of the marginal limit order at each price:

$$\pi_j = \left[p_j - \mathrm{E}(v(x)|x \in \Gamma_j) - g_j\right] \mathrm{Prob}(x \in \Gamma_j) - c_j. \tag{3}$$

Competition drives expected profits from limit orders to zero. As more limit orders are submitted, cumulative depths increase, which causes execution probabilities $\mathrm{Prob}(x \in \Gamma_j)$ to fall and causes expected gross profits conditional on execution, $p_j - \mathrm{E}(v(x)|x \in \Gamma_j)$, to shrink while leaving submission costs the same. In equilibrium the book satisfies a break-even condition: The equilibrium cumulative depths $Q_1, Q_2, \ldots$ set $\pi_j = 0$ at each price p_j with positive depth.

These models proved to be useful for policy purposes. For example, they explain why decimalization reduced market liquidity due to the impact of "penny jumping" on the incentive to submit limit orders.[5] However, these models are also unrealistic in several ways. Most importantly, there is no order type decision. Investors either have an inelastic motive to trade and are willing to pay for immediate execution via market orders, or they are entirely disinterested liquidity providers with no reason to trade other than to be compensated for supplying liquidity via limit orders. The static nature of these models also limits their ability to speak to order flow dynamics. The limit order book changes over time only if structural parameters of the underlying costs and distributions change. Lastly, there is no market power in limit order submission. There are always enough competitive liquidity providers to ensure that the limit order book is break-even rather than having ebbs and flows in limit order profitability.

Empirical evidence Sandås (2001) interprets intraday snapshots of the limit order book as observations of a repeated one-period model. He then conducts the first structural GMM estimation of a limit order model. Two moment conditions are used. The first is a break-even condition. Recognizing that the actual marginal expected profit π_{jt} at any given time t may deviate from zero—either because of delays in the arrival of sufficient limit orders (in which case $\pi_{jt} > 0$) or because of active liquidity demand in the limit order book (in which case $\pi_{jt} < 0$)—the break-even condition is relaxed to mean just that, on average, the expected marginal profit is zero, $\mathrm{E}[\pi_{jt}] = 0$. The second moment condition is rational valuation. Assuming that the conditional value $v(x)$ is linear in the market order size x, Sandås tests an overidentifying restriction that the price impact $v(x)$ implicitly impounded in the cross-section of depths in the limit order book is consistent with the time-series price impact of actual market orders.

Unconditional and conditional versions of the break-even condition are rejected using Sandås's test for actively traded stocks on the Stockholm Stock Exchange. The

[5] See Goldstein and Kavajecz (2000) and Jones and Lipson (2001) for evidence consistent with predictions in Harris (1994) and Seppi (1997).

model's main difficulty in fitting the data is that the estimated impact of order flow implicit in the limit order book is greater than the observed time-series price impact. In other words, the limit order book is, on average, not deep enough to drive average expected profits to zero. One possible interpretation is that limit orders do not arrive fast enough. Supporting the idea of adjusted lags, the expected profits on limit orders are decreasing as the length of time between market orders, during which limit orders can accumulate, is longer. A conditional model, allowing for time variation in price impacts and other variables as functions of changing state variables (e.g., price volatility), fares better than the unconditional (constant parameter) version, but it is still rejected. A second difficulty is that the estimated order execution costs γ_j are negative. This suggests that limit orders are submitted, not by disinterested investors with trading costs, but rather by investors with private trading motives.

2.2. Equilibrium Models with Static Order Choice and a Terminal Penalty

One partial step toward full multiperiod optimization is to introduce a terminal penalty for nonexecution into a static model. Investors presumably dislike trading costs and also dislike deviations from trading targets. This suggests a representation of the investor's problem in which a vector of market orders and limit orders x_i^I is submitted to solve

$$\min_{x_i^I} \; E(g[x(x_i^I, M) - \omega_i] + f[c(x_i^I, x(x_i^I, M))]), \tag{4}$$

where g is a penalty function, given the realized deviation of investor i's actual executed trades $x(x_i^I, M)$ from a personal trading target ω_i, and f is a penalty function for order submission and execution costs $c(x_i^I, x(x_i^I, M))$. The expectation is taken over the random vector M of the aggregate order flow from all investors. The penalty function is a reduced form for the continuation value in the Bellman equation. A shortcoming of this approach is that g is ad hoc rather than derived from an explicit dynamic programming problem.

Kumar and Seppi (1994) is an example of this approach. They model a market in which two different types of traders use limit orders. *Value traders* submit limit orders simply to exploit profit opportunities in the limit order book but do not need to trade per se. In contrast, *liquidity traders* have an active motive to trade in response to random individual liquidity shocks ω_i. Market clearing is a simultaneous move game in which buyers and sellers submit market and limit orders at the same time. Randomness in the trading demand of the liquidity traders leads to price risk for market orders and execution risk for limit orders.

Assuming a quadratic specification for Eq. (4) leads to optimal orders $x_{ij} = b_j\omega_i$ that are linear in the individual trading targets. The coefficient b_j for order type j is a function of the expected costs and probabilities of execution and is identical across investors. After integrating over a continuum of small price-taking liquidity traders and then solving a fixed-point problem for the equilibrium b_j coefficient, the model produces aggregate market and limit order flows that have an endogenous linear factor structure. This factor structure is qualitatively consistent with a block diagonal correlation matrix in which buy (sell) market orders are positively correlated with buy (sell) limit orders. In addition, if repeated over time, the target deviation in period t will induce autocorrelations in order submissions over time, since unfilled orders at date t will roll over into additional trading demand at date $t + 1$. In sum, randomness in the limit order book should have a factor structure, and investors should submit vectors of limit and market orders rather than single orders.

Empirical evidence Cao, Hansch, and Wang (2004) find that different points of the limit order book are cointegrated. Aitken et al. (2005) specifically confirm the use of vector order submissions by institutional investors on the Australian Stock Exchange. Beltran, Giot, and Gramming (2005) find that the first two principal components explain over 90 percent of the limit order book on each side of the market.

2.3. Dynamic Optimal Control Models for Single Agents

Static competition models focus primarily on the shape of the aggregate limit order book rather than on individual investor order submissions. However, order submission strategies themselves are of interest for at least two reasons. First, marketwide order flows M_{jt} are the aggregation of individual investors' order submissions. Thus, dynamic equilibrium models (discussed in Section 2.4) focus on order submissions rather than on the shape of the book. Second, the growth of automated algorithmic trading has stimulated interest in order submissions purely as an optimal control problem. Theoretical and numerical analysis in Harris (1998), Angel (1992), and Obizhaeva and Wang (2005) solves for optimal trading strategies that minimize expected costs for a risk-neutral investor. In this work the dynamics of aggregate order flows M_{jt} are deemed exogenous.

Empirical evidence The earliest empirical studies of limit orders focus on execution costs rather than on order submission decisions. Harris and Hasbrouck (1996) estimate expected trading costs for actual orders, while Handa and Schwartz (1996) use a back-testing approach in which hypothetical executions are simulated for fictitious small orders given actual price time series. Both studies find that, conditional on execution, limit orders have costs that are favorable to market orders but that costs associated with nonexecution can be significant. More recently, Nevmyvaka et al. (2005) use a mean/variance criterion to evaluate various back-tested limit order submission strategies where these strategies are contingent on market conditions.

2.4. Multiperiod Equilibrium Models

Recent research represents limit order markets as sequential games rather than as static batch markets. Foucault (1999), Parlour (1998), Foucault, Kadan, and Kandel (2005), Goettler, Parlour, and Rajan (2005a, 2005b, 2007), and Rosu (2005) take this approach. All of these models embed a discrete choice order submission problem in a variant of a dynamic multiagent bargaining game. Risk neutral investors arrive sequentially and submit orders to maximize their expected gains from trade. In particular, the investor arriving at date t values the asset as the sum of an investor-specific random private value y_t plus possibly a random common component v_t. The order submission decision is formulated as a discrete choice problem with a penalty for nonimmediate execution. Investors choose whether to use market orders or limit orders rather than being assumed to use a particular order type.

Investors in these models have local temporal market power in providing liquidity. This market power comes from two sources. First, quantity constraints restrict the number of shares any one investor can submit as limit orders. This prevents investors from individually driving the book to the break-even competitive depths. Second, only a small number of investors (often just one) are monitoring the market on any given date t and are able to act in real time. Investors who are not "present"—in that they are not actively monitoring the market or in that they have not yet arrived—cannot respond to the actions of investors who are present. This creates a window of time $[t, \tau]$, between t and the next time, τ, a competitor reacts, during which the only direct constraints on the market power in liquidity provision of investor t are the price and time priority of limit orders already in the book. As a result, there are too few liquidity providers—in contrast to the competitive batch models and their deep break-even books. Paradoxically, in equilibrium the shortage of liquidity leads not only to positive expected profits for some limit orders but also, in other cases, to "desperate" limit order submissions that, while optimal, have *negative* expected profits.

The main goal of this line of research is to model endogenous order choice and the resulting patterns of order flow autocorrelation. An influential early impetus to this work was empirical evidence on intraday order submissions on the Paris Bourse in Biais, Hillion, and Spatt (1995). In their study, orders are classified in terms of "aggressiveness," ranging from market orders that "walk the book" and move prices (most aggressive) to limit orders placed behind the inside quotes (least aggressive). Using this schema, Biais, Hillion, and Spatt (1995) document two important facts. First, order submissions are contingent on the "state" of the market. For example, a wide inside bid–ask spread increases the probability of price-improving limit orders and reduces the probability of market orders. Second, order submissions are autocorrelated. For example, there is a "diagonal effect" whereby orders with a particular level of aggressiveness tend to be followed by similar orders. Subsequent research has confirmed these empirical regularities in many different markets.[6]

The order flow and trade dynamics in these multiperiod models are derived from intertemporal bargaining by buyers and sellers on opposite sides of the market and intertemporal competition by traders on the same side of the market. Investors arrive and make trading decisions asynchronously, which precludes Bertrand competition since future investors cannot respond contemporaneously to the actions of earlier investors. However, imperfect intertemporal competition is still possible since the knowledge that more investors will arrive in the future affects the trades to which rational investors agree

[6]See Griffiths et al. (2000) for the Toronto Stock Exchange, Ranaldo (2004) for the Swiss Stock Exchange, Cao, Hansch, and Wang (2004) for the Australian Stock Exchange, and related research discussed below.

at earlier dates. Thus, an investor submitting a limit buy at date t competes indirectly with future potential buyers. If her bid is not sufficiently attractive, future sellers will submit limit sells in the hope of trading with future buyers rather than trading with the date t limit buy. Thus, intertemporal competition imposes dynamic incentive compatibility constraints on limit order submissions: Limit prices must be set such that at least some future traders will choose to trade with existing limit orders rather than submitting limit orders of their own on the other side of the market. In other words, bids must be set so that, for at least some future seller, the "bid in the hand is worth more than an ask in the bush," where the continuation value of the potential future ask itself depends endogenously on incentive compatibility constraints involving potential trading decisions of investors at even more distant future dates.

Modeling chains of incentive compatibility constraints is difficult. The first models to do this for limit order markets were Foucault (1999) and Parlour (1998). A number of models followed that differ from each other in the progressive complexity and realism of the investor decisions and information sets and, specifically, in their assumptions about what happens after limit orders are submitted: How long do limit orders last before being cancelled? How frequently do investors return and modify their orders? These timing assumptions determine the bargaining power of the investor at date t relative to investors who arrived in the past and relative to investors who will arrive in the future.

Foucault (1999) identifies price quotation as an essential aspect of dynamic limit order trading. In particular, at what prices will investors post limit orders? To keep his analysis tractable, limit orders are assumed to survive for just one period. If unfilled after one period, they are exogenously cancelled. This timing assumption effectively turns limit orders into "take it or leave it" offers of liquidity to the next arriving investor. Foucault also assumes that the common value process v_t evolves on a binomial tree with equiprobable increments σ or $-\sigma$ and that the private value y_t takes one of two possible values, L or $-L$. Thus, there are four possible fundamental states for the arriving investor: $(+\sigma, +L)$, $(-\sigma, +L)$, $(+\sigma, -L)$, and $(-\sigma, -L)$. The resulting order submission and trade dynamics are intuitive. If the limit order book is empty, arriving investors with positive (negative) private values post limit buy (sell) orders in hopes of trading with a negative (positive) private value investor next period. The challenge is to determine the equilibrium bid and ask prices where limit orders will be posted when the book is empty. The fact that there are only four possible states next period and the fact that buyer and seller valuations can, given particular parameters, be ranked leads to two equations in two constant quote spreads, $a^* = A_t^* - v_t$ and $b^* = v_t - B_t^*$, above and below the (changing) common value v_t. The solution is the stationary equilibrium spreads.

The Foucault model does not make realistic empirical predictions about order flow dynamics. Indeed, given the one-period limit order shelf life, there is at most one limit order in the book at any time. Rather, the main result is an analysis of the impact of Copeland and Galai (1983) "picking off" risk on the equilibrium mix of limit and market orders. Increased common value volatility weakly increases the bid–ask spread, which reduces the number of states in which investors submit market orders to trade with existing limit orders, thereby lowering the welfare gains from consummated trades.

The intuition is that when value volatility is low, the required compensation for the risk of being picked off is sufficiently small that limit sells from a low private value $-L$ investor at t are executed in both the $(+\sigma, +L)$ and $(-\sigma, +L)$ states at $t+1$. However, when volatility is high and the compensation for picking-off risk must be large, then limit sells at the ask $v_t + a^*$ are only executed in the $(+\sigma, +L)$ state, not in the $(+L, -\sigma)$ state. In particular, an investor with a valuation $v_t - \sigma + L$ submits a limit buy at $v_t - \sigma - b^*$ despite the presence of a limit sell in the book. Thus, higher asset volatility increases the proportion of limit order submissions, reduces the welfare gains from consummated trades, and widens the bid–ask spread.

Empirical evidence Ranaldo (2004) and others confirm that the inside limit order bid–ask spread is indeed increasing in price volatility. Furthermore, Ahn, Bae, and Chan (2001) find that the volume of limit order submissions is increasing in price volatility. These results are consistent with Foucault's prediction. An alternative explanation, however, is that, rather than measuring potential picking-off risk from fundamental valuation randomness, high lagged volatility may instead simply reflect the mechanical effect that prices are more volatile in thin markets. In this case, the observed positive volatility/limit order submission correlation could be spurious, in that high volatility may indicate a thin book and a profitable trading opportunity, which stimulates increased submission of limit orders.

Handa, Schwartz, and Tiwari (2003) derive and test another prediction of the Foucault model: The bid–ask spread should be greater in "balanced" markets than in unbalanced markets with unequal numbers of (high private value) buyers or (low private value) sellers.[7] In unbalanced markets, the scarce type of traders have greater market power, which lets them extract most of the gains-from-trade. Since they extract these gains-from-trade irrespective of whether they post limit orders directly or simply threaten to do so and thereby coerce more advantageous limit orders from their more numerous, desperate-to-trade counterparties, the result is that bid–ask spreads should be tighter in unbalanced markets. This prediction is confirmed empirically for the CAC40 stocks on the Paris Bourse.

Parlour (1998) models dynamic queue formation as another essential aspect of limit order trading. In particular, when will investors choose to join an existing queue of limit orders? Holding bid and ask quotes fixed for tractability, investors decide whether, given the current book, to submit a limit order of their own or to submit a market order. Limit orders in Parlour (1998) are long-lived and remain in the book indefinitely. This leads to a rich set of possible book dynamics as limit orders accumulate and are executed over time. This allows for more detailed predictions about state-contingent order flow autocorrelations than does the three-state book in Foucault (1999). Limit orders are risky because they only execute if enough market orders arrive in the future to execute them plus all of the limit orders with priority ahead of them in the queue. In the model, investors trade to shift consumption between two dates given differences in their

[7]The Foucault bid–ask spread is, strictly speaking, a "shadow" spread between an actual limit order and a hypothetical order on the other side of the market rather than an actual spread between two concurrent limit orders.

intertemporal rates of substitution. Investors with extreme time preferences have large gains to trade and endogenously demand liquidity from investors with less extreme time preferences. The critical time preference where the optimal order changes depends endogenously on the state of the limit order book.

The main result in Parlour (1998) is that the autocorrelations of transactions and order flow submissions reproduce a version of the diagonal effect: Market orders become more likely after market orders on the same side of the market. The intuition is that market buys, for example, reduce the available liquidity at the ask, thus making future liquidity provision at the ask more profitable, thereby shifting the critical time preference and causing more future sellers to choose to submit limit sells rather than market sells. More generally, serial correlation in order flow is shown to arise from liquidity dynamics as well as from informed trading.

Empirical evidence The synergy between theory and empirics has been particularly fruitful in research into order submission dynamics. Taking advantage of the recent willingness of exchanges worldwide to provide order flow data, the empirical literature has disentangled and identified multiple factors driving order flows at different frequencies. Ellul et al. (2007) find strong positive serial correlation in orders at high frequencies (the diagonal effect) but negative autocorrelation at lower frequencies. They interpret this as waves of competing order flows arriving in quick succession in response to market events (e.g., due to mimicking, competition, and order splitting) within a stable cycle of random liquidity depletion and replenishment.

For the most part, reduced-form regressions have been used to test qualitative predictions about order submissions. An exception is Hollifield, Miller, and Sandås (2004), who derive and test structural restrictions on optimal order submissions in a model with sequentially arriving investors. Consider an investor who arrives at a date t with a high total common plus private valuation $v_t + y_t$ and who is restricted to submit at most a single limit order or market order for q_t shares. Given the existing book and the parameters of the prevailing market environment, the investor's expected profit per share using a buy order at price p_j is

$$\pi_t(p_j, q_t) = \psi_t(p_j, q_t)(v_t + y_t - p_{jt}^{\text{trade}}) + \xi_t(p_j, q_t) - c, \tag{5}$$

where $\psi_t(p_j, q_t)$ is the expected fraction of the order that will eventually be filled, p_{jt}^{trade} is the limit price p_j (for a limit order) or the volume-weighted execution price (for a market order), $\xi_t(p_j, q_t)$ is the expected picking-off risk due to future expected changes in the common value component given order execution, and c is an order submission cost.

The fact that the expected profit for each different order is linear in the private value y_t—with a slope equal to order j's expected fill ratio $\psi_t(p_j, q_t)$—means the optimal order submission strategy has a simple representation: There will be a set of intervals in the private values y for which different orders' profit lines are maximal. For each of these intervals, the order corresponding to the maximal profit line is, by construction, optimal. These optimal orders will be ordered as follows: Market buys are optimal given very high private valuations because they have the greatest slope/expected fill ratio $\psi(p_j, q_t)$. Limit buys with progressively lower bids and progressively lower expected fill ratios are optimal for realized private valuations in progressively lower intervals. A symmetric result holds for sell orders.

The key testable insight is that the thresholds delimiting these intervals—which are computed by equating the expected profit lines for the adjoining optimal orders—should be monotone decreasing as the expected fill ratios fall. The HMS statistic tests the monotonicity of estimated thresholds using empirical estimates of $\widehat{\psi}(p_j, q_t)$ and $\widehat{\xi}_t(p_j, q_t)$ in (5).[8] Using a single Swedish stock to illustrate their methodology, the monotonicity restriction is rejected using buy and sell orders jointly. It is not known, unfortunately, how general this rejection is for other stocks. However, Hedvall, Niemeyer, and Rosenqvist (1997) and Ranaldo (2004) also find reduced-form evidence of asymmetries in investor behavior on the two sides of the market.

Foucault, Kadan, and Kandel (2005) combine endogenous quote determination on a multiprice grid, as in Foucault (1999), with queuing behavior given long-lived orders, as in Parlour (1998). This allows for tradeoffs between limit order price choices and execution waiting times. Limit orders are again infinitely lived and cannot be cancelled or changed. Investors' heterogeneous preferences for immediacy are captured by an explicit penalty on waiting time. Analytic expressions are obtained for the equilibrium trading strategies and the expected times until execution, but at the cost of several strong assumptions. Investors arrive sequentially and alternate deterministically between buyers and sellers. There is no quantity choice (all orders are for one share), and only quote-improving limit order submissions are allowed. In particular, limit order submissions deeper in the book are not allowed, by assumption. The effect of these assumptions is that the inside spread becomes a sufficient statistic for the state of the limit order books. Price priority reduces to something we might call *spread priority*: The equilibrium execution priority of a limit order—irrespective of which side of the market it is on—increases the smaller the spread the order causes. On the same side of the market, this is automatic given price priority, but, on the other side, it follows from alternating buyers and sellers and the quote-improving restriction.

The goal of their analysis is to develop predictions about the temporal properties of order submissions and trades rather than about order flow autocorrelation. A result that is directly relevant to the conditional autoregressive duration of transactions (see Engle and Russell 1998) is that the frequency of transactions is weakly decreasing in the bid–ask spread. This is a consequence of the fact that both patient and impatient investors use market orders when the spread is at its minimum, but only impatient investors use market order when the spread is wider. Limit order books in the model also have "holes," ranges of prices that investors jump over when submitting limit orders. Holes are a common feature of empirical limit order books (e.g., see Biais, Hillion, and

[8]This is just a test of order submission optimality, since no market-clearing condition is imposed requiring the fitted individual investor optimal orders to aggregate up to market order flows that are consistent with the empirically estimated $\widehat{\psi}(p_j, q_t)$ and $\widehat{\xi}_t(p_j, q_t)$ functions.

Spatt 1995). This leads to the concept of *resiliency*, which is measured as the probability that enough limit orders will arrive to return the book to the minimum bid–ask spread before the next transaction. Intuitively, the more potential holes there are, the fewer limit orders it takes to tighten the spread.[9] The analysis also delivers comparative static results about "fast" and "slow" markets as measured by the frequency of order arrivals. For example, slower markets are shown here to have narrower spreads and to be more resilient.

Rosu (2005) models a continuous-time market similar to Foucault, Kadan, and Kandel (2005), but with the innovation that investors can dynamically modify limit orders in real time. The result is the first fully dynamic model of a limit order market. This is in contrast to previous models in which the market is dynamic but the individual investor decision problem is static. The ability to modify limit orders in real time is important because now the number of investors actively present in the market varies randomly and, in particular, can be more than just one. Consequently, liquidity providers are no longer local monopolists constrained solely by intertemporal competition. Now there is also contemporaneous competition, as in the competitive batch models. Surprisingly, rather than complicating the model, the analysis is actually simplified due to a key insight: In equilibrium all investors with limit buys in the limit order book must have equal expected utilities (and analogously for investors with limit sells). Otherwise, with continuous prices, lower utility investors would revise their limit orders to undercut higher utility orders by an infinitesimal amount.

Rather than leading to Bertrand competition, the Rosu equilibrium has agents placing limit orders at different prices in the book. Arriving patient investors who wish to sell fill in the book starting from the maximal ask price followed by quote-improving limit orders. Limit orders are placed at prices such that there is no incentive for agents who previously submitted orders to undercut the new limit orders. This sequential undercutting endogenizes one of the assumptions in Foucault, Kadan, and Kandel (2005). More generally, the number of buyers and sellers with outstanding limit orders at each date t is a sufficient statistic for the state of the limit order book.

Rosu's analysis leads to predictions about the shape of the limit order book, order flow autocorrelation, and the temporal properties of orders and trades. As in Rock (1996) and the other batch models, the shape of the limit order book depends on the probability distribution for arriving market orders. For example, sufficiently high probabilities of large (multiunit) orders can lead to hump-shaped limit order books. Rosu also models patient and impatient investor arrival rates separately. This leads to a more intuitive result about the effect of fast markets: High impatient trader arrival rates on one side of the market lead to tighter spreads on the other side of the market. Lastly, the limit order book is full when the "gravitational pull" of using a market order to trade with the best quote on the other side of the market outweighs the price improvement (net of expected waiting cost) from a limit order. A new phenomenon in Rosu is "fleeting" limit orders. Once the book is full, a patient investor on one side of the

[9]There is some ambiguity about the notion of resiliency in the model. While holes lead to rapid spread recovery when limit orders arrive, they also cause rapid spread deterioration when market orders arrive.

quotes may submit a short-lived trial limit order at an intermediate price, proposing to "split the difference" with the patient investor on the other side of the market. This is one possible explanation for very short-lived limit orders documented in Hasbrouck and Saar (2002).

Empirical evidence Causality in the relation between execution time and limit order submissions runs in both directions. On the one hand, Lo, MacKinlay, and Zhang (2002) use survival analysis to show that limit order execution times are decreasing in the aggressiveness of limit prices. This is both a mechanical consequence of price priority rules and the potentially endogenous effect of aggressive order inducing latent demand for trade (i.e., aggressive limit orders reward investors on the other side of the market for submitting market orders rather than limit orders). On the other hand, the premise in Foucault, Kadan, and Kandel (2005) and Rosu (2005) is that investors care about execution time and that expectations about execution time affect order submissions. Tkatch and Kandel (2006) use a simultaneous equations specification to test for a causal impact of expected execution time on the decision of which orders are submitted while controlling for the causal impact of aggressiveness on execution time. They find that investors do appear to care about the expected execution time when trading equities and bonds on the Tel Aviv Stock Exchange.

Goettler, Parlour, and Rajan (2005a) model limit order trading dynamics with a large decision set. Investors can submit multiple limit orders at different prices and choose order quantities. This step forward in terms of realism comes at the cost of analytic tractability. The equilibrium must be computed numerically. The difficulty is that the many order submission possibilities cause the dimensionality of the information set to explode. For example, if there are L possible depths at N possible prices, then the number of possible states of the limit order book is L^N. Even numerically the curse of dimensionality can be severe.

Investors arrive sequentially to trade a risky asset that has a random common value component v_t and an investor-specific private value component y_t. The total value an investor receives/gives up on execution of an order at a date $\tau \geq t$ is $v_\tau + y_t$ per share traded—where the common value component changes over time but an investor's private value is fixed. The size of each investor's feasible trade is also bounded by a random variable z_t. The sequence of investor types (y_t, z_t) is uncorrelated over time. Given the cumulative limit order book L_t at the time she arrives, investor t submits a vector of market and limit orders X. As in Hollifield, Miller, and Sandås (2004), unexecuted limit orders are subject to stochastic cancellation over time, which acts like a discount rate. Making the cancellation probability a function of limit order mispricing relative to the changing common value is a reduced form for market monitoring by limit order submitters.

Investors submit orders to maximize their expected gain-from-trade. While this is a one-time decision for individual investors, their optimization takes into account random order cancellation and internalizes the impact of their orders on the dynamics of future investors' trading decisions. An equilibrium is a fixed point in the execution probability function μ_t^e and the expected common value conditional on order execution function Δ_t^v (i.e., the risk of being picked off). Since these are high dimensional functions, the model is solved based on a numerical algorithm which limits the updating of probabilities and strategies to the set of numerically recurrent states.

The model produces the richest set of conditional order flow dynamics yet derived. Perhaps as important, the analysis illustrates the fundamental differences between quote-driven markets—such as intermediated dealer markets and limit order markets in which only disinterested value traders provide liquidity—and order-driven limit order markets. For example, the common value v_t is frequently outside of the inside bid and ask quotes in the numerical simulations. Moreover, this is not solely due to stale quotes. When the sell side of the book is thin and the buy side is deep, potential buyers with a large positive private value y_t optimally submit limit buys at prices $p_j > v_t$. Such orders encourage future investors to submit market sells rather than limit sells and yet are still profitable relative to investor t's private value so long as $v_t < p_j < v_t + y_t$.

Empirical evidence Lo and Sapp (2005) extend the empirical methodology on order choice by considering the order size decision jointly with the order aggressiveness decision. Using a simultaneous equations probit model, they find that aggressiveness and size are negatively correlated. This study is also noteworthy for using data from the foreign exchange market. As in equity markets, FX limit order submitters appear to trade off execution probability against price concessions.

2.5. Limit Orders and Private Information

Kyle (1985) and Glosten and Milgrom (1985) have been the workhorse frameworks for adverse selection in securities markets. However, both make strong assumptions about the interaction between information and liquidity. In particular, liquidity providers are taken to be uninformed, while informed investors demand liquidity via market orders. Similarly, the intuition in Copeland and Galai (1983) is that infrequently monitored limit orders are susceptible to being picked off by later, better-informed investors. The first formal limit order models, Rock (1996) and Glosten (1994), also treat market orders as potentially informed and limit orders as uninformed.[10]

The recent focus on endogenous order choice has led to interest in rational expectations equilibria in which informed investors use both limit and market orders. This is a hard problem, but there has been some progress. One early model with informed price-contingent orders is Chakravarty and Holden (1995). If there is uncertainty about where uninformed investors will supply liquidity on the other side of the market (or about the random market orders from noise traders with batched market clearing), then strategic informed investors may use limit orders as insurance to bound the (random) price at which their market orders will trade. Another early informational model is Kumar and Seppi (1994). Given that (as discussed in section 2.2) uninformed investors trade

[10]Limit orders are equally vulnerable to being picked off by investors with private information and by investors who can condition on subsequent public news faster than limit orders can be cancelled. In either case, the information set of the market order submitter is superior to the information on which uninformed limit orders are conditioned at the time they are submitted. Of course, the mechanism through which information is revealed (and the limit order book is updated over time) is very different if information is announced or if it must be inferred from trading.

using packages mixing market and limit orders, informed investors must trade using the same mix of market and limit orders to avoid detection. More recently, Kaniel and Liu (2006) investigated the choice between market and limit orders by informed investors and patient uninformed investors. In their model, informed investors use limit orders when private information is sufficiently persistent. This extends earlier partial equilibrium order submission results in Angel (1992) and Harris (1998) to an equilibrium setting. Indeed, Bloomfield, O'Hara, and Saar (2005) argue that informed traders are actually natural liquidity suppliers. In an experimental market they find that informed traders initially demand liquidity via market orders but then switch to provide liquidity via limit orders. Because informed traders know the value of the asset, they are the first to know when prices have adjusted to a level such that limit orders cannot be "picked off."

Goettler, Parlour, and Rajan (2007) numerically solve the first dynamic model of limit orders with asymmetric information. Briefly, this is a continuous-time game in which agents arrive randomly and may trade one share in an open electronic limit order market. Investors value the asset for its cash flows (the common value) and for portfolio motives (private value). The structure of the game differs from the earlier Goettler, Parlour, and Rajan (2005a) model in two significant respects. First, the individual investor trading problem is now dynamic: Agents revisit the market probabilistically, at which time they may revise or cancel previous orders. Thus, the model accounts for the endogenous order-cancellation option. Second, there is endogenous acquisition of asymmetric information. Before the start of trade, investors decide whether or not to pay a fixed fee to receive private information in the future. Investors with the lowest private motive for trade, dubbed *speculators,* have the highest willingness to pay for information. This is intuitive since their strategies are most affected by small changes in the value of the asset. On average, the speculators are liquidity suppliers; therefore limit orders are on average submitted by informed traders. The same "race to trade" by informed investors, as in Holden and Subrahmanyam (1992), operates to mitigate adverse selection in the limit order book. Interestingly, there is an inverse relationship between the informativeness of the limit order book and the volatility of the cash flow common value. When the underlying common value is volatile, informed traders are less likely to supply liquidity and do so at more conservative prices. As a result, the limit order market acts as a volatility multiplier: Small changes in underlying asset volatility lead to larger changes in transaction price volatility. In addition, the correlation between fundamental value changes and changes in the transitory component of prices (i.e., the difference between the transaction price and the common value)—which can bias asset pricing variables such as estimated betas—can vary cross-sectionally with stocks' common value volatilities.

Empirical evidence Research into the information content of limit order submissions has largely concentrated on high frequency return predictability. The initial evidence was mixed. Biais, Hillion, and Spatt (1995) find that price revisions move in the direction of previous limit order flows. This suggests that later investors infer information from prior limit order submissions. However, Griffiths et al. (2000) find a significant price impact of nonmarketable limit orders in the opposite direction. More recent evidence, however, supports the hypothesis that limit orders are used by informed investors and, thus, reveal information. Cao, Hansch, and Wang (2004) find that lagged limit order book imbalances are informative about future price changes. Kaniel and Liu (2006) actually find evidence that informed traders may use limit orders more frequently than market orders.

One weakness with high frequency return predictability evidence is that it is unclear *what* limit orders are informative about. For example, Kavajecz and Odders-White (2004) suggest that limit orders may, in part, be informative about pockets of future liquidity rather than about future fundamentals. However, Berber and Caglio (2005) avoid this critique by investigating order submissions around events prone to private information (e.g., earnings announcements) and find that the direction of limit order flow is correlated with subsequent realized events. For example, more buy limit orders are placed before positive earnings announcements. Lastly, while most of the evidence relates to *directional* information about the mean of subsequent prices, Foucault, Moinas, and Theissen (2005) find that the depth of the limit order book on Euronext Paris can be used to forecast future price volatility.

3. MARKET DESIGN

No one, to date, has formulated the mechanism design problem to which a dynamic limit order market is the solution. Thus, it is difficult to evaluate whether the limit order market structure is optimal. A complete mechanism design analysis would need to address a number of questions. Given the similarity between limit order markets and multiunit auctions, does the discriminatory execution of limit orders prevent potential manipulation of uniform price mechanisms, as in Back and Zender (1993)? Does time priority discourage collusion by liquidity providers, as in Dutta and Madhavan (1997)? However, some progress has been made on three market design issues: the robustness of limit order markets to competition, the welfare properties of limit order markets, and optimal limit order transparency. A related set of market design issues involves comparisons of limit order markets with dealer markets and call markets.

3.1. Competition and Limit Order Markets

Glosten (1994) comes closest to addressing the optimal market design question. He demonstrates that competitive limit order markets provide the maximal liquidity in the presence of adverse selection and monopsonistic liquidity demand. This leads to a striking result: Under certain conditions, limit order markets are competition-proof—the entry of a rival market cannot profitably improve the liquidity provided by a competitive limit order market—and inevitable—the entry of a limit order market can provide additional liquidity if existing markets earn nonnegative profits on liquidity provision. The intuition is as follows: In the model there are competitive risk neutral liquidity providers and a single liquidity demander who maximizes quasi-convex preferences over shares and cash balances. Given her market power, the monopsonistic liquidity demander decides how much to trade based on the marginal cost of liquidity.[11] Thus, when trading on multiple competing liquidity supply schedules, the liquidity demander splits up her total trade x to equate marginal costs in all markets in which she trades (up to any caps on how much a liquidity provider will trade). For liquidity providers, the expected profit from providing the Qth incremental share of aggregate liquidity is an upper-tail expectation, given the asset value conditional on the information revealed by the total amount traded. Since competition among risk neutral liquidity providers in a stand-alone limit order market drives these expected profits to zero, the entry of a new rival market providing additional liquidity at any particular marginal cost level can only drive the expected profit negative. Similarly, a stand-alone liquidity supply schedule that earns nonnegative expected profits, but that differs from the competitive limit order book, must have at least one price where the expected marginal profit from incremental liquidity is positive. A limit order market can then enter and profitably provide liquidity at that point.

The worldwide ascendancy of limit order markets appears to validate Glosten's result, but inevitability is not assumption-free. Thus, the full reach of the inevitability result is still an open theoretical question. For example, although both market order and limit order quantities are endogenously derived in Glosten (1994), the order type choice is exogenous. The optimal mechanism with endogenous order type choice is not known. There are, however, other caveats to limit order inevitability about which more is known.

One caveat is that noninformational trading costs are empirically significant. Huang and Stoll (1997) estimate that order-processing costs account for over 80 percent of the bid–ask spread. Parlour and Seppi (2003) specifically consider heterogeneous noninformational submission costs and find that the impact on intermarket competition is quite different from that of adverse selection. Unlike asymmetric information costs, which depend on information revealed by the total trade of the active investor across all markets, order submission costs are independent of what happens on other markets. Parlour and Seppi (2003) extend Seppi (1997) specifically to model competition between a hybrid limit order market—with both a limit order book and a specialist who can provide ex post price improvement by undercutting the limit order book after the market order has arrived—and a pure limit order market with no specialist. They find multiple equilibria in which the outcome depends on the tie-breaking "preferencing" rules investors use to split orders between the two markets when indifferent. In particular, equilibria exist in which the hybrid market dominates the pure limit order market and in which the two markets coexist. Foucault and Melkveld (2005) use a similar analysis to show that, with time priority (rather than pro rata rationing as in Glosten 1994), the cumulative limit order depth with multiple competing pure limit order markets can exceed that of a single pure limit order market.

A second caveat is that equilibrium outcomes depend on who is trading as well as on institutional structure. Changing the characteristics of traders can lead to different

[11] In contrast, competitive liquidity demanders in a batch market would trade based on the price of the marginal share.

outcomes with the same market structure. The extent of the differences can be illustrated using the model of Seppi (1997). His model gives the equilibrium in a stand-alone pure limit order market (PLM) with value traders and one active trader and also the equilibrium in a stand-alone hybrid limit order market (HLM) with value traders, one active trader, and a specialist who offers ex post price improvement by undercutting the limit order book after the market order arrives but before limit orders are executed. An institutionalized "last mover" advantage is not, however, necessary to implement the HLM equilibrium. Under certain conditions, the HLM equilibrium outcome can also be implemented on a pure limit order market without a specialist. Consider what happens when the person who would have been the specialist—who we call here the *would-be specialist*—joins the other traders in a pure limit order market. In particular, suppose the would-be specialist continues to monitor the market in real time but is stripped of his ability to ex post undercut the limit order book by interposing his order in between market orders and existing limit orders.

***Proposition* 1** *If (i) the active trader is not limited to market orders but can submit a single limit order or market order and (ii) if the would-be specialist retains the specialist's bilateral bargaining power vis-à-vis the active trader,*[12] *then the HLM equilibrium can be implemented on a pure limit order market.*

The difficulty in implementing the HLM equilibrium is that the would-be specialist cannot undercut limit orders unilaterally on a pure limit order market. To circumvent this difficulty requires the active trader's cooperation. The active trader submits a marketable limit order (rather than a market order) that crosses with limit orders up through a quantity-appropriate stop-out price, at which point the unexecuted residual is posted as a limit order. The would-be specialist monitors the market and, seeing the advantageously priced limit order at the stop-out price, submits a market order to clean up the residual limit order using the same liquidity supply schedule he would as the specialist in a hybrid market. The active trader knows this schedule and, given that the would-be specialist retains the bargaining power, submits the right residual order at the appropriate stop-out price given the total amount she wants to trade. The active trader is willing to enable the would-be specialist's undercutting of the limit order book because this reduces her overall trading costs relative to trading with limit orders at even worse prices.[13] The limit order traders, knowing that the would-be specialist and the active investor will cooperate this way, rationally submit the HLM (rather than the PLM) limit order quantities. Thus, although the would-be specialist cannot unilaterally implement the HLM equilibrium—he has no special status on a PLM entitling him to intervene in

[12]Assumptions (i) and (ii) simplify the bargaining problem between the would-be specialist and the active trader. The assumption that the active trader can only submit a single limit order keeps her from tricking the would-be specialist into providing liquidity and then returning to trade again. Similarly, the fact that the active trader actively wants to trade is assumed to prevent her from submitting credible "take it or leave it" offers to extort better liquidity from the would-be specialist, who only trades to earn a profit.

[13]Biais, Hillion, and Spatt (1995) find evidence of investors posting marketable limit orders to draw out unposted (or hidden) liquidity on the Paris Bourse. Short-lived fleeting limit orders in Hasbrouck and Saar (2002) may also be "advertising" by would-be specialists that they are present and monitoring the market.

the mechanical crossing of a market order with limit book—the HLM equilibrium can be collectively implemented. Thus, market institutions are not uniquely associated with equilibrium outcomes. In particular, the allocation implemented on a pure limit order market depends critically on the sophistication of the active traders and the presence or absence of a would-be specialist.

A third caveat, mentioned in Glosten (1994), is the absence of direct communication between traders. Communication is clearly an important channel for information aggregation and contracting in dealer markets. The impact of reduced communication on limit order market inevitability is, however, unclear. On the one hand, communication may intensify informational asymmetries by reducing the amount of anonymous trading noise in which informed traders can hide. On the other hand, communication may also reduce the incentive to acquire information. We also note that in a dynamic context, there is some limited scope for communication in limit order markets. Hasbrouck and Saar (2002) empirically document a large number of fleeting limit orders, which are placed and then immediately cancelled, which, they suggest, may be a communication device to negotiate and propose possible divisions of gains-from-trade.

3.2. Imperfect Competition

An institutional mechanism that performs well under perfect competition may perform less well under oligopolistic or monopolistic conditions. The asynchronous trading models discussed in Section 2.4 analyze intertemporal imperfect competition in limit order markets. Biais, Martimort, and Rochet (2000) present an elegant analysis of contemporaneous imperfect competition. A group of N risk-neutral liquidity providers precommit to quotation schedules to provide liquidity. After the schedules are posted, a risk-averse investor arrives with both private inventory motives and private cash flow information. She decides how much to trade and then splits up her market orders to trade optimally across the various quoted schedules. As previously shown in Bernhardt and Hughson (1997), competition in price schedules need not lead to zero profits for the liquidity providers. Given adverse selection, price schedules are quantity sensitive, and, given order splitting, the competition (unlike in Kyle 1985) is not of the "all or nothing" type that leads to Bertrand competition. The Biais et al. model establishes the existence and uniqueness[14] of a symmetric equilibrium in convex schedules (i.e., the price paid for the marginal share is increasing in the order size) where the liquidity providers earn positive profits. As the number of competitors grows, the equilibrium converges in the limit to the competitive limit order market in Glosten (1994).

The model provides one of the first characterizations of limit order books in a static noncompetitive environment. The fact that the liquidity schedules are convex means that

[14]While the equilibrium is unique within the class of convex schedules and the equilibrium in convex schedules is an equilibrium within the class of all schedules, it is not established that the equilibrium is unique within the larger class.

they are equivalent to a collection of limit orders. To see this, note that the total payment $T_i(x_i)$ associated with a market order x_i to market maker i can be written as

$$T_i(x_i) = \int_0^{x_i} t_i(z)dz, \tag{6}$$

where $t_i(z)$ is the marginal price of the zth unit. If the schedule is convex, then the marginal prices $t_i(z)$ are increasing the quantity z, just as for a schedule of limit orders. Thus, in a static setting, a limit order market is effectively equivalent to a call market in which order schedules are constrained to be convex. The analysis also illustrates that intermarket competition in liquidity provision and cost-minimizing order splitting in the absence of priority rules can mimic intramarket competition between liquidity providers on a limit order market with priority rules. However, the model cannot be viewed as competing ECNs since the quotation schedule submitted by an individual strategic liquidity supplier will not be the same as the aggregate schedule submitted by multiple investors on an ECN.

Instead of modeling competition between markets, Viswanathan and Wang (2002) ask whether liquidity demanders would prefer trading in an oligopolistic dealer market or trading in an oligopolistic limit order market. In each market alternative, liquidity providers compete by quoting price schedules, and then the liquidity demander splits up her total trade across the competing schedules. In the dealer market, customer market orders are executed at a uniform price; in the limit order market, market orders are executed in a discriminatory fashion. The assumption of a finite number N of liquidity providers with inventory costs means liquidity providers have market power. This leads to *bid shading*—that is, paying less than their actual marginal valuations for shares bought (and, analogously, overcharging for shares sold). The aggregate limit order book price schedule has a zero-quantity spread and bid shading that decreases at larger quantities. In contrast, the dealership market schedule is steeper but has no zero-quantity spread. As a result, small orders receive better execution in the dealer market, while larger orders receive better execution in the limit order market.

The welfare analysis is conducted ex ante before the realized shares traded is known. For a large family of bounded market order probability distributions, the expected selling proceeds are always greater in the limit order market. Thus, risk neutral liquidity demanders prefer oligopolistic limit order markets over oligopolistic dealer markets. However, the greater concavity (convexity) of the dealer market total proceeds (cost) for sell (buy) orders, given the steeper price schedules, means there is some level of volatility aversion such that risk averse liquidity demanders will prefer trading in an oligopolistic dealer market.

3.3. Dealer Markets

Limit order markets and dealer markets are the two dominant forms of financial markets today, so understanding the similarities and differences between them is important. Back and Baruch (2007) prove an equivalence result for dynamic limit order markets and a class of dynamic dealer markets when investors can split up their trades over time. Their model is continuous in time and prices and has a strategic long-lived informed trader. The analysis begins by noting that discriminatory pricing and ex ante liquidity provision in a competitive limit order market means that limit prices are upper-tail conditional expectations: A market order for a block of x shares is executed in a discriminatory fashion at a sequence of limit prices, where the limit price for the qth share of the order is $E_t(v|x_t^L \geq q)$, given the informed trader's strategy x_t^L in a limit order market at date t. In contrast, uniform pricing and ex post liquidity provision in a competitive dealer market implies that market-clearing prices are simple conditional expectations: A market order for x is entirely executed at the break-even value $E_t(v|x_t^D = x)$, given the informed trader's strategy x_t^D in a dealer market at date t. Next, the possibility is introduced of a *worked block*, which is a rapid sequence of one-share market orders submitted essentially instantaneously. In this case, when a dealer sees the qth one-share market order arrive within a given instant, she can only condition on the knowledge that the total worked order size is at least q. Thus, the dealer executes the qth unit at the upper-tail expectation $E_t(v|x_t^{WO} \geq q)$, given the informed trader's strategy x_t^{WO} for submitting work blocks in a dealer market at date t. The main result is that whatever outcomes can be implemented on a limit order market can also be implemented in a dealer market if investors use worked blocks.

3.4. Welfare

Separate from whether limit order markets are immune to competition is the question of whether limit order markets are socially desirable. The question here is not which mechanism minimizes the cost of liquidity but, rather, which is more efficient in allowing investors to realize gains-from-trade. Thus, market power and private information, which led to transfers between agents, can be ignored unless they impede efficient trades.

Answers to the efficiency question require measures of the investor costs and benefits from trading. Hollifield et al. (2006) use the first-order condition for the optimal order choice from Hollifield, Miller, and Sandås (2004) to recover a probability distribution over investors' private values implied by observed order submissions. The model is estimated using data from the Vancouver Stock Exchange. The model is then used to compute and compare the realized gains-from-trade from actual trading and the maximum possible gains-from-trade in a frictionless benchmark. The results suggest that there is substantial variation in private values[15] and that the VSE limit order trading mechanism achieves 90 percent of the maximum possible gains-from-trade.

These results are dramatic, but they are also subject to some caveats: The structural estimation assumes that arriving investors only submit orders once and that there is no asymmetric information. The fact that VSE stocks are generally thinly traded has the advantage of emphasizing strategic interactions in the market but also the disadvantage that ignored informational asymmetries may be substantial. Treating differences

[15]This is consistent with Handa, Schwartz, and Tiwari (2003), who use GMM to estimate the deep parameters of a Foucault model for the Paris Bourse. Their implied gains-to-trade are also large.

in information as differences in private values may cause the estimated dispersion in private values to be overstated.

In numerical simulations in Goettler, Parlour, and Rajan (2005b), an open limit order market achieves 92 percent of a theoretical benchmark with no frictions. The paper does not derive the optimal trading mechanism with private values and asymmetric information, but it does find that social welfare with limit orders is better than under several alternate incentive-compatible mechanisms.

These welfare comparisons are conservative, since both papers take the set of traders participating in the market as given. It is reasonable to suppose, however, that investor arrival frequencies might increase if the costs of trading go down. In other words, the composition of investors who choose to trade in a market may be determined, in part, by the market design. Lastly, other aspects of a market may also be important for welfare. For example, markets provide a public externality in the form of price discovery.

3.5. Robustness

Market failure occurs when there is no market-clearing price for liquidity. It is well known from Glosten (1989) that adverse selection problems can cause competitive dealer markets to fail when uninformed traders are price sensitive. Glosten (1994) shows the same is true for limit order markets. Given asymmetric information, there may not be enough price-sensitive uninformed demand to support any price schedule with a noninfinite slope. Portniaguina, Bernhardt, and Hughson (2006) show that limit order markets can fail even in the absence of adverse selection problems. They extend Seppi (1997) by making market orders price sensitive. The intuition for market failure is that if the limit order book is too thin, then price-elastic market order submitters will scale back their market order submissions. However, as the endogenous distribution of submitted market order quantities shifts toward zero, the probability of limit order execution falls, which, given ex ante limit order submission costs, leads to fewer limit orders and, thus, a thinner book. If market order submissions are sufficiently elastic, the limit order book may fail. As an example, they show that, in a hybrid market, cutting the tick size can lead to market failure, since a smaller tick makes it easier for the specialist to undercut the book, which, in equilibrium, makes the book thinner.

3.6. Transparency

Optimal limit order transparency has recently begun to receive attention.[16] In a limit order market, transparency is a continuum going from a *closed book*, in which the public knows nothing about the book, to intermediate cases, in which investors can choose to hide part of their orders (e.g., via iceberg orders) to an *open book* with real-time order disclosure. In terms of the granularity of information disclosed, exchanges might reveal aggregated depths at all prices or at just a subset of prices. They might even reveal individual orders themselves. Order information is sometimes accompanied by investor

[16]Rindi (2002) considers transparency in a rational-expectations framework.

identity information (e.g., broker codes). This can be useful if traders are differentially informed so that reputation matters.

Baruch (2005) constructs a static model of a hybrid market with a specialist in which liquidity traders and possibly an informed trader submit market orders. Limit order traders submit price-contingent orders, and the specialist sets a *stop-out price* at which the market clears. If the limit order book is open, then liquidity suppliers compete more fiercely and, *ceteris paribus*, submit more aggressive orders. A counterbalancing effect is that a deeper book encourages the informed trader to submit larger orders, increasing adverse selection. The competition effect outweighs the adverse selection effect, and (under specified conditions) displaying the limit order book is good for market order traders. They benefit both from a smaller price impact of their orders and because prices reveal more information. In sum, limit order traders and specialists extract fewer informational rents when the book is open.

Empirical evidence In 2002, OpenBook allowed off-exchange investors to see the whole NYSE limit order book instead of just the best bids and offers. Boehmer, Saar, and Yu (2005) find that order submission strategies appear to change. In particular, there is a higher cancellation rate and a shorter time to cancellation for limit orders once the book is open. The volume executed by floor brokers and specialists declined, suggesting that investors substituted away from floor brokers to limit orders and crowded out the specialists, consistent with the Baruch (2005) predictions. Further, characteristics of overall market quality, such as the price impact of orders and price efficiency, improved. This result may not be true for a pure limit order book: Madhavan, Porter, and Weaver (2005) show that the move to transparency on Toronto led to a decrease in overall liquidity and an increase in transaction costs and volatility. Simaan, Weaver, and Whitcomb (2003) find that market makers compete more aggressively when they can post anonymous limit orders on ECNs.

Foucault, Moinas, and Thiessen (2005) use a natural experiment on Euronext for an event study on identity information disclosure. In 2001 Euronext stopped displaying trader IDs publicly. An important intuition from Copeland and Galai (1983) is that limit order submitters give away free options for others to trade at their limit prices. The value of these trading options is increasing in the underlying price volatility. Thus, strategic liquidity suppliers will condition the spread between their limit buy and sell orders on any private information they have about future price volatility. Uninformed liquidity suppliers then attempt to infer volatility information from the limit order book. Specifically, they undercut this spread if they believe the spread in the book is too large and match it if they believe that the spread correctly reflects future price volatility. If the market is transparent, liquidity suppliers who potentially have information about future price movements will sometimes bluff and post wide spreads, even if they know that they are unwarranted, to increase their profits. However, if there is anonymity, then they will only post wide spreads when the price is indeed going to be more volatile (i.e., they cannot bluff about their information). Thus, the introduction of anonymity can lead to both improved liquidity (the informed liquidity traders do not bluff) in terms of on average lower spreads and less informative quotes. The idea that limit orders impound forward-looking information about future volatility is also tested in Foucault, Moinas, and Theissen (2005). As noted earlier, they find that the depth of the limit order book on Euronext Paris does forecast future price volatility.

4. QUESTIONS FOR FUTURE RESEARCH

There is still much we do not know about limit order markets. In terms of the basic modeling of optimal trading strategies and market equilibrium, only very stylized environments have been studied thus far. Joint decisions about order aggressiveness and quantity have not been fully modeled, and the role of optimal monitoring strategies in limit order trading is unexplored territory. The interplay between the use of limit orders and market orders and information aggregation also still needs to be worked out more fully. For example, how can order flow correlations due to liquidity dynamics be distinguished from order splitting and correlated trading on private information? An indication that limit order modeling is still in its infancy is that empirical research has largely focused on testing qualitative predictions of theory but not structural functional forms. In the few exceptions, such as Sandås (2001), the structural model is usually rejected. Much as the "equity premium puzzle" stimulated a wave of asset pricing theory, microstructure theory and empirics might benefit from greater attention to the quantitative and structural predictions of theory. For example, what individual investor order submission strategies aggregate into the observed aggregate order flow process?

The integration of trading strategies and portfolio optimization is still to be done. Since order execution depends on the arrival of counterparties, anything that affects future investors' willingness to trade can change the price/execution probability trade-off, including systematic marketwide events. Some questions here are: How do investors value the riskiness of particular trading strategies? How does the fact that investors trade groups of stocks affect their order submission decisions vis-à-vis an investor trading just one stock? If investors have a demand for certain generic stock characteristics (e.g., growth/value, industry) rather than for a specific stock, how does that affect their order submission choices across stocks?

A fundamental question of interest to financial economists is why investors trade. Limit order submissions are potentially a useful window through which to observe investor heterogeneity (e.g., private trading motives, urgency for trading). This suggests, for example, potential interaction between limit order book characteristics and liquidity-based asset pricing.

Optimal market design and competition between markets pose some timely questions and issues. As competition between demutualized profit-seeking exchanges intensifies, market design will be one front in that competition. Theory can provide guidance to regulators, customers, and the exchanges themselves. Some important questions still outstanding are: To what social welfare problem is a limit order market the solution? What are the welfare and competitiveness properties of limit order markets with random liquidity provision (via customer limit orders) as well as random liquidity demand? What is the theoretical basis for the apparently good welfare performance of limit order markets with asynchronous dynamic trading? Does information get aggregated more quickly via trading in limit order markets or in dealer markets? How do different transparency regimes and other market design decisions affect the efficiency and competitiveness of limit order markets? The large number of natural experiments involving changes in market design in different exchanges means that these questions can be examined both theoretically and empirically. A challenging question for structural estimation would be to see if the deep structural parameters of the trading economy are unchanged given changes in market institutions.

Theoretical modeling may also help with some significant methodological challenges in empirical limit order research. One challenge is data summary and representation. To handle the enormous order flow datasets, observations are typically aggregated. However, absent clear theoretical guidance, the appropriate form of aggregation is not known. Another challenge is that many observables from limit order markets are endogenous and are determined simultaneously. Attempts to deal with endogeneity, such as Tkatch and Kandel (2006) and Lo and Sapp (2005), would benefit from more realistic theory that could identify theoretically justifiable exogenous instruments.

References

Ahn, H., K. Bae, and K. Chan. 2001. Limit Orders, Depth and Volatility: Evidence from the Stock Exchange of Hong Kong, *Journal of Finance* 56, 767–788.

Aitken, M., N. Almeida, F. Harris, and T. McInish. 2005. Order Splitting and Order Aggressiveness in Electronic Trading. Working paper, Wake Forest University.

Amihud, Y., and H. Mendelson. 1986. Asset Pricing and the Bid–Ask Spread, *Journal of Financial Economics* 17, 223–249.

Anand, A., S. Chakravarty, and T. Martell. 2004. Empirical Evidence on the Evolution of Liquidity, Choice of Market versus Limit Orders by Informed Traders. Working paper, Syracuse University.

Angel, J. 1992. Limit versus Market Orders. Working paper, Georgetown University.

Back, K., and S. Baruch. 2007. Working Orders in Limit Order Markets and Floor Exchanges, *Journal of Finance* 62, 1589–1621.

Back, K., and J. Zender. 1993. Auctions of Divisible Goods: On the Rationale for the Treasury Experiment, *Review of Financial Studies* 6, 733–764.

Baruch, S. 2005. Who Benefits from an Open Limit-Order Book? *Journal of Business* 78, 1267–1306.

Beltran, H., P. Giot, and J. Gamming. 2005. Commonalities in the Order Book. Working paper, Catholic University of Louvain.

Berber, A., and C. Caglio. 2004. Order Submission Strategies and Information: Empirical Evidence from the NYSE. Working paper, University of Lausanne.

Bernhardt, D., and E. Hughson. 1997. Splitting Orders, *Review of Financial Studies* 10, 69–101.

Biais, B., L. Glosten, and C. Spatt. 2005. Market Microstructure: A Survey of Microfoundations, Empirical Results, and Policy Implications, *Journal of Financial Markets* 8, 217–264.

Biais, B., P. Hillion, and C. Spatt. 1995. An Empirical Analysis of the Limit Order Book and the Order Flow in the Paris Bourse, *Journal of Finance* 50, 1655–1689.

Biais, B., D. Martimort, and J. Rochet. 2000. Competing Mechanisms in a Common Value Environment, *Econometrica* 68, 799–837.

Bloomfield, R., M. O'Hara, and G. Saar. 2005. The "Make or Take" Decision in an Electronic Market: Evidence on the Evolution of Liquidity, *Journal of Financial Economics* 75, 165–199.

Boehmer, E., G. Saar, and L. Yu. 2005. Lifting the Veil: An Analysis of Pre-Trade Transparency at the NYSE, *Journal of Finance* 60, 783–815.

Brennan, M., and A. Subrahmanyam. 1996. Market Microstructure and Asset Pricing: On the Compensation for Illiquidity in Stock Returns, *Journal of Financial Economics* 41, 441–464.

Cao, C., O. Hansch, and X. Wang. 2004. The Informational Content of an Open Limit Order Book. Working paper, Pennsylvania State University.

Chakravarty, S., and C. Holden. 1995. An Integrated Model of Market and Limit Orders, *Journal of Financial Intermediation* 4, 213–241.

Cohen, K., S. Maier, R. Schwartz, and D. Whitcomb. 1981. Transaction Costs, Order Placement Strategy, and Existence of the Bid–Ask Spread, *Journal of Political Economy* 89, 287–305.

Copeland, T., and D. Galai. 1983. Information Effects on the Bid–Ask Spreads, *Journal of Finance* 38, 1457–1469.

Demsetz, H. 1968. The Cost of Transacting, *Quarterly Journal of Economics* 82, 33–53.

Dutta, P., and A. Madhavan. 1997. Competition and Colusion in Dealer Markets, *Journal of Finance* 52, 245–276.

Easley, D., S. Hvidkjaer, and M. O'Hara. 2002. Is Information Risk a Determinant of Asset Returns? *Journal of Finance* 57, 2185–2221.

Ellul, A., C. Holden, P. Jain, and R. Jennings. 2007. Determinants of Order Choice on the New York Stock Exchange. Working paper, Indiana University.

Engle, R., and R. Ferstenberg. 2006. Execution Risk. Working paper, New York University.

Engle, R., and J. Russell. 1998. Autoregressive Conditional Duration: A New Model for Irregularly Spaced Transaction Data, *Econometrica* 66, 1127–1162.

Foucault, T. 1999. Order Flow Composition and Trading Costs in a Dynamic Limit Order Market, *Journal of Financial Markets* 2, 99–134.

Foucault, T., and A. Menkveld. 2008. Competition for Order Flow and Smart Order Routing Systems. Working paper, *Journal of Finance* 63, 119–158.

Foucault, T., O. Kadan, and E. Kandel. 2005. The Limit Order Book as a Market for Liquidity, *Review of Financial Studies* 18, 1171–1217.

Foucault, T., S. Moinas, and E. Thiessen. 2005. Does Anonymity Matter in Electronic Limit Orders Markets? Working paper, HEC.

Glosten, L. 1989. Insider Trading, Liquidity and the Role of the Monopoly Specialist, *Journal of Business*, 62, 211–235.

Glosten, L. 1994. Is the Electronic Open Limit Order Book Inevitable? *Journal of Finance* 49, 1127–1161.

Glosten, L., and P. Milgrom. 1985. Bid, Ask, and Transaction Prices in a Specialist Market with Heterogeneously Informed Traders, *Journal of Financial Economics* 21, 123–144.

Goettler, R., C. Parlour, and U. Rajan. 2005a. Equilibrium in a Dynamic Limit Order Market, *Journal of Finance* 60, 2149–2192.

Goettler, R., C. Parlour, and U. Rajan. 2005b. Information Acquisition in a Limit Order Market. Working paper, Carnegie Mellon University.

Goettler, R., C. Parlour, and U. Rajan. 2007. Microstructure effects and Asset Pricing. Working paper, UC Berkeley.

Goldstein, M., and K. Kavajecz. 2000. Eighths, Sixteenths, and Market Depth: Changes in Tick Size and Liquidity Provision on the NYSE, *Journal of Financial Economics* 56, 125–149.

Griffiths, M., B. Smith, A. Turnball, and R. White. 2000. The Costs and Determinants of Order Aggressiveness, *Journal of Financial Economics* 56, 65–88.

Handa, Puneet, and Robert A. Schwartz. 1996. Limit Order Trading, *Journal of Finance* 51, 1835–1861.

Handa, P., R. Schwartz, and A. Tiwari. 2003. Quote Setting and Price Formation in an Order Driven Market, *Journal of Financial Markets* 6, 461–489.

Harris, L. 1994. Minimum Price Variations, Discrete Bid–Ask Spreads and Quotation Sizes, *Review of Financial Studies* 7, 149–178.

Harris, L. 1998. Optimal Dynamic Order Submission Strategies in Some Stylized Trading Problems, *Financial Markets, Institutions & Instruments* 7, 1–76.

Harris, L. 2003. *Trading & Exchanges: Market Microstructure for Practitioners*, Oxford University Press, Oxford.

Harris, L., and J. Hasbrouck. 1996. Market vs. Limit Orders: The SuperDOT Evidence on Order Submission Strategy, *Journal of Financial and Quantitative Analysis* 31, 213–231.

Harris, L., and V. Panchapagesan. 2005. The Information Content of the Limit Order Book: Evidence from NYSE Specialist Trading Decisions, *Journal of Financial Markets* 8, 25–67.

Harrison, J. Michael, and David M. Kreps. 1978. Speculative Behavior in a Stock Market with Heterogeneous Expectations, *Quarterly Journal of Economics* 92, 323–336.

Hasbrouck, J. 2007. *Empirical Market Microstructure*. Oxford University Press, Oxford.

Hasbrouck, J., and G. Saar. 2002. Limit Orders and Volatility in a Hybrid Market: The Island ECN. Working paper, New York University.

Hedvall, K., J. Niemeyer, and G. Rosenqvist. 1997. Do Buyers and Sellers Behave Similarly in a Limit Order Book? A High-Frequency Data Examination of the Finnish Stock Exchange, *Journal of Empirical Finance* 4, 279–293.

Holden, C., and A. Subrahmanyam. 1992. Long-Lived Private Information and Imperfect Competition, *Journal of Finance* 47, 247–270.

Hollifield, B., R. Miller, and P. Sandås. 2004. Empirical Analysis of Limit Order Markets, *Review of Economic Studies* 71, 1027–1063.

Hollifield, B., R. Miller, P. Sandås, and J. Slive. 2006. Estimating the Gains from Trade in Limit Order Markets, *Journal of Finance* 16, 2753–2804.

Huang, R., and H. Stoll. 1997. The Components of the Bid–Ask Spread: A General Approach, *Review of Financial Studies* 10, 1035–1064.

Irvine, P., G. Benston, and E. Kandel. 2000. Liquidity Beyond the Inside Spread: Measuring and Using Information in the Limit Order Book. Working paper, Emory University.

Jain, P. 2005. Financial Market Design and the Equity Premium: Electronic versus Floor Trading, *Journal of Finance* 60, 2955–2985.

Jones, C., and M. Lipson. 2001. Sixteenths: Direct Evidence on Institutional Execution Costs, *Journal of Financial Economics* 59, 253–278.

Kaniel, R., and H. Liu. 2006. What Orders Do Informed Traders Use? *Journal of Business* 79, 1867–1913.

Kavajecz, K. 1999. A Specialist's Quoted Depth and the Limit Order Book, *Journal of Finance* 54, 747–771.

Kavajecz, K., and E. Odders-White. 2004. Technical Analysis and Liquidity Provision, *Review of Financial Studies* 17, 1043–1071.

Kumar, P., and D. Seppi. 1994. Limit and Market Orders with Optimizing Traders. Working paper, Carnegie Mellon University.

Kyle, A. 1985. Continuous Auctions and Insider Trading, *Econometrica* 53, 1315–1335.

Kyle, A. 1989. Informed Speculation with Imperfect Competition, *Review of Economic Studies* 56, 317–355.

Lo, A., A. MacKinlay, and J. Zhang. 2002. Econometric Models of Limit-Order Executions, *Journal of Financial Economics* 65, 31–71.

Lo, I., and S. Sapp. 2005. Price Aggressiveness and Quantity: How Are They Determined in a Limit Order Market? Working paper, University of Western Ontario.

Madhavan, A. 2000. Market Microstructure: A Survey, *Journal of Financial Markets* 3, 205–258.

Madhavan, A., D. Porter, and D. Weaver. 2005. Should Securities Markets Be Transparent? *Journal of Financial Markets* 8, 265–287.

Nevmyvaka, Y., M. Kearns, M. Papandreou, and K. Sycara. 2005. Electronic Trading in Order-Driven Markets: Efficient Execution, *E-Commerce Technology: Seventh IEEE International Conference*, 190–197.

Obizhaeva, A., and J. Wang. 2005. Optimal Trading Strategy and Supply/Demand Dynamics. Working paper, MIT.

O'Hara, M. 1995. *Market Microstructure Theory*, Blackwell, Oxford.

Parlour, C. 1998. Price Dynamics in Limit Order Markets, *Review of Financial Studies* 11, 789–816.

Parlour, C., and D. Seppi. 2003. Liquidity-Based Competition for Order Flow, *Review of Financial Studies* 16, 301–343.

Pastor, L., and R. Stambaugh. 2003. Liquidity Risk and Expected Stock Returns, *Journal of Political Economy* 111, 642–685.

Portniaguina, E., D. Bernhardt, and E. Hughson. 2006. Hybrid Markets, Tick Size and Investor Trading Costs, *Journal of Financial Markets* 9, 433–447.

Ranaldo, A. 2004. Order Aggressiveness in Limit Order Book Markets, *Journal of Financial Markets* 7, 53–74.

Ready, M. 1999. The Specialist's Discretion: Stopped Orders and Price Improvement, *Review of Financial Studies* 12, 1075–1112.

Rindi, B. 2002. Transparency, Liquidity and Price Formation. Working paper, Bocconi University.

Rock, K. 1996. The Specialist's Order Book and Price Anomalies. Working paper, Harvard University.

Rosu, I. 2005. A Dynamic Model of the Limit Order Book. Working paper, University of Chicago.

Sandås, P. 2001. Adverse Selection and Competitive Market Making: Empirical Evidence from a Limit Order Market, *Review of Financial Studies* 14, 705–734.

Seppi, D. 1997. Liquidity Provision with Limit Orders and a Strategic Specialist, *Review of Financial Studies* 10, 103–150.

Simaan, Y., D. Weaver, and D. Whitcomb. 2003. Market Maker Quotation Behaviour and Pre-Trade Transparency, *Journal of Finance* 58, 1247–1267.

Swan, P., and P. Westerholm. 2006. Market Architecture and Global Exchange Efficiency. Working paper, University of Sydney.

Tkatch, I., and E. Kandel. 2006. Demand for the Immediacy of Execution: Time *Is* Money. Working paper, Georgia State University.

Viswanathan, S., and J. Wang. 2002. Market Architecture: Limit-Order Books versus Dealership Markets, *Journal of Financial Markets* 5, 127–167.

SECTION 3

Financial Intermediary Structure

Overview by Mitchell Berlin
Federal Reserve Bank of Philadelphia

1. INTRODUCTION

The contributions in this section address the theory of intermediation from an industrial organization perspective. The following three chapters are surveys of recent research on the traditional core questions in industrial organization as applied to financial intermediation. What factors determine the boundaries, size, and internal structure of firms? How does market structure affect the strategies and performance of firms? Of course, these questions are interrelated. In any industry, equilibrium firm size and structure affect the equilibrium market structure and performance, and vice versa.

Why, then, should you read these chapters rather than turn directly to the *Handbook of Industrial Organization*? One of the hard-won insights of the last 25 years of progress in industrial organization is that although game theory and contract theory provide useful unifying frameworks for thinking about many of the traditional questions in industrial organization, very few general statements apply, in general, across industries. We can learn about an individual industry only by detailed theoretical and empirical studies of the industry itself, and the financial services industry is no exception.

Two features of the financial services industry must be taken into account by all researchers in the field:

1. Financial intermediaries are intimately involved in the production and interpretation of information, which economists have long understood to have important implications for both the structure and performance of firms and markets. Issues

related to the production of information—notably, the difficulties of appropriating the returns to the production of information and the agency problems that arise when information production is delegated—run through all three chapters.

2. Financial services are among the most widely regulated industries throughout the world, and the general trend worldwide has been toward deregulation. Both regulation and the process of deregulation seriously complicate matters for researchers who would like to draw conclusions about the equilibrium structure of financial markets. Even where restrictions have been lifted or eased, the present structure of financial firms still reflects the legacy of past restrictions. And, as noted in Chapter 4 by Philip Strahan (in his account of the implications of bank mergers) and in Chapter 6 Amar Gande (in his account of the competitive effects of commercial bank entry into investment banking), the long-run effects of changes in competitive conditions may differ significantly from the short-run effects.

I should comment on the particular selection of topics covered in the three chapters. The authors, who are all prominent contributors to the literatures they survey, and I have used two main criteria for selecting topics. First, we have tried to highlight segments of the literature that have been particularly active and productive in recent years. Second, the authors have attempted to avoid extensive overlap with other recent surveys of the literature, notably Gorton and Winton's (2003) excellent survey of the field. Inevitably, there are active areas of research that neither previous surveys nor the present chapters have covered in detail. I address a couple of these at the end of this overview. For the most part, the chapters focus on commercial banks and only incidentally touch on other types of financial intermediaries, such as insurance companies, mutual funds, and finance companies. Thus, it is often convenient to use the term *bank* rather than the more cumbersome term *financial intermediary*. However, many of the issues faced by commercial banks and addressed in these chapters are also relevant to other types of financial intermediaries.

2. OVERVIEW OF THE CHAPTERS

In Chapter 4, Philip Strahan examines two main issues. In the first section of the chapter, he asks, What are the implications of bank size and structure and for lending behavior? Both deregulation and technological developments have led to a dramatic increase in the size and scope of financial services firms and to a significant increase in industry concentration in the last decade. In addition to the effects of these changes on the price and quantity of credit, Stahan examines the evidence for the feasibility of relationship lending in a deregulated marketplace.[1]

[1]Although he discusses the relevant theoretical developments, Strahan focuses primarily on the empirical literature; the theoretical underpinnings of the modern theory of financial intermediation are addressed at length in other parts of this handbook.

I won't try to convey the subtleties of his analysis, but Strahan's broad conclusion is that the weight of the evidence suggests that increases in bank size lead to greater availability of credit and greater efficiency in lending. However, it is difficult to disentangle the effects of the structural changes themselves from the effects of the factors underlying the structural changes, notably deregulation and technological developments. Strahan provides a very careful and nuanced analysis of the mixed evidence relating bank size and the availability of small business loans and relationship loans. He makes the important methodological point that the empirical literature has been hampered by the difficulty of identifying exogenous instruments that would permit the researcher to differentiate supply-driven changes in market structure from demand-driven changes.

In his second section, Strahan asks, What is the rationale for the joining of deposit taking and making loans? This question can be viewed as a variant of the traditional IO concern with the underlying economics of vertical integration, although (perhaps surprisingly) the intermediation literature has actually borrowed very little from IO theories of vertical integration. Since this is one of the central questions in the theory of intermediation, it is also surprising that the empirical work on this question is so scarce. This is a very active but still small literature that has yet to reach the stage where definite, or even highly qualified, conclusions can be drawn.

In Chapter 5, Loretta Mester examines the evidence for economies of scale and scope in banking, using the methodology of estimating cost and profit functions. This methodology is an essentially independent way of addressing empirically many of the same concerns as the empirical literature surveyed by Strahan, notably the likely effects of regulatory changes that permit both larger banks and more concentration in banking markets. One advantage of estimating cost and profit functions is that this methodology permits a researcher to extrapolate equilibrium outcomes, even in recently deregulated markets. Another advantage is that this methodology permits the researcher to distinguish the different sources of competitive advantage, for example, to differentiate profits that arise from low-cost production from a more profitable product mix.

Mester notes that until very recently, banking economists have confronted a serious dilemma in trying to interpret the central result of a generation of efficiency studies, the finding that economies of scale in banking were exhausted at implausibly low levels. Finding scale economies that were exhausted at levels below $500 million in assets posed an empirical conundrum, given the growth of very large banks in the 1980s and 1990s.[2]

In addition to providing an extensive discussion of the methodological issues in carrying out efficiency studies, Mester surveys recent studies that revise the earlier estimates of scale economies dramatically upward, consistent with observed trends in size and concentration in the banking industry. Interestingly, a significant share of the scale economies uncovered by recent researchers arises only when the models take explicit account of the intermediary functions of banks. In the *intermediation approach*, the

[2]She also identifies two other conundrums: (1) the relatively slow entry by commercial banks into nonbanking markets, despite falling regulatory barriers, and (2) the low empirical estimates of productivity growth in banking firms during the 1990s, despite evidence of significant technological advance.

model takes explicit account of risk taking and financial capital. The large estimated economies of scale appear only when measures of the cost of capital and financial capital are included explicitly in the estimations, evidence of diversification gains that permit large banks to act as more efficient risk takers.

The predominant finding in the efficiency literature is that there is little evidence of scope economies. As Mester notes, this may provide a partial explanation for her second conundrum, the relatively slow pace with which banks have expanded into activities beyond banking. However, the difficulty of using the available data to define inputs and outputs in a way that is consistent with modern theories of intermediation is a weakness of much of the efficiency literature. These measurement problems may also obscure potential scope economies.

In Chapter 6, Amar Gande examines the optimal scope of activities and the optimal structure of the financial firm, focusing on the joining of lending and underwriting. Underwriting is one nonbanking activity that banks have entered on a widespread scale; they have expanded their presence in investment banking markets with each relaxation of regulatory restrictions, culminating in the full removal of Glass–Steagall restrictions in 1999.

Gande's broad conclusion from a careful survey of the empirical literature—both the historical literature from the pre–Glass–Steagall period and the more recent empirical literature—is that significant efficiency gains are realized when lending and underwriting are joined. Empirically, bank entry is associated with lower underwriting fees and better pricing, and the largest effects are found for smaller and more informationally opaque borrowing firms. Gande's preferred interpretation of these results is that they are driven by scope economies; the information that banks gain about borrowers when they act as lenders is also useful when they act as underwriters. However, he cautions that disentangling this efficiency explanation from an alternative explanation that emphasizes the effects of increased competition in the market for underwriters with bank entry will require longer-term evidence.

Gande also concludes that evidence for conflicts of interest—in which lenders use their inside knowledge to exploit investors—is weak. In principle, evidence of conflicts of interest could take two forms. First, it might take the form of greater investor losses on bank-underwritten issues. The literature provides essentially no evidence for this type of direct effect. Second, evidence of conflicts could take the form of organizational decisions by banks, for example, the use of affiliated firms to underwrite risky issues or the design of underwriting syndicates to mitigate potential conflicts. Although some researchers claim to have found indirect evidence of conflicts of interest through such organizational choices, Gande argues that the evidence should be interpreted with caution.

3. PROMISING AVENUES FOR FUTURE RESEARCH

Each of the three chapters in this section points readers toward potentially fruitful directions for future investigation. In particular, the optimal internal organizational structure of financial intermediaries appears to be a particularly promising area for future research. The chapters also touch on interesting institutional structures that are external to the banking firm yet play a significant role in the intermediation process, notably lending syndicates and credit bureaus.

3.1. Internal Organization and Intermediation

One of the most fertile areas for future investigators concerns the optimal internal structure of financial intermediaries. Researchers have made much more progress in understanding the effects of bank size and market concentration on lending behavior and bank efficiency than they have in understanding the factors governing the internal organizational choices of banks.

In Chapter 4, Strahan surveys the evidence that large banks are primarily transactional lenders, while small banks are more likely to be relationship lenders. However, he also cites recent findings that raise a question: Can large banks seek an optimal mix of transactional and relationship lending by an appropriate design of their internal organization, in particular, by decentralizing decision making? This is an intriguing question because most theoretical investigations have concluded that there is a basic incompatibility between competitive markets and loan relationships. The incompatibility has two roots. In most models, relationship lending is infeasible without cross-subsidies, for example, cross-subsidies across time periods or between different groups of customers. Such cross-subsidies are infeasible in fully competitive markets. In addition, large organizations, which appear to be the inevitable outcome of competition, may have disadvantages in processing soft information.

Boot and Thakor (2000) were the first to argue that the mix between transactional and relationship lending might be a strategic choice for banks and that this choice might be affected by the degree of competition among banks.[3] Their analysis of a monopolistically competitive banking market makes the interesting argument that greater competition among banks might actually *increase* relationship lending by inducing banks to attempt to differentiate their loan products. Whether large banks confronting aggressive competitors can feasibly provide relationship banking services through decentralization, or whether they would optimally choose to do so, is an important open question.[4]

In Chapter 5, Mester highlights recent research that explicitly incorporates distinct managerial objectives into the estimation of cost and profit functions, thus enriching the efficiency literature by incorporating modern agency theory. For example, Hughes et al. (2003) find that the degree of managerial entrenchment in the purchasing firm affects whether asset acquisitions through mergers or asset sales increase or decrease bank efficiency. This result suggests that an intensive study of how different managerial incentive structures and different internal organizational choices affect bank efficiency

[3] Boot and Thakor also discuss the different effects of increased competition between banks and competition from capital markets.

[4] Degreyse and Ongena (2007) provide some preliminary empirical evidence from Norway.

may be a fruitful area of research. In particular, it would be interesting to know whether, and how, scale economies are affected by the internal organizational choices of the bank.

3.2. External Organization and Intermediation

3.2.1. Loan Syndicates

In Chapter 6, Gande discusses a number of contributions that examine the structure of underwriting syndicates for clues about potential conflicts of interest when banks act as underwriters. But syndicates, in which multiple intermediaries cooperate to provide or secure funds for a single firm, are intrinsically interesting institutional structures in their own right.

Lending syndicates have received increasing attention from researchers in recent years, mainly because syndicated lending has increased rapidly as a share of total bank lending. Researchers have viewed the syndicated loan as a type of hybrid that has features of both a relationship loan and a transactional loan. From one angle, borrowing from a lending syndicate can be viewed as a structured way for a firm to overcome its exclusive reliance on a single bank and to reduce the holdup problems that arise in exclusive lending relationships.[5] This immediately raises a question: What is the optimal number of lenders, and how should holdings be distributed among the lenders?

In an incomplete contracting setting, Bolton and Scharfstein (1996) argue that coordination problems make it more difficult for multiple lenders to renegotiate debt. This generates an interesting and plausible tradeoff: Multiple lenders reduce the likelihood of strategic default by borrowers who are capable of repaying their loan but increase the likelihood of inefficient liquidations of borrowers who default involuntarily. Bolton and Scharfstein (1996) argue explicitly that their theory is best interpreted as a model of loan syndicates.

A number of researchers have examined syndicate structure in light of Bolton and Scharfstein's model, but the evidence is as yet mixed. Some researchers claim to have found explicit evidence that syndicates are designed to make renegotiation more difficult. Esty and Megginson (2003) find that syndicated project finance loans made to firms in nations with weak creditor rights and weak legal enforcement are typically made by larger and less concentrated syndicates. Their interpretation is that syndicate structure is designed to deter strategic default by raising the costs of renegotiating the loan when formal legal channels are ineffective.[6] Sufi (2004) finds that for his

[5]In Chapter 5, Strahan discusses the problems of exclusive loan relationships and the empirical research on multiple-lender arrangements. This literature provides substantial support for the view that firms use multiple lenders, in part, to overcome holdup problems.

[6]Esty and Megginson (2003) drop all single-lender project loans from their sample, creating a potential selection bias. There is also a question of interpreting their result in light of Bolton and Scharfstein's model, which assumes the existence of a legal technology in which lenders can seize and liquidate assets when they are not repaid. It is not obvious that this assumption is satisfied in nations with impaired creditor rights or weak legal enforcement or that greater coordination problems among creditors increase the likelihood that the assumption will be satisfied. To be a fully coherent explanation, the summary indices of the legal environment would have to be disentangled so that these issues can be resolved.

subsample of loans to firms with debt ratings, syndicates are larger for speculative-grade firms than for investment-grade firms.[7] Most interestingly, he also finds that larger syndicate size reflects the addition of lenders with small loan shares, consistent with the view that syndicates are explicitly designed to raise the costs of loan renegotiations by adding potential holdouts. Sufi argues that although greater default risk is associated with both strategic default and involuntary default, forestalling strategic default is the empirically more important consideration, at least for syndicated loans to rated firms.

At the same time, there is convincing evidence that renegotiation of syndicated loans is common and that the ease of renegotiation is a valuable feature for many syndicates. Preece and Mullineaux (1996) find that the positive-announcement effect of a new loan declines with syndicate size, declining to zero when the syndicate has more than three members. This evidence suggests that the ease with which a loan can be renegotiated is a valuable component of the monitoring technology.[8] Numerous researchers document the prevalence of restrictive covenants in syndicated loans, as in single-lender bank loans.[9] Confirming practitioner claims, Dichev and Skinner (2002) provide formal empirical evidence that loan covenants are binding much of the time and that approximately 30 percent of syndicated loans are actually restructured in their sample (which includes both rated and unrated firms).[10] Interestingly, they find that the vast majority of restructurings involve technical defaults, that is, covenant violations, rather than a restructuring of the essential terms of the loan (interest payments, principle, maturity, or collateral).

Although it is premature to reconcile the conflicting strands of empirical evidence concerning the role of renegotiation in syndicate design, some preliminary thoughts are possible. First, Sufi's (2004) finding that syndicates are designed to create barriers to renegotiation concerns the largest firms that borrow on the syndicated loan market, firms with debt ratings. According to Sufi (2007), the average number of lenders for such firms is over 9, well beyond the range where Preece and Mullineaux (1996) find positive-announcement effects. Loans to large, rated firms are at the transactional end of the relationship/transaction spectrum, and flexibility and ease of renegotiation may be less important for such loans. Second, a syndicate can be designed to limit opportunities to renegotiate the central terms of the loan while retaining monitoring through binding, but renegotiable, covenants. This is feasible because restructuring the central terms of the loan (interest, principle, maturity, and collateral) requires unanimity, while renegotiation of covenants usually requires a majority or supermajority of

[7]Lee and Mullineaux (2004) find the *opposite* result for a sample similar to Sufi's. Sufi ascribes the difference in their results to differences in their empirical specification, notably that Lee and Mullineaux do not control for borrower size. Although I find Sufi's econometric argument in favor of including borrower size convincing—higher-risk firms are significantly smaller than lower-risk firms on average—there are other differences in the two empirical specifications. At this point in time, resolution of the conflicting results remains an open question.

[8]Smith and Warner (1979) were the first to argue that monitoring through covenants that are often renegotiated is an essential feature of private debt, and Berlin and Mester (1992) were the first to model this process formally.

[9]See, for example, Bradley and Roberts (2004), Dichev and Skinner (2002), and Sufi (2004).

[10]Unfortunately, Dichev and Skinner (2002) do not discuss the structure of their loan syndicates.

the lenders. When covenants are renegotiated, a fringe of small lenders need not be decisive. While this account is broadly consistent with the existing evidence, there are many open questions about the role of renegotiation in the structure of loan syndicates.[11]

There is greater consensus about the relationship between the informational opacity of the borrower and syndicate structure. For example, Sufi (forthcoming) provides evidence that more opaque borrowers tend to borrow from smaller syndicates, in which lead banks hold a larger share and which are composed of lenders located near the borrower. These results are consistent with the view that syndicates are designed to ensure that the lead lender has sufficient incentives to monitor the borrower.[12]

3.2.2. Credit Bureaus

The credit bureau is another organizational structure external to the banking firm that can both affect and be affected by the competitive structure of the market. For the most part, serious progress in the study of credit bureaus has been theoretical; the empirical difficulties of identifying the separate effects of credit bureaus within a complex financial system are formidable.[13]

A key effect of a credit bureau, whether private or government-run, is to promote competition by breaking down banks' informational monopolies. For example, Pagano and Jappelli (1993) present a pure adverse-selection model, in which banks have an informational advantage in lending to local customers but can't lend profitably to distant borrowers or to borrowers who have just entered their local market. Pagano and Jappelli find that banks are willing to form a credit bureau voluntarily—or to pay a private credit bureau to collect and disburse information about customers—only when profitable lending to mobile customers outweighs the rents lost from captive local customers. This model makes the interesting prediction that the incentives to form credit bureaus voluntarily are higher when borrowers are more mobile.[14]

This basic tradeoff reappears in subsequent models by Padilla and Pagano (1997) and Padilla and Pagano (2000), which also incorporate borrower incentives to make a high effort (moral hazard) in addition to adverse selection. In this setting, firms will make a higher effort when they expect to capture a large share of the future informational rents, but only if effort actually increases these informational rents.

The two main conclusions of these models are (1) credit bureaus do improve borrowers' incentives, but (2) this improvement may require restrictions on the types of

[11]The precise role of restrictions on loan sales by syndicate members, which Lee and Mullineaux (2004) find in a majority of the syndicated loans, is a particularly interesting area for further research.

[12]Similar results are found in Denis and Mullineaux (2000), Esty and Megginson (2003), and Lee and Mullineaux (2004).

[13]Recent work by Brown and Zehnder (2007) suggests that laboratory studies may be valuable for empirically examining the role of credit bureaus.

[14]Although a straightforward geographic interpretation is both apt and realistic, the term *local customer* may simply refer to any customer with whom a bank has a preexisting relationship. If customers have a range of reasons why they might choose to change banks, customers can be considered more mobile (in the sense of the model) when switching costs *not* related to informational capture are low.

information that can be shared. In particular, in banking markets that are highly competitive ex ante, borrower incentives improve only if the credit bureau limits the type of information it provides about the borrowers. In Padilla and Pagano (2000), the credit bureau must provide only information about the borrower's history of defaults, which depends on both the borrower's type and his or her effort. If the credit bureau provided potential lenders with enough information to infer a borrower's type accurately, then a previous default would not affect a future lender's willingness to lend. In this case, the borrower couldn't affect future lenders' inference about his or her type through greater effort, and information sharing would yield the lowest possible level of effort.[15] However, if the borrower's default history is affected both by the borrower's type and effort, a credit bureau that provides information only about the firm's default history will improve the borrower's incentives.

The basic idea in Padilla and Pagano (2000)—that overcoming adverse selection might exacerbate moral hazard—has also been used by Vercammen (1995) to explain why credit bureaus might choose to limit lender access to only recent information. Elul and Gottardi (2007) present a particularly striking result that welfare can be improved if the fact of a borrower's default is stricken from the public record. In a variant of Diamond's (1989) model of reputation, Elul and Gottardi show that if high-risk borrowers are permitted to reenter the market eventually following a default, the gain in output may outweigh the weakening of incentives. Note, it is essential that the lenders "forget" not just "forgive" past defaults. In Elul and Gottardi's model, lenders would never voluntarily forgive and choose to lend to known, high-risk borrowers.

4. CONCLUSION

I believe the authors in this section have successfully conveyed a sense of the exciting advances that researchers have made in the preceding decade in understanding the structure of financial intermediaries and the markets in which they compete. I hope they have also succeeded in communicating the great gaps in our knowledge that still exist and that they have also provided some useful hints about hopeful ways to fill these gaps. If so, they have carried out their assigned task.

References

Berlin, Mitchell, and Loretta J. Mester. 1992. Debt Covenants and Renegotiation, *Journal of Financial Intermediation* 2, 95–133.

Bolton, Patrick, and David S. Scharfstein. 1996. Optimal Debt Structure and the Number of Creditors, *Journal of Political Economy* 104, 1–25.

Boot, Arnoud W. A., and Anjan V. Thakor. 2000. Can Relationship Banking Survive Competition, *Journal of Finance* 55, 670–713.

[15]While this result is interesting theoretically and the underlying idea has more general application, its empirical significance is suspect. It requires banks to have private information about a borrower (that can be communicated to the credit bureau at reasonable cost) that is *very* informative about his or her future probability of default, apart from the borrower's default history.

Bradley, Michael, and Michael R. Roberts. 2004. The Pricing and Structure of Corporate Debt Covenants. Working paper, Duke University.

Brown, Martin, and Christian Zehnder. "Credit Registries, Relationship Lending, and Loan Repayment," *Journal of Money, Credit, and Banking* 39(8), December 2007, 1883–1919.

Degryse, Hans, and Steven Ongena. 2007. "The Impact of Competition on Bank Orientation," *Journal of Financial Intermediation* 16, 399–424.

Dennis, Steven A., and Donald J. Mullineaux. 2000. Syndicated Loans, *Journal of Financial Intermediation* 9, 404–426.

Diamond, Douglas W. 1989. Reputation Acquisition in Debt Markets, *Journal of Political Economy* 97, 828–862.

Dichev, Ilia D., and Douglas J. Skinner. 2002. Large-sample Evidence on the Debt Covenant Hypothesis, *Journal of Accounting Research* 40, 1091–1123.

Elul, Ronel and Piero Gottardi, "Bankruptcy: Is It Enough to Forgive or Must We Also Forget?" Working paper 07-10, Federal Reserve Bank of Philadelphia.

Esty, Benjamin C., and William L. Megginson. 2003. Creditor Rights, Enforcement, and Debt Ownership Structure: Evidence from the Global Syndicated Loan Market, *Journal of Financial and Quantitative Analysis* 30, 37–59.

Gorton, Gary, and Andrew J. Winton. 2003. Financial Intermediation, in George Constantinides, Milton Harris, and Rene Stulz (eds.), *Handbooks in the Economics of Finance, Volume IA: Corporate Finance*. Elsevier Science, Burlington, MA.

Hughes, Joseph P., William W. Lang, Loretta J. Mester, Choon-Geol Moon, and Michael S. Pagano. 2003. Do Banks Sacrifice Value to Build Empires? Managerial Incentives, Industry Consolidation, and Financial Performance, *Journal of Banking and Finance* 27, 417–447.

Lee, Sang Whi, and Donald J. Mullineaux. 2004. Monitoring, Financial Distress, and the Structure of Commercial Lending Syndicates, *Financial Management*, 107–130.

Padilla, A. Jorge, and Marco Pagano. 1997. Endogenous Communication Among Lenders and Entrepreneurial Incentives, *Review of Financial Studies* 10, 205–236.

Padilla, A. Jorge, and Marco Pagano. 2000. Sharing Default Information as a Borrower Disciplinary Device, *European Economic Review* 44, 1951–1980.

Pagano, Marco, and Tullio Jappelli. 2003. Information Sharing in Credit Markets, *Journal of Finance* 158, 1693–1718.

Preece, Dianna, and Mullineaux, Donald J. 1996. Monitoring, Loan Renegotiability, and Firm Value: The Role Lending Syndicates, *Journal of Banking and Finance* 20, 577–593.

Smith, Clifford W., and Jerold B. Warner. 1979. On Financial Contracting: An Analysis of Bond Covenants, *Journal of Financial Economics* 7, 117–161.

Sufi, Amir. 2004. Agency and Renegotiation in Corporate Finance: Evidence from Syndicated Loans. Working paper, MIT.

Sufi, Amir. 2007. Information Asymmetry and Financing Arrangements: Evidence from Syndicated Loans, *Journal of Finance* 62, 629–668.

Vercammen, James A. 1995. Credit Bureau Policy and Sustainable Reputation Effects in Credit Markets, *Economica* 62, 461–478.

CHAPTER 4

Bank Structure and Lending: What We Do and Do Not Know

Philip E. Strahan
Boston College, Wharton Financial Institutions Center, National Bureau of Economic Research

1. INTRODUCTION

This chapter summarizes empirical studies linking the structure of commercial banks to their ability to lend. By structure, I mean the *size* of banks and the way banks are financed with *deposits*. I offer the reader my perspectives on what we can and cannot conclude from a very large body of research. I make no promise, however, to cite or discuss every contribution.

The theory of financial intermediation generally and banking specifically began by emphasizing the intermediary's role in collecting information about borrowers and using that information to solve financial contracting problems related to adverse selection and moral hazard (e.g., Leland and Pyle 1977). As an intermediary, the bank pools funds from a large number of small and uninformed investors. Given the relatively limited information of these investors, we can expect banks to be financed mainly with debt (Townsend 1979). Because the bank plays the role of loan monitor on behalf of depositors, Diamond (1984) asks: Who monitors the monitor? His theory predicts that this second-order monitoring problem (i.e., the cost of delegation) can be minimized through diversification. The monitoring cost exists to the extent that the bank may default on its debt; as the well-diversified bank's loan *portfolio* becomes safer, the probability of full repayment of debt increases, hence delegated monitoring costs decrease. In a nutshell, safety and soundness improves the banker's incentives. So theory suggests that banks should be large, well diversified, and financed mainly with debt.

More recent models of lending, however, have focused on the need for banks and borrowers to forge long-term relationships. Information attained over the course of time can be used by the bank to make sensible credit allocation decisions, thus increasing credit access to otherwise-opaque firms. However, information generated by such relationships (so-called "soft" information) is hard to verify. Thus, within large organizations it may be costly to provide strong incentives to bank lending officers to make investments in relationships. Stein (2002) predicts, for example, that small and decentralized organizations (e.g., small banks) can more effectively invest in soft information than can large and centralized organizations (e.g., large banks). Thus, theory suggests a *potential tradeoff* associated with bank size. Bigger banks may be better lenders overall, but there may be a segment of the lending market—lending to small firms, where relationships matter most—in which small banks have an edge.

Beyond size, a second central characteristic of banks—as opposed to other intermediaries—has to do with their role in the payments system and as issuers of liquid deposits. Theorists have attempted to understand the marrying of illiquid bank loans with liquid bank deposits. Some models are based on liquidity insurance that may, for example, make banks vulnerable to catastrophic runs (e.g., Diamond and Dybvig 1983). Other models argue that the bank's capital structure is shaped by the illiquidity of the loan portfolio (e.g., Calomiris and Kahn 1991, Flannery 1994, and Diamond and Rajan 2001). In contrast, Fama (1985) argues that deposits, because of their central role in the payments system, give banks unique information that enables them to lend to opaque borrowers. All of these models (and others mentioned later) are struggling to find a synergy between bank deposits and bank loans that explains why they seem to go together, not just here and now, but across a wide range of different economies and across time. The stability of the basic structure of banks is especially impressive, given the growth of banking regulation and the increased role of government safety nets as well as the rapid deepening of securities markets over the past two decades (see, e.g., Mishkin and Strahan 1998).

In this chapter, I review the empirical studies related to these two central aspects of bank structure—their size and their role as deposit takers—and ask how this structure affects their ability to lend. I make no attempt to review theory, although I mention some prominent theoretical ideas as motivation for the empirical tests that have been done. To be more specific, in Section 2 I ask: What is the relationship between bank size and lending? Is there evidence in the data indicating a tradeoff between size in reducing delegated monitoring costs versus smaller banks' better ability to lend on "soft information"? I then turn in Section 3 to deposit/lending synergies. What do we know empirically about the interactions between the lending and deposit-taking sides of the banking business? Does the evidence support the various theories explaining why banks combine lending and deposits? Are deposit–lending synergies really important? If so, then we will continue to see banking in the traditional form going forward. If not, what will banks look like in the future?

The goal of this chapter is to suggest what we do and do not know from existing empirical evidence. Where are the controversies? What are the holes in the empirical literature? That is, what should researchers be doing to advance the literature? I come back to these questions in the conclusion.

2. BANK SIZE AND LENDING

2.1. Do Large Banks Lend More Than Small?

Diamond's seminal article on delegated monitoring implies that banks ought to be large and well diversified. The empirical research supports this broad prediction, in that the majority of banking assets are owned by large banks. For example, in 2000 in the United States, 85 percent of assets in the banking system were held by banking organizations (highest-level bank holding companies or stand-alone banks) with more than $1 billion in assets. Even in 1980, before banking deregulation and the resulting industry consolidation, 70 percent of assets were held by these large banking companies (Table 1). Outside the United States, Berger, Hasan, and Klapper (2004) report that in 21 developed nations, the market share of banks with assets above $1 billion averaged 65 percent. In a sample of 28 developing nations, they find that the share held by large banks rose to 74 percent, although for this group the cutoff for defining a large bank was reduced to $100 million to reflect the smaller average size of these economies.[1] So, broadly consistent with Diamond, even though most banks are small, most banking assets are held by large and well-diversified institutions.

[1]These statistics were computed during the 1994–2000 period.

TABLE 1 Domestic Asset Share, by Assets of the Banking Organization (year 2000 $s)

Year	Under $100 million (1)	$100 million to $1 billion (2)	$1 billion to $10 billion (3)	Over $10 billion (4)
1980	9.9%	19.5%	34.9%	35.7%
1981	10.0%	19.1%	35.2%	35.6%
1982	9.4%	18.2%	33.5%	38.8%
1983	8.7%	18.0%	32.6%	40.6%
1984	8.4%	17.9%	31.0%	42.7%
1985	8.1%	17.5%	26.7%	47.7%
1986	7.2%	16.4%	26.0%	50.4%
1987	7.0%	16.2%	24.9%	51.9%
1988	6.5%	15.9%	25.2%	52.4%
1989	6.2%	15.5%	24.2%	54.1%
1990	6.1%	15.9%	23.9%	54.1%
1991	6.0%	16.3%	24.4%	53.2%
1992	5.9%	16.5%	23.4%	54.2%
1993	5.7%	16.2%	20.9%	57.2%
1994	5.2%	15.5%	19.2%	60.2%
1995	4.7%	14.6%	19.1%	61.6%
1996	4.2%	14.4%	18.8%	62.6%
1997	3.8%	13.6%	17.2%	65.3%
1998	3.4%	12.6%	16.4%	67.6%
1999	3.2%	12.3%	16.7%	67.8%
2000	2.9%	11.9%	14.8%	70.4%

Size cutoffs are based on the asset size of the highest-level bank holding companies' total assets (foreign plus domestic), in constant year 2000 dollars. Nominal dollars were converted using the Consumer Price Index.

Research also has established clearly that larger banks lend a greater fraction of their assets than do very small banks. For example, DeYoung, Hunter, and Udell (2004) report that in 2001 the smallest banks—those with under $100 million in assets—held 59 percent of their assets in loans, while larger banks held between 62 percent and 66 percent of their assets in loans.[2] Differences in the amount of lending are less consistent, however, across size categories for banks with assets above the $100 million threshold. Large banks also tend to hold less capital per dollar of assets; hence, differences in the amount of lending supported by a given amount of *capital* between large and small banks are even larger than differences in the percentage of assets held as loans. To the extent that bank capital represents the scarce factor limiting bank lending capacity, these facts suggest that an increase in the average size of banks would come with more lending.

[2] Differences across size categories were smaller in 1980.

The difference between large and small bank lending is especially striking with respect to lending to businesses. For example, Demsetz and Strahan (1997) report a correlation of 0.3 between the log of bank assets and the ratio of commercial and industrial loans to assets, based on a sample of large, publicly traded banks. DeYoung, Hunter, and Udell (2004) report that 25 percent of loans at the largest banks (over $10 billion in assets) are composed of business loans, compared to only 17 percent of loans for the smallest (nonrural) banks. Banks also appear to *increase* their lending, both as a percentage of capital and as a percentage of assets, after size-increasing mergers and acquisitions (M&As). For example, in a sample of M&As between large banks, Akhavein, Berger, and Humphrey (1997) find lending increases from 56.4 percent of assets before the merger to 63.3 percent after.

If large banks really are better lenders than small, then why do we see so many small banks? One answer is that regulation and government subsidies have supported small banks. For instance, restrictions on geographical expansion, central bank liquidity support and payments system activities, and deposit insurance have consistently provided larger subsidies to small banks than to large banks. Consistent with government support being an important factor, White (1998) documents that until the early 1980s small banks in the United States consistently fought for, and won, increases in the coverage of deposit insurance. Small banks have also doggedly fought for continued Federal Reserve activities within the payments system, particularly with regard to the paper check clearing business (McAndrews and Strahan 2002).

These subsidies have been declining in recent years with deregulation of restrictions on bank branching and interstate banking and with the gradual inflation-induced erosion of deposit insurance coverage, which has been limited to accounts under $100,000 since it was last raised in 1980.[3] Over these same years, both the market share and relative profitability of small banks have declined in the United States.[4] For example, beginning in 1988 and continuing without abatement, the average return on shareholder's equity (book-value based) has been lowest among the smallest banks (Table 2). And between 1980 and 2000, the market share of the smallest banking companies (those with less than $100 million in assets, year 2000 dollars) fell from about 10 percent to less than three percent.[5] Still, many analysts continue to argue that small banks have a future, and the reason given typically has to do with their comparative advantage in offering credit to certain segments of the lending market.

2.2. Do Large Banks Lend Differently from Small Banks?

Despite the fairly strong evidence that large banks lend more than small banks (especially to businesses), there is a growing body of research suggesting that large and small banks may serve different kinds of borrowers. First, as noted, large banks focus on

[3] As of this writing, small banks have been lobbying for increases in deposit insurance coverage.

[4] For evidence that changes in banking structure and small vs. large bank profits are related specifically to banking deregulation, see Jayaratne and Strahan (1998) and Kroszner and Strahan (1999).

[5] The adjustment for inflation means that the smallest banking organizations in the year 2000 had assets of under $100 million, whereas the smallest banking organization in 1980 had assets of under $48 million.

TABLE 2 Median ROE, by Assets of the Banking Organization (year 2000 $s)

Year	Under $100 million (1)	$100 million to $1 billion (2)	$1 billion to $10 billion (3)	Over $10 billion (4)	Profit differential, largest – smallest (4) – (1)
1980	13.3%	12.8%	12.4%	12.8%	–0.6%
1981	12.9%	11.6%	12.1%	11.5%	–1.4%
1982	12.3%	12.0%	12.1%	10.9%	–1.4%
1983	11.4%	12.1%	11.9%	10.8%	–0.6%
1984	10.3%	11.9%	12.6%	12.8%	2.5%
1985	9.8%	12.8%	12.9%	12.7%	2.9%
1986	8.3%	12.1%	13.1%	12.9%	4.6%
1987	8.2%	11.5%	12.0%	7.4%	–0.7%
1988	8.9%	11.3%	12.7%	15.4%	6.4%
1989	9.3%	11.4%	12.0%	13.9%	4.6%
1990	8.9%	10.5%	10.6%	10.2%	1.3%
1991	9.2%	10.7%	10.9%	10.7%	1.5%
1992	11.0%	12.5%	13.3%	13.3%	2.3%
1993	11.1%	12.7%	13.7%	15.6%	4.5%
1994	10.6%	12.1%	13.4%	15.6%	5.0%
1995	10.2%	11.7%	12.9%	14.4%	4.2%
1996	10.2%	12.0%	13.6%	15.5%	5.3%
1997	9.9%	11.9%	13.7%	15.8%	5.9%
1998	9.3%	11.5%	13.3%	14.7%	5.4%
1999	9.1%	11.8%	14.3%	15.8%	6.7%
2000	9.0%	11.1%	13.2%	13.9%	4.9%

Size cutoffs are based on the asset size of the highest-level bank holding companies total assets (foreign plus domestic), in constant year 2000 dollars. Nominal dollars were converted using the Consumer Price Index.

business lending, whereas smaller banks tend to make more real estate loans (DeYoung, Hunter, and Udell 2004). For business lending, large banks seem to concentrate on large and well-established borrowers. These kinds of businesses tend to have relatively long track records with audited financial statements, and thus credit decisions can be made using "hard information," which Petersen (2004) characterizes as information that is quantifiable and comparable across borrowers and that need not be collected in person. Small banks, in contrast, seem to devote more of their business lending to smaller and less well-established firms. That is, small banks seem to specialize in lending based on "soft information." While there is no bright line that delineates the distinction between hard and soft information, one can think of loans based on soft information as the classic character loan, where the lender relies on knowledge about the business owner's integrity or local reputation for reliability. Such soft information is both difficult to compare across borrowers and hard to quantify and is therefore difficult or costly to verify by outsiders.

Lending based on soft information, because it is private to the banker, generates a potential tradeoff for borrowers. Concentrating their business with a single lender minimizes information production costs and the costs of monitoring loans over time. But private information attained over the course of time may tempt lenders to hold up the firm in order to extract rents (Rajan 1992 and Sharpe 1990). That is, a bank with private information can threaten to restrict credit to a borrower and use this threat to earn profits (for example, by increasing the price of the loan). Switching to an alternate source of credit will be expensive for the small borrower under these circumstances because a new lender would not have access to the same information as the current lender. Hence, the current lender can earn rents on its superior information. Ongena and Smith (2000) and Farinha and Santos (2002) study the duration of bank–borrower relationships in Norway and Portugal, respectively. Both studies find that the probability that a relationship ends increases with the age of the relationship (positive duration dependence), consistent with the idea that as firms mature their need for banking relationships declines. Similarly, Houston and James (1996) study publicly traded firms in the United States and find that larger firms, older firms, and firms with access to public debt are more likely to have multiple banking relationships than other firms.

While theory does not make sharp predictions about the duration of banking relationships and about the extent to which a firm concentrates its borrowing, empirical evidence suggests that small and young firms tend to concentrate their borrowing initially. Petersen and Rajan (1994) use data from the 1987 National Survey of Small Business Finance (NSSBF) to show that small firms tend to borrow from a single financial services provider and that the tendency toward concentration decreases with firm size and age. They also find that credit availability, as measured by the ability of a small firm to avoid very expensive late payment on trade credit, increases with both credit concentration and the duration of the bank–borrower relationship. Petersen and Rajan (1994) find a very weak link from the relationship variables to the interest rate on loans, however, arguing that limited credit availability manifests itself in the form of credit rationing rather than higher prices. In a similar study using the same data, Berger and Udell (1995) argue that lines of credit (as opposed to mortgage or equipment leases, for example) ought to reflect relationship capital more than loans secured by property or equipment. And they find that both the interest rate and the probability that a credit line is secured decline with the length of the bank–borrower relationship, although they also limit their sample to floating-rate loans (in contrast to Petersen and Rajan). Bharath et al. (2007) find that even for large borrowers, past relationships increase a bank's probability of capturing future business and that pricing of loans is lower when the firm has had a prior relationship with the bank. Moreover, Sufi (2007) finds that banks chosen to participate in syndicated loans to a large borrower are more likely to have had a prior relationship with the borrower. Taken as a whole, these results suggest that relationships improve credit availability at both the extensive (credit rationing) and intensive (price) margins and that relationships affect the allocation of lenders to borrowers.

Results outside the United States are somewhat less clear. For example, Degryse and Van Cayseele (2000) find that interest rates on loans to small Belgian firms increase, rather than decrease, with the duration of the bank–borrower relationship. This effect, however, is small for firms borrowing under lines of credit, where relationship formation is likely to be more important. Also, they find that collateral is less commonly used as the length of a relationship increases, perhaps suggesting that relationships may be able to substitute for hard assets to solve borrower control problems. Harhoff and Korting (1998) analyze loans to small firms in Germany. Consistent with results from the United States, they find that small firms concentrate their borrowing, that concentration declines with firm size, and that credit availability increases with the duration of a firm's relationship with the lender. Specifically, collateral use declines with relationship duration and trade credit paid late declines with concentration of credit, although like Petersen and Rajan (but in contrast to Berger and Udell 1995) they find no link between relationship duration and the interest rate, even focusing exclusively on lines of credit.

In studies of relationship lending, authors typically control for all observable measures of borrower risk, such as leverage, credit history, cash flow, and firm age. Hence, the significance of the bank relationship variables (e.g., duration) in regressions predicting loan contract terms suggests that lenders over time attain private information that can be used to improve credit availability.[6] Because the information is private, however, its exact nature is hard to pin down. For example, it is difficult to determine whether relationship-based information is private to the bank or to the specific loan officer working for the bank. To the extent that lending officers possess this information, a potential agency problem arises. Models such as that of Stein (2002) assume the latter interpretation, thus creating a potential conflict between the bank and the loan officer. With this interpretation, Stein's model suggests that in organizations (banks) with many layers between the principal (the CEO of the bank or the bank shareholder) and the agent (the loan officer), the agent loses full authority to make decisions. In such an environment, the loan officer runs the risk that her investment in soft information will go to waste (because, for example, her recommendation to approve a "character" loan is vetoed by upper management). Thus, her incentive ex ante to make investments in soft information are reduced. In contrast, in a small bank—in the extreme a bank where the CEO is the loan officer—the loan officer reaps the full benefit of her investments in soft information and thus has much stronger incentives to make such investments.

[6]One potential concern with this interpretation, however, is the maintained assumption that the duration or longevity of a banking relationship has to do with information production by the bank rather than some otherwise-unobservable characteristic of the borrower. Firms that are able to continue to borrow from the same bank, year after year, for example, may simply be better firms. This seems like a plausible alternative interpretation. The ideal empirical test would involve exogenous shocks to relationship duration, such as what might occur following a bank merger or failure. Slovin, Sushka, and Polonchek (1993) use the failure of Continental Illinois as such a shock. They find that the stock returns of a sample of large borrowers fell when investors learned of the likely failure of Continental Illinois and then rebounded following news of a full FDIC bailout of the bank's creditors. They also find that the results are concentrated among borrowers where Continental acted as the lead manager (of a syndicated loan) or as a direct lender (as opposed to cases in which Continental acted as a participant lender only). Using data from Norway, Karceski, Ongena, and Smith (2004) find that the stock price of firms borrowing from acquiring banks increases, while the stock price of borrowers in the target bank decreases following bank mergers. They argue that lending policies are more likely to move toward those of the acquiring bank. Together, these studies suggest that there are some costs even to large borrowers of switching banks, thus supporting the idea that bank relationships are valuable and are costly to replace.

What is the empirical evidence to support this argument? First, small banks devote more of their lending resources to small business loans than do large banks (see, e.g., Berger and Udell 1996, Peek and Rosengren 1998, and Strahan and Weston 1998). This pattern seems to be true not just in the United States but more broadly throughout the world (Berger, Klapper, and Udell 2001). On its face, this evidence supports Stein's model. But there are also much simpler explanations: Small banks may be precluded from lending to large borrowers because of the need to maintain a well-diversified loan portfolio. Or small banks may not be able to offer the array of services that larger clients demand, such as debt and equity underwriting.[7]

Beyond the simple comparisons of the amount of loans held by large and small banks, evidence suggests that loan contract terms made by large banks are consistently different from loan contract terms made by small banks. Berger and Udell (1996) show, for example, that loans originated by large banks tend to have lower interest rates and are less likely to be secured by collateral than *similarly sized* bank loans originated by small banks. The inference that they draw from these facts is that large-bank borrowers are higher quality (and thus less reliant on soft information and relationships) than small-bank borrowers (hence the lower rates and lower likelihood of observing secured loans from large banks). This interpretation is clearly possible and supports the idea of some market specialization—large banks with the better-established firms and small banks with the less well-established ones. Unfortunately, the loan-level data used in this study contain no information about the borrower. So there are two potential explanations for the result. One is that the nature of the borrowers differs. But a second possibility is that large banks offer better terms (lower rates, less collateral) to their borrowers than do smaller banks, perhaps because large banks have lower costs and operate in more competitive markets.[8] Or perhaps large banks make bigger loans to firms of a given size and credit quality than do small banks. In a more recent study, Carter, McNulty, and Verbrugge (2004) show that the overall yield tends to be lower on loans made by large banks, compared to loans made by small banks. Again, however, the interpretation of this finding is difficult because we have little knowledge about the characteristics of borrowers.

Several studies have recently been able to test for systematic differences in the kinds of *borrowers* served by large and small banks as well as differences in the information used by banks of varying sizes to make lending decisions. Berger, Miller, et al. (2004) find that borrowers from small banks tend to be smaller; they tend to be closer geographically to their bank; they are less likely to do business with their bank using telephone or mail; and they tend to have a longer-duration relationship with their banker. Cole, Goldberg, and White (2004) find that large banks tend to base lending decisions on

[7]In the United States, the competitive disadvantage for small banks is potentially growing in recent years because commercial banks are now able to provide capital market services such as bond and equity underwriting following passage of the 1999 Financial Services Modernization Act. Recent studies suggest that information collected through banks' commercial lending business may reduce the costs of underwriting debt and equity securities. See Drucker and Puri (2004), Narayanan, Rangan, and Rangan (2004), Schenone (2004), Sufi (2004), and Yasuda (forthcoming).

[8]For example, small rural banks are more likely to be located in concentrated local markets.

systematic and verifiable information, such as the borrower's credit history, leverage, and cash flow. Loan decisions made by small banks, in contrast, seem somewhat more responsive to relationship variables. Thus, it seems that small banks are more apt to use soft information—invisible to the econometrician—in allocating credit.

Consistent with the idea that different-sized banks lend to different classes of borrowers, Brickley, Linck, and Smith (2003) demonstrate that small banks are more likely to operate in small and rural markets relative to large banks, that they are more likely to have concentrated ownership and have greater ownership by officers and directors (most of whom live in the local community), and that they are more likely to focus their business in a concentrated geographical market. Banks focusing on relationship lending are more apt to value personal contact with borrowers; hence the need for geographical concentration. And focusing on relationship lending worsens internal agency problems, as in Stein (2002); hence the need for more concentrated and local ownership. Thus, Brickley et al. argue that these facts support the notion that small banks focus on business where close proximity to the customer (borrower) is important and where close ties between loan officers and bank equity holders is also important. However, they do not provide any direct evidence linking bank lending to size.

Berger, Klapper, and Udell (2001) study lending in Argentina and find, consistent with the other studies, that smaller borrowers are more likely to borrow from small banks and from domestic banks. Mian (2006) studies the lending behavior of large foreign banks in Pakistan and finds that these banks tend to lend mainly to large firms located in major cities. All of these facts suggest that small (and domestic) banks are more apt to specialize in lending based on soft information than are large (and foreign) banks. A particularly interesting result in Mian (2006) is that domestic banks in Pakistan are much more likely to restructure a troubled loan using a private workout, whereas foreign banks are more prone to use the courts. Relationship lenders (domestic banks) are in a better position to work out loans privately, whereas nonrelationship lenders (large foreign banks) use formal legal procedures. Consistent with this argument, Esty (2004) and Qian and Strahan (2005) both find that the foreign banks' ownership share of loans is greater in countries with lower costs of using the legal system (e.g., lower legal formalism). Mian even finds that *within* the set of foreign banks, those closest "culturally" to the Pakistani borrower—i.e., Asian banks—are more likely to lend to small and rural borrowers and are least likely to resolve default using the courts.

Large banks have also adopted automated underwriting technologies ("credit scoring") more aggressively than smaller banks (Akhavein, Frame, and White 2001). This fact may, in part, reflect an economy of scale in technology adoption. But to the extent that small banks specialize in soft information and relationship lending, their incentive to invest in these technologies is clearly less than large banks.

2.3. Bank Size, Organization Structure, and Lending

So size seems to affect how banks process information, which suggests a meaningful tradeoff associated with size. Large banks are better diversified and thus can lend more per dollar of capital, and they can lend to larger borrowers. Small banks, however, may be better able to make character loans. A few studies suggest, however, that the story is a bit more complicated. A large banking organization may be able to reap the benefits of small size (without losing the diversification advantages of large size) by breaking up its operations into small affiliate banks. Strahan and Weston (1998), for example, find that while the ratio of small business loans to assets does decline with bank size, this ratio does not change with the number of banks owned by a bank holding company. Their results suggest that a one-bank holding company would make the same amount of small business loans as a two-bank holding company with the same-size banks. But the two-bank holding company gains diversification advantages because capital can flow easily between the two affiliates (Houston, James, and Marcus 1997).

Berger and Miller, et al. (2004) report similar results. Recall the many differences between small-bank and large-bank borrowers. They find, however, *no effect* of the size of the holding company on any borrower attribute, once the lending bank's size is taken into account. Thus, a small subsidiary of a large-bank holding company seems to lend to the same kinds of borrowers and using the same sort of information as stand-alone small banks.

Does this mean that a bank can improve its ability to process soft information by changing its internal organization structure? Perhaps. Liberti (2004) studies internal changes at a single large bank aimed at increasing the discretion granted to lending officers. He finds that after these structural changes occur, individual loan officer behavior changes relative to a control sample of loan officers whose incentives did not change. In particular, the loan officers that were given greater discretion devote more time to their customers and receive fewer complaints after the change in organization structure. Thus, consistent with Stein (2002), it seems that bankers invest more in relationships when the need to justify these investments formally to higher levels of management is reduced. The deeper question that remains unanswered is whether large banks can have it both ways. Are there organization structures that can allow them to achieve diversification and yet continue to be able to make relationship loans as effectively as small banks?[9]

2.4. How Does Bank Size Affect Credit Availability?

The most important question motivated by the links between size and bank lending, both for policy as well as research, is whether the size distribution of banks within a market affects credit availability. Given the rapid consolidation of the banking industry during the 1990s, has consolidation led to changes in credit supply?

The existing research suggests, first, that the two key *drivers* of consolidation—deregulation of restrictions on bank expansion and the advent of information

[9]Kroszner and Rajan (1997) document that market forces do sometimes shape organization structure to mitigate potential agency problems. They show that during the pre–Glass-Steagall era, banks' efforts to gain a foothold in the securities underwriting business were mitigated by investor perceptions of potential conflicts of interest. By altering their organization structure—specifically by setting up affiliated investment banking subsidiaries with separate and nonoverlapping boards of directors—commercial banking organizations were able to gain market share over both stand-alone investment banks as well as commercial banks underwriting securities directly (i.e., without setting up a separate affiliate).

technologies that enhance scale economies—have themselves tended to *improve* credit supply.[10] For example, Jayaratne and Strahan (1998) and Stiroh and Strahan (2003) show that following deregulation of restrictions on in-state branching in the United States, the market share of large banks increased (because of consolidation) and, at the same time, the price of credit declined. These papers argue that the decline in loan prices came about both because bank costs declined and because competition became more vigorous after deregulation. Dick (2006) finds increased quality of bank output followed deregulation of restrictions on bank branching at the federal level by studying the impact of the 1994 Interstate Banking and Branching Efficiency Act.[11]

Similar beneficial effects also seem to come with regulatory openness outside the United States. Demiurguc-Kunt, Laeven, and Levine (2004), for example, study cross-border differences in the interest rate spreads between loans and deposits. They find that restrictions on the entry of foreign banks (as well as broader measures of banking market openness) increase these intermediation spreads, presumably because domestic banks face less competitive pressure when foreign bank entry is discouraged. This result, however, seems to be subsumed by a broader measure of how well a country protects property rights. Interestingly, they also show (although they do not emphasize) that countries that restrict foreign entry (as well as countries with weak protection of property rights) tend to have banking systems where small banks are relatively more prevalent.

In France, banking deregulation in the mid-1980s was followed by better credit availability to bank-dependent industries (Betrand, Schoar, and Thesmar, 2004). Relaxation of restrictions on cross-border banking in Europe in the early 1990s, as in the United States, was followed by bank consolidation and, if anything, better credit availability. Cetorelli (2004), for instance, argues that the enhanced competition following this European banking reform led to better credit availability. As evidence, he shows that average firm size declined after reform and that this decline was concentrated in bank-dependent industries. Cetorelli and Strahan (2006) report similar evidence in the United States, where the relative importance of small firms in local economies increased after the removal of restrictions on interstate banking. This last evidence is very indirect but suggests that small, bank-dependent firms gain when banking competition is enhanced through removal of regulatory barriers to entry.

Advances in technology have also spurred bank consolidation because of economies of scale. And large banks have consistently adopted new technologies before small banks, including credit scoring (Akhavein, Frame, and White 2001), securitization (Minton, Sanders, and Strahan 2004), and Internet banking (Furst, Lang, and Nolle 2002). Large banks also take greater advantage of mundane technologies such as telephone and mail relative to smaller banks (Berger and Miller, et al. 2004). At the same time, these technologies plausibly enhance credit availability. For example, securitization reduces the all-in funding costs of loans, particularly credit card loans and home mortgages (see Allen, McAndrews, and Strahan 2002). Credit scoring seems to be

[10]For a comprehensive review of the causes and consequences of bank consolidation, see Berger, Demsetz, and Strahan (1999).

[11]For a more complete discussion of the effects of banking competition on lending and credit availability, see Berger, Demiurguc-Kunt, et al. (2004).

associated with higher levels of lending to small business and also seems to increase the ability of banks to price risks, thereby leading to less credit rationing (Frame, Srinivasan, and Woosley 2002, Berger, Frame, and Miller 2001).

While large banks may have greater incentive to invest in information technologies due to large fixed costs, information exchanges offer an example of how small banks may be able to reap the benefits of such technologies efficiently. These information exchanges, such as Dun and Bradstreet in the United States, collect information on potential borrowers' credit history and make that information available to all potential lenders, irrespective of size, at low cost. Kallberg and Udell (2003) find that D&B's measure of a firm's payment history adds marginal explanatory power to a failure prediction model that includes credit quality variables such as leverage and liquidity ratios. These exchanges also support the development of credit-scoring technologies, and cross-border research suggests that their use improves credit availability (Jappelli and Pagano 1999).[12]

So both deregulation that opens markets and better information technologies seem to improve credit supply, but both of these phenomena are closely linked to the relative importance of large banks. This correlation creates the empirical challenge of trying to isolate the effects of size per se on the availability of bank credit. One approach that has been attempted in a number of studies is to estimate changes in the amount or price of credit following banking consolidation. Most of these studies focus on credit to small businesses (or, often, the amount of loans that are small), based on the idea that small banks have a comparative advantage in this kind of lending for the reasons outlined earlier. The empirical results are mixed, which in my judgment reflects three factors. First, as already mentioned, changes in the size distribution are in part driven by regulatory and technological factors that likely have independent effects on credit supply. Second, the effects of disturbances to banking relationship following M&A activity may be large initially, but these short-run effects seem to dissipate over time. Third, bank consolidation is driven both by supply-side factors (e.g., the effort to lower costs via economies of scale) and by demand-side factors (e.g., removing excess capacity). Demand factors are hard to take fully into account statistically and thus can make clean interpretation of results very difficult. I come back to this point in the conclusion to this chapter.

To be specific, some studies find that the amount of small loans held on the balance sheets of consolidated banks declines relative to the amount held by the pro-forma bank created by force merging the two banks before the actual merger (e.g., Peek and Rosengren 1998, Berger, Saunders, et al. 1998). Another study finds an *increase* in small loans held when two small banks merge and a negative but not statistically significant change when large banks buy small banks (Strahan and Weston 1998). Outside the United States, Sapienza (2002) analyzes how mergers in Italy affect bank lending. The advantage of this study is that loan-level data are available, allowing the author to track the fortunes of individual borrowers over time, both before and after a merger or acquisition has occurred. Sapienza finds that after acquisitions of banks with small market shares, interest rates tend to fall for continuing borrowers. She interprets this result as

[12]For a review of the effects of technology on banking more broadly, see Berger (2003).

consistent with better efficiency after the M&A and hence lower prices. However, when an M&A transaction leads to a large increase in local-market concentration, interest rates tend to rise rather than fall. And small borrowers of target banks seem less likely to borrow money from the merged bank.

A difficulty with many of these M&A studies is that they consider the effects of consolidation only in the short run, typically one to three years after the merger. Focarelli and Panetta (2003) find large initial declines in deposit interest rates due to increased market power following mergers of Italian banks but that these declines are fully eliminated after just three years. (This study does not consider loan rates.) They therefore emphasize the importance of distinguishing initial from long-run consequences of consolidation. Just as deposit supply may respond elastically in the longer run, so may credit supply. First, displaced borrowers will tend to seek alternative sources of credit from other banks operating in the market. Second, entry of new banks may be encouraged by higher prices. Both of these effects, in fact, have been found in the data. For example, Berger, Saunders, et al. (1998) show that initial reductions in small lending following an M&A transaction is offset by credit supplied by other banks in the same local market. Germaise and Moskowitz (2004) find that reductions in competition following some bank mergers did reduce loan supply but that these deleterious effects dissipate after about three years. DeYoung, Goldberg, and White (1998) find that de novo banks focus their lending on small businesses, and Berger, Bonime, Goldberg and White (2004) find that the formation of de novo banks is higher in markets that have experienced consolidation. Thus, new banks may be entering the market, in part, to serve small businesses that have been displaced in the wake of consolidation.

Like the M&A studies, cross-market tests for effects of bank size on credit are also mixed. Avery and Samolyk (2004) use the local market (MSA or rural country), rather than the bank, as the relevant unit of observation to test how total lending to small business within a market varies with consolidation. Their approach incorporates not only the effects of the M&A on the parties to the transaction, but also the effects of market adjustments to any changes or disruptions in credit supply. Again, however, the results are mixed and hard to draw strong conclusions from because they find very different results for two sample periods. During the 1994–97 period, they find a negative correlation between small business lending and consolidation activity across markets. But during the 1997–2000 period, they find a positive correlation between consolidation activity and small business lending. Black and Strahan (2002) find no correlation between state-level bank consolidation activity and the rate of formation of new business incorporations. And they find the rate of new incorporations is significantly *lower* in states with more small banks. This result seems to indicate, if anything, that credit is *more* available to small businesses when banks are larger. But this inference is again indirect because there are no data that link the rate of business incorporations to bank lending.

Several studies can, and do, link credit availability *directly* to the presence of small banks in the local market. These studies use data from the 1993 National Survey of Small Business Finance (NSSBF), which includes data on loan interest rates, borrower characteristics, and other financing variables, such as information on trade credit. Because implied interest rates on late payments on trade credit are extremely high, this variable is a good indicator that separates credit constrained from unconstrained small firms. Unfortunately, two studies using late payments on trade credit reach quite different conclusions with the same data. Jayaratne and Wolken (1999) regress the fraction of trade credit paid late on the fraction of assets held by banks in the local market with under $300 million in assets (and firm-specific variables). They find *no effect* of this measure of small-bank importance on credit constraints (or on the likelihood that small firms have a line of credit). In contrast, Berger and Miller, et al. (2004), in an instrumental variables setup, link the size of a borrower's bank to the fraction of trade credit paid late. Their approach is conceptually similar to Jayaratne and Wolken's because the key identifying instrument is the median bank size in the borrower's local market. However, this paper finds a strong *positive effect* of bank size on late trade credit payment, suggesting that small borrowers forced to use a large bank (because of the market they happen to find themselves in) are more credit constrained than borrowers able to use small banks. To complicate matters further, Berger, Rosen, and Udell (2007) find a *negative effect* of large-bank deposit share on loan rates using the same NSSBF data.

3. DEPOSIT–LENDING SYNERGIES

Both researchers and policymakers have taken the central defining characteristic of a bank as an intermediary that combines lending and deposit taking. Given the prevalence of this structure across time and across different economies, theoreticians have put forth several explanations for its success. These explanations are based on the following ideas. First, banks may have an information advantage from their role in the payments system (i.e., by offering checking accounts to potential borrowers), relative to competing intermediaries. Beyond information, some deposits—"core deposits"—may be relatively insensitive to changes in market yields, thereby allowing banks to offer borrowers insurance against credit shocks that other lenders could not. Second, banks offer liquidity to their customers in both the lending and deposit-taking businesses that may motivate combining these two products in the same institution. Also related to liquidity, bank loans reduce debt capacity by virtue of their lack of liquidity. By funding themselves with deposits that create the risk of a catastrophic run, banks may be able to increase their ability to borrow.

3.1. Do Deposits Make Banks Better Lenders?

Imagine a bank that provides all of the payments services to a small business. Each day the small business makes and receives payments, in the form of checks as well as currency. These payments flows will obviously reflect the current state of business; and if the small firm uses a single bank for all of its financial needs, the bank will have the opportunity to know before anyone else if the firm is having problems. Does this potential information advantage give the payment-providing bank the ability to offer credit on better terms than other banks or nonbank intermediaries? We know that small firms do concentrate their borrowing with a single financial service firm and that these firms usually borrow from commercial banks. More than 80 percent of borrowing from financial institutions comes from commercial banks (Petersen and Rajan 1994). Petersen and Rajan also report that more than half of small-firm borrowing comes from lenders where they have a deposit account (or some other form of financial service).

More generally, Nakamura (1993) argues that small banks lending to small businesses are especially well suited to use checking account information. In contrast, the payments activities of large firms are both too complex and too dispersed to be of much value to a potential bank lender. Bank loan officers at small banks may have the opportunity to draw accurate inferences about a business's payroll, receipts, and collection of accounts based on flows through the checking account. In fact, Nakamura argues that this advantage both explains small banks' relative emphasis on small business lending and suggests that small banks will continue to play an important role despite consolidation trends in the industry. As evidence, he shows that the annual rate of turnover of deposits at large banks (i.e., the ratio of checks drawn plus checks deposited to total deposits) is up to 50 times as high as at small banks. However, there is no direct evidence in this study that small banks actually use checking account information in lending. Cole, Goldberg, and White (2004) offer some direct evidence consistent with Nakamura's conjecture. They find that for small firms applying to borrow from small banks, the likelihood of approval increases with the presence of a deposit relationship; no such result, however, is evident when small firms borrow from large banks.

For large firms, Carey, Post, and Sharpe (1998) compare lending by commercial banks with lending by unregulated finance companies, whose funding relies primarily on commercial paper rather than on deposits. In this sample, they find little difference between bank borrowers and finance company borrowers in measures of firm opacity, such as borrower size, market-to-book ratio, sales growth, or age (years in *Compustat*). Carey et al. do find that bank borrowers have higher R&D-to-sales ratios than finance company borrowers, but this result is not robust across specifications. They also find that finance company borrowers, while not more opaque, appear riskier in observable ways (e.g., higher leverage). Their findings suggest, at least for large firms, that banks have no particular *informational* advantage relative to other intermediaries. Similarly, Billett, Flannery, and Garfinkel (1995) show that equity prices rise significantly with loan announcements, irrespective of whether the lender is a bank or a nonbank.[13]

For small firms, loan pricing and credit availability *do not* seem lower for those borrowing from the bank that holds their checking account, relative to those borrowers using other banks for payments services. Cole (1998), for example, finds no link between the presence of a checking account and the probability that a firm will be granted credit from a bank. Oddly, however, he finds a positive and significant relationship between the presence of a savings account and the probability that credit is extended, although it seems unlikely that this result has anything to do with information. Petersen and Rajan (1994) find no relationship between borrower deposits and the

[13]They find, however, that the credit rating of the lender affects the equity response to loan announcements. Lenders with better ratings elicit more positive-announcement effects.

interest rate charged (holding constant the length of the bank–borrower relationship). Berger and Miller, et al. (2004) find no link between the presence of a checking account and the fraction of trade credit paid late, a measure of credit availability to the firm.

In a unique case study of a single bank, Mester, Nakamura, and Renault (2007) do provide some concrete evidence that information from the checking account may be helpful in lending. They analyze data on checking account balances for a sample of small borrowers over time at a single Canadian bank. They show a high correlation between changes in borrower's checking account balances and the bank's valuation of the borrower's accounts receivable and inventories (typically used to secure short-term bank loans). This correlation is higher for borrowers with an exclusive relationship with the bank. Moreover, this bank seems to use changes in its assessment of the value of receivables and inventory to identify troubled loans. Moreover, according to Udell (2004), finance companies that lend with accounts receivable as collateral sometimes require borrowers to set up a special checking account to take payment on the receivables, thus potentially providing the finance company with the same information flows available to a bank. These results suggest, in an indirect but plausible way, that information from checking accounts may be valuable to lenders and that nonbank lenders may also be able to find ways to acquire information from payment flows.

Berlin and Mester (1999) present a model in which bank core deposits provide them a source of funding that is supplied inelastically with respect to economic shocks. They show that this kind of funding allows a bank to insure borrowers against credit shocks, whereas an intermediary funded with, say, commercial paper, would not be able to offer this insurance. Borrowers value this contract either because they are risk averse or because they face costly financial distress. Thus, the deposit franchise of banks gives them an advantage in lending that is unrelated to an information advantage. As evidence, Berlin and Mester show that interest rates on bank loans are less sensitive to economy-wide credit shocks (e.g., corporate bond spreads, changes in unemployment) when the originating bank holds more core deposits (defined as deposits under $100,000). This evidence echoes an earlier study of bank loan commitments in which Berger and Udell (1992) show that borrowers with loan commitments face less credit rationing during business cycle downturns. Berger and Udell, however, do not tie their results to bank deposits.

3.2. Banks as Liquidity Providers

The most prominent attribute of banking that has motivated theorists is probably banks' role as liquidity providers. Diamond and Dybvig (1983) model a bank as a mechanism to allow investors to finance illiquid but high-return projects while insuring against unpredictable early-period consumption demands through pooling. The cost of this arrangement is the possibility of a bank run. While this model does not suggest a true synergy between lending and deposits, it does begin to consider links between the two sides of the banking business. Later models argue explicitly that the illiquid nature of bank loans affects the optimal capital structure for banks. For example, Calomiris and Kahn (1991) and Diamond and Rajan (2001) argue that demandable deposits, by making the bank vulnerable to a destructive run, improve incentives for monitoring loans and avoiding the temptation to exploit uninformed depositors. Similarly, Flannery (1994) argues that very short-term maturity of deposits improves bank incentives; for example, asset substitution problems are contained by short debt maturity. Moreover, Calomiris and Kahn emphasize that the "sequential service constraint," whereby deposits are paid on a first-come, first-served basis, strengthen monitoring incentives for informed depositors. Thus, the nature of the bank loan portfolio shapes the structure of its deposits.

Conversely, Myers and Rajan (1998) argue that because banks are funded with very liquid debt and have such high leverage, they need to hold some illiquid assets to mitigate the risk of expropriation or fraud. It is simply too easy for a banker to "steal" when assets are highly liquid. In a sense, their model is an argument against the pure "narrow bank" in which deposits are backed 100 percent by low-risk and highly liquid government securities. In essence, they argue that too much liquidity on the asset side is dangerous because it becomes too easy for funds to be expropriated quickly. Although not an empirical article, Myers and Rajan argue that the historical development of commercial banking supports their model. Banks historically emerged as payments providers only; the bank began as a "money changer." These money changers held high levels of reserves, and the main risk perceived at the time had to do with fraud rather than bank runs. Myers and Rajan argue that the money changers enhanced their reputation for honesty by engaging in lending in the local community.

Morgan (2002) finds some modern evidence consistent with the flavor of Myers and Rajan. He uses the probability that a bank will have a different rating from the two major rating agencies as a measure of "opacity" and finds that this measure increases with a bank's trading assets. On its face this result seems odd because, in contrast to the illiquid lending business, trading assets are carried on bank balance sheets at market value. The high level of liquidity in trading assets, however, makes it hard for outsiders to judge a banks' risk because the nature of these assets can be altered too easily and quickly. Perhaps most convincing, he finds that this effect increases as a bank's leverage increases (capital–asset ratio decreases). This makes sense because the incentive for insiders to engage in asset substitution or looting increases with leverage.

Kashyap, Rajan, and Stein (2002) argue that banks provide liquidity to customers in both the lending and deposit-taking sides of their business. On the lending side, lines of credit give borrowers the option to take down funds on demand up to a specified amount over a specified period of time. Similarly, demand deposit accounts give depositors the option to convert their funds to cash at any time. These two businesses subject the bank to the risk of having to be able to supply liquidity at short notice. Kashyap, Rajan, and Stein argue that this liquidity risk is costly because it forces the bank to operate with a surplus of cash that yields low returns and may bring agency costs of the sort modeled in Myers and Rajan (1998). By combining these two products within the same institution, however, the bank can minimize these liquidity costs as long as liquidity demand by depositors is less than perfectly correlated with liquidity demands by borrowers.

Given all of this theory linking lending to deposits through banks' role as liquidity providers, it is surprising how little empirical evidence actually attempts to test these ideas. The early idea of Diamond and Dybvig, which emphasized the potential for liquidity-driven bank runs, has not been supported by historical evidence. For example, Gorton (1988) looked back at the banking crises in the United States in the nineteenth and early twentieth centuries and found that these instances were associated with concern over bank solvency.[14]

Kashyap, Rajan, and Stein offer evidence consistent with their model by showing first that banks are more active issuers of lines of credit (especially unsecured lines), compared to finance companies or other intermediaries. Even more convincing, when asked whether their firm had required financing needs to cover seasonal or unexpected credit needs, 70 percent of small firms responded by mentioning a commercial bank, while just 1 percent of respondents mentioned a finance company. Consistent with their results, Harjoto, Mullineax, and Yi (2006) study loans to large firms, finding that commercial banks are more likely than investment banks to provide loan commitment contracts that expose the lender to potential liquidity risk. And Gatev and Strahan (2004) argue that the market for backup lines of credit to large commercial paper issuers is similarly dominated by banks. Moreover, Kashyap et al. also show that banking organizations that hold more demand deposits as a fraction of the balance sheet also have greater off-balance-sheet unused commitments to lend, again as a fraction of the balance sheet.

Saidenberg and Strahan (1999) and Gatev and Strahan (2004) argue that during periods of market crisis, this deposit–lending synergy becomes especially strong. In particular, they emphasize periods of market uncertainty in which investors become less willing to hold risky debt. During these so-called "flights to quality," commercial paper spreads widen (as do other credit spreads), which leads firms to draw funds from backup lines of credit from banks. Gatev and Strahan show that during these periods, the supply of deposits to banks increases. Most of these inflows are concentrated in transaction deposits. And, among banks, those with the largest transaction deposit base experience the greatest inflows of funds (Gatev, Schuermann, and Strahan, 2006). Thus, banks can offer liquidity insurance best because when the cash is needed (from, for example, commercial paper issuers), it is in the bank (from depositors looking for safety).

4. CONCLUSION

After all of this research, what do we know and what is left? With respect to size and lending, we know that large banks lend more than smaller banks and that large banks focus more on business lending and lending to larger customers than do smaller banks. We also know that changes in the regulatory and technological landscape have tipped the balance in favor of large banks, leading to an increase in their market share through

[14]Gorton and Winton (2003) review the literature on bank panics and systemic crises.

consolidation. The evidence also suggests that these broad evolutionary changes toward more openness and better technology have increased credit supply.

What is much harder to judge is whether changes in the bank size distribution per se have affected credit supply, especially to small and young borrowers, whose access to credit improves if they are able to forge long-term relationships with banks. The empirical evidence seems to indicate that small banks have been more apt to engage in relationship loans, but *one should not conclude that credit availability will fall as the market share of small banks declines*. One major challenge to most studies is the problem that the bank size distribution is endogenously driven by demand conditions in credit markets. Sorting out the effects of loan demand from loan supply is a continuing challenge to all empirical research (in banking and elsewhere). Consider, for example, studies of consolidation that link bank M&As to small business lending. These studies would like to be able to draw an inference about how loan supply to small business changes following an M&A transaction. The difficulty is controlling for demand conditions, which plausibly lie at the heart of the motivation to consolidate in the first place.

Here is an example. Suppose, as the research suggests, that following a merger the following three things happen: First, the size of the consolidating banks increases, leading to a decline in the market share of small banks in the local economy. Second, loans to small businesses held by the consolidated bank decline (or, perhaps, lending to small business in the whole market declines). Third, new banks enter this market after the consolidation, and these new banks focus on serving small firms. What do these facts tell us about credit availability? One possibility is that the consolidation lowered *credit supply to small customers*, whose unsatisfied demand, through increased prices, drew new banks into the market. Another possibility, however, is that the process was driven by *unsatisfied demand by large firms*! Here's how: Prior to the initial consolidation, large firms in the local economy may have had unmet credit demands due to a paucity of large-bank capacity in the area. This demand created a profit opportunity for a large bank to enter via an M&A. So the large bank buys the small bank to begin serving the local needs of the large firms. Thus, after the M&A the newly consolidated firm's ratio of small loans to assets falls. If the new bank reallocates sufficient resources toward large customers, there may be a temporary decline in credit to smaller firms, which in turn generates an incentive for de novo banks to enter. According to this second scenario, small business lending did not fall because large banks can't serve them efficiently. Instead, small business lending fell because of relatively strong loan demand by large firms. The key problem in interpreting the facts is the difficulty of fully accounting for ways in which loan demand may drive market structure.

How can you rule out alternative "demand side" explanations? The truth is that it is not easy. One needs to find *plausibly exogenous* variation in the bank-size distribution, meaning changes in bank size that are not related to loan demand. In my view, changes in banking market structure following M&As are not plausibly exogenous to credit demands. One recent paper, however, uses changes in lending concentration in local markets that stem from *large-bank* mergers with operations in many markets to find exogenous variation in competitive conditions (Germaise and Moskowitz, 2004).

To understand the idea, consider the 1996 merger of Wells Fargo and First Interstate, two large banks with operations across the state of California. The Germaise and Moskowitz empirical test focuses on how lending concentration at the neighborhood level changes following transactions like this one and then traces out the effects of these (exogenous) changes in concentration on credit supply there. Their identifying assumption is that a merger between very large banks like Wells Fargo and First Interstate would not be affected by loan demand conditions at the very local level. And they find that increased concentration following large-bank mergers is followed by higher lending rates, reduced property values, and even higher levels of crime.

Here are two other examples of clever ways to find plausibly exogenous variation in loan supply. While neither study relates directly to the issues of bank structure and lending, the authors' strategies in finding exogenous variation in credit supply illustrate how future research on structure ought best to proceed. Peek and Rosengren (2000) study lending by Japanese banks' U.S. subsidiaries during the banking crisis of the 1990s in Japan. They argue that the massive declines in capital and profits at Japanese banks reduced their willingness to supply loans to borrowers in California. The key identifying assumption (which I regard as plausible) is that loan demand in California is different from loan demand in Japan. In other words, the financial condition of the Japanese banks had little or nothing to do with demand conditions in California. They find very different lending behavior of U.S. banks in California from Japanese bank subsidiaries in California.

In the second study, Ashcraft (2005) finds an equally clever way to isolate loan supply changes by studying lending by *healthy* subsidiaries of bank holding companies that were closed by the FDIC. Under the so-called source-of-strength doctrine, one bank's liabilities to the FDIC become the liability of other banks held by the same BHC. Ashcraft provides evidence that the FDIC caused these healthy banks to close (rather than the normal instance where banks close due to poor performance), so any change in lending following the closure likely reflects reduced supply rather than weak demand. Like Peek and Rosengren, he finds large real effects of declines in bank credit supply.

With respect to deposit–lending synergies, there seems to be much more theory than evidence, beyond the obvious (but nevertheless important) observation that banks have historically been structured combining these two functions. Calls for narrow banking, which recommend breaking the payments and lending franchises of banks into two separate entities, have not been heeded. Under this alternative arrangement, the payments entity would look like a money market mutual fund, whereas the lending entity would look like a finance company. As noted earlier, information-based arguments have support in some studies but not others. It is simply not clear yet, for example, whether banks gain an informational advantage over competing intermediaries by virtue of their access to payments information. We need more "case studies" such as that of Mester et al. that might allow us to see exactly how a bank uses information from checking account flows. Liquidity explanations for deposit–lending synergies also appear promising, but again there is only limited empirical evidence focusing mainly on the U.S. banking system.

References

Akhavein, Jalal, Allen N. Berger, and David Humphrey. 1997. The Effects of Bank Megamergers on Efficiency and Prices: Evidence from the Profit Function, *Review of Industrial Organization* 12, 95–139.

Akhavein, Jalal, W. Scott Frame, and Lawrence J. White. 2001. The Diffusion of Financial Innovations: An Examination of the Adoption of Small Business Credit Scoring by Large Banking Organizations. Federal Reserve Bank of Atlanta. Working paper no. 2001-9.

Allen, Franklin, James J. McAndrews, and Philip E. Strahan. 2002. E-Finance: An Introduction, *Journal of Financial Services Research* 22(1/2), 5–27.

Ashcraft, Adam. 2005. Are Banks Really Special? New Evidence from the FDIC-Induced Failure of Healthy Banks, *American Economic Review* 95(5), 1712–1730

Avery, Robert B., and Katherine A. Samolyk. 2004. Bank Consolidation and Small Business Lending: The Role of Community Banks. *Journal of Financial Services Research* 25(2/3), 291–326.

Berger, Allen N. 2003. The Economic Effects of Technological Progress: Evidence from the Banking Industry. *Journal of Money, Credit and Banking* 35, 141–176.

Berger, Allen N., and Gregory F. Udell. 1992. Some Evidence on the Empirical Significance of Credit Rationing, *Journal of Political Economy* 100(5), 1047–1068.

Berger, Allen N., and Gregory F. Udell. 1995. Relationship Lending and Lines of Credit in Small Firm Finance, *Journal of Business* 68, 351–382.

Berger, Allen N., and Gregory F. Udell. 1996. Universal Banking and the Future of Small Business, in A. Saunders and I. Walter (eds.), *Financial System Design: The Case for Universal Banking*. Irwin, Burr Ridge, IL, pp. 559–627.

Berger, Allen N., Rebecca S. Demsetz, and Philip E. Strahan. 1999. The Consolidation of the Financial Services Industry: Causes, Consequences, and Implications for the Future, *Journal of Banking and Finance* 23(2–4), 135–194.

Berger, Allen N., W. Scott Frame, and Nathan Miller. 2001. Credit Scoring and the Availability, Price, and Risk of Small Business Credit, Federal Reserve Bank of Atlanta. Working paper no. 2001-6.

Berger, Allen N., Iftekar Hasan, and Leora F. Klapper. 2004. Further Evidence on the Link Between Finance and Growth: An International Analysis of Community Banking and Economic Performance, *Journal of Financial Services Research* 25(2/3), 169–202.

Berger, Allen N., Anil K. Kashyap, and Joseph M. Scalise. 1995. The Transformation of Banking: What a Long Strange Trip It's Been, *Brookings Papers on Economic Activity* 55, 218.

Berger, Allen N., Leora F. Klapper, and Gregory F. Udell. 2001. The Ability of Banks to Lend to Informationally Opaque Small Businesses, *Journal of Banking and Finance* 25, 2127–2167.

Berger, Allen N., Richard J. Rosen, and Gregory F. Udell. 2007. The Effect of Market Size Structure on Competition: The Case of Small Business Lending, *Journal of Banking and Finance* (forthcoming).

Berger, Allen, N., Seth Bonime, Lawrence Goldberg, and Lawrence J. White. 2004. The Dynamics of Market Entry: The Effects of Mergers and Acquisitions on Entry in the Banking Industry, *Journal of Business* 77, 797–834.

Berger, Allen N., Asli Demirguc-Kunt, Ross Levine, and Joseph G. Haubrich. 2004. Bank Concentration and Competition: An Evolution in the Making, *Journal of Money, Credit and Banking* 36(3, part 2), 433–452.

Berger, Allen, Nathan Miller, Mitchell Petersen, Raghuram Rajan, and Jeremy Stein. 2005. Does Function Follow Form? Evidence from the Lending Practices of Large and Small Banks, *Journal of Financial Economics* 76(2), 237–269

Berger, Allen N., Anthony Saunders, Joseph M. Scalise, and Gregory F. Udell. 1998. The Effects of Bank Mergers and Acquisitions on Small Business Lending, *Journal of Financial Economics* 50, 187–229.

Berlin, Mitchell, and Loretta J. Mester. 1999. Deposits and Relationship Lending, *Review of Financial Studies* 12(3), 579–607.

Bertrand, Marianne, Antoinette Schoar, and David S. Thesmar. 2007. Bank Deregulation and Industry Structure: Evidence from the French Banking Reforms in 1985, *Journal of Finance* 62(2), 597–628.

Bharath, Sreedhar, Sandeep Dahiya, Anthony Saunders, and Anand Srinivasan. 2007. So What Do I Get? The Bank's View of Lending Relationships, *Journal of Finance Economics* 85(2), 787–821.

Billett, Matthew T., Mark J. Flannery, and Jon A. Garfinkel. 1995. The Effect of Lender Identity on a Borrowing Firm's Equity Return, *Journal of Finance* 50(2), 699–718.

Black, Sandra, and Philip E. Strahan. 2002. Entrepreneurship and Bank Credit Availability, *Journal of Finance* 57(6), 2807–2833.

Brickley, James A., James S. Linck, and Clifford W. Smith. 2003. Boundaries of the Firm: Evidence from the Banking Industry, *Journal of Financial Economics* 70, 351–383.

Calomiris, Charles, and Charles Kahn. 1991. The Role of Demandable Debt in Structuring Optimal Banking Arrangements, *American Economic Review* 81(3), 497–513.

Carey, Mark, Mitch Post, and Steven A. Sharpe. 1998. Does Corporate Lending by Banks and Finance Companies Differ? Evidence on Specialization in Private Debt Contracting, *Journal of Finance* 53(3), 845–878.

Carter, David A., James E. McNulty, and James A. Verbrugge. 2004. Do Small Banks Have an Advantage in Lending? An Examination of Risk-Adjusted Yields on Business Loans at Large and Small Banks, *Journal of Financial Services Research* 25(2/3), 232–252.

Cetorelli, Nicola. 2004. Real Effects of Bank Competition, *Journal of Money, Credit and Banking* 36(3, part 2), 543–558.

Cetorelli, Nicola, and Philip E. Strahan. 2006. Finance as a Barrier to Entry: Bank Competition and Industry Structure in U.S. Local Markets, *Journal of Finance* 61(1), 437–461.

Cole, Rebel A. 1998. The Importance of Relationship to the Availability of Credit, *Journal of Banking and Finance* 22(6/8), 959–977.

Cole, Rebel A., Lawrence G. Goldberg, and Lawrence J. White. 2004. Cookie Cutter vs. Character: The Micro Structure of Small Business Lending by Large and Small Banks, *Journal of Financial and Quantitative Analysis* 39(2), 227–251.

Degryse, Hans, and Patrick Van Cayseele. 2000. Relationship Lending with a Bank-Based System: Evidence from European Small Business Data, *Journal of Financial Intermediation* 9(1), 90–109.

Demestz, Rebecca S., and Philip E. Strahan. 1997. Diversification, Size and Risk at U.S. Bank Holding Companies, *Journal of Money, Credit and Banking* 29, 300–313.

Demirguc-Kunt, Asli, Luc Laeven, and Ross Levine. 2004. Regulations, Market Structure, Institutions and the Cost of Financial Intermediation, *Journal of Money, Credit and Banking* 36(3, part 2), 593–622.

DeYoung, Robert, Lawrence G. Goldberg, and Lawrence J. White. 1998. Youth, Adolescence and Maturity of Banks: Credit Availability to Small Business in an Era of Banking Consolidation, *Journal of Banking and Finance* 23, 463–492.

DeYoung, Robert, William C. Hunter, and Gregory F. Udell. 2004. The Past, Present and Future for Community Banks, *Journal of Financial Services Research* 25(2/3), 85–134.

Diamond, Douglas. 1984. Financial Intermediation and Delegated Monitoring, *Review of Economic Studies* 51, 393–414.

Diamond, Douglas, and Philip H. Dybvig. 1983. Bank Runs, Deposit Insurance and Liquidity, *Journal of Political Economy* 91(3), 401–419.

Diamond, Douglas, and Raghuram Rajan. 2001. Liquidity Risk, Liquidity Creation and Financial Fragility: A Theory of Banking, *Journal of Political Economy* 91, 401–419.

Dick, Astrid. 2006. Nationwide Branching and Its Impact on Market Structure, Quality and Bank Performance, *Journal of Business* 79(2).

Drucker, Steven, and Manju Puri. 2004. On the Benefits of Concurrent Lending and Underwriting, 2005, *Journal of Finance* 60, 2763–2799.

Esty, Benjamin C. 2004. When Do Foreign Banks Finance Domestic Projects? New Evidence on the Importance of Legal and Financial Systems. Mimeo.

Fama, Eugene F. 1985. What's Different About Banks? *Journal of Monetary Economics* 15, 29–39.

Farinha, Luisa A., and Joao A. C. Santos. 2002. Switching from Single to Multiple Lending Relationships: Determinants and Implications, *Journal of Financial Intermediation* 11(2), 124–151.

Flannery, Mark. 1994. Debt Maturity and the Deadweight Costs of Leverage: Optimally Financing Banking Firms, *American Economic Review* 84, 320–331.

Focarelli, Dario, and Fabio Panetta. 2003. Are Mergers Beneficial to Consumers? Evidence from the Market for Bank Deposits, *American Economic Review* 93(4), 1152–1172.

Frame, W. Scott, Aruna Srinivasan, and Lynn Woosley. 2002. The Effect of Credit Scoring on Small Business Lending, *Journal of Money, Credit and Banking* 33, 813–825.

Furst, Karen, William H. Lang, and Daniel Nolle. 2002. Internet Banking, *Journal of Financial Services Research* 22, 95–117.

Gatev, E., and P. E. Strahan. 2006. Bank's Advantage in Hedging Liquidity Risk: Theory and Evidence from the Commercial Paper Market, *Journal of Finance* 61(2), 867–892.

Gatev, E., T. Schuermann, and P. E. Strahan. 2006. How Do Banks Manage Liquidity Risk? Evidence from the equity and deposit and markets in the Fall of 1998, in Mark Carey and René Stulz (eds.), *Risks of Financial Institutions*, Chicago IL: University of Chicago Press, 105–127.

Germaise, Mark J., and Tobias J. Moskowitz. 2004. Bank Mergers and Crime: The Real and Social Effects of Credit Market Competition. Mimeo.

Gorton, Gary. 1988. Banking Panics and Business Cycles, *Oxford Economic Papers* 40(4), 751–781.

Gorton, Gary, and Andrew Winton. 2003. Financial Intermediation, in George M. Constantinides, Milton Harris, and Rene M. Stulz (eds.), *Handbook of the Economics of Finance*. Elsevier.

Harhoff, Dietmar, and Timm Korting. 1998. Lending Relationships in Germany: Empirical Evidence from Survey Data, *Journal of Banking and Finance* 22, 1317–1353.

Harjoto, Maretno, Donald J. Mullineaux, and Ha-Chin Yi. 2006. Loan Pricing at Investment versus Commercial Banks, *Financial Management*, Winter, 49–70.

Houston, Joel, and Christopher James. 1996. Bank Information Monopolies and the Mix of Private and Public Debt Claims, *Journal of Finance* 51(6), 1863–1889.

Houston, Joel, Christopher James, and David Marcus. 1997. Capital Market Frictions and the Role of Internal Capital Markets in Banking, *Journal of Financial Economics* 46, 135–164.

Jappelli, Tullio, and Marco Pagano. 1993. Information Sharing in Credit Markets, *Journal of Finance* 48, 1693–1718.

Jappelli, Tullio, and Marco Pagano. 2002. Information Sharing, Lending and Defaults: Cross-Country Evidence, *Journal of Banking and Finance* 36, 2017–2045.

Jayaratne, Jith, and Philip E. Strahan. 1998. Entry Restrictions, Industry Evolution and Dynamic Efficiency: Evidence from Commercial Banking, *Journal of Law and Economics* 41(1), 239–274.

Jayaratne, Jith, and John Wolken. 1999. How Important Are Small Banks to Small Business Lending? New Evidence from a Survey of Small Firms, *Journal of Banking and Finance* 23, 427–458.

Kallberg, Jarl G., and Gregory F. Udell. 2003. The Value of Private Sector Credit Information Sharing: The U.S. Case, *Journal of Banking and Finance* 27, 449–469.

Karceski, Jason, Steven Ongena, and David C. Smith. 2005. The Impact of Bank Consolidation on Commercial Borrower Welfare, with Jason Karceski and Steven Ongena, *Journal of Finance* 2043–2082.

Kashyap, Anil K., Raghuram G. Rajan, and Jeremy C. Stein. 2002. Banks as Liquidity Providers: An Explanation for the Coexistence of Lending and Deposit-Taking, *Journal of Finance* 57(1), 33–73.

Kroszner, Randall, and Raghuram Rajan. 1997. Organization Structure and Credibility: Evidence from Commercial Bank Securities Activities Before the Glass-Steagall Act, *Journal of Monetary Economics* 39, 475–516.

Kroszner, Randall S., and Philip E. Strahan. 1999. What Drives Deregulation? Economics and Politics of the Relaxation of Bank Branching Restrictions, *Quarterly Journal of Economics* 114(4), 1437–1467.

Leland, Haynes, and David E. Pyle. 1977. Information Asymmetries, Financial Structure and Financial Intermediation, *Journal of Finance* 32(2), 371–387.

Liberti, Jose Maria. 2004. Initiative, Incentives and Soft Information: How Does Delegation Impact the Role of Bank Relationship Managers? Mimeo.

McAndrews, James J., and Philip E. Strahan. 2002. Deregulation, Correspondent Banking, and the Role of the Federal Reserve, *Journal of Financial Intermediation* 11, 320–343.

Mester, Loretta, Nakamura, Leonard, and Micheline Renault. 2007. Checking Accounts and Bank Monitoring, *Review of Financial Studies* 20, 529–556.

Mian, Atif. 2006. Distance Constraints: The Limits of Lending in Poor Economies, *Journal of Finance* 61(3), 1465–1505.

Minton, Bernadette A., Anthony Sanders, and Philip E. Strahan. 2004. The Rise of Securitization: Efficient Contracting or Regulatory Arbitrage? Mimeo.

Mishkin, Frederic S., and Philip E. Strahan. 1998. What Will Technology Do to Financial Structure?, in Robert Litan and Anthony Santomero (eds.), *The Effect of Technology on the Financial Sector*. Brookings-Wharton Papers on Financial Services, pp. 249–287.

Morgan, Donald P. 2002. Rating Banks: Risk and Uncertainty in an Opaque Industry, *American Economic Review* 92(4), 874–888.

Myers, Stewart C., and Raghuram G. Rajan. 1998. The Paradox of Liquidity, *Quarterly Journal of Economics* 113(2), 733–771.

Nakamura, Leonard. 1993. Commercial Bank Information: Implications for the Structure of Banking, in Michael Klausner and Lawrence J. White (eds.), *Structural Change in Banking*. Irwin, Burr Ridge, pp. 131–160.

Narayanan, R., Rangan K., and Rangan, N. 2004. The Value of Commercial Banks' Private Debt Underwriting Reputation in Public Underwriting. Mimeo.

Ongena, Steven, and David C. Smith. 2000. The Duration of Banking Relationships, *Journal of Financial Economics* 61, 449–475.

Peek, Joseph, and Eric S. Rosengren. 1998. Bank Consolidation and Small Business Lending: It's Not Just Size That Matters, *Journal of Banking and Finance* 22, 799–820.

Peek, Joseph, and Eric S. Rosengren. 2000. Collateral Damage: Effects of the Japanese Bank Crisis on Real Activity in the U.S., *American Economic Review* 90(1), 30–45.

Petersen, Mitchell. 2004. Information: Hard and Soft. Northwestern Kellogg School of Management mimeo.

Petersen, Mitchell, and Raghuram Rajan. 1994. The Benefits of Firm–Creditor Relationships: Evidence from Small-Business Data, *Journal of Finance*, 49, 3–37.

Qian, Jun, and Philip E. Strahan. 2007. How Law and Institutions Shape Financial Contracts: The Case of Bank Loans, *Journal of Finance* 62(6), 2803–2834.

Rajan, R. 1992. Insiders and Outsiders: The Choice Between Informed and Arm's-Length Debt, *Journal of Finance* 47, 1367–1400.

Saidenberg, Marc R., and Philip E. Strahan. 1999. Are Banks Still Important for Financing Large Businesses? Federal Reserve Bank of New York's *Current Issues in Economics and Finance* 5(12).

Sapienza, Paola. 2002. The Effects of Bank Mergers on Loan Contracts, *Journal of Finance* 57, 329–367.

Schenone, Carola. 2004. The Effect of Banking Relationships on the Firm's IPO Underpricing, *Journal of Finance* 59(6), 2903–2958.

Sharpe, Steven. 1990. Asymmetric Information, Bank Lending and Implicit Contracts: A Stylized Model of Customer Relationship, *Journal of Finance* 45, 1069–1087.

Slovin, M., M. Sushka, and J. Polonchek. 1993. The Value of Bank Durability: Borrowers as Bank Stakeholders, *Journal of Finance* 48(1), 247–266.

Stein, Jeremy. 2002. Information Production and Capital Allocation: Hierarchical vs. Decentralized Firms, *Journal of Finance* 57, 1891–1921.

Stiroh, Kevin J., and Philip E. Strahan. 2003. Competitive Dynamics of Competition: Evidence from U.S. Banking, *Journal of Money, Credit and Banking* 35(5), 801–828.

Strahan, Philip E., and James P. Weston. 1998. Small Business Lending and the Changing Structure of the Banking Industry, *Journal of Banking and Finance* 22(2–6), 821–845.

Sufi, Amir. 2007. Agency and Renegotiation in Corporate Finance: Evidence from Syndicated Loans, *Journal of Finance* 62(2), 629–668.

Sufi, Amir. 2004. Does Joint Production of Lending and Debt Underwriting Help or Hurt Firms? A Fixed Effects Approach, MIT mimeo.

Townsend, Robert M. 1979. Optimal Contracts and Competitive Markets with Costly State Verification, *Journal of Economic Theory* 21, 1–29.

Udell, Gregory. 2004. *Asset-Based Finance: Proven Disciplines for Prudent Lending*. Commercial Finance Association, New York.

White, Eugene. 1998. The Legacy of Deposit Insurance: The Growth, Spread, and Cost of Insuring Financial Intermediaries, in Michael Bordo, Claudia Goldin, and Eugene White (eds.), *The Defining Moment*. University of Chicago Press, Chicago.

Yasuda, Ayako. 2005. Do Bank Relationships Affect the Firm's Underwriter Choice in the Corporate Bond Market? *Journal of Finance* 60(3), 1259–1292.

CHAPTER 5

Optimal Industrial Structure in Banking*

Loretta J. Mester
Federal Reserve Bank of Philadelphia and the Wharton School, University of Pennsylvania

*The views expressed here are those of the author and do not represent the views of the Federal Reserve Bank of Philadelphia or of the Federal Reserve System.

1. INTRODUCTION AND MOTIVATION

The banking industry has been undergoing a significant restructuring over the last several years. Since the mid-1980s, the number of commercial banks has fallen by over 7,000 (from 14,407 in 1985 to 7,303 in Septemper 2007) as a result of failures and, especially, mergers. According to FDIC statistics, there were about 12,000 mergers, an average of 430 per year, between 1985 and 2007.[1] The average asset size of banks has also increased, because assets are being redistributed from smaller banks to larger ones. In real terms, the average asset size of U.S. banks has quadrupled since 1985 and in 2007 was over $1 billion. Bank of America, the largest bank holding company in the United States (as of September 2007) has $1.3 trillion in consolidated commercial banking assets. Another result of consolidation is that by some measures, banking is becoming more concentrated. According to data from commercial bank reports of condition and income, the largest 10 banks in the United States were holding over half of the United States banking industry's assets in 2007, compared to 25 percent in 1985. Banks with assets over $5 billion (in 2007 dollars) were holding about 81 percent of total U.S. banking industry assets in 2007, compared with 53 percent in 1985, and banks with more than $10 billion (in 2007 dollars) in assets were holding 78 percent of industry assets in 2007, compared with about 45 percent in 1985.

Consolidation is a global phenomenon. There has been a considerable amount of merger activity not only in the United States but in other countries. The Group of Ten study (2001) of consolidation in 13 countries in the 1990s indicates that of 7,304 financial mergers, 61 percent involved banks, and the number of banks fell in almost every country.[2]

The consolidation in the financial services industry has raised some conundrums.

Conundrum 1 The consolidation in the banking industry has created some very large banks; indeed, as of September 30, 2007 there were three bank holding companies in the United States with over $1 trillion in assets. Bank managers say that one of their motivations in consolidating is to capture scale economies, that is, efficiencies gained from operating at a large scale, but much of the literature suggests these economies are exhausted at relatively small sizes.

Conundrum 2 The Gramm-Leach-Bliley Act of 1999 repealed the Glass-Steagall prohibitions against mixing commercial banking with investment banking and allowed commercial banks into other nonbank activities (such as insurance). Under Gramm-Leach-Bliley, an institution must form a bank holding company (BHC) and then convert the BHC into a financial holding company (FHC) before engaging in nontraditional activities. As of February 2, 2008, there were 648 FHCs; most were created from

[1] FDIC (2007).

[2] Only in Belgium, Japan, and Australia did the number of banks rise in the 1990s, Japan because of a change in definition and Belgium by just two banks. Although the number of banks in Australia increased from 34 in 1990 to 44 in 1999, the report characterizes the banking industry in Australia as highly concentrated. In 1999, the five largest banks in Australia held 74 percent of deposits, while the five largest banks in the United States held 27 percent of deposits. (As of 2007, the largest five banks in the United States held 44 percent of industry deposits and 48 percent of industry assets.)

long-standing BHCs rather than de novo. Many are small; most are not engaged in nonbanking activities. Indeed, fewer commercial banks have moved into those areas than was anticipated when the act was passed.

Conundrum 3 Official government statistics suggest that productivity in the banking industry rose at a slower rate from 1994 to 2005 than that in the rest of the corporate sector. This seems somewhat surprising given the technological advances that have been made in banking over the last two decades.[3]

One goal of the research agenda on optimal bank productive efficiency and industrial structure is to answer some fundamental questions in financial industry restructuring, such as what motivates bank managers to engage in mergers and acquisitions, and to evaluate the costs and benefits of consolidation, which is essentially an empirical question. The most recent literature has begun to shed light on these three puzzles via several advances in modeling bank production, which are then brought to data. These advances include recognizing that the level of risk is an endogenous choice of bank managers and that financial capital is an input into bank production. Models that allow for managerial preferences that differ from cost minimization and profit maximization and that allow managers to trade off risk against return have been developed and estimated. The models can be used to help in understanding the motivation and outcomes of banking industry consolidation.

Consolidation is a potential positive for the industry and economy to the extent that it eliminates inefficient banks and results in a healthier banking system via better diversification of risks. Positives potentially include the following.

1. *More efficient scale or product mix* Scale or scope economies exist if the average cost of production declines as the size or number of products increases, respectively. Average cost might decline as the size of the bank increases if there are significant fixed costs that can be spread over larger operations. Technological change has afforded banks new tools of financial engineering (e.g., derivatives, off-balance-sheet guarantees, and risk management) that may be more efficiently produced by larger institutions. Also, new delivery methods for banking services (e.g., online banking, phone centers, ATMs) favor larger banks that can spread the fixed costs of setting up such systems over larger volumes, implying lower average costs of production. With respect to product mix, if there are cost complementarities among products (e.g., joint use of inputs, such as marketing), then producing multiple products in the same bank can be efficient.
2. *Better diversification over product lines and/or across geographic markets* The price of risk taking falls via diversification, and there is some evidence that United States acquiring banks bid more for targets when the M&A would lead to significant diversification gains (Benston, Hunter, and Wall 1995).

[3]According to Berger and Mester (2003), government agencies typically measure productivity by the ratio of an output index to an input index. Updating the statistics reported in Berger and Mester (2003), average annual growth in labor productivity (measured by output per employee-hour) in commercial banking (NAICS Code 52211) was 1.57 percent over 1994–2005, compared to 4.39 percent in manufacturing, 2.45 percent in nonfarm businesses, and 2.88 percent in nonfinancial corporations. These data indicate banking productivity is rising at a slower pace than the productivity of the rest of the corporate sector.

3. *Higher X-efficiency* Even firms that are operating at the efficient scale of operations and producing the efficient mix of products might not be doing so in a manner that minimizes costs; for example, managers may be wasting some of the firm's inputs or diverting some for their own benefit. Consolidation can help rid the industry of such X-inefficiency to the extent that more efficient firms take over less efficient firms and are able to extend efficient operations to the target. In many U.S. M&As, a larger, more efficient institution takes over a smaller, less efficient institution, and acquiring banks are more cost efficient than target banks on average (Pilloff and Santomero 1998).

But consolidation could also be a negative for the industry and economy. It could result in a less competitive banking system, concentrating market power in a handful of very large institutions, or reduce the supply of funds to small firms by driving community banks out of business. To the extent that banks can be "too big to fail," consolidation might be motivated by banks' desire to exploit the underpriced federal safety net. Using 1990 data on U.S. bank holding companies, Hughes and Mester (1993) found evidence of such a "too big to fail" size advantage: For banks with greater than $6.5 billion in assets, an increase in size, holding default risk and asset quality constant, significantly lowers the uninsured deposit price. Consolidation might be motivated by a desire to maximize managers' objectives and therefore not be socially optimal. But even if consolidation is motivated by a desire to maximize shareholder value, it need not be socially optimal. While shareholder value can be raised via more efficient production, it can also be raised via higher prices if banks' market power rises via consolidation.

Systemic risk problems might also increase as a result of consolidation. Adverse shocks to a large bank can be transmitted across the financial system, since a large bank has more linkages to other banks. As discussed in the G10 report (2001) on consolidation, evidence shows that interdependencies between large and complex banking organizations have increased in the last 10 years in the United States and Japan and are beginning to do so in Europe. These increases are correlated with consolidation (but a causal link has not been established). According to the G10 report, the interdependencies most associated with consolidation include interbank loans, market activities such as over-the-counter derivatives, and payment and settlement systems.

Research suggests that consolidation in the latter half of the 1990s was not driven by the cleanup of failed or failing banks, since bank performance was very good (Berger and Mester 2003); thus, it is a trend rather than merely a response to cyclical events.[4] Instead, changes in the banking environment appear to be important factors spurring consolidation. These include technological progress, improvements in financial

[4]The mid-1980s to early 1990s was a time of relatively poor performance of U.S. banks. Performance problems with loans to less developed countries and in commercial real estate markets led to performance problems at U.S. banks and a "credit crunch" in the early 1990s. This was the first phase of the consolidation trend, and the number of banks fell by almost 20 percent between 1984 and 1991. After the credit crunch period, the banking industry had much better performance. Profits and efficiency rose, the ratio of nonperforming loans to total loans fell, and risk taking and deposit market concentration remained constant (see Berger and Mester 2003).

condition, which allowed for more voluntary M&As, deregulation of geographic and product restrictions on banking, which allowed the industry to evolve into the structure that would have existed had the restrictions not been imposed, and excess capacity in the industry or particular markets. International consolidation (globalization) of markets also has been a factor. Transfer of securities, goods, and services in international markets creates demand for financial services in international markets, spurring cross-border M&As. Banks can also achieve the dual goals of risk diversification and new sources of funds by cross-border expansion. But these potential benefits must be weighed against the costs, which include having to deal with different regulatory regimes and corporate and national cultural differences.

The research on optimal bank productive efficiency and industrial structure can help in evaluating the extent to which consolidation yields cost and revenue benefits or, instead, whether it is a way that agency problems within the firm are manifested, whether consolidation is attractive to managers because they gain from "building empires" and controlling larger banks, and whether large banks allow managers to consume "agency goods," such as reduced effort and risk avoidance. In helping us understand the motivation for consolidation, the research can also help guide policy regarding consolidation in the industry.

The rest of this chapter is organized as follows. Section 2 discusses the concepts used in evaluating banking firm and industry productive efficiency. Section 3 discusses empirical implementation of the concepts. Section 4 discusses measurement issues that must be confronted when bringing the concepts to data. Section 5 discusses the main empirical findings in the literature related to each concept. Section 6 concludes.

2. EFFICIENCY CONCEPTS

In investigating the optimal structure of the banking industry and its efficiency, one must start with a concept of optimization. As a general definition, efficiency is a measure of deviation between actual performance and desired performance. Thus, efficiency must be measured relative to an *objective function*. A fundamental decision in measuring financial institution efficiency is which concept to use, and the choice will depend on the question being asked.

The concept chosen should be related to *economic* optimization in reaction to market prices and competition, rather than being based solely on the use of technology. We can ask whether the bank is maximizing the amount of output it produces given its inputs or is minimizing the amount of inputs it uses to produce a given level of output—that is, whether it is operating on its production frontier—but that is a question about *technological* optimization. This is less interesting from an economic perspective, since it ignores values. It cannot account for allocative inefficiency in misresponding to relative prices in choosing inputs and outputs, and it is difficult to compare firms that tend to specialize in different inputs or outputs, because there is no way to compare one input or output with another without the benefit of relative prices. There is also no way to determine whether the output being produced is optimal without value information on the outputs. Instead, we would like to investigate questions of *economic* optimization.[5]

For example, is the bank minimizing its costs of production given its choice of inputs, taking input prices as given? Is the bank maximizing its profits given its choice of inputs and outputs, taking input and output prices as given? A bank might be operating on its production frontier (i.e., not wasting resources), and so be *technically* efficient, but it could still be *allocatively* inefficient if it is choosing the wrong mix of inputs given the relative prices of those inputs. Similarly, the bank could be technically and allocatively efficient in producing its chosen level of output, but it could be choosing the wrong level of output in order to maximize profits.

Figure 1 presents a simple two-input, one-output case of firm production. The figure shows an isoquant—the combinations of inputs x_1 and x_2 (say, labor and capital) it takes to make output level y_0. Firm B is technically efficient, since it is operating on the isoquant. Firm A is inefficient, since it is operating interior to the isoquant. That is, Firm A is using more of inputs x_1 and x_2 to produce y_0 than an efficient firm would use. But note that Firm B could do better as well. Firm B could lower its costs of producing y_0 by using a different combination of the inputs, given their prices w_1 and w_2. Namely, given the prices of the inputs, Firm B would minimize its cost of producing y_0 by operating at point O. Firm B should use more x_1 and less of x_2. Since we want to capture such allocative inefficiency, we want to focus on the economic concepts of cost minimization and profit maximization, which are based on economic optimization in reaction to market prices and competition, rather than based solely on the use of technology.

There are different aspects to economic optimization. Most of the literature focuses on cost minimization. But from a performance standpoint, one might also investigate whether the bank is producing the optimal outputs in terms of profitability and firm value. For this, one can study the profit function (and, less commonly, the revenue function). This is important to the extent that bank output quality is a significant choice variable for the bank. If revenue losses more than counteract cost savings, the choice is not profit maximizing. Profit efficiency includes revenue benefits from improving product mix and can reflect the benefits of improved diversification.

Newer studies acknowledge the fact that the objectives of firm management may differ from cost minimization and profit maximization and try to incorporate this into efficiency measurement. These papers focus on more market-based definitions of efficiency, for example, operation on a risk–return frontier.

Three main types of efficiency are measured: scale, scope, X-efficiency. They are used to address questions pertaining to different aspects of bank structure.

What is the optimal scale of operations of the bank? This is pertinent to the issue of optimal structure in terms of number of firms in the industry. Is banking a natural monopoly? *Scale economies* are usually measured with respect to bank costs and refer to how the bank's scale of operations (its size) is related to cost—what percentage increase in costs occurs with a 1 percent increase in scale. A firm is operating at constant returns

[5]For further discussion see Berger and Mester (1997) and Mester (2003).

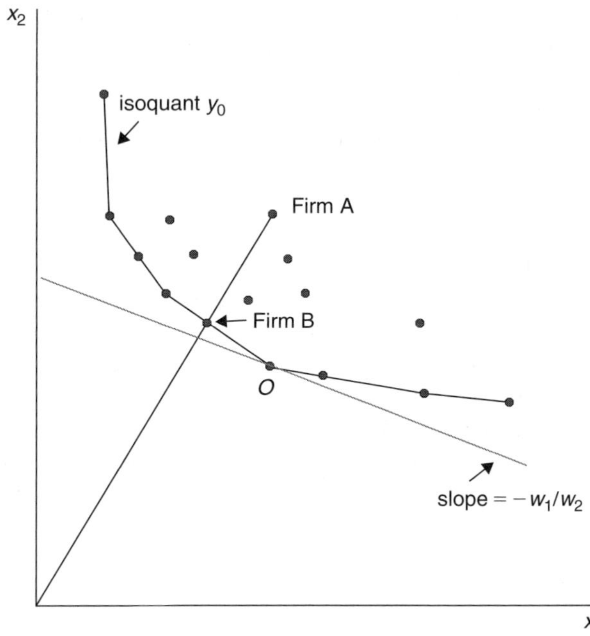

FIGURE 1 Two-input one-output isoquant.

to scale if, for a given mix of products, a proportionate increase in all its outputs would increase its costs by the same proportion; a firm is operating with scale economies if a proportionate increase in scale leads to a less-than-proportionate increase in cost; a firm is operating with scale diseconomies if a proportionate increase in scale leads to a more-than-proportionate increase in cost. For single-product firms, operating at the point of constant returns to scale implies operating at minimum average cost.

What is the efficient mix of outputs in banking? That is, what's the optimal combination of products to minimize cost (or maximize profits)? This is pertinent to the issue of universal banking and the mixing of commercial and investment banking in the aftermath of Gramm-Leach-Bliley. *Scope economies* are usually measured with respect to bank costs and refer to how the bank's choice of multiple product lines is related to cost. A firm producing multiple products enjoys scope economies if it is less costly to produce those products together in a single entity than it would be to separate production into specialized firms.[6] A potential source of such scope economies is the opportunity to cross-market new and existing products to customers. For example, the merger of Citibank with Travelers, which had bought Smith Barney (which had bought Salomon), brought together commercial banking, securities, and insurance products. On the other

[6]Note, I have defined *scale economies* and *scope economies* relative to the costs of production, but they could just as well have been defined relative to the bank's revenues or profits.

hand, the cost of integrating disparate computer systems in order to take advantage of such potential cross-marketing opportunities might mitigate any scope economies.

Given the technology, what percent of banks are using the best-practice methods of production, that is, are operating on the efficient frontier? *X-efficiency* measures how productive the firm is in its use of inputs to create output. The concept refers to the dispersion of costs (profits, revenues) in any given size/product mix class. If all firms in an industry are producing the scale and combination of outputs that minimize the average cost of production, then the total cost of producing the industry's output is minimized, and the industry is producing the efficient combination and level of products, provided each firm is using its inputs efficiently. Firms that exhibit cost X-inefficiency are either wasting some of their inputs (technical inefficiency) or are using the wrong combination of inputs to produce outputs (allocative inefficiency) or both. Management ability (or lack thereof) may be a source of X-inefficiency, but managerial preferences might be another source, to the extent that managers can pursue objectives that differ from those of stockholders. For example, managers might derive utility, U, from having large staffs or other perquisites, as well as high profits, so that $U = U(\pi, E)$, where π is profits and E is expenditure on labor (or other inputs). Some studies of commercial banks and savings and loans have found evidence of such "expense-preference" behavior; others have found evidence of "empire building," that is, pursuit of inefficient mergers to gain larger scale and presumably prestige (see Edwards 1977, Mester 1989a, 1989b, Mester 1991, and Hughes, et al. 2003).

How has the production technology shifted over time (*technological change*), and how has productivity changed over time? *Productivity* is a combination of a shift in the best-practice frontier and in dispersion from the frontier (X-inefficiency).

These concepts can be focused more specifically on the optimality of particular aspects of bank strategy. For example, Berlin and Mester (1998) provide evidence on whether relationship lending is efficient. Banks are able to smooth loan rates for their borrowers with which they have formed a long-term relationship. Berlin and Mester (1998) find that loan-rate smoothing in response to a shock to a small business borrower's credit risk is not efficient, but in response to an interest-rate shock such loan-rate smoothing is efficient.

3. EMPIRICAL IMPLEMENTATION

3.1. Bank Production

To bring efficiency concepts to bear in investigating the optimal structure of the banking firm, one must begin with a theory of the banking firm. That is, what do banks do? Most of the literature applies traditional microeconomic theory of firm production to banking firms—a bank is a factory producing financial services (like a factory makes widgets). The newer literature takes seriously the bank as a financial intermediary that differs from other types of firms. Factors important for banks that have generally been ignored in much of the literature include the bank's choice of risk and diversification of assets, asset quality and its feedback on the bank's input prices, and the bank's financial capital structure. The newer literature combines the theory of financial intermediation with the microeconomics of bank production (see Hughes, et al. 2000, Hughes 1999, Hughes, et al. 1999, and Hughes, Mester, and Moon 2001).

In the standard application of efficiency analysis to banking, bank production decisions do not affect bank risk. The bank is assumed to take the entire price of its outputs and inputs as given. This rules out the possibility that scale-related improvements in diversification could lower the cost of borrowed funds and induce banks to alter their exposure to risk. In contrast, the newer research recognizes the bank's role as a monitor and producer of information and the bank as a manager of risk. The theory of the banking firm emphasizes the bank's role in producing information about its borrowers. Hence, output measures should attempt to proxy for these aspects of banking. One study, Mester (1992), directly accounted for the monitoring and screening role of banks in measuring bank output by treating loans purchased and originated loans as separate outputs entailing different types of screening and by treating loans held on balance sheet and loans sold as separate outputs entailing different types of monitoring.

The bank's choice of capital structure (funding choices regarding capital and debt) and its strategic decisions regarding asset quality vary with production decisions. Thus, part of the input and output prices a bank faces are not exogenous—the risk premium in these prices is partly endogenous as it depends on the bank's production choices. This affects the modeling of banking production and therefore the measurement of scale economies and scope economies (Hughes, et al. 2000, Hughes 1999). But in standard efficiency studies, the bank is assumed to choose a production plan to minimize cost and maximize profits *given* the prices of inputs and outputs (including the required return on shareholders' equity). That is, the standard assumption is that the required return on debt and equity is independent of production decisions of the firm. The higher moments of cost and profit are assumed not to vary across banks. In newer research, banks are modeled as taking actions that will maximize their market value. Since production decisions affect bank risk, they affect the discount rate applied to evaluating discounted present value. Production decisions that increase expected profit but also the discount rate applied to that profit may not increase the bank's market value. The optimal production choices depend not only on the expected profits they generate but also on the variability of the profit stream generated. The newer research tries to evaluate the tradeoff between expected return and the riskiness of that return.

The newer theory also recognizes that bank managers may be making production decisions that do not maximize value because of agency problems between owners and managers. The researcher has data on the decisions managers are actually making, which need not be value-maximizing decisions. Measurement of scale economies and scope economies and X-efficiency should take this into account.

3.2. Cost Minimization

The second step in empirical implementation is to decide which optimization goal to investigate, such as, cost, profits, and revenue. The earliest literature assumed that the bank produced a single output. Once techniques were developed for measuring scale economies and scope economies at multiproduct firms (Baumol, Panzar, and Willig 1982), these techniques were applied to financial institutions.

In a cost function, variable costs depend on the prices of variable inputs, the quantities of variable outputs, any fixed inputs or outputs, and environmental factors, as well as an error term. If the error term includes only random error and not the possibility of X-inefficiency, then the estimated cost function is an *average-practice cost function*, describing the average relationship between costs, outputs, and input prices. If the error term includes a term representing random error and a term representing X-inefficiency, then the estimated cost function is a *best-practice frontier*, which indicates the cost for a bank to produce using the best practices under ideal conditions. (Note, this does not necessarily represent the best possible practice, merely the best practice observed among banks in the sample. See Berger and Mester, 1997.) Such a cost function is often written in logarithmic form:

$$\ln C_i = \ln f(y_i, w_i, z_i, h_i) + u_i + v_i, \tag{1}$$

where C measures variable costs, w is the vector of prices of variable inputs, y is the vector of quantities of variable outputs, z indicates the quantities of any fixed netputs (inputs or outputs, such as physical plant, which cannot be changed quickly), h is a set of environmental or market variables that may affect performance (e.g., regulatory restrictions) but are not a choice for firm management, u_i denotes an inefficiency factor that may raise costs above the best-practice level, and v_i denotes the random error that incorporates measurement error and luck that may temporarily give firms high or low costs. The inefficiency factor u_i incorporates both allocative inefficiencies from failing to react optimally to relative prices of inputs, w, and technical inefficiencies from employing too much of the inputs to produce y.

The function f denotes some functional form and represents the best-practice frontier. The term $u_i + v_i$ is treated as a composite error term: v_i is a two-sided error, since random measurement error or luck can be positive or negative, and u_i is a one-sided (positive) error, since inefficiency means higher costs. The various X-efficiency measurement techniques use different methods to identify the inefficiency term, u_i, as distinct from the random error term, v_i.

Scale economies measure the percentage change in costs per 1 percent increase in all the outputs, as given by the frontier. Consider composite output bundle y^0, and suppose $y = ty^0$. Then

$$\text{SCALE} = \frac{f}{\dfrac{df}{\left(\dfrac{dt}{t}\right)}} = \frac{f}{\sum_{i=1}^{N} \dfrac{\partial f}{\partial y_i} y_i} = \frac{1}{\sum_{i=1}^{N} \dfrac{\partial \ln f}{\partial \ln y_i}} = \frac{1}{\sum_{i=1}^{N} \dfrac{\partial \ln C}{\partial \ln y_i}}, \tag{2}$$

where N = number of outputs.

There are scale economies (i.e., increasing returns to scale) if SCALE > 1; scale diseconomies (i.e., decreasing returns to scale) if SCALE < 1; and constant returns to scale if SCALE = 1. Note that for single-product firms, choosing y such that SCALE = 1 minimizes the average cost of production.

Scope economies measure whether it is less costly for a multiproduct firm to produce the outputs together than for single-product firms to produce the products, as given by the frontier:

$$\text{SCOPE}(y_1, \ldots, y_N) = \frac{[f(y_1, 0, \ldots, 0) + f(0, y_2, 0, \ldots, 0) + \cdots + f(0, \ldots 0, y_N)] - f(y_1, y_2, \ldots, y_N)}{f(y_1, y_2, \ldots, y_N)} \quad (3)$$

Several criticisms have been leveled at the scope economies measure. First, it requires evaluation of the cost function at zero-output levels. This rules out certain functional forms, such as the translog, in which outputs appear in logarithmic form. Researchers have handled this either by replacing the zero output with a very small positive number or by selecting a functional form that permits zero-output levels (e.g., the hybrid translog function, which replaces ln y_i in the translog cost function with y_i transformed by the Box–Cox metric, i.e., $[(y_i^\lambda - 1)/\lambda]$, where λ is a parameter to be estimated).

A more telling criticism of the conventional measure of scope economies is that it requires the cost function to be evaluated at zero-output levels even if all firms in the sample are producing positive levels of each output, as they often are in banking studies. So the scope measure involves extrapolation outside the sample. This problem is not resolved by functional forms such as the hybrid translog, which permit evaluation at zero output. Mester (1991) proposes a new measure, within-sample scope economies, which avoids extrapolation:

$$\text{WSC}(y_1, \ldots, y_N) = \frac{\begin{array}{c}\{[f(y_1 - (N-1)y_1^{\min}, y_2^{\min}, \ldots, y_N^{\min}) + f(y_1^{\min}, y_2 - (N-1)y_2^{\min}, y_3^{\min}, \ldots, y_N^{\min}) + \cdots \\ \cdots + f(y_1^{\min}, \ldots, y_{N-1}^{\min}, y_N - (N-1)y_N^{\min})] - f(y_1, y_2, \ldots, y_N)\}\end{array}}{f(y_1, y_2, \ldots, y_N)} \quad (4)$$

where $y_i^{\min}$ is the minimum value of y_i in the sample. The specialized firms in the within-sample measure produce positive amounts of each output but tend to specialize in one or the other.

The cost *X-inefficiency* of any bank i would be measured relative to the best-practice frontier. Note that the best-practice frontier refers to the best practice observed in the sample and not true minimum cost, which is not observable. Conceptually, the cost inefficiency of bank i measures the percentage increase in cost of bank i, adjusted for random error, relative to the estimated cost needed to produce bank i's output vector if the firm were as efficient as the best-practice firm in the sample facing the same exogenous variables (w, y, z, h).[7] It can be thought of as the proportion of costs or resources

[7]To see this, note that, ignoring random error, $u_i = \ln C_i - \ln f(y_i, w_i, z_i, h_i)$.

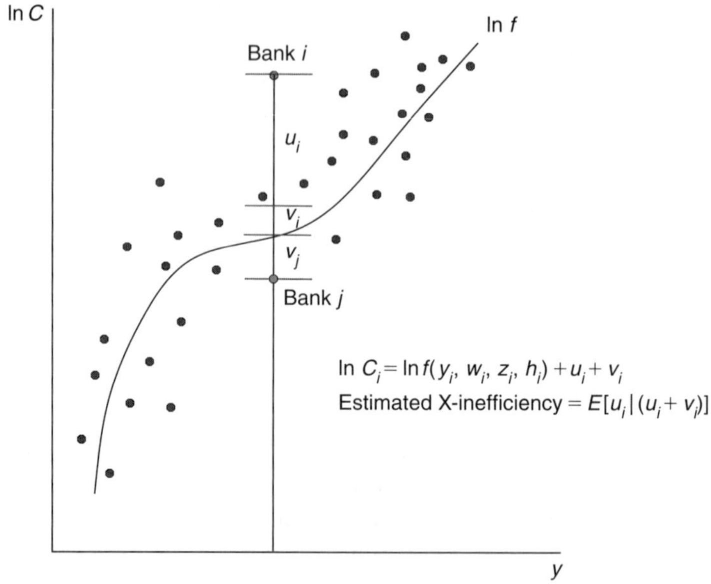

FIGURE 2 Cost frontier and X-inefficiency u_i.

that are used inefficiently or wasted. Figure 2 shows an example. The estimated cost frontier is given by $\ln f$. Bank j is fully efficient. Its actual cost lies below the frontier, due to random error. Bank i is inefficient. The difference in bank i's cost and the frontier value at the same y is due to both random error, v_i, and inefficiency, u_i. Cost inefficiency would include both technical inefficiency (operating in the interior of the production possibilities frontier) and allocative inefficiency (operating at a point on the production possibilities frontier that is not cost-minimizing).

If time-series or panel data are available, then *productivity growth* can be measured. Productivity growth is a combination of technological change, which is given by shifts in the frontier over time, and changes in inefficiency, which are changes in dispersion around the frontier. Berger and Mester (2003) define cost productivity growth as the change in cost from period t to period $t + k$, holding constant the exogenous environmental variables, which they term "business conditions," at their period-t levels. It is important to control for these business conditions to avoid attributing a change in costs that is not due to bank managers' decisions or skill to a change in productivity.

3.3. Profit Maximization

The bank should minimize the cost of producing a given output bundle, but that output bundle should be chosen to maximize profits. Standard profit efficiency measures how close a firm is to producing the maximum possible profit given a particular level of input prices and output prices (and fixed netputs and environmental variables). In contrast to the cost function, the standard profit function specifies variable profits in place of variable costs and takes variable output prices as given, rather than holding all output quantities statistically fixed at their observed, possibly inefficient, levels. That is, the dependent variable in the profit function allows for consideration of revenues that can be earned by varying outputs as well as inputs. Output prices are taken as exogenous, allowing for inefficiencies in the choice of outputs when responding to these prices or to any other arguments of the profit function.

The standard profit function, in log form, is

$$\ln(\pi + \theta)_i = \ln g(p_i, w_i, z_i, h_i) - u_{\pi i} + v_{\pi i}, \tag{5}$$

where π is the variable profits of the firm, θ is a constant added to every firm's profit so that the natural log is taken of a positive number, p is the vector of prices of the variable outputs, $v_{\pi i}$ represents random error, and $u_{\pi i}$, represents inefficiency that reduces profits.

Similar to cost X-inefficiency, profit X-inefficiency is defined as that amount of profit that is not being earned compared to the predicted maximum profit that could be earned if the firm were as efficient as the best-practice firm. Thus, it is the percentage of profits that is left on the table, so to speak. Similar to cost productivity growth, profit productivity growth is the change in profit from period t to period $t + k$, holding constant the exogenous environmental variables ("business conditions") at their period-t levels.

As discussed in Berger and Mester (1997), profit efficiency is a more comprehensive measure of performance than is cost efficiency, since it accounts for errors on the output side as well as those on the input side. It is based on the economic goal of profit maximization, which requires that the same amount of managerial attention be paid to raising a marginal dollar of revenue as to reducing a marginal dollar of costs. That is, a firm that spends \$1 additional to raise revenues by \$2, all else held equal, would appropriately be measured as being more profit efficient but might inappropriately be measured as being less cost efficient. Note that cost efficiency evaluates performance, holding output constant at its current level, which generally will not correspond to an optimum. A firm that is relatively cost efficient at its current output may or may not be cost efficient at its optimal output, which typically involves a different scale and mix of outputs. Standard profit efficiency embodies the cost inefficiency deviations from the optimal point as well as revenue inefficiencies.[8]

3.4. More Complicated Objectives

As discussed earlier, the standard concepts of cost minimization and profit maximization may not be the only goals being pursued by the firms' managers, and some studies have

[8] Berger and Mester (1997) discuss another type of profit efficiency: alternative profit efficiency. This concept is based on estimates of the alternative profit function, which substitutes output levels for output prices in the specification of the profit function. This function is estimated to provide additional information when the maintained assumptions underlying the standard profit function do not hold. It may provide useful information if there are unmeasured differences in output qualities across firms, outputs are not completely variable, output markets are not perfectly competitive, or output prices are not accurately measured.

incorporated more complicated objectives. Explicitly recognizing the tradeoff between return and risk, where risk is a choice variable of the firm, would seem to be an important consideration for financial institutions (see Hughes 1999, Hughes, et al. 2000, and Hughes, Mester, and Moon 2001). For example, an increase in a bank's scale of operations may allow it to reduce its exposure to both credit and liquidity risk through diversification. All else equal, this could mean scale economies in risk management costs. But all else is not equal: By reducing the risk attached to any given production plan, better diversification can decrease the marginal cost of risk taking and lead banks to take on more risk to earn a greater return. Not accounting for risk when specifying the production structure can obscure scale economies, since additional risk taking is costly in terms of the additional resources needed to manage the risk and the higher risk premium that has to be paid to attract uninsured funding. When exposure to risk is influenced by production decisions, then cost minimization and profit maximization need not coincide with value maximization. Estimates of efficiency that are derived from cost and profit functions may be mismeasured, since they do not penalize suboptimal choices of risk and quality that then affect prices. Moreover, if the managers are able to make choices in their own interest rather than on behalf of the owners of the firm (the stockholders), that is, if the market for corporate control does not discipline managers, then the choices of risk versus return need not be value maximizing either. Recognition that managers make decisions introduces the possibility of agency problems that also need to be considered in measuring efficiency.

If firms take risk as well as profit into account when making production decisions, then the model of production against which efficiency is evaluated would need to include this. Hughes, et al. (1996, 2000) construct a model of firm production that incorporates the risk–return tradeoff. Managers' most preferred production plan maximizes a utility function that accounts for how the probability distribution of profit depends on the production plan. Duality theory is used to derive the most preferred input and profit demand equations from the expenditure function. These demand functions are those that maximize the managers' utility function. The managers' demand for financial capital can also be estimated along with the input and profit demand equations.[9]

Hughes, Mester, and Moon (2001) develop measures of efficiency based on the expected return–risk tradeoff implied by the production model. ER is the firm's predicted profit, as calculated from the estimated profit-share equation from the model, divided by the firm's equity level. RK is the standard error of predicted profit divided by equity. The authors show that ER and RK are systematically related to the market value of equity for the subsample of publicly traded banks, so they can be used to derive market return efficiency measures. A risk–return frontier is then estimated:

$$\mathrm{ER}_i = \Gamma_0 + \Gamma_1\,\mathrm{RK}_i + \Gamma_2\,\mathrm{RK}_i^2 + v_i - u_i, \tag{6}$$

[9]The functional forms for the utility-maximizing input and profit equations can be derived from the almost-ideal demand system. These equations are conditioned on the level of financial capital. A second stage can be added to the utility maximization problem to determine the bank mangers' choice of financial capital, and this demand function can be estimated along with the input and profit demand equations.

where v_i is a two-sided error term representing random error and u_i is a one-sided error term representing inefficiency. An inefficiency measure based on this frontier would give the increase in expected return that would occur if the firm moved to the frontier, holding risk constant. That is, it identifies lost potential return given the firm's level of return risk. One can identify the group of banks that are most efficient (say, the quarter of banks with the lowest levels of measured inefficiency) as those that are value-maximizing banks.[10]

We can generalize the efficient frontier given in Eq. (6) so that it applies to more complicated objectives (see Hughes, et al. 2000). If X_i denotes a measure of the financial performance of firm i (e.g., profit or the market value of its assets) and G_i denotes a measure defining the peer group used to compare firm i's financial performance (e.g., risk or the market value of assets), the general form of the frontier, which gives the highest potential value of X_i given G_i, is

$$X_i = \alpha_0 + \alpha_1 G_i + \alpha_2 (G_i)^2 + v_i - u_i, \tag{7}$$

where v_i is a two-sided random error term with zero mean and u_i is a one-sided error term representing inefficiency. (Note that more flexible function forms than the quadratic could be specified.) For example, financial performance, X, might be measured by predicted profit from an estimated model and G might be measured by risk (e.g., the firm's interest-rate beta) or by size (e.g., its equity or asset level). Note that for any G, the optimality of the choice of G is not taken into account when measuring efficiency. That is, if G is risk, then a firm's performance would be compared only to those taking on the same level of risk. The firm would not be penalized for a suboptimal choice of risk that lowered performance.

Expense preference is one particular form of X-inefficiency, in which firm managers are assumed to derive utility from choosing a greater-than-efficient (i.e., cost-minimizing or profit-maximizing) level of one or more of the firm's inputs, usually labor. That is, the managerial utility function is $U = U(\pi, E)$, where E represents expenditures on the input.

Tests for expense preference are based on estimating input demand functions or cost functions. The functional forms are derived explicitly from the utility function, which depends on the underlying production function of the firm. Edwards (1977) derived the

[10]Hughes, et al. (1996) present two other efficiency measures. Instead of holding risk constant and comparing the bank's expected return to the expected return it would have if it were on the frontier and had the same level of risk, these measures compare the bank's expected return and risk with the expected return and risk it would have if it moved to the frontier along the shortest path to the frontier. This shortest path is along the ray that is orthogonal to the frontier. These measures have a drawback, in that they cannot account for random error's effect on the placement of the bank relative to the frontier.

Hughes, Mester, and Moon (2001) present two additional efficiency measures. For publicly traded bank holding companies they derive an efficiency measure based on estimating a frontier that relates the market value of assets to the book value of assets, and they derive another efficiency measure based on estimating a frontier that relates the market value of equity to the book value of equity. These measures indicate the bank holding company's lost potential market value of equity or assets based on the book value of equity or assets, respectively.

demand-for-labor equation for a firm using a Cobb–Douglas production function and exhibiting expense preference for labor. Mester (1989b) generalizes expense preference tests to allow for less restrictive production structures and the presence of expense preference toward any input, not just labor. Note that the derived tests in both of these studies cannot give firm-specific measures of inefficiency. Rather, they are tests of whether a group of firms is showing expense preference toward any input.

4. MEASUREMENT

Even after the appropriate concept or goal against which efficiency is to be evaluated is chosen, certain issues need to be confronted before the estimates can be obtained. These include estimation technique, specification of the functional form of the frontier, variables to include in the frontier, and data-measurement issues.

4.1. Estimation Techniques

Different methods have been developed to identify the inefficiency component from the random noise component in frontier estimation. Common frontier efficiency estimation techniques are data envelopment analysis (DEA), free disposable hull analysis (FDH), the stochastic frontier approach, the thick frontier approach, and the distribution-free approach. The first two of these are nonparametric techniques, and the latter three are parametric methods (see Berger and Mester 1997 for further discussion of these techniques).

My preference is for the parametric techniques. The nonparametric methods generally ignore prices and can, therefore, account only for technical inefficiency in using too many inputs or producing too few outputs (as discussed earlier). Another drawback is that they usually do not allow for random error in the data, assuming away measurement error and luck as factors affecting outcomes (although some progress is being made in this regard by using bootstrapping methods). In effect, they disentangle efficiency differences from random error by assuming that random error is zero! To see the effect of measurement error, consider Figure 3. The true data for a set of banks are given by the squares. The true frontier for this set of banks is indicated by the dashed line. The measured data for these banks are indicated by the circles. The frontier determined by DEA using the measured data is given by the solid line. Now consider Banks B and C. The researcher using DEA and ignoring measurement error would conclude that Bank C is not on the frontier and that Bank B is more efficient than Bank C. But the data are measured with error, and Bank C is actually more efficient than Bank B. The researcher would not know the true data but would need to allow for the possibility that the data are measured with error to avoid erroneous conclusions.

In the parametric methods, a bank is labeled inefficient if it is behaving less than optimally with respect to the specified goal (e.g., costs are higher or profits are lower) than the frontier value. The estimation methods differ in the way u_i is disentangled

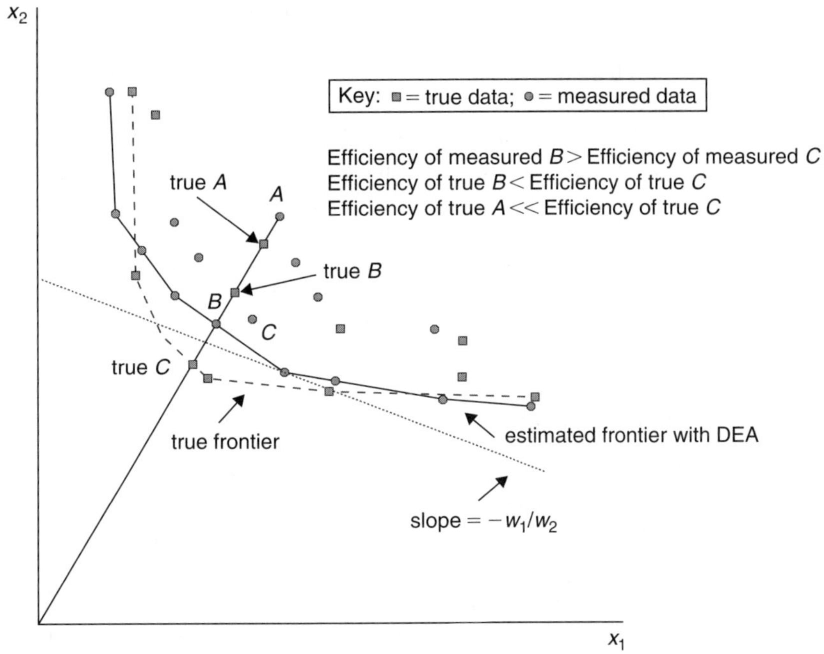

FIGURE 3 Effect of measurement error on estimated inefficiency.

from the composite error term $u_i + v_i$. A drawback of the parametric methods is that assumptions must be made about the shape of the frontier and the distribution of the inefficiency term. However, sufficient flexibility can usually be introduced so that the stochastic methods dominate the nonparametric methods in my opinion.

In the *stochastic frontier approach*, the inefficiency and random error components of the composite error term are disentangled by making explicit assumptions about their distributions. The random error term, v_i, is assumed to be two-sided (usually normally distributed), and the inefficiency term, u_i, is assumed to be one-sided (usually half-normally distributed). The parameters of the two distributions are estimated and can be used to obtain estimates of firm-specific inefficiency. The estimated mean of the conditional distribution of u_i given $u_i + v_i$ (i.e., $\hat{u}_i \equiv \hat{E}(u_i|(u_i + v_i))$) is usually used to measure inefficiency. The distributional assumptions of the stochastic frontier approach are fairly arbitrary, and sometimes the residuals are not skewed in the direction predicted by the assumptions of the stochastic frontier approach, so estimates are not obtainable.

If panel data are available, some of these maintained distributional assumptions can be relaxed, and the *distribution-free approach* may be used. This method assumes that there is a core efficiency or average efficiency for each firm over time. The core inefficiency is distinguished from random error (including any temporary fluctuations in inefficiency) by assuming that core inefficiency is persistent over time, while random errors tend to average out over time. In particular, a cost or profit function is estimated for each period of a panel dataset. The residual in each separate regression is composed of both inefficiency, u_i, and random error, v_i, but the random component, v_i, is assumed to average out over time, so an estimate of the inefficiency term, $\hat{u}$, is always the average of a firm's residuals from all of the regressions = average $(u_i + v_i)$ = average (u_i).[11] The reasonableness of the maintained assumptions about the error term components depends on the length of the period studied. If too short a period is chosen, the random errors might not average out, in which case random error would be attributed to inefficiency (although truncation can help). If too long a period is chosen, the firm's core efficiency becomes less meaningful because of changes in management and other events; that is, it might not be constant over the time period.

4.2. Functional Form, Variable Selection, and Variable Measurement

The next step in the parametric estimation methods is the choice of functional form for the frontier, including variable selection and measurement. The most popular form in the literature for cost and profit functions is the translog. The Fourier-flexible functional form augments the translog by including Fourier trigonometric terms, which makes it more flexible than the translog. Berger and Mester (1997) found only a small difference in average efficiency and very little difference in efficiency dispersion or rank between cost or profit efficiency estimates based on the translog functional form and those based on the Fourier-flexible functional form. While formal statistical tests indicated that the coefficients on the Fourier terms were jointly significant at the 1 percent level, the average improvement in goodness of fit was small and was not significant, from an economic point of view.

Once the objective and functional form are selected, the next decision is the variables to include in the function and proxies for those variables. Ideally, the frontier to be estimated should be derived from first principles. For example, if the objective is cost minimization, the cost function should be derived based on the specified production technology. Variables to include in the cost function would be those indicated by the theory of duality: output levels, input prices, netputs (factors that the firm cannot vary over the short run, which are measured in levels), and environmental variables (to account for differences across the firms' environments or markets, which may affect performance but are not a choice for firm management). For example, Hughes, et al. (2000) derive the profit and input demand functions by applying Shephard's Lemma to the managerial expenditure function (based on the almost-ideal demand system), which is dual to the managerial utility maximization problem, in which managers trade off risk and return. These equations include revenue terms, the tax rate, and risk terms, which would not be included in the functions were the managers maximizing

[11]For banks with very low or very high $\hat{u}$, an adjustment (called *truncation*) is made to assign less extreme values of $\hat{u}$ to these banks, since extreme values may indicate that random error, v_i, has not been completely purged by averaging.

profits. Hence, the coefficients on these terms offer a test of profit maximization versus utility maximization.[12] Other models would lead to other specifications.

In any of the estimation techniques, X-efficiency is essentially the residual. This means that omitted variables (or extraneous variables) can have large effects on measured efficiency. Specification of included variables is important, since the methodology depends on comparing the firm's cost or profit or market value, etc., to those of a best-practice firm operating at the same level of the exogenous variables included in the frontier. That is, the exogenous variables determine the reference set for the firm whose efficiency is being measured. If something extraneous is included in the frontier specification, then one might mislabel a firm as efficient because the estimation would be comparing firms in too narrow a reference set and not the entire set of relevant firms. For example, if two firms differ only in that one's CEO is blond and one is a brunette—which I'm assuming is unrelated to efficiency!—then we would want to consider these two firms in the same reference set and compare their costs to one another. If we included CEO hair color in the cost function as a dummy variable, we would preclude such a comparison. We might want to include in the specification of the frontier variables that account for differences in the environment in which the firm operates that are exogenous to the firm's decision making but that may affect performance. For instance, we might want to include variables that account for demand, such as income growth in the firm's market, or whether the firm is located in an urban or rural market. Then in measuring efficiency, the urban firms would be compared to other urban firms and the rural firms to rural firms. But note that the manager's potentially inefficient choice of where to set up shop—in a rural or an urban market—would not be penalized. The alternative is to leave the variable out of the frontier specification but then determine whether the efficiency estimates are correlated with the variable. For example, Mester (1993, 1996, 1997) and Berger and Mester (1997) have looked at correlations between efficiency measures and various exogenous factors. Judgment has to be used about the better way to proceed, including the variables as part of the frontier or excluding them and looking at correlations.

4.3. Special Issues in Banking

Judgment also has to be used when applying efficiency techniques to certain industries. The special issues that arise in applying the techniques to the banking industry are suggestive of some of the problems and issues that can arise in efficiency estimation in general. In banking, an important issue has been how to measure outputs and inputs. There has been some disagreement in the literature over what a commercial bank is actually producing. Two general approaches have been taken: the "production" approach and the "intermediation" approach (also called the "asset" approach).

The production approach focuses on the bank's operating costs, that is, the costs of labor (employees) and physical capital (plant and equipment). The bank's outputs are

[12]Hughes, et al. (2000) reject the hypothesis of profit maximization using 1989–1990 data on United States banks that reported at least $1 billion in assets as of the last quarter of 1998.

measured by the number of each type of account, such as commercial and industrial loans, mortgages, and deposits, because it is thought that most of the operating costs are incurred by processing account documents and debiting and crediting accounts; inputs are labor and physical capital.

The "intermediation" approach considers a financial firm's production process to be one of financial intermediation, that is, the borrowing of funds and the subsequent lending of those funds. Thus, the focus is on total costs, including both interest and operating expenses. Outputs are measured by the dollar volume of each of the bank's different types of loans, and inputs are labor, physical capital, deposits and other borrowed funds, and, in some studies, financial capital.[13] The studies on X-efficiency in banking have tended to use the intermediation approach.

Theoretically, to compare one firm's efficiency to another's, we would like to compare each firm's cost of producing the *same* outputs. For banks, significant characteristics are loan quality, which reflects the amount of monitoring the bank does to keep the loan performing, and the riskiness of the bank's portfolio. Unless these characteristics are controlled for, one might conclude a bank was producing in a very efficient manner if it were spending far less to produce a given output level, but its output might be highly risky and of a lower quality than that of another bank. It would be wrong to say a bank was efficient if it were scrimping on the credit evaluation needed to produce sound loans. Thus, recent studies have included quality and nonperforming loans in the specifications of cost and profit functions. Hughes, et al. (2000) derive the risk–return tradeoff explicitly from a utility maximization model rather than just augmenting the cost and profit functions with risk and quality measures. See Hughes (1999) for further discussion.

Unfortunately, there are likely to be unmeasured differences in quality because the banking data do not fully capture the heterogeneity in bank output. The amount of service *flow* associated with financial products is by necessity usually assumed to be proportionate to the dollar value of the *stock* of assets or liabilities on the balance sheet, which can result in significant mismeasurement. For example, commercial loans can vary in size, repayment schedule, risk, transparency of information, type of collateral, covenants to be enforced, etc. These differences are likely to affect the costs to

[13] A slight variation on the intermediation approach, which has been used in some studies, is to distinguish between transactions deposits, which are treated as an output, since they can serve as a measure of the amount of transactions services the bank produces, and purchased or borrowed funds (such as federal funds or large CDs purchased from another bank), which are treated as inputs, since the bank does not produce services in obtaining these funds. The strict intermediation approach would consider the transactions services produced by the bank as an intermediate output, something that must be produced along the way toward the bank's final output of earning assets. Hughes and Mester (1993) empirically tested whether deposits should be treated as an input or output and found support that they should be treated as an input in their study.

Another approach that has been taken less often is the "value-added" approach, which considers all liabilities and assets of the bank to have at least some of the characteristics of an output. Still another approach, taken in Mester (1992), is to consider the bank's output to be its loan origination and loan-monitoring services, since these outputs are more closely related to the theory of financial intermediation. The outputs specified were: loans originated, loans purchased, loans originated or purchased earlier and held on balance sheet, and loans sold.

the bank of loan origination, ongoing monitoring and control, and financing expense. Unmeasured differences in product quality may be incorrectly measured as differences in cost inefficiency.

Another issue raised in recent papers in the bank efficiency literature is the treatment of financial capital.[14] As discussed in Berger and Mester (1997), a bank's insolvency risk depends not only on the riskiness of its portfolio but on the amount of financial capital it has to absorb losses. Insolvency risk affects bank costs and profits via the risk premium the bank has to pay for uninsured debt, through the intensity of risk management activities the bank undertakes, and (as discussed in Hughes 1999 and Hughes, et al. 2000) through the discount rate applied to future profits. Thus, the bank's financial capital should be considered when studying efficiency. To some extent, controlling for the interest rates paid on uninsured debt helps account for differences in risk, but these rates are imperfectly measured.

Even apart from risk, a bank's capital level directly affects costs by providing an alternative to deposits as a funding source for loans. In most studies, interest paid on debt (deposits) is counted as a cost, but dividends paid are not. On the other hand, raising equity typically involves higher costs than raising deposits. If the first effect dominates, measured costs will be higher for banks using a higher proportion of debt financing; if the second effect dominates, measured costs will be lower for these banks.

Studies that have considered financial capital include the level of capital rather than its price. Including the price assumes that banks on the frontier are selecting the cost-minimizing level of capital. This might not be the case because of regulations that set a minimum capital-to-asset ratio or because of risk aversion on the part of bank managers. See Hughes and Mester (1993) for further discussion.

To summarize, the preceding review discusses some of the steps that need to be followed in implementing efficiency measurement. The main steps involve choosing the efficiency concept, that is, firm objective function (this includes specification of the production function of the firm), estimation technique, functional form, and variables and their proxies.

5. EMPIRICAL FINDINGS IN THE LITERATURE

There is a vast literature on efficiency at commercial banks, and there have been several comprehensive reviews of the literature (e.g., Berger, Hunter, and Timme 1993, Berger and Humphrey 1997, and Berger 2003). Here, I focus on several overall impressions that can be drawn from the literature rather than presenting a comprehensive review.

5.1. Scale Economies

The evidence on scale economies has been changing over time as more complicated and realistic models have been applied to the data. Early studies using data from the 1980s

[14]The discussion of the role of financial capital is taken mainly from Berger and Mester (1997).

failed to find scale economies beyond a very small bank size—up to about $100 million in assets. Later studies using data from the 1990s have found scale economies in a range of up to about $10 billion. And the latest studies (e.g., Berger and Mester 1997, Hughes, Mester, and Moon 2001, Bossone and Lee 2004), which incorporate banks' risk preferences and financial capital into bank production models, find scale economies for the very largest banks in the sample, up to at least $25 billion in assets. For example, Berger and Mester (1997) incorporated asset quality and financial capital into the cost function and, using the sample of almost 6,000 U.S. commercial banks that were in continuous existence over the six-year period 1990–1995, found significant cost scale economies for banks in each size class, with estimates suggesting that the typical bank would have to be two to three times larger in order to maximize cost scale efficiency for its product mix and input prices.

The difference in results between the earlier and later studies may partly reflect improvements in the technologies used for bank intermediation and the relaxation of geographic restrictions on competition. Improvements in information processing, automated loan systems, and credit scoring may have reduced costs of extending loans more for large banks than for smaller banks. The removal of geographic branching restrictions may have made it less costly to become large.

There also may be some measurement issues involved. Studies that have focused on smaller banks and studies that have focused on larger banks have tended to find scale economies exhausted at different sizes. For example, studies that used only banks with under $1 billion in assets (and used the standard approach, which did not incorporate risk or financial capital) usually found average costs to be minimized between about $75 million and $300 million in assets, while studies that used only banks with over $1 billion in assets usually found the minimum average cost point to be between $2 billion and $10 billion in assets (see Berger, Hunter, and Timme 1993). This suggests that a single function may not be able to incorporate both large- and small-bank technologies or that some important factor that varies with bank size is excluded from the model. There is conflicting evidence on this point. McAllister and McManus (1993) found that the translog is not a good global approximation to banks of all sizes. Berger and Mester (1997) found that while the coefficients on the Fourier terms in the Fourier-flexible functional form were jointly significantly different from zero, the improvement in the goodness of fit of the Fourier over the translog was small and not economically significant. Both functional forms yield essentially the same average level and dispersion of measured efficiency, and both ranked the individual banks in almost the same order.

But the later studies' finding of significant scale economies likely also reflects improvements in the methods used to measure scale economies—in particular, accounting for the bank's choice of risk and financial capital. As discussed in Hughes, Mester, and Moon (2001), the standard model ignores the fact that bank risk is endogenous. A larger scale of operations may allow the bank to be better diversified. Better diversification can lead to reduced liquidity risk on the liability side of the balance sheet and reduced credit risk on the asset side of the balance sheet, which can mean reduced costs of risk management. The bank might be able to economize on financial capital, a relatively expensive source of funds, to the extent that diversification lowers banks' insolvency risk. Also, the cost of funds might decline as banks grow in size if large depositors and other creditors perceive that regulators consider some banks are "too big to fail."[15]

Better diversification leading to reduced marginal cost of risk-taking and reduced marginal cost of risk management, all else equal, is the usual diversification effect. But all else is not necessarily equal, because risk taking is endogenous. Banks might respond to the lower cost of risk management by taking on more risk. In turn, banks may have to spend more to manage the increased risk. This risk-taking effect may offset the diversification effect, and the potential economies that follow from scale-related diversification may be obscured. Thus, to unmask scale economies due to better diversification it is important to incorporate risk into the analysis. It is also important to account for the fact that bank managers need not be holding the level of financial capital that minimizes costs. As discussed in Hughes and Mester (1998), financial capital is the bank's own bet on its management of risk, so it provides a credible signal to depositors and creditors of the resources allocated to preserve capital and reduce insolvency risk. As a bank's scale increases, its loan portfolio and deposit base become more diversified. Diversification reduces the cost of the signaling, since the same degree of protection against financial distress can be attained at a lower capital-to-asset ratio. Larger scale also reduces the level of the signal required, to the extent that outsiders infer the bank's level of diversification from the bank's scale of operations, which is observable.

Using 1989 and 1990 data on U.S. banks with assets over $1 billion, Hughes and Mester (1998) find evidence that financial capital is a signal of risk, that banks do not hold the cost-minimizing level of capital, that the level of capitalization increases less than proportionally with assets, and that there are significant scale economies at even the largest banks in the sample (which is $74 billion).

Hughes, Mester, and Moon (2001) undertake a systematic study of bank-cost models and find that estimated scale economies depend critically on how banks' capital structure and risk taking are modeled. Using 1994 data on highest-level bank holding companies in the United States, they find that a standard cost function that omits equity capital and a standard cost function that incorporates capital structure and the cost of capital both generally yield estimates of constant returns to scale across bank holding companies in the sample. However, regressing the bank-specific scale economies measures on variables accounting for sources of risk taking and diversification, they show that better diversification is associated with larger scale economies, while increased risk taking is related to smaller scale economies. They also find that a proportional variation in size and diversification, controlling for sources of risk taking, yields a statistically and economically significant increase in scale economies and that, by the criterion of cost minimization, smaller banks overutilize capital while larger banks underutilize capital. These results suggest that scale economies might be masked by the banks' endogenous choice of risk, which needs to be modeled.

[15]Hughes and Mester (1993) find evidence of "too big to fail": For large banks, an increase in size, holding default risk, and asset quality constant is associated with a significantly lower price of uninsured deposits.

Hughes, Mester, and Moon (2001) verify this by estimating the managers' most preferred production model that includes equity capital, in addition to debt, and models bank managers as maximizing utility as a function of expected profits and risk. This allows banks to be value maximizers rather than profit maximizers and allows the bank's production choices to reflect risk management concerns. Calculating the change in cost as output is expanded so as to maximize utility, they find that banks have large scale economies that increase with size. Since agency problems between owners and managers might mean utility-maximizing managers might not choose value-maximizing production plans, the value-maximizing banks are identified as those that make efficient risk–return tradeoffs. Restricting attention to the most efficient quarter of banks in each of five size groups and calculating the change in cost as output is expanded so as to maximize utility, they again find that banks have large scale economies that increase with size. By incorporating capital structure and risk taking into models of bank production they have uncovered the scale economies that are often cited by merging banks but that can be obscured in the standard models, which ignore the endogeneity of the bank's choice of risk.

Hughes, et al. (2000) also measure scale economies along the value-maximizing expansion path using 1990 data on banks with greater than \$1 billion in assets. Banks in all size quartiles were found to be operating with significant scale economies.

Bossone and Lee (2004) apply the methods of Hughes and Mester (1998) and Hughes, Mester, and Moon (2001) to study the relationship between productive efficiency and the size of the financial system. Using a sample of 875 commercial banks from 75 countries, they estimate a cost function and measure scale economies, allowing for the banks' endogenous choice of risk and financial capital. (For comparison, they also estimate the standard measure of scale economies, which does not incorporate risk and financial capital). Size of the financial system is proxied by three measures: absolute size, which is the sum of domestic credit, domestic deposits, foreign assets, and foreign liabilities of the banking system; relative size or financial depth, which is the ratio of absolute size to the level of GDP; and financial market size, which is stock market capitalization to GDP × stock market total value traded to GDP × stock market turnover to GDP. They find the presence of significant scale economies that are increasing with the size of the financial system, for each of the three measures of size. (Similar to the results in Hughes, Mester, and Moon (2001), these scale economies are not uncovered using the standard cost function, which doesn't incorporate risk and financial capital.) They also find that small banks in larger financial systems are more cost efficient than small banks in small systems and that scale economies are less variable across bank size, holding the financial system size constant, than they are across financial system size, holding bank size constant. They interpret their findings as evidence of what they call "systemic scale economies," that is, economies derived from operating in a larger financial system. For example, it might be less costly for a bank operating in a large financial system if a larger payment system charges lower fees to banks using its services or if a larger financial system makes it easier to diversify across products or geography, thereby allowing banks to save on capital costs.

The papers discussed suggest that scale can confer economic benefits. But the degree of benefits can vary across the type of expansion. Hughes, et al. (1999) find that the economic benefits of consolidation are strongest for those banks engaged in interstate expansion and, in particular, interstate expansion that diversifies banks' macroeconomic risk. Hughes, et al. (2003) find evidence that an increase in assets by internal growth (in contrast to acquisition) is associated with better performance at most banks, consistent with the existence of scale economies. They also find that at banks without entrenched management, both asset acquisitions (e.g., via merger) and asset sales are associated with improved performance; but at banks with entrenched managers, asset sales are associated with smaller improvements, and asset acquisitions are associated with worse performance.[16] This suggests that while there are value-enhancing incentives to merge, they may be subordinated to the incentives to build larger institutions, from which entrenched managers can gain perquisites.

5.2. Scope Economies

Most studies have not found strong evidence of scope economies, either between traditional commercial banking products or between on-balance-sheet and off-balance-sheet bank products. This is not to say that deregulation that permits banks to expand the types of products they can offer could not enable banks to take advantage of potential scope economies. Still, it is difficult to find evidence of strong scope economies in the literature, with a few exceptions. Mester (1991) found evidence of diseconomies of scope for mutual savings and loans using 1982 data on California S&Ls, but Mester (1993), using 1991 data on U.S. S&Ls, found scope economies between traditional outputs—these results are consistent with the hypothesis that the removal of interest rate ceilings in 1986 reduced the ability of mutual S&L managers to pursue their own goals.

Mester (1992) measures outputs based on an information-theoretic approach: loan origination, monitoring, selling, and buying. These outputs involve different levels of credit evaluation and loan monitoring. Loans originated or purchased before the current date t and loans originated at t and held are the traditional outputs of a bank. Loans bought at time t and loans originated at time t and sold are less traditional. She finds diseconomies of scope between the traditional banking services and nontraditional services.

Berger, Hancock, and Humphrey (1993), using data on U.S. banks from 1984 to 1989, find evidence of scope economies based on the profit function. The profit function measure takes into account not only cost gains from joint production but also revenue gains perhaps derived from cross-selling. They test whether the optimal quantity of every output is positive for all the price vectors observed in the data and find that, for most firms, this is true. This contrasts with Berger, Humphrey, and Pulley (1996), who estimated a revenue function using 1978–1990 data on United States banks and found no evidence of revenue scope economies between loans and deposits.

[16]Entrenchment is found to be related to higher levels of managerial ownership, better investment opportunities, higher inefficiency, and smaller asset size.

5.3. X-Efficiency

Research on cost X-efficiency in banking generally finds large inefficiencies on the order of 20–25 percent or more of total banking industry costs when the stochastic methods are used.[17] That is, achievement of X-efficiency (elimination of X-inefficiency) at the average bank could produce about a 20–25 percent cost savings, making this an important source of inefficiency in banking. Although 20 percent seems quite large and perhaps too large to sustain in a reasonably competitive industry, I note that similar levels of inefficiency are found in studies of manufacturing and other industries. The conclusion from the earlier literature that found constant returns to scale but high levels of X-inefficiency was that managerial inefficiencies outweighed the inefficiencies related to scale and scope. However, with the latest studies finding significant scale economies, this conclusion need not be the case.

Berger and Mester (1997) estimate both cost X-efficiencies and profit X-efficiencies. The mean cost efficiency from their preferred model is 0.868, suggesting that about 13.2 percent of cost is wasted on average, relative to a best-practice firm. The mean profit inefficiency is much larger, suggesting that 50 percent of potential profits that could be earned by a best-practice bank are lost to inefficiency. They also find considerably more variation in profit inefficiency among the banks than in cost inefficiency, with many banks achieving higher or higher profit efficiency than the average. As with scale economies measurement, how financial capital is modeled affects estimates of X-efficiency. They find that profit X-inefficiency was much higher when equity capital was excluded in the profit function. Instead of 50 percent inefficiency, the estimates indicate 90 percent inefficiency.

Berger and Mester (1997) also investigate the relationship between their X-efficiency estimates and various aspects of the banks, their markets, and their regulation that are potential correlates of efficiency that are at least partially exogenous. The characteristics investigated fall into six categories: bank size, organizational form and corporate governance, other bank characteristics, market characteristics, state geographic restrictions on competition, and primary federal regulator. Both multiple regression and single-variable regressions were estimated. A few robust relationships were uncovered. Large and small banks appear to be equally cost X-efficient, but large banks are less profit X-efficient, suggesting it is harder to efficiently generate revenues as a bank grows in size. Higher risk, as measured by the standard deviation of return on assets, is associated with lower X-efficiency. Greater market power is associated with lower cost X-efficiency and greater profit X-efficiency. But the basic conclusion from this analysis was that the correlates of efficiency are still largely unknown: 25 explanatory variables explain only about 7 percent of the variance of measured cost efficiency and 35 percent of the variables of measured profit efficiency.

Hughes, et al. (2003) measure market-value inefficiency by the bank's shortfall ratio, which gives the shortfall of a bank's market value from its highest potential market value as a proportion of the bank's book-value investment in its assets, net of goodwill. The

[17] When the nonparametric DEA method is used, there is a greater range of findings from 10 percent to 50 percent.

measure is derived by stochastic frontier techniques to fit the frontier of market value on book value (i.e., replacement cost) of assets. They find an average shortfall of 19 percent.

Koetter (2004) studies the efficiency of German banks over the period 1995–2001 using the managerial utility-maximization model of Hughes, et al. (2000). He finds average inefficiency measured relative to the risk–return frontier to be quite low, around 5 percent.

5.4. Productivity

There are fewer studies of productivity in banking. Using data on banks from the late 1970s and 1980s, most studies find negative cost productivity growth, on the order of −1 percent per year. Using panel data on 661 top-tier bank holding companies continuously in existence during 1991–1997, Stiroh (2000) found small cost productivity improvements of between 0.05 percent and 0.47 percent annually, depending on the definitions of output and the method of measurement. But the literature suggests that bank size matters. Some studies find increased productivity growth (in terms of costs or profits) in the early 1980s for large banks (due to shifts in the best-practice frontier) but not for small banks. For example, Humphrey and Pulley (1997) found that profits of larger banks in the sample (with assets over $500 million) increased by 12 percent between the 1977–1981 period and the 1981–1984 period. Decomposing this change, they found that it results from a shift in the profit function and changes in business condition, particularly deposit deregulation. Only business conditions accounted for the rise in large banks' profits from 1981–1984 to 1985–1998. For smaller banks (assets of $100 million to $500 million), there was little increase in profits between 1977–1981 and 1981–1984. Wheelock and Wilson (1999) used linear programming techniques (DEA) and decomposed the change in productivity into the change in efficiency and the shift in efficient frontier. They found that banks on the frontier improved over the period 1984–1993 but that productivity declined, on average, during this period because of reductions in efficiency. Smaller banks (assets below $300 million), in particular, were unable to adapt to changes in technology, regulation, and competitive condition and fell further away from the efficient frontier.[18]

Berger and Mester (2003) look at both cost and profit productivity, where productivity is measured as a combination of technological change and changes in inefficiency, holding constant the exogenous environmental variables. They find that during 1991–1997, cost productivity in the banking industry worsened while profit productivity improved substantially and concluded this was because revenue-based productivity changes are not accounted for in measuring cost productivity. Banks have been offering wider varieties of financial services and have been providing additional convenience, which may have raised costs but also raised revenues by more than the cost increases. They also found that banks involved in merger activity might be responsible for their main findings. The merging banks had greater cost productivity deterioration and profit

[18]Berger and Mester (2003) discuss several other studies of bank productivity.

productivity improvements than other banks. Merging banks may have also improved their profit performance, on average, by shifting their portfolios into investments with higher risk and higher expected return to take advantage of the diversification gains from mergers, as suggested by the work of Hughes, et al. (1996) and Hughes, Mester, and Moon (2001).

6. CONCLUSION

One goal of the research agenda on optimal bank productive efficiency is to answer some fundamental questions about financial industry restructuring. The results from this literature shed light on the consolidation trend in the commercial banking industry and suggest some answers to the three conundrums posed in the introduction.

Conundrum 1 In contrast to the earlier literature, new bank production models that incorporate banks' choice of risk and financial capital and that explicitly consider how banks' production decisions influence their riskiness have uncovered scale economies at very large banks. This is consistent with the consolidation trend, which is creating very large banks and helps resolve the inconsistency between the earlier literature's finding of constant returns to scale and the reality of consolidation. Diversification benefits appear to be a source of these scale economies. The cost of risk taking decreases with size. If banks respond to the reduced price by taking on more risk, then the standard models would not be able to uncover scale economies.

Conundrum 2 There is little evidence of scope economies in the literature, which may explain why banks have not responded to the Gramm-Leach-Bliley Act's relaxation of the barriers to offering nontraditional activities along with traditional commercial bank activities. This can only be a tentative conclusion, however, since the literature on this topic is thin. Partly this reflects a lack of data on institutions that are mixing these products, since the restrictions on product mix have only recently been repealed.

Conundrum 3 It is true that banks experienced a worsening of cost productivity in the 1990s. This might seem at odds with the technological changes that have occurred in banking. But a focus on cost productivity is misleading. At the same time cost productivity worsened, banks experienced an increase in profit productivity. This is consistent with banks' offering wider varieties of financial services and additional convenience, which may have raised costs but raised revenues more. Merging banks had greater cost productivity deterioration and profit productivity improvements than other banks. Their better profit productivity gains might also reflect their ability to take advantage of diversification benefits.

References

Akhavein, Jalal D., Allen N. Berger, and David B. Humphrey. 1997. The Effects of Megamergers on Efficiency and Prices: Evidence from a Bank Profit Function, *Review of Industrial Organization* 12, 95–139.

Baumol, William J., John C. Panzar, and Robert D. Willig. 1982. *Contestable Markets and the Theory of Industry Structure*. New York: Harcourt Brace Jovanovich.

Benston, George J., William C. Hunter, and Larry D. Wall. 1995. Motivations for Bank Mergers and Acquisitions: Enhancing the Deposit Insurance Put Option versus Earnings Diversification, *Journal of Money, Credit and Banking* 27, 777–788.

Berger, Allen N. 2003. The Economic Effects of Technological Progress: Evidence from the Banking Industry, *Journal of Money, Credit, and Banking* 35, 141–176.

Berger, Allen N., and David B. Humphrey. 1997. Efficiency of Financial Institutions: International Survey and Directions for Future Research, *European Journal of Operational Research* 98, 175–212.

Berger, Allen N., and Loretta J. Mester. 1997. Inside the Black Box: What Explains Differences in the Efficiencies of Financial Institutions? *Journal of Banking and Finance* 21, 895–947.

Berger, Allen N., and Loretta J. Mester. 2003. Explaining the Dramatic Changes in Performance of U.S. Banks: Technological Change, Deregulation, and Dynamic Changes in Competition, *Journal of Financial Intermediation* 12, 57–95.

Berger, Allen N., Diana Hancock, and David B. Humphrey. 1993. Bank Efficiency Derived from the Profit Function, *Journal of Banking and Finance* 17, 317–347.

Berger, Allen N., David B. Humphrey, and Lawrence B. Pulley. 1996. Do Consumers Pay for One-Stop Banking? Evidence from an Alternative Revenue Function, *Journal of Banking and Finance* 20, 1601–1621.

Berger, Allen N., William C. Hunter, and Stephen G. Timme. 1993. The Efficiency of Financial Institutions: A Review and Preview of Research Past, Present, and Future, *Journal of Banking and Finance* 17, 221–249.

Berlin, Mitchell, and Loretta J. Mester. 1998. On the Profitability and Cost of Relationship Lending, *Journal of Banking and Finance* 22, 873–897.

Bossone, Biagio, and Jong-Kun Lee. 2004. In Finance, Size Matters: The "Systemic Scale Economies" Hypothesis, *IMF Staff Papers* 51, 19–46.

Edwards, Franklin R. 1977. Managerial Objectives in Regulated Industries: Expense-Preference Behavior in Banking, *Journal of Political Economy* 85, 147–162.

FDIC. 2007. Historical Statistics on Banking, Table CB02, Changes in Number of Institutions, FDIC-Insured Commercial Banks and Statistics on Depository Institutions.

Group of Ten. 2001. Report on Consolidation in the Financial Sector. www.bis.org.

Hughes, Joseph P. 1999. Incorporating Risk into the Analysis of Production, Presidential Address to the Atlantic Economic Society, *Atlantic Economic Journal* 27, 1–23.

Hughes, Joseph P., and Loretta J. Mester. 1993. A Quality- and Risk-Adjusted Cost Function for Banks: Evidence on the "Too-Big-To-Fail" Doctrine, *Journal of Productivity Analysis* 4, 293–315.

Hughes, Joseph P., and Loretta J. Mester. 1998. Bank Capitalization and Cost: Evidence of Scale Economies in Risk Management and Signaling, *Review of Economics and Statistics* 80, 314–325.

Hughes, Joseph P., Loretta J. Mester, and Choon-Geol Moon. 2001. Are Scale Economies in Banking Elusive or Illusive? Evidence Obtained by Incorporating Capital Structure and Risk-Taking into Models of Bank Production Checking Accounts and Bank Monitoring, *Journal of Banking and Finance* 25, 2169–2208.

Hughes, Joseph P., William W. Lang, Loretta J. Mester, and Choon-Geol Moon. 1996. Efficient Banking Under Interstate Branching, *Journal of Money, Credit, and Banking* 28, 1043–1071.

Hughes, Joseph P., William Lang, Loretta J. Mester, and Choon-Geol Moon. 1999. The Dollars and Sense of Bank Consolidation, *Journal of Banking and Finance* 23, 291–324.

Hughes, Joseph P., William W. Lang, Loretta J. Mester, and Choon-Geol Moon. 2000. Recovering Risky Technologies Using the Almost Ideal Demand System: An Application to U.S. Banks, *Journal of Financial Services Research* 18, 5–27.

Hughes, Joseph P., William W. Lang, Loretta J. Mester, Choon-Geol Moon, and Michael S. Pagano. 2003. Do Banks Sacrifice Value to Build Empires? Managerial Incentives, Industry Consolidation, and Financial Performance, *Journal of Banking and Finance* 27, 417–447.

Humphrey, David B., and Lawrence B. Pulley. 1997. Banks' Responses to Deregulation: Profits, Technology, and Efficiency, *Journal of Money, Credit, and Banking* 29, 73–93.

Koetter, Michael. 2004. The Stability of Efficiency Rankings When Risk Preferences Are Different. Tjalling C. Koppmans Research Institute Discussion Paper No. 04-08, Utrecht School of Economics, University of Utrecht.

McAllister, Patrick H., and Douglas McManus. 1993. Resolving the Scale Efficiency Puzzle in Banking, *Journal of Banking and Finance* 17, 389–405.

Mester, Loretta J. 1989a. Owners versus Managers: Who Controls the Bank? *Business Review*, Federal Reserve Bank of Philadelphia (May/June), 13–23.

Mester, Loretta J. 1989b. Testing for Expense Preference Behavior: Mutual versus Stock Savings and Loans, *RAND Journal of Economics* 20, 483–498.

Mester, Loretta J. 1991. Agency Costs Among Savings and Loans, *Journal of Financial Intermediation* 1, 257–278.

Mester, Loretta J. 1992. Traditional and Nontraditional Banking: An Information-Theoretic Approach, *Journal of Banking and Finance* 16, 545–566.

Mester, Loretta J. 1993. Efficiency in the Savings and Loan Industry, *Journal of Banking and Finance* 17, 267–286.

Mester, Loretta J. 1996. A Study of Bank Efficiency Taking into Account Risk Preferences, *Journal of Banking and Finance* 20 (July), 1025–1045.

Mester, Loretta J. 1997. Measuring Efficiency at U.S. Banks: Accounting for Heterogeneity Is Important, *European Journal of Operational Research* 98, 230–242.

Mester, Loretta J. 2003. Applying Efficiency Measurement Techniques to Central Banks. Working paper no. 03-13, Federal Reserve Bank of Philadelphia.

Pilloff, Steven J., and Anthony M. Santomero. 1998. The Value Effects of Bank Mergers and Acquisitions, in Y. Amihud and G. Miller (eds.), *Bank Mergers and Acquisitions*. Kluwer Academic, Boston.

Stiroh, Kevin J. 2000. How Did Bank Holding Companies Prosper in the 1990s? *Journal of Banking and Finance* 24, 1703–1745.

Vander Vennet, Rudi. 1996. The Effect of Mergers and Acquisitions on the Efficiency and Profitability of EC Credit Institutions, *Journal of Banking and Finance* 20, 1531–1558.

Wheelock, David C., and Paul W. Wilson. 1999. Technical Progress, Inefficiency, and Productivity Change in U.S. Banking, 1984–1993, *Journal of Money, Credit, and Banking* 31, 212–234.

CHAPTER 6

Commercial Banks in Investment Banking

Amar Gande
Southern Methodist University

I thank Mitchell Berlin for his thoughtful comments and help in focusing this chapter. Given that the scope of the chapter is limited to the activities of commercial banks in investment banking, I apologize for any relevant papers that may have been omitted inadvertently or represented inadequately in this chapter.

Abstract

In many countries, commercial banks routinely conduct investment banking activities, such as helping their customers in bringing new debt and equity issues to the market. However, in the United States, after the Glass-Steagall Act was passed in 1933, commercial banks were not allowed to underwrite securities, for almost six decades. In 1989, Congress allowed commercial banks to underwrite corporate securities in a limited manner through Section 20 subsidiaries. In November 1999, with the repeal of the Glass-Steagall provisions through the Financial Modernization Act of 1999, all restrictions for underwriting securities were removed.

This chapter starts with a brief description of the main benefits (information advantages and scope economies) and the main costs of combining lending with underwriting (conflicts of interest and information monopoly rents). It summarizes the underlying theory for these benefits and costs and presents empirical evidence. In examining the commingling of lending and underwriting, this chapter attempts to provide specific answers to the following questions that have preoccupied researchers in recent times: (1) Should commercial banks be allowed to underwrite securities? (2) If commercial banks were to be allowed to underwrite securities, in what organizational form should they underwrite securities? (3) Do commercial banks, with prior access and superior information about firms to whom they lend (from loan-monitoring activities), have an unfair advantage in underwriting that can result in their monopolizing the market and drive investment houses out of underwriting securities, especially in the longer term?

We end this chapter with a summary of the main results from the literature and a few suggestions for future research.

1. INTRODUCTION

Universal banking, in which banks act as a one-stop shop for customers, is practiced in many countries in the world. For example, commercial banks in Germany routinely conduct investment banking activities, such as helping their customers in bringing new debt and equity issues to the market. However, in the United States, since the Banking Act of 1933 (also known as the Glass-Steagall Act), commercial banks were not allowed to underwrite securities for more than 60 years. There were two main concerns for the proponents of the Glass-Steagall Act: (1) Combining lending with underwriting presents a significant conflict of interest for a commercial bank. For example, a bank may be tempted to underwrite the securities of a lower-quality issuer, certify it as a higher-quality issue, and use those proceeds to retire its existing loans to the issuing firm. (2) Combining lending with underwriting increases the risk of the banking system as a whole, which could lead to more bank failures in the future.

In November 1999, all restrictions for underwriting securities were removed with the enactment of the Financial Modernization Act of 1999 (also known as the Gramm-Bleach-Bliley (GLB) Act), which repealed the Glass-Steagall Act. However, despite many previous attempts (prior to the GLB Act) to repeal the Glass-Steagall Act, the best that Congress was able to do was to allow (since 1989) a commercial bank to underwrite corporate securities in a limited manner through a Section 20 subsidiary. Not all commercial banks can establish Section 20 affiliates, and special permission must be received from the Federal Reserve. For example, J.P. Morgan, Inc., was allowed by the Federal Reserve to create a separate Section 20 subsidiary (J.P. Morgan Securities) through which it can engage in investment banking activities in a restricted manner so as not to violate the Section 20 of the Banking Act of 1933.[1]

In this chapter, we focus on the main costs and benefits of allowing commercial banks into investment banking activities and specifically into underwriting of corporate (debt and equity) securities. The basic distinction we draw between a commercial bank and an investment bank (which we refer to as investment house for the remainder of this chapter) is that an investment house underwrites securities but does not make loans, whereas a commercial bank does both. For example, J.P. Morgan would have been considered a typical commercial bank and Goldman Sachs a typical investment house prior to the passage of the Financial Modernization Act of 1999, which allowed commercial banks to acquire investment banks, and vice versa.

We examine both the theory and the empirical evidence on the tradeoffs in combining lending with underwriting of securities. While there are some early reviews on this subject, there is no recent comprehensive review that captures the current body of knowledge in this rapidly growing area of research.[2]

The main costs of combining lending with underwriting that we discuss in this paper are: (1) conflicts of interest (e.g., a commercial bank faces a conflict of interest to inflate issuer quality while underwriting a borrower's securities and using the proceeds to retire

[1]Section 20 of the Banking Act of 1933 stated, "No member bank shall be affiliated in any manner described in subsection (b) of section 221a of this title with any corporation, association, business, trust, or other similar organization engaged principally in the issue, floatation, underwriting, public sale, or distribution at wholesale or retail or through syndicate participation of stocks, bonds, debentures, notes, or other securities." Legally, these Section 20 subsidiaries do not violate Section 20 of the Banking Act of 1933 as long as a minority (i.e., less than 50%) of the total revenues they generate comes from ineligible or "gray area" securities activities, such as underwriting corporate debt and equity securities (the only eligible securities activities up until 1987 were underwriting new issues of Treasury bills, notes, and bonds, underwriting municipal general obligation bonds, and private placements of all bonds and equities). To avoid legal challenges, the Federal Reserve initially set the revenue limit at a very conservative 5% in 1987, which was subsequently raised to 10% in 1989, and finally to 25% by end of 1996. These Section 20 subsidiaries were also subject to an extensive set of firewalls (28 in number as of the end of 1996) that limit the information, resource, and financial linkages between the Section 20 subsidiary, the bank holding company, and the commercial banking subsidiary.

[2]Earlier reviews on this subject, such as Mester (1996), Rajan (1996), and Santos (1998), do not have the benefit of the newer empirical findings in this literature (which are summarized in this paper) and predate recent regulatory changes in securities underwriting in the United States (e.g., the repeal of the Glass-Steagall Act as a consequence of the Financial Services Modernization Act of 1999). The recent review on financial intermediation, a topic broader than the one reviewed here, by Gorton and Winton (2003) mentions a handful of these studies, without any details, under "other issues" (see p. 532). In writing this chapter, we have made a conscious attempt to avoid unnecessary duplication with these reviews.

its existing loans to the same borrower[3] (see Saunders 1985 and Benston 1990 for a detailed discussion of various types of conflicts of interest faced by commercial banks)), and (2) lock-in effects, in which a commercial bank exploits the information developed over the life of a lending relationship to extract monopoly profits (see Sharpe 1990, James 1992, and Rajan 1992) and to exclude outside underwriters from competing for the firm's business.[4]

The main benefits of combining lending and underwriting that can result in efficiency gains at the commercial bank level are: (1) information advantages (e.g., commercial banks acquire private information in monitoring loans,[5] and such proprietary information may be reused by commercial banks to certify a security issue of the same firm (see Puri 1999)), while investment houses must expend costly resources to produce information on the issuer; and (2) economies of scope (e.g., if there is a fixed-cost component to both lending and underwriting of securities for the same firm, combining these functions lowers the information production costs, since this fixed cost is incurred only once (see Kanatas and Qi 2003 for a model of information scope economies)).

While examining the empirical evidence on the costs and benefits, we attempt to provide specific answers to three questions on combining lending and underwriting that have preoccupied researchers in recent times. Notwithstanding the passage of the Financial Modernization Act of 1999, which repealed the Glass-Steagall Act, these questions remain relevant, since researchers continue to examine the merits of such legislation, and similar regulations are potentially forthcoming (e.g., commingling of

[3]More generally, any ongoing relationship can be the basis for conflicts as evidenced in scandals, such as those involving stock analyst research and investment banking (e.g., maintaining inflated stock ratings to win investment banking business). The focus here is on the conflicts of interest due to underlying lending relationship with the issuer prior to the commercial bank underwriting the issuer's securities.

[4]An additional concern underlying the passage of the Glass-Steagall Act was that the commingling of investment and commercial banking increased the riskiness of banks and endangered the solvency of the banking system. White (1986) analyzed this issue and found that commercial banks with securities operations were not riskier (in that they did not have higher earning variance or lower capital ratios) than commercial banks without such operations. Moreover, this study found that commercial banks with securities operations were less likely to fail than commercial banks with no such operations. Also, see Yu (2002) and Akhigbe and Whyte (2004) for evidence on risk changes in the financial services industry following the passage of the Gramm-Leach-Bliley Act of 1999 that effectively repealed the separation of commercial and investment banking functions. One would require a longer-time series to evaluate risk changes from combining lending and underwriting than the data used in the latter two studies.

[5]Several theoretical models highlight the unique monitoring functions of commercial banks (e.g., Diamond 1984, Ramakrishnan and Thakor 1984, Fama 1985). These studies generally argue that commercial banks have the incentives and a comparative advantage in monitoring debt contracts. For example, Diamond (1984) contends that banks have scale economies and comparative cost advantages in information production that enable them to undertake superior debt-related monitoring. Ramakrishnan and Thakor (1984) show that banks as information brokers can improve welfare by minimizing the costs of information production and moral hazard. Fama (1985) argues that bank loans are a form of inside debt, since a commercial bank has access to information that is not publicly available. Several empirical studies also provide evidence on the uniqueness of bank loans, e.g., James (1987), Lummer and McConnell (1989), and Billett, Flannery, and Garfinkel (1995). Also see James and Smith (2000) and Saunders (2002) for comprehensive reviews of why banks are considered "special" (or "unique").

banking and commerce, i.e., banks owning corporations, and vice versa, a topic not addressed here). Apart from regulatory concerns, the evidence is also relevant to basic issues in the theory of financial intermediation, which seeks to explain the optimal structure of intermediaries that produce information about firms (among other matters).

The first question, which gained substantial media coverage in the United States (during periods surrounding the Great Depression, 1933–34, the latter part of the 1980s, and much of the 1990s) is: Should commercial banks be allowed to underwrite corporate securities? We provide in Section 2.4 a summary of the empirical evidence on whether the efficiency gains (from information advantages and scope economies) are larger than the costs in underwriting corporate securities (e.g., see Ang and Richardson 1994, Puri 1994, Kroszner and Rajan 1994, Puri 1996, and Gande et al. 1997 for early evidence on this question). The empirical evidence broadly suggests that the efficiency gains largely outweigh the costs, and hence commercial banks should be allowed to underwrite corporate securities, a view that paved the way for the passage of the Financial Modernization Act of 1999, which repealed the Glass-Steagall Act.

It could be argued that the empirical evidence on efficiency gains from combining lending and underwriting may be explained alternatively by the effect of bank competition. Moreover, since the long-run (market structure) and short-run (entry) effects of bank competition could be different, it is important to disentangle the effects of heightened competition in markets where commercial banks compete from the effects of banks' real cost advantages. We devote Section 3 to a discussion of the effects of commercial bank entry into the market for corporate securities underwriting, the difficulties in empirically disentangling the effects of heightened bank competition from banks' real cost advantages, and how empirical studies may control for changes in bank competition in analyzing the efficiency gains from combining lending and underwriting.

The second question (which is closely related to the first question) is, if commercial banks are allowed to underwrite debt securities, in what organizational form should they underwrite securities? For example, should commercial banks be allowed to underwrite corporate securities in-house (through an internal securities department within the commercial bank) or through an affiliate (a separately incorporated company that is organized as a subsidiary of the commercial bank), or should the commercial banks decide for themselves? This question has been central to the Glass-Steagall debate (which barred commercial banks from underwriting securities since the days of the Great Depression until recently) in the United States. When banks were initially allowed to underwrite corporate securities in the late 1980s, the extant regulation focused on using the affiliate structure as a tool to reduce potential conflicts of interest. That is, commercial banks were allowed to underwrite securities through Section 20 subsidiaries, with extensive "firewalls" (numbering 28 in 1996) between the parent holding company, the bank subsidiary, and the Section 20 subsidiary.

In Section 2.6, we discuss the empirical evidence on whether an affiliate structure is net beneficial as compared to an in-house underwriting, if one were to compare the loss of beneficial effects (in terms of efficiency gains) vis-à-vis the amelioration of conflicts of interest (see, e.g., Puri 1996 and Kroszner and Rajan 1997 for empirical evidence on this question). While there is no clear consensus, interestingly the revealed preference of bank holding companies' overwhelming choice to merge their investment banking operations into the bank (i.e., in-house) rather than use separate subsidiaries (i.e., affiliates) provides strong evidence of banks' views about the relative inefficiency of keeping their investment banking operations separate. We end Section 2.6 with recent empirical evidence on the efficacy of other external organizational forms in potentially reducing conflicts of interest, such as underwriting syndicates.

The third question is whether banks, with prior access and superior information about firms to whom they lend, have an unfair advantage in underwriting that can result in their monopolizing the market and can drive investment houses out of underwriting corporate securities, especially in the longer term. We examine in Section 3 the effect of commercial bank entry into securities underwriting on ex ante yield spreads, underwriter spreads, and market concentration. We revisit the empirical evidence on efficiency gains from combining lending and underwriting and see to what extent it may be explained by the effect of bank competition. We also discuss the difficulties in disentangling the effects of heightened bank competition from banks' real cost advantages and how the empirical studies typically control for changes in bank competition in analyzing the efficiency gains from combining lending and underwriting. Since the long-run and short-run effects of bank competition could be different, we summarize the evidence on the announcement effects surrounding the enactment of the Financial Modernization Act of 1999 repealing the Glass-Steagall Act as a proxy for the longer-term effects as perceived by the stock markets. Overall, the evidence suggests that commercial bank entry has been pro-competitive.

Section 4 presents a concluding summary of the main results from the literature along with a few suggestions for future research.

2. TRADEOFFS IN COMBINING LENDING AND UNDERWRITING

In this section, we describe the costs and benefits of combining lending and underwriting. We also attempt to answer the first question, whether commercial banks should be allowed to underwrite securities, by examining the available evidence on whether the benefits outweigh the costs.

2.1. Costs of Combining Lending and Underwriting

The main costs of combining lending with underwriting that we discuss here are (1) conflict of interest that a commercial bank faces to inflate issuer quality while underwriting a borrower's securities and using the issue proceeds to retire its existing loans to the same borrower, and (2) information monopoly rents; that is, a commercial bank may "lock in" its client over the longer term and extract profits from such a relationship as a result of an information monopoly based on private information generated through the loan-monitoring activities.

2.1.1. Conflict of Interest

Commercial banks have been effectively prohibited from underwriting corporate securities from 1933 until recently by the Glass-Steagall provisions of the Banking Act of 1933,[6] amidst concerns that combining the underwriting of these securities with lending activities presented a potential conflict of interest that was detrimental to investors. For example, by underwriting securities they privately know to be questionable (e.g., based on information obtained during the loan-monitoring process) and by requiring that the proceeds from the issue be used to pay down loans, commercial banks may protect their own interest at the expense of outside investors in the newly issued securities. See Saunders (1985) and Benston (1990) for a detailed discussion of various types of conflicts of interest faced by commercial banks. Since investment houses do not engage in loan making, they are not subject to the type of a conflict of interest described here (see footnote 3 for other types of conflicts faced by investment houses in recent times, which are not a subject of this paper).

2.1.2. Information Monopoly Rents

A concern of combining lending with underwriting is that a commercial bank may "lock in" its client over the longer term and extract profits from such a relationship as a result of an information monopoly based on private information generated through the loan-monitoring activities. In the presence of such an information monopoly, firms cannot easily switch to other lenders, since outside lenders may face a winner's-curse problem if they choose to lend at later stages to a borrowing firm. See Sharpe (1990), James (1992), and Rajan (1992) for details.

The empirical studies typically control for information monopoly rents by specifically testing whether their results hold in subsamples where information monopoly rents are expected to be higher, such as firms that have multiple security issues underwritten during a sample period and smaller and lower-credit-rated firms (see Section 2.4).

[6]The Glass-Steagall provisions of the Banking Act of 1933 (Sections 16, 20, 21, and 32) were passed amidst allegations of abuses by commercial banks, recorded in the Pecora Committee investigations (U.S. Senate Committee on Banking and Currency, 1933–1934). These hearings focused specifically on the potentially conflict-laden abusive practices at securities affiliates of the two most prominent national banks, National City Company and Chase Securities Company. The presumption of these investigations was that abuses at these two banks were representative of a systematic underwriting of poorer-quality securities by all commercial banks with securities operations as a group. For a major critique of the facts underlying the Pecora Committee's findings and the Glass-Steagall Act, see Benston (1989). Also see Benston (1990) for specific cases from the Pecora hearings often cited as examples of abusive practices. In fact, Benston argues that few stand up to close scrutiny, since these practices could be interpreted as examples of bad business judgment rather than as abuses (pp. 96, 103).

2.2. Benefits of Combining Lending and Underwriting

The main benefits of combining lending and underwriting that we discuss here are (1) information advantages; that is, commercial banks acquire private information in monitoring loans (see footnote 5), and such proprietary information may be used advantageously by them as compared to investment houses who have to pay for any information on the issuer, and (2) economies of scope; for example, if there is a fixed-cost component to both lending and underwriting of securities for the same firm, combining these functions lowers the information production costs, since this fixed cost is incurred only once.

We consider scope economies and information advantages to be distinct benefits, since it is possible to have scope economies without there being an information advantage for commercial banks relative to investment houses. For example, if an investment bank is able to structure private debt or a bridge loan (from institutional investors) for a client whose securities they underwrite, to the extent they do not monitor such private debt or a bridge loan (since it is distributed to institutional investors), they are unlikely to have an information advantage even though they may be able to realize some scope economies due to savings from fixed costs. Simply put, an information advantage may lead to scope economies, but scope economies, do not require an information advantage.

2.2.1. Information Advantages

It is well known that commercial banks acquire private information in monitoring loans (see footnote 5). For example, commercial banks inspect factory premises and inventory, or they may be privy to investment opportunities available to the firm. In contrast, investment houses do not have access to such information, and they expend costly resources for any information on the issuer. Since much of this information is reusable, it may permit the bank to certify a security issue better than investment houses, as is formally modeled in Puri (1999), which we discuss in Section 2.3.

This information advantage of commercial banks provides interesting testable empirical implications of commercial banks versus investment house underwritings. For example, one can weigh the information advantage of a commercial bank against its conflict of interest and analyze whether combining lending and underwriting is net beneficial to the issuer. Several papers test this wedge between information advantage and the conflict of interest of commercial bank underwritings vis-à-vis comparable investment house underwritings (see Section 2.4 for details).

2.2.2. Scope Economies

The basic idea of scope economies is that if there is a fixed-cost component to both lending and underwriting of securities for the same firm, combining these functions lowers the information production costs, since this fixed cost is incurred only once. An example of such a fixed cost is that associated with establishing a "relationship," that is, an initial evaluation of a firm's credit worthiness by a commercial bank (or an investment house);

the commercial bank (or the investment house) need not incur this relationship-building cost in subsequent dealings with this firm. In contrast, having securities underwritten by a specialized underwriter—that is, an investment house—commits the firm to a new relationship cost if the firm previously sought a loan from a commercial bank. See Kanatas and Qi (2003) for a model of information scope economies, where information costs incurred in learning about a firm in the process of underwriting their securities need not be fully incurred again when making a bank loan to the same firm.

We discuss evidence of scope economies and the relative importance of the type of relationship that a client has with a bank (e.g., lending relationship or underwriting relationship, especially, prior to a securities underwriting) in Section 2.5.

2.3. Theory

While commercial banks obtain private information on the borrower-issuer relatively costlessly from the loan-monitoring process, investment houses must expend resources in collecting information. As a result, high information collection costs can induce investment houses to produce less information than commercial banks, despite potential reputation losses from "uninformed certification" (see Puri 1999 for a theoretical derivation of these effects). Commercial banks are therefore likely to be better informed than investment houses, and their underwritings can have a stronger "certification effect."

Puri (1999) argues that this potentially stronger certification effect (as a result of the information advantage described in Section 2.2.1) has to be weighed against a "conflict of interest effect" (described in Section 2.1.1), arising from commercial banks' incentives to misuse private information through their lending activities. Rational investors anticipate which intermediary type has a higher net certification effect (defined as the certification effect net of any conflict of interest) and price securities accordingly. In particular, if investors perceive that conflicts of interest are strong, it is likely that commercial bank–underwritten securities will be priced lower (have higher yields) than similar investment-house underwritten securities. Alternatively, if conflicts of interest appear to be small, commercial bank–underwritten issues will be priced higher (have lower yields).[7]

We next turn our attention to empirical evidence on the net certification effect.

2.4. Empirical Evidence from Debt Underwritings

We next describe the empirical studies on the certification–conflict of interest debate. We then examine whether the organizational form of underwriting of securities influences the magnitude of these effects.

[7] Here we described the theory behind the certification and conflict of interest effects. For theory papers that examine the potential for commercial banks and investment banks to coexist, as well as the implications of such a scenario, see Boot and Thakor (1997), Kanatas and Qi (1998, 2003), Puri (1999), and Rajan (2002). We discuss some of these papers in the context of commercial bank entry into the securities underwriting market in Section 3.

2.4.1. Ex Post Default Performance

The early studies in this area, such as Ang and Richardson (1994), Kroszner and Rajan (1994), and Puri (1994), assessed conflicts of interest by examining ex post default performance of securities underwritten by commercial banks as compared to similar securities underwritten by investment houses in the pre–Glass-Steagall era. The basic premise these papers test is, if conflicts of interest are indeed present in the case of debt securities underwritten by commercial banks, then such securities are likely to default more ex post than similar debt securities underwritten by investment banks (since investment banks do not make loans, they are not subject to such conflicts of interest). In contrast to such assertions, these studies find that commercial bank–underwritten securities had a better default record than investment house–underwritten securities (despite the potential conflicts of interest that were present). That is, commercial–bank underwritten debt issues defaulted less than investment house–underwritten issues.

This result holds across different issuer types, such as domestic corporate, foreign corporate, and foreign government bonds, and across different credit rating classifications, such as investment- and noninvestment-grade issues. In particular, the difference in ex post default performance between commercial bank and investment house underwritings is larger for noninvestment-grade debt issues as compared to investment-grade debt issues, which suggests that commercial banks did not systematically fool naive investors into investing in securities that later turned out to be of low quality. Interestingly enough, the evidence in these studies indicates that the Pecora Committee may have wrongfully condemned an entire industry based on alleged questionable practices at two banks, which were found in these studies to have issued bonds of lesser quality than other commercial bank affiliates, but no worse than those of the investment houses.

The aforementioned studies provide a useful first step in assessing conflicts of interest. However, the mere presence of conflicts of interest is not problematic if investors rationally price such conflicts. That is, even if the aforementioned studies found that commercial bank–underwritten debt securities defaulted more than investment house–underwritten securities, and if investors rationally paid less for the securities underwritten by commercial banks, then one could conclude that no regulatory action (such as prohibiting commercial banks from underwriting corporate securities) was required. A comparison of the ex ante offering prices would help answer whether there were any conflicts of interest, and if so whether investors rationally priced them in. The next set of studies adopt such an ex ante approach.

2.4.2. Ex Ante Price (Yield) Performance

Puri (1996) and Gande et al. (1997) were the earliest studies to adopt an ex ante (rather than an ex post) assessment of conflicts of interest. Puri (1996) examines data pertaining to the pre–Glass-Steagall period (1927–29), whereas Gande et al. (1997) examine data pertaining to a more recent time period (1993–95), when commercial banks were allowed to underwrite debt securities in a limited manner through Section 20 subsidiaries.[8] Both studies find that commercial bank–underwritten debt issues generated lower yields (i.e., higher prices) than similar investment bank–underwritten issues, suggesting that conflicts of interest were minimal and that commercial bank underwritings played a valuable certification role.

In essence, Puri (1996) regresses ex ante yield spread[9] (defined as the premium of the stated ex ante yield to maturity of a debt security over the ex ante yield to maturity of a Treasury security of comparable maturity) for underwritings during the pre–Glass-Steagall period (1927–29) on an indicator variable that takes a value of 1 if a commercial bank is the lead or sole underwriter (and zero otherwise) and a set of control variables that includes issue size, and whether it is a new issue. She performs a variety of subsample tests (such as new versus seasoned issues, investment- versus noninvestment-grade securities, and in-house underwritings versus affiliate underwritings), and conducts several robustness tests.

Puri concludes that there was no evidence of conflicts of interest in commercial bank–underwritten issues in the pre–Glass-Steagall period. On the contrary, investors perceived commercial banks as being valuable certifiers of firm value since they were willing to pay higher prices (i.e., accept lower yields), as evidenced by the magnitude and sign of the indicator variable that captures commercial bank underwritings, for securities underwritten by commercial banks relative to those underwritten by investment houses. Furthermore, the lowering of the yields for commercial bank–underwritten securities as compared to investment houses was higher for new versus seasoned issues and for noninvestment-grade securities versus investment-grade securities, attesting to the valuable role of commercial bank certification for such junior and information-sensitive securities.

A sharper test of the conflicts of interest would require controlling for the underlying lending relationship, since the source of the commercial bank's conflict of interest is its preexisting lending relationship with the issuer at the time of underwriting. That is, two factors are important in designing a sharper test of conflicts of interest: (1) The commercial bank who is underwriting an issuer's securities should have a loan outstanding on its financial books to the same issuer prior to the time of underwriting; (2) the commercial bank should be using the underwritten issue proceeds to pay down its existing debt to the same issuer. Unfortunately, such an analysis was extremely difficult in the pre–Glass-Steagall period, since data on the underlying lending relationship was not available, and the information on the purpose of issue, while stated, was extremely noisy, given that stringent disclosure rules (such as those provided in

[8]In 1987, the Federal Reserve permitted commercial banks to set up special Section 20 investment banking subsidiaries. Not all banks can establish Section 20 affiliates, and special permission must be received from the Federal Reserve. In 1987, the Federal Reserve gave the first permission to a commercial bank to underwrite commercial paper, municipal revenue bonds, and securitization issues. In 1989, corporate bond underwriting was permitted for the first time, as was corporate equity underwriting in 1990. See footnote 1 for additional details on the Section 20 subsidiaries.

[9]*Yield spread* as defined here is sometimes also referred to as *net yield* in the literature.

the Securities Act of 1934) did not exist. Hence the studies in the pre–Glass-Steagall period, such as Puri (1996), relied on whether the underwriter was a commercial bank or an investment house, without controlling for the underlying lending relationship. However, this biases the results toward the null hypothesis of no difference in yield spreads between commercial bank and investment house underwritings. See footnote 5 in Puri (1996) for details.

Gande et al. (1997) provide a sharper test of conflicts of interest because they use lending data for more recent data (1993–1995) in the post–Glass-Steagall period, which corresponds to a time period when commercial banks were allowed to underwrite debt securities in a limited manner through Section 20 subsidiaries (see footnote 1 for details). Specifically, Gande et al. focus on the use of proceeds of debt issues (i.e., whether the issue proceeds were being used to refinance existing bank debt or for other purposes), using an empirical methodology similar to Puri (1996). They posit (and test) that a potential conflict of interest exists only when the proceeds of a debt issue are being used to refinance existing bank debt and the underwriter is a commercial bank whose loans are being refinanced.

They find no evidence of conflicts of interest (i.e., no difference in yield spreads on similar debt issues underwritten by Section 20 subsidiaries and investment houses) when the debt issue is used to repay bank debt. Where debt securities are issued for purposes other than repaying existing bank debt, and where the commercial bank that underwrites the issue through its Section 20 affiliate retains a significant lending stake, yield spreads are reduced by 42 basis points (per unit of the natural log of the commercial bank's outstanding loans, in millions of dollars, to the issuer) for noninvestment-grade issues as compared to similar securities underwritten by investment houses. Thus, the results support earlier findings from the pre–Glass-Steagall studies of a dominant net certification effect of commercial bank underwritings.

In a recent study, Yasuda (2005) examines the value of banking relationships for the firm's underwriter choice in the corporate bond market. She uses a unique dataset consisting of 1,535 U.S. domestic corporate bond issues from 1993–97, where she accounts for the significance of roles played by banks in syndicated loans. Using a framework that allows imputation of unobserved fees conditional on the choice of underwriter (a nested multinomial logit model),[10] she models the firm's underwriter-choice problem and measures the effect of banking relationships on the choice of underwriter, both when the banks are chosen and when they are not. She finds that existing bank relationships have positive and statistically significant effects on a firm's underwriter choice, especially for junk bond issuers and first-time issuers. She finds the strength of the banking relationship matters. Specifically, she finds that serving as arranger of past loan transactions has the strongest effect on underwriter choice, whereas serving merely as a participant on a loan syndicate has no effect.

[10]This model is a generalization of the multinomial logit model (also called *conditional logit model*), both developed by McFadden (1974) and discussed in Maddala (1983). The nested logit model relaxes the irrelevance of independent alternatives (IIA) property of the logit model by structuring the decision process as a tree or nest structure. The IIA assumption implies that odds ratios in multinomial logit models are independent of other choices, which is inappropriate in many instances, including the one studied here.

The preceding study complements Schenone (2004), which examines IPO underpricing and pre-IPO banking relationships, which are discussed in Section 2.5.1.

In summary (so far), investors perceived debt securities underwritten by commercial banks to be of a higher quality, ex ante. This result of a higher ex ante quality by investors for commercial bank–underwritten debt securities (based on yield spread differentials) supports the results regarding ex post quality (based on default performance). Collectively, the empirical evidence from the foregoing studies suggests that investors, on average, behaved rationally in pricing securities and that concerns about exploitation of conflicts of interest were minimal as compared to the valuable benefit that commercial banks bring to the issuers, especially small and lower-credit-rated issuers, while underwriting their debt securities.

One may argue that so far the efficiency gains from combining lending with underwriting may be attributable to the changes in competition for the underwriting of corporate securities. Specifically, the observed results (e.g., lowering of yield spreads for commercial bank–underwritten securities relative to comparable investment bank–underwritten securities) may be due entirely to the effects of heightened bank competition with the entry of commercial banks into securities underwriting rather than to any real cost advantages at the bank level resulting from efficiency gains. Moreover, since the short-run (entry) and long-run (market structure) effects of bank competition could be different, it is important to disentangle the effects of competition from efficiency gains. Since this is an important issue, we devote all of Section 3 to it, summarizing the evidence on commercial bank entry into the corporate securities underwriting market in 1989 (as a proxy for short-run effects) and the evidence on announcement effects surrounding the enactment of the Financial Modernization Act of 1999, which repealed the Glass-Steagall Act (as a proxy for long-run effects).

2.5. Empirical Evidence from Equity Underwritings

In the previous section, we focused on debt underwritings. Here we summarize evidence from equity underwritings, since they provide the same incentive effects, in terms of conflicts of interest, as debt underwritings. For example, a commercial bank facing a conflict of interest due to its underlying lending relationship with a borrower is equally likely to underwrite the borrower's debt or equity issue and to use the proceeds to repay its existing debt. Thus, ignoring evidence from equity underwritings is equivalent to precluding the equity channel of commercial bank conflict of interest. Moreover, not all firms (e.g., small issuers) may be able to access public debt markets, but they may be able to access public equity markets. Hence, analyzing equity underwritings enlarges the spectrum of firms in a sample. Finally, we are interested not only in whether there are efficiency gains from combining lending and underwriting but also in the importance of prior relationships (such as lending and underwriting) in determining the magnitude of the efficiency gains. Data on equity underwritings is available for a longer time period than for debt underwritings.

We first present evidence from initial public offerings (IPOs). These studies use the underpricing of the issue (i.e., initial-day return of the security once it is publicly traded), corresponding to the ex ante yield used in the studies that examine debt underwritings. We follow this with similar evidence from seasoned equity offerings (SEOs).

2.5.1. Initial Public Offerings

Hebb (2002) examines the pricing characteristics of initial public offerings underwritten by commercial banks from 1995 to 1998. He argues that since IPO underpricing is directly related to ex ante uncertainty, then if the market rationally perceives an underwriting commercial bank to have a conflict of interest, these securities should have more underpricing than noncommercial bank–underwritten initial public offerings (IPOs). On the other hand, if the market believes that commercial bank involvement signals firm quality, less underpricing should be observed. He tests this hypothesis and finds that the underpricing of commercial bank–underwritten initial public offerings in which the firm had a previous banking relationship with the underwriter is significantly less than those underwritten by investment houses.

One caveat of this study is that their data does not contain information on the exact nature of this relationship. That is, an indicator variable (created from prospectus and other public sources) that captures whether a previous commercial banking relationship exists between one of the underwriters and the IPO firm is used in making inferences about conflicts of interest. However, this variable does not state whether an actual loan was made by the underwriting commercial bank to the issuer and, if so, whether that loan is outstanding at the time of the IPO for it to be a potential source of conflict of interest. Later studies (e.g., Schenone 2004, discussed later) use refined data on the pre-IPO relationship between the issuer and the underwriter.

Fields, Fraser, and Bhargava (2003) examine differences in total issuance costs (gross spread plus underpricing) of 4,566 IPOs underwritten during 1991–97. They find that the total issuance costs are significantly lower for commercial bank IPOs. The lower cost for commercial bank IPOs is attributable to less severe underpricing for these issues. Gross spreads generally do not differ between commercial bank and investment bank issues. Since it is possible that commercial bank–underwritten issues may underperform in the long run, they examine this issue and find that commercial bank–underwritten issues have superior long-run performance than comparable investment bank–underwritten issues. Their results show no strong evidence of any conflicts of interest.

The foregoing study complements Hebb (2002) by examining a longer time series and also provides evidence on long-term performance of commercial bank–underwritten securities vis-à-vis investment bank–underwritten securities. One caveat for this study is that it does not condition on the existence of any underlying lending relationship (the source of potential conflict of interest), even though such data were available for the 1991–97 sample period.

Schenone (2004) investigates whether lending relationships established prior to a firm's IPO mitigate the information-asymmetry problem that first-time issuers face and consequently reduce IPO underpricing. She constructs a unique dataset that matches the firm's pre-IPO banking institution with the firm's IPO underwriter. In particular, using this dataset, she can establish whether the firm's pre-IPO bank could have managed the firm's IPO and, further, whether it did manage it or not. In essence, Schenone compares the list of pre-IPO banks for a firm (during a period up to five years prior to the IPO) with the list of all the institutions (obtained from Securities Data Corporation (SDC) New Issues database) that managed an IPO (as a book runner, lead manager, or manager) at the time the IPO firm is going public, and she evaluates whether a pre-IPO bank could have managed the firm's IPO directly or indirectly through a Section 20 subsidiary.[11] In her sample of IPOs from 1998–2000, she finds that firms with an established banking relationship with a bank that could have taken the firm public exhibit 17% lower underpricing than firms without a banking relationship with a potential IPO underwriter and that the results are robust to controlling for the firm's endogenous selection of pre-IPO banking institution. She classifies the pre-IPO banking relationship as a lending relationship or an underwriting relationship (e.g., the bank underwrote the firm's prior debt issue) and finds that lending relationships are more valuable than underwriting relationships in terms of their impact on lowering the IPO underpricing.

The fact that Schenone's sample corresponds to high-technology startups during the Internet bubble period warrants two observations: First, the sample period may be somewhat special, and hence it would help to understand whether one obtains similar results in other time periods. Second, it is important to know whether this phenomenon is partially reversed subsequently. That is, it would be helpful to know whether the long-term performance of the IPOs with a pre-IPO lending relationship or a pre-IPO underwriting relationship is superior to comparable IPOs with no pre-IPO banking relationships.

As before, the empirical evidence from the preceding studies suggests that investors, on average, behaved rationally in pricing securities. Thus, concerns about exploitation of conflicts of interest were outweighed by the valuable benefit that commercial banks bring to the issuers, especially for IPO issuers, for whom the information asymmetry about future prospects is the highest. In addition, the evidence shows that pre-IPO lending relationships are more valuable than pre-IPO underwriting relationships, at least for debt issues prior to the IPO.

2.5.2. Seasoned Equity Offerings

Using underwriting data of seasoned equity offerings from 1994–97, Narayanan, Rangan, and Rangan (2004) find that the total issuance costs (underpricing plus underwriter spread) is lower when a lending bank comanages the issue with a reputable investment bank. Their interpretation of this result is that lending banks comanage to reduce perceptions of conflicts of interest. We discuss this study in more detail in Section 2.6.2.

Using a sample of SEOs from 1996–2001, Drucker and Puri (2005) find that when a financial intermediary concurrently lends to an issuer and underwrites the firm's SEO,

[11] See pages 2911–2912 of the paper for more details on the classification of whether a pre-IPO bank could or could not have underwritten a firm's IPO.

the issuer benefits through lower financing costs and through receiving lower underwriter fees and lower loan yield spreads. This is particularly for noninvestment-grade issuers, for whom the informational economies of scope are likely to be large.[12] They show that concurrent lending also helps underwriters build relationships, increasing the probability of receiving current and future business. This study also highlights the importance of prior lending relationships in more general terms (thus complementing Schenone 2004 and Yasuda 2005). Specifically, they show that issuers with prior lending relationships receive lower underwriter spreads; for the underwriter, a prior lending relationship increases the likelihood of receiving the underwriter business from the issuer. Their results are robust to a variety of matching procedures based on Heckman, Ichimura, and Todd (1997, 1998).

The empirical evidence from the foregoing studies suggests that there are clear benefits to a lending relationship, which can be interpreted as evidence of scope economies and that the certification effect is larger than the conflict of interest effect. In addition, the pricing benefits that empirical studies show are prima facie evidence that a firm is not being hurt by implicit tying arrangements, such as concurrent lending.[13] This is most notable for firms that are most likely to be subject to commercial banks' market power, such as small firms and lower-credit-rated (and hence high-risk) firms.

While we have so far presented empirical evidence on conflicts of interest (or the lack thereof) from U.S. studies based on corporate debt and equity markets, there are numerous other studies that look at non-U.S. data and arrive at similar conclusions, that is, that there is minimal evidence on conflicts of interest around the world. See, for example, Ber, Yafeh, and Yosha (2001) for evidence from Israel, Hebb and Fraser (2002) for evidence from Canada, Konishi (2002) for evidence from Japan, and Hebb and Fraser (2003) for evidence from the United Kingdom.

Similarly, there are studies that examine U.S. data from other (than corporate debt and equity) markets and arrive at a similar conclusion vis-à-vis conflicts of interest faced by a commercial bank in such a setting. See, for example, Saunders and Stover (2004) for evidence from the municipal bond market, Allen et al. (2004) for evidence on bank advisory services to target firms in a mergers and acquisitions transaction, and Li and Masulis (2004) for evidence from venture capital investments by IPO underwriters.

2.6. Organizational Form of Underwriting

While there is no strong evidence of conflicts of interest from the previous sets of studies, a few papers examined how commercial banks have responded to minimizing

[12]The definition of *concurrent lending* that is adopted in this study is that if a firm receives a loan from the underwriter of the SEO between six months prior to and within six months after the SEO, they classify the loan as a *concurrent loan* and the SEO as a *concurrent deal*.

[13]The existing laws on tying arrangements (see Section 106 of the Bank Holding Company Act Amendments of 1970) "do not prohibit a bank from granting credit or providing any other product to a customer based solely on a desire or a hope (but not a requirement) that the customer will obtain additional products from the bank or its affiliates in the future." In any case, clients are expected to be free to "use their own bargaining power" to seek a bundle of banking services.

perceptions of conflicts of interest based on the organizational form of underwriting. These broadly follow two such organizational forms to minimize perceptions of conflicts of interest: (1) an internal form: affiliate (rather than in-house) underwritings, and (2) an external form: syndicated (as a comanager) rather than lead commercial bank underwriter.

2.6.1. Affiliate Structure

Whether a commercial bank underwrites in-house or through an affiliate can affect its incentives. Specifically, when commercial banks make loans and underwrite securities in-house, the flow of private information from the loan department to the underwriting department is likely to be stronger and the certification effect higher.[14] This distinction is traditionally drawn between the German and the U.K. models of banking (see, for example, Saunders and Walter 1994, p. 85). Puri (1996) finds that in-house underwritings do not lead to greater conflicts of interest than underwriting through affiliates in the pre–Glass-Steagall period. In fact, she finds that in-house underwritings reduce yields (obtain higher prices) relative to investment houses more than affiliate underwritings do, suggesting a stronger net certification effect for in-house underwritings as compared to affiliate underwritings.

Kroszner and Rajan (1997) also examine pre–Glass-Steagall data, and they conclude that conflicts of interest led commercial banks to evolve to an affiliate structure to underwrite securities. However, one needs to be cautious about such an interpretation, for the following reasons. First, regulations favored an affiliate structure. Only after the 1927 McFadden Act were national banks explicitly allowed to underwrite securities. Additionally, affiliates could be chartered under state law as limited liability corporations; could help evade interstate branching restrictions; had no minimal capital requirements; and could do almost anything "except solemnize marriages and perform religious ceremonies" (U.S. Senate, 1934, p. 4776). Finally, this study had no access to direct lending data. Since both departments and affiliates could lend to firms, better prices for affiliate underwritings might simply reflect that affiliates lent more than departments to issuers in their sample. This would support a certification rather than a conflict of interest effect. In contrast, since only banks can lend, it is easier to interpret which effect dominates by comparing commercial bank and investment house underwritings, as in Puri (1996), or by gathering direct lending data, as in Gande et al. (1997) and subsequent studies; both approaches indicate a dominant certification effect.

While there is no clear consensus from the preceding studies, interestingly the revealed preference of bank holding companies' overwhelming choice to merge their investment banking operations into the bank (i.e., in-house) rather than use separate subsidiaries (i.e., affiliates) following the passage of the GLB Act provides strong

[14] In addition, an analysis of the choice of the in-house versus affiliate form of underwriting as an effective commitment device against conflicts of interest is of interest to policymakers since it may provide a rationale for the structural restrictions that governments often impose on firms in regulated industries, such as the "firewalls" to separate the lending and underwriting operations in the post–Glass-Steagall period.

evidence of banks' views about the relative inefficiency of keeping their investment banking operations separate and indirect evidence that conflicts of interest are relatively small compared to efficiency gains from in-house underwritings.

2.6.2. Syndicate Structure

Using underwriting data of seasoned equity offerings from 1994–97, Narayanan, Rangan, and Rangan (2004) examine the use of syndicate structure by lending banks. They argue that by comanaging with a reputable investment house (rather than lead managing by themselves), commercial banks obtain independent certification of the issue, allowing them to mitigate any adverse pricing consequences that they might otherwise face due to perceptions of conflicts of interest. They present evidence that when lending banks comanage issues, they lower the total issuance costs for their loan clients.[15]

Song (2004) examines the decision of lead investment banks to organize hybrid syndicates (where commercial banks participate as comanagers) versus pure investment bank syndicates using corporate debt issues from 1991–96. Using a switching simultaneous-equations model described in Maddala (1983, p. 282), she shows that clients served by hybrid syndicates are "special."[16] For example, their debt issues are more difficult to float, as evidenced by the fact that hybrid syndicates serve clients that are smaller, have lower common stock rankings (i.e., have more information asymmetry), have less prior access to capital markets, and rely more on bank loans, and issue proceeds are more likely to be used for the purpose of repaying bank debt. She presents evidence supporting an enhancement of underwriting services as the economic rationale of syndication between incumbent investment banks and entrant commercial banks. She concludes that the combined lending and underwriting capacity of commercial banks enhances the certification function of hybrid syndicates and that the reputation of a lead investment bank as an independent third party alleviates the conflicts of interest of commercial banks through hybrid syndicates.

The results of both these studies suggest that the benefits of bank entry to issuing firms are by no means limited to the cases where commercial banks lead the syndicates; they do extend to cases where they comanage with an independent reputable investment house. Apart from Narayanan, Rangan, and Rangan's (2004) interpretation that the syndicate structure is designed to reduce perceived conflicts of interest, for which the evidence is weak (see later), it appears that bank's primary role within the syndicate is to provide valuable certification. Alternatively, it may be an artifact of the change in

[15] *Total issuance costs* is defined as the sum of issue underpricing and gross spread. *Issue underpricing* is computed as the return from buying at the offer price and selling as of close on the day of the offer. *Gross spread*, expressed as a percentage, is the sum of the underwriting fee, management fee, and selling concession per share divided by the offer price.

[16] The unique feature of this model is that it permits the analysis of both exogenous and endogenous factors affecting syndicate formation. It also allows the evaluation of resulting underwriting services while recognizing that the observed syndicate distributions are not random. This is the so-called *endogenous switching problem*.

competition introduced by commercial bank entry (see Section 3 for details) and the propensity of a client to switch (or not to switch) its underwriter rather than having anything to do with conflicts of interest. For example, if a client is likely to switch from an incumbent investment bank to an entrant commercial bank, wouldn't the lead investment bank cooperate and invite the entrant commercial bank to join the syndicate rather than lose a client?

Clearly, more research is needed to identify the sources of value creation from inducting a commercial bank into an underwriting syndicate, how significant conflicts of interest really are as a driving force in syndicate formation, and other factors that determine the decision of a lead investment bank to cooperate and invite a commercial bank to join the syndicate. These factors could include the threat that the customer might switch to a commercial bank or a quid pro quo on future deals, among other reasons.

On the last question of how significant are the conflicts of interest, it appears there is no strong evidence in either of the aforementioned studies that containing conflicts of interest is a major factor affecting syndicate formation or structure. For example, while Narayanan, Rangan, and Rangan (2004) present some evidence that the total issuance costs for comanaged issues is lower than those of lead-managed issues (i.e., where lending bank is the lead underwriter), is it due to the small sample size of lead-managed issues? That is, it would be helpful to better understand how the preponderance of comanaging security issues by lending banks relative to lead-managing by themselves in their sample (see p. 557: "the proportion of syndicate comanager roles to lead manager roles for lending banks is about three times higher that for nonlending banks") influences the conclusions of their study.

In Song (2004), the evidence on conflicts of interest is based on the idea that when a commercial bank is the lead underwriter, with or without other commercial banks as comanagers in a syndicate, clients suffer price discounts (i.e., have a higher net yield, also known as the *yield spread*), whereas hybrid clients do not suffer any price discounts. However, in the net yield regressions of the subsample where the commercial bank is the lead underwriter (in their Table VIII), the evidence for conflicts of interest are not statistically significant at traditional levels, suggesting that the evidence of conflicts of interest is rather weak.[17]

Overall, the fact that syndicates bring complementary abilities of rival underwriters to enhance the underwriting service of clients (e.g., in terms of lower net yields or lower total issuance costs) is undisputable. Whether there are significant conflicts of interest to start with and whether the lowering of such conflicts of interest is a fundamental driver of syndicate formation is still not clear, and this issue needs more empirical work.

In the next section, we examine other evidence on efficiency gains from combining lending with underwriting, such as how the market viewed the commercial bank

[17] More specifically, the coefficient of an indicator variable that denotes whether the purpose of a bond issue is to refinance bank debt is not statistically significant, and the coefficient of this indicator variable, interacted with the size of the natural log of the underwriter loans, is positive and statistically significant only at a p-value of 16% (t-stat 1.41).

entry into the securities underwriting market in 1989, in terms of its impact on underwriter spreads, ex ante yields, and market concentration, and in terms of capital market reactions to the announcement of the Financial Modernization Act of 1999, which effectively repealed the Glass-Steagall Act.

3. COMPETITIVE EFFECTS OF COMMERCIAL BANK ENTRY INTO SECURITIES UNDERWRITING

In this section we examine the third question, that is, whether commercial banks, with access to superior information (from loan-monitoring activities as described in the previous section) about firms to whom they lend, have an unfair advantage in underwriting that can result in their monopolizing the market.

3.1. Theory

If combining lending with underwriting results in larger efficiency gains for commercial banks (e.g., due to their information advantage in the loan-monitoring process) as compared to investment banks, a commercial bank entry into the market for corporate securities underwriting could be beneficial to the issuer if the commercial bank passes on those efficiency gains (or at least a part of them) to the issuer. Such a view could be developed based on the framework in Puri (1999), discussed previously.

However, even in a competitive environment, where any efficiency gains are passed on fully to the issuers, Kanatas and Qi (2003) show that an issuer may not be strictly better off. In their model, a universal bank offers both lending and underwriting (i.e., raising capital), thereby economizing on such costs to the benefit of their customers. However, those cost savings also have a downside by enabling universal banks to capture their customers' future business. That is, a universal bank has less incentive to provide the costly efforts that will aid the successful marketing of their clients' securities (e.g., if the capital raising was unsuccessful, a universal bank can offer a loan to its client and not incur the relationship cost, whereas using a specialized investment bank triggers a relationship cost for that client). Thus, an issuer trades off the benefit from economies of scope from a universal bank with a higher likelihood of a specialized investment bank's selling its securities successfully.

So the effect of commercial bank entry on the issuer in terms of whether it lowers the yields or underwriter spreads is finally an empirical question.

3.2. Empirical Evidence on Commercial Bank Entry in 1989

Gande, Puri, and Saunders (1999) was the earliest study that examined the competitive effects of commercial bank entry into the corporate debt underwriting market.

3.2.1. Underwriter Spreads

Gande, Puri, and Saunders (1999) analyze how underwriter spreads (defined as the difference between the offered amount and the proceeds to the issuer, expressed as a percentage of the offered amount) were influenced by commercial bank entry into the underwriting of corporate securities. They state that underwriter spreads are determined by two major factors. The first factor relates to distribution costs, information production costs, and other costs, including compensation for the risk carried in underwriting a security issue. The second factor is the competitive element in the market, that is, whether markets are fully competitive or whether there are some "monopoly" rents to underwriters. They argue that on the one hand, commercial bank entry can make markets more competitive, leading to reduced underwriter spreads. On the other hand, large, well-capitalized banks could monopolize the debt-underwriting market, leading to increased underwriter spreads. They test for this and find that commercial bank entry significantly reduced underwriter spreads in the corporate debt market. For example, the underwriter spreads for debt issues dropped on average by 24 basis points after commercial bank entry, which is statistically significant (at the 1% level) and economically significant (the average debt underwriter spreads was 132 basis points in their sample period, 1985–1996).

Moreover, they show that the reduction in underwriter spreads is strongest among lower-rated (i.e., noninvestment-grade debt) and smaller debt issues, with banks underwriting a relatively larger proportion of such issues. To further ensure that other factors are not contributing to these declines in underwriter spreads, such as greater ease of distribution and lower information production costs, they compare and contrast the trends in the corporate bond market, where banks had a significant market share (16.28% by dollar volume and 20.42% by number of issues by 1996—see Table 2 of their paper), to that in equity (IPO and SEO) markets, where banks had not yet made major inroads by 1996. Interestingly, they find that while Section 20 deregulation appears to have resulted in a significant decline in underwriting spreads in the corporate bond market, similar declines were not apparent in equity markets.[18]

3.2.2. Ex Ante Yields

Gande, Puri, and Saunders (1999) argue that banks differ from investment houses in that they can obtain information about a firm through their loan-monitoring activities. If banks are more credible certifiers than investment houses, for example, because of better information at their disposal, then bank-underwritten securities will have better prices (lower yields) than will securities underwritten by investment houses, as long as

[18]See Daniels and Vijayakumar (2001), who document an increase in competition in the underwriting of municipal revenue bonds as a result of commercial bank entry when all municipal revenue bonds became eligible for commercial banks to underwrite starting in 1987. Also, see Silber (1979) for a summary of the empirical evidence prior to 1987, when banks were permitted (starting in 1968) to underwrite in a limited manner certain types of municipal revenue bonds (for housing, university, and dormitory purposes).

bank entry does not increase the degree of market concentration and banks' power over issuers. Bank entry can therefore force investment houses to expend more resources and produce more information about issuing firms, resulting in better prices (and lower yields) for the market as a whole.

They test whether bank entry affects ex ante yield spreads of corporate bond issues, and they find that ex ante yield spreads have declined (rather than increased) with bank entry and that this decline is most apparent in smaller issues.

3.2.3. Market Concentration

Gande, Puri, and Saunders (1999) find that bank entry into the corporate debt market has lowered market concentration. However, they state that one must be cautious in interpreting this result, since it was somewhat early (at the time of their study) to assess the long-term impact of bank underwriting on market concentration.

The sample for the foregoing study ends in 1996, prior to the relaxation of the revenue cap (from 10% to 25%), which made it feasible for banks to acquire investment banks since 1997. This also predates the enactment of the Financial Modernization Act of 1999.

One could argue that this evidence captures the short-run (entry) effect of bank competition, which can be quite different from the long-run (market structure) effect. In other words, while the early evidence suggests that bank entry has been pro-competitive, whether bank entry will have an anticompetitive long-term effect, pushing traditional investment houses out of the market, remains to be seen. The long-run effects of bank entry can be studied in one of the following two ways: (1) Analyze a long-time series of data, for instance, 10 years' worth of data (i.e., 1999–2008), or (2) examine the announcement effects for the enactment of the Financial Modernization Act of 1999 as a proxy for the long-term effects. Since we do not as yet have a sufficiently long time series, we use the latter approach in Section 3.3.

An implication of the evidence just presented is that some or all of the evidence of efficiency gains from Section 2 may be attributable to the heightened bank competition. In other words, how would one disentangle the effects of bank competition from banks' real cost advantages, and how might empirical studies control for changes in bank competition in analyzing the efficiency gains from combining lending and underwriting? While this is a rather difficult problem to solve, one possibility is for empirical studies to include a proxy for market concentration, such as a Herfindahl Index to control for changes in bank competition. Another alternative would be to include a time trend or a market share variable, such as the one used in the Gande, Puri, and Saunders (1999) study.

3.3. Empirical Evidence on the Financial Modernization Act of 1999

On November 12, 1999, President Bill Clinton signed the Financial Modernization Act of 1999, essentially eliminating the separation of commercial banking, investment banking, and insurance activities in the United States. Now, for the first time in six decades, these activities can be integrated within a general financial services firm (such as "the Citigroup") in the United States.[19]

Interestingly, numerous studies have examined the capital market reaction of investment banks, commercial banks, and insurance companies to the passage of the Financial Modernization Act of 1999. The results of these studies (described later) provide a capital markets perspective to the net benefits of elimination of the separation of commercial banking, investment banking, and insurance activities in the United States. Additionally, they can help us understand whether financial convergence is expected to add value through better utilization of scope economies (or increased monopoly rents due to reduced competition, especially in the longer term), reduce value due to perceptions of conflicts of interest, or maintain somewhat of a status quo, resulting in at most a redistribution of wealth from one institution type to another.

Carow and Heron (2002) and Hendershott, Lee, and Tompkins (2002) find a strong positive response among insurance companies and investment banks and no significant response among commercial banks. Larger institutions in all three financial sectors earn higher abnormal returns. Additionally, better-performing banks earn higher abnormal returns. These studies conclude that financial convergence can add value through synergies and that large players are needed to exploit scope economies.

There are several caveats to this analysis. First, to the extent that the Financial Modernization Act was partially anticipated, the observed capital market reactions reflect only the unanticipated, or "surprise," part of the announcement of the passage of the act. One would have expected that investors rationally capitalized prior to the passage of the act the anticipated net benefits based on their estimate of the likelihood ($\hat{p}$; where $0 \leq \hat{p} \leq 1$) of passage of the act. In other words, the capital market reactions on November 12, 1999, reflect the portion of the net benefits that were not yet capitalized, that is, those that result from updating from $\hat{p}$ to 1. While these studies try to identify legislative dates leading up to the passage of the act and add the announcement effects on those dates to that of passage of the act, it is unclear whether this set of events fully encompasses the changes in investor expectations vis-à-vis the likelihood of enactment of the act. Second, the capital market reactions provide a snapshot at the time of passage of the act. Whether these effects are permanent or transitory can lead to significantly different inferences. That is, at the very least one would like to know if there are reversals of the capital market reactions in the weeks following the passage of the act. Finally, whether there are any confounding institution-specific events that coincided with passage of the act. If so, the capital market reactions need to be adjusted for any such confounding institution-specific events. Consequently, due to the preceding caveats, one needs to be somewhat cautious in making inferences concerning the economic effects based solely on the capital market reactions to enactment.

[19]For an excellent discussion of the causes and consequences of the consolidation of the financial services industry, see Berger, Demsetz, and Strahan (1999).

4. CONCLUSION

The evidence summarized in this chapter suggests that the evidence for conflicts of interest in combining lending with underwriting is unconvincing and that there are clear benefits to commercial bank underwritings due to the bank's ability to achieve economies of scope and to certify the issuer better than investment houses, which translates to lowering the cost of financing for the issuer. While there appears to be no consensus on whether specific organization forms of underwriting are required and whether these forms reduce perceptions of conflict of interest, one could argue that this is not a major concern given the weak evidence for significant conflicts of interest in the first place.

The value of a banking relationship appears to be largest for noninvestment-grade, small, and IPO firms, for whom one would ex ante expect the benefit of bank monitoring to be highest. There also is evidence to suggest that prior lending relationships help obtain future underwriting business. If so, one may see an increase in lending by banks, which can be an additional benefit, especially for noninvestment-grade and small firms with growth opportunities.

Initial evidence on bank entry into the securities underwriting market suggest a pro-competitive effect. Whether this remains the case in the longer term remains to be seen. Capital market reactions to the enactment of the Financial Modernization Act may not be a good proxy for the long-run effects of commercial bank entry since the announcement effects may be understated due to partial anticipation of enactment.

Some suggestions for future research include examining whether combining lending and underwriting increases or decreases the risk both at the bank level as well as at the country level and analyzing the dynamics of syndicate formation over and beyond the papers discussed here.

References

Allen, L., J. Jagtiani, S. Peristiani, and A. Saunders. 2004. The Role of Bank Advisors in Mergers and Acquisitions, *Journal of Money Credit and Banking* 36(2), 197–224.

Akhigbe, A., and A. M. Whyte. 2004. The Gramm-Leach-Bliley Act of 1999: Risk Implications for the Financial Services Industry, *Journal of Financial Research* 27(3), 435–446.

Ang, J. S., and T. Richardson. 1994. The Underwriting Experience of Commercial Bank Affiliates Prior to the Glass-Steagall Act: A Reexamination of Evidence for Passage of the Act, *Journal of Banking and Finance* 18(2), 351–395.

Ber, H., Y. Yafeh, and O. Yasha. 2001. Conflict of Interest in Universal Banking: Bank Lending, Stock Underwriting, and Fund Management, *Journal of Monetary Economics*, 47(1), 189–218.

Berger, A. N., R. S. Demsetz, and P. E. Strahan. 1999. The Consolidation of the Financial Services Industry: Causes, Consequences, and Implications for the Future, *Journal of Banking and Finance* 23(2–4), 135–194.

Benston, G. J. 1989. *The Separation of Commercial and Investment Banking: The Glass-Steagall Act Revisited and Reconsidered*. St. Martins Press, New York.

Benston, G. J. 1990. *The Separation of Commercial and Investment Banking*. Oxford University Press, New York.

Billett, M. T., M. T. Flannery, and J. A. Garfinkel. 1995. The Effect of Lender Identity on a Borrowing Firm's Equity Return, *Journal of Finance* 50(2), 699–718.

Boot, A., and A. Thakor. 1997. Banking Scope and Financial Innovation, *Review of Financial Studies* 10(4), 1099–1131.

Carow, K. A., and R. A. Heron. 2002. Capital Market Reactions to the Passage of the Financial Services Modernization Act of 1999, *Quarterly Review of Economics and Finance* 42(3), 465–485.

Daniels, K. N., and J. Vijayakumar. 2001. The Competitive Impact of Commercial Bank Underwriting on the Market for Municipal Revenue Bonds, *Journal of Financial Services Research* 20(1), 57–75.

Diamond, D. W. 1984. Financial Intermediation and Delegated Monitoring, *Review of Economic Studies* 51(3), 393–414.

Drucker, S., and M. Puri. 2005. On the Benefits of Concurrent Lending and Underwriting, *Journal of Finance* 60(6), 2763–2799.

Fama, E. F. 1985. What's Different About Banks? *Journal of Monetary Economics* 15(1), 29–39.

Fields, P., D. Fraser, and R. Bhargava. 2003. A Comparison of Underwriting Costs of Initial Public Offerings by Investment and Commercial Banks, *Journal of Financial Research* 26(4), 517–534.

Gande, A., M. Puri, and A. Saunders. 1999. Bank Entry, Competition, and the Market for Corporate Securities Underwriting, *Journal of Financial Economics* 54(2), 165–195.

Gande, A., M. Puri, A. Saunders, and I. Walter. 1997. Bank Underwriting of Debt Securities: Modern Evidence, *Review of Financial Studies* 10(4), 1175–1202.

Gorton, G., and A. Winton. 2003. Financial Intermediation, G. M. Constantinides, M. Harris, and R. M. Stulz (eds.), *Handbook of the Economics of Finance*. Elsevier North Holland, Amsterdam.

Hebb, G. M. 2002. Conflict of Interest in Commercial Bank Equity Underwriting, *Financial Review* 37(2), 185–205.

Hebb, G. M., and D. R. Fraser. 2002. Conflict of Interest in Commercial Bank Security Underwritings: Canadian Evidence, *Journal of Banking and Finance* 26(10), 1935–1949.

Hebb, G. M., and D. R. Fraser. 2003. Conflict of Interest in Commercial Bank Security Underwritings: United Kingdom Evidence, *Quarterly Journal of Business and Economics* 42(1–2), 79–95.

Heckman, J., H. Ichimura, and P. Todd. 1997. Matching as an Econometric Evaluation Estimator: Evidence from Evaluating a Job Training Programme, *Review of Economic Studies* 64(4), 605–654.

Heckman, J., H. Ichimura, and P. Todd. 1998. Matching as an Econometric Evaluation Estimator, *Review of Economic Studies* 65(2), 261–294.

Hendershott, R. J., D. E. Lee, and J. G. Tompkins. 2002. Winners and Losers as Financial Service Providers Converge: Evidence from the Financial Modernization Act of 1999, *Financial Review* 37(1), 53–72.

James, C. 1987. Some Evidence on the Uniqueness of Bank Loans, *Journal of Financial Economics* 19(2), 217–235.

James, C. 1992. Relationship-Specific Assets and the Pricing of Underwriter Services, *Journal of Finance* 47(5), 1865–1885.

James, C., and D. Smith. 2000. Are Banks Still Special? New Evidence on Their Role in the Capital-Raising Process, *Journal of Applied Corporate Finance* 13, 52–63.

Kanatas, G., and J. Qi. 1998. Underwriting by Commercial Banks: Incentive Conflicts, Scope Economies, and Project Quality, *Journal of Money, Credit, and Banking* 30(1), 119–133.

Kanatas, G., and J. Qi. 2003. Integration of Lending and Underwriting, *Journal of Finance* 58(3), 1167–1191.

Konishi, M. 2002. Bond Underwriting by Banks and Conflicts of Interest: Evidence from Japan During the Prewar Period, *Journal of Banking and Finance* 26(4), 767–793.

Kroszner, R. S., and R. G. Rajan. 1994. Is the Glass-Steagall Act Justified? A Study of the U.S. Experience with Universal Banking Before 1933, *American Economic Review* 84(4), 810–832.

Kroszner, R. S., and R. G. Rajan. 1997. Organization Structure and Credibility: Evidence from Commercial Bank Securities Activities Before the Glass-Steagall Act, *Journal of Monetary Economics* 39(3), 475–516.

Li, X., and R. W. Masulis. 2004. Venture Capital Investments by IPO Underwriters: Certification or Conflict of Interest? Vanderbilt University working paper.

Lummer, S. L., and J. J. McConnell. 1989. Further Evidence on the Bank Lending Process and the Capital-Market Response to Bank Loan Agreements, *Journal of Financial Economics* 25(1), 99–122.

Maddala, G. S. 1983. *Limited-Dependent and Qualitative Variables in Econometrics*. Cambridge University Press, Cambridge.

McFadden, D. 1974. The Measurement of Urban Travel Demand, *Journal of Public Economics* 3(4), 303–328.

Mester, L. 1996. Repealing Glass-Steagall: The Past Points the Way to the Future, *Federal Reserve Bank of Philadelphia Business Review* (July/Aug), 3–18.

Narayanan, R. P., K. P. Rangan, and K. R. Rangan. 2004. The Role of Syndicate Structure in Bank Underwriting, *Journal of Financial Economics* 72(3), 555–580.

Puri, M. 1994. The Long-Term Default Performance of Bank-Underwritten Security Issues, *Journal of Banking and Finance* 18(2), 397–418.

Puri, M. 1996. Commercial Banks in Investment Banking: Conflict of Interest or Certification Role? *Journal of Financial Economics* 40(3), 373–401.

Puri, M. 1999. Commercial Banks as Underwriters: Implications for the Going-Public Process, *Journal of Financial Economics* 54(2), 133–163.

Rajan, R. G. 1992. Insiders and Outsiders: The Choice Between Informed and ARM's-Length Debt, *Journal of Finance* 47(4), 1367–1400.

Rajan, R. G. 1996. The Entry of Commercial Banks into the Securities Business: A Selective Survey of Theories and Evidence, in I. Walter and A. Saunders (eds.), *Universal Banking: Financial System Design Reconsidered*. Irwin, Chicago.

Rajan, R. G. 2002. An Investigation into the Economics of Extending Bank Powers, *Journal of Emerging Market Finance* 1(2), 125–156.

Ramakrishnan, R., and A. Thakor. 1984. Information Reliability and a Theory of Financial Intermediation, *Review of Economic Studies* 51(3), 415–432.

Santos, J. 1998. Commercial Banks in the Securities Business: A Review, *Journal of Financial Services Research* 14(1), 35–60.

Saunders, A. 1985. Conflicts of Interest: An Economic View, in I. Walter (ed.), *Deregulating Wall Street*. John Wiley & Sons, New York.

Saunders, A. 2002. *Financial Institutions Management: A Modern Perspective*, 4th ed. Irwin, Chicago.

Saunders, A., and R. D. Stover. 2004. Commercial Bank Underwriting of Credit-Enhanced Bonds: Are There Certification Benefits to the Issuer? *Journal of International Money and Finance* 23(3), 367–384.

Saunders, A., and I. Walter. 1994. *Universal Banking in the U.S.* Oxford University Press, New York.

Schenone, C. 2004. The Effect of Banking Relationships on the Firm's IPO Underpricing, *Journal of Finance* 59(6), 2903–2958.

Sharpe, S. 1990. Asymmetric Information, Bank Lending, and Implicit Contracts: A Stylized Model of Customer Relationships, *Journal of Finance* 45(4), 1069–1087.

Silber, W. H. 1979. Municipal Revenue Bond Costs and Bank Underwriting: A Survey of the Evidence, in *Monograph Series in Finance and Economics*. Salomon Brothers Center for the Study of Financial Institutions.

Song, W. L. 2004. Competition and Coalition Among Underwriters: The Decision to Join a Syndicate, *Journal of Finance* 59(5), 2421–2444.

White, E. N. 1986. Before the Glass-Steagall Act: An Analysis of the Investment Banking Activities of National Banks, *Explorations in Economic History* 23(1), 33–55.

Yasuda, A. 2005. Do Bank Relationships Affect the Firm's Underwriter Choice in the Corporate-Bond Underwriting Market? *Journal of Finance* 60(3), 1259–1292.

Yu, L. 2002. On the Wealth and Risk Effects of the Glass-Steagall Overhaul: Evidence from the Stock Market. Working paper, New York University.

SECTION 4

Mutual Funds

Overview by Sudipto Bhattacharya

London School of Economics

Mutual funds play a very visible and growing role in financial markets. The proliferation of mutual funds is part of a more general trend involving a growing importance of institutional investors. Total assets under management in the U.S. market have evolved from \$50 billion and 500 funds in 1975 to \$10 trillion and 9,000 mutual funds being offered today.[1] Following this trend, research in finance has increasingly devoted efforts to understanding mutual funds focusing on their added value in particular. A question that has been looked at extensively is whether mutual funds, and particularly the actively managed funds outperform the market.

The three chapters in this section seek to shed light on this question, but more broadly they analyze three issues that are central to the debate on the role and added value of mutual funds. Each is addressed by one of the chapters.

The first issue, the performance measurement of mutual funds, is addressed in Chapter 7, by Lehmann and Timmermann. The persistence of rankings across mutual funds makes this an important issue. Lehmann and Timmermann focus in particular on methodological (econometric) questions related to the power of econometric tests in trying to assess the performance of mutual funds.

The second issue focuses on the behavior of the investors in mutual funds. How do they choose among mutual funds? This is analyzed in Chapter 8, by Zheng. She

[1] SEC. 2007. Key note address by Andrew J. Donohue, director Division of Investment Management SEC, at 2007 Mutual Fund and Investment Management Conference.

addresses several questions, including the following. To what extent do these choices depend on the past performance and fees (fee structures) of the funds? What is the role of brokers? And how do funds seek to affect investor choices and behavior?

The third issue relates to the incentives of mutual fund managers. Investing in mutual funds is in essence a delegation of investment decisions by investors to fund managers. The question then is what the incentives of fund managers are, and how can these be aligned with those of the investors? Recent scandals involving mutual funds that had given privileges to some and had hidden (high) fee structures are prominent examples of potential divergence of interests. This is the focus of Chapter 9, by Bhattacharya, Dasgupta, Guembel, and Prat. They particularly point at herding and churning behavior by fund managers, in response to ex post (reputational) incentives.

Together these chapters provide a rather comprehensive picture of the insights that the ongoing work on mutual funds has produced. They are critical though cautious about the added value of mutual funds to investors, particularly when it comes to actively managed funds. Zheng concludes that "overall, empirical findings suggest that investors on average are better off investing in a low-cost index fund than in actively managed funds." She also highlights potential agency problems between funds and investors. In this context she points out that fund managers are aware of investor behavior and choose to develop strategies accordingly. The distorting incentives of fund managers highlighted in Chapter 9 are consistent with Zheng's views.

Addressing the question of superior performance more directly, Lehmann and Timmermann are also cautious. They conclude that the lack of statistical power in evaluating relative performances across funds is to be expected. Overall, these three chapters help uncover the intricacies of the functioning of mutual funds, which have become so ubiquitous in today's financial markets.

CHAPTER 7

Performance Measurement and Evaluation

Bruce Lehmann
University of California, San Diego

Allan Timmermann
University of California, San Diego

HANDBOOK OF FINANCIAL INTERMEDIATION AND BANKING

Abstract

This chapter considers performance measurement and evaluation for managed funds. Similarities and differences—both in econometric practice and in interpretation of outcomes of empirical tests—between performance measurement and conventional asset pricing models are analyzed. We also discuss how inference on "skill" is affected when fund managers have market-timing information. Performance testing based on portfolio weights is also covered, as is recent developments in Bayesian models of performance measurement that can accommodate errors in the benchmark asset pricing model.

1. INTRODUCTION

Mutual funds are managed portfolios that putatively offer investors a number of benefits. Some of them fall under the rubric of economies of scale, such as the amortization of transactions and other costs across numerous investors. The most controversial potential benefit, however, remains the possibility that some funds can "beat the market." The lure of active management is the modern equivalent of alchemy, with the transformation of lead into gold replaced by hope that the combination of specialized insights and superior information can result in portfolios that can outperform the market. Hence, mutual fund performance evaluation—and, more generally, the evaluation of the performance of managed portfolios—is all about measuring performance to differentiate those managers who truly add value through active management from those who do not.

How would a financial economist naturally address this question? The answer lies in a basic fact that can be easily overlooked amid the hyperbole associated with the alleged benefits of active management: Mutual funds simply represent a potential increase in the menu of assets available to investors. Viewed from this perspective, it is clear which tools of modern finance should be brought to bear on performance evaluation: (1) the theory of portfolio choice and, to a lesser extent, the equilibrium asset pricing theory that follows, in part, from it and (2) the no-arbitrage approach to valuation.

Indeed, there are many similarities between the econometrics of performance measurement and that of conventional asset pricing. Jensen's alpha is just mispricing in asset pricing models, we test for their joint significance using mean-variance efficiency tests or Euler equations, benchmark portfolios are the (conditionally) mean-variance efficient portfolios implied by such models, and stochastic discount factors appear in both settings. Similarly, the distinction between predictability in performance and its converse of no persistence must often be handled with care in both settings.

The mechanical difference between the two settings lies in the asset universe: managed portfolios with given weights in the performance literature as opposed to individual securities or portfolios chosen by financial econometricians, not by portfolio managers, in the asset pricing literature. This mechanical difference is of paramount economic importance. It is the fact that regularities observed in the moments of the returns of managed portfolios are the direct consequence of explicit choices made by the portfolio manager that makes the setting so different. To be sure, corporate officers, research analysts, investors, traders, and speculators all make choices that affect the stochastic properties of individual asset and aggregate portfolio returns. However, they do not do so in the frequent, routine, and direct way that is the norm in the high-turnover world of active portfolio management. The finance literature is littered with examples of ways in which the direct impact of investment choices makes concerns like stochastic betas and the measurement of biases in alphas first-order concerns.

Managed portfolios are therefore not generic assets, which makes performance evaluation distinct from generic applications of modern portfolio theory in some dimensions. Chief among these is the question of whether active managers add value, making the premise that active managers do not add value to the natural null hypothesis. Another difference is in the kind of abilities we imagine that active managers who do add value possess: market timing ability as opposed to skill in security selection. In contrast, rejections of the null hypothesis in asset pricing theory tests are typically attributed to failures of the model. Others include the economic environment—that is, the industrial organization of the portfolio management industry—confronting managers, the need for performance measures that are objective and, thus, not investor specific, and differences in the stochastic properties of managed portfolio returns as compared with individual assets and generic passive portfolios.

The fact that managed portfolios' performance is the outcome of fund managers' explicit choices also opens up the possibility of studying these choice variables explicitly when data are available on a time series of portfolio weights. Tests for the optimality of a fund manager's choice of portfolio weights are available in these circumstances, although it is difficult to use this type of data in a meaningful way unless the manager's objective function is known. This is a problem, for example when assessing pension funds' asset liability management unless data are available not just on asset holdings but also on liabilities.

This chapter focuses on the methodological themes in the literature on performance measurement and evaluation and only references the empirical literature sparingly, chiefly to support arguments about problems with existing methods. We do not aim to provide a comprehensive survey of the empirical literature, which would call for a different chapter altogether.

The outline of the remainder of the chapter is as follows. Section 2 establishes theoretical performance benchmarks in the context of investors' marginal investment decisions, discusses sources of benchmarks, and introduces some performance measures in common use. Section 3 provides an analysis of performance measurement in the presence of market timing and time variations in the fund manager's risk exposures. As part of our analysis, we cover a range of market timing specifications that entertain different notions of the form that the market timer's information signals take. Section 4 studies performance measurement when portfolio weights are observed. Section 5 falls under the broad title of the cross section of managed portfolio returns. It covers standard econometric approaches and test statistics for detecting abnormal performance both at the level of individual funds and also for the cross section of funds or subgroups of (ranked) funds. Finally Section 6 discusses recent Bayesian contributions to the literature, and Section 7 concludes.

2. THEORETICAL BENCHMARKS

Our analysis of the measurement of the performance of managed portfolios begins with generic investors with common information and beliefs who equate the expected marginal cost of investing (in utility terms) with expected marginal benefits. Without being specific about where it comes from, assume that an arbitrary investor's indirect utility of wealth, W_t, is given by $V(W_t, \mathbf{x}_t)$, where $\mathbf{x}_t$ is a generic state vector that might include other variables (including choice variables) that impinge on the investor's asset allocation decision, permitting utility to be state dependent and nonseparable. Let p_{it} and d_{it} be the price and dividend on the ith asset (or mutual fund), respectively, while the corresponding gross rate of return is given by $R_{it+1} = (p_{it+1} + d_{it+1})/p_{it}$. The marginal conditions for this investor are given by

$$E\left[\frac{V'(W_{t+1}, \mathbf{x}_{t+1})}{V'(W_t, \mathbf{x}_t)} R_{it+1} | I_t\right] \equiv E[m_{t+1} R_{it+1} | I_t] = 1, \tag{1}$$

where I_t is information available to the investor at time t. We assume there is a riskless asset with return R_{ft+1} (known at time t) and so $E[m_{t+1}|I_t] = R_{ft+1}^{-1}$.

The investment decisions of any investor who maximizes expected utility can be characterized by a marginal decision of this form. The denominator is given by $V'(W_t, \mathbf{x}_t)p_{it}$—the ex post cost in utility terms of investing a little more in asset i, and the numerator is given by $V'(W_{t+1}, \mathbf{x}_{t+1})(p_{it+1} + d_{it+1})$, the ex post marginal benefit from making this incremental investment. Setting their expected ratio to 1 ensures that the marginal benefits and costs of investing are equated. Note that nothing in this analysis relies on special assumptions about investor preferences or about market completeness.

Now consider the population projection of the intertemporal marginal rate of substitution of this investor $m_{t+1} = V'(W_{t+1}, \mathbf{x}_{t+1})/V'(W_t, \mathbf{x}_t)$ on the $N-$vector of returns $\mathbf{R}_{t+1}$ of risky assets with returns that are not perfectly correlated:

$$\begin{aligned} m_{t+1} &= \delta_{0t} + \delta_t' \mathbf{R}_{t+1} + \varepsilon_{mt+1} \\ &= R_{ft+1}^{-1} + \delta_t'(\mathbf{R}_{t+1} - E[\mathbf{R}_{t+1}|I_t]) + \varepsilon_{mt+1} \\ &= R_{ft+1}^{-1} + \text{Cov}(\mathbf{R}_{t+1}, m_{t+1}|I_t)' \text{Var}(\mathbf{R}_{t+1}|I_t)^{-1}(\mathbf{R}_{t+1} - E[\mathbf{R}_{t+1}|I_t]) + \varepsilon_{mt+1}, \end{aligned} \tag{2}$$

where, assuming $\boldsymbol{\iota}$ is an $N \times 1$ vector of 1s,

$$\begin{aligned} \delta_t &= \text{Var}(\mathbf{R}_{t+1}|I_t)^{-1}\text{Cov}(\mathbf{R}_{t+1}, m_{t+1}|I_t) \\ &= \text{Var}(\mathbf{R}_{t+1}|I_t)^{-1}(E[\mathbf{R}_{t+1} m_{t+1}|I_t] - E[\mathbf{R}_{t+1}|I_t]E[m_{t+1}|I_t]) \\ &= \text{Var}(\mathbf{R}_{t+1}|I_t)^{-1}(\boldsymbol{\iota} - E[\mathbf{R}_{t+1}|I_t]R_{ft+1}^{-1}). \end{aligned} \tag{3}$$

It is convenient to transform δ_t into portfolio weights via $\omega_{\delta t} = \delta_t/\delta_t'\iota$, with associated returns $R_{\delta t+1} = \omega_{\delta t}'\mathbf{R}_{t+1}$. In terms of the (conditional) mean/variance efficient set, the weights of portfolio δ are given by

$$\begin{aligned}
\omega_{\delta t} &= \frac{\operatorname{Var}(\mathbf{R}_{t+1}|I_t)^{-1}(\iota - E[\mathbf{R}_{t+1}|I_t]R_{ft+1}^{-1})}{\iota'\operatorname{Var}(\mathbf{R}_{t+1}|I_t)^{-1}(\iota - E[\mathbf{R}_{t+1}|I_t]R_{ft+1}^{-1})} \\
&= \frac{\operatorname{Var}(\mathbf{R}_{t+1}|I_t)^{-1}[\iota - E(\mathbf{R}_{t+1}|I_t)R_{ft+1}^{-1}]}{(c_t - bR_{ft+1}^{-1})} \\
&= \frac{R_{ft+1}}{R_{ft+1} - E[R_{0t+1}|I_t]}\omega_{0t} - \frac{E[R_{0t+1}|I_t]}{R_{ft+1} - E[R_{0t+1}|I_t]}\omega_{st} \\
&= \omega_{0t} + \frac{E(R_{0t+1}|I_t)}{E(R_{0t+1}|I_t) - R_{ft+1}}(\omega_{st} - \omega_{0t}),
\end{aligned} \tag{4}$$

where $\omega_{0t} = \operatorname{Var}(\mathbf{R}_{t+1}|I_t)^{-1}\iota/c_t$ is the vector of portfolio weights of the conditional minimum variance portfolio, R_{0t+1} is the corresponding minimum variance portfolio return, $c_t = \iota'\operatorname{Var}(\mathbf{R}_{t+1}|I_t)^{-1}\iota$, $b_t = \iota'\operatorname{Var}(\mathbf{R}_{t+1}|I_t)^{-1}E(\mathbf{R}_{t+1}|I_t)R_{ft+1}^{-1}$, and $\omega_{st} = \operatorname{Var}(\mathbf{R}_{t+1}|I_t)^{-1}E(\mathbf{R}_{t+1}|I_t)/b_t$ is the weight vector for the maximum squared Sharpe ratio portfolio.

None of the variables in this expression for the conditional regression coefficients δ_t are investor specific. All investors who share common beliefs about the conditional mean vector and covariance matrix of the N asset returns and who are on the margin with respect to these N assets will agree on the values of the elements of δ_t, irrespective of their preferences, other traded and nontraded asset holdings, or any other aspect of their economic environment. Put differently, portfolio δ is the optimal portfolio of these N assets for hedging fluctuations in the intertemporal marginal rates of substitution of any marginal investor. Similarly, all investors who are marginal with respect to these N assets will perceive that expected returns satisfy

$$E[\mathbf{R}_{t+1} - \iota R_{ft+1}|I_t] = \beta_{\delta t}E[\mathbf{R}_{\delta t+1} - \iota R_{ft+1}|I_t], \tag{5}$$

since δ is a conditionally mean-variance efficient portfolio.[1]

There is another way to arrive at the same benchmark portfolios: the application of the no-arbitrage approach to the valuation of risky assets. Once again, begin with N risky assets with imperfectly correlated returns. Asset pricing based on the absence of arbitrage typically involves three assumptions in addition to the definition of an

[1] What is lost in the passage from the intertemporal marginal rate of substitution to portfolio δ? The answer is simple: While the realizations of m_{t+1} are strictly positive since it is a ratio of marginal utilities, the returns of portfolio δ need not be strictly positive since its weights need not be positive (i.e., portfolio δ might have short positions). As a practical matter, the benchmark portfolios used in practice seldom have short positions.

arbitrage opportunity:[2] (1) Investors perceive a deterministic mapping between end-of-period asset payoffs and underlying states of nature s; (2) agreement on the possible; and (3) the perfect-markets assumption. The first condition is met almost by construction if investors identify states with the array of all possible payoff patterns. The second asserts that no investor thinks any state is impossible since such an investor would be willing to sell an infinite number of claims that pay off in that state. The perfect markets—that is, the absence of taxes, transactions costs, indivisibilities, short sales restrictions, or other impediments to free trade—is problematic since it is obviously impossible to sell managed portfolios short to create zero-net-investment portfolios.

Fortunately, there is an alternative to the absence of short sale constraints that eliminates this concern. Any change in the weights of a portfolio that leaves its cost unchanged is a zero-net-investment portfolio. Hence, arbitrage reasoning can be used when there are investors who are long the assets under consideration. All that is required to implement the no-arbitrage approach to valuation is the existence of investors with long positions in each asset who can costlessly make marginal changes in existing positions. In unfettered markets, the substitution possibilities of a few investors can replace the marginal decisions of many when the few actively seek arbitrage profits in this asset menu.

It is now a simple matter to get from these assumptions to portfolio δ. The absence of arbitrage coupled with some mild regularity conditions (such as investors prefer more to less) when there is a continuum of possible states implies the existence of strictly positive state prices, not necessarily unique, that price the N assets under consideration as in

$$p_{it} = \int \psi_{t+1}(s)\,[p_{it+1}(s) + d_{it+1}(s)]\,ds, \tag{6}$$

where s indexes states and $\psi_{t+1}(s)$ is the (not necessarily unique) price at time t of a claim that pays one dollar if state s occurs at time $t+1$ and zero otherwise. Letting $\pi_{t+1}(s)$ denote the (conditional) probability at time t that state s will occur at time $t+1$, this expression may be rewritten as

$$\begin{aligned} p_{it} &= \int \pi(s)\frac{\psi_{t+1}(s)}{\pi_{t+1}(s)}\,[p_{it+1}(s) + d_{it+1}(s)]\,ds \\ &\equiv \int \pi_{t+1}(s)m_{t+1}(s)\,[p_{it+1}(s) + d_{it+1}(s)]\,ds \qquad (7) \\ &\equiv E[m_{t+1}(p_{it+1} + d_{it+1})|I_t], \end{aligned}$$

where $m_{t+1}(s) = \psi(s)/\pi(s)$ is a strictly positive random variable—that is, both state prices and probabilities are strictly positive—with realizations given by state prices per unit probability, which is termed a *stochastic discount factor* in the literature. All that remains is to project any stochastic discount factor m_{t+1} that reflects common beliefs $\pi_{t+1}(s)$—where the word *any* reflects the fact that state prices need not be unique—onto the returns of the N assets to recover portfolio δ.

[2]We have ignored the technical requirement that there be at least one asset with positive value in each state because managed portfolios and, for that matter, most traded securities are limited-liability assets.

As was already noted, there is at least one reason for taking this route: to make it clear that the existence of portfolio δ does not require all investors to be on the margin with respect to these N assets. Many, even most, investors may be inframarginal, but some investors must be (implicitly) making marginal decisions in these assets for this reasoning to apply. Chen and Knez (1996) reach the same conclusion in their analysis of arbitrage-free performance measures.[3]

These considerations make portfolio δ a natural candidate for being the benchmark portfolio against which investment performance should be measured for investors who are skeptical regarding the prospects for active management. It is appropriate for skeptics precisely because managed portfolios are given zero weight in portfolio δ. Put differently, this portfolio can be used to answer the question of whether such investors should take small positions in a given managed portfolio.[4] As noted earlier, it is an objective measure, in that investors with common beliefs about the conditional mean vector and covariance matrix will agree on the composition of δ. Thus, we have identified a reasonable candidate benchmark portfolio for performance measurement.

What benchmark portfolio is appropriate for investors who are not skeptical about the existence of superior managers? One answer lies in an observation made earlier: Such investors would naturally think that managed portfolios represent a nontrivial enlargement of the asset menu. That is, portfolio δ would change in its composition because it would place nonzero weight on managed portfolios if they truly added value by improving investors' ability to hedge against fluctuations in their intertemporal marginal rate of substitution. Like the managed-portfolio-free version of δ, it is an objective measure for investors who share common beliefs about conditional means, variances, and covariances of returns in this enlarged asset menu.

2.1. Sources of Benchmarks

There is an apparent logical conundrum here: It would seem obvious that managed portfolios either do or do not improve the investment opportunities available to investors. The answer, of course, is that it is difficult in practice to estimate the weights of portfolio δ with any precision. The required inputs are the conditional mean vector $E[\mathbf{R}_{t+1}|I_t]$ and the conditional covariance matrix $\mathrm{Var}(\mathbf{R}_{t+1}|I_t)$ of these N assets. Unconditional mean stock returns cannot be estimated with precision due to the volatility of long-lived asset returns, and the estimation of conditional means adds further complications.

[3]More precisely, they search for performance measures that satisfy four desiderata: (1) The performance of any portfolio that can be replicated by a passively managed portfolio with weights based only on public information should be zero; (2) the measure should be linear (i.e., the performance of a linear combination of portfolios should be the linear combination of the individual portfolio measures); (3) it should be continuous (i.e., portfolios with similar returns state by state should have similar performance measures); and (4) it should be nontrivial and assign a nonzero value—that is, a positive price—to any traded security. They show that these four conditions are equivalent to the absence of arbitrage and the concomitant existence of state prices, or, equivalently, strictly positive stochastic discount factors.

[4]This point is not quite right as stated because investors can only make marginal changes in one direction when they cannot sell managed portfolios short. The statement is correct once one factors in the existence of an investor who is long the fund in question and can make marginal changes in both directions.

Unconditional return variances and covariances are measured with greater precision, but the curse of dimensionality associated with the estimation of the inverse of the conditional covariance matrix limits asset menus to 10 or 20 assets at most—far fewer than the number of securities in typical managed portfolios.

This is one reason why benchmark portfolios are frequently specified in advance according to an asset pricing theory. In particular, most asset pricing theories imply that intertemporal marginal rates of substitution are linear combinations of particular portfolios. The Sharpe–Lintner–Mossin critical asset pricing model (CAPM) implies that m_{t+1} is linear in the return of the market portfolio of all risky assets. In the consumption CAPM, the single index is the portfolio with returns that are maximally correlated with aggregate consumption growth, sometimes raised to some power. Other asset pricing models imply that m_{t+1} is linear in the returns of other portfolios. In the CAPM with nontraded assets, the market portfolio is augmented with the portfolio of traded assets with returns that are maximally correlated with nontraded-asset returns. The indices in the intertemporal CAPM are the market portfolio plus portfolios with returns that are maximally correlated with the state variables presumed to drive changes in the investment opportunity set. The arbitrage pricing theory (APT) also specifies that m_{t+1} is (approximately) linear in the returns of several portfolios, well-diversified portfolios that are presumed to account for the bulk of the (perhaps conditional) covariation among asset returns.

In practice, chosen benchmarks typically reflect the empirical state of asset pricing theory and constraints on available data. For example, we do not observe the returns of "all risky assets"—that is, aggregate wealth—but stock market wealth in the form of the S&P 500 and the CRSP value-weighted index is observable and, at one time, appeared to price most assets pretty well. Before that, the single index market model was used to justify using the CRSP equally weighted index as a market proxy, while the APT motivates the use of multiple well-diversified portfolios. The empirical success of models like the three-factor Fama–French model a market proxy along with size and market-to-book portfolios as benchmarks, and, more recently, the putatively anomalous returns to momentum portfolios, have been added to the mix as a fourth factor.

Irrespective of the formal justification, such benchmarks take the form of a weighted average of returns on a set of factors f_{kt+1}:

$$m_{t+1} = \sum_{k=1}^{K} \omega_{kt} f_{kt+1}, \tag{8}$$

where this relation differs from the projection in Eq. (2) in having no error term. That is, the stochastic discount factor is an exact linear combination of observables. In the case of the multifactor benchmarks, the weights are usually treated as unknowns to be estimated, as is the case with portfolio δ, save for the fact that there are only K weights to be estimated in this case. This circumstance arises because most multifactor models, both the APT and the ad hoc models like the Fama–French model, do not specify the values of risk premiums, which are intimately related to the weights ω_{kt}. In contrast, equilibrium models do typically specify the relevant risk premiums and, implicitly, the weights

ω_{kt}. For example, letting R_{mt+1} be the return on the market portfolio, the stochastic discount factor in the CAPM is given by:

$$m_{t+1} = \frac{1 - E[R_{mt+1} - R_{ft+1}|I_t][R_{mt+1} - E(R_{mt+1}|I_t)]}{R_{ft+1}}. \quad (9)$$

As noted by Dybvig and Ingersoll (1982), the CAPM implicitly places constraints on the sample space of market returns R_{mt+1}: The stochastic discount factor must be positive, and so

$$E[R_{mt+1} - R_{ft+1}|I_t][R_{mt+1} - E(R_{mt+1}|I_t) < 1$$

must hold for all dates and states.

Another source of benchmark portfolios arises from specification of determinants of the betas computed with respect to portfolio δ. At various times, security characteristics, such as firm value, the ratio of market to book equity, price-earnings and price-dividend ratios, momentum variables, and alternative leverage ratios, have been thought of as cross-sectional determinants of expected stock returns. To see how a priori specification of the determinants of betas facilitates the identification of benchmark portfolios, let $\mathbf{Z}_t$ denote an $N \times M$ matrix, the rows of which consist of vectors z_{it} composed of attributes of the ith security. Consider the population projection of $\beta_{\delta t}$ on $\mathbf{Z}_t$ in the cross section

$$\beta_{\delta t} = \mathbf{Z}_t \mathbf{\Pi}_{\delta t} + \eta_{\delta t}, \quad (10)$$

and substitute this projection into the return equation

$$\begin{aligned} \mathbf{R}_{t+1} - \iota R_{ft+1} &= \beta_{\delta t}(\mathbf{R}_{\delta t+1} - \iota R_{ft+1}) + \epsilon_{\delta t+1} \\ &= (\mathbf{Z}_t \mathbf{\Pi}_{\delta t} + \eta_{\delta t})(\mathbf{R}_{\delta t+1} - \iota R_{ft+1}) + \epsilon_{\delta t+1} \\ &= \mathbf{Z}_t \lambda_{zt+1} + \upsilon_{t+1}, \end{aligned} \quad (11)$$

where $\lambda_{zt+1} = \mathbf{\Pi}_{\delta t}(\mathbf{R}_{\delta t+1} - \iota R_{ft+1})$ and $\upsilon_{t+1} = \eta_{\delta t}(\mathbf{R}_{\delta t+1} - \iota R_{ft+1}) + \epsilon_{\delta t+1}$. Since $\mathbf{Z}_t$ is orthogonal to $\eta_{\delta t}$ by construction, $\mathbf{Z}_t$ will be orthogonal to $\eta_{\delta t}(\mathbf{R}_{\delta t+1} - \iota R_{ft+1})$ if the elements of $\eta_{\delta t}$ are uncorrelated with the risk premium $E[\mathbf{R}_{\delta t+1} - \iota R_{ft+1}|I_t]$. Hence, the returns of portfolio δ are a linear combination of returns to security characteristics that can be estimated via cross-sectional regression of $\mathbf{R}_{t+1} - \iota R_{ft+1}$ on $\mathbf{Z}_t$ when the risk premium of portfolio δ is uncorrelated with the unmodeled changes in betas computed with respect to it.

2.2. A First Pass at Performance Measurement

What does all of this have to do with portfolio performance measurement? To answer this, consider a portfolio manager who manages a portfolio called p comprised of these N assets. The manager uses information I_{pt} to choose the weights ω_{pt}. Suppose that the information available to the manager is contained in the investor's information set I_t (i.e., $I_{pt} \subseteq I_t$). Would an investor whose portfolio holdings have been chosen to satisfy the marginal conditions $E[m_{t+1}R_{it+1}|I_t] = 1$ find it desirable to divert some of the investment in the original N assets to this managed portfolio? The answer is clearly no: The investor could have chosen ω_{pt} as part of the original portfolio because $\omega_{pt} \in I_{pt} \subseteq I_t$, since

$$E[m_{t+1}R_{pt+1}|I_t] = E[m_{t+1}\omega'_{pt}\mathbf{R}_{t+1}|I_t] = \omega'_{pt}E[m_{t+1}\mathbf{R}_{t+1}|I_t] = 1. \tag{12}$$

Now consider the case in which the manager has access to information not available to the investor so that $w_{pt} \notin I_{pt} \subseteq I_t$. In this case, the Euler equation need not hold—that is, $E[m_{t+1}R_{pt+1}|I_t]$ need not equal 1—if the information is available to investors only through the managed portfolio p.

In particular, consider the (conditional) population projection of $R_{pt+1} - R_{ft+1}$ on $R_{\delta t+1} - R_{ft+1}$ and a constant:

$$R_{pt+1} - R_{ft+1} = \alpha_{pt} + \beta_{pt}(R_{\delta t+1} - R_{ft+1}) + \varepsilon_{pt+1}, \tag{13}$$

where α_{pt} and β_{pt} are conditioned on I_t, the information available to the investor and not the potentially richer information in the hands of the portfolio manager. Now consider the Euler equation for p evaluated at the intertemporal marginal rate of substitution (or, equivalently, the stochastic discount factor) after p has been added to the asset menu:

$$\begin{aligned} 0 &= E[m_{t+1}(R_{pt+1} - R_{ft+1})|I_t] = E[m_{t+1}(\alpha_{pt} + \beta_{pt}(R_{\delta t+1} - R_{ft+1}) + \varepsilon_{pt+1})|I_t] \\ &= R^{-1}_{ft+1}\alpha_{pt} + E[m_{t+1}\varepsilon_{pt+1}|I_t], \end{aligned} \tag{14}$$

which implies that

$$\alpha_{pt} = -R_{ft+1}E[m_{t+1}\varepsilon_{pt+1}|I_t]. \tag{15}$$

Large values of α_{pt} imply correspondingly large values of $E[m_{t+1}\varepsilon_{pt+1}|I_t]$, suggesting correspondingly large gains from adding p to the asset menu in terms of hedging fluctuations in marginal utilities. Put differently, δ_{pt}, the coefficient on R_{pt+1} from the (conditional) population regression of m_{t+1} on $\mathbf{R}_{t+1}$ and R_{pt+1}, is given by

$$\delta_{pt} = \frac{E[\varepsilon_{mt+1}\varepsilon_{pt+1}|I_t]}{\mathrm{Var}(\varepsilon_{pt+1}|I_t)} = \frac{E[m_{t+1}\varepsilon_{pt+1}|I_t]}{\mathrm{Var}(\varepsilon_{pt+1}|I_t)} = -\frac{\alpha_{pt}}{R_{ft+1}\mathrm{Var}(\varepsilon_{pt+1}|I_t)} \tag{16}$$

from the usual omitted-variables formula. Large values of δ_{pt} also imply better marginal utility hedging, and δ_{pt} will be nonzero if and only if α_{pt} is nonzero.

The regression intercept α_{pt} is called the *conditional Jensen measure* in the performance evaluation literature, the unconditional version of which was introduced in Jensen (1968, 1969).[5] It has a simple interpretation as the return on a particular zero-net-investment portfolio: that obtained by purchasing one dollar of portfolio p and financing

[5]Interestingly, Jensen did not motivate the use of the CRSP equally weighted portfolio solely by reference to the CAPM. He coupled this justification with the observation that its returns would approximate well the returns on aggregate wealth if returns follow a single-factor model, implicitly making his reasoning a progenitor of one-factor versions of the equilibrium APT.

this acquisition by borrowing $1-\beta_{pt}$ dollars at the riskless rate and by selling β_{pt} dollars of portfolio δ short. The Sharpe ratio of this portfolio is

$$\frac{\alpha_{pt}}{\sqrt{\text{Var}(\varepsilon_{pt+1}|I_t)}},$$

which is proportional to the t-statistic for the difference of α_{pt} from zero (the Sharpe ratio of any zero-net-investment portfolio is its expected payoff scaled by the standard deviation of its payoff). This Sharpe ratio is called the Treynor–Black (1973) appraisal ratio.

This role for the regression intercept also suggests that performance evaluation via Jensen measures is fraught with hazard. A nonzero value of α_{pt} could also reflect benchmark error. That is, α_{pt} would typically be nonzero if portfolio δ is not (conditionally) mean-variance efficient even if the portfolio manager has no superior information and skill. Hence, it is often difficult to tell if one is learning about the quality of the manager or the quality of the benchmark when examining Jensen regressions. This is why the strictly correct interpretation of nonzero intercepts is that the mean-variance tradeoff based on portfolio δ and the riskless asset can be improved by augmenting the asset menu to include portfolio p as well, not that the managed portfolio outperforms the benchmark.

As noted earlier, portfolio δ might include or exclude portfolio p. The exclusion of portfolio p from the asset menu corresponds to a thought experiment in which hypothetical investors with no investment in this portfolio are using portfolio δ to evaluate the consequences of adding a small amount of portfolio p to the asset menu. Similarly, the inclusion of portfolio p in the asset menu used to construct portfolio δ corresponds to a thought experiment in which hypothetical investors who have a position in portfolio p are assessing whether they have invested the correct amount in it. In the language of hypothesis testing, the former approach corresponds to a Lagrange multiplier test of the null hypothesis of no abnormal performance, while the latter corresponds to a Wald test when testing the hypothesis that the weight on p should be zero. The pervasive adoption of the former approach in the performance evaluation literature probably reflects general skepticism in the profession on the economic value of active management. It is as though we believe that asset prices are set in an efficient market but that the market for active managers who earn abnormal fees is inefficient.

Finally, the Sharpe ratio to which we referred earlier represents a nonbenchmark-based approach to performance measurement. In its conditional form, the Sharpe ratio of portfolio p is given by

$$\frac{E[R_{pt+1} - R_{ft+1}|I_t]}{\sqrt{\text{Var}[R_{pt+1}|I_t]}},$$

which is the conditional mean return divided by its standard deviation of a dollar invested in portfolio p that is financed by borrowing a dollar at the riskless rate. The Sharpe ratio got its start in Sharpe (1966) as a simple and intuitive measure of how far a given portfolio was from the mean/variance efficient frontier.

Over time, it has become clear that the measurement of the distance between a given portfolio and the mean/variance efficient frontier is quite a bit more subtle, involving Jensen's alpha in an unexpected way (see, e.g., Jobson and Korkie 1982 and Gibbons, Ross, and Shanken 1989). We noted earlier that α_{pt} is the expected return of a portfolio that is long one dollar of portfolio p and short β_{pt} dollars of portfolio δ and $1-\beta_{pt}$ dollars of the riskless asset, which makes it a costless and zero-beta portfolio. As such, it is a means to get to the mean/variance efficient frontier through a suitable combination of the N given assets, the riskless asset, and this costless zero-beta portfolio. This reasoning extends to M additional managed portfolios in a straightforward way.

This has left the Sharpe ratio in a sort of intellectual limbo. The simple intuition has survived, and the practitioner literature and, perhaps more importantly, performance measurement in practice often refers to the Sharpe ratio. It has fallen out of fashion in the academic literature since we now understand its deficiencies much better. It is simply not the case that managed portfolio A is better than B if its Sharpe ratio is higher, because the distance to the frontier depends on portfolio alphas and residual variances and covariances, not on the mean and variance of overall portfolio returns. Benchmark-based performance measurement is the focus of the academic literature, and practitioners who use Sharpe ratios generally do so in conjunction with Jensen alphas, often under the rubric of tracking error.

3. PERFORMANCE MEASUREMENT AND MARKET TIMING

The conditional Jensen regression (13) differs from the original in Jensen (1968, 1969) in only two details: the Jensen alpha α_{pt} and portfolio beta β_{pt} are conditional and not unconditional moments, and the benchmark portfolio is δ and not "the market portfolio of all risky assets" underlying the CAPM. There is an important commonality with the original since it is natural to decompose returns into two components, that related to benchmark or market returns—that is, $\beta_{pt}(R_{\delta t+1} - R_{ft+1})$—and that unrelated to them—that is, $\alpha_{pt} + \varepsilon_{pt+1}$. By analogy with the older parlance, we can term the first component the return to market timing, and, under this interpretation, the second component must reflect the rewards to security selection. The distinction between market timing and security selection permeates both the academic and practitioner literatures on performance attribution and evaluation.

The impact of real or imagined market timing ability on performance measurement depends on whether the return-generating process experiences time variation. That is, the benchmark beta β_{pt} might change because of time variation in individual security betas and not because the manager is attempting to time the market. Similarly, the expected returns of portfolio p might also change if $E[R_{\delta t+1} - R_{ft+1}|I_t]$ varied over time. Moreover, the manager might choose to make portfolio betas shift along with changes in benchmark portfolio volatility or other higher moments. Accordingly, we must distinguish between the case in which excess benchmark returns are serially independent from the perspective of uninformed portfolio managers and those in which there is serial dependence (predictability) based on public information. We deal with these cases in turn, and we shall do so often in what follows.

Accordingly, consider first the case in which the manager of portfolio p does not attempt to time the market and the conditional benchmark risk premium is time invariant—that is,

$$E[R_{\delta t+1} - R_{ft+1}|I_t] = E[R_{\delta t+1} - R_{ft+1}].$$

Since the fund has a constant target beta β_p, the original unconditional Jensen regression,

$$R_{pt+1} - R_{ft+1} = \alpha_p + \beta_p(R_{\delta t+1} - R_{ft+1}) + \epsilon_{pt+1}, \tag{17}$$

is related to that from the conditional Jensen regression (13) via

$$\epsilon_{pt+1} = \alpha_{pt} - \alpha_p + \varepsilon_{pt+1}, \tag{18}$$

where $\alpha_p \equiv E[\alpha_{pt}]$ is the unconditional Jensen performance measure. This is a perfectly well-posed regression with potentially serially correlated and heteroskedastic disturbances, although there are economic settings in which market efficiency requires $\alpha_{pt} - \alpha_p$ to be unpredictable. Hence, one can estimate α_p and β_p consistently in these circumstances, and so the Jensen measure correctly measures the rewards to security selection.

Unsuccessful market timing efforts complicate performance attribution, but not performance measurement per se, when expected excess benchmark returns are constant. If the manager shifts betas but has no market timing ability, the composite error ϵ_{pt+1} in the population is now given by

$$\epsilon_{pt+1} = \alpha_{pt} - \alpha_p + (\beta_{pt} - \beta_p)(R_{\delta t+1} - R_{ft+1}) + \varepsilon_{pt+1}, \tag{19}$$

which has unconditional mean zero because

$$\begin{aligned} E[\epsilon_{pt+1}] &= E[\alpha_{pt} - \alpha_p + (\beta_{pt} - \beta_p)(R_{\delta t+1} - R_{ft+1}) + \varepsilon_{pt+1}] \\ &= E[(\beta_{pt} - \beta_p)(R_{\delta t+1} - R_{ft+1})] \\ &= \mathrm{Cov}[\beta_{pt}, R_{\delta t+1} - R_{ft+1}] \end{aligned} \tag{20}$$

is equal to zero unless the manager has market timing ability. Once again, the unconditional Jensen regression will yield consistent estimates of the unconditional beta β_p and Jensen measure α_p.[6] The residual, however, is no longer solely a reflection of the security selection component of returns.

[6]The fact that the residual is conditionally heteroskedastic and, perhaps, serially correlated due to the $\alpha_{pt} - \alpha_p$ and $(\beta_{pt} - \beta_p)(R_{\delta t+1} - R_{ft+1})$ terms suggests that some structure might be placed on their stochastic properties to draw inferences about their behavior. An example of this sort is presented in the next section.

Problems crop up when managers engage in efforts to time the market and they are successful (on average) in doing so. Once again, the unconditional Jensen measure is given by (17):

$$\begin{aligned}\alpha_p &= E[R_{pt+1} - R_{ft+1} - \beta_p(R_{\delta t+1} - R_{ft+1})] \\ &= E[\alpha_{pt} + (\beta_{pt} - \beta_p)(R_{\delta t+1} - R_{ft+1}) + \varepsilon_{pt+1}] \\ &= E[\alpha_{pt}] + \mathrm{Cov}[\beta_{pt}, R_{\delta t+1} - R_{ft+1}].\end{aligned}$$

So the sign and magnitude of the unconditional alpha depend on the way in which the manager exploits market timing ability. The coefficient α_p will measure the reward to security selection only if the manager uses this skill to give the portfolio a constant beta, in which case ϵ_{pt+1} correctly measures the return to security selection.

Otherwise, the Jensen measure will reflect both market timing and security selection ability when managers are successful market timers, thus breaking the clean decomposition of returns into security selection and market timing. The Jensen alpha will be positive if the manager uses market timing to improve portfolio performance—that is, to have a higher expected return than what can be gained solely from security selection ability—by setting

$$\mathrm{Cov}[\beta_{pt}, R_{\delta t+1} - R_{ft+1}] > 0.$$

But the Jensen measure alone cannot be used to decompose performance into market timing and security selection components. Similarly, market timing efforts can yield a negative Jensen alpha when the manager tries to make the fund countercyclical by setting

$$\mathrm{Cov}[\beta_{pt}, R_{\delta t+1} - R_{ft+1}] < 0.$$

This last possibility is not a pathological special case: Managers with market timing ability who minimize portfolio variance for a given level of unconditional expected excess returns will tend to have portfolio betas that are negatively correlated with benchmark risk premiums. The observation that a negative estimate of Jensen's alpha can result from market timing skills has been made by, inter alia, Jensen (1972), Admati and Ross (1985), and Dybvig and Ross (1985).

Performance measurement and attribution is even more complicated when there is serial dependence in returns from the perspective of managers without market timing ability. The reason is obvious: Such managers can make their betas dependent on conditional expected excess benchmark returns. That is, managed portfolios can have time-varying expected returns and betas conditional on public information, not just private information. In particular, $\mathrm{Cov}[\beta_{pt}, R_{\delta t+1} - R_{ft+1}]$ need not be zero even in the absence of market timing ability since

$$\begin{aligned}\mathrm{Cov}[\beta_{pt}, R_{\delta t+1} - R_{ft+1}] &= E[(\beta_{pt} - \beta_p)[(R_{\delta t+1} - R_{ft+1}) - E(R_{\delta t+1} - R_{ft+1}|I_t)]] \\ &\quad + E[(\beta_{pt} - \beta_p)[E(R_{\delta t+1} - R_{ft+1}|I_t) - E(R_{\delta t+1} - R_{ft+1})]] \\ &= \mathrm{Cov}[\beta_{pt}, R_{\delta t+1} - R_{ft+1}|I_t] + \mathrm{Cov}[\beta_{pt}, E(R_{\delta t+1} - R_{ft+1}|I_t)]\end{aligned} \tag{21}$$

can be nonzero in the presence of both market timing ability, which makes the first term nonzero, and portfolio betas that are correlated with shifts in the benchmark risk premium, which makes the second term nonzero. Once again, there is no simple decomposition of portfolio returns into security selection and market timing components based on managed portfolio returns alone when returns are predictable on the basis of public information.

Successful market timing and, to a lesser extent, serial dependence in returns engenders more than just problems with the measurement of security selection and market timing ability per se. First, the distinction between conditional and unconditional moments is a subtle and important one. Successful market timers may produce portfolios with superior conditional risk/reward ratios that appear to be inferior when viewed unconditionally. After all, informed managers will of necessity substantially alter the composition of their portfolios when their information warrants doing so, while their uninformed counterparts are staying the course, with the result that the return of the actively managed portfolio appears to be more volatile to the uninformed eye. Reaction to public information that changes the conditional mean and covariance structure of returns can do so as well. Second, this volatility created by successful active management makes for decidedly nonnormal returns. The beta of a successful market timer will be correlated with the subsequent benchmark return. Even if benchmark returns are normally distributed, the product of the benchmark return and the beta with which it is correlated will not be normally distributed. In some of the models in the next section, benchmark returns are normally distributed and betas are linear in benchmark returns, resulting in managed portfolio returns that are the sum of normally distributed and chi squared distributed terms. The latter are skewed to the right and bounded from below. For both kinds of reasons, portfolio means and variances are not "sufficient statistics" for the return distributions produced by the portfolio manager.

3.1. Alternative Models of Market Timing

Since market timing complicates performance measurement and attribution, it is perhaps unsurprising that methods for dealing with it have been one of the main preoccupations of the literature. These come in two basic flavors: simple modifications of the Jensen regression to deal with successful market timing, and the time-varying expected returns and models in which signals to informed managers are drawn from analytically convenient distributions. We discuss these issues in turn.

As it happens, it is possible to improve on the Jensen regression in a very simple way. Treynor and Mazuy (1966) pointed to an adjustment to deal with potential market timing ability by asking a simple question: When will market timing be most profitable relative to a benchmark? Their answer was equally simple: Market timers will profit both when returns are large and positive and when they are large and negative if they increase betas when they expect the market to rise and shrink or choose negative betas when they expect the market to fall. Since squared returns will be large in both circumstances, modifying the Jensen regression to include squared benchmark returns can facilitate the measurement of both market timing and security selection ability.

Accordingly, consider the Treynor–Mazuy quadratic regression:

$$R_{pt+1} - R_{ft+1} = a_p + b_{0p}(R_{\delta t+1} - R_{ft+1}) + b_{1p}(R_{\delta t+1} - R_{ft+1})^2 + \zeta_{pt+1},$$

and suppose that the manager has a constant unconditional beta $\overline{\beta}_p$, so $\beta_{pt} = \overline{\beta}_p + \xi_{\beta_{pt}}$ is a choice variable for the manager and not the conditional beta based on public information as in Eq. (13).[7] Substitution of this variant of the conditional Jensen regression into the normal equations for the quadratic regression reveals that the unconditional projection coefficients b_{0p} and b_{1p} are given by

$$\begin{aligned}
\begin{pmatrix} b_{0p} \\ b_{1p} \end{pmatrix} &= \left[\mathrm{Var}\begin{pmatrix} R_{\delta t+1} - R_{ft+1} \\ (R_{\delta t+1} - R_{ft+1})^2 \end{pmatrix}\right]^{-1} \mathrm{Cov}\left[R_{pt+1} - R_{ft+1}, \begin{pmatrix} R_{\delta t+1} - R_{ft+1} \\ (R_{\delta t+1} - R_{ft+1})^2 \end{pmatrix}\right] \\
&= \begin{pmatrix} \overline{\beta}_p \\ 0 \end{pmatrix} + \frac{1}{\sigma_\delta^2 \sigma_{4\delta} - \sigma_{3\delta}^2} \begin{pmatrix} \sigma_{4\delta} & -\sigma_{3\delta} \\ -\sigma_{3\delta} & \sigma_\delta^2 \end{pmatrix} \\
&\quad \times \begin{pmatrix} \mathrm{Cov}[\xi_{\beta_{pt}}, (R_{\delta t+1} - R_{ft+1})^2] + \mathrm{Cov}[\alpha_{pt}, R_{\delta t+1} - R_{ft+1}] \\ \mathrm{Cov}[\xi_{\beta_{pt}}, (R_{\delta t+1} - R_{ft+1})^3] + \mathrm{Cov}[\alpha_{pt}, (R_{\delta t+1} - R_{ft+1})^2] \end{pmatrix} \\
&\equiv \begin{pmatrix} \overline{\beta}_p \\ 0 \end{pmatrix} + \begin{pmatrix} \gamma_{0p} \\ \gamma_{1p} \end{pmatrix},
\end{aligned} \tag{22}$$

where $\sigma_{3\delta}$ and $\sigma_{4\delta}$ are the unconditional skewness and kurtosis of excess benchmark returns, respectively. Similarly, the quadratic regression intercept a_p is given by

$$a_p = \alpha_p + \mathrm{Cov}[\xi_{\beta_{pt}}, R_{\delta t+1} - R_{ft+1}] - \gamma_{0p} E[R_{\delta t+1} - R_{ft+1}] - \gamma_{1p} E[(R_{\delta t+1} - R_{ft+1})^2]. \tag{23}$$

[7] The target beta could be time-varying as long as its value is known by uninformed investors.

As was the case earlier, it is convenient to separate the analysis into two cases: that in which excess benchmark returns are serially independent, and that in which they are serially dependent. We discuss these cases in turn.

Before doing so, however, we must address the role of α_{pt} in understanding market timing skills. To the best of our knowledge, no paper in the performance evaluation literature has contemplated the possibility that the conditional Jensen measure α_{pt} is correlated with the conditional moments of future excess benchmark returns, probably because selection skills have been thought to deliver, at best, constant expected returns and not because there are economic reasons for thinking that security selection prospects are not correlated with fluctuations in benchmark volatility and skewness. A better reason for assuming that these correlations are zero is implicit in the observation that security selection is a zero-beta trading activity, suggesting that active managers would probably control the portfolio beta so as to make it so. Accordingly, it seems reasonable to suppose the covariance terms involving α_{pt} are equal to zero in what follows.

That said, these relations conceal a somewhat surprising result when excess benchmark returns are serially independent. In this case, the two bias terms are given by

$$\begin{pmatrix} \gamma_{0p} \\ \gamma_{1p} \end{pmatrix} = \frac{1}{\sigma_\delta^2 \sigma_{4\delta} - \sigma_{3\delta}^2} \begin{pmatrix} \sigma_{4\delta} & -\sigma_{3\delta} \\ -\sigma_{3\delta} & \sigma_\delta^2 \end{pmatrix} \begin{pmatrix} \mathrm{Cov}[\xi_{\beta_{pt}}, (R_{\delta t+1} - R_{ft+1})^2] \\ \mathrm{Cov}[\xi_{\beta_{pt}}, (R_{\delta t+1} - R_{ft+1})^3] \end{pmatrix},$$

which will be nonzero only if $\xi_{\beta_{pt}}$ is correlated with next period's square and/or cubed excess returns, except for singularities in these equations. That is, only a manager who possesses market timing ability can shift portfolio betas in this fashion. Unfortunately, this ability to detect market timing does not translate into clean measures of market timing ability because the beta shifts cannot be inferred from returns alone without further assumptions. One simply cannot separately identify the three moments related to systematic risk exposure—that is, $\overline{\beta}_p$, $\mathrm{Cov}[\xi_{\beta_{pt}}, (R_{\delta t+1} - R_{ft+1})^2]$, and $\mathrm{Cov}[\xi_{\beta_{pt}}, (R_{\delta t+1} - R_{ft+1})^3]$—from b_{0p} and b_{1p} alone without additional restrictions.

3.1.1. Gaussian Signals and Returns

Admati et al. (1986) put additional structure on the problem to measure market timing ability within this framework.[8] They assume that the manager observes excess benchmark returns with error and that both the signal and benchmark returns are normally distributed. They show that b_{1p} equals the ratio of the risk-aversion parameter to the variance of the noise of the market timing signal under these assumptions.

[8]Admati et al. (1986) also provide a different formulation in which both the quality of the timing and selectivity information can be deduced. Unfortunately, their result requires an extremely large number of regressors—the levels, squares, and cross-products of individual security and benchmark returns—to be included in a set of cross-sectional and time-series regressions, rendering this approach infeasible.

They then observe that the residual from the Treynor–Mazuy regression has conditional heteroskedasticity related to excess benchmark returns. They show that the coefficient from the regression of ζ^2_{pt+1} on $(R_{\delta t+1} - R_{ft+1})^2$ is equal to the ratio of the squared risk-aversion parameter to the variance of the noise of the market timing signal, which they can use in conjunction with b_{1p} to disentangle the two. Finally, they note that a nonzero intercept will correctly indicate the presence of security selection ability under their assumptions but that its quality cannot be determined since it can only be used to measure the sum $\alpha_p + \mathrm{Cov}[\xi_{\beta_{pt}}, R_{\delta t+1} - R_{ft+1}]$ and not its components.

One can gain additional insight into the Treynor–Mazuy regression by reparameterizing the problem slightly. In particular, substitute the unconditional projection of excess benchmark returns on $\xi_{\beta_{pt}}$,

$$R_{\delta t+1} - R_{ft+1} = \mu_\delta + \pi_p \xi_{\beta_{pt}} + \upsilon_{\delta t+1}, \tag{24}$$

into the bias terms:

$$\begin{pmatrix} \gamma_{0p} \\ \gamma_{1p} \end{pmatrix} = \frac{1}{\sigma^2_\delta \sigma_{4\delta} - \sigma^2_{3\delta}} \begin{pmatrix} \sigma_{4\delta} & -\sigma_{3\delta} \\ -\sigma_{3\delta} & \sigma^2_\delta \end{pmatrix} \tag{25}$$

$$\times \begin{pmatrix} \pi^2_p \sigma_{3\xi} + \pi_p \mu_\delta \sigma^2_\xi + E[\xi_{\beta_{pt}} \upsilon^2_{\delta t+1}] \\ \pi^3_p \sigma_{4\xi} + \mu_\delta \pi^2_p \sigma_{3\xi} + \pi_p \mathrm{Cov}[\xi^2_{\beta_{pt}}, \upsilon^2_{\delta t+1}] + 2\pi_p E[\xi^2_{\beta_{pt}} \upsilon^2_{\delta t+1}] + \mu_\delta \mathrm{Cov}[\xi_{\beta_{pt}}, \upsilon^2_{\delta t+1}] \end{pmatrix}.$$

As is readily apparent, one determinant of the complexity of the inference problem is the possibility of conditional heteroskedasticity in the projection relating ex post excess benchmark returns to beta shifts. In the absence of such dependence, the bias terms reduce to

$$\begin{pmatrix} \gamma_{0p} \\ \gamma_{1p} \end{pmatrix} = \frac{1}{\sigma^2_\delta \sigma_{4\delta} - \sigma^2_{3\delta}} \begin{pmatrix} \sigma_{4\delta} & -\sigma_{3\delta} \\ -\sigma_{3\delta} & \sigma^2_\delta \end{pmatrix} \begin{pmatrix} \pi^2_p \sigma_{3\xi} + \pi_p \mu_\delta \sigma^2_\xi \\ \pi^3_p \sigma_{4\xi} + \mu_\delta \pi^2_p \sigma_{3\xi} + 2\pi_p \sigma^2_\xi \sigma^2_\upsilon \end{pmatrix}.$$

This is further simplified if normality of $\xi_{\beta_{pt}}$ and $\upsilon_{\delta t+1}$ is assumed along the lines of Admati et al. (1986). Normality simplifies matters considerably, the resulting symmetry implying that $\sigma_{3\delta} = \sigma_{3\xi} = 0$ and the absence of excess kurtosis leading to $\sigma_{4\delta} = 3\sigma^4_\delta$ and $\sigma_{4\xi} = 3\sigma^4_\xi$. Under these conditions, the bias terms are given by

$$\begin{pmatrix} \gamma_{0p} \\ \gamma_{1p} \end{pmatrix} = \begin{pmatrix} \mu_\delta \pi_p \frac{\sigma^2_\xi}{\sigma^2_\delta} \\ \pi^3_p \frac{\sigma^4_\xi}{\sigma^4_\delta} + \pi_p \frac{2\sigma^2_\xi \sigma^2_\upsilon}{3\sigma^4_\delta} \end{pmatrix} = \begin{pmatrix} \mu_\delta \frac{\pi_p \sigma^2_\xi}{\sigma^2_\delta} \\ \pi_p \frac{\pi^2_p \sigma^4_\xi}{\sigma^4_\delta} + \frac{2}{3} \frac{\pi_p \sigma^2_\xi}{\sigma^2_\delta} \frac{\sigma^2_\delta - \pi^2_p \sigma^2_\xi}{\sigma^2_\delta} \end{pmatrix}$$

$$\equiv \begin{pmatrix} \frac{\mu_\delta}{\sigma^2_\delta} \theta_p \\ \frac{\pi_p}{3\sigma^4_\delta} \theta^2_p + \frac{2}{3\sigma^2_\delta} \theta_p \end{pmatrix}, \tag{26}$$

where

$$\theta_p = \pi_p \sigma_\xi^2 = \mathrm{Cov}[\xi_{\beta_{pt}}, R_{\delta t+1} - R_{ft+1}]$$

is the bias term preventing estimation of Jensen's alpha in the Jensen regression. The Treynor–Mazuy intercept is biased as well: While $\mathrm{Cov}[\xi_{\beta_{pt}}, R_{\delta t+1} - R_{ft+1}]$ is positive in this model, so are γ_{0p} and γ_{1p}, and, hence, a_p is of unknown sign.

Next we exploit the conditional heteroskedasticity in the quadratic regression residual. In our notation, the residual is given by

$$\zeta_{pt+1} = (\xi_{\beta_{pt}} - \gamma_{0p})(\pi_p \xi_{\beta_{pt}} + \upsilon_{\delta t+1}) - \pi_p \sigma_\xi^2 + \mu_\delta \xi_{\beta_{pt}} - b_{1p}[(\pi_p \xi_{\beta_{pt}} + \upsilon_{\delta t+1})^2 - \sigma_\delta^2] + \varepsilon_{pt+1}, \tag{27}$$

when $\alpha_{pt} = \alpha_p$ and there is conditional heteroskedasticity in the Treynor–Mazuy regression related to excess benchmark returns, as was observed by Admati et al. Consider the population value of the squared quadratic regression residual on excess benchmark returns and their squares:

$$\zeta_{pt+1}^2 = \kappa_{0p} + \tau_{0p}(R_{\delta t+1} - R_{ft+1}) + \tau_{1p}(R_{\delta t+1} - R_{ft+1})^2 + \eta_{pt+1},$$

which differs from Admati et al. (1986) in the inclusion of $R_{\delta t+1} - R_{ft+1}$ on the right-hand side. An exceptionally tedious calculation reveals that τ_{1p} and τ_{2p} are given by

$$\begin{pmatrix} \tau_{0p} \\ \tau_{1p} \end{pmatrix} = \begin{pmatrix} 2\mu_\delta \sigma_\xi^2 - 2\mu_\delta \frac{\pi_p^2 \sigma_\xi^4}{\sigma_\delta^2} \\ \frac{2}{3}[4\gamma_{1p}^2 \sigma_\delta^2 - 8\gamma_{1p}\pi_p \sigma_\xi^2 + \sigma_\xi^2 + 3\frac{\pi_p^2 \sigma_\xi^4}{\sigma_\delta^2}] \end{pmatrix}$$
$$\equiv \begin{pmatrix} 2\mu_\delta \sigma_\xi^2 - 2\mu_\delta \frac{\theta_p^2}{\sigma_\delta^2} \\ \frac{2}{3}[4\gamma_{1p}^2 \sigma_\delta^2 - 8\gamma_{1p}\theta_p + \sigma_\xi^2 + 3\frac{\theta_p^2}{\sigma_\delta^2}] \end{pmatrix},$$

where τ_{0p} is also given by $2\mu_\delta \sigma_\xi^2(1 - R_\delta^2)$, where R_δ^2 is the coefficient from the projection of $R_{\delta t+1} - R_{ft+1}$ on $\xi_{\beta_{pt}}$ (i.e., Equation (24)). These quadratic equations can be solved for σ_ξ^2 and θ_p in yet another tedious calculation. The two solutions are given by:

$$\theta_p = \gamma_{1p}^2 \sigma_\delta^2 \pm \frac{\sqrt{\gamma_{1p}^2 \sigma_\delta^2 \mu_\delta^3 (3\mu_\delta \tau_{1p} - \tau_{0p})}}{2\sqrt{2}\mu_\delta^2},$$

$$\sigma_\xi^2 = \gamma_{1p}^2 \sigma_\delta^2 + \frac{3}{8\mu_\delta}(\mu_\delta \tau_{1p} + \tau_{0p}) \pm \frac{\sqrt{\gamma_{1p}^2 \sigma_\delta^2 \mu_\delta^3 (3\mu_\delta \tau_{1p} - \tau_{0p})}}{2\sqrt{2}\mu_\delta^2}.$$

The remaining parameters are now easily obtained by noting that $\pi_p = \theta_p / \sigma_\xi^2$ and obtaining $\overline{\beta}_p$ and α_p, substituting θ_p into Eq. (26). In addition, γ_{1p} is completely determined by π_p and θ_p, and so there is a cross-equation restriction relating b_{1p}, τ_{0p}, and τ_{1p} that can be tested using the appropriate χ^2 statistic.

Despite the need for making strong assumptions to arrive at these results, it is remarkable that we can infer a range of economically interesting parameters from a set of simple, conditionally heteroskedastic regressions.

Matters are more complicated still when returns are serially dependent. The first point echoes one made in the previous section: Time variation in expected returns can make a portfolio manager without skill look like a successful market timer. That is, the covariance terms

$$\begin{pmatrix} \mathrm{Cov}[\xi_{\beta_{pt}}, (R_{\delta t+1} - R_{ft+1})^2] \\ \mathrm{Cov}[\xi_{\beta_{pt}}, (R_{\delta t+1} - R_{ft+1})^3] \end{pmatrix}$$

$$= \begin{pmatrix} \mathrm{Cov}[\xi_{\beta_{pt}}, E[(R_{\delta t+1} - R_{ft+1})^2 | I_t]] + \mathrm{Cov}[\xi_{\beta_{pt}}, (R_{\delta t+1} - R_{ft+1})^2 | I_t] \\ \mathrm{Cov}[\xi_{\beta_{pt}}, E[(R_{\delta t+1} - R_{ft+1})^3 | I_t]] + \mathrm{Cov}[\xi_{\beta_{pt}}, (R_{\delta t+1} - R_{ft+1})^3 | I_t] \end{pmatrix}$$

can be nonzero in the absence of true market timing ability when there is serial dependence in excess returns, since $\xi_{\beta_{pt}}$ can be chosen by the manager to move with $E[(R_{\delta t+1} - R_{ft+1})^2 | I_t]$ and $E[(R_{\delta t+1} - R_{ft+1})^3 | I_t]$.[9] Hence, it is no longer the case that $b_{1p} \neq 0$ only if the manager possesses market timing ability.

Little can be done about this problem without a priori information on time variation in the distribution of excess benchmark returns. Suppose we know both the conditional mean and variance of excess benchmark returns, perhaps in the form of models of the form

$$\mu_{\delta t} = E[R_{\delta t+1} - R_{ft+1} | I_t] = f(z_t, \theta)$$

and

$$\sigma_{\delta t}^2 = E[(R_{\delta t+1} - R_{ft+1} - \mu_{\delta t})^2 | I_t] = g(z_t, \theta),$$

where $z_t \in I_t$ and θ is a vector of unknown parameters. Rewrite the Treynor–Mazuy quadratic regression with the linear and quadratic terms in deviations from conditional means:

$$\begin{aligned} R_{pt+1} - R_{ft+1} \\ = E_p + b_{0p}^*(R_{\delta t+1} - R_{ft+1} - \mu_{\delta t}) + b_{1p}^*[(R_{\delta t+1} - R_{ft+1} - \mu_{\delta t})^2 - \sigma_{\delta t}^2] + \zeta_{pt+1}, \end{aligned}$$

[9] In addition, a manager with true selection skill can appear to be a market timer as well since $\mathrm{Cov}(\alpha_{pt}, E[(R_{\delta t+1} - R_{ft+1})^2 | I_t])$ and $\mathrm{Cov}(\alpha_{pt}, E[(R_{\delta t+1} - R_{ft+1})^3 | I_t])$ can be nonzero as well. Our earlier argument suggests that we should not be so concerned about spurious market timing measures from this source.

where E_p is the unconditional mean return of the managed portfolio. Similarly, rewrite the unconditional projection in Eq. (24) in terms of $R_{\delta t+1} - R_{ft+1} - \mu_{\delta t}$:

$$R_{\delta t+1} - R_{ft+1} = \mu_{\delta t} + \pi_p^* \xi_{\beta_{pt}} + \upsilon_{\delta t+1}^*, \tag{28}$$

where the projection coefficient π_p^* is generally different from π_p since μ_δ is replaced by $\mu_{\delta t}$ in this projection. In these circumstances, managed portfolio returns are given by

$$\begin{aligned} R_{pt+1} - R_{ft+1} &= \alpha_{pt} + \beta_{pt}(R_{\delta t+1} - R_{ft+1}) + \varepsilon_{pt+1} \\ &= \alpha_{pt} + \beta_{pt}(\mu_\delta + \pi_p^* \xi_{\beta_{pt}} + \upsilon_{\delta t+1}^*) + [\beta_{pt}(\mu_{\delta t} - \mu_\delta)] + \varepsilon_{pt+1}, \end{aligned} \tag{29}$$

where the term in square brackets—that is, $\beta_{pt}(\mu_{\delta t} - \mu_\delta)$—is the incremental term in the conditional Jensen regression over that in the independently distributed case. Hence, the quadratic regression coefficients are given by

$$\begin{aligned} \begin{pmatrix} b_{0p}^* \\ b_{1p}^* \end{pmatrix} = & \left[\mathrm{Var} \begin{pmatrix} R_{\delta t+1} - R_{ft+1} \\ (R_{\delta t+1} - R_{ft+1})^2 \end{pmatrix} \right]^{-1} \\ & \mathrm{Cov} \left[R_{pt+1} - R_{ft+1}, \begin{pmatrix} R_{\delta t+1} - R_{ft+1} - \mu_{\delta t} \\ (R_{\delta t+1} - R_{ft+1} - \mu_{\delta t})^2 - \sigma_{\delta t}^2 \end{pmatrix} \right] \\ = & \left[\mathrm{Var} \begin{pmatrix} R_{\delta t+1} - R_{ft+1} \\ (R_{\delta t+1} - R_{ft+1})^2 \end{pmatrix} \right]^{-1} \\ & \times E \Big[[\alpha_{pt} + \beta_{pt}(\mu_\delta + \pi_p^* \xi_{\beta_{pt}} + \upsilon_{\delta t+1}^*) \\ & + \varepsilon_{pt+1}] \begin{pmatrix} R_{\delta t+1} - R_{ft+1} - \mu_{\delta t} \\ (R_{\delta t+1} - R_{ft+1} - \mu_{\delta t})^2 - \sigma_{\delta t}^2 \end{pmatrix} \Big] + \left[\mathrm{Var} \begin{pmatrix} R_{\delta t+1} - R_{ft+1} \\ (R_{\delta t+1} - R_{ft+1})^2 \end{pmatrix} \right]^{-1} \\ & E \left[\beta_{pt}(\mu_{\delta t} - \mu_\delta) \begin{pmatrix} R_{\delta t+1} - R_{ft+1} - \mu_{\delta t} \\ (R_{\delta t+1} - R_{ft+1} - \mu_{\delta t})^2 - \sigma_{\delta t}^2 \end{pmatrix} \right] \\ = & \begin{pmatrix} \bar{\beta}_p \\ 0 \end{pmatrix} + \frac{1}{\bar{\sigma}_\delta^2 \bar{\sigma}_{4\delta} - \bar{\sigma}_{3\delta}^2} \begin{pmatrix} \bar{\sigma}_{4\delta} & -\bar{\sigma}_{3\delta} \\ -\bar{\sigma}_{3\delta} & \bar{\sigma}_\delta^2 \end{pmatrix} \\ & \times E \left[\xi_{\beta_{pt}}(\mu_{\delta t} + \pi_p^* \xi_{\beta_{pt}} + \upsilon_{\delta t+1}^*) \begin{pmatrix} \pi_p^* \xi_{\beta_{pt}} + \upsilon_{\delta t+1}^* \\ (\pi_p^* \xi_{\beta_{pt}} + \upsilon_{\delta t+1}^*)^2 - \sigma_{\delta t}^2 \end{pmatrix} \right], \end{aligned}$$

where the bars over the variance and covariance terms represent the unconditional expectation of the corresponding time-varying conditional moments. While this expression bears a formal resemblance to Eq. (22), it is still potentially corrupted with spurious market timing both because $\xi_{\beta_{pt}}$ is uncorrelated with $\upsilon_{\delta t+1}^*$ but need not be independent of it and because $\xi_{\beta_{pt}}^2$ and $\xi_{\beta_{pt}} \upsilon_{\delta t+1}^*$ can be correlated with $\mu_{\delta t}$ as well. Accounting for the serial dependence in excess benchmark returns alone is insufficient to solve the problem posed by spurious market timing.

One way out of this conundrum is to break the beta-shift terms $\xi_{\beta_{pt}}$ into two components, one that reflects the expected portfolio beta given public information and another that represents the manager's market timing efforts beyond that which can be accounted for with public information. Put differently, we took the target beta to be constant earlier, but we could just as easily have made it time-varying, as in

$$\beta_{pt} = \overline{\beta}_{pt} + \xi_{\beta_{pt}} \equiv \overline{\beta}_p + \varsigma_{\beta_{pt}} + \xi_{\beta_{pt}}, \tag{30}$$

where $\varsigma_{\beta_{pt}}$ has mean zero conditional on public information I_t. As was the case with $\mu_{\delta t}$ and $\sigma^2_{\delta t}$, we will treat $\varsigma_{\beta_{pt}}$ as an observable even though it is modeled, usually as a projection on time t information, in actual practice. Measurement of this component of beta fluctuations eliminates spurious market timing biases in the simple Jensen measure since

$$R_{pt+1} - R_{ft+1} = \alpha_{pt} + \overline{\beta}_p(R_{\delta t+1} - R_{ft+1}) + \varsigma_{\beta_{pt}}(R_{\delta t+1} - R_{ft+1}) + \varepsilon_{pt+1} \tag{31}$$

and $\alpha_p = E[\alpha_{pt}]$ and $\overline{\beta}_p$ can be estimated without bias when the manager does not possess market timing ability and $\varsigma_{\beta_{pt}}(R_{\delta t+1} - R_{ft+1})$ is observed. The words *without bias* are replaced by *consistently* when $\varsigma_{\beta_{pt}}$ is not observed but can be estimated consistently. Ferson and Schadt (1996) assume that both $\overline{\beta}_{pt}$ and $\varsigma_{\beta_{pt}}$ are postulated to be linear projections on conditioning and study a version of the Treynor–Mazuy quadratic regression that takes the form

$$\begin{aligned} R_{pt+1} - R_{ft+1} \\ &= \alpha_{pt} + \overline{\beta}_{pt}(R_{\delta t+1} - R_{ft+1}) + \varsigma_{\beta_{pt}}(R_{\delta t+1} - R_{ft+1}) + b^*_{1p}(R_{\delta t+1} - R_{ft+1})^2 + \varepsilon_{pt+1}. \end{aligned} \tag{32}$$

Similarly, we can refine the Treynor–Mazuy regressions while simultaneously weakening the assumption regarding the observability of replacing observation of $\varsigma_{\beta_{pt}}$. In particular, augmenting the quadratic regression with the assumption that $\text{Cov}[\varsigma_{\beta_{pt}}, \sigma^2_{\delta t}] = \text{Cov}[\varsigma_{\beta_{pt}}, \sigma_{3\delta t}] = 0$ solves the market timing problem, in that, since $\varsigma_{\beta_{pt}}$ is in the time t public information set,

$$\begin{aligned} \begin{pmatrix} b^*_{0p} \\ b^*_{1p} \end{pmatrix} &= \left[\text{Var}\begin{pmatrix} R_{\delta t+1} - R_{ft+1} \\ (R_{\delta t+1} - R_{ft+1})^2 \end{pmatrix}\right]^{-1} \\ &\quad E\left\{(\overline{\beta}_p + \varsigma_{\beta_{pt}})E\left[\begin{pmatrix} (R_{\delta t+1} - R_{ft+1} - \mu_{\delta t})^2 \\ (R_{\delta t+1} - R_{ft+1} - \mu_{\delta t})^3 \end{pmatrix} | I_t\right]\right\} \\ &\quad + \left[\text{Var}\begin{pmatrix} R_{\delta t+1} - R_{ft+1} \\ (R_{\delta t+1} - R_{ft+1})^2 \end{pmatrix}\right]^{-1} \\ &\quad E\left[\xi_{\beta_{pt}}(\mu_{\delta t} + \pi^*_p\xi_{\beta_{pt}} + \upsilon^*_{\delta t+1})\begin{pmatrix} \pi^*_p\xi_{\beta_{pt}} + \upsilon^*_{\delta t+1} \\ (\pi^*_p\xi_{\beta_{pt}} + \upsilon^*_{\delta t+1})^2 - \sigma^2_{\delta t} \end{pmatrix}\right] \end{aligned}$$

$$= \begin{pmatrix} \overline{\beta}_p \\ 0 \end{pmatrix} + \frac{1}{\overline{\sigma}_\delta^2 \overline{\sigma}_{4\delta} - \overline{\sigma}_{3\delta}^2} \begin{pmatrix} \overline{\sigma}_{4\delta} & -\overline{\sigma}_{3\delta} \\ -\overline{\sigma}_{3\delta} & \overline{\sigma}_\delta^2 \end{pmatrix}$$

$$\times E\left[\xi_{\beta_{pt}} (\mu_{\delta t} + \pi_p^* \xi_{\beta_{pt}} + \upsilon_{\delta t+1}^*) \begin{pmatrix} \pi_p^* \xi_{\beta_{pt}} + \upsilon_{\delta t+1}^* \\ (\pi_p^* \xi_{\beta_{pt}} + \upsilon_{\delta t+1}^*)^2 - \sigma_{\delta t}^2 \end{pmatrix} \right]$$

$$= \begin{pmatrix} \overline{\beta}_p \\ 0 \end{pmatrix} + \begin{pmatrix} \gamma_{0p}^* \\ \gamma_{1p}^* \end{pmatrix}.$$

In so doing, we have recovered the earlier result that $b_{1p}^* = \gamma_{1p}^*$ will be nonzero if and only if the manager possesses market timing ability.

A few additional moment conditions will permit us to recover the results we obtained earlier for the case of serially independent returns. If the lack of correlation between $\xi_{\beta_{pt}}$ and $\upsilon_{\delta t+1}^*$ is strengthened to independence, the bias terms reduce to

$$\begin{pmatrix} \gamma_{0p}^* \\ \gamma_{1p}^* \end{pmatrix} = \frac{1}{\overline{\sigma}_\delta^2 \overline{\sigma}_{4\delta} - \overline{\sigma}_{3\delta}^2} \begin{pmatrix} \overline{\sigma}_{4\delta} & -\overline{\sigma}_{3\delta} \\ -\overline{\sigma}_{3\delta} & \overline{\sigma}_\delta^2 \end{pmatrix} \begin{pmatrix} \pi_p^2 \overline{\sigma}_{3\xi} + \pi_p E[\mu_{\delta t} \sigma_{\xi t}^2] \\ \pi_p^3 \overline{\sigma}_{4\xi} + \pi_p^2 E[\mu_{\delta t} \sigma_{3\xi t}] + 2\pi_p E[\sigma_{\xi t}^2 \sigma_{\upsilon t}^2] \end{pmatrix}, \tag{33}$$

and so the bias terms are structurally identical to γ_{0p} and γ_{1p} if $\mu_{\delta t}$ is uncorrelated with $\sigma_{3\xi t}$ and $\sigma_{\xi t}^2$ and if $\sigma_{\xi t}^2$ is uncorrelated with $\sigma_{\upsilon t}^2$. Similarly, normality of $\xi_{\beta_{pt}}$ and $\upsilon_{\delta t+1}$ further simplifies the bias terms to

$$\begin{pmatrix} \gamma_{0p}^* \\ \gamma_{1p}^* \end{pmatrix} = \begin{pmatrix} \overline{\mu}_\delta \pi_p \frac{\overline{\sigma}_\xi^2}{\overline{\sigma}_\delta^2} \\ \pi_p^3 \frac{\overline{\sigma}_\xi^4}{\overline{\sigma}_\delta^4} + \pi_p \frac{2\overline{\sigma}_\xi^2 \overline{\sigma}_\upsilon^2}{3\overline{\sigma}_\delta^4} \end{pmatrix} \equiv \begin{pmatrix} \frac{\overline{\mu}_\delta}{\overline{\sigma}_\delta^2} \overline{\theta}_p \\ \frac{\pi_p}{3\overline{\sigma}_\delta^4} \overline{\theta}_p^2 + \frac{2}{3\overline{\sigma}_\delta^2} \overline{\theta}_p \end{pmatrix}, \tag{34}$$

where

$$\overline{\theta}_p = \pi_p \overline{\sigma}_\xi^2 = \mathrm{Cov}[\xi_{\beta_{pt}}, R_{\delta t+1} - R_{ft+1}]$$

is the average bias term preventing consistent estimation of Jensen's alpha. The conditional heteroskedasticity analysis goes through as written, with starred and barred quantities once again replacing their unadorned counterparts.

3.1.2. Period-Weighting Measures

Returning to the case of time-invariant risk exposures and risk premiums, Grinblatt and Titman (1989) point to circumstances in which Jensen-like alphas will correctly signal the presence of managerial skill in a model with the same basic structure as Admati et al. (1986). A good starting point is the Jensen regression with time-invariant alphas and betas. As is well known, the least-squares estimator of the Jensen alpha is a linear combination of managed portfolio returns:

$$\widehat{\alpha}_p = \sum_{t=1}^{T} \omega_{\alpha t}(R_{pt+1} - R_{ft+1}),$$

with weights that satisfy

$$\sum_{t=1}^{T} \omega_{\alpha t} = 1$$

$$\sum_{t=1}^{T} \omega_{\alpha t}(R_{\delta t+1} - R_{ft+1}) = 0.$$

Grinblatt and Titman (1989) point out that the least-squares weights are only one linear combination with these features: Any intercept estimator based on weights that satisfy these constraints will provide an unbiased estimate of the regression intercept (which will generally not be equal to the Jensen alpha in the presence of market timing ability) as long as it has weights of order $1/T$. They termed the estimators in this class *period-weighting measures* because each of the weights $\omega_{\alpha t}$ gives a potentially different weight to each observation, and they searched for estimators that improve on the Jensen alpha under the normality assumptions made in Admati et al. (1986).

Period-weighting measures are given by

$$\widehat{\alpha}_p^{GT} = \sum_{t=1}^{T} \omega_{\alpha t}(R_{pt+1} - R_{ft+1}) = \sum_{t=1}^{T} \omega_{\alpha t}[\alpha_{pt} + \beta_{pt}(R_{\delta t+1} - R_{ft+1}) + \varepsilon_{pt+1}],$$

and their associated expectations $\alpha_p^{GT} = E[\widehat{\alpha}_p^{GT}]$ are given by

$$\begin{aligned}\alpha_p^{GT} &= \sum_{t=1}^{T} E\left[\omega_{\alpha t}(\alpha_{pt} + \beta_{pt}(R_{\delta t+1} - R_{ft+1}) + \varepsilon_{pt+1})\right] \\ &= \sum_{t=1}^{T} E\left[\omega_{\alpha t}(\alpha_{pt} + \varepsilon_{pt+1})\right] + \sum_{t=1}^{T} E\left[\omega_{\alpha t}\beta_{pt}(R_{\delta t+1} - R_{ft+1})\right].\end{aligned}$$

Now suppose that the weights are chosen to be functions of the normally distributed excess benchmark returns alone. Uncorrelated random variables are independent under joint normality, so the first term is an unbiased estimate of the expected alpha as before because

$$\alpha_p^{GT} = \sum_{t=1}^{T} \omega_{\alpha t} E\left[\alpha_{pt} + \varepsilon_{pt+1}\right] + \sum_{t=1}^{T} E\left[\omega_{\alpha t}\beta_{pt}(R_{\delta t+1} - R_{ft+1})\right]$$
$$= \alpha_p + \sum_{t=1}^{T} E\left[\omega_{\alpha t}\beta_{pt}(R_{\delta t+1} - R_{ft+1})\right], \tag{35}$$

as was the case for the Jensen measure. In this model, the bias term can be rewritten as

$$\alpha_p^{GT} = \alpha_p + \sum_{t=1}^{T} E\left[\omega_{\alpha t}(\overline{\beta}_p + \xi_{\beta_{pt}})(R_{\delta t+1} - R_{ft+1})\right]$$
$$= \alpha_p + \sum_{t=1}^{T} E\left[\omega_{\alpha t}\xi_{\beta_{pt}}(R_{\delta t+1} - R_{ft+1})\right] \tag{36}$$

because

$$\sum_{t=1}^{T} \omega_{\alpha t}(R_{\delta t+1} - R_{ft+1}) = 0.$$

If, in addition, the weights $\omega_{\alpha t}$ are strictly positive, this bias term is positive as well, since the substitution of the projection

$$\xi_{\beta_{pt}} = \pi_\beta(R_{\delta t+1} - R_{ft+1} - \mu_\delta) + \upsilon_{\beta t+1}$$

into Eq. (36) yields

$$\alpha_p^{GT} = \alpha_p + \sum_{t=1}^{T} E\left[\omega_{\alpha t}\left[\pi_\beta(R_{\delta t+1} - R_{ft+1} - \mu_\delta) + \upsilon_{\beta t+1}\right](R_{\delta t+1} - R_{ft+1})\right]$$
$$= \alpha_p + \sum_{t=1}^{T} E\left[\omega_{\alpha t}(R_{\delta t+1} - R_{ft+1})E\left[\pi_\beta(R_{\delta t+1} - R_{ft+1} - \mu_\delta) + \upsilon_{\beta t+1}|R_{\delta t+1} - R_{ft+1}\right]\right]$$
$$= \alpha_p + \sum_{t=1}^{T} E\left[\omega_{\alpha t}(R_{\delta t+1} - R_{ft+1})\pi_\beta(R_{\delta t+1} - R_{ft+1} - \mu_\delta)\right]$$
$$= \alpha_p + \sum_{t=1}^{T} \pi_\beta E\left[\omega_{\alpha t}(R_{\delta t+1} - R_{ft+1})^2\right] > 0,$$

where the transition from the penultimate to the last line follows from the constraint

$$\sum_{t=1}^{T} \omega_{\alpha t}(R_{\delta t+1} - R_{ft+1}) = 0$$

and where $\alpha_p^{GT} > 0$ because $\omega_{\alpha t} > 0$ implies

$$\omega_{\alpha t}(R_{\delta t+1} - R_{ft+1})^2 > 0.$$

Once again, $\widehat{\alpha}_p^{GT}$ does not measure the degree of ability or whether it is of the market timing or security selection variety. Grinblatt and Titman's insight was that positive period-weighting measures are positive in the presence of skill in this setting.

3.1.3. Directional Information

Merton (1981) and Henriksson and Merton (1981) provide a framework for testing market timing skills when forecasters make directional forecasts that produces another variant of the Treynor–Mazuy regression. That is, they study market timers who may have information on whether excess benchmark returns $R_{\delta t+1} - R_{ft+1}$ are expected to be positive or negative and not on their magnitudes. The market timing strategies assumed by them are particularly simple: The portfolio beta is set to the high value β_h when the benchmark is predicted to exceed the riskless rate and to the low value β_ℓ when the expected excess benchmark return is negative.

This structure makes it easy to analyze the impact of market timing on performance measurement. There are four states of the world, *hu*, *hd*, ℓu, and ℓd, where *u* denotes states in which $R_{\delta t+1} \geq R_{ft+1}$ and where *d* denotes states in which $R_{\delta t+1} < R_{ft+1}$. Beta choices are concordant with realized benchmark returns in states *hu* and ℓd—that is, a high beta when the benchmark return exceeds the riskless rate and a low beta when the expected excess benchmark return is negative—and discordant in states *hd* and ℓu since the betas move in the opposite direction from benchmark returns in these states. To facilitate the analysis, let π_{hu}, π_{hd}, $\pi_{\ell u}$, and $\pi_{\ell u}$ denote the probabilities of the corresponding states and let $\pi_u = \pi_{hu} + \pi_{\ell u}$ and $\pi_d = \pi_{hd} + \pi_{\ell d}$ so that $\pi_u + \pi_d = 1$.

The managed portfolio return is still described by the conditional Jensen regression, but the model for portfolio betas takes a particularly simple form in this case. The conditional beta in up markets is equal to β_h with probability $\frac{\pi_{hu}}{\pi_u}$ and equals β_ℓ with probability $\frac{\pi_{\ell u}}{\pi_u}$, while the down-market beta is equal to β_h with probability $\frac{\pi_{hd}}{\pi_d}$ and equals β_ℓ with probability $\frac{\pi_{\ell d}}{\pi_d}$. Now consider the regression of portfolio returns on both the up-market excess benchmark return $(R_{\delta t+1} - R_{ft+1})^+$ and the down-market excess benchmark return $(R_{\delta t+1} - R_{ft+1})^-$:

$$R_{pt+1} - R_{ft+1} = \alpha_p + \beta_p^+(R_{\delta t+1} - R_{ft+1})^+ + \beta_p^-(R_{\delta t+1} - R_{ft+1})^- + \varepsilon_{pt+1}, \qquad (37)$$

where β_p^+ and β_p^- are the up- and down-market portfolio betas, respectively. As is readily apparent, the up- and down-market betas as well as the average beta are given by

$$\begin{aligned}\beta_p^+ &= \frac{\pi_{hu}}{\pi_u}\beta_h + \frac{\pi_{\varrho u}}{\pi_u}\beta_\varrho \\ \beta_p^- &= \frac{\pi_{hd}}{\pi_d}\beta_h + \frac{\pi_{\varrho d}}{\pi_d}\beta_\varrho \\ \overline{\beta}_p &= (\pi_{hu} + \pi_{hd})\beta_h + (\pi_{\varrho u} + \pi_{\varrho d})\beta_\varrho.\end{aligned} \tag{38}$$

Moreover, the conditions under which the manager has market timing ability takes a particularly simple form, since

$$\begin{aligned}\beta_p^+ - \overline{\beta}_p &= \left[\frac{\pi_{hu}}{\pi_u} - (\pi_{hu} + \pi_{hd})\right]\beta_h + \left[\frac{\pi_{\varrho u}}{\pi_u} - (\pi_{\varrho u} + \pi_{\varrho d})\right]\beta_\varrho \\ &= (1 - \pi_u)\left[\frac{\pi_{hu}}{\pi_u} + \frac{\pi_{\varrho d}}{\pi_d} - 1\right](\beta_h - \beta_\varrho)\end{aligned} \tag{39}$$

is positive if and only if $\frac{\pi_{hu}}{\pi_u} + \frac{\pi_{\varrho d}}{\pi_d} > 1$, or equivalently, if $\frac{\pi_{hu}}{\pi_u} > \frac{\pi_{hd}}{\pi_d}$. Since $\beta_p^- - \overline{\beta}_p$ must be negative if $\beta_p^+ - \overline{\beta}_p$ is positive, the covariance between betas and subsequent excess benchmark returns is positive as well in this case, and so only managers whose information and behavior are such that $\frac{\pi_{hu}}{\pi_u} + \frac{\pi_{\varrho d}}{\pi_d} > 1$ possess market timing ability. This makes intuitive sense: The concordant probabilities have to be larger than the discordant ones or betting on the up- and down-market betas is a losing proposition. Note also that α_p is the expected return to selection because the covariance between betas and subsequent excess benchmark returns is embedded in the fitted part of the regression.

This first version of this regression in Merton (1981) looks more like Treynor–Mazuy regression. Instead of having up- and down-market excess benchmark returns on the right-hand side as in Eq. (37), the regressors in the original model are $R_{\delta t+1} - R_{ft+1}$ and $-(R_{\delta t+1} - R_{ft+1})^-$. This reparameterization of Eq. (37) is given by

$$R_{pt+1} - R_{ft+1} = \alpha_p + b_{1p}(R_{\delta t+1} - R_{ft+1}) - b_{2p}(R_{\delta t+1} - R_{ft+1})^- + \varepsilon_{pt+1}, \tag{40}$$

which is related to Eq. (37) via

$$\begin{aligned}R_{pt+1} - R_{ft+1} &= \alpha_p + \beta_p^+(R_{\delta t+1} - R_{ft+1})^+ + \beta_p^-(R_{\delta t+1} - R_{ft+1})^- + \varepsilon_{pt+1} \\ &= \alpha_p + \beta_p^+(R_{\delta t+1} - R_{ft+1})^+ + \beta_p^+(R_{\delta t+1} - R_{ft+1})^- \\ &\quad - \beta_p^+(R_{\delta t+1} - R_{ft+1})^- + \beta_p^-(R_{\delta t+1} - R_{ft+1})^- + \varepsilon_{pt+1} \\ &= \alpha_p + \beta_p^+(R_{\delta t+1} - R_{ft+1}) - (\beta_p^+ - \beta_p^-)(R_{\delta t+1} - R_{ft+1})^- + \varepsilon_{pt+1}.\end{aligned} \tag{41}$$

The expressions for β_p^+ and β_p^- in (41) imply that b_{1p} and b_{2p} are given by

$$b_{1p} = \beta_p^+ = \frac{\pi_{hu}}{\pi_u}\beta_h + \frac{\pi_{\ell u}}{\pi_u}\beta_\ell$$

$$b_{2p} = \beta_p^+ - \beta_p^- = \left[\frac{\pi_{hu}}{\pi_u} + \frac{\pi_{\ell d}}{\pi_d} - 1\right](\beta_h - \beta_\ell), \tag{42}$$

and so $b_{2p} \neq 0$ if and only if the manager possesses market timing ability. Merton (1981) provided an elegant economic interpretation of b_{1p} and b_{2p}:b_{1p} is the hedge ratio for replicating the option with returns that are perfectly correlated with the returns to market timing, and b_{2p} is the implicit number of free put options on the benchmark struck at the riskless rate that is generated by the market timing ability of the manager.[10]

3.2. Observable Information Signals

In the analysis so far, the key variable is the timing signal, the variable that causes the manager to bet on market direction. If we observed the signals themselves, we could separate the question of whether the manager has forecasting ability—that is, whether $\frac{\pi_{hu}}{\pi_u} + \frac{\pi_{\ell d}}{\pi_d} > 1$—from that of how it informs the manager's trading strategy—that is, the uses to which the forecast is put. It could be that some managers are good forecasters but are poor at executing appropriate trading strategies or have other unknown motives for trade. Irrespective of the reason, studying the signals or forecasts observed by the manager can be an interesting exercise. Bhattacharya and Pfleiderer (1985) discuss conditions (including symmetry of the underlying conditional payoff distribution) under which a principal can elicit the agent's (fund manager's) true information.

Henriksson and Merton (1981) propose a simple nonparametric method for evaluating prediction signals. The states of the world are the same as outlined earlier—that is, *hu*, *hd*, *ℓu*, and *ℓd*—but *h* and *ℓ* refer to positive and negative market timing signals, respectively, not to high and low betas. For the concordant pairs *hu* and *ℓd*, $\frac{\pi_{hu}}{\pi_u} + \frac{\pi_{\ell d}}{\pi_d} = 1$ if and only if the signal is of no value, and $\frac{\pi_{hu}}{\pi_u} + \frac{\pi_{\ell d}}{\pi_d} > 1$ if it has positive value; as noted by Henriksson and Merton (1981), $\frac{\pi_{hu}}{\pi_u} + \frac{\pi_{\ell d}}{\pi_d} < 1$ also has positive value in the perhaps unlikely event that one recognizes that the forecasts are perverse. Then adding up restrictions for up and down probabilities—that is, $\pi_u + \pi_d = 1$—under the null hypothesis of no market timing ability imply that $\frac{\pi_{hu}}{\pi_u} = \frac{\pi_{hd}}{\pi_d}$ and $\frac{\pi_{\ell u}}{\pi_u} = \frac{\pi_{\ell d}}{\pi_d}$, or, in other words, that the high and low signals are independent of whether ex post excess benchmark returns are positive or negative.

Now consider a sample based on this implicit experiment: the 1s and 0s corresponding to positive *h* signals and negative *ℓ* signals and those corresponding to whether the observed excess benchmark returns are positive or negative. A sample of size T will then have T_{hu}, T_{hd}, $T_{\ell u}$, and $T_{\ell d}$ observations in the cells corresponding to each state of the world, with $T = T_{hu} + T_{hd} + T_{\ell u} + T_{\ell d}$ and with $T_u = T_{hu} + T_{\ell u}$ and $T_d = T_{hd} + T_{\ell d}$

[10]Ferson and Schadt (1996) develop a version of this market timing model when betas are time-varying but the expected excess benchmark portfolio return and its volality are constant.

observations in the up and down cells, respectively. Suppose that returns are independently and identically distributed under the null hypothesis, a condition that is a bit stronger than is necessary, so that the up and down probabilities are constant over time. If the null hypothesis is true, independent of the up and down probabilities, the sample proportions respect

$$\frac{\pi_{hu}}{\pi_u} = E\left[\frac{T_{hu}}{T_{hu} + T_{\ell u}}\right] = E\left[\frac{T_{hd}}{T_{hd} + T_{\ell d}}\right] = \frac{\pi_{hd}}{\pi_d}$$
$$= E\left[\frac{T_{hu} + T_{hd}}{T}\right] = \pi_h.$$

Henriksson and Merton (1981) used this independence—that is, $\pi_{hu} = \pi_h \pi_u$ and $\pi_{hd} = \pi_h \pi_d$—to calculate the conditional probability of receiving one cell count from the other three. This computation is facilitated by partitioning the sample into T_{hu}, T_h, T_u, and T_d. Then the probability of receiving T_{hu} concordant up-market pairs given the other three cell counts is given by

$$\begin{aligned}\Pr[T_{hu} = N_{hu}|T_u, T_d, T_h] &= \frac{\Pr[T_{hu} = N_{hu}, T_h = N_h|T_u, T_d]}{\Pr[T_h = N_h|T]} \\ &= \frac{\Pr[T_{hu} = N_{hu}, T_{hd} = N_h - N_{hu}|T_u, T_d]}{\Pr[T_h = N_h|T]} \\ &= \frac{\Pr[T_{hu} = N_{hu}|T_u]\Pr[T_{hd} = N_h - N_{hu}|T_d]}{\Pr[T_h = N_h|T]}.\end{aligned}$$

This holds because the high/low split is independent of the up/down split in the absence of market timing ability. The reason for repartitioning the sample in this fashion is now obvious: Each probability is that of a binomial random variable with the same probability π_h. Hence, the probability is given by

$$\begin{aligned}\Pr[T_{hu} = N_{hu}|T_u, T_d, T_h, \pi_h] &= \frac{\Pr[T_{hu} = N_{hu}|T_u, \pi_h]\Pr[T_{hd} = N_h - N_{hu}|T_d, \pi_h]}{\Pr[T_h = N_h|T, \pi_h]} \\ &= \frac{\binom{T_u}{T_{hu}}\pi_h^{T_{hu}}(1-\pi_h)^{T_u - T_{hu}}\binom{T_d}{T_h - T_{hu}}\pi_h^{T_h - T_{hu}}(1-\pi_h)^{T_d-(T_h - T_{hu})}}{\binom{T}{T_h}\pi_h^{T_h}(1-\pi_h)^{T-T_h}} \\ &= \frac{\binom{T_u}{T_{hu}}\binom{T_d}{T_{hd}}}{\binom{T}{T_h}} = \frac{T_h!T_\ell!T_u!T_d!}{T_{hu}!T_{\ell u}!T_{hd}!T_{\ell d}!T!},\end{aligned} \tag{43}$$

independent of the high signal probability π_h. The test is therefore distribution-free under the null hypothesis so long as the up probability π_u is constant. Henriksson and Merton (1981) point out that this ratio follows a hypergeometric distribution, which makes sense because this distribution is appropriate for experiments that differ in one detail for binomial experiments: A sample is first drawn at random from some overall population without replacement and is then randomly sorted into successes and failures.

In this application, T is the size of the population, T_h is the size of the random sample, T_{hu} is the number of successes, and T_{hd} is the number of failures. Cumby and Modest (1987) noted that the Henriksson/Merton test statistic is identical to Fisher's exact test for 2×2 contingency tables since

		Realization		
		Up	*Down*	*Sum*
Prediction	*High*	T_{hu}	T_{hd}	T_h
	Low	$T_{\ell u}$	$T_{\ell d}$	T_ℓ
	Sum	T_u	T_d	T

They also noted that there is a convenient normal approximation to the test of the moment condition $E\left[\frac{T_{hu}}{T} - \frac{T_h}{T}\frac{T_u}{T}\right] = 0$ that is given by

$$\frac{T_{hu} - \frac{T_h}{T}\frac{T_u}{T}}{\sqrt{\frac{T_h T_\ell T_u T_d}{T^2(T-1)}}} \sim N(0,1). \tag{44}$$

Pesaran and Timmermann (1992) show how to extend the analysis to more than two outcomes.

4. PERFORMANCE MEASUREMENT AND ATTRIBUTION WITH OBSERVABLE PORTFOLIO WEIGHTS

This state of affairs is somewhat unsatisfying and reflects the fact that returns are being asked to do a lot of work. The theory is straightforward and beautiful: All marginal investors agree that performance should be judged relative to portfolio δ, a specific conditionally mean-variance efficient portfolio. Unfortunately, the identification of an empirical analog of this portfolio is problematic, and it is likely that much of the evidence on fund performance reflects the inadequacy of benchmarks and not the abilities of fund managers. Moreover, and perhaps more importantly, fund returns are being asked to tell us both the fund's normal performance—that is, the appropriate expected return given its normal exposure to risk—as well as any abnormal performance due to security selection skill or market timing ability. In addition, the role played by parametric assumptions such as normality in dealing with this problem is worrisome. In the absence of a priori information about time variation in expected benchmark returns and fund risk exposures, performance evaluation based solely on fund and benchmark returns is simply not feasible. Performance evaluation is somewhat less problematic when it is plausible to assume that risk exposures are constant a priori, leaving benchmark error as the principle source of difficulty.

Of course, simplest of all is the case in which managers are judged on the basis of excess returns over an explicit benchmark. It is noteworthy that compensation contracts are increasingly taking this form and that managed portfolio performance is now routinely reported relative to an explicit benchmark irrespective of the nature of the manager's compensation. This change in best practice is a very real measure of the considerable impact that the academic performance evaluation literature has had on the portfolio management industry.

In fact, performance evaluation via the difference between the managed portfolio and benchmark returns contains an implicit model of the division of labor between two hypothetical (and, often, real) active portfolio managers: a market timer and a stock picker.[11] The stock picker chooses a portfolio of these N assets called δ^S, which is structured to have a beta of 1 on δ because its performance is measured relative to δ. That is, its return is given by

$$R^S_{\delta t+1} = R_{\delta t+1} + \alpha_{pt} + \varepsilon_{pt+1}, \tag{45}$$

where $\alpha_{pt} = E[R^S_{\delta t+1} - R_{\delta t+1}|I_t]$ correctly measures the conditional expected excess return produced by the stock picker. The quantity $R^S_{\delta t+1} - R_{\delta t+1} = \alpha_{pt} + \varepsilon_{pt+1}$ is called the *tracking error* in portfolio δ^S (with respect to its benchmark δ). The market timer takes this portfolio as given and determines the fraction ω_{pt} of the overall portfolio p that is allocated to portfolio δ^S at time t and the fraction $1 - \omega_{pt}$ that is allocated to the riskless asset. Hence, the overall return on p is given by

$$R_{pt+1} = (1 - \omega_{pt})R_{ft+1} + \omega_{pt}R^S_{\delta t+1}. \tag{46}$$

We have a division of labor and a benchmark for evaluating the performance of one of the laborers. What is missing is a benchmark for the market timer, a measure of normal performance for the asset allocation choice. For simplicity, suppose that the normal or strategic asset allocation—the passive portfolio that would be chosen by the manager of the overall portfolio in the absence of attempts to time the market—is an allocation of ω^n_{pt} to portfolio δ^S and $1 - \omega^n_{pt}$ to the riskless asset. Clearly any measure of the performance of the market timer should involve $\omega_{pt} - \omega^n_{pt}$, the market timer's policy tool, and how it moves with benchmark returns.

Armed with this additional datum, the overall return to p can be rewritten as

$$\begin{aligned} R_{pt+1} &= (1 - \omega_{pt})R_{ft+1} + w_{pt}R^S_{\delta t+1} \\ &= R_{ft+1} + \omega_{pt}(R^S_{\delta t+1} - R_{ft+1}) \\ &= R_{ft+1} + \omega^n_{pt}(R^S_{\delta t+1} - R_{ft+1}) + (\omega_{pt} - \omega^n_{pt})(R^S_{\delta t+1} - R_{ft+1}), \end{aligned} \tag{47}$$

which is almost, but not quite, in a form suitable for assessing the performance of the market timer. The missing element is the substitution of the return of the security

[11] Obviously, the more correct term here is *asset picker* or *security selector*. Both seem awkward, and *stock picker* is the term of art in the profession.

selection portfolio δ^S into this expression, which yields

$$\begin{aligned} R_{pt+1} &= R_{ft+1} + \omega^n_{pt}(R_{\delta t+1} + \alpha_{pt} + \varepsilon_{pt+1} - R_{ft+1}) \\ &\quad + (\omega_{pt} - \omega^n_{pt})(R_{\delta t+1} + \alpha_{pt} + \varepsilon_{pt+1} - R_{ft+1}) \\ &= [R_{ft+1} + \omega^n_{pt}(R_{\delta t+1} - R_{ft+1})] + \omega^n_{pt}[\alpha_{pt} + \varepsilon_{pt+1}] \\ &\quad + [(\omega_{pt} - \omega^n_{pt})(R_{\delta t+1} - R_{ft+1})] + [(\omega_{pt} - \omega^n_{pt})(\alpha_{pt} + \varepsilon_{pt+1})]. \end{aligned} \tag{48}$$

Note that this expression is perfectly compatible with the conditional Jensen regression with $\beta_{pt} = \omega_{pt}$, $\omega_{pt}\alpha_{pt}$ equal to the conditional Jensen alpha and $\omega_{pt}\varepsilon_{pt+1}$ equal to the residual return. Note also that observation of the portfolio weights ω_{pt} and ω^n_{pt} are equivalent to observation of the conditional and target betas, respectively, in these circumstances.

This simple portfolio arithmetic was introduced in Brinson, Hood, and Beebower (1986) and provides a nearly perfect decomposition of returns into economically relevant components. The first term in square brackets is the normal portfolio return, the return on the portfolio in the absence of active management. The second term is the return to security selection, which is given by the portfolio tracking error, since the stock picker is measured relative to the benchmark portfolio δ. The third term is a natural measure of the performance of the market timer: the product of $\omega_{pt} - \omega^n_{pt}$, the deviation from the normal weight that is chosen by the manager, and the excess return on the benchmark portfolio. The choice of the benchmark portfolio makes sense: The use of δ^S would mix market timing ability with the security selection skill of the stock picker. Of course, this ambiguity is merely pushed into the fourth term in square brackets: the product of the asset allocation choice of the market timer $\omega_{pt} - \omega^n_{pt}$ and the tracking error of the stock picker $\alpha_{pt} + \varepsilon_{pt+1}$.

This residual component $(\omega_{pt} - \omega^n_{pt})(\alpha_{pt} + \varepsilon_{pt+1})$ cannot be clearly assigned to either active manager, which is why we termed this decomposition *nearly perfect*. This circumstance arises because the market timing portfolio is the stock picker's portfolio δ^S, not the benchmark portfolio. In fact, the residual would vanish if the tools of active management were modified so that the market timer used the benchmark portfolio, since the decomposition would be given by

$$\begin{aligned} R_{pt+1} &= (1 - \omega_{pt})R_{ft+1} + \omega^n_{pt}R^S_{\delta t+1} + (\omega_{pt} - \omega^n_{pt})(R_{\delta t+1} - R_{ft+1}) \\ &= [R_{ft+1} + \omega^n_{pt}(R_{\delta t+1} - R_{ft+1})] + \omega^n_{pt}[\alpha_{pt} + \varepsilon_{pt+1}] \\ &\quad + [(\omega_{pt} - \omega^n_{pt})(R_{\delta t+1} - R_{ft+1})], \end{aligned} \tag{49}$$

which cleanly allocates overall return to strategic or normal asset allocation, security selection, and market timing. Actual managed portfolios can sometimes use this decomposition because their market timers use index futures markets to effect market timing bets, and the allocations to their stock pickers are permitted to drift away from normal weights with infrequent reallocations when the cumulative deviation grows sufficiently large. Of course, the residual will be small when the allowable deviations from strategic asset allocations as well as the returns to security selection are small, conditions that frequently obtain in actual practice.

Of course, the universe of assets is seldom broken down into only two asset classes or sectors. The decomposition into J asset classes is straightforward:

$$R_{pt+1} \equiv \sum_{j=1}^{J} \omega_{pjt} R_{jt} \equiv \sum_{j=1}^{J} \omega^{n}_{pjt} R_{njt} + \sum_{j=1}^{J} \omega^{n}_{pjt}(R_{jt} - R_{njt}) + \sum_{j=1}^{J} (\omega_{pjt} - \omega^{n}_{pjt}) R_{njt} + \sum_{j=1}^{J} (\omega_{pjt} - \omega^{n}_{pjt})(R_{jt} - R_{njt}), \tag{50}$$

where ω_{pjt} and ω^{n}_{pjt} are the actual and normal or strategic asset allocations of portfolio p, respectively, and R_{jt} and R_{njt} are the corresponding actual and benchmark asset class returns. This relation can be rewritten in the excess-return form when the riskless asset, often termed *cash* in common parlance, is one of the asset classes.

This decomposition of the performance of active managers into market timing and security selection components across asset classes or sectors is called *performance attribution*, and it is now widely used in actual practice. This division of labor also roughly reflects the management structure at many, if not most, large pension funds, although the market timing or tactical asset allocation is often done passively. Their investment policy statements typically carve up the asset menu into a number of asset classes and choose explicit benchmarks against which asset class returns are measured with no beta adjustment, corresponding to a structure in which asset class managers are hired and instructed to remain fully invested in the asset class since their performance will be measured against the asset-class-specific benchmark. Moreover, they often specify both the normal or strategic asset allocation weights and the permissible amounts by which the actual asset allocations are allowed to deviate from the normal ones, which corresponds to a short-run or tactical asset allocation or managers who choose asset class exposures and sit one level above the asset class managers. In addition, it is now common for fiduciaries to read performance attribution reports that make routine reference to tracking errors and risk exposures. It is fair to say that performance measurement and attribution along these lines is one of the many dimensions in which financial economics has had an effect, and a beneficial one at that, on real-world investment practice.

Note that there is an implicit assumption about the investment opportunity set in this management structure. Asset class managers can look at correlations within asset classes, and market timers can consider comovements across benchmarks, but neither has the incentive to consider the covariances between each asset class benchmark and individual security returns in other asset classes. In fact, they have a disincentive to do so because they are typically rewarded according to benchmarks that make no provision for such correlations. Hence, it is imperative that the asset class definitions be narrow enough so that the fund does not unintentionally overlook valuable diversification opportunities. Put differently, carving up the asset menu into asset classes with specific benchmarks creates another potential source of benchmark error when

$$R_{\delta t+1} - R_{ft+1} \neq \sum_{j=1}^{J} \omega_{pjt}^{n} R_{njt}. \tag{51}$$

While we are unaware of any empirical evidence on this question, a cursory examination of the investment policy statements of large public U.S. pension funds suggests that such breakdowns are quite refined and probably do not result in materially inferior diversification.

The extent to which performance attribution can be usefully employed depends on whether one is viewing the portfolio from inside the fund or from the outside. Clearly, this method cannot be used without information on actual and normal or strategic asset allocations along with actual and benchmark asset class returns. Data on all of these quantities can be obtained within the fund when it has an explicit investment policy governing asset allocation and benchmarks. The academic perspective, however, is typically external to the fund, and so which of these data are available hinges on what has been reported to the data source. Actual and benchmark asset class returns along with the actual allocation were available in the two main academic applications of these tools, Brinson, Hood, and Beebower (1986) and Brinson, Singer, and Beebower (1991), who studied 82 U.S. pension funds, and Blake, Lehmann, and Timmermann (1999), who examined 306 UK pension funds. Neither study had data on normal or strategic asset allocations.

While our emphasis is on methods and not on empirical evidence, there are two results that are both quite striking and of great relevance for performance measurement and attribution. The first concerns the extent to which performance measurement based on tracking error results in managers actually setting betas equal to 1. Lakonishok, Shleifer, and Vishny (1992) found sample equity betas to be tightly clustered about 1—raw beta estimates and not betas significantly different from 1 at some significance level—in a sample of U.S. pension fund stock portfolios, and Blake, Lehmann, and Timmermann (1999) found similar results for their sample of UK pension funds. That is, managers typically have the incentive to set betas to 1, and the evidence suggests that they are good at doing so. The second broad result concerns market timing. Brinson, Hood, and Beebower (1986) found that only one out of the 96 U.S. pension funds they studied had positive—not statistically significant at some confidence level but simply positive—market timing measures. Similarly, Blake, Lehmann, and Timmermann (1999) found that roughly 80 percent of the 306 UK pension funds they examined had negative market timing measures, with the average return from market timing (at −34 basis points per annum) was statistically significant at conventional levels. Put differently, pension fund managers have typically attempted to time the overall market or individual asset classes, but they have been unsuccessful in doing so.

This last observation has had a profound impact on beliefs about the extent to which managed portfolios benefit from market timing. Many pension funds now follow the passive market timing strategy based on mechanical rebalancing rules, letting their asset class managers—that is, those engaged in security selection—implicitly choose increased pension fund exposure to asset classes when they outperform their benchmarks and lower exposures after underperformance. Other pension funds manage their "traditional" assets this way but buy explicit market timing services from hedge funds, with performance being measured against Treasury bills. That is, a generation of pension fund investment consultants has used this evidence to persuade their clients to forego market timing or to treat it as an asset class with a strict performance standard.

In any event, external performance measurement and attribution with data on actual asset allocations along with actual and benchmark asset class returns requires a model for the strategic or normal asset allocation. Brinson et al. use sample averages of portfolio weights as the normal portfolio weights:

$$\omega_{pjt}^{n} = \omega_{pj}^{n} = \sum_{t=1}^{T} \omega_{pjt}/T, \tag{52}$$

which is a reasonable definition if the fund has a stable de facto asset allocation. However, asset allocations that drift in a particular direction, as was the case in the UK pension funds by Blake, Lehmann, and Timmermann (1999), make this assumption untenable. The models they explored include a linear trend in normal portfolio weights,

$$\omega_{pjt}^{n} = \omega_{pj1} + (t/T)(\omega_{pjT} - \omega_{pj1}), \tag{53}$$

identical strategic asset allocations across funds at a point in time:

$$\omega_{pjt}^{n} = \sum_{p=1}^{P} \omega_{pjt}^{n}, \tag{54}$$

where P is the number of pension funds in the sample, which implicitly assumes zero timing ability for the funds as a whole.[12]

Returning for simplicity to the case of two assets, recall that the portfolio weights w_{pt} and w_{pt}^{n} are equal to the conditional and target betas, respectively, of a portfolio managed in this fashion. This observation suggests that tests for the presence of market timing ability can be based on the conditional and unconditional projections (24) and (28). Consider first the baseline case in which both ω_{pt} and ω_{pt}^{n} are observed for a particular asset class so that $\xi_{\beta_{pt}} = \beta_{pt} - \overline{\beta}_{pt} = \omega_{pt} - \omega_{pt}^{n}$. Since $\xi_{\beta_{pt}}$ is the innovation in the conditional portfolio beta given publicly available information (i.e., $E[\xi_{\beta_{pt}}|I_t] = 0$),

[12]Other alternatives are the error components model used to summarize the stochastic properties of asset class weights in Blake, Lehmann, and Timmermann (1999) and the asset allocation guidelines of the funds with public investment policy statements. Neither approach has been tried in the literature to the best of our knowledge.

the projection of benchmark returns on $\xi_{\beta_{pt}}$ is given by

$$R_{\delta t+1} - R_{ft+1} = \pi_0 + \pi_p \xi_{\beta_{pt}} + \upsilon_{\delta t+1}, \tag{55}$$

with $\pi_p \neq 0$ if and only if the manager possesses market timing ability in great generality. In particular, benchmark excess returns can have arbitrary serial dependence so long as this does not affect the ability of least squares to estimate π_p consistently.[13] This is an obvious consequence of the assumption that both β_{pt} and $\overline{\beta}_{pt}$ are observed via ω_{pt} and ω^n_{pt}.

Of course, we typically observe ω_{pt} but not ω^n_{pt}, which corresponds to observations on β_{pt} but not on $\overline{\beta}_{pt}$ and, hence, not on $\xi_{\beta_{pt}}$. The unobservability of ω^n_{pt} is a subtle problem because its strategic nature suggests that most of its fluctuations occur at low frequencies. That is, π_p in Eq. (55) is given by

$$\begin{aligned}\pi_p &= \frac{\text{Cov}\,(\mu_{\delta t}, \overline{\beta}_{pt} + \xi_{\beta_{pt}})}{\text{Var}[\beta_{pt}]} + \frac{E[(R_{\delta t+1} - R_{ft+1} - \mu_{\delta t})(\overline{\beta}_{pt} + \xi_{\beta_{pt}})]}{\text{Var}[\beta_{pt}]} \\ &= \frac{\text{Cov}\,(\mu_{\delta t}, \overline{\beta}_{pt})}{\text{Var}[\beta_{pt}]} + \frac{\text{Cov}\,(R_{\delta t+1} - R_{ft+1}, \xi_{\beta_{pt}})}{\text{Var}[\beta_{pt}]}\end{aligned} \tag{56}$$

The first term is the bias due to predictability of benchmark returns and the absence of observations on $\overline{\beta}_{pt}$, while the second term is nonzero if and only if market timing is present. Note that only the conditional first moment of excess benchmark returns (and not higher moments) is relevant here, one of the benefits of the observability of β_{pt} under these assumptions.

As in our earlier discussion of the Treynor–Mazuy regressions, there are three approaches to dealing with the bias term in this regression. The first is to assume it away via constancy of $\mu_{\delta t}$ and/or $\overline{\beta}_{pt}$, or $\text{Cov}[\mu_{\delta t}, \overline{\beta}_{pt}] = 0$. Alternatively, one can postulate a model for $\widehat{\mu}_{\delta t}$ and rewrite Eq. (55) in terms of $R_{\delta t+1} - R_{ft+1} - \widehat{\mu}_{\delta t}$, which requires model errors—that is, nonzero values of $E[R_{\delta t+1} - R_{ft+1} - \widehat{\mu}_{\delta t}|I_t]$—to be uncorrelated with $\overline{\beta}_{pt}$. Finally, we can postulate a model for the target beta $\overline{\beta}_{pt} = f(\mathbf{z}_t, \theta)$, where $\mathbf{z}_t \in I_t$ is publicly available conditioning information and θ is a vector of unknown parameters that can be estimated consistently since consistent estimation of $\overline{\beta}_{pt}$ implies consistent estimation of $\xi_{\beta_{pt}}$.[14]

[13]The residual in this projection inherits the serial correlation properties of excess benchmark returns. That is,

$$E[\upsilon_{\delta t+1}|I_t] = E[R_{\delta t+1} - R_{ft+1}|I_t] - \pi_0 = \mu_{\delta t} - \mu_\delta,$$

which would typically be assumed to be well behaved. Typical bounds on higher-order dependence would then yield consistency of least squares in this application.

[14]Note that this last approach requires that $f(z_t, \theta)$ be incorporated in Eq. (55) in the restricted fashion,

$$R_{\delta t+1} - R_{ft+1} = \pi_0 + \pi_p[\omega_{pt} - f(\mathbf{z}_t, \theta)] + \upsilon_{\delta t+1},$$

if the goal is to mimic Eq. (55) exactly because the required regressor is $\xi_{\beta_{pt}}$. However, the natural desire to correct for serial correlation in $\upsilon_{\delta t+1}$ would normally militate in favor of including $\mathbf{z}_t$ or suitable functions of $\mathbf{z}_t$ as regressors.

Graham and Harvey (1996) adopt a variant of this last approach that works instead with changes in actual asset allocations and $\mathbf{z}_t$ as additional regressors, as in

$$R_{\delta t+1} - R_{ft+1} = \pi_z^{*\prime}\mathbf{z}_t + \pi_p^*\triangle\omega_{pt} + v_{\delta t+1}^*,$$

where a test of the hypothesis $\pi_p^* = 0$ is a test of the hypothesis that portfolio weight changes Granger-cause (i.e., predict) benchmark excess returns. This projection is conveniently analyzed by considering the two unconditional population projections:

$$\mu_{\delta t} = \phi_\delta' z_t + e_{\delta t},$$
$$\overline{\beta}_{pt} - \overline{\beta}_{pt-1} - \xi_{\beta_{pt-1}} = \phi_w'\mathbf{z}_t + e_{wt}$$

since

$$\begin{aligned}
\pi_p^* &= \frac{\text{Cov}\,(R_{\delta t+1} - R_{ft+1} - \phi_\delta'\mathbf{z}_t, \triangle\omega_{pt} - \phi_w' z_t)}{\text{Var}[\triangle\omega_{pt} - \phi_w'\mathbf{z}_t]} \\
&= \frac{\text{Cov}[\mu_{\delta t} - \phi_\delta'\mathbf{z}_t, \triangle\overline{\beta}_{pt} - \xi_{\beta_{pt-1}} - \phi_w'\mathbf{z}_t] + \text{Cov}\,(R_{\delta t+1} - R_{ft+1}, \xi_{\beta_{pt}})}{\text{Var}[\xi_{\beta_{pt}} + e_{wt}]} \\
&= \frac{\text{Cov}[e_{\delta t}, e_{wt}]}{\text{Var}[\sigma_\xi^2 + \sigma_{e_w}^2]} + \frac{\text{Cov}(R_{\delta t+1} - R_{ft+1}, \xi_{\beta_{pt}})}{\sigma_\xi^2 + \sigma_{e_w}^2},
\end{aligned} \tag{57}$$

where the bias term depends on the correlation of the projection errors. A priori confidence in the merits of this specification involves a belief that the bias is small and that $\triangle\overline{\beta}_{pt}$ is close to an innovation sequence, thus mitigating the main source of serial correlation in this specification.

Another test of market timing when portfolio weights are observed is suggested by the Henriksson and Merton (1981) analysis of the fidelity between signals and outcomes given at the end of the previous section. An interesting special case is that of tactical asset allocation in which the manager allocates 100 percent to the benchmark portfolio when placing an up-market bet and 100 percent to the riskless asset when placing a down-market bet. This corresponds to Eq. (38), with $\beta_h = 1$ and $\beta_\varrho = 0$ and with up, down, and expected betas of $\beta_p^+ = \frac{\pi_{hu}}{\pi_u}$, $\beta_p^- = \frac{\pi_{hd}}{\pi_d}$, and $\overline{\beta}_p = \pi_h$, respectively. Accordingly, evaluating the performance of tactical asset allocation with observable portfolio weights that take on only the values 1 and 0 is equivalent to the evaluation of prediction signals given in the previous section. Hence, inference for the hypothesis $\frac{\pi_{hu}}{\pi_u} + \frac{\pi_{\varrho d}}{\pi_d} = 1 \Leftrightarrow \frac{\pi_{hu}}{\pi_u} = \frac{\pi_{hd}}{\pi_d}$ can proceed based on the hypergeometric distribution for, while that for the hypothesis $\pi_{hu} = \pi_h\pi_u$ can be based on an asymptotic normal approximation.

More generally, we can use observed portfolio weights to evaluate implicitly the fidelity of market timing signals using the Henriksson–Merton approach. If we assume that up and down markets have constant probabilities and that the manager has a constant target beta, $\omega_{pt} - \omega_p$ will be perfectly correlated with the signal since the manager will have a beta above the mean—that is, $\beta_{pt} > \overline{\beta}_p$—in the high-signal state and one below the mean in the low-market state. When the strategic asset allocation and, hence, the target beta are observed, which is possible in some cases through examination of investment policy statements, the cell counts can be based on the sign of $\omega_{pt} - \omega_p$ and inference can be based on the hypergeometric distribution in Eq. (43). If it is not, the cell counts can be based on the sign of $\omega_{pt} - \overline{\omega}_p$, where $\overline{\omega}_p = \frac{1}{T}\sum_{t=1}^{T} \omega_{pt}$, and inference can be based on the normal approximation (44) since $\overline{\omega}_p \to \omega_p$ in probability under a set of general conditions.

Grinblatt and Titman (1993) implement period-weighting measures when portfolio weights are observed under the assumption that uninformed investors perceive expected asset returns to be constant over time and returns to be independently and identically distributed. In this circumstance, changes in portfolio weights should not be correlated with future returns. In contrast, informed investors will adjust portfolio weights in anticipation of future returns, and, if their information is valid, portfolio-weight changes should be correlated with future returns. The exact form of the relation will depend on the way in which the informed investor's information and preferences interact to produce a portfolio decision rule. That said, the unconditional covariance between portfolio weights and future returns should be positive under the weak assumption that portfolio weights are increasing in each asset's conditionally expected return. A simple test for the presence of performance ability can be based on the sum of the covariances between portfolio weights and asset returns across all assets in the universe:

$$\text{Cov} = \sum_{j=1}^{N} (E[\omega_j R_j] - E[\omega_j]E[R_j]). \tag{58}$$

This is equal to the expected return of the investor's actual portfolio minus the expected return if portfolio weights and returns were uncorrelated. The second term also acts as a risk adjustment since it gives the expected return on a portfolio with the same average risk as the actual portfolio.

Equation (58) can equivalently be rewritten in one of two ways:

$$\text{Cov} = \sum_{j=1}^{N} E\left[\omega_j(R_j - E[R_j])\right] \tag{59}$$

or

$$\text{Cov} = \sum_{j=1}^{N} E\left[(\omega_j - E[\omega_j])R_j\right]. \tag{60}$$

Since ω_j and R_j are observed, these expressions point to two types of additional information that can be used to produce period-weighting measure estimates described in the previous section.

The first of these expressions in Eq. (59) requires an estimate of the (unconditional) expected return, $E[R_j]$. Given the assumption that returns are independent and identically distributed (iid), a natural way to proceed is to use average future returns on these assets, making this approach much like an event study, in that returns from outside the event window—the performance measurement period in this case—measure normal performance. Abnormal performance arises when these assets earn higher returns when they are in the investor's portfolio than at other times.

The second expression in Eq. (60) requires instead an estimate of the expected portfolio weight, ω_j. This formulation is more problematic because serial dependence in weights—such as that produced, for example, by momentum or contrarian investment strategies—causes sample period-weighting measures to be biased. If the serial dependence in momentum or contrarian portfolio weights is short-lived, such biases can be mitigated or eliminated by introducing a lag between return and expected portfolio weight measurement. For example, if weights are covariance stationary, each observed weight is an unbiased estimate of expected portfolio weights. If weights and returns are K dependent—that is, if they are independent when K periods separate their measurement—there is no such bias. Hence, Grinblatt and Titman recommend setting $E[\omega_j] = \omega_{jt-K}$, resulting in period-weighting estimates of the form

$$\widehat{\text{Cov}}_\omega = \frac{1}{T}\sum_{j=1}^{N}\sum_{t=K}^{T}(\omega_{jt} - \omega_{jt-K})R_{jt},$$

and they use the same idea for expected returns by setting $E[R_j] = R_{jt+K}$ in the revised estimate:

$$\widehat{\text{Cov}}_R = \frac{1}{T}\sum_{j=1}^{N}\sum_{t=1}^{T-K}\omega_{jt}(R_{jt} - R_{jt+K}).$$

Each of these measures will converge to zero provided fund managers use no information with predictive content regarding future returns when setting their portfolio weights and returns are not predictable for uninformed investors. That said, $\widehat{\text{Cov}}_\omega$ makes for simpler inference than $\widehat{\text{Cov}}_R$, since its returns are serially uncorrelated when individual asset returns are serially uncorrelated as well. In contradistinction, the overlapping returns implicit in $\widehat{\text{Cov}}_R$ make its returns $K - 1$ dependent when individual asset returns are serially uncorrelated. Hence, the test statistic based on $\widehat{\text{Cov}}_\omega$ is a simple test of the null hypothesis that a mean is zero.

4.1. Should Investors Hold Mutual Funds?

A key question from an investor's point of view is whether—and by how much—to invest in one or more mutual funds. Suppose we cannot reject the null hypothesis that a particular fund's alpha equals zero, although its point estimate indicates a sizeable skill level. This is a likely outcome of many empirical tests due to the weak power of these tests. Does this mean that the investor should hold none of his portfolio in the mutual fund? Clearly this is not implied by the outcome of the statistical test, which is based on a discrete-loss function that is typically very different from the underlying utility function. Statistical tests do not in general trade off the cost of wrongly including an investment in a mutual fund versus wrongly excluding it.[15] Conversely, suppose we reject the null hypothesis that the portfolio weight on the mutual fund(s) equals zero. Then how much should be invested in such funds?

The investor's decision of whether to hold mutual funds at all is naturally set up as a test on the portfolio weights when data on these are available. When investors have mean-variance preferences, constructing such a test and deriving its properties are quite straightforward and can be based on a simple regression approach to portfolio selection that minimizes the squared deviations between the excess returns on a constructed portfolio and the excess returns implicit in the unity vector, ι, c.f. Britten-Jones (1999). As shown by Britten-Jones, this minimization can be implemented through a projection of ι on excess returns on the risky assets and mutual funds, excluding an intercept term. To this end, define the $N + P$–vector of period–$t + 1$ excess return on all risky assets extended to include a set of P mutual funds as $\widetilde{\mathbf{r}}_{t+1} = (\mathbf{R}'_{t+1}\ \mathbf{R}'_{pt+1})' - \iota R_{ft+1}$, and let $\widetilde{\mathbf{r}} = (\mathbf{r}_1 \mathbf{r}_2 \ldots \mathbf{r}_T)'$ be the $T \times (N + P)$ matrix of stacked returns. The projection proposed by Britten-Jones is

$$\iota = \widetilde{\mathbf{r}}\beta + \mathbf{u}. \tag{61}$$

The resulting vector of estimated coefficients,

$$\widehat{\mathbf{b}} = (\widetilde{\mathbf{r}}'\widetilde{\mathbf{r}})^{-1}\widetilde{\mathbf{r}}'\iota, \tag{62}$$

gives—up to a proportionality factor—the weights of the mean-variance efficient portfolio of risky assets. Using the scaling $\widehat{\mathbf{b}}/\iota'\widehat{\mathbf{b}}$, we get the maximum Sharpe ratio (tangency) portfolio,

$$\frac{\overline{\Sigma}^{-1}\,\overline{\mathbf{r}}}{1'\overline{\Sigma}^{-1}\,\overline{\mathbf{r}}},$$

where $\overline{\mathbf{r}} = \widetilde{\mathbf{r}}'\iota/T$ is the sample mean, while the (maximum-likelihood) sample covariance matrix is

$$\overline{\Sigma} = \frac{(\widetilde{\mathbf{r}} - 1\overline{r}')'(\widetilde{\mathbf{r}} - 1\overline{r}')}{T}.$$

Suppose that there are P mutual funds under consideration (the last P assets in the vector of excess returns, $\widetilde{\mathbf{r}}$). Then the restriction that the investor should entirely exclude mutual funds from the portfolio takes the form

$$\mathbf{\Gamma b} = \mathbf{0},$$

where the $P \times (N + P)$ matrix of restrictions, $\mathbf{\Gamma}$, is given by

$$\mathbf{\Gamma} = \begin{pmatrix} \mathbf{0}_{P\times N} & \mathbf{I}_P \end{pmatrix}.$$

[15] Although in principle one could make the critical level used to define the nominal size of the statistical test a function of the relative cost of type I and type II errors, this does not resolve the problem that the hypothesis testing uses a discrete decision, whereas the investor's utility function is generally assumed to be continuous.

Assuming that returns are joint normally distributed and iid, Britten-Jones shows that this restriction can be tested through the F-statistic:

$$\frac{(\mathrm{SSR}_r - \mathrm{SSR}_u)/P}{\mathrm{SSR}_u/(T-N-P)}, \tag{63}$$

where SSR_u is the sum of squared residuals implied by the unrestricted regression underlying the coefficient estimates in Eq. (62), SSR_r is the sum of squared residuals from estimation of regression (62) subject to the restriction that $\boldsymbol{\Gamma}\mathbf{b} = \mathbf{0}$. This test statistic has an exact central F distribution with P and $T - N - P$ degrees of freedom.

4.2. Determining the Optimal Holdings in Mutual Funds

When preferences outside the mean-variance class are considered and we are also interested in answering the second question—namely, how much to invest in mutual funds—a more general approach is called for. We illustrate a simple method valid in a single-period setting where dynamic programming concerns can be ignored. Let W_t, W_{t+1} be an investor's current and future wealth and suppose that the investor evaluates utility from future wealth through the function $U(W_{t+1})$. Returns on traded risky assets and mutual funds are again given by $\widetilde{\mathbf{R}}_{t+1} = (\mathbf{R}'_{t+1}\ \mathbf{R}'_{pt+1})'$, while $\widetilde{\boldsymbol{\omega}}_t = (\omega'_t\ \omega'_{pt})'$ is the associated vector of portfolio holdings. Future wealth associated with a given set of portfolio holdings is simply

$$W_{t+1} = W_t(\widetilde{\boldsymbol{\omega}}'_t\widetilde{\mathbf{R}}_{t+1}),$$

while the investor's optimization problem is to maximize expected utility conditional on current information, I_t:

$$\max_{\omega_t}\ E[U(W_t(\widetilde{\boldsymbol{\omega}}'_t\widetilde{\mathbf{R}}_{t+1}))|I_t].$$

The portfolio weights on the mutual funds can be obtained from the last P elements of ω_t corresponding to the mutual fund returns.

For example, in the earlier example with mean-variance preferences,

$$E[U(W_{t+1})|I_t] = E[W_{t+1}|I_t] - \frac{\gamma}{2}\mathrm{Var}\,(W_{t+1}|I_t),$$

where γ is the absolute risk aversion. This gives a closed-form solution (c.f. Ait-Sahalia and Brandt (2001)):

$$\widetilde{\boldsymbol{\omega}}_t = \Sigma_t^{-1}\iota\frac{\gamma W_t - \iota'\Sigma_t^{-1}\mu_t}{\gamma W_t\iota'\Sigma_t^{-1}\iota} + \frac{\Sigma_t^{-1}\mu_t}{\gamma W_t},$$

where $\Sigma_t = \mathrm{Var}(\widetilde{R}_{t+1}|I_t)$ and $\boldsymbol{\mu}_t = E(\widetilde{R}_{t+1}|I_t)$. Since (conditional) population moments are unknown, in practice sample estimates of these moments, $\widehat{\Sigma}$ and $\widehat{\boldsymbol{\mu}}$, are typically plugged in to get estimated weights, as follows:

$$\widehat{\omega}_t = \widehat{\Sigma}_t^{-1}\iota \frac{\gamma W_t - \iota'\widehat{\Sigma}_t^{-1}\widehat{\mu}_t}{\gamma W_t \iota'\widehat{\Sigma}_t^{-1}\iota} + \frac{\widehat{\Sigma}_t^{-1}\widehat{\mu}_t}{\gamma W_t}.$$

This of course ignores the sampling errors in the moment estimates. Furthermore, due to the nonlinearity in the mapping from $\widehat{\Sigma}$ and $\widehat{\boldsymbol{\mu}}$ to $\widehat{\boldsymbol{\omega}}_t$, it is not possible to identify which predictors $\mathbf{z}_t \in I_t$ are important to portfolio holdings by inspecting the predictability of the mean, variance of returns.

Rather than adopting a two-stage approach that first estimates a model for the predictive distribution of returns and then plugs in the resulting parameter estimates in the equation for the optimal weight, Ait-Sahalia and Brandt suggest modeling the portfolio weights directly as a function of the predictor (or state) variables, $\mathbf{z}_t$. To this end let the portfolio policy function map $\mathbf{z}_t$ into optimal asset holdings:

$$\widetilde{\boldsymbol{\omega}}_t = \omega(\mathbf{z}_t). \tag{64}$$

Of course, in general both the functional form of the optimal portfolio policy $\omega(\mathbf{z}_t)$ and the form of the predictability of returns are unknown. One way to deal with this that avoids the curse of dimensionality is to follow Ait-Sahalia and Brandt (2001) and assume that the portfolio policy depends on only the state variables through a single index, $\mathbf{z}_t{}'\beta$:

$$\max_{\omega_t} E[U(W_t(\widetilde{\boldsymbol{\omega}}_t'\widetilde{\mathbf{R}}_{t+1}))|\mathbf{z}_t'\boldsymbol{\beta}],$$

$$\omega_t = \omega(\mathbf{z}_t{}'\boldsymbol{\beta};\boldsymbol{\beta}).$$

This is a semiparametric approach that assumes a parametric (linear) index function but allows for a flexible (nonparametric) policy function.

Differentiating the optimization problem with respect to $\widetilde{\boldsymbol{\omega}}_t$ and using $\widetilde{\boldsymbol{\omega}}_t = \omega(X_t'\beta;\beta)$ gives the conditional moment condition

$$E[Q_{t+1}(\beta)|\mathbf{z_t}] = E[U'(W_t(\omega(\mathbf{z}_t'\beta;\beta)'\widetilde{\mathbf{R}}_{t+1}))\widetilde{\mathbf{R}}_{t+1}|\mathbf{z}_t'\beta] = 0.$$

This can be estimated via generalized method of moments (GMM), using instruments $g(\mathbf{z}_t)$:

$$\min_{\beta} E[Q_{t+1}(\beta)\otimes g(\mathbf{z}_t)]'W\,E[Q_{t+1}(\beta)\otimes g(\mathbf{z}_t)]$$

where $W = \text{Cov}(Q_{t+1} \otimes g(\mathbf{z}_t))^{-1}$ is again some weighting matrix.

Alternatively, one can approximate the policy function, in Eq. (64), using a series expansion such as

$$\widetilde{\omega}_{it} = \widetilde{\omega}_{0i} + \sum_{j=1}^{n_z} \widetilde{\omega}_{1ij} z_{jt} + \sum_{j=1}^{n_z} \sum_{k=1}^{n_z} \widetilde{\omega}_{2ijk} z_{jt} z_{kt}, \tag{65}$$

where n_z is the number of z-variables. Again the parameters of the policy function can be estimated using GMM.

5. THE CROSS SECTION OF MANAGED PORTFOLIO RETURNS

What makes the econometrics of performance measurement and its economic setting different from that of conventional asset pricing? After all, Jensen's alpha is just mispricing in asset pricing models, we test for their joint significance using mean-variance efficiency or Euler equation tests, benchmark portfolios are the (conditionally) mean-variance efficient portfolios implied by such models, and stochastic discount factors appear in both settings. Similarly, the distinction between serially dependent and independent returns must often be handled with care in both settings.

A key difference is in the interpretation of rejections of the null hypothesis: Researchers often interpret rejections of the null hypothesis for managed portfolios as a reflection of managerial skill, while rejections of the null hypothesis in asset pricing theory tests are typically attributed to failures of the model. Most papers that evaluate the performance of managed portfolios simply do not treat the finding of economically and statistically significant alphas as an indication that the benchmark is not conditionally mean-variance efficient. Most papers that evaluate the performance of asset pricing models simply do not treat the finding of economically and statistically significant alphas as an indication that the test assets are underpriced or overpriced.

What makes the stochastic properties of this universe of test assets different from the passive—that is, unmanaged—portfolios typically employed in asset pricing theory tests? The answer probably lies in the commonalities among portfolio managers arising from the comparatively small range of investment styles and asset classes into which the universe of securities is partitioned. The portfolios used in asset pricing theory tests are formed according to different principles. In some cases, researchers seek dispersion across population-conditional betas to facilitate more precise estimation of any risk premiums, which reflects a concern for inferences about the implications of the model under the null hypothesis that it is true. Many tests are based on portfolios formed on the basis of security characteristics that proved to be correlated with the alphas from earlier asset pricing models, reflecting a concern for inference when the null hypothesis is false. Others are based on portfolios chosen because the underlying test assets were thought to have low correlation conditional on the benchmark in question: Industry and commodity portfolios have been chosen for this reason at different times.

The commonalities among the trading strategies of portfolio managers make for potential differences in each of these dimensions. The dispersion of conditional betas across funds is quite small, probably because performance is typically measured relative to an explicit or implicit benchmark, which gives the manager strong incentive to maintain beta close to 1 on that benchmark. Management styles are often highly correlated with security attributes as well, and so managers have to take bets that are different from the characteristics portfolios used by financial econometricians in order to justify management fees. Finally, the very commonalities among trading strategies suggest that residual correlations are likely to be higher in the managed portfolio setting than in asset pricing theory tests. Of these, the second one is likely to be second order, but the first and third are of first-order importance.

5.1. Inference in the Absence of Performance Ability

Consider first the setting in which it is known a priori that the excess returns of N securities are independently and identically distributed over time from the perspective of uninformed investors. As before, let portfolio δ be the mean-variance efficient portfolio based on these N assets. Portfolio δ has constant weights under these assumptions, and its excess returns are given by

$$\mathbf{R}_{t+1} - \iota R_{ft+1} = \beta_\delta(\mathbf{R}_{\delta t+1} - \iota R_{ft+1}) + \varepsilon_{\delta t+1},$$

where $E[\varepsilon_{\delta t+1}|I_t] = 0$.

Managers, however, need not have portfolio weights that are constant, and the extent and manner in which their weights vary over time depend on whether they believe they have skill at market timing or security selection. Managers who do not believe they have market timing ability but who think they possess skill at selection will tend to choose fixed-weight portfolios if they believe there are constant expected returns to selection, but they will have portfolios with time-varying weights if they believe that the returns to selection vary across stocks over time.[16] In terms of the conditional Jensen regression, these managers will choose time-invariant betas and will believe they have time-varying Jensen alphas. Managers who believe they have market timing ability will also generically vary their weights over time so that their betas and, if they have skill at selection, their alphas will vary over time.

Only tests of the skill of managers of the first kind—those with no timing ability and who know it but who falsely think they possess skill at security selection with constant expected returns—are completely straightforward in these circumstances. Such managers believe that their portfolios satisfy the Jensen regression with constant conditional betas:

$$R_{pt+1} - R_{ft+1} = \alpha_p + \beta_p(R_{\delta t+1} - R_{ft+1}) + \epsilon_{pt+1}, \tag{66}$$

[16]Constant expected returns to selection will not lead to fixed-weight portfolios if managers have implicit hedging demands, such as those that can arise from different compensation schemes.

where the manager believes that $\alpha_p = E[\boldsymbol{\omega}'_p \varepsilon_{\delta t+1} | I_{pt}] = \boldsymbol{\omega}'_p E[\varepsilon_{\delta t+1} | I_{pt}]$ and the residual $\epsilon_{pt+1} = \omega'_p \varepsilon_{\delta t+1}$ is homoskedastic. Hence, the null hypothesis that the manager of portfolio p does not have skill at selection can be tested with the simple t-test, which goes by the name of the Treynor–Black appraisal ratio in the performance evaluation literature, as was noted earlier.

Similarly, a joint test to show if such P funds have skill at selection involves the P regressions:

$$\mathbf{R}_{pt+1} - \iota R_{ft+1} = \alpha_p + \beta_p(\mathbf{R}_{\delta t+1} - \iota R_{ft+1}) + \epsilon_{pt+1},$$

where the natural null hypothesis is

$$H_0 : \alpha_p = \mathbf{0}. \tag{67}$$

If returns are normally distributed, this hypothesis can be tested via

$$\frac{T(T-P-1)}{P(T-2)} \frac{\widehat{\alpha}'_p \widehat{\mathbf{S}}^{-1}_{\epsilon_p} \widehat{\alpha}_p}{1 + \widehat{\phi}^2_\delta} \sim F(P, T-P-1),$$

where $\widehat{\alpha}_p$, $\widehat{\mathbf{S}}_{\epsilon_p}$ is the sample covariance matrix of the residuals and $\widehat{\phi}^2_\delta$ is the sample squared Sharpe ratio of the benchmark portfolio that is given by $\widehat{\phi}_\delta = \frac{\overline{R_\delta - R_f}}{s_\delta}$, where

$$\overline{R_\delta - R_f} = \sum_{t=1}^{T} (R_{\delta t+1} - R_{ft+1})/T$$

and

$$s^2_\delta = \sum_{t=1}^{T} (R_{\delta t+1} - R_{ft+1})^2/(T-1) - \left(\overline{R_\delta - R_f}\right)^2$$

are the sample mean and variance of benchmark returns, respectively. Jobson and Korkie (1982) and Gibbons, Ross, and Shanken (1989) showed that this statistic follows an exact F-distribution with P numerator and $T - P - 1$ denominator degrees of freedom. In large samples, we can dispense with normality, since the statistic

$$T \frac{\widehat{\alpha}'_p \widehat{\mathbf{S}}^{-1}_{\epsilon_p} \widehat{\alpha}_p}{1 + \widehat{\phi}^2_\delta} \sim \chi^2(P) \tag{68}$$

is distributed as χ^2 with P degrees of freedom asymptotically, although it is common to use the associated F-statistic formulation as a sort of ad hoc small-sample correction. This is a conventional mean-variance efficiency test where the test assets are managed portfolios.

Managers might believe they do not have timing ability but that they possess time-varying selection skill. Such managers will generically choose portfolios with time-varying weights, and they will believe that their returns satisfy

$$\begin{aligned} R_{pt+1} - R_{ft+1} &= \omega'_{pt}(\mathbf{R}_{t+1} - \iota R_{ft+1}) = \omega'_{pt}\beta_\delta(\mathbf{R}_{\delta t+1} - \iota R_{ft+1}) + \omega'_{pt}\,\varepsilon_{\delta t+1} \\ &= \alpha_p + \beta_p(\mathbf{R}_{\delta t+1} - \iota R_{ft+1}) + \alpha_{pt} - \alpha_p + \varepsilon_{pt+1} \\ &\equiv \alpha_p + \beta_p(\mathbf{R}_{\delta t+1} - \iota R_{ft+1}) + \epsilon_{pt+1}, \end{aligned}$$

where the manager believes $\alpha_{pt} = E[\omega'_{pt}\,\varepsilon_{\delta t+1}|I_{pt}] = \omega'_{pt}E[\varepsilon_{\delta t+1}|I_{pt}] \neq 0$. If the manager is right, $\alpha_{pt} > 0$, $\alpha_p = E[\alpha_{pt}] > 0$, and $\epsilon_{pt+1} = \omega'_{pt}\varepsilon_{\delta t+1}$ is a heteroskedastic and serially correlated error term. If the manager is wrong, $\alpha_{pt} = \alpha_p = 0$ and $\epsilon_{pt+1} = \omega'_{pt}\varepsilon_{\delta t+1}$ is generically a heteroskedastic and serially dependent, but not serially correlated, error term.

The principles governing hypothesis testing are a bit different under the null hypothesis of no skill at security selection. The least-squares estimates $\widehat{\alpha}_p$ and $\widehat{\beta}_p$ are given by

$$\widehat{\alpha}_p = \alpha_p + \frac{1+\widehat{\phi}_\delta^2}{T}\sum_{t=1}^{T}\epsilon_{pt+1} - \frac{\overline{R_\delta - R_f}}{T}\sum_{t=1}^{T}\left(R_{\delta t+1} - R_{ft+1}\right)\epsilon_{pt+1}, \tag{69}$$

and, since $\varepsilon_{\delta t+1}$ is independently and identically distributed, its variance converges to

$$\begin{aligned} \mathrm{Var}(\widehat{\alpha}_p) \to \frac{1}{T}\Big\{&(1+\phi_\delta^2)^2E\left[\epsilon_{pt+1}^2\right] - 2(1+\phi_\delta^2)\overline{R_\delta - R_f}\,E\left[(R_{\delta t+1} - R_{ft+1})\epsilon_{pt+1}^2\right] \\ &+ \overline{R_\delta - R_f}^2\,E\left[(R_{\delta t+1} - R_{ft+1})^2\epsilon_{pt+1}^2\right]\Big\}, \end{aligned} \tag{70}$$

which obviously depends on the extent to which $\epsilon_{pt+1}^2 = (\omega'_{pt}\varepsilon_{\delta t+1})^2$ is related to $R_{\delta t+1} - R_{ft+1}$ and $(R_{\delta t+1} - R_{ft+1})^2$. This is, of course, the familiar heteroskedasticity-consistent estimator of the variance of $\mathrm{Var}(\widehat{\alpha}_p)$. If the portfolio weights are independent of market conditions, the variance simplifies to

$$\mathrm{Var}(\widehat{\alpha}_p) \to \frac{(1+\phi_\delta^2)^2\sigma_{\epsilon_p}^2}{T},$$

just as it did in the conditionally homoskedastic case, and so inference can be based on the large-sample χ^2 statistic in Eq. (68), since normality of asset returns does not deliver normally distributed managed portfolio returns when weights are time-varying.

As it happens, the case in which managers believe they have time-varying skill is identical to that in which they believe they have market timing ability when they do not possess skill in either dimension. That is, the Jensen residual when managers feel they have both market timing and stock picking ability is given by

$$\epsilon_{pt+1} = \alpha_{pt} - \alpha_p + (\beta_{pt} - \beta_p)(R_{\delta t+1} - R_{ft+1}) + \varepsilon_{pt+1},$$

where

$$E[\alpha_{pt} - \alpha_p] = E[(\beta_{pt} - \beta_p)(R_{\delta t+1} - R_{ft+1})] = 0$$

under the null hypothesis. Hence, irrespective of whether conditional heteroskedasticity arises from attempts at selection that are dependent on market conditions or attempts at market timing, the joint hypothesis that P alphas are zero can be tested via the χ^2 statistic:

$$T\frac{\widehat{\alpha}_p'\widehat{\mathbf{S}}_{\epsilon_p}^{*}\widehat{\alpha}_p}{1+\widehat{\phi}_\delta^2} \sim \chi^2(P), \tag{71}$$

where $\widehat{\mathbf{S}}_{\epsilon_p}^{*}$ is given by:

$$\widehat{\mathbf{S}}_{\epsilon_p}^{*} = \frac{1}{T}\left[(1+\phi_\delta^2)^2\widehat{\mathbf{S}}_{\epsilon_p} - 2(1+\phi_\delta^2)\overline{R_\delta - R_f}\,\widehat{\mathbf{S}}_{R_\delta\epsilon_p} + \overline{R_\delta - R_f}^2\widehat{\mathbf{S}}_{R_\delta^2\epsilon_p}\right],$$

$$\widehat{\mathbf{S}}_{R_\delta\epsilon_p} = \frac{1}{T}\sum_{t=1}^{T}(R_{\delta t+1} - R_{ft+1})\widehat{\epsilon}_{pt+1}\widehat{\epsilon}_{pt+1}'; \ \widehat{\mathbf{S}}_{R_\delta^2\epsilon_p} = \frac{1}{T}\sum_{t=1}^{T}(R_{\delta t+1} - R_{ft+1})^2\widehat{\epsilon}_{pt+1}\widehat{\epsilon}_{pt+1}',$$

which makes $\widehat{\mathbf{S}}_{\epsilon_p}^{*}$ the heteroskedasticity-consistent equivalent of $\widehat{\mathbf{S}}_{\epsilon_p}$.

Little is changed if we dispense with the assumption that returns are identically distributed over time while maintaining the assumption of serial independence. From the perspective of the Jensen regression, there is one more potential source of conditional heteroskedasticity related to market conditions if returns are not identically distributed unconditionally. For this reason, too, it would appear that conservative inference suggests the use of the heteroskedastic-consistent χ^2 statistic in Eq. (71).

Serial dependence in returns from the perspective of uninformed investors can create additional complexities although it need not do so: Changes in betas due to time variation in expected returns do not bias Jensen alphas unless

$$\text{Cov}[\overline{\beta}_{pt}, R_{\delta t+1} - R_{ft+1}] = E[\varsigma_{\beta_{pt}}\mu_{\delta t}] \neq 0,$$

where $\overline{\beta}_{pt} = \overline{\beta}_p + \varsigma_{\beta_{pt}}$ is the conditional beta based on public information, not on market timing ability. Unfortunately, any beta change of the form $\varsigma_{\beta_{pt}} = k(\mu_{\delta t} - \mu_\delta)$ will cause this assumption to fail, biasing the Jensen alpha upward on the natural hypothesis $k > 0$.

One general strategy for dealing with this problem is to attempt to measure $\varsigma_{\beta_{pt}}$, or, more precisely, that portion of $\varsigma_{\beta_{pt}}$ that is correlated with expected benchmark returns $\mu_{\delta t}$. To this end, Ferson and Schadt (1996) propose modeling time variation in mutual fund betas as projections onto observed conditioning information, as in

$$\overline{\beta}_{pt} = \overline{\beta}_p + \pi'_{\overline{\beta}}(\mathbf{z}_{pt} - \mu_z) + e_{\overline{\beta}t},$$

where the identifying assumption is that

$$E[e_{\overline{\beta}t}(R_{\delta t+1} - R_{ft+1})] = E[e_{\overline{\beta}t}(R_{\delta t+1} - R_{ft+1})] = 0,$$

and so the alpha from the revised Jensen regression,

$$E[R_{pt+1} - R_{ft+1} = \alpha_p + \overline{\beta}_p(R_{\delta t+1} - R_{ft+1}) + \pi'_{\overline{\beta}}(\mathbf{z}_{pt} - \mu_z)(R_{\delta t+1} - R_{ft+1}) + \epsilon_{pt+1},$$

is purged of the effects of time variation in conditional benchmark betas related to public information under these assumptions. Hence, this model can be estimated by ordinary least squares and the inference procedures identified earlier can be applied to them without modification.

The Treynor–Mazuy regression, coupled with the same sorts of simplifying assumptions, provides another avenue for dealing with serial dependence. As is obvious, this resolution can work here because there is no timing ability under the null hypothesis. Accordingly, consider the Treynor–Mazuy quadratic regression

$$R_{pt+1} - R_{ft+1} = a_p + b_{0p}(R_{\delta t+1} - R_{ft+1}) + b_{1p}(R_{\delta t+1} - R_{ft+1})^2 + \zeta_{pt+1}$$

along with the unconditional population projection

$$R_{\delta t+1} - R_{ft+1} = \mu_\delta + \pi_\varsigma \varsigma_{\beta_{pt}} + \upsilon^\varsigma_{\delta t+1}, \tag{72}$$

where the residual $\upsilon^\varsigma_{\delta t+1}$ is purged of the correlation of $\varsigma_{\beta_{pt}}$ with expected excess benchmark returns. Now assume that excess benchmark returns $R_{\delta t+1} - R_{ft+1}$ and beta innovations $\varsigma_{\beta_{pt}}$ are jointly normally distributed and strengthen the lack of correlation between $\upsilon^\varsigma_{\delta t+1}$ and $\varsigma_{\beta_{pt}}$ to independence.[17] Substitution of Eq. (72) into the normal equations of this variant of the quadratic regression reveals that the unconditional

[17]This assumption is not entirely innocuous because both $\upsilon^\varsigma_{\delta t+1}$ and $\varsigma_{\beta_{pt}}$ would typically be serially dependent in this setting. The aim of this assumption is to eliminate any role for dependence between the possibly time-varying higher comments of $\upsilon^\varsigma_{\delta t+1}$ and $\varsigma_{\beta_{pt}}$.

projection coefficients b_{0p} and b_{1p} are given by

$$\begin{aligned}
\begin{pmatrix} b_{0p} \\ b_{1p} \end{pmatrix} &= \left[\text{Var} \begin{pmatrix} R_{\delta t+1} - R_{ft+1} \\ (R_{\delta t+1} - R_{ft+1})^2 \end{pmatrix} \right]^{-1} \text{Cov} \left[R_{pt+1} - R_{ft+1}, \begin{pmatrix} R_{\delta t+1} - R_{ft+1} \\ (R_{\delta t+1} - R_{ft+1})^2 \end{pmatrix} \right] \\
&= \begin{pmatrix} \sigma_\delta^2 & 0 \\ 0 & 3\sigma_\delta^4 \end{pmatrix}^{-1} \text{Cov} \left[(\overline{\beta}_p + \varsigma_{\beta_{pt}})(R_{\delta t+1} - R_{ft+1}) + \epsilon_{pt+1}, \begin{pmatrix} R_{\delta t+1} - R_{ft+1} \\ (R_{\delta t+1} - R_{ft+1})^2 \end{pmatrix} \right] \\
&= \begin{pmatrix} \overline{\beta}_p \\ 0 \end{pmatrix} + E \begin{pmatrix} \varsigma_{\beta_{pt}}(\mu_\delta + \pi_\varsigma \varsigma_{\beta_{pt}} + \upsilon_{\delta t+1}^\varsigma)(\pi_\varsigma \varsigma_{\beta_{pt}} + \upsilon_{\delta t+1}^\varsigma) \\ \varsigma_{\beta_{pt}}(\mu_\delta + \pi_\varsigma \varsigma_{\beta_{pt}} + \upsilon_{\delta t+1}^\varsigma)[(\pi_\varsigma \varsigma_{\beta_{pt}} + \upsilon_{\delta t+1}^\varsigma)^2 - \sigma_\delta^2] \end{pmatrix} \\
&= \begin{pmatrix} \overline{\beta}_p \\ 0 \end{pmatrix} + \frac{\pi_\varsigma \sigma_\xi^2}{\sigma_\delta^2} \begin{pmatrix} \mu_\delta \\ \frac{2}{3} \end{pmatrix} \equiv \begin{pmatrix} \overline{\beta}_p \\ 0 \end{pmatrix} + \begin{pmatrix} \gamma_{0p}^\varsigma \\ \gamma_{1p}^\varsigma \end{pmatrix}.
\end{aligned} \tag{73}$$

And the corresponding intercept a_p is, under the null hypothesis, given by

$$\begin{aligned}
a_p &= \text{Cov}[\xi_{\beta_{pt}}, R_{\delta t+1} - R_{ft+1}] - \gamma_{0p}^\varsigma E[R_{\delta t+1} - R_{ft+1}] - \gamma_{1p}^\varsigma E[(R_{\delta t+1} - R_{ft+1})^2] \\
&= \pi_\varsigma \sigma_\xi^2 - \pi_\varsigma \sigma_\xi^2 \frac{\mu_\delta^2}{\sigma_\delta^2} - \pi_\varsigma \sigma_\xi^2 \frac{2}{3} \frac{\mu_\delta^2 + \sigma_\delta^2}{\sigma_\delta^2} \\
&= \pi_\varsigma \sigma_\xi^2 \left[\frac{1}{3} - \frac{5}{3} \phi_\delta^2 \right].
\end{aligned}$$

Now b_{1p} can be used to solve for $\pi_\varsigma \sigma_\xi^2$, which can, in turn, be used to solve for $\overline{\beta}_p$, and the null hypothesis

$$H_0 : a_p = \pi_\varsigma \sigma_\xi^2$$

can be tested using the delta method to calculate the standard error for $\widehat{a}_p - \widehat{\pi}_\varsigma \widehat{\sigma}_\xi^2$. The extension to P funds is straightforward.

We have taken the benchmark portfolio as known when it is, in fact, a construct based on stochastic discount factors if one follows the route leading in Section 2.[18] We can adopt one of two variants of the stochastic discount factor approach, one based on the moment condition (1) and the other based on the moment condition (4) defining portfolio δ. We describe these methods in turn.

The first approach treats the identification of the stochastic discount factor as a modeling problem. That is, we can model the stochastic discount factor as being given by

[18] The case in which the stochastic discount factor is a portfolio of given portfolios can be handled by replacing the single-index Jensen and Treynor–Mazuy regressions with multifactor ones in which there are separate betas on each given portfolio. The main complications are notational complexity coupled with the potential for the benchmark portfolio so constructed to have realizations that are not strictly positive.

some functional form,

$$m_{t+1} = g(\mathbf{x}_{t+1}, \theta_m) + \varepsilon^g_{mt+1},$$

where $\mathbf{x}_{t+1}$ is a set of state variables that help determine the realization of the family of stochastic discount factors defined by $E[\varepsilon^g_{mt+1}\mathbf{R}_{t+1}|I_t] = 0$ and θ_m is a set of unknown parameters. These parameters can be estimated by exploiting the conditional moment conditions,

$$\iota = E[m_{t+1}\mathbf{R}_{t+1}|I_t] = E[[g(\mathbf{x}_{t+1}, \theta_m) + \varepsilon^g_{mt+1}]\mathbf{R}_{t+1}|I_t] = E[g(\mathbf{x}_{t+1}, \theta_m)\mathbf{R}_{t+1}|I_t]. \tag{74}$$

Multiplying both sides of Eq. (74) by $\mathbf{z}_t \in I_t$ and taking unconditional expectations yields

$$\begin{aligned}\iota\mathbf{z}'_t = \; & E[g(\mathbf{x}_{t+1}, \theta_m)\mathbf{R}_{t+1}|I_t]\mathbf{z}'_t = E[g(\mathbf{x}_{t+1}, \theta_m)\mathbf{R}_{t+1}\mathbf{z}'_t|I_t] \\ & \Rightarrow E[\iota\mathbf{z}'_t] = E[g(\mathbf{x}_{t+1}, \theta_m)\mathbf{R}_{t+1}\mathbf{z}'_t],\end{aligned}$$

and so the sample analog of this moment condition can be used to estimate θ_m. The null hypothesis that the manager of portfolio p has no skill at security selection or market timing implies that

$$E[\mathbf{z}_t] = E[g(\mathbf{x}_{t+1}, \widehat{\theta}_m)\mathbf{z}_t R_{pt+1}], \tag{75}$$

and this hypothesis can be tested using the delta method to calculate the standard error of the difference. Alternatively, the vector of asset returns can be augmented with R_{pt+1} via $\mathbf{R}^*_{t+1} = (\mathbf{R}'_{t+1}\ R_{pt+1})'$, and the model can be estimated via the unconditional moment condition,

$$E[\iota\mathbf{z}'_t] = E[g(\mathbf{x}_{t+1}, \theta_m)\mathbf{R}^*_{t+1}\mathbf{z}'_t], \tag{76}$$

and the null hypothesis can be tested by examining the difference

$$E[\mathbf{z}_t] = E[g(\mathbf{x}_{t+1}, \widehat{\theta}^*_m)R_{pt+1}\mathbf{z}_t] \tag{77}$$

using the delta method once again. Other GMM tests can be constructed in a similar fashion.

Alternatively, we can construct the empirical analog of portfolio δ by using the sample analog of the moment conditions (4). This approach seems more natural: One usually thinks of m_{t+1} as being *the* stochastic discount factor implied by some asset pricing model, whereas performance evaluation requires only the portfolio of these assets that is the best hedge for any m_{t+1}, which is portfolio δ. Since it is convenient to use the variant of the moment conditions for portfolio δ that works with m_{t+1} as opposed to

$m_{t+1} - E[m_{t+1}|I_t] = m_{t+1} - R_{ft+1}^{-1}$, the defining moment conditions are given by

$$\boldsymbol{\iota} = E[\mathbf{R}_{t+1}(\mathbf{R}'_{t+1}\boldsymbol{\delta}_t + \varepsilon_{mt+1})|I_t] = E[\mathbf{R}_{t+1}\mathbf{R}'_{t+1}|I_t]\boldsymbol{\delta}_t,$$

where $\boldsymbol{\delta}_t$ is the vector of weights defining portfolio δ prior to normalizing them to sum to 1. Here, too, we require a model for the time-varying weight vector $\boldsymbol{\delta}_t$ of the form

$$\boldsymbol{\delta}_t = \mathbf{h}(\mathbf{z}_t, \boldsymbol{\theta}_\delta),$$

where $\boldsymbol{\theta}_\delta$ is a set of unknown parameters. Once again, the parameters of this model can be estimated via the unconditional moment conditions

$$E[\boldsymbol{\iota}] = E[\mathbf{R}_{t+1}\mathbf{R}'_{t+1}\mathbf{h}(\mathbf{z}_t, \boldsymbol{\theta}_\delta)]$$

using GMM. For example, Chen and Knez (1996) examine the natural model

$$\boldsymbol{\delta}_t = \mathbf{h}(\mathbf{z}_t, \boldsymbol{\theta}_\delta) = \boldsymbol{\omega}^* \mathbf{z}_t, \tag{78}$$

where $\boldsymbol{\omega}^*$ is a suitably conformable matrix of constants. Tests of the null hypothesis can be based on Eqs. (75) and (76) by substituting $\mathbf{R}'_{t+1}\mathbf{h}(\mathbf{z}_t, \boldsymbol{\theta}_\delta)$ for $g(\mathbf{x}_{t+1}, \boldsymbol{\theta}_m)$.

5.2. Power of Statistical Tests for Individual Funds

There are good reasons to be concerned about power in performance evaluation. Economic reasoning suggests that superior performance should not be pervasive across the universe of fund managers. Statistical reasoning suggests that the substantial noise in long-lived asset returns makes it difficult to measure performance reliably in the best of circumstances. We discuss these issues in turn.

Long-lived asset returns can typically be decomposed into systematic risk that cannot be eliminated via diversification and unsystematic risk that cannot be diversified away. The decomposition of stock returns into common factors and idiosyncratic disturbances is the basis of the arbitrage pricing theory of Ross (1976, 1977). Two or three factors account for the bulk of time-series and cross-sectional variation in bonds of different maturities. Similarly, currencies are essentially uncorrelated, conditional on two or three currencies. Thus it is not an accident that market timing ability is distinguished from skill at security selection among practitioners; the former corresponds to systematic risk and the latter to diversifiable risk.

Security selection cannot pervade the asset universe. If a manager could successfully identify many assets with positive or negative alphas, then a well-diversified portfolio that tilted toward the former and away from the latter (or sell them short if feasible) would systematically outperform the benchmark. Any manager with such ability would be able to charge a fee roughly equal to the amount of outperformance and we would routinely observe consistent positive differences between gross and net returns. We do not observe such behavior in the universe of managed portfolios.

Skill at security selection across segments of the asset universe cannot pervade the manager universe either. If there were many managers who could consistently identify assets with positive or negative alphas in different securities, investors would systematically outperform the benchmark by holding diversified portfolios of funds. That is, diversification across funds can replace diversification across assets in these circumstances. Once again, it would be easy to identify portfolios of managed portfolios with consistent positive differences between gross and net returns. We do not observe such behavior in the universe of portfolio managers.

Market timing ability cannot be pervasive because of the number of opportunities to time the market. Market volatility provides managers with many opportunities to profit by buying on average before the relevant benchmark portfolio appreciates and selling on average before its value declines. Even if managerial skill were only slightly better than a coin toss, the sheer number of coin tosses would result in consistently positive performance on a quarterly or annual basis. Once again, we would observe consistently positive performance among market timers if this were the case. Managers might have "infrequent" market timing success, but this would be hard to distinguish from good luck unless, of course, it was "frequent," which this argument says it cannot be.

What do we actually observe? Studies based on managed portfolios for which there is information on asset allocations along the lines of Eq. (48) consistently reveal two facts: Measured market timing almost never contributes positively to portfolio performance, and the distribution of measured security selection skill across portfolios appears to be roughly symmetric and centered around zero. That is, we seldom observe successful market timers, and we cannot tell if the good performance of successful stock pickers represents good luck or good policy.

The appropriate null hypothesis may be "no abnormal performance," but this observation implies that "abnormal performance" is not the appropriate alternative hypothesis. Rather the natural alternative hypothesis is that K out of P funds can outperform the benchmark in a given fund universe, with K small relative to P. Devising power tests against such an alternative is challenging.

The volatility of long-lived asset returns figured prominently in this reasoning. Covariances are measured well in high-volatility environments, but means are measured poorly. Market timing ability involves covariances, and security selection skill is measured by means. The inability to find the former suggests that it is not a widespread skill, and observed standard errors of alphas reflect the imprecision with which they are estimated. We can learn more about the latter through simulation.

Two features of long-lived asset returns have special relevance for the question at hand: their extraordinary volatility, and the fact that they can be decomposed into systematic and unsystematic risk. We can assess the comparative difficulty of this problem by answering the following question. Suppose we are given the population Treynor–Black appraisal ratio of a managed portfolio along with the population Sharpe ratio of the benchmark. How long would we have to observe the fund in order to have a given probability of rejecting the null hypothesis that the fund exhibits abnormal performance? That is, what is the power of the t-test for the Jensen alpha evaluated at different sample sizes? To answer this question, we follow the analysis of Blake and Timmermann (2002).

As was noted earlier, the t-statistic for the Jensen alpha is given by

$$t(\widehat{\alpha}_p) = \frac{\sqrt{T}\widehat{\alpha}_p}{(1+\phi_\delta^2)\sigma_{\epsilon_p}},$$

which is normally distributed when the returns are normally distributed and ϕ_δ^2 and σ_{ϵ_p} are known. If we are trying to assess the impact of volatility on tests for abnormal performance (i.e., that $\alpha_p \neq 0$, as would be appropriate if we were concerned with the prospect of significant underperformance, corruption of alpha due to market timing ability, or benchmark error), we would consider two-sided tests with critical values of $c/2$ and we would want to assess the probability of detection,

$$\Pr\left[\sqrt{T}\frac{\widehat{\alpha}_p}{(1+\phi_\delta^2)\sigma_{\epsilon_p}} > z_{1-c/2}\right] = \Phi\left[t(\widehat{\alpha}_p) - z_{1-c/2}\right] + \Phi\left[-t(\widehat{\alpha}_p) - z_{1-c/2}\right], \tag{79}$$

as a function of sample size T. Alternatively, we would seek a one-sided interval with critical value c if we thought Jensen's alpha is measured without bias and we were not concerned with underperformance, for which

$$\Pr\left[\sqrt{T}\frac{\widehat{\alpha}_p}{(1+\phi_\delta^2)\sigma_{\epsilon_p}} > z_{1-c}\right] = \Phi\left[t(\widehat{\alpha}_p) - z_{1-c}\right]$$

is the probability of detection.

To be concrete, suppose we are given a managed portfolio with a Treynor–Black appraisal ratio of 0.1—which corresponds to an appraisal ratio of 0.1 or −0.1 for the two-sided test—and a benchmark Sharpe ratio of zero. These numbers could be generated by a growth stock fund with a beta of 1 on a passive growth stock index with a volatility of 4.5 percent per month, which, when coupled with an R^2 of 0.9, would imply that the portfolio has a residual standard deviation of 1.5 percent. Hence, this fund would have an alpha of 0.15 percent per month and an annualized alpha of 1.8 percent. In this low-signal-to-noise-ratio environment, a one-sided test is associated with the following tradeoff between statistical power and sample size:

Power	Required sample size (T)
10%	13 (1.085 years)
25%	94 (7.83 years)
50%	270 (22.5 years)

while the corresponding two-sided test yields a tradeoff between sample size and power of

Power	Required sample size (T)
10%	43 (3.6 years)
25%	165 (13.8 years)
50%	385 (30.1 years)

As these numbers clearly indicate, it takes many months to be able to detect positive or abnormal performance with any reliability.

Similarly, we can examine the somewhat higher signal-to-noise-ratio environment with an appraisal ratio of 0.2 (and −0.2 for the two-sided test), which corresponds to an alpha of 3.6 percent per year in the numerical example given earlier. In this case, the tradeoff between power and sample size is given by

Power	Required sample size (T)
10%	4 (0.3 years)
25%	24 (2.0 years)
50%	68 (5.7 years)

while the corresponding two-sided test yields a tradeoff of

Power	Required sample size (T)
10%	12 (1.0 years)
25%	42 (3.5 years)
50%	96 (8.0 years)

While the probability of detection is considerably higher in this case, the case remains that it is remarkably difficult to be confident that a managed portfolio has a Treynor–Black appraisal ratio of 0.2, a number that most managers would be thrilled to attain. This difficulty in detecting abnormal performance with any statistical precision is why we emphasized the significant benefits associated with the acquisition of other information, such as portfolio weight data, to supplement return data.

5.3. Inference for Multiple Funds

The presence of literally thousands of actively managed funds raises the natural question of whether individual funds or (sub-)groups of funds can outperform their benchmarks. Given this large number of funds, whether outperformance is the result of skill or luck can be very difficult to detect. The Bonferroni bound can be used to establish an upper bound on the probability of superior performance of the very best fund among a large set of P funds. Suppose we are considering the performance of P funds through the t-statistics of their alpha estimates. The Bonferroni bound computes the probability that at least one of these is exceeds some critical value, $t_{\max}$ (in practice the largest value observed in the cross section):

$$\begin{aligned}\Pr(\text{at least one } t_i > t_{\max}) &= 1 - \Pr\left(\bigcap_{i=1}^{P} (t_i < t_{\max})\right)\\ &\leq 1 - \left(1 - \sum_{i=1}^{P} \Pr(t_i \geq t_{\max})\right)\\ &= \sum_{i=1}^{P} \Pr(t_i \geq t_{\max})\\ &= P\Phi(t_{\max}), \text{ or}\\ \Pr(\text{at least one } t_i \geq t_{\max}) &\leq \min(1, P\Phi(t_{\max})),\end{aligned}$$

where $\Phi(.)$ is the complementary cumulative distribution function of the individual student-t-statistics. Unfortunately, the Bonferroni bound is known to be conservative and may thus fail in detecting genuine abnormal performance. The reason is that it is robust to any correlation patterns across the P performance statistics, including patterns for which inference is very difficult.

An alternative, semiparametric approach that accounts for the correlation structure in fund returns through their exposure to a set of common benchmark portfolios factors but does not require explicitly modeling the covariance structure in fund-specific residuals has been proposed by Kosowski et al. (2006). They argue that the question of skill versus luck can be addressed in many different ways, depending on how large a fraction of funds one tests abnormal performance for. The hypothesis that the manager of the very best fund among a larger universe of P funds cannot produce a positive alpha takes the form

$$H_0 : \max_{p=1,\ldots,P} \alpha_p \leq 0 \quad \text{and} \quad H_A : \max_{p=1,\ldots,P} \alpha_p > 0.$$

More broadly, one may want to rank a group of funds by their alpha estimates and ask whether the top 5 percent, say, of funds outperform. Let i^* be the rank of the fund corresponding to this percentile. When testing whether this fund manager can pick stocks, the null and alternative hypotheses are

$$H_0 : \alpha_{p^*} \leq 0 \quad \text{and} \quad H_A : \alpha_{p^*} > 0.$$

Since the alpha measure is not pivotal, whereas the estimated t-statistic of $\widehat{\alpha}$, $\widehat{t_{\alpha}}$ is, a bootstrap test based on this statistic is likely to have lower coverage errors. $\widehat{t_{\alpha}}$ has another attractive statistical property: Funds with a shorter history of monthly net returns will have an alpha estimated with less precision and will tend to generate alphas that are outliers. The t-statistic provides a correction for these spurious outliers by normalizing the estimated alpha by the estimated precision of the alpha estimate—it is related to the well-known "information ratio" method of performance measurement of Treynor and Black (1973).

Using this performance measure, the null and alternative hypotheses for the highest-ranked fund are

$$H_0 : \max_{p=1,\dots,P} t_p \leq 0 \quad \text{and} \quad H_A : \max_{p=1,\dots,P} t_p > 0.$$

The joint distribution of the alphas is difficult to characterize and compute. Even if it is known that returns are joint Gaussian, the foregoing test statistics will still depend on the $P \times P$ covariance matrix, which is difficult to estimate with any degree of precision when—as is typically the case—P is large relative to the sample size, T. Furthermore, many funds do not have overlapping return histories, which renders estimation of the covariance matrix infeasible by means of standard methods. Kosowski et al. (2006) propose use of the following bootstrap procedure to test for abnormal performance of a group of funds. In the first step the individual funds' alphas are estimated via ordinary least squares (OLS) using a performance model of the form

$$R_{pt} - R_{ft} = \widehat{\alpha}_p + \widehat{\beta}_p'(R_{\delta t} - R_{ft}) + \widehat{\epsilon}_{p,t}.$$

This generates coefficient estimates, $\{\widehat{\alpha}_p, \widehat{\beta}_p\}_{p=1}^{P}$, time series of residuals, $\{\widehat{\epsilon}_{p,t}, t = 1, T_p, p = 1, \dots, P\}$, as well as the t-statistic of alpha, $\widehat{t_{\widehat{\alpha}}}$. Bootstrapped residuals can be resampled by drawing a sample with replacement from the fund i residuals, thus creating a new time series, $\{\widehat{\epsilon}_{p,t}^{b}, t = s_1^b, s_2^b, \dots, s_{T_p}^b\}$. Each bootstrap sample has the same number of residuals (e.g., the same number of time periods, T_p) as the original sample for each fund p. This resampling procedure is repeated for all bootstrap iterations, $b = 1, \dots, B$.

For each bootstrap iteration, b, a time series of (bootstrapped) net returns is constructed for each fund, imposing the null hypothesis of zero true performance ($\alpha_p = 0$, or, equivalently, $\widehat{t_{\widehat{\alpha}}} = 0$), letting $s_1^b, s_2^b, \dots, s_{T_p}^b$ be the time reordering imposed by resampling the residuals in bootstrap iteration b:

$$\{R_{pt}^b - R_{ft}^b = \widehat{\beta}_i(R_{\delta t} - R_{ft}) + \widehat{\epsilon}_{p,t}^{b}\ ,\ t = s_1^b, s_2^b, \dots, s_{T_p}^b\}. \tag{80}$$

By construction, these artificially generated returns have a true alpha of zero, since we have imposed alpha to be zero. Because a given bootstrap draw may have an unusually large number of positive draws of the residual term, however, this can lead to an unusually large estimate of alpha in the OLS regression of the returns in the bth bootstrap sample on an intercept and the benchmark portfolio returns.

Repeating these steps across funds, $p = 1, \dots, P$, and bootstrap iterations, $b = 1, \dots, B$, gives a cross-sectional distribution of the alpha estimates, $\widehat{\alpha}_p^b$, or their t-statistics, $\widehat{t}_{\widehat{\alpha}_p}^{b}$, due to sampling variation, as we impose the null hypothesis of no abnormal performance. Keeping b fixed and letting p vary from 1 to P, we get one draw from the cross-sectional distribution of alpha estimates. These alpha estimates $\{\widehat{\alpha}_1^b, \widehat{\alpha}_2^b, \dots, \widehat{\alpha}_P^b\}$ can be ranked to get an estimate of the maximum value of $\widehat{\alpha}$, $\widehat{\alpha}_{\max}^b$, the cth quantile, $\widehat{\alpha}_{(c)}^b$, and so forth. Repeating this across $b = 1, \dots, B$ produces a distribution of cross-sectional quantiles $\{\widehat{\alpha}_{(c)}^1, \dots, \widehat{\alpha}_{(c)}^B\}$. Comparing the corresponding quantile in the actual data generates a test of whether the top 100c percentage of funds can outperform, based on a statistic such as

$$B^{-1}\sum_{b=1}^{B} I\{\widehat{\alpha}^{b}_{(c)} < \widehat{\alpha}_{(c)}\}.$$

5.4. Empirical Specifications of Alpha Measures

Following the earlier discussion of performance benchmarks, we briefly discuss some benchmarks that have been used extensively in the empirical literature. The class of unconditional alpha measures includes specifications proposed by Jensen (1968), Fama and French (1993), and Carhart (1997). The Carhart (1997) four-factor regression model is

$$R_{pt} - R_{ft} = \alpha_p + b_p(R_{mt} - R_{ft}) + s_p \cdot \mathrm{SMB}_t + g_p \cdot \mathrm{HML}_t + h_p \cdot \mathrm{PR1YR}_t + \varepsilon_{pt}, \quad (81)$$

where SMB_t, HML_t, and $\mathrm{PR1YR}_t$ equal the period t returns on value-weighted, zero-investment factor-mimicking portfolios for size, book-to-market equity, and one-year momentum in stock returns, respectively. The Fama and French alpha is computed using the Carhart model of Equation (81), excluding the momentum factor ($\mathrm{PR1YR}_t$), while the Jensen alpha is computed using the market excess return as the only benchmark:

$$R_{pt} - R_{ft} = \alpha_p + b_p \cdot (R_{mt} - R_{ft}) + \varepsilon_{pt}. \quad (82)$$

Ferson and Schadt (1996) propose modifying the Jensen model of Equation (82) to obtain a class of conditional performance measures that control for time-varying factor loadings as follows:

$$R_{pt} - R_{ft} = \alpha_p + b_p \cdot (R_{mt} - R_{ft}) + \sum_{j=1}^{K} B_{p,j}[z_{j,t-1} \cdot (R_{mt} - R_{ft})] + \varepsilon_{pt}, \quad (83)$$

where $z_{j,t-1}$ is the de-meaned period $(t-1)$ public information variable j and $B_{p,j}$ is the fund's "beta response" to the value of $z_{j,t-1}$.[19] Hence the Ferson and Schadt measure computes the alpha of a managed portfolio, controlling for investment strategies that use publicly available economic information to modify dynamically the portfolio's beta in response to the predictable component of mark returns.

A natural extension of this class is proposed by Christopherson, Ferson, and Glassman (1998), who allow both the alpha and the factor loadings of a fund to

[19] Farnsworth et al. (2001) find that a range of stochastic discount factor models have a mild negative bias when performance is neutral. See also Lynch et al. (2002) for an analysis of the relationship between performance measures and stochastic discount factor models.

vary through time. For example, Jensen model of Equation (82) is modified as follows:

$$R_{pt} - R_{ft} = \alpha_p + \sum_{j=1}^{K} A_{p,j} \cdot z_{j,t-1} + b_p \cdot (R_{mt} - R_{ft}) + \sum_{j=1}^{K} B_{p,j}[z_{j,t-1} \cdot (R_{mt} - R_{ft})] + \varepsilon_{pt}. \tag{84}$$

Most studies have found that the typical fund does not outperform on a risk- and expense-adjusted basis, c.f. Jensen (1968), Carhart (1997), Malkiel (1995), Gruber (1996), and Daniel et al. (1997).

5.4.1. Persistence in Performance

One of the implications of no arbitrage is that we should not expect to find funds that persistently outperform the relevant benchmarks. To see this, note that the no-arbitrage condition

$$E[(R_{pt+1} - R_{ft+1})m_{t+1}|I_t] = 0$$

implies

$$E[(R_{pt+1} - R_{ft+1})(R_{pt} - R_{ft} - (\overline{R}_p - \overline{R}_f))m_{t+1}] = 0,$$

so, on a risk-adjusted basis, returns are serially uncorrelated.

Some studies—inter alia Lehmann and Modest (1987), Grinblatt and Titman (1992), Hendricks, Patel, and Zeckhauser (1993), Brown and Goetzmann (1995), Carhart (1997), and Kosowski et al. (2006)—have found evidence of persistence in fund performance. In particular, there is little doubt empirically that there is persistence among the worst funds' performance, c.f. Carhart (1997). It is more disputed whether funds with superior performance can repeat their past success after accounting for differences in risk exposures and the effects of survivorship bias, c.f. Brown et al. (1992), and Carpenter and Lynch (1999).

One way to model time variations in alpha and beta, pursued by Kosowski (2002), is to assume that these depend on some underlying state (boom and bust, expansion and recession, volatile and calm markets) and to treat this state as unobserved. Suppose that the state follows a Markov chain and that the alpha, beta, and idiosyncratic risk are functions of a single, latent state variable (s_t):

$$R_{pt} - R_{ft} = \alpha_{s_t} + \beta_{s_t}(R_{\delta t} - R_{ft}) + \epsilon_t, \epsilon_t \sim (0, \sigma^2_{s_t}).$$

Conditional on a vector of variables known at time $t-1$, $\mathbf{z}_{t-1}$, the state transition probabilities follow a first-order Markov chain:

$$\begin{aligned} p_t &= P(s_t = 1|s_{t-1} = 1, \mathbf{z}_{t-1}) = p(\mathbf{z}_{t-1}) \\ 1 - p_t &= P(s_t = 2|s_{t-1} = 1, \mathbf{z}_{t-1}) = 1 - p(\mathbf{z}_{t-1}) \\ q_t &= P(s_t = 2|s_{t-1} = 2, \mathbf{z}_{t-1}) = q(\mathbf{z}_{t-1}) \\ 1 - q_t &= P(s_t = 1|s_{t-1} = 2, \mathbf{z}_{t-1}) = 1 - q(\mathbf{z}_{t-1}). \end{aligned}$$

Hence, conditional on being in state s_t, portfolio returns have a normal distribution with mean $\alpha_{s_t} + \beta_{s_t}(R_{\delta t} - R_{ft})$ and variance $\sigma^2_{s_t}$. We assume a constant relationship between the market return and excess returns within each state, but we allow this relation to vary between states. Hence, in certain states, beta is high and the sensitivity to market movements very significant. At other times beta is low and risk is smaller. Information about which state the portfolio is currently in is therefore important for assessing risk and portfolio performance.

6. BAYESIAN APPROACHES

A meaningful decision theoretical framework must use information on the uncertainty surrounding the parameters characterizing a fund's abnormal performance. However, it can also use prior information as a way to account for the noise often dominating parameter estimates. Use of such prior information is akin to shrinkage, a technique that is known to be able to improve on out-of-sample forecasting performance in areas such as construction of covariance matrix estimators, forecast combinations, and portfolio formation.

As an example of this approach, Baks, Metrick, and Wachter (2001) propose a Bayesian setting where investors with mean-variance preference decide whether or not to hold any of their wealth in a single actively managed mutual fund. The setup is as follows. Suppose the common component of asset returns is captured through K benchmark assets (passively managed index funds) with period $-(t+1)$ returns $\mathbf{F}_{t+1}$ and an actively managed fund with returns r_{t+1} that are assumed to be generated by the model

$$r_{t+1} = \alpha + \mathbf{F}'_{t+1}\beta + \varepsilon_{t+1}, \tag{85}$$

where $\varepsilon_{t+1} \sim N(0, \sigma^2)$. The parameters $\alpha, \boldsymbol{\beta}$ are viewed as fixed attributes associated with the fund manager. The question is now how large a fraction of wealth, ω, the investor is willing to allocate to the mutual fund. This question depends in part on the investor's prior beliefs about the manager's ability to generate a positive α, in part on the fund manager's track record. The latter is captured through a $T \times 1$ vector of excess returns, $\mathbf{r}$, while $\mathbf{F}$ is a $T \times K$ matrix of factor returns and ε is a $T \times 1$ vector of residuals. Assuming that return shocks, ε, are iid and normally distributed, we have

$$p(\mathbf{r}|\alpha, \beta, \sigma^2, \mathbf{F}) = N(\alpha\iota_T + \mathbf{F}\beta, \sigma^2\mathbf{I}_T),$$

where again ι_T is a $T \times 1$ vector of 1s and $\mathbf{I}_T$ is the $T \times T$ identity matrix. Baks, Metrick, and Wachter capture prior beliefs concerning α as follows. Let $\mathcal{Z}$ be a random indicator variable that captures whether the manager is skilled ($\mathcal{Z} = 1$) or unskilled ($\mathcal{Z} = 0$), the former having a prior probability of q. Both β and σ are assumed to be independent of whether or not the manager is skilled, so any skills are defined with respect to security selection. This means that the prior for the joint distribution of $(\alpha, \beta, \sigma^2)$ can be factored out as follows:

$$p(\alpha, \beta, \sigma^2) = [p(\alpha|\mathcal{Z} = 0)P(\mathcal{Z} = 0) + p(\alpha|\mathcal{Z} = 1)p(\mathcal{Z} = 1)]p(\beta, \sigma^2). \qquad (86)$$

To get analytical results, Baks, Metrick, and Wachter assume a diffuse prior on β, σ^2, i.e., $p(\beta, \sigma^2) \propto \sigma^{-2}$. The prior for the manager's stock selection skills is determined from the following set of equations:

$$\begin{aligned} p(\mathcal{Z} = 1) &= q \\ p(\mathcal{Z} = 0) &= 1 - q, \\ p(\alpha|\mathcal{Z} = 0, \sigma^2) &= \delta_{\alpha}, \\ p(\alpha|\mathcal{Z} = 1, \sigma^2) &= 2N\left(\alpha, \sigma_{\alpha}^2\left(\frac{\sigma^2}{s^2}\right)\right) I_{\alpha > \underline{\alpha}}, \end{aligned} \qquad (87)$$

where δ_α is the Dirac function that puts full mass at $\alpha = \underline{\alpha}$ and no mass anywhere else, while $I_{\alpha>\underline{\alpha}}$ is an indicator function that equals unity if $\alpha > \underline{\alpha}$ and is zero otherwise. $\alpha < 0$ represents the return expected from an unskilled fund manager, while s^2 is a constant used in the elicitation of priors. Baks, Metrick, and Wachter set $\alpha = -q\sigma_\alpha\sqrt{2/\pi} - \text{fee} - \cos t$, where *fee* is the manager's expected fee and $\cos t$ is the fund's expected transaction costs.

Under these assumptions the posterior distribution of α, $E[\alpha|\mathbf{r}, \mathbf{F}]$, denoted by $\widetilde{\alpha}$, can be computed as the (posterior) expected value of α conditional on the manager's being skilled times the probability that the manager is skilled, plus the value of α if the fund manager is unskilled, $\underline{\alpha}$, times the probability that he is unskilled:

$$\widetilde{\alpha} = \widetilde{q}E[\alpha|\mathcal{Z} = 1, \mathbf{r}, \mathbf{F}] + (1 - \widetilde{q})\underline{\alpha},$$

where $\widetilde{q} = P(\mathcal{Z} = 1|\mathbf{r}, \mathbf{F})$ is the posterior probability that the fund manager is skilled. Both $\widetilde{q}$ and $E[\alpha|\mathcal{Z} = 1, \mathbf{r}, \mathbf{F}]$ need to be computed to assess the value of fund management. Let $\mathbf{X} = (\iota_T \; F)$, so the least-squares estimates of $(\widehat{\alpha} \; \widehat{\beta})$ are given by

$$(\widehat{\alpha} \; \widehat{\beta})' = (\mathbf{X}'\mathbf{X})^{-1}\mathbf{X}'\mathbf{r},$$

while the variance of the maximum likelihood for α conditional on a known residual variance, σ^2, is

$$\text{Var}(\widehat{\alpha}) = \mathbf{e}_1'(\mathbf{X}'\mathbf{X})^{-1}\mathbf{e}_1\sigma^2,$$

where $\mathbf{e}_1 = (1 \; 0 \ldots 0)'$. For a skilled manager ($\mathcal{Z} = 1$), the posterior distribution of α given the data and σ^2 is

$$P(\alpha|\mathcal{Z} = 1, \mathbf{r}, \mathbf{F}, \sigma^2) \propto N(\alpha', \sigma'^2)1_{\alpha > \underline{\alpha}}, \qquad (88)$$

where the posterior parameters are

$$\alpha' = \lambda\widetilde{\alpha} + (1-\lambda)\underline{\alpha},$$
$$\sigma'^2 = \left(\frac{1}{\mathrm{Var}(\widetilde{\alpha})} + \frac{1}{\sigma_\alpha^2(\frac{\sigma^2}{s^2})}\right),$$
$$\lambda^2 = \frac{\sigma'^2}{\mathrm{Var}(\widetilde{\alpha})}.$$

Here α' is the mode of the skilled manager's posterior distribution. This differs from the mean due to the truncation of the distribution of α at $\underline{\alpha}$. Under the assumed normality, Baks, Metrick, and Wachter show that the truncation causes the mode to be a weighted average of the least-squares estimate, $\widehat{\alpha}$, and truncation point, $\underline{\alpha}$, with weights that reflect the precision of the data relative to the precision of the prior, λ. Finally, the posterior precision, σ'^{-2}, is the sum of the precision of the prior and the precision of the data.

Integrating out β and σ^2, the (marginal) posterior distribution for α is proportional to a truncated student-t:

$$p(\alpha|\mathcal{Z}=1,\mathbf{r},\mathbf{F}) \propto t_v\left(\alpha', \frac{\lambda\mathbf{e}_1'(\mathbf{X}'\mathbf{X})^{-1}\mathbf{e}_1 h}{T-K}\right) I_{\alpha>\underline{\alpha}},$$

where

$$h = (\mathbf{r}-\widehat{\mathbf{r}})'(\mathbf{r}-\widehat{\mathbf{r}}) + (1-\lambda)(\widehat{\alpha}-\underline{\alpha})^2(\mathbf{e}_1'(\mathbf{X}'\mathbf{X})^{-1}\mathbf{e}_1)$$

and $\widehat{\mathbf{r}} = \mathbf{X}(\widehat{\alpha}\;\widehat{\beta})$ are the fitted returns. This is all that is required to compute the posterior mean of α, obtained by integrating over $p(\alpha|\mathcal{Z}=1,\mathbf{r},\mathbf{F})$ to the right of the truncation point, $\underline{\alpha}$:

$$E[\alpha|\mathcal{Z}=1,\mathbf{r},\mathbf{F}] = \alpha' + \frac{\lambda\mathbf{e}_1'(\mathbf{X}'\mathbf{X})^{-1}\mathbf{e}_1 h}{T-K-2}\,\frac{t_{T-K}\left(\underline{\alpha};\alpha',\frac{\lambda\mathbf{e}_1'(\mathbf{X}'\mathbf{X})^{-1}\mathbf{e}_1 h}{T-K-2}\right)}{\int_{\underline{\alpha}}^{\infty} t_{T-K}\left(\alpha;\alpha',\frac{\lambda\mathbf{e}_1'(\mathbf{X}'\mathbf{X})^{-1}\mathbf{e}_1 h}{T-K-2}\right)d\alpha}.$$

The posterior probability that the manager is skilled, given the data, is obtained from Bayes' rule:

$$\widetilde{q} = P(\mathcal{Z}=1|\mathbf{r},\mathbf{F}) = \frac{qP(\mathbf{r}|\mathcal{Z}=1,\mathbf{F})}{qP(\mathbf{r}|\mathcal{Z}=1,\mathbf{F}) + (1-q)P(\mathbf{r}|\mathcal{Z}=0,\mathbf{F})}$$
$$= \frac{q}{q+\frac{1-q}{B}},$$

where

$$B = \frac{p(\mathbf{r}|\mathcal{Z}=1,\mathbf{F})}{p(\mathbf{r}|\mathcal{Z}=0,\mathbf{F})}$$

is the odds ratio that a given return is generated by a skilled versus an unskilled manager. The more likely it is that given return data are generated by a skilled manager than by an unskilled manager, the higher is B:

$$B = \frac{t_{T-K-1}\left(\underline{\alpha}; \widehat{\alpha}, \frac{\lambda \mathbf{e}_1'(\mathbf{X}'\mathbf{X})^{-1}\mathbf{e}_1 h(\mathbf{r}-\widehat{\mathbf{r}})'(\mathbf{r}-\widehat{\mathbf{r}})}{(1-\lambda)(T-K-1)}\right)}{t_{T-K-1}\left(\underline{\alpha}; \widehat{\alpha}, \frac{\lambda \mathbf{e}_1'(\mathbf{X}'\mathbf{X})^{-1}\mathbf{e}_1 h(\mathbf{r}-\widehat{\mathbf{r}})'(\mathbf{r}-\widehat{\mathbf{r}})}{(T-K-1)}\right)} \left(2\int_{\underline{\alpha}}^{\infty} t_{T-K}\left(\alpha; \alpha', \frac{\lambda \mathbf{e}_1'(\mathbf{X}'\mathbf{X})^{-1}\mathbf{e}_1 h}{T-K}\right) d\alpha\right).$$

Hence beta is the likelihood ratio of two t-distributions multiplied by a term that accounts for the effect of truncation.

To account for the possibility of investing in multiple actively managed funds, Baks, Metrick, and Wachter (2001) assume that both the likelihood functions and the priors are independent across managers. In this case the posterior distributions are independent across managers, so the computations with multiple active funds do not change.

Letting $(\mathbf{r}_N\ \mathbf{F})$ be the return on N actively managed funds and the K passive index funds, under the assumption that $(\mathbf{r}_N\ \mathbf{F}) \sim N(\widetilde{\mathbf{E}}, \widetilde{\mathbf{V}})$, Baks, Metrick, and Wachter (2001) show that the weights on the actively managed and index funds, $\boldsymbol{\omega} = (\boldsymbol{\omega}_A\ \boldsymbol{\omega}_F)'$ for an investor with mean-variance preferences $U = E[R_p] - (A/2)\mathrm{Var}(R_p)$ over the mean and variance of portfolio returns, $E[R_p]$, $\mathrm{Var}(R_p)$, are given by

$$\begin{pmatrix} \boldsymbol{\omega}_A \\ \boldsymbol{\omega}_F \end{pmatrix} = (1/A)\widetilde{\mathbf{V}}^{-1}\widetilde{\mathbf{E}}. \tag{89}$$

Furthermore, holdings in the actively managed funds can be shown to be given by

$$\boldsymbol{\omega}_A = (1/A)\boldsymbol{\Omega}^{-1}\widetilde{\boldsymbol{\alpha}}, \tag{90}$$

where $\boldsymbol{\Omega}^{-1}$ is diagonal with exclusively positive elements. This means that an active fund is held if and only if the posterior mean of its alpha estimate is strictly positive.

In their empirical analysis, Baks, Metrick, and Wachter (2001) find that a frequentist analysis of the performance of the best fund managers cannot reject the null hypothesis that none of the fund managers is skilled (and hence that nothing should be invested in their funds). In contrast, the Bayesian analysis finds that even small prior probabilities of skill translate into some holdings in actively managed funds. The reason for this seemingly contradictory result is related to the weak power of statistical tests against small positive values of α, which are nevertheless economically important.[20]

6.1. Asset Mispricing and Investment in Mutual Funds

Pastor and Stambaugh (2002a, 2002b) extend this analysis to allow for the possibility of mispricing relative to a factor-pricing benchmark, such as a multifactor model. Hence

[20]It may also be a consequence of implicitly placing strong prior probabilities that some funds outperform the benchmark. With many funds with parameters that are treated as independent a priori and a posteriori, it must be the case that the prior probability that a small number of funds outperform is overwhelming when there are many funds in the sample.

investors view manager skill not just in relation to a set of benchmark portfolio returns but also with respect to a set of nonbenchmark assets' returns that are tracked by a set of passive index funds. In this setting investors also are endowed with priors about possible mispricing.

Common components in asset returns are captured through an $m \times 1$ vector of excess returns, $\mathbf{r}_{Nt}$, on m nonbenchmark passive assets and k benchmark returns, $\mathbf{r}_{Bt}$. Returns on the nonbenchmark assets are given by

$$\mathbf{r}_{Nt} = \boldsymbol{\alpha}_N + \mathbf{B}_N \mathbf{r}_{Bt} + \varepsilon_{Nt}, \tag{91}$$

where $E[\varepsilon_{Nt}\varepsilon'_{Nt}] = \Sigma$.

Returns on any fund can now be regressed on the nonbenchmark and benchmark returns:

$$r_{At} = \delta_A + \mathbf{c}'_{AN}\mathbf{r}_{Nt} + \mathbf{c}'_{AB}\mathbf{r}_{Bt} + u_{At}, \tag{92}$$

where $E[u^2_{At}] = \sigma^2_u$ and all innovations are assumed to be Gaussian.

The key difference between nonbenchmark and benchmark returns in Pastor and Stambaugh's analysis lies in the assumption that only the latter are included as priced factors in asset pricing models. Hence, under the null hypothesis that only the benchmark assets are priced, fund performance is naturally measured only with regard to r_{Bt}:

$$r_{At} = \alpha_A + \beta'_A \mathbf{r}_{Bt} + \varepsilon_{At}. \tag{93}$$

Notice that a fund manager with a positive alpha need not be skilled if the positive alpha is due to his holdings of passive assets with nonzero alphas. Thus, if there is a possibility that the benchmark assets do not price the nonbenchmark assets exactly, $\alpha_N \neq \mathbf{0}$, then δ_A in Eq. (92) defined with regard to the full set of passive assets becomes a better measure of skill than α_A in Eq. (93). Using Eq. (91) in Eq. (92) gives the decomposition

$$r_{At} = \underbrace{\delta_A + \mathbf{c}'_{AN}\alpha_N}_{\alpha_A} + \underbrace{(\mathbf{c}_{AN}\mathbf{B}_N + \mathbf{c}'_{AB})}_{\beta'_A}\mathbf{r}_{Bt} + \underbrace{c_{AN}\varepsilon_{Nt} + u_{At}}_{\varepsilon_{At}},$$

so

$$\alpha_A = \delta_A + c'_{AN}\alpha_N,$$
$$\beta_A = c_{AN}\mathbf{B}_N + c'_{AB}.$$

The priors assumed by Pastor and Stambaugh are as follows. $\mathbf{B}_N$ has a diffuse prior, while the prior for Σ is an inverted Wishart, $\Sigma^{-1} \sim W(\mathbf{H}^{-1}, \mathbf{v})$, the prior for σ^2_u is an inverted gamma, that is, $\sigma^2_u \sim v_0 s^2_0 / \chi^2_{v_0}$, where $\chi^2_{v_0}$ is a chi square variate with v_0 degrees of freedom. Finally, given σ^2_u, the prior for $\mathbf{c}_A = (c'_{AN}\ c'_{AB})'$ is Gaussian. The specific values of the parameters assumed for these priors are derived using empirical Bayes methods.

Turning to the skill and mispricing priors, Pastor and Stambaugh assume that, conditional on Σ, the prior for α_N is

$$\alpha_N|\Sigma \sim N\left(0, \sigma^2_{\alpha_N}\frac{\Sigma}{s^2}\right),$$

where $E[\Sigma] = s^2\mathbf{I}_m$ is a diagonal matrix. Here σ_{α_N} is the (marginal) prior standard deviation of α_N (assumed to be identical across all nonbenchmark assets). Clearly, if $\sigma_{\alpha_N} = 0$, then $\alpha_N = \mathbf{0}$ and the investor has full confidence in the benchmark assets' ability to price the nonbenchmark assets. The greater the value of σ_{α_N}, the higher the chance of mispricing of these assets, although since the prior distribution of α_N is centered at zero, in expectation the investor always thinks there is no bias in the pricing model.

Pastor and Stambaugh assume that investors' prior beliefs about managers' skills follow a similar distribution:

$$\delta_A|\sigma^2_u \sim N\left(\delta_0, \frac{\sigma^2_u}{E[\sigma^2_u]}\sigma^2_\delta\right).$$

The scaling by $\sigma^2_u/E[\sigma^2_u]$ ensures that if σ^2_u is high, meaning that little of the variation in a fund's returns is explained by the passive portfolios, then a larger value of abnormal performance, δ_A, becomes more likely. δ_0, the mean of the residual performance adjusted for risk exposure to the benchmark and nonbenchmark assets, reflects the performance, net of cost, of a truly unskilled fund manager. Hence it is given by the monthly equivalent to the fund's expense ratio and its turnover times a roundtrip cost of 1 percent:

$$\delta_0 = \frac{-1}{12}(\text{expense} + 0.01 \times \text{turnover}).$$

Letting $\mathbf{R} = (\mathbf{R}_N\ \mathbf{R}_B)$ be the $T \times (n + k)$ matrix of sample data on the passive index portfolios and r_{T+1} be the vector of fund returns in the following period, the posterior predictive distribution is obtained as

$$p(r_{T+1}|\mathbf{R}) = \int_\theta p(r_{T+1}|\mathbf{R}, \boldsymbol{\theta})p(\boldsymbol{\theta}, \mathbf{R})d\boldsymbol{\theta}, \tag{94}$$

where $p(\boldsymbol{\theta}|\mathbf{R})$ is the posterior distribution of the parameters, $\boldsymbol{\theta}$.

In their empirical analysis, Pastor and Stambaugh (2002b) find that both prior beliefs about managers' skills and prior beliefs about pricing models are important to investors' decision of whether or not to invest in actively managed funds. An investor with complete confidence in the benchmark asset pricing model (CAPM) who is ruling out the possibility of a nonzero value of α_A naturally only invests in market-index funds. If this investor admits the possibility that returns may be explained by p passive funds, even when believing with full confidence that $\delta_A = 0$, this investor is willing to hold some money in actively managed funds, provided that it is not possible to invest directly in the passive funds. The logic is of course that when investors cannot hold the benchmark or nonbenchmark assets directly, actively managed funds can track the benchmark portfolios with smaller errors than passively managed funds. Hence even investors who are skeptical about the possibility of managerial skill may choose to invest in actively managed mutual funds.

7. CONCLUSION

In fits and starts, the finance profession has come a long way since the pioneering work of Jensen (1968, 1969, 1972), Sharpe (1966), and Treynor and Mazuy (1966). To be sure, many of the issues discovered in this early work remain: in particular, the twin problems of the identification and measurement of appropriate benchmarks and the biases in performance measures arising from market timing. Yet we have learned much about the precise form these problems take and we have developed new methods and new sources of information. And the markets have learned much as well: the pervasive use of benchmark-based performance measurement and attribution in the mutual fund and pension fund industries are a testament to the impact of academic research.

We know that the theoretically appropriate benchmark is a portfolio, δ, which need not come from some equilibrium asset pricing model. It can come from the theory of portfolio choice: portfolio δ is the mean variance efficient portfolio that hedges the intertemporal marginal rates of substitution of any investor who is on the margin with respect to each asset chosen by the performance evaluator even if the investors invest in many other assets not included in the analysis. It can come from the hypothesis that markets are arbitrage-free, which is a necessary but not a sufficient condition for optimal portfolio choice: after all, nobody would be a marginal investor in an asset menu that permitted investors to eliminate their budget constraints. We know this because the basic question of performance measurement turns out to be quite simple: are the managed portfolios under evaluation worth adding to the asset menu chosen by the evaluator? To be sure, the optimal benchmark remains the Holy Grail, if only because the moments – in particular, the conditional and unconditional first moments of asset returns – required for its identification are hard to measure with any precision. However, much progress has been made on identifying the asset menus that are hard for managed portfolios to beat.

We also know quite a bit about the problem of market timing, ignoring the benchmark identification issue. When asset returns are not predictable based on public information, market timing efforts cause problems for performance evaluation based on Jensen-type measures only when it is successful, modulo sampling error. Moreover, Treynor-Mazuy-type measures can detect the presence of successful market timing when present and, when returns and shifts in betas to exploit market timing opportunities are jointly normally distributed, it is possible to measure both Jensen-type alphas and the quality of market timing information. Matters are more complicated when returns are predictable based on public information but the same basic results obtain when it is possible to characterize the predictability of excess benchmark returns and betas from the perspective of an uninformed investor. To be sure, these developments are mostly of academic interest, in part because of an important empirical development: the availability of data beyond managed portfolio returns.

In particular, much recent research has exploited newly available data on asset allocations and individual security holdings.[21] Asset allocation data make it reasonably straightforward to see whether managers are successful market timers by seeing whether they tilt toward an asset class before it does well and away before it does poorly. The empirical record for pension funds is clear on this score: successful market timers are rare, if not nonexistent. Individual portfolio holdings make it reasonably straightforward to see whether managers tilt toward individual securities before they go up in price and away before they decline, although there is no clear distinction between market timing and security selection in this case. Most importantly, these observations make it clear that the data are being overworked when managed portfolio returns are asked to reveal both normal performance and abnormal performance of both the security selection and market timing variety.

And it seems that the impact of academia on best practice in the industry would appear to have largely solved the problem of market timing as well. Managers are typically measured against explicit benchmarks, eliminating the problem of estimating betas when the target beta of a fund is unity by contract. Moreover, the gap between the practitioner and academic communities has narrowed considerably given the performance measurement and attribution procedures that now pervade industry. Future analyses of managed portfolio performance may well be largely free of the problem of market timing.

This suggests that future research will have more to say about the performance of managed portfolios than about the tools we use to measure it. To be sure, methodology will continue to be a focus of the academic literature as evidenced, for example, in the emergence of a Bayesian literature on performance evaluation. The main point remains that research over the last four decades has made it much easier to answer the central question of performance measurement: do managed portfolios add to the investment opportunities implicit in sensible benchmark portfolios?

References

Admati, A., and S. Ross. 1985. Measuring Investment Performance in a Rational Expectations Equilibrium Model, *Journal of Business* 58, 1–26.

Admati, A. R., S. Bhattacharya, P. Pfleiderer, and S. A. Ross. 1986. On Timing and Selectivity, *Journal of Finance* 41, 715–730.

Ait-Sahalia, Y., and M. W. Brandt. 2001. Variable Selection for Portfolio Choice, *Journal of Finance* 56, 1297–1351.

Baks, K. P., A. Metrick, and J. Wachter. 2001. Should Investors Avoid All Actively Managed Mutual Funds? A Study in Bayesian Performance Evaluation, *Journal of Finance* 56, 45–85.

Berk, J., and R. Green. 2004. Mutual Fund Flows and Performance in Rational Markets. Working paper, Carnegie Mellon University.

[21] For a comprehensive study making use of data on mutual funds' securities holdings, see Wermers (2000).

Bhattacharya, S., and Pfleiderer, P. 1985. Delegated Portfolio Management, *Journal of Economic Theory* 36, 1–25.

Blake, D., B. Lehmann, and A. Timmermann. 1999. Asset Allocation Dynamics and Pension Fund Performance, *Journal of Business* 72, 429–462.

Blake, D., and A. Timmermann. 2002. Performance Benchmarks for Institutional Investors: Measuring, Monitoring and Modifying Investment Behaviour, in J. Knight and S. Satchell (eds.), *Performance Measurement in Finance*. Butterworth Heinemann, London, pp. 108–140.

Brinson, G. P., L. R. Hood, and G. L. Beebower. 1986. Determinants of Portfolio Performance, *Financial Analysts Journal* (July–August), 39–48.

Brinson, G. P., B. D. Singer, and G. L. Beebower. 1991. Determinants of Portfolio Performance II: An Update, *Financial Analysts Journal* (May–June), 40–48.

Britten-Jones, M. 1999. The Sampling Error in Estimates of Mean-Variance Efficient Portfolio Weights. *Journal of Finance* 54, 655–671.

Brown, S. J., and W. N. Goetzmann. 1995. Performance Persistence, *Journal of Finance* 50, 679–698.

Brown, S. J., W. Goetzmann, R. G. Ibbotson, and S. A. Ross. 1992. Survivorship Bias in Performance Studies, *Review of Financial Studies* 5, 553–580.

Carhart, M. 1997. On Persistence in Mutual Fund Performance, *Journal of Finance* 52, 57–82.

Carpenter, J., and A. W. Lynch. 1999. Survivorship Bias and Attrition Effects in Measures of Performance Persistence, *Journal of Financial Economics* 54, 337–374.

Chen, H. L., N. Jegadesh, and R. Wermers. 2000. An Examination of the Stockholdings and Trades of Fund Managers, *Journal of Financial and Quantitative Analysis* 35, 343–368.

Chen, Z., and P. J. Knez. 1996. Portfolio Performance Measurement: Theory and Applications, *Review of Financial Studies* 9, 511–555.

Christopherson, J. A., W. E. Ferson, and D. A. Glassman. 1998. Conditioning Manager Alphas on Economic Information: Another Look at the Persistence of Performance, *Review of Financial Studies* 11(1), 111–142.

Connor, G., and R. Korajczyk. 1986. Performance Measurement with the Arbitrage Pricing Theory: A New Framework for Analysis, *Journal of Financial Economics* 15, 373–394.

Cumby, R. E., and D. M. Modest. 1987. Testing for Market Timing Ability. A Framework for Forecast Evaluation. *Journal of Financial Economics* 19, 169–189.

Daniel, K., M. Grinblatt, S. Titman, and R. Wermers. 1997. Measuring Mutual Fund Performance with Characteristic-Based Benchmarks, *Journal of Finance* 52, 1035–1058.

Dybvig, P. H., and J. E. Ingersoll. 1982. Mean-Variance Theory in Complete Markets, *Journal of Business* 55, 233–251.

Dybvig, P., and S. Ross. 1985. Differential Information and Performance Measurement Using a Security Market Line, *Journal of Finance* 40, 383–399.

Fama, E. F. and K. R. French. 1993. Common Risk Factors in the Returns on Stocks and Bonds, *Journal of Financial Economics* 33, 3–56.

Farnsworth, H., W. Ferson, D. Jackson, and S. Todd. 2001. Performance Evaluation with Stochastic Discount Factors, *Journal of Business* 75, 473–583.

Ferson, W. E., and R. W. Schadt. 1996. Measuring Fund Strategy and Performance in Changing Economic Conditions, *Journal of Finance* 51, 425–461.

Gibbons, Michael R., Stephen A. Ross, and Jay Shanken. 1989. A Test of the Efficiency of a Given Portfolio, *Econometrica* 57, 1121–1152.

Graham, J., and Harvey, C. 1996. Market Timing Ability and Volatility Implied in Investment Newsletters' Asset Allocation Recommendations, *Journal of Financial Economics* 42, 397–421.

Grinblatt, M., and S. Titman. 1989. Portfolio Performance Evaluation: Old Issues and New Insights, *Review of Financial Studies* 2, 393–422.

Grinblatt, M., and S. Titman. 1992. The Persistence of Mutual Fund Performance, *Journal of Finance* 47, 1977–1984.

Grinblatt, M., and S. Titman. 1993. Performance Measurement Without Benchmarks: An Examination of Mutual Fund Returns, *Journal of Business* 66, 47–68.

Gruber, M. J. 1996. Another Puzzle: The Growth of Actively Managed Mutual Funds, *Journal of Finance* 51, 783–810.

Hendricks, D., J. Patel, and R. Zeckhauser. 1993. Hot Hands in Mutual Funds: Short-Run Persistence of Relative Performance 1974–1988, *Journal of Finance* 48, 93–130.

Henriksson, R. D., and R. C. Merton. 1981. On Market Timing and Investment Performance II: Statistical Procedures for Evaluating Forecasting Skills, *Journal of Business* 54, 513–533.

Jensen, M. 1968. The Performance of Mutual Funds in the Period 1945–1964, *Journal of Finance* 23, 389–416.

Jensen, M. 1969. Risk, the Pricing of Capital Assets, and the Evaluation of Investment Performance, *Journal of Business* 42, 167–247.

Jensen, M. 1972. Optimal Utilization of Market Forecasts and the Evaluation of Investment Portfolio Performance, in G. Szego and K. Shell (eds.), *Mathematical Methods in Investment and Finance*. North Holland, Amsterdam.

Jobson, J. D., and B. Korkie. 1982. Potential Performance and Tests of Portfolio Efficiency, *Journal of Financial Economics* 10, 433–456.

Kosowski, R. 2002. Do Mutual Funds Perform When It Matters Most to Investors? U.S. Mutual Fund Performance and Risk in Recessions and Booms 1962–2000. Working paper, INSEAD.

Kosowski, R., A. Timmermann, R. Wermers and H. White. 2006. Can Mutual Fund "Stars" Really Pick Stocks? New Evidence from a Bootstrap Analysis, *Journal of Finance* 61, 2551–2595.

Lakonishok, J., A. Shleifer, and R. W. Vishny. 1992. The Structure and Performance of the Money Management Industry, *Brooking Papers: Microeconomics*, 339–379.

Lehmann, B., and D. Modest. 1987. Mutual Fund Performance Evaluation: A Comparison of Benchmarks and Benchmark Comparisons, *Journal of Finance* 42, 233–265.

Lynch, A. W., J. Wachter, and W. Boudry. 2002. Does Mutual Fund Performance Vary Over the Business Cycle? NBER discussion paper.

Mackinlay, A. C., and M. Richardson. 1991. Using the Generalized Method of Moments to Test Mean-Variance Efficiency, *Journal of Finance* 46, 511–527.

Malkiel, B. G. 1995. Returns from Investing in Equity Mutual Funds 1971 to 1991, *Journal of Finance* 50, 549–572.

Merton, R. C. 1981. On Market Timing and Investment Performance I: An Equilibrium Theory of Value for Market Forecasts, *Journal of Business* 54, 363–406.

Pastor, L., and R. F. Stambaugh. 2002a. Mutual Fund Performance and Seemingly Unrelated Assets, *Journal of Financial Economics* 63, 315–349.

Pastor, L., and R. F. Stambaugh. 2002b. Investing in Equity Mutual Funds, *Journal of Financial Economics* 63, 351–380.

Pesaran, M. H., and A. Timmermann. 1992. A Simple Nonparametric Test of Predictive Performance, *Journal of Business and Economic Statistics* 10, 461–465.

Ross, S. A. 1976. The Arbitrage Theory of Capital Asset Pricing, *Journal of Economic Theory* 3, 343–362.

Ross, S. A. 1977. Risk, Return, and Arbitrage, in I. Friend and J. L. Bicksler (eds.), *Risk and Return in Finance*. Ballinger, Cambridge, MA.

Sharpe, W. 1966. Mutual Fund Performance, *Journal of Finance* 39, 119–138.

Treynor, J. L., and F. Black. 1973. How to Use Security Analysis to Improve Portfolio Selection, *Journal of Business* 46, 66–86.

Treynor, J., and K. Mazuy. 1966. Can Mutual Funds Outguess the Market? *Harvard Business Review* 44, 131–136.

CHAPTER 8

The Behavior of Mutual Fund Investors

Lu Zheng
Paul Merage School of Business, University of California, Irvine

Abstract

This chapter reviews findings on the behavior of mutual fund investors. It first outlines the evidence on how fund investors choose among many funds in the marketplace and how aggregate fund flows relate to market returns. It then explores the investment performance of mutual fund investors. Finally, it discusses investor externality as well as possible interactions between behavioral patterns of fund investors and strategies of mutual funds.

1. INTRODUCTION

The mutual fund industry has grown dramatically over the past several decades. In the first quarter of 2005, mutual fund assets worldwide were $16.13 trillion, with $8.8 trillion in the U.S. market.[1] In the United States, mutual funds have become one of the major investment and savings vehicles for individual investors: More than 50 percent of U.S. households invest in mutual funds, which in turn own more than 20 percent of the U.S. equity market.[2] Since many individual investors rely on mutual fund investments for retirement income and educational funding for their children, the performance of mutual fund investments is essential to the financial well-being of U.S. households. Consequently, the quality of decisions made by fund investors has profound welfare implications for these investors and the U.S. economy in general. Given the importance of these investments, the behavior of mutual fund investors is an important area of research.

Investor behavior in general is an important stream of research in behavioral finance. This field of research examines how certain groups of investors behave, for example, what types of securities they hold and how these investors trade over time (Barberis and Thaler 2003). The mutual fund industry provides a useful laboratory in which researchers study the trading behavior of individual investors. Because most funds (share classes) are held primarily by individuals, mutual fund money flows reveal the investment decisions of individual investors. Studies on the behavior of mutual fund investors contribute to the growing literature on investor behavior.

Furthermore, the behavior of fund investors has significant implications for the soundness of the mutual fund industry in particular and the stability of financial markets in general. Voting with money, mutual fund investors exert great influence on the activities of mutual funds. The rationality of fund flows is thus crucial to ensuring a well-functioning and competitive mutual fund industry. Moreover, the large shares of financial markets held by mutual funds suggest that the trading behavior of mutual fund investors may have significant impact on asset prices, especially if fund investors display common sentiment and trade in the same directions. Understanding the behavior of mutual fund investors sheds light on the functioning of the fund industry and the financial markets.

Research on mutual fund behavior is facilitated by the accessibility of data on mutual fund returns, total net assets, and other fund characteristics.[3] Over the years, researchers have studied the determinants of investors' fund selection decisions and the outcomes of their investment choices. Academic studies also explore how mutual fund flows reflect investor sentiment and how they are related to asset prices. Recent studies have further

[1] According to "Worldwide Mutual Fund Assets and Flows: First Quarter 2005" by Investment Company Institute.

[2] According to "Trends in Mutual Fund Investing," July 2005, by Investment Company Institute, an Investment Company Institute survey report, and the "Flow of Funds Account" by the Board of Governors of the Federal Reserve System.

[3] Among many datasets, the most accessible and widely used is the CRSP mutual fund database, which was initially compiled by Mark Carhart for his dissertation at the University of Chicago.

examined how the trading behavior of some investors affects fund performance and thus returns to other investors. Another important finding is that the mutual fund industry is well aware of the behavioral patterns in fund flows and adopts strategies in response to the observed investor behavior.

This chapter reviews the most recent research findings related to the behavior and performance of mutual fund investors. The findings provide an understanding of individual investment decisions and generate an ongoing debate on the rationality of certain types of investor behavior. This chapter also reviews the evidence on investor externality and discusses possible interactions between behavioral patterns of fund investors and the investment strategies of mutual funds. These dynamics provide insight into additional potential economic consequences of mutual fund investor behavior.

The rest of the chapter is organized as follows. Section 2 reviews evidence related to the investment behavior of mutual fund investors. Section 3 discusses the findings regarding the investment performance of fund investors. Section 4 considers the evidence on investor externality. Section 5 discusses the strategies of mutual funds and fund companies in response to fund flows. Section 6 concludes the chapter.

2. EXAMINING INVESTOR BEHAVIOR USING FUND FLOWS

Fund flows reveal the investment decisions of mutual fund investors. The availability of data to estimate fund flows makes it possible for researchers to infer many investment decisions of mutual fund investors as a group. This section reviews two streams of research regarding the behavior of mutual fund investors. The first stream of research considers how investors choose among many funds in the marketplace. Specifically, this research explores how fund flows are related to fund characteristics such as past fund performance, fund fees and expenses, taxes, search costs and advertising, and fund corporate governance. This research provides insight into individual decision making and yields significant implications for the welfare of mutual fund investors as well as the strategies of mutual funds. The second stream of research considers how mutual fund flows on an aggregate level relate to marketwide price movements. The related findings from this area of research have implications for overall market stability.

2.1. Estimating Mutual Fund Flows

Due to data availability, most studies do not have access to the actual amount of purchases and redemptions of funds, so they estimate net mutual fund flows from reported fund returns and total net asset values (e.g., Gruber 1996 and Zheng 1999). Dollar net flow (new money) is typically defined as the change in total net asset value minus the appreciation in the fund assets, as follows:

$$\text{Flow}_{i,t} = \text{TNA}_{i,t} - \text{TNA}_{i,t-1}(1 + R_{i,t}),$$

where $TNA_{i,t}$ is the total net assets of fund i at the end of period t and $R_{i,t}$ is the total return, including dividends and capital gains distributions, of fund i in period t. The calculation of net flow by this method makes two assumptions. First, it assumes that distributed dividends and capital gains are reinvested. Second, it assumes that all cash flows occur at the end of each period.

Since large funds are likely to incur relatively large cash flows in terms of dollar amount, most studies use a relative measure of net flow, scaling the dollar net flow by the beginning of period total net asset, as follows:

$$\text{Percentage Flow}_{i,t} = (\text{TNA}_{i,t} - \text{TNA}_{i,t-1}(1 + R_{i,t}))/\text{TNA}_{i,t-1} = \text{Flow}_{i,t}/\text{TNA}_{i,t-1}.$$

This percentage flow measures new money as a growth rate and takes into account the size of a fund. Some studies adjust for merger activity in their estimates of cash flows (e.g., Zheng 1999), because cash flows due to merger activities do not usually reflect voluntary investment decisions by fund investors.

2.2. The Decision to Choose Among Mutual Funds

2.2.1. Past Fund Performance

Investors of actively managed mutual funds seek to select funds with strong expected future performance based on observed fund characteristics. In identifying factors that affect fund cash flows, many researchers have documented evidence that investors chase past fund performance. Starting in the 1970s, researchers have uncovered evidence that cash flows to mutual funds are positively related to these funds' past performances, indicating that investors view past fund performance as a useful predictor of future fund performance. Beyond the generally positive relationship, recent empirical work documents an intriguing nonlinear cash flow response to past fund performance, in which investors pour money into past winners but do not withdraw proportionately from past losers.

Earlier studies on cash flows document a positive linear relationship between fund performance and investor cash flows. Several studies, including Spitz (1970), Smith (1978), Lakonishok et al. (1992), and Patel, Zeckhauser, and Hendricks (1994), report that funds with better performance incur higher subsequent cash flows. However, recent papers indicate that the relationship between fund cash flows and past fund performance is not linear. This body of research, including Ippolito (1992), Gruber (1996), Chevalier and Ellison (1997), Goetzmann and Peles (1997), Sirri and Tufano (1998), and Del Guercio and Tkac (2001), indicates that funds with strong past performance attract a high inflow of new money; however, funds with poor past performance do not suffer a proportionate outflow of money.

Figure 1 illustrates the nonlinear relationship between fund flows and past fund performance using a sample of U.S. diversified equity funds from 1970 to 1999. In each quarter, funds are ranked into deciles according to their excess returns over the stock market returns. Average new money growth as a percentage of total net assets (TNA) is calculated for each performance decile. Figure 1 plots the average new money growth

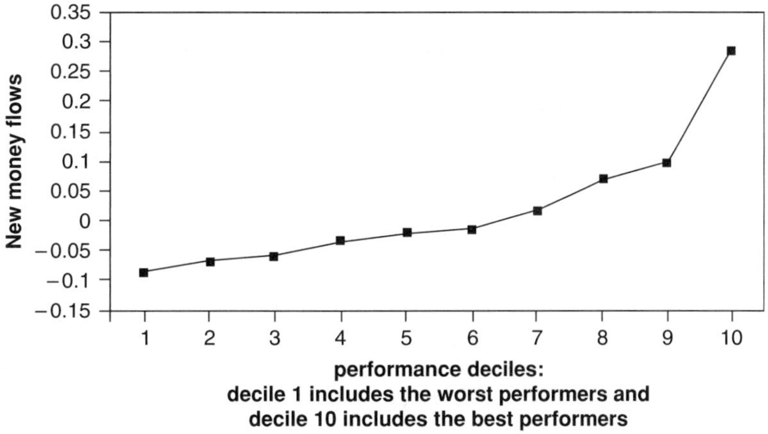

FIGURE 1 New money flows of past performance deciles. This figure plots the average quarterly new money flows for deciles of funds based on the previous one-year excess returns over the stock market return. Decile 10 consists of funds with best past performance, and decile 1 consists of funds with worst past performance. The sample includes diversified U.S. equity funds covered in the CRSP mutual fund database from 1970 to 1999.

for each decile across all quarters. The relationship depicted in Figure 1 indicates a disproportionate inflow of new money into the top performance decile and a less pronounced relationship between new money flow and past fund performance for funds that performed poorly in the past. The pattern is similar if these rankings are based on alternative performance measures, such as Jensen's alpha (Jensen 1968), Fama–French three-factor alpha (Fama and French 1993), and Carhart four-factor alpha (Carhart 1997).

Further research shows that the fund family structure magnifies the flow benefit of a stellar past performance. Why is this so? Consider that most mutual funds are members of fund families. Empirical findings suggest that top-performing funds not only attract more new money into themselves but also into other funds in the same fund family. Nanda, Wang, and Zheng (2004) document such a positive spillover effect from a star fund to other funds in the family. By contrast, they find no spillover effect from a poorly performing fund. Khorana and Servaes (2004) also find a positive relationship between fund family market shares and the presence of a star fund in the family.

However, the observed nonlinear cash flow response to past fund performance is at odds with the empirical findings regarding the relationship between past and future fund performance. Empirical evidence suggests that strong performers may or may not do well in the future, but poor performers will most likely continue to perform poorly.[4] Consequently, it may seem perplexing that investors move money into past strong performers but do not move money out of past poor performers.

[4]For evidence on performance persistence, see, for example, Grinblatt and Titman (1992), Elton et al. (1993), Hendricks, Patel and Zeckhauser (1993), Goetzmann and Ibbotson (1994), S. Brown and Goetzmann (1995), Christopherson, Ferson, and Glassman (1998), Elton, Gruber, and Blake (1996), Carhart (1997), H-L. Chen, Jegadeesh, and Wermers (2000), Teo and Woo (2001), and Kacperczyk, Sialm, and Zheng (2005a).

To explain this behavioral pattern, let's first consider behavior related to mutual funds that perform poorly. One reason for staying with a poor performer may be the transaction costs involved in switching between funds, as proposed by Ippolito (1992), Sirri and Tufano (1998), and Huang, Wei, and Yan (2007). Sirri and Tufano (1998) further point out that search costs and the marketing effort to promote good performers and obscure poor performers may explain the nonlinear flow response to past fund performance.

A second reason why investors may stick with poor performers is that funds can abandon investment strategies that underperform. Lynch and Musto (2003) argue that funds respond to bad performance by replacing the personnel or techniques that yielded this performance. They show that strategy changes occur only after bad performance and that bad performers who change strategy have dollar flows and future performances that are less sensitive to past performance.

Yet another reason for keeping a poor performer is that investors may adjust their beliefs to support past decisions. Goetzmann and Peles (1997) apply the theory of cognitive dissonance to investment behavior to propose that investors bias their perceptions about past fund performance to feel good about the efficacy of their choices. Using questionnaire responses from fund investors, they find that investor recollections of past fund performance are consistently biased above actual past fund performance.

Gruber (1996) suggests that the insufficient response to poor past fund performance could be due to the existence of a "disadvantaged clientele." Among these investors, some are unsophisticated and are influenced by advertising or advice from brokers. Others are constrained due to the rules of their pension plans or due to tax considerations. Berk and Xu (2004) show that funds performing poorly two years in a row experience significantly less outflow than funds performing poorly only for a year, indicating a constrained investor clientele.

There may be several reasons why investors stay with poor performers. But what leads them to put more money into strong past performers, despite unclear evidence that the strong performance will continue? One reason for this behavior is that investors may apply a representativeness heuristic. In general, when faced with uncertain choices, people use heuristics or rules of thumb to make judgments (Tversky and Kahneman 1974). They believe small samples are overly representative of the population from which they are drawn (Tversky and Kahnemann 1971). Choosing a mutual fund from thousands of funds in the market is a decision fraught with uncertainty. Using a representativeness heuristic when buying mutual funds, investors may view a fund's recent performance as overly representative of a fund manager's skill and, thus, of the fund's future prospects. Kliger, Levy, and Sonsino (2003) report experimental evidence that investors move more money into funds with strong past performance, even in cases where past performance conveys no information regarding investment ability.

A second reason why investors chase strong past performers despite mixed empirical evidence regarding performance persistence is that the mixed results are caused by an overflow of rational investors moving money into such funds. Berk and Green (2004) suggest that the lack of performance persistence for strong performers is actually a result of investors chasing past performance. New money flows to the fund to the point at which expected excess returns going forward are competitive because there are decreasing returns to scale for managers in deploying their superior investment ability. Their model shows that chasing past fund performance can be rational even within the context of a lack of empirical evidence on the performance persistence of mutual funds.

While there is an ongoing debate on the rationality of investors in their reactions to past fund performance, a recent study further questions the rationality of a group of generally sophisticated investors. Elton, Gruber, and Busse (2004) suggest that index fund investors, generally viewed as relatively sophisticated, do not respond sufficiently to past fund characteristics in a setting where these fund characteristics strongly predict future fund performance. Analyzing a sample of 52 S&P 500 index funds, they show that future fund performance and other fund characteristics, such as fees, risk and tax efficiency, are all highly predictable. However, they show that investors do not respond to past performance as much as one would expect based on rational behavior.

In short, investors show a nonlinear pattern of response to past fund performance. While their decisions do not correlate with empirical findings regarding the relationship between past and future performance for funds, researchers have proposed several explanations for why investors invest the way they do.

2.2.2. Fund Fees and Expenses

Investment costs decrease the returns to fund investors and thus should be a natural concern when investors select among mutual funds. The direct costs of investing in mutual funds include load charges and commissions paid when investors purchase or sell mutual funds as well as annual operating expense ratios applied to assets under management. If fund managers are not skilled at investing, such expenses reduce expected returns for investors. Empirical evidence indicates that even before load charges are deducted, load funds do not outperform no-load funds (e.g., Morey 2003 and Bergstresser, Chalmers, and Tufano 2005). Moreover, researchers have documented a negative relationship between a fund's operating expense ratio and its performance (e.g., Gruber 1996 and Carhart 1997). Thus, it is sensible for investors to avoid funds with load charges and high operating expenses.

A number of papers examine how investors consider load charges and annual expense ratios when investing in mutual funds. While empirical findings indicate a generally negative relationship between fund flows and total fund fees, further analyses suggest that fund investors respond differently to different forms of fees: They learn to avoid salient, in-your-face fees more quickly than they do obscure fees. Experimental evidence also suggests that investors are usually unable to assess the tradeoff between different fees charged by mutual funds.

When making investment decisions, do investors take load charges and annual expense ratios into account? Woerheide (1982) finds no significant correlation between fund flows and load charges/expense ratios for a sample of 44 funds from 1972 to 1976. Analyzing a sample of 690 funds from 1971 to 1990, Sirri and Tufano (1998) document a negative relation between fund flows and total fund expenses, indicating that investors avoid funds with high total expenses. Specifically, they calculate total fund expense as the expense ratio plus the up-front load amortized over seven years, the average holding period for equity mutual funds.

On the other hand, survey and experimental evidence suggests that investors are unable to assess the different forms of costs of investing in mutual funds. For example, Wilcox (2003) finds that 46 of 50 potential investors in his study overemphasize loads relative to expense ratios. Alexander, Jones, and Nigro (1998) document that less than 20 percent of 2,000 surveyed mutual fund investors could give an estimate of the expenses incurred for their largest mutual fund holding. Furthermore, despite empirical evidence to the contrary, 84 percent of the respondents in their study believed that mutual funds with higher expenses earned average or above-average returns.

In another study, Barber, Odean, and Zheng (2005) find that investors are more sensitive to salient, in-your-face fees, like front-end loads and commissions, than to operating expenses. Analyzing mutual fund flows from 1970 to 1999, they find consistently negative relations between fund flows and front-end load fees. They also document a negative relation between fund flows and commissions charged by brokerage firms. In contrast, they find no relation (or a perverse positive relation) between fund flows and operating expenses.

Figures 2 and 3 plot the average new money growth for two partitions of a sample of diversified U.S. equity funds on the basis of front-end loads and expense ratios, respectively. Figure 2 shows that funds without front-end loads enjoy higher growth rates. In contrast, Figure 3 indicates a nearly monotonic positive relationship between expenses and new money growth rates, with high-expense funds showing the highest growth rates. This relationship is explored by Barber, Odean, and Zheng (2005), who find that mutual fund marketing and advertising costs account for the positive relation between fund flows and expenses. Overall these results suggest that investors would benefit from a greater understanding and awareness of mutual fund expenses. To improve cost disclosure, in 2004 the U.S. Securities and Exchange Committee adopted an amendment

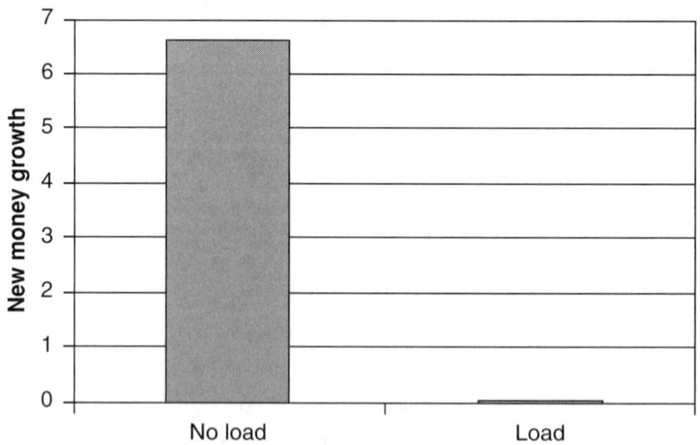

FIGURE 2 Cash flow response to front-end load charges. This figure plots the average quarterly new money flows for no load and load funds, respectively. The sample includes diversified U.S. equity funds covered in the CRSP mutual fund database from 1970 to 1999.

Source: Barber, Odean, and Zheng (2005).

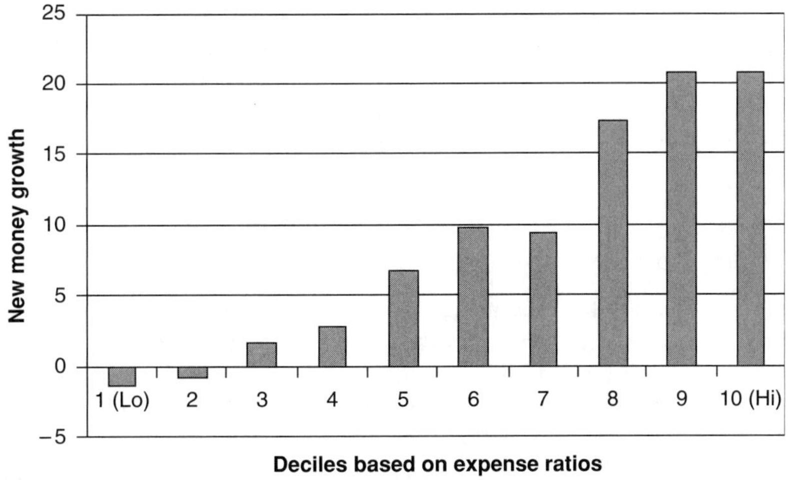

FIGURE 3 Cash flow response to annual expense ratios. This figure plots the average quarterly new money flows for deciles of funds based on the previous disclosed annual expense ratios. Decile 10 consists of funds with highest expense ratios, and decile 1 consists of funds with lowest expense ratios. The sample includes diversified U.S. equity funds covered in the CRSP mutal fund database from 1970 to 1999.
Source: Barber, Odean, and Zheng (2005).

requiring funds to disclose the cost in dollars associated with an investment of $1,000, based on the fund's actual periodic expenses.

2.2.3. Taxes

Taxes can have a significant impact on the returns of mutual fund investors. Tax law requires mutual funds in the United States to pass dividends and realized capital gains through to fund investors and to allocate these distributions equally across all shares, regardless of when the shares were purchased. Investors, in turn, pay taxes on the distributed dividends and capital gains. As a result, the after-tax return of investing in a mutual fund may differ substantially from the pretax return. Several studies have demonstrated that higher realized and potential tax burdens are associated with significantly lower subsequent cash flows to a fund. This finding suggests that at least a group of sophisticated investors are aware of the tax effect on their net investment returns and base their investment decisions accordingly. However, the prevalence of tax awareness among taxable mutual fund investors and the welfare loss due to investors' not following strategies to maximize their after-tax returns are open issues.

Barclay, Pearson, and Weisbach (1998) find that tax-sensitive investors are deterred by the overhang of unrealized gains, which increase future capital gains realizations. They show that fund managers thus have incentives to reduce the overhang in order to attract new investors.

In another study, Bergstresser and Poterba (2002) examine the relationship between after-tax returns of mutual funds and subsequent cash flows to these funds. Assuming tax rates that apply to hypothetical upper-income taxable investors, they construct after-tax returns for a large sample of equity mutual funds from 1993 to 1999. They report a 19.1 percent average annual pretax return, versus a 16.0 percent average annual after-tax return for the sample period. They further find a negative relationship between the tax burden and subsequent flows into a fund as well as a negative relationship between the capital gain overhang and subsequent fund flows.

2.2.4. Search Costs and Advertising

Collecting and processing information about fund performance, fees, and other fund characteristics is costly for mutual fund investors. Search costs vary for different investors and thus are difficult to measure. Nevertheless, if search costs are significant, investors would purchase funds that are less costly for them to identify. Empirical evidence shows that fund flows are significantly higher for funds that are more visible. Theoretical work further indicates that search costs can explain the nonlinear flow–performance relationship and substantial price differentiation among relatively homogeneous funds.

If search costs affect investor purchase decisions, information dissemination on the part of mutual funds may attract new investors by lowering their search costs. Several studies document a positive relationship between fund flows and funds' marketing and advertising effort, indicating that on average investors flock to funds that are more heavily marketed or advertised. However, although marketing and advertising expenses may benefit those investors who otherwise would not identify the fund, the effect of these expenses on existing shareholders is unclear, especially in cases where existing shareholders bear such cost by paying 12b-1 fees. Further research is necessary to assess the overall welfare effect of marketing and advertising expenses.

Sirri and Tufano (1998) point out that search costs can affect investors' decisions, with investors selecting those funds that are easier or less costly for them to identify. Using mutual fund complex size, marketing and distributing expenses, and the extent of media coverage as proxies for search costs, they find a relationship between search costs and fund flows for a sample of 690 U.S. equity funds from 1971 to 1990. In another study, Huang, Wei, and Yan (2005) show that search costs and transaction costs can explain the nonlinear flow–performance relationship. Hortacsu and Syverson (2004) show that small search costs can explain the substantial price differentiation across the S&P 500 index funds.

Since search costs affect investor purchase decisions, information dissemination by mutual funds can increase flows for such funds. Khorana and Servaes (2004) and Barber, Odean, and Zheng (2005) find that fund 12b-1 fees are positively related to fund flows or fund family market share. Gallaher, Kaniel, and Starks (2005) document that print advertising expenditures of mutual fund families have a positive but nonlinear correlation with flows into fund families, with the top advertisers receiving disproportionately high cash inflows.

A number of studies document direct evidence that cash flows into funds are positively related to advertisements and media attention. Jain and Wu (2000) analyze fund flows to 294 equity mutual funds advertised in *Barron's* or *Money* magazine. Compared to a matched control group, such funds receive significantly larger cash flows, despite a lack of evidence for future superior performance of such funds. Cronqvist (2003) examines retirement fund advertising in Sweden and finds a similar positive relationship between fund advertisements and subsequent fund flows. Reuter and Zitzewitz (2006) find that mutual fund recommendations published between 1996 and 2002 in five top media outlets in the United States are correlated with new money growth ranging from 6 to 15 percent in the subsequent 12 months, even after controlling for a variety of fund characteristics.

2.2.5. The Role of Brokers

Empirical findings assert that load funds do not outperform no-load funds, even before deducting load charges. Why do investors pay extra distributional fees to buy load funds? What benefits do professional brokerage services provide to fund investors? Although academic research has uncovered certain influence of brokers on investor behavior, so far researchers have identified little evidence of benefits provided by brokers to investor decisions.

However, as acknowledged by researchers, a more complete analysis of the value of brokers and financial advisors will require information about the less tangible aspects of brokerage services. For example, brokers may help customize investor portfolios to their risk preference and may increase investor comfort with their investment decisions. Moreover, to assess fully the value added by brokers, researchers need to know what investment choices these same investors in the brokered channel would have made without advice from brokers.

In one study, Zhao (2004) studies the role of brokers and financial advisors by examining cash flows into load vs. no-load funds. He finds evidence that load funds with higher loads tend to have larger cash flows, suggesting that brokers and financial advisors play a significant role in the investment decision-making process. Unfortunately, the evidence also suggests that brokers and financial advisors may act in their self-interest rather than that of their investors by selling funds with high loads. He also documents that brokers and financial advisors direct investors into smaller funds and that brokered funds exhibit higher cash flow sensitivity to past performance than do no-load funds.

Bergstresser, Chalmers, and Tufano (2005) also examine the effect of brokers on investor decisions and returns. They find that brokered funds charge higher nondistributional fees, display lower raw and risk-adjusted returns, even before deducting distribution charges, and exhibit no better asset allocation skill than their no-load counterparts. They also find that the cash flows of brokered funds are more likely to chase past fund performance. Christoffersen, Evans, and Musto (2005) compare the cash flow pattern of captive brokers (those associated with mutual funds) to that of unaffiliated brokers. They find that the sensitivity of redemptions to past poor performance is much higher among unaffiliated broker funds than captive broker funds, demonstrating an influence of brokers on the fund investor decision making.

One documented benefit of brokerage is tax counseling. Starks, Yong, and Zheng (2006) find that funds associated with brokerage firms display more tax-loss selling behavior at the end of the year, suggesting that brokers provide tax counseling to investors. This finding suggests that it could be useful to explore the potential non performance-related value provided by brokers, such as investment education and additional services.

In examining the influence of advertising and broker advice on investor decisions, researchers find that demographics are correlated with the influence these factors yield on investment decisions. For example, Malloy and Zhu (2004) find evidence that investors located in less affluent, less educated, and ethnic minority neighborhoods invest more in funds with high load fees. Merging individual accounts data from a large discount brokerage firm with U.S. Census data, they aggregate investment choices by zip code and examine how the characteristics of each zip code relate to investor decisions. Their finding is consistent with the hypothesis in Gruber (1996) that a "disadvantaged clientele" will direct money based on brokerage advice and advertising.

2.2.6. Corporate Governance and Disclosure

Following the SEC investigations of mutual fund activities, a flurry of papers studied the governance and regulation aspect of mutual funds. However, the current research has focused on funds' internal governance mechanism. The issue of whether mutual fund investors care about fund governance has received little attention. If investors are aware of and act on fund governance issues, fund flows may serve as an external governance mechanism. Future research is needed to shed light on this issue. For now, only a couple of recent papers show preliminary evidence that some investors seem to act on the governance measures.

Ge and Zheng (2004) suggest that investors value frequent portfolio disclosure by analyzing the relationship between portfolio disclosure frequency and new money growth. Controlling for other fund characteristics, they compare new money flows for funds providing voluntary quarterly disclosure to flows for funds providing mandatory semiannual disclosure. They document a nonlinear response of new money flows to disclosure frequency with respect to past performance. Specifically, they find that more frequent disclosure is associated with higher new money flows for funds with poor past performance. However, the positive relationship weakens and becomes insignificant for funds with better past performance.

Wellman and Zhou (2005) document some evidence that investors purchase and redeem funds based on fund governance. The authors examine Morningstar Stewardship Grades that measure fund governance according to five criteria: board quality, regulatory issue, manager incentives, fees, and corporate culture. They find that cash flows into 357 diversified U.S. equity funds receiving a good governance grade are higher than those into funds receiving a poor grade. Their study also finds that funds with good governance grades significantly outperform funds with poor grades both before and after grade publication.

2.3. Mutual Fund Flows and Aggregate Market Returns

The foregoing research provides some understanding of the factors investors consider when selecting among mutual funds. Another stream of research looks at how mutual fund investments in aggregate affect market returns. The findings from this stream of research have implications for financial market stability, since some have expressed concern over the potential effect of the dramatic expansion of the mutual fund industry on financial markets overall. In particular, some question whether positive-feedback trading (buy when prices rise and sell when prices fall) by mutual fund investors may exacerbate price declines during market downturns.

Analyses at the monthly/quarterly frequency indicate a significant contemporaneous correlation between aggregate fund flows and stock market returns. To disentangle causality, researchers exploit daily flow data and demonstrate that the contemporaneous daily correlation between flows and returns are due to market return responding to fund flows. Further research indicates that fund flows reflect investor sentiment and are related to asset prices. Evidence on positive-feedback trading on market returns is only found at the daily frequency.

Warther (1995) is one of the first researchers to examine the relationship between aggregate fund flows and aggregate security returns. Analyzing monthly aggregate mutual fund net sales and security returns from 1984 to 1993 for different categories of funds, he finds strong evidence that fund flows are correlated with the current returns of the securities held by the funds. However, he finds no support that mutual fund investors follow a positive-feedback trading strategy. Boyer and Zheng (2003) also document a strong contemporaneous correlation between aggregate fund flows and stock market returns using quarterly flow data for funds from 1952 to 2004.

To better understand the causality between fund flows and returns, Edelen and Warner (2001) use daily flow data for a sample of 424 U.S. equity funds. They document a positive concurrent daily relationship between fund flows and market returns. Additional tests using intraday returns suggest that the positive concurrent relationship is caused mainly by returns responding to flows. They also document that aggregate flow follows market returns, with a one-day lag, indicating a common response to news or positive-feedback trading.

In another study, Goetzmann and Massa (2003) examine the relationship between daily flows of Fidelity S&P index funds and S&P 500 index returns from 1993 to 1997. Because index fund managers typically invest new money immediately in the market, these funds allow more precise identification of the day on which flows could affect market prices, which is essential in determining the causality between flows and returns. They document a strong same-day relationship between flows into index funds and the movement of the S&P 500 index. They show that the correlation is likely due to investor flows' affecting market returns rather than market returns causing flows.

Aggregate mutual fund flows reflect the investment decisions of individual investors as a group and thus may serve as a proxy for investor sentiment. Goetzmann, Massa, and Rouwenhorst (1999) document evidence of a negative correlation between daily fund flows into equity mutual funds and money market funds/precious metal funds, suggesting that fund flows reflect investor sentiments regarding equity premiums. In another study, S. Brown et al. (2002) construct a sentiment index using daily Japanese and U.S. mutual fund flows. They show that, in both markets, exposure to the sentiment factor is priced. The Japanese flow data indicate a negative correlation between flows to foreign equity funds and those to domestic equity funds. Indro (2004) shows that aggregate mutual fund flows are significantly correlated with other investment sentiment measures, including sentiment survey data from American Association of Individual Investors and a sentiment index based on independent investment newsletters from Investor Intelligence.

Overall, empirical evidence suggests that aggregate fund flows reflect investor sentiment and affect the price level of the stock market. There is some evidence of positive-feedback trading, but only at the very short horizon.

3. INVESTMENT PERFORMANCE OF MUTUAL FUND INVESTORS

Because mutual funds have become a major investment and savings vehicle for U.S. investors, the performance of these investments is essential for the financial well-being of individual investors. The growth of data companies such as Morningstar and Lipper and the explosion of books and articles on mutual funds reflect tremendous demand for detailed mutual fund information and investment advice. Given this interest in learning how to invest wisely in mutual funds, how do mutual fund investors actually perform? Beginning with Jensen (1968), many researchers have documented a significant negative abnormal return (after deducting the expense ratio) for the average mutual fund. The average risk-adjusted return of actively managed mutual funds is inferior to that of a low-cost index fund (Gruber 1996). However, return for investors can differ significantly from the average fund return because managers' investment skills are not priced, and investors can choose to invest in funds with high expected risk-adjusted returns to the extent they are able to forecast fund performance. Unfortunately, the average investor dollar return measured by TNA-weighted fund return is similar to the equal-weighted fund return (Zheng 1999). Thus, research suggests that mutual fund investors overall would do better to invest in a low-cost index fund.

While investor returns overall do not yield superior results, do some types of mutual fund investors fare better than others? Researchers document evidence that cash flows of sophisticated investors earn better returns than the average mutual fund because these investors can choose to invest with skilled managers at little cost. Specifically, new money flows are able to predict future fund performance over the short horizon. The predictability of fund performance is shown to be related to the momentum in stock returns. However, new money flows do not earn superior returns in the long run. Furthermore, stock styles that receive more fund flows tend to underperform in the long run.

Among many other empirical findings, Gruber (1996) reports monthly cash-flow-weighted abnormal returns for 227 actively managed equity funds from 1985 to 1994. He shows that the risk-adjusted returns are positive for the portfolio of funds that received net inflows of new money and negative for the portfolio of funds that experienced net outflows of new money over the short term. His evidence suggests that sophisticated investors act on predictors of future fund performance and that new money flows earn positive abnormal returns.

In an independent paper, Zheng (1999) investigates the performance of newly invested money using a sample of 1,826 diversified U.S. equity funds from 1970 through 1993. Using several measures of performance, she compares the performance of portfolios formed on the basis of past new money flow signals and finds that funds that receive more new money perform significantly better over the subsequent short horizon than those that lose money. This finding supports a "smart money" hypothesis, suggesting that investor purchase and redemption decisions predict future fund performance over the short term, especially for small funds. However, this effect is short-lived, since the performance of the "new money" portfolios shows a mean-reverting pattern over time. This finding is consistent with the argument in Berk and Green (2004) that increased fund size due to flows is associated with a decline in fund performance.

Figure 4 plots the performance of positive and negative new money portfolios for different holding periods up to 36 months. In general, the performance of the positive new money portfolio deteriorates over time, and the performance of the negative new money portfolio improves over time. After month 30, the negative new money portfolio outperforms the positive new money portfolio. This mean-reversion pattern demonstrates the short-term property of investor forecasts.

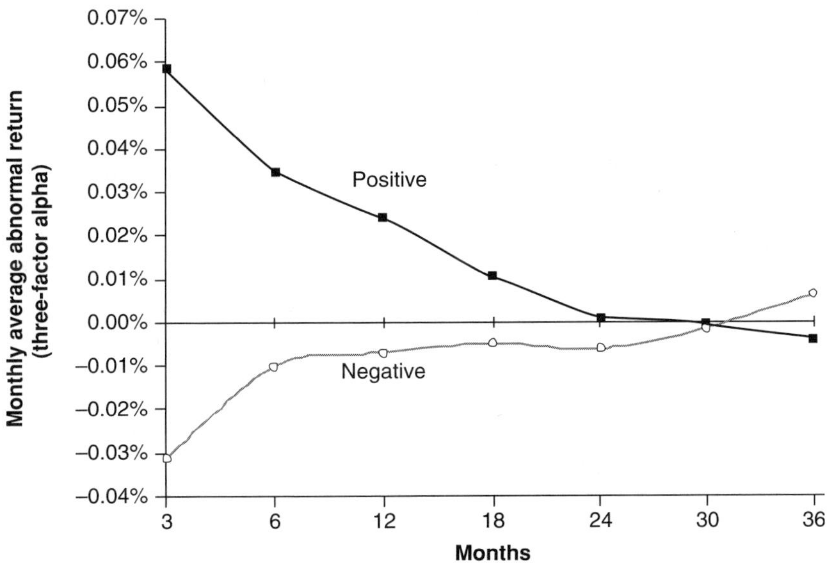

FIGURE 4 Performance of positive and negative new money portfolios for different holding periods. This figure plots the monthly average Fama–French three-factor alpha for the positive and negative new money portfolios of diversified U.S. equity material funds for different holding periods up to 36 months.
Source: Zheng (1999).

Both Gruber (1996) and Zheng (1999) suggest that the "smart money" effect is closely related to the persistence of fund performance. Zheng (1999) conjectures that one possible explanation for the "smart money" effect is the momentum in stock returns documented in Jegadeesh and Titman (1993). Sapp and Tiwari (2004) reexamine the "smart money" effect, controlling explicitly for the momentum in stock returns for a sample of diversified U.S. funds from 1970 to 2000. They show that the "smart money" effect can be explained largely by the Carhart momentum factor (Carhart 1997) and conclude that fund investors do not appear to be able to identify superior fund managers. An alternative interpretation of their finding is that actively managed open-end funds provide a way for investors to exploit return momentum with low transaction costs.

Wermers (2003) and Berndardt, Davies, and Westbrook (2005) suggest another explanation for the positive association between fund flows and subsequent short-term performance. They argue that funds use cash inflows to increase their existing positions and thus push up the prices of these stocks and fund returns through their own trades. They conclude that superior performance of past winners (or funds that receive inflows) is likely caused by flow-related trades rather than managers' investment skills.

Using a sample of British funds that report monthly purchases and redemptions, Keswani and Stolin (2008) document a significant "smart money" effect. They find that "new money" portfolios significantly outperform the TNA-weighted portfolio of all funds, even after controlling for the momentum factor, suggesting that new money performs better than old money. They also find evidence that funds with high net flows outperform funds with low net flows. Additional tests indicate that the "smart money" effect is mainly due to fund inflows rather than to fund outflows and is driven by flows from both individual and institutional investors.

Focusing on the long-run performance of investor decisions, Lamont and Frazzini (2005) show that investors reallocate through mutual funds to stocks that have low future returns. For each stock, they calculate the change in mutual fund ownership due to fund flows, assuming that fund managers allocate the flows to stocks based on their previously disclosed holdings. They find that reallocations into stocks through mutual funds reflect small investor sentiment and decrease total long-term returns for investors.

Overall, empirical findings suggest that investors on average are better off investing in a low-cost index fund than in actively managed mutual funds. While there is evidence that some sophisticated investors can earn superior returns following a short-term investment strategy, the longer-term performance of investor cash flows is less promising.

4. INVESTOR EXTERNALITY

The investment behavior of certain investors can affect fund performance and thus returns to other investors. This section reviews evidence on two types of investor externality.

The first type of investor externality is caused by liquidity trades of fund investors. Open-end mutual funds provide liquidity to investors at little direct cost. Unfortunately, the resulting uninformed, liquidity-motivated trading by mutual funds can have a negative impact on fund returns and thus returns to other investors. Empirical findings provide evidence on the effect of such liquidity costs. Moreover, empirical evidence further indicates that, since some investors tend to trade more than others, the composition of investor clientele can affect fund performance and cause a wealth transfer between fund shareholders. This finding questions the structure of mutual funds as an investment vehicle for heterogeneous shareholders. Meanwhile, research also suggests that by adopting different fee structures, mutual funds attract different investor clienteles.

The second type of investor externality is caused by mispricing of fund net asset value, which is calculated using closing security prices. When the closing prices do not fully reflect the available information on the values of the underlying securities, some investors trade on the arbitrage opportunities, at the expense of long-term investors in the fund. Stale-price arbitrage is especially pronounced among mutual funds holding foreign securities. Researchers have documented significant empirical evidence of such an effect and have recommended fair-value pricing rules to preclude the arbitrage opportunities.

Although investor externalities affect fund returns, they are not disclosed explicitly to investors. A recent study, Kacperczyk, Sialm, and Zheng (2005b), estimates the overall impact of unobserved actions, including investor externality, on fund performance.[5] They find a substantial cross-sectional heterogeneity and time-series persistence in such an impact, demonstrating that unobserved activities of some funds persistently destroy value, while unobserved activities of other funds create value.

4.1. Liquidity Costs

Edelen (1999) shows how liquidity-motivated trading affects fund performance, using a sample of 166 open-end mutual funds. He estimates the extent of liquidity-motivated trading using data on fund flows and trading activities from the N-SAR filings. He documents a significant negative relationship between investor flows and a fund's abnormal return, indicating that fund shareholders bear an indirect cost of providing liquidity. Controlling for the indirect cost of providing liquidity improves the average annual fund abnormal return by more than 1 percent. Rakowski (2002) provides additional empirical evidence on the negative relationship between liquidity costs and fund performance, using cash flow volatility as estimated from daily fund flows to measure liquidity cost.

Related evidence indicates that fund size can affect its performance. J. Chen et al. (2004) examine economies of scale in actively managed mutual funds using a sample of diversified equity funds from 1962 to 1999.[6] Empirical tests show that a fund's performance is inversely correlated with its lagged size, after controlling for fund style and other fund characteristics. Additional tests indicate that the diseconomies of scale of

[5] The impact of unobserved actions also includes trading costs, agency costs, and interim trading benefits.
[6] They exclude funds with less than $15 million in total assets.

fund performance are related to liquidity, because the effect is most pronounced among "small-cap" funds, or those that invest in small, illiquid stocks.

The possibility of investor externality and the existence of different investor types suggest that the composition of clientele can affect a fund's performance. For example, shareholders who trade implicitly impose the cost of their liquidity demands onto other shareholders in the fund. In one study, Johnson (2004) suggests a wealth transfer from low-cost to high-cost shareholders. He analyzes a proprietary database that includes all shareholder transactions within and across all funds in one no-load mutual fund family between 1994 and 2000. He shows that observable shareholder characteristics predict whether an account will be short term or long term. Moreover, simulations show that the liquidity costs imposed on the fund by the expected short-term shareholders are significantly greater than those imposed by the expected long-term shareholders.

Nanda, Wang, and Zheng (2003) provide additional empirical evidence on how investor clientele composition affects fund performance by analyzing the introduction of multiple share classes for a fund. In the 1990s, many funds with front-end loads introduced additional share classes to give investors the choice of paying back-end charges and/or annual fees instead of front-end loads. The authors show that introducing new share classes results in more new money and attracts investors with a shorter investment horizon and greater sensitivity to past fund performance. Consistent with the liquidity cost hypothesis, they document a decline in fund performance about two years after introducing the new classes. Further analysis indicates that the decrease in fund performance is related to changes in overall fund cash flow volatility and fund size after attracting new investor clientele.

Drawing on the adverse effects of liquidity costs and fund size, researchers have developed theoretical models to explain mutual fund fee structures as well as to provide rational explanations for empirical findings. These models take into account the interaction between investor activities and fund performance and management strategies. In one such model, Chordia (1996) argues that load charges dissuade redemptions and induce a separating equilibrium in which short-term investors cluster at no-load funds and long-term investors willingly invest in load funds to avoid the liquidity costs due to other investor externality. In a related study, Nanda, Narayanan, and Warther (2000) model management fees that are endogenously determined by competitive fund managers who anticipate the effects of fees on investor flows and subsequent earnings. The model shows how the existence of multiple investor clienteles with differing liquidity and marketing needs and heterogeneous managerial abilities gives rise to a variety of open-end fund structures. As discussed earlier, Berk and Green (2004) derive a rational model of active fund management that explains flow and performance patterns. An important premise of their model is decreasing returns to scale in deploying investment abilities due to liquidity-related costs and limited resources in identifying investment opportunities.

Investors holding mutual funds in taxable accounts face an additional externality from the trading of other investors. For example, Dickson, Shoven, and Sialm (2000) demonstrate that shareholder flows affect after-tax returns of mutual funds. They outline a negative effect of redemptions on after-tax returns because funds may be forced to liquidate assets and distribute taxable capital gains to their shareholders. Conversely, they outline a positive effect of new investors on the after-tax returns of existing investors through dilution of unrealized capital gains. Simulation results show that tax-related externalities between fund shareholders are important determinants of the after-tax performance of equity mutual funds and that tax-management can significantly affect after-tax returns of mutual funds.

4.2. Stale-Price Arbitrage

Since mutual funds collect buy and sell orders at the end of the day and transact at the net asset value calculated using closing security prices, the closing prices might not fully reflect the most recent available information. The possibility of stale pricing opens up the opportunity for some investors to perform stale-price arbitrages. In addition, brokers sometimes permit investors to place orders after the close of the market. These transactions decrease returns to long-term investors in the mutual fund.

A number of studies examine the extent of such stale-price arbitrage losses for mutual funds. Chalmers, Edelen, and Kadlec (2001) show that NAV mispricing can be exploited to form profitable trading strategies in domestic and foreign equity funds. Goetzmann, Ivkovich, and Rouwenhorst (2004) illustrate that mutual funds are exposed to speculative traders through their comparison of day-trading vs. buy-and-hold strategies, with day-trading funds outperforming by more than 20 percent per year. Greene and Hodges (2002) show that NAV arbitrage activities of open-end international equity funds hurt the returns of passive long-term shareholders by 48 basis points annually. Using a comprehensive dataset, Zitzewitz (2003) estimates that, due to NAV arbitrage activities, investors in international equity funds lost an average 56 basis points annually during the late 1990s. Academic studies (e.g., Chalmers, Edelen, and Kadlec 2001, Goetzmann, Ivkovic, and Rouwenhorst 2001, Ciampi and Zitzewitz 2001, and Zitzewitz 2003) further discuss methodologies of estimating fair-value prices. To prevent such arbitrage activities, the SEC adopted fair-value pricing rules for mutual funds in 2003.

5. STRATEGIES OF MUTUAL FUNDS

The revenue of open-end mutual funds is usually a fixed percentage of their total net assets. To maximize revenue, fund management seeks to maximize total assets under management. Evidence suggests that the mutual fund industry exploits the patterns in fund flows to increase total assets under management. For example, fund management pursues strategies that increase their chances of having top performance rankings, to take advantage of the strong response of fund flows to stellar past performance. Researchers have discovered such behavior at both the fund and the fund family level. There is also evidence that fund managers follow trading strategies that focus only on the short-term performance, in response to the sensitivity of fund flows to short-term fund performance. Furthermore, the mutual fund industry set their fees, both the level and the form, in response to the price sensitivity of their investors. The preceding evidence suggests that the mutual fund industry is well aware of investor behavior and develops strategies in response to patterns in fund flows.

The nonlinear relationship between fund flows and past fund performance suggests a disproportionate benefit from a star performance and provides a convex, call-option-like incentive to fund management. K. Brown, Harlow, and Starks (1996) discuss the tournament phenomenon, in which rational managers revise the composition of their portfolios conditioned on their relative yearly performance to increase their chances of winning the performance tournament and attracting more new money. Specifically, they hypothesize that managers with extremely poor relative performance at midyear have incentives to increase their portfolio risk more in the latter part of the year than do managers with extremely good relative performance. Analyzing the performance and portfolio risk of 334 funds with a "growth" investment objective from 1976 to 1991, they find that midyear losers have higher fund return volatility in the latter part of a year than do midyear winners. They also show that this effect is stronger for newer, less well-established funds.

Chevalier and Ellison (1997) establish a direct link between risk taking by fund managers and the estimated incentives from the flow–performance relationship. They argue that the response of fund flows to past performance is an implicit incentive contract. Using a semiparametric model, they estimate the shape of the flow–performance relationship for a sample of growth and growth-income funds from 1982 to 1992. They then use estimated flow–performance functions to construct a measure of the incentive to alter portfolio risk toward the end of the year. They show that funds indeed alter their portfolio riskiness between September and December in a manner consistent with the estimated incentive to maximize their expected flows. Their estimates also indicate that incentives to alter riskiness are stronger for newer funds.

Investment behavior at the fund family level is also affected by the incentive to attract cash flows. Nanda, Wang, and Zheng (2004) indicate that some fund families adopt strategies to increase the likelihood of creating a star fund in order to maximize their overall cash flows. Using a sample of diversified equity funds from 1992 to 1998, they show a family spillover effect. That is, a fund's net new cash flows are positively affected by the stellar performance of other funds within the same family. Moreover, they find that families with higher variation in investment strategies across funds are more likely to generate star performance. They argue that the spillover effect encourages lower-ability families to pursue star-creating strategies. Consistent with their conjecture, fund families with high variation in investment strategies across funds significantly underperform low-variation families.

Gaspar, Massa, and Matos (2006) explore the concept of *cross-fund subsidization*, in which fund families strategically transfer performance across member funds to favor those more likely to increase overall family profits. Using a sample of actively managed equity mutual funds from the top 50 U.S. fund families, they examine whether fund families enhance the performance of "high-value" funds at the expense of "low-value" funds. "High- (low-) -value" funds are those that contribute more (less) to the total family profit. A fund's value is determined by fee levels, year-to-date performance, and fund age. Their empirical analysis indicates a higher performance gap between "high-value" and "low-value" funds within a fund family than between similar funds across fund families. Further analysis suggests that favoritism in the allocation of hot initial public offerings (IPOs) and the use of opposite trades across funds within a family might explain this performance difference.

In another study that examines the strategies of fund managers, Cooper, Gulen, and Rau (2005) provide disturbing evidence that fund managers change fund names strategically to take advantage of the suboptimal behavior of investors. They identify a sample of 296 equity mutual funds that have changed names to take advantage of a "hot" category association. For these funds, they find significantly positive abnormal fund flows of about 20 percent in the subsequent year. The abnormal return exists even for funds whose holdings do not match the style implied by their new name.

As further insight into the interaction between fund investor and manager behavior, Jin (2005) suggests that by chasing short-term fund performance, fund flows induce mutual fund managers to follow investment strategies that pursue short-term trading profits. Using a mutual fund dataset with information on portfolio holdings and fund managers, he establishes a link between short-term performance pressure (the sensitivity of flow to past performance) and fund managers' strategies to focus on short-horizon investments (the average remaining holding periods of securities or fund turnover). Further tests of causality suggest that these fund managers' short investment horizons are caused by their investors' short horizons. In other words, fund managers respond to the investor inclination to chase strong performers.

Barber, Odean, and Zheng (2005) document that over the past 40 years, the average operating expense charged by mutual funds has steadily increased, while the proportion of funds charging front-end load fees and the level of those load fees have both declined. They suggest that this pattern reflects an industry adapting to investor avoidance of front-end loads by embedding fees into less salient operating expenses.

Christoffersen and Musto (2002) show evidence at the fund level that fees are set in response to the price sensitivity of their subset of investors. In a setting of money market funds, where fund fees largely explain fund net returns, they find that funds raise the level of fees after experiencing heavy outflows, which result in a decrease in the price sensitivity of their remaining investors. Their finding indicates that investor behavior is an important determinant of mutual fund fees.

While the academic literature has paid more attention to how strategies of mutual funds exploit the behavioral patterns in fund flows, it is not fair to say that all strategies derived from fund flows have negative effects on investor returns. Funds also adopt investment strategies that improve the welfare of investors through observing fund flow responses. For example, funds on average have improved on tax management and transparency of disclosure to fund investors. Also, paying close attention to fund performance per se is in the interest of investors. In either the positive or the negative case, investor behavior reflected in fund flows seems to have a significant impact on the strategies of mutual funds. Consequently, the rationality of investor behavior has important implications for the functioning of the mutual fund industry.

6. CONCLUSION

Mutual funds provide a useful and informative setting in which to examine the behavioral patterns of individual investors. The literature on mutual fund investor behavior contributes to a growing stream of research focused on exploring why and how investors make their investment decisions. Research that investigates the rationality underlying investment behavior can shed light on issues of concern in behavioral finance. Moreover, understanding how mutual fund investors behave has great implications for investor welfare and asset prices, given the large amount of wealth invested in mutual funds by U.S. households.

Although mutual funds were designed largely to simplify investment decisions of individual investors, the sheer number of such funds creates a new challenge in terms of fund selection. Despite clear advice from academic finance, evidence indicates that individual investors would benefit from more guidance on their investment decisions. Educating financially unsophisticated investors is thus an important but unfortunately complex task. A first step toward an effective educational program is understanding the behavior and motivations of these investors. The research presented in this chapter provides a foundation for such an understanding.

References

Alexander, Gordon J., Jonathan D. Jones, and Peter J. Nigro. 1998. Mutual Fund Shareholders: Characteristics, Investor Knowledge, and Sources of Information, *Financial Services Review* 7, 301–316.

Barber, Brad M., Terrance Odean, and Lu Zheng. 2005. Out of Sight, Out of Mind: The Effect of Expenses on Mutual Fund Flows, *Journal of Business* 78(6), 2095–2120.

Barberis, Nicholas, and Richard Thaler. 2003. A Survey of Behavioral Finance, in George Constantinides, Milton Harris, Rene Stulz (eds.), *Handbook of the Economics of Finance*. Elsevier B.V.

Barclay, Michael J., Neil D. Pearson, and Michael S. Weisbach. 1998. Open-End Mutual Funds and Capital-Gains Taxes, *Journal of Financial Economics* 49, 3–43.

Bergstresser, Daniel, John M. R. Chalmers, and Peter Tufano. 2005. Assessing the Costs and Benefits of Brokers in the Mutual Fund Industry. Working paper, Harvard Business School.

Bergstresser, Daniel, and James Poterba. 2002. Do After-Tax Returns Affect Mutual Fund Inflows? *Journal of Financial Economics* 63, 381–414.

Berk, Jonathan B., and Richard C. Green. 2004. Mutual Fund Flows and Performance in Rational Markets, *Journal of Political Economy* 112(6), 1269–1295.

Berk, Jonathan B., and Jing Xu. 2004. Persistence and Fund Flows of the Worst-Performing Mutual Funds. Working paper, Haas School of Business, University of California, Berkeley.

Bernhardt, Dan, Ryan Davies, and Harvey Westbrook. 2005. Smart Fund Managers? Stupid Money? Working paper, University of Illinois.

Boyer, Brian, and Lu Zheng. 2003. Who Moves the Market? A Study of Stock Prices and Investment Cashflows. *Investor Flows and Stock Market Returns*, University of Michigan.

Brown, Keith C., W. V. Harlow, and Laura T. Starks. 1996. Of Tournaments and Temptations: An Analysis of Managerial Incentives in the Mutual Fund Industry, *Journal of Finance* 51, 85–110.

Brown, Stephen J., and William N. Goetzmann. 1995. Performance Persistence, *Journal of Finance* 50, 679–698.

Brown, Stephen J., William N. Goetzmann, Takato Hiraki, Noriyoshi Shiraishi, and Masahiro Watanabe. 2002. Investor Sentiment in Japanese and U.S. Daily Mutual Fund Flows. Working paper, Yale University.

Carhart, Mark M. 1997. On Persistence in Mutual Fund Performance, *Journal of Finance* 52, 57–82.

Chalmers, John M. R., Roger M. Edelen, and Gregory B. Kadlec. 2001. On the Perils of Security Pricing by Financial Intermediaries: The Wildcard Option in Transacting Mutual Fund Shares, *Journal of Finance* 56(6), 2209–2236.

Chen, Hsiu-Lang, Narasimhan Jegadeesh, and Russ Wermers. 2000. The Value of Active Mutual Fund Management: An Examination of the Stockholdings and Trades of Fund Managers, *Journal of Financial and Quantitative Analysis* 35, 343–368.

Chen, Joseph, Harrison Hong, Ming Huang, and Jeffrey D. Kubik. 2004. Does Fund Size Erode Fund Performance: The Role of Liquidity and Organization, *American Economics Review* 94, 1276–1302.

Chevalier, Judith, and Glenn Ellison. 1997. Risk-Taking by Mutual Funds as a Response to Incentives, *Journal of Political Economy* 105, 1167–1200.

Chordia, Tarun. 1996. The Structure of Mutual Fund Charges, *Journal of Financial Economics* 41, 3–39.

Christoffersen, Susan E. K., Richards Evans, and David Musto. 2005. The Economics of Mutual-Fund Brokerage: Evidence from the Cross Section of Investment Channels. Working paper, McGill University.

Christoffersen, Susan, and David K. Musto. 2002. Demand Curves and the Pricing Money Management, *Review of Financial Studies* 15(5), 1499–1524.

Christopherson, Jon A., Wayne Ferson, and Debra A. Glassman. 1998. Conditioning Manager Alphas on Economic Information: Another Look at the Persistence of Performance, *Review of Financial Studies* 11, 111–142.

Ciampi, Peter, and Eric Zitzewitz. 2001. Fair Value Pricing to Solve the NAV Predictability Problem. FT Interactive Data White Paper.

Cooper, Michael, Huseyin Gulen, and P. Raghavendra Rau. 2005. Changing Names with Style: Mutual Fund Name Changes and Their Effects on Fund Flows, *Journal of Finance* 60, 2825–2838.

Cronqvist, Henrik. 2003. Advertising and Portfolio Choice. Working paper, Ohio State University.

Del Guercio, Dianne, and Paula A. Tkac. 2001. Star Power: The Effect of Morningstar Ratings on Mutual Fund Flows, *Journal of Financial and Quantitative Analysis* 37, 523–557, University of Oregon.

Dickson, Joel M., John B. Shoven, and Clemens Sialm. 2000. Tax Externalities of Equity Mutual Funds, *National Tax Journal* 53(3,2), 607–628.

Edelen, Roger M. 1999. Investor Flows and the Assessed Performance of Open-End Mutual Funds, *Journal of Financial Economics* 53, 439–466.

Edelen, Roger M., and Jerold B. Warner. 2001. Aggregate Price Effects of Institutional Trading: A Study of Mutual Fund Flow and Market Returns, *Journal of Financial Economics* 59, 195–220.

Elton, Edwin J., Martin J. Gruber, and Christopher R. Blake. 1996. The Persistence of Risk-Adjusted Mutual Fund Performance, *Journal of Business* 69, 133–157.

Elton, Edwin J., Martin J. Gruber, and Jeffrey A. Busse. 2004. Are Investors Rational? Choices Among Index Funds, *Journal of Finance* 59, 261–288.

Elton, Edwin J., Martin J. Gruber, Sanjiv Das, and Matthew Hlavka. 1993. Efficiency with Costly Information: A Reinterpretation of Evidence for Managed Portfolios, *Review of Financial Studies* 6, 1–22.

Fama, Eugene F., and Kenneth R. French. 1993. Common Risk Factors in Returns on Stocks and Bonds, *Journal of Financial Economics* 33, 3–56.

Gallaher, Steven, Ron Kaniel, and Laura Starks. 2005. Madison Avenue Meets Wall Street: Mutual Fund Families, Competition and Advertising. Working paper, University of Texas at Austin.

Gaspar, Jose-Miguel, Massimo Massa, and Pedro Matos. 2006. Favoritism in Mutual Fund Families? Evidence of Strategic Cross-Fund Subsidization, *Journal of Finance* 19(2), 633–685.

Ge, Weili, and Lu Zheng. 2004. The Frequency of Mutual Fund Portfolio Disclosure. Working paper, University of Michigan.

Goetzmann, William N., and Roger G. Ibbotson. 1994. Do Winners Repeat? Patterns in Mutual Fund Performance, *Journal of Portfolio Management* 20, 9–17.

Goetzmann, William N., Zoran Ivkovic, and Geert K. Rouwenhorst. 2004. Day Trading International Mutual Funds: Evidence and Policy Solutions, *Journal of Financial and Quantitative Analysis* 36(3), 287–309.

Goetzmann, William N., and Massimo Massa. 2003. Index Funds and Stock Market Growth, *Journal of Business* 76, 1–28.

Goetzmann, William N., Massimo Massa, and Geert K. Rouwenhorst. 1999. Behavorial Factors in Mutual Fund Flows. Working paper, Yale University.

Goetzmann, William N., and Nadav Peles. 1997. Cognitive Dissonance and Mutual Fund Investors, *Journal of Financial Research* 20, 145–158.

Greene, Jason T., and Charles W. Hodges. 2002. The Dilution Impact of Daily Fund Flows on Open-End Mutual Funds, *Journal of Financial Economics* 65, 131–158.

Grinblatt, Mark, and Sheridan Titman. 1992. Performance Persistence in Mutual Funds, *Journal of Finance* 47, 1977–1984.

Gruber, Martin. 1996. Another Puzzle: The Growth in Actively Managed Mutual Funds, *Journal of Finance* 51, 783–810.

Hendricks, Darryll, Jayendu Patel, and Richard Zeckhauser. 1993. Hot Hands in Mutual Funds: The Persistence of Performance 1974–1988, *Journal of Finance* 48, 93–130.

Hortacsu, Ali, and Chad Syverson. 2004. Product Differentiation, Search Costs and Competition in the Mutual Fund Industry: A Case Study of S&P 500 Index Funds, *Quarterly Journal of Economics* 119, 403–456.

Huang, Jennifer, Kelsey D. Wei, and Hong Yan. 2007. Participation Costs and the Sensitivity of Fund Flows to Past Performance, *Journal of Finance* 62(3), 1273–1311, University of Texas at Austin.

Indro, Daniel. 2004. Does Mutual Fund Flow Reflect Investor Sentiment? *Journal of Behavioral Finance* 5, 105–115.

Ippolito, Richard A. 1992. Consumer Reaction to Measures of Poor Quality: Evidence from the Mutual Fund Industry, *Journal of Law and Economics* 35, 45–70.

Jain, Prem C., and Joanna Shuang Wu. 2000. Truth in Mutual Fund Advertising: Evidence on Future Performance and Fund Flow, *Journal of Finance* 55, 937–958.

Jegadeesh, Narasimhan, and Sheridan Titman. 1993. Returns to Buying Winners and Selling Losers: Implication for Stock Market Efficiency, *Journal of Finance* 48, 65–91.

Jensen, Michael C. 1968. The Performance of Mutual Funds in the Period 1945–1964, *Journal of Finance* 23, 389–416.

Jin, Li. 2005. How Does Investor Short-Termism Affect Mutual Fund Manager Short-Termism? Working paper, Harvard Business School.

Johnson, Woodrow T. 2004. Predictable Investment Horizons and Wealth Transfers Among Mutual Fund Shareholders, *Journal of Finance* 59, 1979–2012.

Kacperczyk, Marcin, Clemens Sialm, and Lu Zheng. 2005a. On the Industry Concentration of Actively Managed Equity Mutual Funds, *Journal of Finance* 60(4), 1983–2011.

Kacperczyk, Marcin, Clemens Sialm, and Lu Zheng. 2005b. Unobserved Actions of Mutual Funds, *Review of Financial Studies*, forthcoming.

Keswani, Aneel, and David Stolin. 2008. Which Money Is Smart? Mutual Fund Buys and Sells of Individual and Institutional Investors, *Journal of Finance* 63(1), 85–118, Cass Business School.

Khorana, A., and H. Servaes. 2004. Conflicts of Interest and Competition in the Mutual Fund Industry. Working paper, Georgia Institute of Technology.

Kliger, Doron, O. Levy, and D. Sonsino. 2003. On Absolute and Relative Performance and the Demand for Mutual Funds—Experimental Evidence. *Journal of Economic Behavior and Organization* 52(3), 341–363. The Wharton School.

Lakonishok, Josef, Andrei Shleifer, Robert W. Vishny, Oliver Hart, and George L. Perry. 1992. The Structure and Performance of the Money Management Industry, *Brookings Papers on Economic Activity. Microeconomics* 339–391.

Lamont, Owen, and Andrea Frazzini. 2005. Dumb Money: Mutual Fund Flows and the Cross Section of Stock Returns, *Journal of Financial Economics*, forthcoming.

Lynch, Anthony W., and David K. Musto. 2003. How Investors Interpret Past Fund Returns, *Journal of Finance* 58(5), 2033–2058.

Malloy, Christopher, and Ning Zhu. 2004. Mutual Fund Choices and Investor Demographies. Working paper, London Business School.

Morey, Matthew R. 2003. Should You Carry the Load? A Comprehensive Analysis of Load and No-Load Funds out of Sample Performance, *Journal of Banking and Finance* 27(7), 1245–1271.

Nanda, Vikram, M. P. Narayanan, and Vincent Warther. 2000. Liquidity, Investment Ability and Mutual Fund Structure, *Journal of Financial Economics* 57, 417–443.

Nanda, Vikram, Z. Jay Wang, and Lu Zheng. 2003. The ABCs of Mutual Funds: A Natural Experiment on Fund Flows and Performance. Working paper, University of Michigan.

Nanda, Vikram, Z. Jay Wang, and Lu Zheng. 2004. Family Values and the Star Phenomenon: Strategies of Mutual Fund Families, *Review of Financial Studies* 17(3), 667–698.

Patel, Jayendu, Richard Zeckhauser, and Darryll Hendriks. 1994. Investment Flows and Performance: Evidence from Mutual Funds, Cross-Border Investments, and New Issues in Japan, Europe, and International Financial Markets, *Analytic and Empirical Perpectives*, New York: Cambridge University Press.

Rakowski, David. 2002. Fund Flow Volatility and Performance. Working paper, Georgia State University.

Reuter, Jonathan, and Eric Zitzewitz. 2006. Do Ads Influence Editors? Advertising and Bias in the Financial Media, *Quarterly Journal of Economics*, 121(1), 197–227.

Sapp, Travis, and Ashish Tiwari. 2004. Does Stock Return Momentum Explain the "Smart Money" Effect? *Journal of Finance* 59, 2605–2622.

Sirri, Erik, and Peter Tufano. 1998. Costly Search and Mutual Fund Flows, *Journal of Finance* 53, 1589–1622.

Smith, Keith V. 1978. Is Fund Growth Related to Fund Performance? *Journal of Portfolio Management* 4, 49–54.

Spitz, Edward A. 1970. Mutual Fund Performance and Cash Inflows, *Applied Economics* 2, 141–145.

Starks, Laura, Li Yong, and Lu Zheng. 2006. Tax Loss Selling and the January Effect: Evidence from Municipal Bond Closed-End Funds, *Journal of Finance* 61(6), 3049–3067.

Teo, Melvyn and Woo, Sung-Jun. 2001. Persistence in Style-Adjusted Mutual Fund Returns. Working paper, Harvard University.

Tversky, Amos, and Daniel Kahnemann. 1971. Belief in the Law of Small Numbers, *Psychological Bulletin* 76, 105–110.

Tversky, Amos, and Daniel Kahneman. 1974. Judgment Under Uncertainty. Heuristics and Biases, *Science* 211, 453–458.

Warther, Vincent. 1995. Aggregate Mutual Fund Flows and Security Returns, *Journal of Financial Economics* 39, 209–235.

Wellman, Jay, and Jian Zhou. 2005. Corporate Governance and Mutual Fund Performance: A First Look at the Morningstar Stewardship Grades. Working paper, University of Binghamton.

Wermers, Russel. 2003. Is Money Really "Smart"? New Evidence on the Relation Between Mutual Fund Flows, Manager Behavior, and Performance Persistence. Working paper, University of Maryland.

Wilcox, Ronald T. 2003. Bargain Hunting or Star Gazing? Investors' Preferences for Stock Mutual Funds, *Journal of Business* 76, 645–663.

Woerheide, Walt. 1982. Investor Response to Suggested Criteria for the Selection of Mutual Funds, *Journal of Financial and Quantitative Analysis* 17, 129–137.

Zhao, Xinge. 2004. The Role of Brokers and Advisors Behind Investments into Load Funds. Working paper, College of William and Mary.

Zheng, Lu. 1999. Is Money Smart? A Study of Mutual Fund Investors' Fund Selection Ability, *Journal of Finance* 54, 901–933.

Zitzewitz, Eric. 2003. How Widespread Is Late Trading in Mutual Funds? Working paper, Stanford University.

CHAPTER 9

Incentives in Funds Management: A Literature Overview

Sudipto Bhattacharya
London School of Economics

Amil Dasgupta
London School of Economics

Alexander Guembel
Oxford University

Andrea Prat
London School of Economics

This article is a revised version of an invited lecture delivered at the Jornadas di Economia Conference of the Banco Central di Uruguay on 30th and 31st of July 2001. We thank the officers of the bank and other conference participants for their comments.

Abstract

We review several recent theoretical models of principals and agents and delegation, including those of cheap talk cum expertise and career concerns, in the context of delegated portfolio management, as well as empirical evidence pertaining to the incentives and behaviors of fund managers and analysts choosing or advising on the allocations of others' investments among diverse assets. We focus in particular on the resulting efficiency (from the investors' perspective), in terms of risk taking, as well as on considering the possibility of herding or churning behavior in delegated trading. Key general equilibrium (pricing) implications of these issues are also noted.

1. INTRODUCTION

In most major capital markets the role of institutional investors—such as mutual funds and pension funds as well as insurance companies and banks—has been increasing over time, dramatically so in the last two decades, so that by now investments channeled via these institutions and their fund managers amount to half or more of the value of assets traded in many equity markets, for example. In other markets, such as those for public bonds, commercial paper, and currencies, the importance of institutional investor trades is even greater. As such, it is important to ask if the incentive structures to which these fund managers are subject lead them to invest and trade over time in the interests of their principals, leading to market allocations and prices that are efficient in some (Pareto) sense, or whether existing market mechanisms might lead to phenomena such as excessive risk taking, churning (trading without any informational justification), and herding behavior (where funds follow others' trades, ignoring their own information) that may exacerbate the volatility of fund flows and possibly prices in capital markets, as some have suggested.

In this chapter we try to provide an overview of the existing theoretical literature pertaining to these themes, focusing in particular on normative and positive models of optimal and observed fund manager performance contracts as well as on other incentives, such as their career concerns over time. We also refer to some recent evidence regarding issues such as herding (or not) by fund managers and analysts. Concerns regarding performance fees and their impact on incentives of delegated fund managers were expressed quite early in the United States, in the form of legislation that significantly restricted the form of these fees. In particular, the Investment Advisers Act of 1940 and its Amendment in 1970 prohibited fund manager compensation schemes from diverging from linear functions of fund returns (including fixed fees per unit of investment), possibly relative to the returns on a fixed market index.

At a conceptual level, this regulation anticipated the literature on optimal risk sharing and preference similarity when optimal-sharing rules are linear in total payoff (Ross 1973), and corporate finance results on excessive risk taking (Jensen and Meckling 1976) given limited-liability (convex) fee contracts for fund managers, as is commonly the case for performance fee contracts in many hedge funds. Key analytical implications of these regulations were analyzed in Modigliani and Pogue (1975). These regulations were seriously relaxed in 1998, with free contracting allowed for funds with wealthy and sophisticated investors; see Das and Sundaram (2002), who have also questioned the utility of the prior restrictions on freedom of contracting and noted that rewards for fund managers that are increasing and convex functions of portfolio returns may encourage more informed trading by agents and thus benefit the fund investors.

In Section 2 of this chapter we discuss the (emerging) theory of fund managers' contractual and other incentives, starting with a brief discussion of principal-agent models in contract theory, moving on to general contracts based on managers' portfolio positions and returns to those based on returns only or on the relative performance vis-à-vis other funds, as in some models of their career concerns, to issues concerning herding and churning in richer settings, with managers having dynamic reputational concerns and endogenous price formation. In Section 3 we examine some empirical evidence on these issues. In Section 4 we conclude.

2. THEORIES OF INCENTIVES FOR FUND MANAGERS AND INFORMATIVE EXPERTS

2.1. Principal-Agent Models: Effort Choice, Delegation, and Screening

Theoretical models of interactions and contracting among principals and agents taking actions or advising them to choose actions have been in development over the last three decades, and these may be classified as follows along the dimensions of the private or nonverifiable versus contractible nature of the agent's information and actions at different stages of the game, describing their choices of messages and costly actions. At the ex ante stage, agents are endowed with different qualities of potential private information regarding the future returns on a risky (set of) asset(s). Their heterogenous qualities may be privately and asymmetrically known to the agents, the case of adverse selection, or be symmetrically known to the agents and principals (syndicates of fund investors) and subject to learning over time, the case of career concerns. Alternatively, otherwise-homogeneous agents may need to exert privately observed and costly effort/investment to acquire increasing levels of quality in forecasting asset returns. At the interim stage, agents make portfolio choices across the risky asset(s) and riskless ones, which affect the portfolio returns to their funds' investors as well as agents' rewards, which are also a function of the realized returns on the risky assets and are assumed to be verifiable. Agents' interim portfolio choices may or may not be contractible. Their rewards may be not only explicit contractual payoffs but also implicit, in terms of termination prospects (outflows from and inflows to their managed fund).

A key tool in analyzing such environments with asymmetric information across the principals and their agents is the so-called *revelation principle*, which basically asserts that an agent's choices of her ex ante contract and ex ante cum interim actions—which together with resulting final payoffs affect her rewards—can be viewed as her optimally choosing (a) to tell the truth about her ability and then her interim information, given the contractually mandated (interim) verifiable action set and ex ante contract choice for each set of agent types, as well as (b) her nonverifiable equilibrium action(s). For example, consider the following two-asset mean-variance portfolio choice problem, in which the gross returns at time $t = 2$ on investments made at $t = 0$ are $r > 1$ on the riskless asset, and, on the risky asset, R distributed as a normal (M, V) variate with $M > r$, the prior distribution. At the interim date $t = 1$, the agent comes to know the realization of S, her private signal on R: $S = R + e$, where e is normal, $\text{cov}(R, e) = 0$, with its quality being $Q = 1/\text{var}(e)$, which is also private information to the agent ex ante. Alternatively, her Q could be an increasing function of some privately chosen action (effort E) by the agent at $t = 0$. The principal, being the collective (syndicate) of investors in the fund, designs the optimal contract(s) for the agent(s) that is based on mutually observable, verifiable information only that seeks to maximize her own ex ante expected utility, subject to the agent's choices at each stage being incentive compatible as described by the revelation principle, and her ex ante expected utility—which is affected by her costly actions—being at or above a reservation level (for desired agents), which may depend on her privately known type or quality level.

2.2. Optimal Contracts Based on Verifiable Portfolio Composition Choices and Returns

Per the revelation principle, at $t = 0$ the agent declares $q(Q)$ about her quality Q, and then at $t = 1$ she announces $s(S, q, Q)$ regarding her interim signal S in order to maximize her ex ante as well as interim expected utilities, given her reward function $Z(R, s, q)$. She also implements the contractually mandated portfolio choice rule of investing $X(s, q)$ in the risky asset and $(W - X)$ in the riskless asset, giving rise to the overall portfolio return

$$P = [X^* R + (W - X)^* r], \tag{1}$$

where W is the wealth of the syndicate of fund investors. For example, in the Bhattacharya and Pfleiderer (1985) model,

$$X(s, q) = [\{m(s, q) - r\}^* h(s, q)]/A, \tag{2}$$

where A equals the investors' (aggregated) constant absolute risk-aversion coefficient, $m(,,)$ is the conditional mean of R given $\{q, s\}$—$m(s, q) = \text{expectation}[R|Q = q, S = s]$—and $h(s, q) = h(q) = 1/\text{var}[R|Q = q]$ is the precision on R. Then a menu of agents' contracts defined by appropriately chosen functions $\{B(\,), C(\,), D(\,)\}$ so that

$$Z(R, s, q) = [B(q) - D(q)^* C(|R - m(s, q)|)], \tag{3}$$

$\{B, D\} > 0$, with $C(.)$ being an increasing, strictly convex function, leads to (a) truth-telling about S—$s(S, q, Q) = S$ being optimal for the agent for all $\{S, q, Q\}$—and (b) truth-telling regarding Q at $t = 0$, with the agents' equilibrium expected utilities $\text{EU}(Q)$ equaling their reservation or outside utilities $O(Q)$ for a large class of increasing $O(Q)$ functions. Otherwise, when $O(Q)$ is sufficiently concave, $\text{EU}(Q)$ can at least equal the chord from the lowest value $O(Q)$ to $O(Q^*)$, Q^* being the minimum desirable level of Q. Note that (i) $Z(R, S, Q)$ need not be increasing in R or in P the ex post returns on agents' chosen portfolio; (ii) $Z < 0$ is possible; and (iii) optimal (second-best) risk sharing is ignored, even vis-à-vis an agent who shares the same class of (negative exponential) utility functions. We shall reconsider the issue of limited liability for the agent later; as for optimal risk sharing, they [BP] assumed a principal who is much larger than the agent, having far greater wealth and risk tolerance, so their screening contracts are approximately first-best.

Later work has reconsidered this tradeoff and also allowed for moral hazard regarding the agent's choice of Q.[1] Dybvig, Farnsworth, and Carpenter (2001) extend this type of problem to the multiasset case, without restrictions on the contracting space and allowing contracts also to be contingent on the signal announcement. Assuming logarithmic utility functions for the agent and the principal and a general class of portfolio choice rules $X(s)$, Dybvig, Farnsworth, and Carpenter find that in their numerical solutions (a) the agent's reward is lower when $m(s)$ is close to the prior mean M of R and the realized R is close to $m(s)$, in order to encourage effort for higher Q, but also that (b) the agent is heavily penalized when the realized R differs from her declared mean of $m(s)$ on either side of it, much as in Bhattacharya and Pfleiderer (1985). Indeed, this second feature of their optimal contract is, for realistic parameter values, qualitatively greater than the first by an order of magnitude, so their agent's payoff Z can be nonincreasing in R and even in the portfolio return P, owing primarily to this qualitative feature.

Empirically, fund managers' reward functions Z, which may be nonincreasing vis-à-vis their portfolio returns P, are rare. In the realm of performance fee contracts, which are monotonically increasing functions of P, Das and Sundaram (2000) concluded that reward functions for fund manager agents, which are increasing and convex functions of the portfolio return P achieved by them, may lead to easier self-selection (as well as learning over time) about their forecasting abilities among agents differing in their quality of information, by encouraging aggressively risk-taking portfolio strategies on their part (initially). In contrast, the papers of Rajan and Srivastava (1999) and Palomino and Prat (2003) derive result(s) on the optimality of bonus contracts, having two levels of flat fees over two different regions of the portfolio returns (P) space. Rajan and Srivastava assume a complete market with risk-averse participants; Palomino and Prat assume a cost of privately chosen effort that enables their agents to access assets with higher levels of risky returns; both assume limited liability for agents.

2.3. Returns-Based and Relative Performance-Based Contracts

A large class of models considers the preceding set of problems in a setting where contracts cannot be conditioned on portfolio composition. Stoughton (1993) explores linear and quadratic contracts in a setting in which Q is not an a priori known type

[1] Kihlstrom (1988) provides one of the first treatments of moral hazard in a simple model with two states and two signals.

but is acquired via privately chosen and costly effort by the agent, which is induced by her reward function, now $Z(R)$. This obviously makes the agency problem harder to resolve, because fund managers can now undo some (or all) of the contract's intended effects by changing the portfolio composition. This problem is most extreme when contracts are linear. Stoughton (1993) finds that a quadratic contract approaches the first-best.[2]

Fund managers may, of course, be rewarded based on returns relative to those of benchmark portfolios, which can be taken from a passive index or a set of other actively managed portfolios. Moreover, relative-performance incentives may be provided explicitly through compensation that is linked directly to relative performance or implicitly through relative-performance-contingent fund flows. We discuss each of these in turn. In all of these cases the manager's reward is a function of (relative) portfolio returns but not of portfolio composition. Career concerns typically introduce an element of relative performance when portfolio composition is observable, though not directly contracted on. Relative performance or portfolio composition may then affect investors' beliefs about a manager's ability. We discuss this type of model in Section 2.4.

Admati and Pfleiderer (1997) considered the use of linear-compensation contracts based on relative returns on common market indices, and they found this device to be of very limited use. One of the reasons is that a passive benchmark per se does not make it easier to satisfy the manager's incentive compatibility constraint: A manager can completely undo the payoff effects that benchmarking has by changing the portfolio composition.[3] Maug and Naik (1996) and Guembel (2005b) consider wage contracts that explicitly reward a manager on the basis of his performance relative to another fund manager, instead of a passive index. A single active manager (Maug and Naik) or multiple active managers (Guembel) must incur a cost of becoming privately informed about asset payoffs, and the compensation contract needs to provide the corresponding incentives. A manager now cannot undo the effect of benchmarking, because the precise composition of the benchmark depends on other managers' portfolio choices, and is thus unknown to a manager who does not acquire information. This tightens the manager's incentive compatibility constraint and allows more efficient contracting.

Heinkel and Stoughton (1994) present a dynamic model in which a fund manager's compensation is contingent only on absolute performance but contracts can be terminated, which provides implicit relative-performance incentives. When the manager–investor relationship is subject to both moral hazard and an adverse selection problem regarding inherent ability, a pooling contract may be optimal at the initial date so that all fund managers regardless of ability (except for a few very high types) receive a flat fee. Incentives are then provided implicitly through the threat of terminating the relationship in response to poor performance. This contracting arrangement reduces the

[2]Dybvig, Farnsworth, and Carpenter (2001) argue that a quadratic contract does not approach the first-best in terms of the certainty equivalent.

[3]Ou-Yang (2003) argues that benchmarks can perform a more useful role in a multiperiod (continuous time) context because the contracting space is enriched by the time dimension. Benchmarks should then be time varying.

agency rent that managers capture at the initial date. As asymmetric information about fund manager ability is reduced over time, implicit incentives are replaced by explicit incentives in the form of a performance-contingent fee. This captures the empirical fact that contracts for mutual fund managers typically reward managers on the basis of net asset value under management, in an environment where fund inflows and outflows are sensitive to past performance.

A number of papers have investigated the implications of explicit and implicit relative-performance incentives regarding risk taking by managers and equilibrium asset pricing. Hvide and Kristiansen (2003) suggest that this aspect of fund managers' rewards, which are likely to be more important for younger managers (see Heinkel and Stoughton 1994), may lead to excessive risk taking by funds, for only a few funds at the top receive increased new financing. The game among fund managers takes on the characteristics of a "winner takes all" tournament among potentially many agents. This generates managerial compensation that is convex in relative performance and therefore leads to excessive (relative to current investors' preferences) risk taking. This appears to be the case empirically (see Brown, Harlow, and Starks 1996 and Chevalier and Ellison 1997). In Section 3 we consider the empirical evidence in Chevalier and Ellison (1999) on the relationships among terminations of fund managers by funds and the various aspects of their past returns performance, portfolio choices, and personal attributes.

Relative performance–based incentives can lead to excessive risk taking, even when compensation is not convex in relative performance, as in a "winner takes all" tournament. This has been shown in the context of optimal explicit relative performance–based contracts (Guembel 2005b) and implicit incentives provided through fund flows (Palomino 2005). Both papers consider a setting where asset prices are determined endogenously in a market microstructure framework based on Kyle (1985) and fund managers trade strategically, taking into account their effect on asset prices. Because managers have market power over their private information, they restrain their trades so as not to reveal too much information. On the other hand, this motive becomes less important when managers are more strongly compensated on the basis of their relative performance, because fund managers then care more about submitting similar-sized trades than they care about holding back their information. In the limiting case where compensation puts the same weight on a manager's own performance as on another manager's performance, trade sizes become infinitely large.

Since fund owners are assumed to be risk neutral in Guembel (2005b), the cost of overly aggressive trade consists of the dissipation of informational rents alone. More generally, excessively risky trade may also result in the suboptimal allocation of risk to fund owners. This problem is considered in Kapur and Timmermann (2005), who also allow agents' rewards to be based on their relative portfolio performances among multiple fund managers, but in a market environment without any private information for agents. They conclude that if fund managers are rewarded only according to their performance relative to the average of other funds', then in the only symmetric Nash equilibrium, their demands for risky assets would cause all risk premia to fall to zero, a state in which risk-averse fund owners would (unlike fund managers) not wish to invest at all in risky assets. In this context, it is useful to note that, unlike in the moral hazard problem of unobserved effort choices by agents facing (perfectly) correlated output shocks, where relative-performance contracts can be optimal, greater unobserved risk taking by fund managers does not—unlike more effort undertaken by the agents—have an unambiguously positive effect on the funds' risk-averse principals, since the impact of a higher agent action is no longer a first-order stochastically dominant shift in random output, here the portfolio return P.

One implication of most models that allow for differential ability of fund managers is that fund performance should exhibit considerable long-term persistence. Empirically, however, there is little evidence for persistence beyond short horizons (see, for example, Carhart 1997). Berk and Green (2004) address this issue and show that differential ability does not necessarily lead to persistence in performance when fund managers face decreasing returns to scale. In that case investors rationally allocate funds to those managers who performed well in the past and thereby demonstrated superior ability. The resulting increase in their amount of funds under management then drives down returns such that, in equilibrium, any excess return is competed away, and hence any persistence in performance disappears.

2.4. Conformist Trading: The Roles of Career Concerns

Recent literature on experts and career concerns has considered the possibility of imitative behavior on the part of fund managers and security analysts.[4] This is part of a substantial academic effort that has been devoted over the past decade to the theoretical modeling and empirical analysis of conformism among economic agents. Before proceeding to explicate the link to fund manager incentives, it is worth briefly outlining the terms of the broader discussion.

The literature now differentiates between two different phenomena: *information cascades* and *herd behavior*, both of which lead to (varying degrees) of conformism. According to Smith and Sorensen (2000), *information cascades* constitute (permanently) incomplete learning and involve a sequence of individuals who all completely neglect their (valuable) private information in equilibrium, while *herds* involve a sequence of agents who happen to take the same action, though they still condition their behavior on their signals. A cascade, therefore, implies a herd according to this classification, but not vice versa. There is general agreement in the literature on the meaning of cascades, but not so on herds.[5] In order to avoid confusion, we shall refer to purely imitative (and thus uninformative) behavior as cascades and other weaker forms of behavior as *partial* cascades.

Two main mechanisms have been proposed to explain cascades in rational settings. The first mechanism arises purely from social learning and was originally proposed by Banerjee (1992) and Bikhchandani, Hirshleifer, and Welch (1992, henceforth BHW).

[4]Security analysts' rewards are not typically linked explicitly to their forecast errors, and incentives are largely provided implicitly through career concerns. Considerable parts of this section are therefore also applicable to security analysts' incentives regarding herding in their forecasts.

[5]For example, Chari and Kehoe (2004) define herds as "incorrect cascades," thus implying that herds are a specific manifestation of cascades, rather than vice versa.

The essence of this mechanism is an information externality, which arises because the observation of predecessors' decisions influences the actions of successors, but this fact is not taken into account by these predecessors in making their decisions. In these social learning models, depending on the information structure, cascades arise when the observation of the actions of predecessors influence the beliefs of successors sufficiently that they neglect their private information entirely. Actions thus cease to be informative, and learning stops in equilibrium.

The original work of Banerjee and BHW gave rise to a large literature that used their crucial insight to study a large class of applications.[6] However, the canonical social learning models fail to reflect a key feature of (efficient) financial markets, namely, the (quick) adjustment of prices to new information reflected in a sequence of trades. As Avery and Zemsky (1998) have noted, this feature of financial markets makes it impossible (Proposition 3) to rationalize full imitative behavior in the form of an information cascade in equilibrium among investors (principals). The usual social learning mechanism for cascades breaks down because the (noisy) information regarding future payoffs revealed by such a sequence of trades would already be reflected in the evolving market price of the traded asset, thus making it always optimal for a trader who has (new) private information to exploit that information.

In one scenario a weaker form of conformist behavior can arise via partial cascades (Avery and Zemsky call these *herds*). This can be justified with more complex information structures involving higher-order uncertainty about traders' quality of information, or composition vis-à-vis these qualities, at a point in time. If this aspect of a market can vary randomly without its becoming common knowledge and traders' informative private signals can be heterogeneous, then an equilibrium involving a partial cascade trading sequence could arise, even with trades by principals, and also manifest itself largely in trading flows rather than in prices.[7]

The second mechanism for conformism relates more directly to fund manager incentives and was first proposed by Scharfstein and Stein (1990). In this paper they consider a setting in which managers and the market are both uncertain of their qualities as forecasters and private signals of the smart (informed) forecasters are perfectly correlated. The signals of dumb (uninformed) forecasters are independently distributed noisy random variables. They show that there exist equilibria in which the expert who makes the second choice mimics the first one who acts on her signal honestly, irrespective of her own signal. The (equilibrium) rationale is that the second expert's posterior evaluation as (likelihood of being) an (informative) expert is higher if the ex post outcome is in accord with a unanimous evaluation by both experts, rather than just one of them, given the differential correlation structures of signals among smart and dumb experts. The

[6]See Bikhchandani, Hirshleifer, and Welch (1998) for a survey.

[7]Two other methods to support statistical information cascades in financial markets have been proposed by Lee (1998) and by Chari and Kehoe (2004). In both of these papers, however, a cascade (partial or full) arises only when the market breaks down and traders exit (or do not enter) the market. This occurs either because, as in Lee, the transaction costs to trade are high relative to information precision or because, as in Chari and Kehoe, information arrives exogenously over time and the benefit of waiting to trade on this information may not exceed the cost of waiting for it.

core of the mechanism hinges, therefore, on the reputational (career) concerns of fund managers.

Scharfstein and Stein's seminal work has led to a number of papers on modeling the career concerns of experts. A survey of the large literature on experts in general is beyond the scope of this paper.[8] Instead, we briefly survey a smaller number of papers that build on Scharfstein and Stein's basic insight to model conformism (or the lack thereof). Avery and Chevalier (1999) build directly on Scharfstein and Stein's model. They preserve most of the assumptions but allow the agents to receive an informative signal about this type and show that the resulting equilibrium depends on the precision of this signal. If the signal is imprecise, the original Scharfstein and Stein behavior results. If, however, the signal is very precise, agents acting second act in a contrarian manner with positive probability (in a mixed-strategy equilibrium), thus violating the complete (cascading) conformism of Scharfstein and Stein. A mixed strategy for the follower arises also in Trueman (1994), where analysts who have full-type knowledge make sequential forecasts. Contrarian behavior also arises in Effinger and Polborn (2001). They show that if a uniquely high-quality expert is valued much more highly than one of two (or many), then the second expert reports her own signal when it is different from the (honest) report of the first, but she makes a false report different from the first one when they both receive separately the same private signal, that is, she is "consensus averse." However, Graham (1999) constructs a testable variant of Scharfstein and Stein (1990) and provides structural empirical tests that support the hypothesis that imitative behavior due to reputational concerns occurs among investment newsletters.

The original work of Scharfstein and Stein, as well as the various extensions we have just discussed, restricts attention to partial equilibrium settings. In the context of (efficient) financial markets, they could thus be thought to be potentially vulnerable to the Avery and Zemsky (1998) critique, as originally applied to statistical learning models. However, the recent work of Dasgupta and Prat (2005) suggest that the reputational conformism mechanism is robust in the face of the informational role of prices. They consider a standard asset pricing model, à la Glosten and Milgrom (1985), in which informed traders are fund managers with differing precisions of information who care both about their trading profits (as in the standard model) and (possibly infinitesimally) about their reputation for being able to identify undervalued assets. They show that in such a setting there are no equilibria in which prices reveal all information, even after an infinite number of trades. The reputational concerns of agents endogenously restrict the informativeness of prices, which in turn ensures that conformist behavior due to reputational concerns is optimal along the equilibrium path. In any equilibrium, if agents trade according to their signal sufficiently often, public information becomes precise, thus diminishing trading incentives while simultaneously identifying a particular subset of actions as being reputation-enhancing, independent of private signals. At some point, agents start conforming and prices no longer reveal any information. Thus,

[8]This literature includes, for example, the well-known work of Prendergast and Stole (1996) on the dynamic incentives of managers within firms, various applications (e.g., Prat 2005), and theoretical generalizations (e.g., Ottaviani and Sorensen 2006).

in sharp contrast to Avery and Zemsky's result in the standard model that cascades are impossible, the presence of even small amounts of career concerns make cascades *inevitable*.

To conclude our discussion of conformism, we briefly comment on a third notion, *investigative herding*, which is sometimes discussed in parallel with statistical or reputation-based imitative behavior. The idea of investigative herding, or conformism in the collection of information, was first noted by Froot, Scharfstein, and Stein (1992).[9] They observed that if traders had short horizons and could not wait to earn benefits from mispricing relative to liquidation value, they may all prefer to "herd" on collecting information along the same dimension. This is because in order for a trading strategy to be profitable, it is necessary that others trade based on the same information, thus leading to such information's being incorporated into prices (for profitable unwinding). When various forms of information exist, this creates *strategic complementarities* in the collection of specific types of information. Thus, it is possible to see equilibria in which all agents collect some specific type of information (for example, short-term information). It is worth noting that such behavior is not imitative behavior in the sense discussed to date here. Investigative herding occurs in simultaneous-move settings and arises purely out of a coordination element in the collection of information. We do not discuss it in detail here.[10] We merely note that fund manager incentives have been viewed in the literature as one way of providing a basis for investigative herding by endogenously providing short horizons for traders. The well-known paper of Shleifer and Vishny (1997), which gave rise to the now-large literature on limits to arbitrage-modeled short-termism as a consequence of delegation. Maug and Naik (1996) and Guembel (2005a, 2005b) provide micro-founded mechanisms by which principal-agent relationships in delegated funds management induce phenomena akin to investigative herding among fund managers.

2.5. Fund Manager Incentives and Uninformed Trading

There has also been concern that incentives created by delegated portfolio management can lead to "excessive" trading by fund managers. For example, it has been argued that they may trade in the absence of any useful information. Such trading has been termed *churning*. A small number of papers has provided formal models of churning. We can classify these papers according to whether the nature of incentives considered are explicit or implicit (via career concerns).

The first formal model of churning was provided by Trueman (1988). Trueman presents a reduced-form career concerns model in which the fund manager's ability is unknown and compensation depends exogenously on performance and on the posterior belief in the fund manager's ability. He shows that there is a churning equilibrium in which uninformed fund managers trade without information in order to impress their investors. More recently, Dasgupta and Prat (2006) provide a micro-founded model

[9]See also Dow and Gorton (1994) and Hirshleifer, Subrahmanyam, and Titman (1994).
[10]For an excellent survey of investigative herding, see Brunnermeier (2001).

of career-concerned fund managers in which churning also arises. Unlike Trueman (1988), Dasgupta and Prat (2006) explicitly model the price effects of the fund manager's actions, and they are thus able to consider general equilibrium implications of fund manager incentives. In particular, they show that churning can lead to substantial endogenous increases in the volume of trade in financial markets.[11] In addition, in Dasgupta and Prat (2006) future managerial compensation depends on the investor's retention decision, which is endogenous, and the optimal contract is derived and shown to be akin to the (noncontingent) contracts observed between mutual funds and their investors.

A parallel set of papers has observed how churning can also arise in a setting of explicit incentives in the absence of career concerns. The first such paper was by Allen and Gorton (1993). In that model fund managers exit the market at uncertain and exogenous times, and a given fund manager may not know whether he is the last delegated trader in a given asset. Uninformed fund managers may, therefore, buy bubble stocks at prices above their known liquidation value in the hope of reselling them before they die—at even higher prices—to other bad fund managers. Their behavior is the result of an optionlike payoff structure under which profits are shared with managers but losses are not. Churning thus creates the possibility of short-term speculative profits for the agent.

Dow and Gorton (1997) also model churning by fund managers in a setting with explicit incentives. In their paper, dumb agents receive no (informative) signals and smart agents sometimes receive perfectly correlated and accurate signals of future payoffs and receive no signals at other times. Each of these agents knows her own type. Dow and Gorton conclude that churning by the smart agents, whom the optimal contracts try to screen in, may be impossible to eliminate with contracts for agents that are subject to a limited liability constraint on their wages (punishments) for trading away from an optimal passive position based on priors in an erroneous direction. Thus, the reward for such trading in the right direction must be limited so that agents who can only churn are not attracted to these jobs, relative to their outside option. If, in addition, the wage for just holding a passive position is limited, the attracted smart agent churns.

Bhattacharya (1999) argues that the assumption that dumb agents give up their outside wages only if they trade, which Dow and Gorton make to limit the wage paid for holding the passive position, appears to be inconsistent with their self-knowledge of being dumb and never having information. He shows that, if the usual assumption is made that all hired agents give up their outside options, then equilibrium contracts (which must screen out the set of dumb agents) do not result in churning by the hired smart agents. He also notes that if smart agents differ sharply from the dumb agents in their outside utilities or smartness can be acquired but only with very costly effort, then equilibrium contracts that screen out the dumb agents, by reducing the payoffs to random lucky trades, may not attract (or motivate effort by the) smart agents; the principal would then not hire any (active) agent and would hold her passive portfolio.

[11] General equilibrium implications of delegated funds management are discussed further later.

Bhattacharya then shows that in such an environment with perfectly correlated signals across smart agents, a *conformity-rewarding payoff structure* that takes relative performance among multiple agents into account, can augment the extent of heterogeneity in the outside utilities (or effort costs) across dumb and smart agents that can be screened. Such a contract rewards agents for active trades in an ex post correct direction if and only if the other agent also traded in the same direction, and it penalizes such a trade otherwise, thus lowering all agents' expected payoffs for churning trades, which helps to discourage dumb agents even when the rewards for correct and conforming trades are higher, in order to attract (motivate) the smart.

An interesting possibility in this context is that such a conformity-rewarding fee contract might lead to attempts by agents to coordinate the directions of their churning trades, based on some sunspot variables, even when they have no payoff-relevant information that is correlated across them, in order to increase their expected payoff from ex post lucky trades. The general equilibrium effects of such coordinated churning would lead to interesting predictions for the volatility of asset prices, for example. We now turn to a brief discussion of the asset pricing implications of the explicit and implicit incentives of fund managers that have already theoretically delineated in the literature.

2.6. General Equilibrium Implications of Fund Manager Incentives

Given the large (and increasing) proportion of assets traded by fund managers, the perverse behavior arising out of explicit and implicit fund manager incentives as just outlined can and must have implications for the general properties of prices and volume in financial markets. Allen (2001) emphasizes the importance of understanding such general equilibrium implications of delegated portfolio management. A small number of papers explicitly consider such implications.

The first such paper is by Brennan (1993), who presents a simple static example of a mean-variance economy in which some traders are fund managers who are rewarded proportionately to their excess return over a benchmark portfolio. Brennan demonstrates that in such a setting asset returns can be described by a simple two-factor model, where the two factors are the market and the benchmark portfolio. Stocks that are more correlated with the benchmark portfolio have lower expected returns.

A number of the papers discussed previously also outline general equilibrium implications. For example, Allen and Gorton's (1993) churning result implies that (short-lived) asset price bubbles may arise in financial markets. Similar results emerge from the agency problems implicit in Allen and Gale (2000). Along a similar vein, the explicit incentives that arise in Dow and Gorton (1997) give rise to high amounts of trading volume and thus help to provide simultaneously a justification for noise trading and a partial resolution of the so-called trading volume paradox.[12]

[12] Asset pricing implications are also implicit in the work of Maug and Naik (1996) and Guembel (2005a, 2005b), as discussed above.

The recent work of Dasgupta and Prat (2005, 2006) explicitly models the general equilibrium implications of implicit (reputational) fund manager incentives. As we have already outlined, Dasgupta and Prat (2006) provide an alternative micro-foundation for the high trading volume observed in financial markets, while Dasgupta and Prat (2005) delineate how the informative role of prices may be endogenously restricted by the presence of reputational concerns on the part of fund managers. In addition, they argue that career concerns by a large fund management industry can lead to *systematic mispricing* of financial assets in which there is institutional trade. This arises because an asset that is bought by a large number of institutions (and thus experiences a price increase) can endogenously develop a *reputational premium*. That is, a reputationally sensitive fund manager may be willing to pay more for such an asset than a trader without career concerns. In the presence of frictions, dealers may be able to extract part of this reputational premium from fund managers, thus leading to (at least short-term) systematic mispricing of some assets.[13]

A recent paper by Cuoco and Kaniel (2001) examines the general equilibrium implications of (explicit) performance fees for fund managers in a richer, continuous-time asset pricing framework with many risky assets. They consider the pricing effects of various exogenously specific fee structures, including ones commonly seen in fund management. They find that fee structures have important effects on portfolio choice for fund managers and thus for market prices. For example, symmetric (fulcrum) fees defined relative to a benchmark portfolio lead to excessive weighting of benchmark stocks by risk-averse fund managers, which in turn leads to higher prices and lower Sharpe ratios for benchmark stocks relative to comparable nonbenchmark stocks. This phenomenon is partially mitigated by asymmetric-performance fees. Such fees create an additional incentive to hold nonbenchmark stocks, to maximize performance rewards and thus balance somewhat (depending on the parameters) the price and Sharpe ratio differences between benchmark and nonbenchmark assets.

The recent work of Vayanos (2003) considers the implications of delegation incentives on liquidity premia. Like Cuoco and Kaniel (2001), he takes the form of compensation for fund managers as given: Fund managers are subject to withdrawals when their fund performs sufficiently badly. Such an incentive structure creates an endogenous and time-varying preference for liquidity, which increases in volatility. Liquidity premia thus increase in volatile periods, investors (endogenously) become more risk averse, and asset correlations can rise.

He and Krishnamurthy (2006) take a distinct micro-founded approach to examining the general equilibrium implications of delegated portfolio management. They embed an idea originally proposed by Holmstrom and Tirole (1997)—that intermediaries who face moral hazard in monitoring must commit some of their own capital to be credible monitors—into a Lucas–Tree asset pricing model in continuous time. The delegated monitor is interpreted to be a hedge fund manager. Investors can invest in equity only through hedge funds but insist that hedge funds put up some of their own capital to maintain their incentives to monitor. In good times, when hedge fund wealth is high, the

[13]Empirical evidence for such mispricing is considered by Dasgupta, Prat, and Verardo (2006).

incentive constraint of hedge fund managers does not bind. However, a negative shock to hedge fund assets can reduce hedge fund managers' wealth to a point where the incentive constraint binds. At this point, investors withdraw money from hedge funds and buy riskless bonds, which, in equilibrium, must be sold by hedge funds. Thus, hedge funds have to take on leveraged equity positions, which leaves them overexposed to dividend fluctuations and leads to higher risk premia, lower risk-free rates, and higher volatility.

The small literature on the asset pricing implications of fund manager incentives raises more questions than it answers. Various hitherto-puzzling stylized facts of asset pricing, such as volatility clusters, may well have roots in underlying agency problems arising from delegated portfolio management. This remains a promising area for further research.

3. EVIDENCE ON THE CHOICES AND REWARDS OF ANALYSTS AND FUND MANAGERS

The richness and complexity of the theoretical possibilities noted earlier suggest that empirical evidence might be essential in resolving questions about the (relative) magnitudes of the effects of different incentives for agents in differing scenarios. Recently, spurred on perhaps by the huge growth of (Western) mutual funds, their increasing role in emerging markets, and the 1997–98 financial crises across Latin America, Russia, and East Asia—which some believe to have been contagious across nonrelated economies—much useful evidence has emerged. We start with evidence on the behavior of forecasters and fund managers in developed equity markets.

Zitzewitz (2001), following on some others, exhaustively analyzes a very large U.S. database of quarterly equity earning forecasts, containing over 800,000 forecasts on more than 7,000 firms, made by nearly 6,000 analysts and brokerage firms and recorded in real time (after lags of one or two days) by these analysts. He finds that their motive for accuracy of forecasts is very significantly modified by their desire to deviate from the evolving consensus forecast, which is clearly supportive of exaggeration (of their own signals), not of herding. The older analysts are less prone to this, and the differences among the qualities or information contents of different analysts' forecasts are very large.

The study of Chevalier and Ellison (1999) on the career concerns of fund managers utilizes data on the termination of managers of U.S. mutual funds and its relationship with their funds' performances as well as risks (on a market model or beta criterion), with the managers' ages serving as proxies for their relative weights on career concerns versus current performance-based fees as well as for uncertainty about their abilities. They show that a fund manager's probability of termination is significantly increased by bad (10 percent negative excess) current and lagged returns, the more so for younger managers. This may correct for their excessive risk-taking incentives, arising from new funds going to a few outliers with positive excess returns. They also show that controlling for fund performance, managers, especially the younger ones, are more likely to be terminated for taking portfolio positions that diverge (in sectoral composition or in riskiness) greatly from the average for that category of funds. This feature is significant at the 5 percent level, given bad performance as well, but the choice of a high degree of unsystematic risk or divergent sectoral portfolios by funds is found to be significantly positively related to their managers' ages, at the 1 percent level, and this appears to be rewarded (via nontermination) only for the older (over 45 years of age) managers if they perform well. For the younger managers, only successful divergence on the market or systematic risk dimension relative to other funds appears to be somewhat rewarded via nontermination, as with older managers. Presumably, excessive risk taking along these lines is something investors can easily adjust for, by taking their own compensating portfolio positions in bond markets, say.

There appears to be strong evidence that excessive (unsystematic) risk taking that is driven by career concern issues, which are more likely to dominate for younger managers, is not very important, in the sense that it is effectively discouraged by the threat of their termination. There seem to be major differences across scenarios in which experts provide advice or "cheap talk," as with equity analysts, as opposed to making delegated investment choices with costly consequences for investors. In particular, the tendency to overdifferentiate oneself by actively exaggerating the import of one's private signal is stronger among young analysts in "cheap-talk" settings.

Another, somewhat less direct, source of empirical evidence regarding fund manager incentives derives from international financial contagion. Calvo and Mendoza (2000) have suggested that, with global diversification of portfolios, the fixed costs of collecting country-specific information have increased relative to the benefits of doing so, thus making herd behavior more likely; it is not clear why this should apply selectively to emerging markets in developing economies only. Dornbusch, Park, and Claessens (2000) survey studies of contagion, or increase in cross-country linkages in asset prices, in exchange rates, and in rates of interest, etc., after (an adverse) shock to a subset of countries, as has often been suggested to have been the case over 1997–98. Clearly, capital flow reversals are very large in magnitude, for example, +\$70 billion in 1996 and −\$100 billion in recalled bank debt in 1997 out of five Southeast Asian countries, but this may have arisen from trade links, or the (foreign) investors' liquidity or capital ratio or value-at-risk (VAR) constraints. A recent study by Forbes and Rigobon (2002) shows little contagion in stock prices across economies that is not explained by fundamentals such as their trade linkages. Some positive evidence for contagion in interest rates exists (Agenor, Aizenman, and Hoffmaister 1999), but any evidence for regional contagion in exchange rates or currency crises is confounded by the possibility of strategic devaluation by countries competing in export markets. Dornbusch, Park, and Claessens remain skeptical regarding evidence suggestive of contagion increasing secularly (as in Bordo and Murshid, 1999).

However, detailed studies of the portfolio reactions of emerging market mutual funds by Froot, O'Connell, and Seasholes (2001) and Kaminsky, Lyons, and Schmukler (2004) provide some evidence of positive-feedback trading or trend following (buying current winners and selling losers), which also appear to increase during regional crises, and also of regional factors in comovements of funds flows increasing in importance over time.

4. CONCLUSION

We have attempted to provide a brief guided tour of recent and emerging literature on the optimal and actual incentive structures facing managers who invest funds on behalf of other investors, primarily in the context of traded securities, as well as on some empirical evidence pertaining to the impact of these incentives on risk taking, exuberance, and herding by these managers. Both the theory and the evidence are rich, nonuniform in stressing the importance of alternative effects and contractual instruments and in the tendency of fund managers and analysts to behave as herds versus as overly exuberant experts striving to differentiate themselves at the cost of exaggeration of their signals. Deserving of further study are the structures of the incentives and information available to, and the resulting impact on the key investment behavior patterns of, alternative classes of investors, such as "arm's-length" fund managers versus relationship-based domestic and foreign bank lenders, as well as market interactions among them in an imperfectly competitive context. We hope to have convinced the reader of both the theoretical intricacies as well as the enormous practical importance of gaining further analytical and empirical understanding of these key concerns, the efficient resolution and regulation of which is vital for the process of globalization.

References

Admati, A., and P. Pfleiderer. 1997. Does It All Add Up? Benchmarks and the Compensation of Active Portfolio Managers, *Journal of Business* 70, 323–351.

Agenor, J-P, J. Aizenman, and A. Hoffmaister. 1999. Contagion, Bank Lending Spreads and Output Fluctuations. Mimeo, The World Bank.

Allen, F. 2001. Do Financial Institutions Matter? *Journal of Finance* 56, 1165–1175.

Allen, F., and D. Gale. 2000. Bubbles and Crises, *Economic Journal* 110, 236–255.

Allen, F., and G. Gorton. 1993. Churning Bubbles, *Review of Economic Studies* 60, 813–836.

Avery, C., and J. Chevalier. 1999. Herding Over the Career, *Economics Letters* 63, 327–333.

Avery, C., and P. Zemsky. 1998. Multidimensional Uncertainty and Herd Behavior in Financial Markets, *American Economic Review* 88, 724–748.

Banerjee, A. 1992. A Model of Herd Behavior, *Quarterly Journal of Economics* 107, 797–817.

Berk, J., and R. Green. 2004. Mutual Fund Flows and Performance in Rational Markets, *Journal of Political Economy* 112, 1269–1294.

Bhattacharya, S. 1999. Delegated Portfolio Management, No Churning, and Relative Performance-Based Incentive cum Sorting Schemes. Mimeo, London School of Economics.

Bhattacharya, S., and P. Pfleiderer. 1985. Delegated Portfolio Management, *Journal of Economic Theory* 36, 1–25.

Bikhchandani, S., D. Hirshleifer, and I. Welch. 1992. A Theory of Fads, Fashion, Customs and Cultural Changes as Information Cascades, *Journal of Political Economy* 100, 992–1026.

Bikhchandani, S., D. Hirshleifer, and I. Welch. 1998. Learning from the Behavior of Others: Conformity, Fads, and Information Cascades, *Journal of Economic Perspectives* 12, 151–170.

Bordo, M., and A. Murshid. 1999. The International Transmission of Financial Crises Before World War II: Was There Contagion? Mimeo.

Brennan, M. 1993. Agency and Asset Pricing. Mimeo, UCLA.

Brown, K. C., W. V. Harlow, and L. T. Starks. 1996. Of Tournaments and Temptations: An Analysis of Managerial Incentives in the Mutual Fund Industry, *Journal of Finance* 51, 85–110.

Brunnermeier, M. 2001. *Asset Pricing under Asymmetric Information: Bubbles, Crashes, Technical Analysis, and Herding*. Oxford University Press, Oxford.

Calvo, G., and E. Mendoza. 2000. Rational Contagion and the Globalization of Securities Markets, *Journal of International Economics* 51, 79–113.

Carhart, M. 1997. On Persistence in Mutual Fund Performance, *Journal of Finance* 52, 57–82.

Chari, V., and P. Kehoe. 2004. Financial Crises as Herds: Overturning the Critiques, *Journal of Economic Theory* 119, 128–150.

Chevalier, J., and G. Ellison. 1997. Risk Taking by Mutual Funds as a Response to Incentives, *Journal of Political Economy* 105, 1167–1200.

Chevalier, J., and G. Ellison. 1999. Career Concerns of Mutual Fund Managers, *Quarterly Journal of Economics* 114, 389–432.

Cuoco, D., and R. Kaniel. 2001. Equilibrium Prices in the Presence of Delegated Portfolio Management. Mimeo, University of Pennsylvania.

Das, S., and R. Sundaram. 2002. Fee Speech: Signalling, Risk-Sharing, and the Impact of Fee Structures on Investor Welfare, *Review of Financial Studies* 15, 1465–1497.

Dasgupta, A., and A. Prat. 2005. Asset Price Dynamics When Traders Care About Reputation. CEPR Discussion Paper No. 5372.

Dasgupta, A., and A. Prat. 2006. Financial Equilibrium with Career Concerns, *Theoretical Economics* 1, 67–94.

Dasgupta, A., A. Prat, and M. Verardo. 2006. Institutional Trade Persistence and Long-Term Equity Returns. Mimeo, London School of Economics.

Dornbusch, R., Y. C. Park, and S. Claessens. 2000. Contagion: How It Spreads and How It Can Be Stopped. Mimeo, The World Bank.

Dow, J., and G. Gorton. 1994. Arbitrage Chains, *Journal of Finance* 49, 819–849.

Dow, J., and G. Gorton. 1997. Noise Trading, Delegated Portfolio Management and Economic Welfare, *Journal of Political Economy* 105, 1024–1050.

Dybvig, P., H. Farnsworth, and J. Carpenter. 2001. Portfolio Performance and Agency. Mimeo, Washington University in Saint Louis.

Effinger, M., and M. Polborn. 2001. Herding and Anti-Herding: A Model of Reputational Differentiation, *European Economic Review* 45, 385–403.

Forbes, K., and R. Rigobon. 2002. No Contagion, Only Interdependence: Measuring Stock Market Co-movements, *Journal of Finance* 57, 2223–2261.

Froot, K., P. O'Connell, and M. Seasholes. 2001. The Portfolio Flows of International Investors, *Journal of Financial Economics* 59, 151–193.

Froot, K., D. Scharfstein, and J. Stein. 1992. Herd on the Street: Information Inefficiencies in a Market with Short-Term Speculation, *Journal of Finance* 47, 1461–1484.

Glosten, L., and P. Milgrom. 1985. Bid, Ask and Transaction Prices in a Specialist Market with Heterogeneously Informed Traders, *Journal of Financial Economics* 14, 71–100.

Graham, J. 1999. Herding Among Investment Newsletters: Theory and Evidence, *Journal of Finance* LIV, 237–268.

Guembel, A. 2005a. Trading on Short-Term Information, *Journal of Institutional and Theoretical Economics* 161, 428–452.

Guembel, A. 2005b. Herding in Delegated Portfolio Management: When Is Comparative Performance Information Desirable? *European Economic Review* 49, 599–626.

He, Z., and A. Krishnamurthy. 2006. Intermediation, Capital Immobility, and Asset Prices. Mimeo, Northwestern University.

Heinkel, R., and N. M. Stoughton. 1994. The Dynamics of Portfolio Management Contracts, *Review of Financial Studies* 7, 351–387.

Hirshleifer, D., A. Subrahmanyam, and S. Titman. 1994. Security Analysis and Trading Patterns When Some Investors Receive Private Information Before Others, *Journal of Finance* 49, 1665–1698.

Holmstrom, B., and J. Tirole. 1997. Financial Intermediation, Loanable Funds, and the Real Sector, *Quarterly Journal of Economics* 112, 663–691.

Hvide, H., and E. Kristiansen. 2003. Risk Taking in Selection Contests, *Games and Economic Behavior* 42, 172–181.

Jensen, M., and W. H. Meckling. 1976. Theory of the Firm: Managerial Behavior, Agency Costs and Ownership Structure, *Journal of Financial Economics* 3, 305–360.

Kaminsky, G., Lyons, R., and S. Schmukler. 2004. Managers, Investors, and Crises: Mutual Fund Strategies in Emerging Markets, *Journal of International Economics* 64, 113–134.

Kapur, S., and A. Timmermann. 2005. Relative Performance Evaluation Contracts and Asset Market Equilibrium, *Economic Journal* 115, 1077–1102.

Kihlstrom, R. E. 1988. Optimal Contracts for Security Analysts and Portfolio Managers, *Studies in Banking and Finance* 5, 291–325.

Kyle, A. 1985. Continuous Auctions and Insider Trading, *Econometrica* 53, 1315–1336.

Lee, I. 1998. Market Crashes and Informational Avalanches, *Review of Economic Studies* 65, 741–759.

Maug, E., and N. Naik. 1996. Herding and Delegated Portfolio Management: The Impact of Relative Performance Evaluation on Asset Allocation. Mimeo, London Business School.

Modigliani, F., and G. A. Pogue. 1975. Alternative Investment Performance Fee Arrangements and Implications for SEC Regulatory Policy, *Bell Journal of Economics* 6, 127–160.

Ottaviani, M., and P. Sørensen. 2006. Professional Advice, *Journal of Economic Theory* 126, 120–142.

Ou-Yang, H. 2003. Optimal Contracts in a Continuous-Time Delegated Portfolio Management Problem, *Review of Financial Studies* 16, 173–208.

Palomino, F. 2005. Relative Performance Objectives in Financial Markets, *Journal of Financial Intermediation* 14, 351–375.

Palomino, F., and A. Prat. 2003. Risk Taking and Optimal Contracts for Money Managers, *RAND Journal of Economics* 34, 113–138.

Prat, A. 2005. The Wrong Kind of Transparency, *American Economic Review* 95, 862–877.

Prendergast, C., and L. Stole. 1996. Impetuous Youngsters and Jaded Oldtimers, *Journal of Political Economy* 104, 1105–1134.

Rajan, U., and S. Srivastava. 1999. Portfolio Delegation with Limited Liability. Mimeo, Carnegie Mellon University.

Ross, S. 1973. Economic Theory of Agency: The Principal's Problem, *American Economic Review* 63, 134–139.

Scharfstein, D., and J. Stein. 1990. Herd Behavior and Investment, *American Economic Review* 80, 465–479.

Shleifer, A., and R. Vishny. 1997. The Limits of Arbitrage, *Journal of Finance* 52, 35–55.

Smith, L., and P. Sorensen. 2000. Pathological Outcomes of Observational Learning, *Econometrica* 68, 371–398.

Stoughton, N. 1993. Moral Hazard and the Portfolio Management Problem, *Journal of Finance* 48, 2009–2028.

Trueman, B. 1988. A Theory of Noise Trading in Securities Markets, *Journal of Finance* 18, 83–95.

Trueman, B. 1994. Analyst Forecasts and Herding Behavior, *Review of Financial Studies* 7, 97–124.

Vayanos, D. 2003. Flight to Quality, Flight to Liquidity, and the Pricing of Risk. Mimeo, London School of Economics.

Zitzewitz, E. 2001. Measuring Herding and Exaggeration by Equity Analysts. Mimeo, Massachusetts Institute of Technology.

SECTION 5

Regulation

Overview by Mark J. Flannery

University of Florida

The four chapters in this section shed light on various aspects of the U.S. regulatory system. The first two discuss the causes and consequences of recent changes in the structure of the U.S. banking industry. The second two address banks' capital decisions and regulatory efforts to control risk through minimum capital requirements.

In Chapter 10, Jones and Critchfield review the path of consolidation within the U.S. banking system over the period 1984–2003. They argue that technical changes and globalization had set the stage for substantial consolidation within the industry by the late 1970s. Yet binding restrictive regulations remained in force. It was not until the thrift crisis created an incentive to encourage previously forbidden merger combinations that the forces of technical change and globalization were permitted to operate. The 1980s' consolidation, therefore, was driven largely by the bank and thrift industries' failing health. By the 1990s, legislation had removed most statutory obstacles to bank mergers, and the consolidation continued, propelled now by healthy industry participants seeking strategic allies and lower operating costs. Jones and Critchfield point out that the number of "community" banks (assets less than $1 billion) fell most sharply, although many still remain in operation.

In predicting the eventual size of the banking system (in terms of number of charters/distinct firms), the authors can use recent information that was unavailable to researchers who had previously addressed the question. They see a decrease in the rate of banking consolidation and predict that roughly 6,500 banks will remain by 2013 (compared to approximately 7,600 in late 2006). Importantly, they predict that the smallest organizations (assets below $100 million) are the only subset of banks whose numbers will actually decline (by nearly 50%). The number of banking firms with more than $100 million in assets is predicted to increase slightly through 2013.

In Chapter 11, Robert DeYoung also explores the evolution of U.S. banks over the past two decades, primarily from the perspective of how banking firms can effectively compete with one another through specialization. DeYoung basically agrees with Jones and Critchfield that the extent of specialization had been limited by government regulatory restrictions. DeYoung discusses how eliminating these restrictions has permitted the industry's basic economic forces to emerge more starkly. Large banks enjoy scale economies that permit them to succeed with price competition, although only when they provide a standardized product based primarily on "hard" (quantifiable) information. In contrast, the small banks' higher operating costs are feasible only if they offer customized, relationship-based products with high value added. Given this specialization, large and small banks should be able to coexist. The danger will be if a firm gets "caught in the middle" and pursues neither strategy effectively.

In Chapter 12, Flannery and Rangan examine the relationship between bank capital and asset risk for the 100 largest banks in the U.S. economy between 1986 and 2001. They show that both book and market measures of bank capital rose substantially after the early 1990s. By 2001, the average large bank holding company had 400 basis points (bps) more of equity capital than required under Basel I. The ratio of equity's *market* value to assets was even higher.

In part, this increase in large U.S. banks' capital ratios derives from worldwide regulatory interest in encouraging more capital, specifically through the Basel Accord of 1988 (Basel I). However, U.S. banks also underwent substantial regulatory changes in the early 1990s. Depositor preference, prompt corrective action, and "constructive ambiguity" all led bank counterparties to feel more at risk than they had been in the preceding decade. Flannery and Rangan's empirical analysis demonstrates a longitudinal improvement in the relation between a bank's risk and the (market-valued) equity capital it holds. They conclude that this finding implies effective market discipline: Counterparties' preferences for safer claims or higher premia on risky claims lead banks to reduce their leverage, in a way that is consistent with the sort of corporate financial theory applied to firms more generally.

Importantly, however, banks are uniquely subject to regulatory capital requirements. Supervisors justify their imposition of minimum capital requirements in either of two ways. First, the government's *insurance* of bank liabilities creates an artificial incentive for bank shareholders to operate with higher equity and to seek high asset volatility. Second, many supervisors believe that a bank's failure—particularly a large bank's failure—would generate negative *external effects* on other firms and even on the economy's real sector. Minimum capital requirements counteract both of these factors, by reducing the probability of default for regulated firms.[1] So an important question becomes the extent to which those regulations effectively constrain bank leverage.

How can we reconcile a need for capital regulation with the observation that banks have held "excess" capital—above their specified regulatory minima—for at least the past decade? Some supervisors view this excess as a cushion protecting the banks from incurring the regulatory costs of falling below regulatory minima. However, Flannery and Rangan point out that such a cushion should be related to the riskiness of bank assets, which it is not. In addition, the extent of excess capital seems extreme if equity capital is much more expensive than debt, as the bankers claim it is.

Chapter 13 (by Kupiec), the final chapter in this section, deals with Basel II, the recently agreed method by which most of the developed economies' financial regulators will regulate their banks' capital in coming years. Basel I constituted a substantial advance in capital regulation for several reasons. First, it was applied uniformly across the major banking nations. Second, it emphasized the idea that adequate capital should reflect the banking book's credit risk exposures (although these exposures were crudely categorized).[2] Third, it incorporated the risks of off-balance-sheet positions in a standardized way. Over time, the limited number of risk weights in Basel I permitted banks to arbitrage capital standards, with the effect that true credit risk exposures may have been larger than they would have been in the absence of risk-based capital standards.

Regulatory arbitrage generated pressure to revise the capital standard. After one or two false starts, the Basel Committee on Bank Supervision (BCBS) produced a 250-page document in June 2004 that completely specified a mechanism for tying required capitalization to a bank's credit risk exposures. This new methodology will be introduced in Europe beginning in 2007. In the United States, Basel II's "advanced internal ratings–based" method for assessing minimum capital adequacy will be applied to 10 or 20 large, sophisticated banking firms. The transition to Basel II will be slower in the United States—starting in 2008 and becoming complete no earlier than 2012. Moreover, after substantial debate among the federal banking agencies, the U.S. implementation of Basel II will include a leverage standard that requires equity capital to exceed a fixed proportion of on-book, total assets. This leverage standard is expected to bind for some banks, negating the risk sensitivity that has been used to justify the new standard.

For the largest banks worldwide, this new system specifies a complex, detailed model that calculates a bank's required capital as a function of its self-reported exposure to default. Motivated implicitly by the notion that these are the most important banks to supervise properly, Kupiec evaluates how this formula is likely to correspond to the BCBS's stated objective of making all banks attain a 99.9 percent annual solvency standard. Using closed-form valuation models and simulations, he concludes that the

[1] It has long been known, however, that limiting leverage need not reduce default probability, since the constrained firm rationally takes on riskier assets (e.g., Kahane [1977]).

[2] Even while it included credit risk, Basel I basically ignored other sources of banking risk, such as interest rate and FX risks.

advanced internal ratings–based formula will likely permit banks to operate with far *less* capital than would be needed to meet this solvency level. Kupiec's analysis does not necessarily imply that Basel II offers no improvement over Basel I. Rather, he warns that the new system's financial models, which deal in tail probabilities, are very sensitive to the underlying assumptions. Observers should not be overly comforted by the apparent precision embodied in the Basel II formula.

CHAPTER 10

Consolidation in the U.S. Banking Industry: Is the "Long, Strange Trip" About to End?

Kenneth D. Jones
FDIC

Tim Critchfield
FDIC

The authors wish to thank Tyler Davis, Ron Kidd, Terry Kissinger, Steve McGinnis, and Chau Nguyen for their valuable assistance. The views expressed in this chapter are those of the authors and not necessarily those of the FDIC. Naturally, any errors are the responsibility of the authors.

In 1995, the Brookings Institution published a paper entitled "The Transformation of the U.S. Banking Industry: What a Long, Strange Trip It's Been."[1] Using a breathtaking array of facts and figures, the paper described in great detail the dramatic changes that had occurred in the U.S. commercial banking industry over the 15 years from 1979 to 1994. The banking industry was transformed during that period, according to the paper (p. 127), by "the massive reduction in the number of banking organizations; the significant increase in the number of failures; the dramatic rise in off-balance-sheet activities; the major expansion in lending to U.S. corporations by foreign banks; the widespread adoption of ATMs; ... and the opening up of interstate banking markets." The paper went on to explain that most of these major changes in banking could be traced to two developments: (1) the extraordinary number of major regulatory changes during the period, from deposit deregulation in the early 1980s to the relaxation of branching restrictions later in the decade; and (2) clearly identifiable innovations in technology and applied finance, including improvements in information processing and telecommunication technologies, the securitization and sale of bank loans, and the development of derivatives markets. Other research would later confirm the paper's assessments and its explanation of the course of events in the banking industry over the period 1979–1994.

Yet, more than a decade after the publication of that paper, data indicate that the transformation of the banking industry is ongoing and that the number of banking organizations continues to decline—though recently there have been signs that the number of organizations is beginning to stabilize. In fact, when we take a closer look at the data, we find that the rate of decline in the number of banking organizations appears to be slowing markedly. Indeed, if the data from the past few years indicate anything about a future direction, the rate of decline can be expected to slow even more over the next five-year period. Moreover, some evidence suggests that this slowdown in the rate of decline might presage a return to a relatively stable population of banking organizations. Such a result would be in sharp contrast to conventional wisdom, which foresees continued consolidation of the banking industry in the United States.

Because this chapter is part of a collective review of the U.S. banking industry's past and an anticipation of its future, many aspects of the industry's transformation are discussed in companion papers.[2] Our focus, therefore, is primarily on industry structure: how it has already changed and how it might evolve in the future. Accordingly, we begin with an updated review of the structural changes that occurred in the industry over the two decades 1984–2003. This should give us a better understanding of the scope of the decline that has taken place. We then review the causes of this decline and the literature on how the decline has affected such things as asset concentration, banking competition, efficiency, profitability, shareholder value, and the availability and pricing of banking

[1] Berger, Kashyap, and Scalise (1995).

[2] In 2004, the FDIC released its findings from a comprehensive research project looking into the future of banking. The study as a whole projects likely trends in the structure and performance of the banking industry and anticipates the policy issues that will confront the industry and the regulatory community in the coming years. Copies of the research papers making up the study can be obtained at http://www.fdic.gov/bank/analytical/future/index.html.

services. After this analysis of the past, we offer some projections of future banking industry structure.

1. OVERVIEW OF STRUCTURAL CHANGE IN THE U.S. BANKING INDUSTRY 1984–2003

Over the two decades 1984–2003, the structure of the U.S. banking industry indeed underwent an almost unprecedented transformation—one marked by a substantial decline in the number of commercial banks and savings institutions and by a growing concentration of industry assets among a few dozen extremely large financial institutions. This is not news. As mentioned earlier, the decline in the number of banking organizations has been going on for more than two decades and has been well documented in the literature.[3] Nevertheless, a brief overview will serve to clarify both the scope of the decline and the increasing concentration of assets among the nation's largest banking organizations.[4]

1.1. Industry Size

At year-end 1984, there were 15,084 banking and thrift organizations (defined as commercial bank and thrift holding companies, independent banks, and independent thrifts).[5] By year-end 2003, that number had fallen to 7,842—a decline of almost 48 percent (Figure 1). Distributed by size, nearly all the decline occurred in the community bank sector (organizations with less than $1 billion in assets in 2002 dollars) and especially among the smallest-size group (less than $100 million in assets in 2002 dollars).[6] Yet the community banking sector still accounts for 94 percent of banking organizations (Figure 2).

Geographically, the decline in the number of banking organizations appears to have been remarkably uniform across a variety of regions and markets. Critchfield et al. (2004),

[3]Discussions about the declining number of banks can be found not only in the paper already mentioned (Berger, Kashyap, and Scalise 1995) but also in Berger, Demsetz, and Strahan (1999), Hughes et al. (1999), and the Group of Ten (2001).

[4]Data limitations at the level of banking organizations restrict our analysis to the years 1984–2003. And because the number of commercial banks alone peaked in 1984 at 14,496, we use that year as the beginning of our discussion of the consolidation trend, even though in certain respects the transformation of the U.S. banking industry may be said to have begun earlier.

[5]The expansion of banking powers over the period we are studying has left few differences between commercial banks and savings institutions (thrifts), so, unless otherwise specified, our analysis combines the two types of institutions. Moreover, we focus on top-tier organizations rather than on individual institutions in order to avoid counting multiple charters belonging to a single corporate entity. The count here for year-end 1984 (15,084) includes all active organizations, whereas Figure 1 (which shows a total of 14,884 organizations for year-end 1984) includes only organizations that filed a financial report at the end of 1984.

[6]Asset size classes have been adjusted for inflation using the GDP price deflator with 2002 as the base year. Hence, the number of banks in 2003 that had less than $100 million in assets is comparable to the number of banks in 1984 that had less than $66 million in assets.

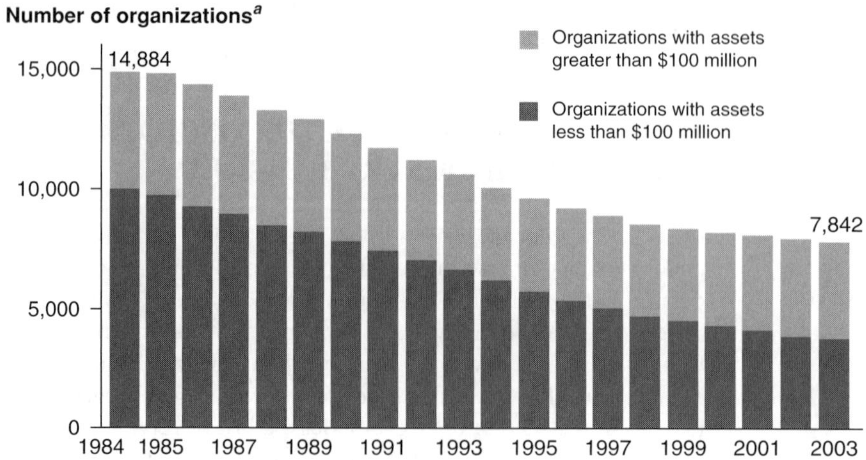

FIGURE 1 Number of banking organizations, 1984–2003.
[a]Count is year-end and includes only organizations that filed a financial report in the fourth quarter.

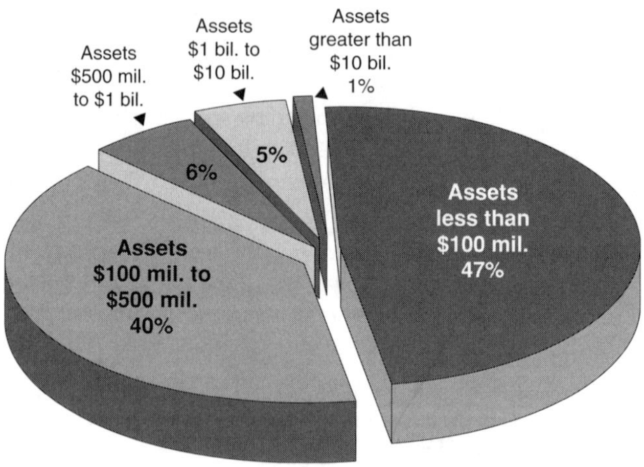

FIGURE 2 Distribution of banking organizations by asset size, year-end 2003.
Note: Percentages may not add to 100 because of rounding.

for example, examined the decline of community banks across four market segments—rural markets, small metropolitan markets, and suburban and urban parts of large metropolitan markets—and found that the declines across all four markets were proportionally similar (Figure 3). The dynamics underlying the declines, however, differed depending on the market. Rural areas, for example, saw proportionally fewer mergers and very little de novo entry in comparison with both small and large metro markets, where a larger number of mergers was partially offset by a larger number of new-bank start-ups.

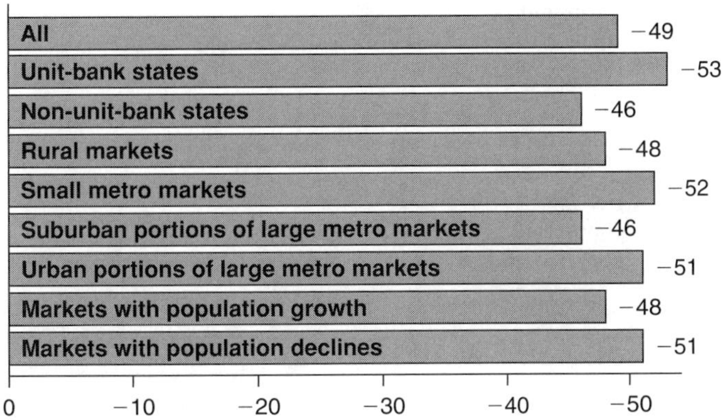

FIGURE 3 Percentage decline in the number of commercial banks, 1985–2003 (unit- vs. non-unit-bank states and across various types of markets).
Source: Critchfield et al. (2004).

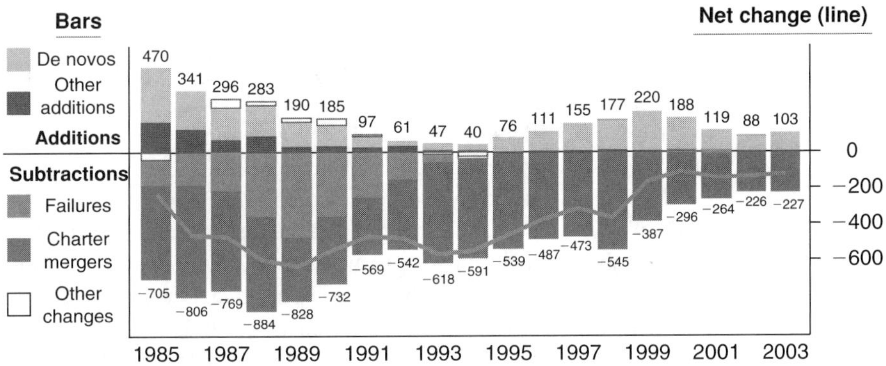

FIGURE 4 Change in the number of banking organizations, 1985–2003.

Overall, the bulk of the decline in the number of organizations between year-end 1984 and year-end 2003 was due to unassisted mergers and acquisitions (see Figure 4, which decomposes the net change in the number of banking organizations into several components).[7] In every year but one, mergers and acquisitions were the single largest contributor to the net decline in banking organizations.[8] During the entire period, 8,122 individual bank and thrift organizations disappeared through unassisted mergers and holding company purchases.

From 1985 through 1992, though, failures also contributed significantly to the decline in the number of banking organizations (Figures 4 and 5). Of the 2,698 bank and

[7]"Other additions" included in Figure 4 were non-FDIC-insured institutions that became FDIC insured, often transferring from state insurance programs in the mid-1980s. "Other changes" were voluntary liquidations of organizations.
[8]The sole exception was 1989, when the savings and loan (S&L) and banking crises were near their peak.

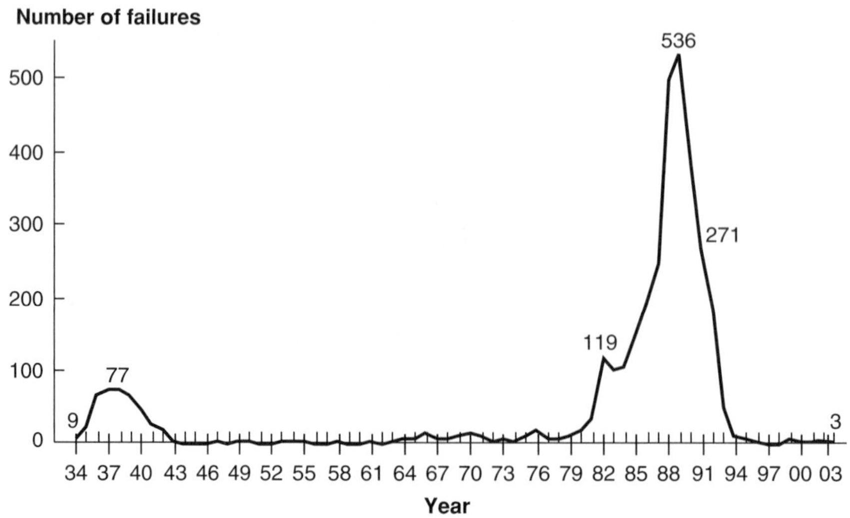

FIGURE 5 Number of commercial bank and savings institution failures, 1934–2003.

thrift closings caused by failure during the entire period 1984–2003,[9] almost 75 percent of them occurred in the five years 1987–1991, when failures averaged 388 per year.[10] In contrast, from 1994 to 2003 only 66 institutions failed—a figure that reflects greatly improved economic conditions and stronger safety-and-soundness regulation.

The decline caused by mergers, acquisitions, and failures was partially offset by the entry of 3,097 new banking organizations between year-end 1984 and year-end 2003. This number is remarkable, given the overriding downward trend. During the entire period, the number of de novo bank entrants averaged 163 per year, even though the creation of new banks was suppressed at the height of the thrift and banking crises. The number of start-up institutions peaked in 1984 and then declined each year until 1993; then, as economic conditions improved and more capital became available, de novo entry into the banking industry resumed and continued through the end of the century. With the beginning of an economic recession in March 2001, the number of new charter formations again began decreasing.

As indicated by the trends in mergers, acquisitions, and failures on the one hand and start-ups on the other hand, the pace of the decline in the number of banking organizations has not been uniform. Indeed, graphing the rate of change reveals a very strong cyclical pattern, with declines occurring at a rate that increased in the 1980s, only to slow in the 1990s (Figure 6). Since 1992 the rate of decline in the number of institutions has trended consistently lower. (This pattern has important implications for our projections on the structure of the industry.)

[9]This number includes not only 2,262 organizations (including multibank holding companies) that were eliminated because of failure but also individual charters that were merged into other charters with FDIC assistance; however, it does not include insolvent institutions that remained open with FDIC financial assistance.

[10]The number of failures peaked in 1989, when 536 banks and thrift institutions failed.

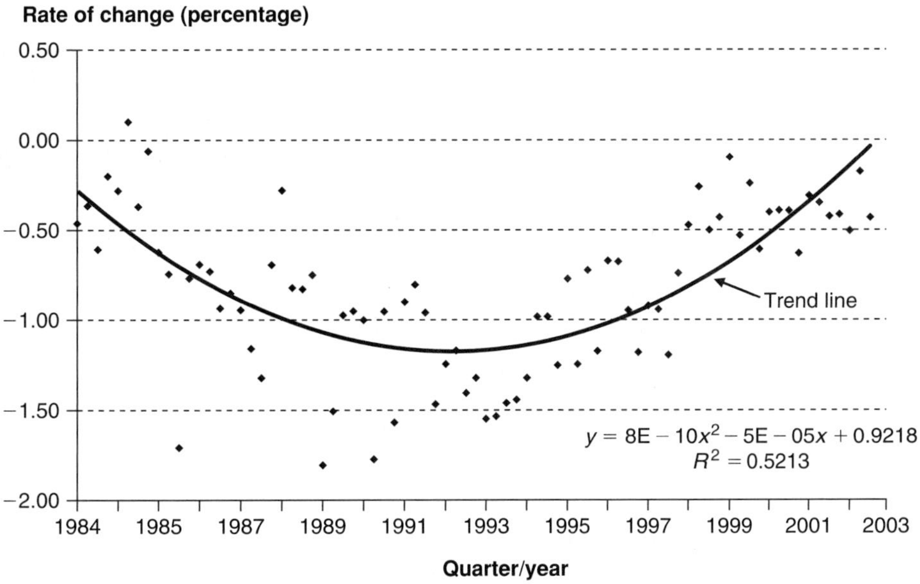

FIGURE 6 Quarterly rate of change in the number of banking organizations, 1984–2003.

1.2. Industry Concentration

At the same time that the number of banking organizations was decreasing, industry assets were increasing. Over the 1984–2003 period, banking industry assets grew from \$3.3 trillion to \$9.1 trillion—an increase of nearly 70 percent in real terms.[11] Existing assets and asset growth, however, were not evenly distributed across the industry but, instead, were becoming more and more concentrated among the nation's largest financial institutions. This trend can be seen in Figure 7, which compares asset share over time for each of five size groups during our period. The asset share of the largest size group—organizations with more than \$10 billion in assets—increased dramatically, rising from 42 percent in 1984 to 73 percent in 2003. In contrast, the share of industry assets held by community banks (organizations with less than \$1 billion of assets) dropped from 28 percent in 1984 to only 14 percent in 2003; and the smallest banks, organizations with less than \$100 million in assets, accounted as a group for only 2 percent of industry assets in 2003—compared with 8 percent in 1984.

In terms of deposits, industry concentration has been equally dramatic: A quarter of the nation's domestic deposits are now controlled by just four organizations (see Table 1), whereas in 1984 that same proportion was held by 42 companies. At year-end 2003, Bank of America Corporation, the largest holder of domestic bank deposits,

[11]We determined real growth by adjusting nominal dollars for inflation using the GDP chain-type price deflator, with 2002 selected as the base year.

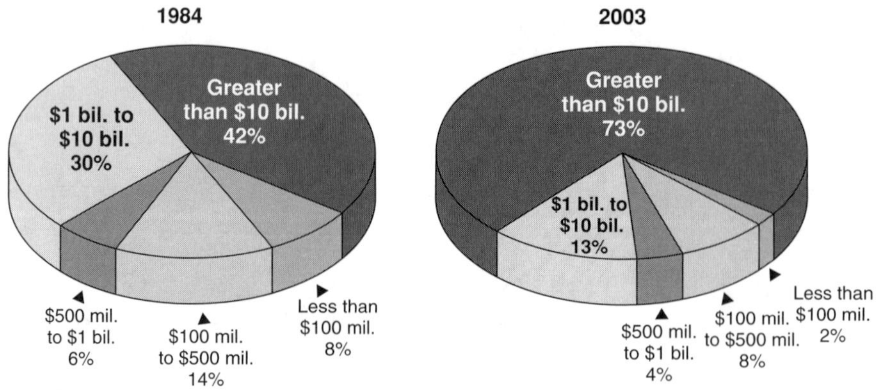

FIGURE 7 Share of banking industry assets by size group, 1984 and 2003.

held approximately $512 billion in domestic deposits (9.8 percent of the industry) and had $870 billion in assets (9.6 percent of the industry).[12] Also at year-end 2003, the 3,683 banking organizations that each held less than $100 million in assets accounted as a group for only $192 billion of industry assets (2 percent, as noted earlier) and $160 billion (3 percent) of domestic deposits.

Analyzing banking industry concentration, Moore and Siems (1998) and Rhoades (2000) found that, despite some recent increases, national and local measures of concentration had remained, on average, relatively low.[13] This was surprising, given that many mergers had been of the within-market type—those most likely to result in increases in concentration. Hence, despite the heightened merger activity among banks over the two decades 1984–2003, it appears that current concentration measures generally remain below the level where monopolistic behavior might manifest itself. Part of the reason may be that deregulatory efforts to lower entry barriers and expand bank powers—helped along by advances in technology—have resulted in an expanded geographic reach of competitors. Competition from nonbank financial market participants also provides an important check on market power. However, Rhoades (2000) does caution that, although MSA (metropolitan statistical area) market concentration remains fairly low on average, it has nonetheless increased substantially since 1984, and the increase suggests that in the future there is likely to be a growing number of MSA markets in which bank merger proposals raise significant competitive issues.

[12]Table 1 has been updated to provide year-end data for 2006. The new data show that at year-end 2006, Bank of America held approximately $605 billion in domestic deposits (9.1 percent of the industry) and had $1.376 trillion in assets (11.6 percent of the industry).

[13]Standard measures of concentration include the Herfindahl–Hirschmann Index (HHI—defined as the sum of the squares of the individual market shares of all banks in the market) and the three-firm concentration ratio (CR3—that is, the percentage of deposits accounted for by the three largest banking organizations in the market).

TABLE 1 Share of Industry Assets and Deposits Held by the Nation's 25 Largest Banking Companies (data as of December 31, 2006)

Ranking	Bank holding companies	Total assets[a] ($ in billion)	Share of industry assets (%)	Cumulative percentage of assets	Domestic deposits ($ in billion)	Share of industry domestic deposits	Cumulative percentage of deposits
1	Bank of America Corporation	1,376	11.60	11.60	605	9.12	9.12
2	JP Morgan Chase & Co.	1,264	10.66	22.26	478	7.21	16.33
3	Citigroup, Inc.	1,121	9.46	31.71	238	3.60	19.93
4	Wachovia Corporation	683	5.76	37.47	389	5.87	25.80
5	Wells Fargo & Company	429	3.62	41.09	287	4.32	30.12
6	Washington Mutual, Inc.	384	3.24	44.33	220	3.31	33.43
7	U.S. Bancorp	222	1.87	46.20	119	1.79	35.22
8	Suntrust Banks, Inc.	183	1.54	47.74	119	1.79	37.01
9	HSBC Holdings, PLC	168	1.42	49.15	77	1.16	38.17
10	Royal Bank of Scotland Group, PLC	164	1.38	50.54	100	1.51	39.68
11	National City Corporation	139	1.17	51.70	78	1.18	40.85
12	Regions Financial Corporation	139	1.17	52.87	93	1.40	42.25
13	Capital One Financial Corporation	134	1.13	54.01	82	1.24	43.49
14	ABN AMRO Holding, N.V.	123	1.03	55.04	58	0.87	44.36
15	BB&T Corporation	117	0.99	56.03	80	1.20	45.56
16	Fifth Third Bancorp	103	0.87	56.90	68	1.02	46.58
17	Banco Santander Central Hispano, S.A.	98	0.82	57.72	57	0.85	47.44
18	State Street Corporation	96	0.81	58.53	11	0.17	47.61
19	PNC Financial Services Group, Inc.	94	0.79	59.32	64	0.97	48.57
20	Countrywide Financial Corporation	93	0.78	60.11	56	0.84	49.42
21	Keycorp	88	0.74	60.85	58	0.87	50.29
22	Bank of New York Company, Inc.	88	0.74	61.59	30	0.45	50.74
23	BNP Paribas	68	0.57	62.16	44	0.66	51.40
24	Northern Trust Corporation	63	0.53	62.69	14	0.22	51.62
25	Comerica Incorporated	59	0.49	63.18	44	0.66	52.28
	Total Top 25 Banking Companies	$7,494	63.18%		$3,466	52.28%	

[a]Nonbank assets are excluded.
Source: FDIC Call Reports and Thrift Financial Reports.

2. FUNDAMENTAL CAUSES OF CONSOLIDATION

Naturally policymakers, academics, and others have wanted to know the "why" of consolidation. Why, after decades of seeming to change so little, did the industry begin to consolidate and restructure itself so dramatically? There is no single reason for the consolidation trend and no single underlying cause. Rather, the trend might best be viewed as the result of a combination of macro- and microeconomic factors: external forces that fundamentally and irrevocably changed the environment in which banks operated, and banks' strategic responses to those environmental forces (ostensibly with the goal of maximizing shareholder value). Previous studies of the consolidation phenomenon have examined and discussed the various factors at considerable length. Berger, Kashyap, and Scalise (1995), Berger, Demsetz, and Strahan (1999), and Shull and Hanweck (2001), in particular, offer broad reviews of the literature.[14]

2.1. Environmental Factors

At the macroeconomic level, consolidation has been driven by exogenous changes in the banking industry's economic environment, and these changes have often worked in concert to encourage consolidation. Foremost among them have been globalization of the marketplace, technological change, deregulation, and major macroeconomic events (such as the thrift and banking crises of the 1980s and the early 1990s and the economic and stock market boom of the late 1990s). Globalization and technological change have been persistent forces for change over the entire period, and deregulation (in its various manifestations) has been a recurring enabling force. In contrast, the strength and influence of major macroeconomic events have varied over time. For example, the economic forces that led to the thrift and banking crises were influential primarily in the middle to late 1980s and early 1990s; by the mid-1990s the crises were over, and bank and thrift failures were no longer a major contributor to industry consolidation. Similarly, the influence of the economic growth and stock market boom of the late 1990s was largely restricted to a specific period. Hence, adding a temporal dimension to the discussion of the external influences on consolidation will help us not only understand the current trend but also formulate expectations about the future.

2.1.1. Globalization and Technology

Globalization began slowly in the aftermath of World War II. After that war, the major economies of the world gradually became more connected and interdependent. This trend toward globalization accelerated in the 1970s and 1980s—in tandem with the beginnings of what would become a revolution in information and telecommunication (ITC) technologies. Indeed, by the end of the twentieth century, technological change

[14]Expanded discussions of the macroeconomic forces driving consolidation can also be found in Rhoades (2000), Hannan and Rhoades (1992), and Boyd and Graham (1998). The microeconomic underpinnings of banking consolidation are discussed in Hughes et al. (2003), Milbourn, Boot, and Thakor (1999), Calomiris and Karceski (1998), and Hughes et al. (1996).

would affect nearly every aspect of the business of banking: the demand for banking services, the character and intensity of sector competition, and the very structure of the industry.[15] Through what has been described as "a protracted series of technology shocks with order-of-magnitude effects on the costs of transmitting and processing information," advances in ITC technologies have created new advantages of scale in production and have lowered barriers to entry.[16]

Dramatically lowered costs and the ability to transmit information almost instantaneously around the globe effectively freed the financial services industry from the constraints of time and place. In the new global financial economy, banks, securities firms, corporations, and even individual investors became able to transfer huge amounts of capital around the globe with the click of a mouse. Yet, while these new technologies enabled financial firms of all types to exploit innovations in financial and economic theory, engineer new products, and implement new techniques for managing risk, they also resulted in a sharply more competitive marketplace for banking and financial services. To survive and prosper, banking organizations needed to respond to this new environment. Consolidation was one response. However, the strict regulatory environment that existed before the 1980s largely precluded any dramatic consolidation within the banking industry. Not until regulatory constraints were relaxed did consolidation of the banking industry begin in earnest.

2.1.2. Deregulation

In the early 1980s, policymakers began a decades-long process of deregulating the banking and thrift industries so that they could be more responsive to marketplace realities (see Table 2).

TABLE 2 Major Legislative and Regulatory Changes Affecting Banking Consolidation

Year	Description
1980	Depository Institutions Deregulation and Monetary Control Act (DIDMCA). Raised federal deposit insurance coverage limit from \$40,000 to \$100,000. Phased out interest-rate ceilings. Allowed depositories to offer negotiable order of withdrawal (NOW) accounts nationwide. Eliminated usury ceilings. Imposed uniform reserve requirements on all depository institutions and gave them access to Federal Reserve services.
1982	Garn-St Germain Act. Permitted money market deposit accounts. Permitted banks to purchase failing banks and thrifts across state lines. Expanded thrift lending powers.
1987	Competitive Equality in Banking Act (CEBA). Allocated \$10.8 billion in additional funding to the Federal Savings and Loan Insurance Corporation (FSLIC). Authorized forbearance program for farm banks. Reaffirmed that the "full faith and credit" of the U.S. Department of the Treasury (Treasury) stood behind federal deposit insurance.

(Continued)

[15]For more detailed discussions of technology and the effects it has had on the restructuring of the financial services sector, see Berger (2003), Berger and DeYoung (2002), the Group of Ten (2001), Hunter (2001), Mishkin and Strahan (1999), and Emmons and Greenbaum (1998).
[16]Emmons and Greenbaum (1998, p. 37).

TABLE 2 *Continued*

Year	Description
1987	Board of Governors of the Federal Reserve System (Federal Reserve) authorized limited underwriting activities for Bankers Trust, J.P. Morgan, and Citicorp, with a 5 percent revenue limit on Section 20–ineligible securities activities.
1989	Financial Institutions Reform, Recovery, and Enforcement Act (FIRREA). Provided $50 billion in taxpayer funds to resolve failed thrifts. Replaced Federal Home Loan Bank Board with the Office of Thrift Supervision to charter, regulate, and supervise thrifts. Restructured federal deposit insurance for thrifts and raised premiums. Reimposed restrictions on thrift lending activities. Directed the Treasury to study deposit insurance reform.
1989	Federal Reserve expanded Section 20 underwriting permissibility to corporate debt and equity securities, subject to revenue limit.
1989	Federal Reserve raised limit on revenue from Section 20–eligible securities activities from 5 percent to 10 percent.
1991	Federal Deposit Insurance Corporation Improvement Act (FDICIA). Directed the Federal Deposit Insurance Corporation (FDIC) to develop and implement risk-based deposit insurance pricing. Required "prompt corrective action" of poorly capitalized banks and thrifts and restricted "too big to fail." Directed the FDIC to resolve failed banks and thrifts in the least costly way to the deposit insurance funds.
1993	Court ruling in *Independent Insurance Agents of America v. Ludwig* allowed national banks to sell insurance from small towns.
1994	Riegle-Neal Interstate Banking and Branching Efficiency Act (Riegle-Neal). Permitted banks and bank holding companies (BHCs) to purchase banks or establish subsidiary banks in any state nationwide. Permitted national banks to open branches or convert subsidiary banks into branches across states lines.
1995	Court ruling in *NationsBank v. Valic* allowed banks to sell annuities.
1996	Court ruling in *Barnett Bank v. Nelson* overturned states' restrictions on bank insurance sales.
1996	Federal Reserve announced the elimination of many firewalls between bank and nonbank subsidiaries within BHCs.
1996	Federal Reserve raised limit on revenue from Section 20–eligible securities activities from 10 percent to 25 percent.
1997	Federal Reserve eliminated many of the remaining firewalls between bank and nonbank subsidiaries within BHCs.
1999	Gramm-Leach-Bliley Financial Modernization Act (GLB). Authorized financial holding companies (FHCs) to engage in a full range of financial services, such as commercial banking, insurance, securities, and merchant banking. Gave the Federal Reserve, in consultation with the Treasury, discretion to authorize new financial activities for FHCs. Gave the Federal Reserve discretion to authorize complementary actives for FHCs. Established the Federal Reserve as the "umbrella" regulator of FHCs. Provided low-cost credit to community banks. Reformed the Community Reinvestment Act. Eliminated the ability of commercial firms to acquire or charter a single thrift in a unitary thrift holding company.
2001	Federal Reserve issued revisions to Regulation K. Expanded permissible activities abroad for U.S. banking organizations. Reduced regulatory burden for U.S. banks operating abroad and streamlined the application and notice process for foreign banks operating in the United States. Allowed banks to invest up to 20 percent of capital and surplus in edge corporations. Liberalized provisions regarding the qualification of foreign organizations for exemptions from the nonbanking prohibitions of Section 4 of the Bank Holding Company Act. Implemented provisions of Riegle-Neal that affect foreign banks.

Sources: Lown et al. (2000), Kroszner and Strahan (2000), and Montgomery (2003).

Over time, these legislative and other deregulatory efforts gradually (albeit haltingly) loosened the constraints on the industry, thus freeing it to cope more effectively with both the new environmental challenges and the heightened competition that resulted. In two areas—banking activities and branching—legislative and regulatory efforts were particularly important for the consolidation trend: Restrictions on permissible banking activities were relaxed, and geographic limitations on branching were removed. The importance of these two efforts is perhaps best illustrated by the spate of interstate mergers that occurred immediately after passage of the Riegle-Neal Interstate Banking and Branching Efficiency Act of 1994 (Figure 8). Although some researchers have argued that much of the merger activity associated with the deregulatory process reflected only pent-up demand that had long been accumulating because of other causal factors, there can be no doubt about the influence of deregulation on the merger wave as it unfolded in the United States: If deregulation in and of itself was not a primary causal factor, it was certainly an essential enabling factor.[17]

2.1.3. Macroeconomic Events

In the 1970s—even before deregulation and before the full effects of the revolution in ITC technologies had been felt—a series of macroeconomic shocks combined with

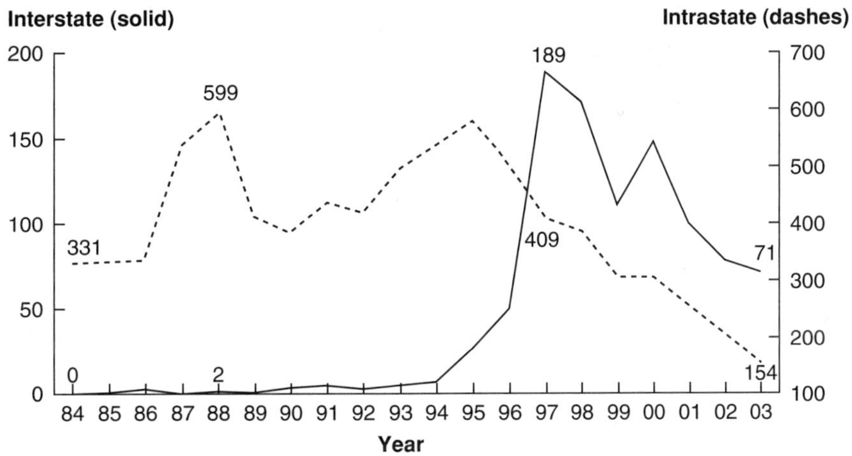

FIGURE 8 Number of commercial bank charter mergers interstate and intrastate, 1984–2003.

[17] As mentioned, the Riegle-Neal Act (along with regional interstate compacts that repealed interstate branching restrictions) had a significant effect on bank merger activity and industry consolidation. In contrast, the latest legislative initiative aimed at modernizing the financial services industry—the Gramm-Leach-Bliley Act of 1999 (GLB)—has not had a similar effect. As explained by Rhoades (2000), GLB provides for cross-industry mergers between banks, securities firms, and insurance companies. However, such combinations are likely to be considered by only the largest banking organizations. Moreover, by definition, the combination of a banking firm and another type of financial services provider does not result in the loss of a bank charter. Hence, the combination will have no effect on the number of banking organizations.

the twin forces of globalization and technology to alter dramatically the economic environment within which banks operated. Indeed, the decade of the 1970s saw the introduction of floating exchange rates, increased volatility in interest rates, oil price shocks, stagflation, and unexpected changes in other real economic and financial variables. These economic conditions, and governmental responses to them, began putting stress on the environment in which banks and thrifts had successfully operated, unchanged, for many decades.

In the early 1980s these stresses were intensified by double-digit inflation and then by the anti-inflationary monetary policies designed to combat it. By mid-decade, wild swings in interest rates, combined with sharp declines in oil and gas prices and in the value of real estate, precipitated a series of rolling regional recessions that wreaked havoc on the nation's S&L and banking industries. The number of failures soared, soon reaching (and then far exceeding) levels that had not been seen since the Great Depression. But as bank failures rose to record levels, so did bank mergers and acquisitions: Federal regulators responded to the growing number of weak and failing depository institutions and shrinking insurance-fund balances by loosening their restrictions on mergers. The FDIC even provided financial support to encourage better-capitalized and profitable banking organizations to acquire weakened or insolvent institutions. As a result, during the 1980s the consolidation movement was particularly strong.

The consolidation of the banking industry continued into, and then through, the 1990s, but it is important to note that the forces driving the trend in the 1990s differed markedly from the forces driving it in the 1980s. Indeed, in many respects the 1980s and the 1990s were the worst of times and the best of times (respectively) for the banking industry. Banks in the 1980s were struggling under harshly unfavorable economic conditions and outdated legislative and regulatory constraints. Many banks and S&Ls were unprofitable. Many failed. In contrast, the middle to late 1990s saw a convergence of several factors that created an environment extremely conducive to merger activity. First, unlike the 1980s, the middle to late 1990s were a period when banks were highly profitable, flush with cash, and reveling in favorable economic and interest-rate environments. In fact, bank performance from 1993 through the end of the decade (and beyond) would set multiple records for profitability (Figures 9 and 10). Second, Riegle-Neal's removal of barriers to interstate banking and branching provided opportunities for many organizations to consolidate operations and pursue geographic diversification through acquisitions. Third, a record-breaking bull market in stocks pushed market valuations of banks and thrifts to unprecedented levels, encouraging many banking firms to use their stock as currency to purchase the hard assets of other banking firms (Figure 11). This was especially the case when managers believed their firms' own stocks were "favorably" priced. Conversely, managers of firms wishing to be acquired were able to maximize firm value by selling out at record market-to-book valuations. While these conditions persisted, consolidation continued at a relatively rapid pace, although it was partially offset by a rise in the number of new bank start-ups.

At the end of the decade, however, several events appeared to have had a markedly dampening effect on bank merger activity and on the pace of industry consolidation.

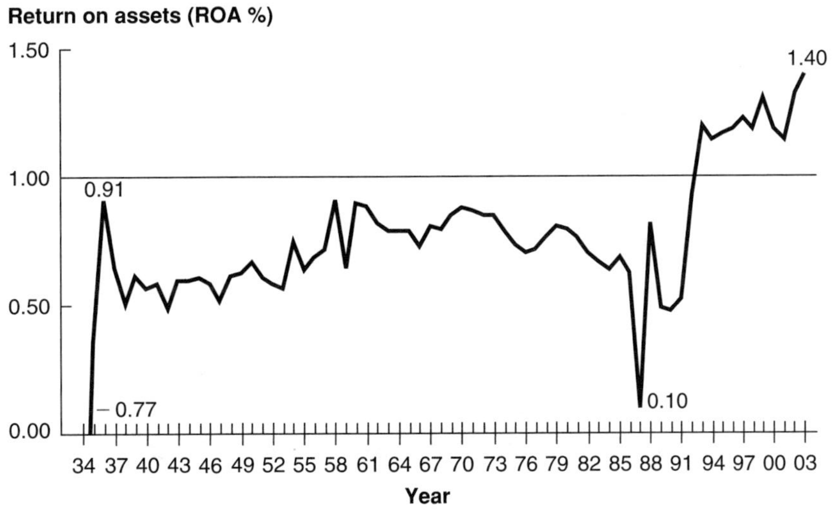

FIGURE 9 Return on assets (percent), commercial banks, 1934–2003.

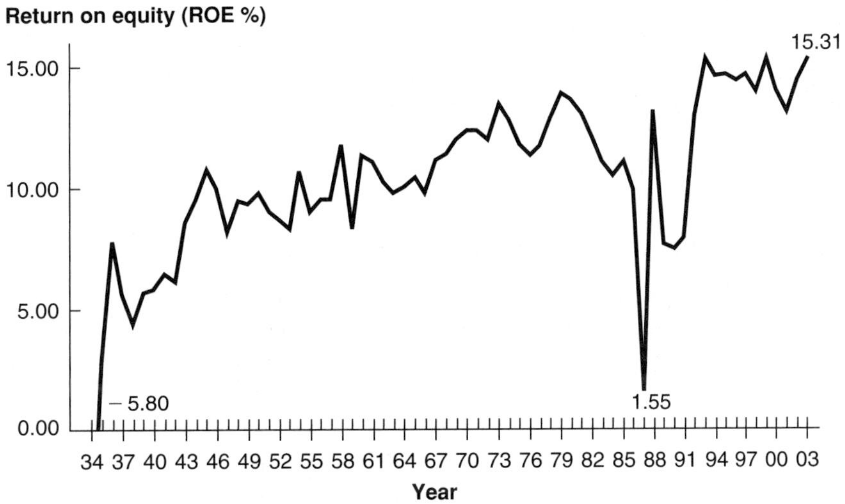

FIGURE 10 Return on equity (percent), commercial banks, 1934–2003.

First, Y2K-related concerns might have caused some merger plans to be postponed until after the beginning of the new millennium. Then, in March 2000, the record run-up in stock prices reversed itself.[18] A year later (in March 2001) the U.S. economy entered a mild recession. Coincident with these adverse economic developments, a significant

[18]For the next several years, all the major stock indexes would fall dramatically; from March 2000 to March 2003, for example, the S&P 500 benchmark fell a cumulative 43 percent.

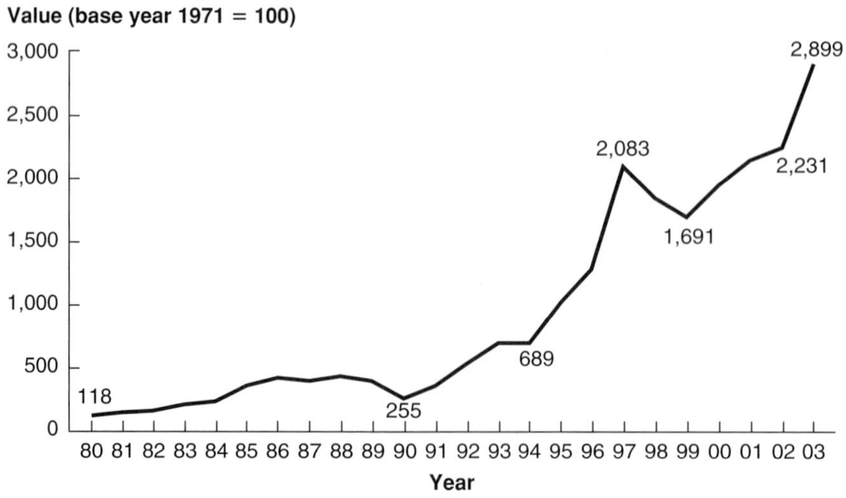

FIGURE 11 Nasdaq bank stock index, 1980–2003.

accounting change in the way mergers were recorded served to discourage stock-funded bank merger transactions.[19] Finally, the terrorist attacks on the World Trade Center and the Pentagon on September 11, 2001, and the subsequent wars in Afghanistan and Iraq adversely affected the broader economic and business environments. Nevertheless, consolidation in the banking industry continued into the twenty-first century, though at a much slower rate.

2.2. Microeconomic Factors in Merger Decisions

As we have just seen, at the macroeconomic level consolidation has been influenced by technology, deregulation, macroeconomic events, and other environmental factors. But it is the microeconomic factors that, in the aggregate, are largely responsible for the consolidation trend. These factors are the individual decisions by banking firms to pursue a merger or acquisition strategy. From a microeconomic perspective, a bank's decision to consolidate charters—to merge with or acquire another firm—should reflect management's chosen strategy for maximizing or preserving firm value in the face of increased competitive pressure stemming from a more market-oriented environment. For example, a merger strategy can be based on value-maximizing motives, such as achieving economies of scale and scope or reducing risk or increasing profits through

[19]Financial Accounting Standards Rule 141 (FAS 141) terminated the use of pooling-of-interest accounting for business combinations after 2001 and required that purchase accounting methodology be used instead. Purchase accounting requires a firm to record goodwill if the market value of net assets acquired is less than the purchase price. Historically goodwill was amortized regularly, but now (under FAS 142) companies must test goodwill (and other intangibles) for impairment once each fiscal year. A finding of impairment may require additional noninterest-expense recognition.

geographic and product diversification. Indeed, in a recent survey of bank management, value-maximizing motives were most often cited as the principal reason to undertake a merger.[20]

A firm's decision to merge, however, may also be influenced by motives that do not necessarily maximize the firm's value. Adverse changes in a bank's competitive environment may compel a banking firm to undertake an acquisition as part of a purely defensive strategy, or merger decisions may be based wholly or partly on the self-serving motives of managers. (Bliss and Rosen 2001 and Ryan 1999, for example, suggest that empire building and increased managerial compensation might be the primary motive behind some bank mergers.) Another motive—suggested by Shull and Hanweck (2001), Penas and Unal (2004), and others—is a desire to obtain "too-big-to-fail" status and the funding and other competitive advantages that seem to accrue to the largest and most complex banking organizations.

Just as economic and regulatory conditions in the 1980s differed significantly from those in the 1990s, some economists have suggested that the motivations behind bank mergers in the 1980s were different from the motivations behind the mergers of the 1990s. Berger (1998, p. 106) observes that

> Consistent with a change in merger motives, many of the merger participants in the 1980s focused on expanding their geographic bases to gain strategic long-run advantage by getting footholds in new locations, rather than on reducing costs or raising profits in the short run. Merger participants in the 1990s appear to be more focused on cutting costs quickly through mergers—for example, they often announce goals for employee layoffs, branch closings, and total cost savings in advance of mergers.

It may well be that merger motives have changed over time. Additional research will undoubtedly help us better understand if this is so.

3. THE EFFECTS OF CONSOLIDATION

Perhaps more important than knowing why consolidation has occurred in the U.S. banking industry is understanding what its effects have been on the banking industry, its shareholders, and the customers served. In theory, globalization, technology, and deregulation should have resulted in a significant increase in competition. Increased competition, in turn, should drive value-maximizing managers to seek greater efficiencies through consolidation. In other words, if profit-oriented managers think that there are economies of scale or scope to be gained or that opportunities exist to replace inefficient managers at other firms or to enhance profitability by servicing customers better, a competitive environment will encourage these managers to seek such economies or opportunities. Of course, the question of consolidation trend has made the banking

[20] Group of Ten (2001).

industry more efficient or a better provider of services to the banking public is an empirical one.

Fortunately, the effects of consolidation have been a particularly active area of empirical research for more than a decade, and a consensus is beginning to form. Table 3 gives a synopsis of these general findings.

TABLE 3 Summary of Recent Empirical Studies on the Causes of Consolidation in the Banking Industry

Empirical finding	Study reference	Summary
Some evidence of increase in market power (share) with some evidence of price effects in concentrated market	Shull and Hanweck (2001), Berger, Demsetz, and Strahan (1999)	Surveyed the literature and found evidence of market power effects (with higher loan rates and lower deposit rates in concentrated markets) in the 1980s. Data for the 1990s, however, suggested a weaker relationship between local market concentration and deposit rates.
	Pilloff (1999)	Found that banks in more concentrated markets earned higher profits and that the number of multimarket contacts was positively related to profitability, suggesting that multimarket contact may reduce competition.
	Prager and Hannan (1998)	Found that a reduction in interest rates on local deposit accounts was associated with horizontal mergers that raised market concentration significantly.
	Simons and Stavins (1998)	Using data for the period 1986–1994, found that after a bank's participation in a merger, a 1.0 percent higher HHI was associated with a 1.2 percent reduction in interest rates on MMDA, a 0.3 percent lower rate on CDs, and lower rates on deposit accounts across the board.
	Moore and Siems (1998)	Found that the relationship between concentration and profitability was much weaker in 1997 than it had been a decade earlier.
	Berger and Hannan (1997)	Found that banks in more concentrated markets charged higher rates on small business loans and paid lower rates on retail deposits.
Some evidence of greater profit efficiencies	Berger (1998), Akhavein, Berger, and Humphrey (1997)	Found that mergers led to an improvement in profit efficiency. The improvement seemed to result from an increase in lending activity (as opposed to security investments) and a more efficient use of capital.
	Boyd and Graham (1998)	Found that being merged "helped" small banks, increasing ROA and decreasing expense measures.

TABLE 3 *Continued*

Empirical finding	Study reference	Summary
Some evidence of improvements from geographic diversity	Group of Ten (2001)	Reviewed the latest research, which suggested that because of geographic diversification, consolidation of banks within the United States was likely to lead to reductions in risk. However, the studies also noted that these positive benefits might be offset by shifts to higher-risk portfolios or by operational risks.
	Berger and DeYoung (2001)	Found that the negative effects of distance tended to be modest in size. This finding suggests that efficient organizations can successfully export their superior skills, policies, and practices to their out-of-state affiliates.
	Hughes et al. (1996, 1999)	Found that when organizations diversified geographically, especially via interstate banking, efficiency tended to be higher and insolvency risk tended to be lower.
Some evidence of improvements in payment system efficiency	Hancock, Humphrey, and Wilcox (1999)	Found substantial scale economies in Fedwire operations and an improvement in cost efficiency of Fedwire from consolidation of processing sites. Suggested results were likely to carry over to consolidation of private-sector processors.
	Adams, Bauer, and Sickles (2002)	Found indications of significant and positive scale economies in the provision of electronic payment processing services by the Federal Reserve (Fedwire, ACH, and Book-Entry securities). Results also showed that during the 1990s, technological change lowered marginal costs significantly.
Some evidence that management may act in self-interest	Hughes et al. (2003)	Found evidence that managerial entrenchment at U.S. bank holding companies was associated with asset sales that yielded smaller improvements and with acquisitions that resulted in worse performance. Suggested that these results were consistent with empire-building strategies that sacrificed value.
	Bliss and Rosen (2001), Gorton and Rosen (1995)	Argued that two primary motives for bank mergers were empire building and increased managerial compensation, especially on the part of managers who were entrenched or insulated from the market.

(*Continued*)

TABLE 3 *Continued*

Empirical finding	Study reference	Summary
	Hadlock, Houston, and Ryngaert (1999)	Found that banks with higher levels of management ownership were less likely to be acquired; argued that this evidence was consistent with an entrenchment hypothesis, which holds that management teams with significant ownership positions block attempts to be acquired at reasonable prices.
Some support for the too-big-to-fail motive	Shull and Hanweck (2001)	Found that the top 10 largest banks paid less for funds than smaller banks and operated with lower capitalization rates.
	Penas and Unal (2004)	Showed that positive bond returns and a decline in credit spreads were related to the incremental size attained in bank mergers by medium-sized banks, those most likely to become large enough to be considered too big to fail.
	Kane (2000)	Showed that in banking megamergers of 1991–98, stockholders of large-bank acquirers gained value when a target institution was large. Argued that the effect of size underscored the possibility that too-big-to-discipline subsidies had distorted deal-making incentives for megabanks.
Some potential for increased systemic risk and safety net expansion	De Nicola and Kwast (2002)	Showed that, among large complex banking organizations during the 1990s, there was a significant upward trend in the degree of interdependency.
	Group of Ten (2001)	Concluded that there were reasons to believe that financial consolidation in the United States had increased the risk that the failure of a large, complex banking organization would be disorderly.
	Saunders and Wilson (1999)	Found a dramatic reduction in bank capital ratios associated with increased safety-net support; also found that the structure and strength of safety-net guarantees might affect risk taking.
BUT—Mixed evidence on cost efficiencies from scale economies	Stiroh (2000)	Examined the improved performance of U.S. BHCs from 1991 to 1997 and found that the gains were due primarily to productivity growth and changes in scale economies. Estimated cost functions showed modest economies of scale present throughout the period, with the largest BHCs showing stronger economies of scale.

TABLE 3 *Continued*

Empirical finding	Study reference	Summary
	Hughes, Mester, and Moon (2001), Hughes et al. (1999), Hughes and Mester (1998)	Claimed to have found evidence of large-scale economies once risk diversification, capital structure, and endogenous risk taking were explicitly considered in the analyses of production.
	Berger, Demsetz, and Strahan (1999)	Extensively reviewed the literature on cost efficiency and found, on the basis of data from the 1980s and early 1990s, little efficiency improvement from mergers and acquisitions. However, cost efficiency effects might depend on the type of merger, the motivations of the managers, and the implementation of the merger.
	Kwan and Wilcox (1999)	Found significant (but still relatively small) expense savings in mergers that occurred in the mid-1990s, after the pure accounting effects on reported expense data were removed.
	Boyd and Graham (1998)	Examined the effects of mergers and found evidence of cost-efficiency gains for only the smallest banks. The gains disappeared quickly with increases in size and were negative for larger banks.
	Peristiani (1997)	Found that acquiring banks in the 1980s achieved moderate improvements in scale efficiency, attributable in part to the fact that the smaller target banks were on average less scale efficient than their acquirers.
Mixed evidence on cost efficiencies from scope economies	Stiroh (2004)	Examined the link between the banking industry's growing reliance on noninterest income and the volatility of bank revenue and profits. Found almost no evidence that this shift offers large diversification benefits in the form of more stable profits or revenue.
	Amel et al. (2002)	In reviewing the literature, found little evidence that mergers yielded significant economies of scope.
	DeLong (2001)	Found that mergers that focused banks geographically and among product types created value, whereas those that diversified generally failed to benefit shareholders.
	Demsetz and Strahan (1997)	Showed that large bank holding companies had better diversification across loan portfolios; it allowed them to operate with greater leverage and engage in more risky (and potentially more profitable) lending without increasing firm-specific risk.

(*Continued*)

TABLE 3 *Continued*

Empirical finding	Study reference	Summary
	Kwan (1998)	Found that securities subsidiaries provided BHCs in the United States with potential benefits of diversification because revenues from the subsidiaries were not highly correlated with revenues from the rest of the BHC.
	Berger, Humphrey, and Pulley (1996)	Found no evidence of statistically significant revenue economies (and only small cost economies) of scope among either small or large banks over the period 1978–1990, even for the most efficient banks.
Little evidence of any significant, permanent increase in shareholder value	Calomiris and Karceski (1998), Pilloff and Santomero (1998)	Reviewed the literature and concluded that although some event studies found that acquirers increased their market value, most studies found that the market value of the acquiring bank declined, whereas that of the target bank increased.
	Houston, James, and Ryngaert (2000)	Found (like previous studies) that the market value of the acquiring bank declined, on average, whereas that of the target bank increased. However, compared with the 1980s, the 1990s were a period of higher average abnormal returns for both bidders and targets. Results also suggested that the realization of anticipated cost savings was the primary source of gains in the majority of recent bank mergers.
	Cornett et al. (2003)	Found that diversifying bank acquisitions earn significantly negative announcement-period abnormal returns for bidder banks, whereas focusing acquisitions earn zero abnormal returns.
Little evidence of lower consumer prices	Shull and Hanweck (2001)	After reviewing prices for retail banking services over the last decade, found no evidence that retail prices had declined. In fact, the evidence suggested the opposite—that consumer prices had increased.
	Kahn, Pennachi, Sopranzetti (2000)	Found that mergers appeared to increase rates on unsecured personal loans charged by all banks in the market in which the merger had taken place. This was consistent with an increase in market power in the market for personal loans. However, the opposite effect was observed for rates on automobile loans.

TABLE 3 *Continued*

Empirical finding	Study reference	Summary
	Prager and Hannan (1998)	Found a reduction in deposit rates attributable to substantial horizontal mergers (mergers between banks competing in the same geographic markets).
Little effect on the availability of services to consumers	Avery et al. (1999)	Found that mergers of banks with branches in the same zip code reduced the number of branches per capita, whereas other mergers had little effect on branch office availability.
	DeYoung, Hasan, and Kirchhoff (1998)	Found that small business lending declined as banks aged and increased in size. But an increase in market concentration was found to have a positive effect on small business lending in urban markets and only a modest negative effect in rural markets.
	Jayaratne and Wolken (1999)	Found (using survey data on small business borrowers) that the probability that a small firm would have a line of credit from a bank did not decrease in the long run when there were fewer small banks in the area.
	Peek and Rosengren (1996, 1998), Strahan and Weston (1996, 1998), Berger, Kashyap, and Scalise (1995)	Found that large banking organizations generally devoted smaller proportions of their assets to small business loans and that mergers between large and small banks resulted in a decrease in small business lending. Mergers between smaller banks, however, did not appear to reduce small business lending.
	Cole, Goldberg, and White (2004)	Found that large banks tended to base their small business loan decisions more on financial ratios than on prior lender–borrower relationships. In contrast, small banks relied to a greater extent on the character of the borrower.

However, we should first note that researchers have faced substantial econometric difficulties in their attempts to test for efficiency and other potential gains from consolidation. Pilloff and Santomero (1998) and Calomiris and Karceski (1998), in particular, have enumerated several methodological pitfalls that make it hard to assess the effects of consolidation accurately. Among the pitfalls are these: (1) Because of increased competition, efficiency gains from mergers might not be reflected in net earnings; (2) lags in performance improvement may be extensive (three to five years), especially for mergers motivated by strategic goals such as diversification rather than by a desire to cut costs; (3) constructing a believable benchmark (for purposes of comparison) in the midst of a merger wave may be difficult; and (4) controlling for multiple causal and motivational factors over time and across mergers may be difficult. In addition to these methodological difficulties, there is likely to be a problem reconciling the findings of studies based on 1980s' data with the findings of studies that use 1990s' data. Furthermore, as our chronological account indicates, the causal factors (and probably the motivations) driving mergers in the 1990s' were very different from those driving mergers in the 1980s. With these qualifications in mind, we now briefly summarize the existing evidence about the effects of consolidation.

On the positive side, findings to date suggest that consolidation has resulted in somewhat greater profit efficiency (profit efficiency measures how close a bank is to earning the maximum profits that a best-practice bank would earn under the same circumstances).[21] According to Berger (1998), profit efficiency is enhanced by mergers because the combined firms generally achieve greater diversification of their risk exposures through a better mix of geographic areas, industries, loan types, and maturity structures. In turn, improved diversification might allow the combined banking organization to undertake a portfolio shift from security investments into consumer and business loans—activities with higher expected values. Hence, profit efficiency would be greater with consolidation because capital is put to better use and because greater geographic diversification tends to reduce risk.[22]

Findings to date also suggest somewhat greater payment-system efficiency (see Hancock, Humphrey, and Wilcox 1999, Adams, Bauer, and Sickles 2002) and, for institutions that have increased their geographic diversification, possibly a lower risk of insolvency (Group of Ten 2001, Berger and DeYoung 2001). Finally, a potential negative effect of the reduced number of banking organizations has been avoided: Access to banking services (including lending to small businesses) seems to have been relatively unaffected (see, for example, Avery et al. 1999, DeYoung, Hasan, and Kirchhoff 1998, Jayaratne and Wolken 1999).

On the other hand, most researchers—especially those focusing on the 1980s and early 1990s—have not been able to identify any of the broad-based improvements in cost efficiency that one might have expected from economies of scale or scope.[23] Given that managers most often cite gains from increased cost efficiency as the primary motivation for strategic consolidations, this finding (or the lack thereof) represents a fairly substantial puzzle. Some researchers have tried to explain away the lack of support for economies of scale by citing measurement and econometric difficulties and a time horizon too short for making observations. And, in fact, a few more recent studies that claim to have overcome some of these obstacles have reported results suggesting that scale-related efficiency gains in the 1990s have been substantial (Hughes, Mester, and Moon 2001, Hughes, Lang, Mester, and Moon 1999, among others). Additional investigations into gains in efficiency will undoubtedly help solve this puzzle.

[21]Berger's (1998) concept of profit efficiency includes not only the cost-efficiency effects of mergers and acquisitions but also the revenue effects of changes in output that occur after a merger.

[22]For additional evidence on increased profit efficiencies, see Akhavein, Berger, and Humphrey (1997) and Boyd and Graham (1998).

[23]A number of studies have found little or no evidence of scale economies. These include Stiroh (2000) and Berger, Demsetz, and Strahan (1999). Additional studies with similar findings are listed in Table 3. For the findings on scope economies, see Stiroh (2004), Amel et al. (2002), DeLong (2001), and Demsetz and Strahan (1997), among others.

In addition to lacking consensus on cost-efficiency gains, empirical work to date has failed to find substantive evidence of other benefits that one might hope consolidation would yield. For example, there is little evidence that either consumers or shareholders have benefited from consolidation in the industry (Shull and Hanweck 2001, Kahn, Pennachi, and Spranzetti 2000, Prager and Hannan 1998). Rather, there is growing evidence that increases in market power at the local level may be adversely affecting consumer prices (for both depositors and borrowers).[24] And as we mention earlier, there is also some evidence that managers may be pursuing mergers and acquisitions for reasons other than maximizing firm value: Researchers who have studied the issue have consistently found support for the idea that empire building and increased managerial compensation are often primary motives behind bank mergers.[25] Finally, findings from several researchers suggest that industry consolidation and the emergence of large, complex banking organizations have probably increased systemic risk in the banking system and exacerbated the too-big-to-fail problem in banking.[26]

Thus, despite the many empirical studies of consolidation in the U.S. banking industry, much uncertainty remains not only about the importance of the various factors behind the merger trend but also about the effects of consolidation on bank shareholders and on those who use banking services. Before we can fully understand either the causes of consolidation or all of its ramifications, more work needs to be done.

4. PROJECTIONS OF BANKING INDUSTRY STRUCTURE

Because banks play an important role in the U.S. financial system, changes in the industry's structure are likely to have widespread effects. Hence, for planning purposes it would be useful if structural changes could be anticipated before they occurred.

4.1. Review of Previous Projections and Their Methodologies

Of the studies that have documented and discussed the decline in the number of banks, several—including Hannan and Rhoades (1992), Nolle (1995), Berger, Kashyap, and Scalise (1995), and Robertson (2001)—have also projected the future size and structure of the banking industry. Most of these projections are based on linear extrapolations from past trends. Although these studies all use somewhat different approaches, they all predicted a sharp decline in the number of commercial banking organizations through the decade of the 1990s and beyond.[27]

In the earliest of these papers, Hannan and Rhoades (1992) approached the task of projecting the future U.S. commercial banking structure by assuming that the national trend would follow past responses to the relaxation of interstate banking regulations

[24]See Shull and Hanweck (2001) and Berger, Demsetz, and Strahan (1999), among others.

[25]See, for example, Hughes et al. (2003), Bliss and Rosen (2001), and Gorton and Rosen (1995).

[26]Support for the too-big-to-fail motive is found in Shull and Hanweck (2001), Penas and Unal (2004), and Kane (2000). Studies on systemic risk include De Nicola and Kwast (2002) and Saunders and Wilson (1999).

[27]To the best of our knowledge, all previous studies excluded thrift organizations and projected only the numbers of commercial banking organizations or institutions.

at the regional level. Accordingly, the authors examined more closely the structural transition to interstate branching experienced by the Southeast and New England over the period 1980–1989.[28] The authors approximated linear trends for each region by calculating an average annual rate of change in the number of commercial banking organizations for the period studied (and for the subperiod 1984–1989). They then assumed that the number of commercial banking organizations in the nation starting in 1989 would change at the rate that had been observed in the two regions. This method projected the number of commercial banking organizations in the United States to be in the range of 5,000 to 6,000 by the year 2010 (depending on the region and period used). For comparative purposes, the authors also based projections on extrapolations from national trends. This resulted in a projection of just over 5,000 commercial banking organizations by 2010.

In addition to extrapolating from regional and national trends, the authors extrapolated from the banking structure observed in the state of California, where intrastate branching had been allowed since 1908. The commercial banking structure in California, they reasoned, would represent a sort of equilibrium case, since the structure there had evolved in the absence of branching restrictions over a long period of time. In this extrapolation, the authors assumed that once all geographic restrictions on branching were lifted, the ratio of commercial banking organizations to bank deposits nationwide would approach the ratio already observed in California. Projections to 2010 based on this approach varied, depending on the period used to formulate the trend. However, according to the authors, the most realistic projection indicated that the U.S. banking industry would eventually shrink to about 3,500 commercial banking organizations.[29]

Given the range of predictions yielded by the different cases, Hannan and Rhoades eventually offered a "best-guess" projection for the year 2010 of 5,500 commercial banking organizations. Regardless of methodology, however, all extrapolations suggested that, even with a continuation of the decline, the long-run equilibrium banking structure in the United States would probably consist of a very large number of banking organizations.

Nolle's 1995 paper likewise attempted to simulate the possible effects on the U.S. banking structure of liberalizing interstate branching restrictions. Using data on the state-by-state pattern of mergers, failures, and entries over the seven-year period 1987–1993, Nolle mechanically projected the number of commercial banks (individually chartered institutions) through the end of the year 2000. He considered two scenarios: an extrapolation from past trends under the assumption that legislation allowing nationwide interstate branching would not be enacted, and a judgmental adjustment of the first

[28]Nolle (1995) reports that by 1984 most of the six New England states had established reciprocal arrangements allowing bank holding companies to own (typically through acquisition) banking subsidiaries in another New England state; by 1987 all six states were participating in these arrangements. Similarly, by 1985 most of the states in the southeastern region of the country had accepted reciprocal arrangements, and by 1988 all of them had.

[29]Extrapolations from the 1980–1989 period actually predicted a slight increase in the number of commercial banking organizations nationwide. The estimate of 3,500 organizations is based on the trend from 1984 to 1989.

scenario assuming that interstate branching legislation would be passed in 1994 and fully enacted by midyear 1997 (this latter scenario proved to be historically accurate).[30] Results from the first scenario (the no-interstate-branching case) indicated a decrease of just under 2,100 banks (to 8,798 institutions) during the period 1994–2000—a decrease equal to about two-thirds of the amount of consolidation observed over the 1987–1993 period. The second extrapolation (the interstate-branching case) suggested that the total additional effect on consolidation of interstate branching would be an additional decline of about 1,000 banks (resulting in an industry total of 7,787 commercial banks in the year 2000). Given these results, Nolle concluded that interstate branching would not fundamentally alter the structure of the nation's commercial banking industry; that is, there would still be thousands of commercial banks and thousands of bank holding companies in existence at the turn of the millennium.

A conclusion similar to those reached by Hannan and Rhoades (1992) and Nolle (1995) was reached by Berger, Kashyap, and Scalise (BKS, 1995) as well, but they used a much more complex methodology. To quantify the possible effects of the removal of all state and federal restrictions on interstate branch banking, BKS constructed an econometric model to explain the distribution of domestic commercial bank assets across organization size classes on a state-by-state basis. In their model, the proportion of banking assets in each size class was assumed to be a function of state demographic variables as well as of a number of independent variables that had been designed to capture differences in the existence and the lifting of regulatory restrictions on statewide and interstate branching as well as on multibank holding company acquisitions.

Using the regressions, BKS then simulated the effects of nationwide interstate banking for 5 years, 10 years, 25 years, and the long term, under two scenarios: first, assuming zero growth of gross domestic banking assets; second, assuming asset growth at the national trend rate over the sample period (1979–1994). For each scenario the authors assumed that nationwide banking occurred immediately (in 1994); they therefore removed all variation among the explanatory variables related to the liberalization of geographic restrictions, except for variables capturing time-since-liberalization effects. These time-effect variables were adjusted for the number of years to be projected in the simulation. The changes in the predicted proportions for each size class for each state were then added to the actual proportions in 1994 to obtain the future value. The predicted shares of domestic banking assets for each size class were then aggregated across the 50 states to obtain a weighted average proportion of assets in each size class at the national level. Finally, BKS obtained an estimate of the number of commercial banking organizations in each size class by dividing the projected total dollar value of assets in each size class by the average size of organizations in that size class in 1994.

Results from the zero-growth simulations indicated that "the removal of all geographic barriers to nationwide banking was likely to result in continued substantial

[30]For his interstate branching scenario, Nolle assumed that no states would choose to opt out of interstate banking or branching provisions; that all multistate, multibank holding companies (MSMBHCs) in existence at midyear 1993 would still be in existence at midyear 1997, when interstate branching was assumed to be fully in effect; and that as a group these MSMBHCs would "branch up" 75 percent of their out-of-home-state subsidiary banks by year-end 2000.

consolidation of the banking industry."[31] Specifically, in this scenario the model predicted that the number of commercial banking organizations would fall by almost 4,000 by 1999, from a total of 7,926 to 4,106—a decline of almost 50 percent over five years. Surprisingly, little change was predicted to occur after 1999. When gross domestic assets were allowed to grow at trend rates, the predicted increase in consolidation in the first five years due to enactment of interstate branching was even greater: The number of commercial banking organizations falls to 3,440. In contrast to the zero-growth simulation—which predicted little consolidation after the first five years—the growth simulation projected the number of organizations as continuing to fall. Under this scenario the number of banking organizations falls to 1,939 in 25 years—a decline of 76 percent from 1994 levels. Notwithstanding these reductions, BKS's simulations still predicted that the banking structure in the United States would be characterized by thousands of small banking organizations. This finding was consistent with the findings of Hannan and Rhoades (1992) and Nolle (1995).

Finally, Robertson (2001) projected the number of commercial banking organizations in each size class by first calculating a transition matrix that indicated the probability that a bank would remain in the same size class from one year to the next, move to a new size class, or leave the industry altogether. After confirming matrix stability, he then applied the transition probabilities from the 1994–2000 transition matrix to the year-end 2000 numbers to obtain estimates for the industry's future size distribution. On the basis of this methodology, Robertson predicted that the number of commercial banking organizations would continue to decline—from 6,750 in 2000 to 4,567 in 2007, for a 32 percent reduction. Like the projections of earlier studies, Robertson's suggested that the number of smaller banking organizations would continue to fall steadily. Indeed, Robertson's simulation predicted that the number of banking organizations with less than $100 million in real assets would decline by nearly 40 percent over the seven-year period he was forecasting.

4.2. New Linear Extrapolations: A Comparison with the Literature

On the basis of earlier studies, then, it seems that we can expect to see further declines in the number of banking organizations, especially in the community banking sector (where the number of organizations with less than $100 million in assets is expected to continue to fall dramatically). Some of the aforementioned projections, however, are based on data that are more than a decade old. We showed earlier that the decline in the number of banking organizations, while ongoing, has slowed appreciably in the last few years. This slowing should have important implications for expectations about the future structure of the banking industry. Consequently, we have formulated new projections of industry structure based on the latest observed trends.

As a starting point, we adhered to the linear approach to project the number of banking organizations in each of five size classes through the year 2013. Our projections are based on the average quarterly net change over the five-year period 1999–2003.

[31] Berger, Kashyap, and Scalise (1995, p. 113).

We chose to focus on only the last five years of data because we believe that the change occurring over this period better reflects the mix of forces affecting the banking industry at the turn of the millennium and that this period is therefore most relevant to anticipating the future direction of the industry's structure. To make our projections comparable with those of earlier studies, we projected both the number of commercial bank organizations and the number of commercial bank and thrift organizations combined. Table 4 presents our five- and ten-year projections. As can be seen in panel A, our linear extrapolations suggest a continuing decline (of 34 organizations per quarter) in the total number of banking and thrift organizations—from 7,842 at year-end 2003 to 7,161 at year-end 2008 and to 6,480 at the end of 2013. The projected decline over five years is 681 organizations (8.7 percent); over ten years, twice that. Projections for commercial bank organizations alone (panel B) show a similar pattern. Interestingly, projections for both groups indicate that the decline will occur exclusively within the smallest size group (organizations with less than $100 million in assets). Our extrapolations from the trends of the past five years indicate that all other size groups will grow by small amounts.

For comparison, Figure 12 contrasts our linear projections for the number of commercial bank organizations with those from earlier studies. Remarkably, Hannan and Rhoades' (1992) "best-guess" 20-year projection for the number of commercial bank organizations in 2010 is not that much different from our own—their 5,500 compared with our 5,847. The projections by BKS (1995) and Robertson (2001), however, suggest significantly more of a decline among commercial bank organizations than is indicated by our linear extrapolation from the data for the last five years.

TABLE 4 Projected Number of Banking Organizations, 2003–2013 (By GDP-deflated asset class)

Number of organizations	Assets < $100M	$100M ≤ assets < $500M	$500M ≤ assets < $1B	$1B ≤ assets < $10B	Assets ≥ $10B	Total
		Panel A. Commercial Banks and Thrifts Combined				
5-year average quarterly change	−50.55	7.85	5.15	2.50	1.00	−34.05
2003	3,683	3,172	481	411	95	7,842
2008	2,672	3,329	584	461	115	7,161
2013	1,661	3,486	687	511	135	6,480
		Panel B. Commercial Bank Organizations Only				
5-year average quarterly change	−43.40	13.50	3.90	2.70	0.60	−22.70
2003	3,219	2,568	335	290	71	6,483
2008	2,351	2,838	413	344	83	6,029
2013	1,483	3,108	491	398	95	5,575

Note: Linear projections based on 5-year average quarterly change (1999–2003).

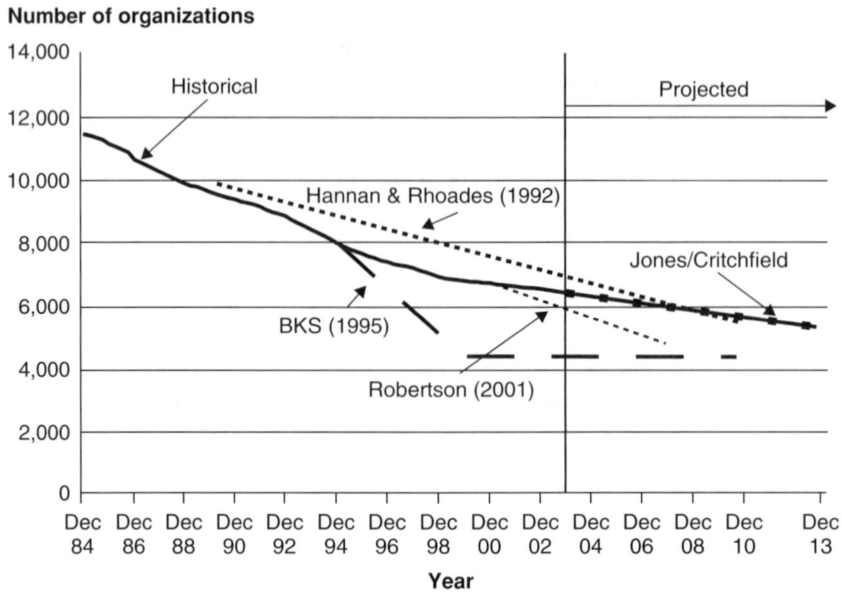

FIGURE 12 Comparison of projections for the commercial bank organizations, 1984–2013.

4.3. Beyond Linear Extrapolations

Although linear extrapolations like those just described provide a simple means of projecting industry structure, Shull and Hanweck (2001) have argued that projections based on simple linear extrapolations of past trends are inadequate because they fail to specify the process generating the structural change. We tend to agree. Although we used the linear approach for illustrative purposes, we believe this approach is somewhat naive because it fails to incorporate all the information contained in the data. Most importantly, it ignores the changing nature of the forces behind the decline in the number of organizations. Consequently, for reasons that will soon become clear, we view our linear projections as representing the lower bound of our estimates of the future size of the banking industry.

To improve on the simple linear extrapolations presented earlier, what is needed is a forecasting methodology that can capture the underlying features of the full time series on banking structure. An extremely general econometric model that promises to do this in a simple and expeditious manner is the autoregressive integrated moving-average time-series model (ARIMA). First developed by Box and Jenkins (1976), this approach to modeling the processes that generate a time series of data has "withstood the test of time and experimentation as a reasonable approach for describing underlying processes that are probably, in truth, impenetrably complex."[32] In simple descriptive terms, this class of models either regresses a time series on its own past values or uses a

[32]Greene (2000, p. 531).

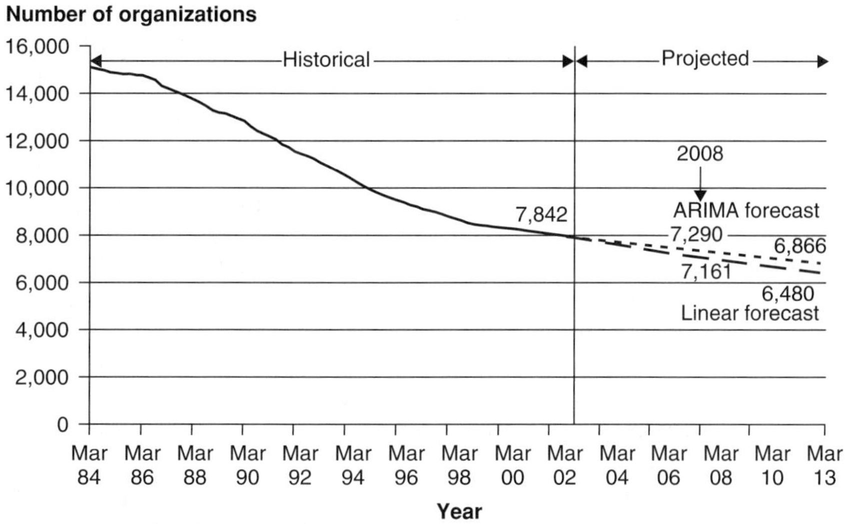

FIGURE 13 Projected number of thrift and commercial bank organizations, 1984–2013.

moving-average process to express a times series as a linear combination of past error terms or does both. In practice, the Box–Jenkins approach to time-series model building has been made relatively easy through the use of modern statistical software. After testing various models for fit, we selected for our forecasting a first-order moving-average model, fit to the second-differenced log of the time series.[33]

Figure 13 illustrates our forecasts of the total number of banking organizations for the years 2004–2013, based on the estimated parameters of our time-series model. As can be seen, we project the consolidation trend in the banking industry as continuing over the next ten years, albeit at a slightly slower pace over the second five-year period. In the near term (the next five years), according to our model, the industry will decline by a total of 552 organizations, from 7,842 at year-end 2003 to 7,290 by the end of 2008 (a decline of 7 percent). By 2013, our forecast shows the banking industry shrinking by an additional 424 organizations, to 6,866 (a 6 percent decline)—for a total reduction of almost a thousand organizations (or slightly more than 12 percent) over the ten-year period.

[33]Given a time series, one can estimate several types of models within the class of ARIMA models. Model selection can then be based on the use of information criteria such as Akaike's information criterion (AIC) or Schwarz's Bayesian criterion (SBC), which seek to identify the "best" model—best in terms of accuracy and efficiency. We chose to use the SBC because of its greater emphasis on parsimony. Among the models tested, we settled on a first-order moving-average model where the model was fit to the second-differenced log of the time series using maximum-likelihood estimation (ARIMA [0,2,1]). Second-differencing was needed to achieve stationarity—an important underlying assumption of model estimation. To confirm stationarity, we examined the autocorrelation and partial correlation functions and conducted a Dickey–Fuller unit root test. See Box, Jenkins, and Reinsel (2000) or Judge et al. (1988) for a more detailed explanation of time-series model estimation and fit. Further details on model selection and testing are available from the authors of the present study.

Although we believe that the forecast based on our moving-average model is a substantive improvement over the forecast obtained through the simple linear extrapolation method, another interpretation of the data suggests that consolidation of the industry is slowing more appreciably than is suggested even by our time-series forecast. Indeed, according to an interpretation presented by Shull and Hanweck (2001), the decades-long consolidation trend in banking may come to an end in the not-too-distant future. Basically, Shull and Hanweck view the structural change in banking as a dynamic and nonlinear process in which a population of banks in a stable state has been subjected to an exogenous shock (or shocks) that causes the population to shift to a new steady-state equilibrium. According to this interpretation, the reduction in the number of banking organizations is characterized as a situation in which an equilibrium banking structure (described by the stability in the number of banking organizations in the United States before 1980) was disturbed by economic, regulatory, and technological changes. The consequent decline reflected a transitional movement toward a new equilibrium structure.

Figure 14 follows Shull and Hanweck in using a phase diagram. It plots the quarterly rate of change in the number of banking organizations against the actual number of organizations for the period 1984–2000. In the diagram we can observe a distinct transitional pattern (as indicated by the trend line) from an equilibrium structure of just over 15,000 organizations (when the rate of change was last near zero) to the current structure of just under 8,000 organizations (at year-end 2000). Indeed, the transitional nature of the plot is quite dramatic. One noteworthy feature of the diagram is that once

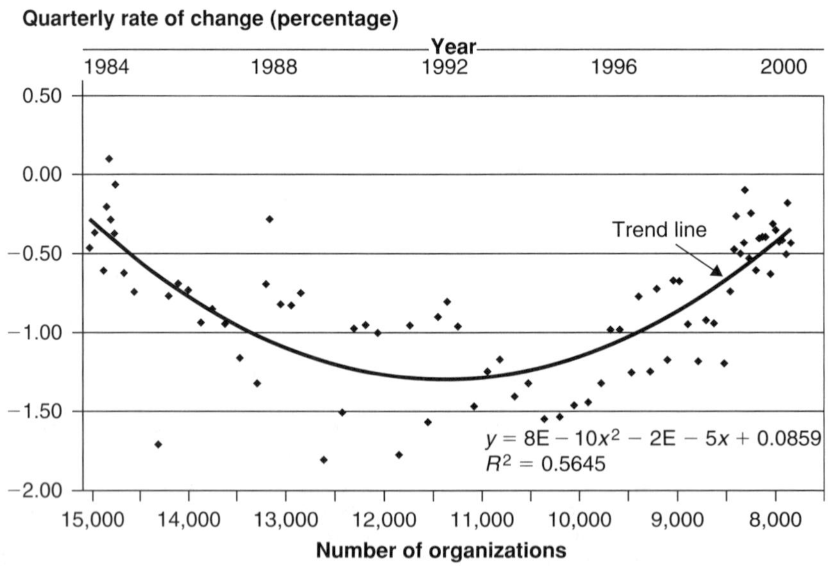

FIGURE 14 Phase diagram of number of commercial bank and thrift organizations, 1984–2000.

the numbers of banking organizations began to decline, they did so first at an increasing rate and then at a decreasing rate. The turning point appears to have been at about 11,500 organizations. This is roughly the size of the industry in mid-1992. Interestingly, that year marked both the end of a national recession and the unofficial end of the S&L and banking crises. And if we layer the phase diagram with a time line, it becomes easy to see how the transition has progressed since 1984.

Extension of the trend line to a point of intersection with the zero-rate-of-change line would indicate that the structure of the banking industry will again reach an equilibrium structure in about five years, at approximately 7,250 organizations (assuming that progression along the trend proceeds unimpeded). The conclusion to be drawn from the phase diagram—that the decline in the number of banking organizations has slowed appreciably and that industry structure is likely to stabilize within the next few years at about 7,250 organizations—is at least numerically consistent with the five-year forecast generated by our moving-average model.

5. CONCLUSION

Considered together, our three forecasts (based on linear extrapolation, time-series modeling, and a phase diagram) imply that in the absence of a new shock to the industry, the U.S. banking industry is likely to retain a structure characterized by several thousand very small to medium-size community bank organizations, a less numerous group of midsize regional organizations, and a handful of extremely large multinational banking organizations. Consistent with projections from earlier studies, our projections indicate that the U.S. banking industry is not likely to resemble the banking industries in countries such as Germany, which have only a handful of universal banks.

Although our forecasts contrast rather sharply with conventional wisdom about the future pace of decline in the number of banking institutions, we believe these projections to be reasonable under current conditions. The major influences of the 1980s, under which the decline accelerated, are no longer relevant. Gone are the high failure rates and other contractionary influences of the thrift and banking crises. Similarly, the effects of the liberalization of interstate banking and branching laws are largely in the past, as are the effects of most other major deregulatory initiatives. Bank holding companies, for example, have already collapsed inefficient multistate, multibank structures, and opportunities for additional gains are limited. This might be especially true for the larger banks (which have been particularly active merger participants) as they become increasingly constrained by state and federal limits on deposit market shares. Also gone are the merger-accommodating atmosphere and the "irrational exuberance" that accompanied the amazing stock market boom of the late 1990s.

In their place is a more uncertain economic environment that has spawned fewer bank mergers and consolidations. Although we believe that sustained industry profitability and competitive pressures will lead to some additional decline in the number of banking organizations going forward, we do not foresee a return to the rate of decline witnessed in the late 1980s and early 1990s. Rather, we see a balance developing between the number of bank start-ups and the number of charter losses due to mergers and acquisitions—with little net change in the number of banking organizations nationwide.

When we first published this article, it ended here.[34] But we have access to 10 additional quarters of data on the number of banking organizations. Table 5 compares our linear and ARIMA forecasts to the actual number of banking organizations through the second quarter of 2006. Figure 15 plots the same information. Both models actually

TABLE 5 Comparison of ARIMA and Linear Forecasts with the Actual Number of Banking Organizations (1st quarter 2004–2nd quarter 2006)

Quarter	Actual count	ARIMA forecast	Linear forecast
Mar–2004	7,808	7,812	7,808
Jun–2004	7,766	7,783	7,774
Sep–2004	7,738	7,753	7,740
Dec–2004	7,700	7,725	7,706
Mar–2005	7,674	7,696	7,672
Jun–2005	7,656	7,667	7,638
Sep–2005	7,657	7,638	7,604
Dec–2005	7,638	7,610	7,570
Mar–2006	7,617	7,582	7,536
Jun–2006	7,591	7,554	7,502

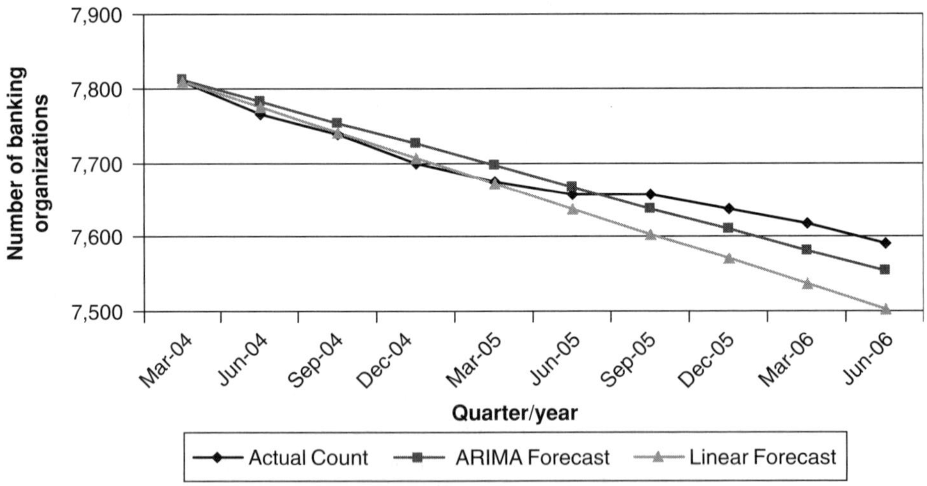

FIGURE 15 Actual vs. forecasted banking organizations, Mar-04 through June-06.

[34]This study first appeared in the FDIC Banking Review (17)4, 31–61.

performed fairly well. At the end of the second quarter of 2006, the actual number of banking organizations was 7,591. Our ARIMA forecast for the same quarter was 7,554, and the linear projection was 7,501. Evidently, consolidation in the banking industry actually occurred at a slower pace than we projected—an observation that only reinforces our conclusion that the population of banking organizations in the United States may stabilize over the next decade. In other words, it just might be that the consolidation trend in banking—that "long, strange trip"—is nearing an end.

References

Adams, Robert M., Paul W. Bauer, and Robin C. Sickles. 2002. Scope and Scale Economies in Federal Reserve Payment Processing. Working paper 02-13, Federal Reserve Bank of Cleveland.

Akhavein, J. D., A. N. Berger, and D. B. Humphrey. 1997. The Effects of Megamergers on Efficiency and Prices: Evidence from a Bank Profit Function, *Review of Industrial Organization* 12(1), 95–139.

Amel, Dean, Colleen Barnes, Fabio Panetta, and Carmelo Salleo. 2002. Consolidation and Efficiency in the Financial Sector: A Review of the International Evidence. Finance and Economics Discussion Series. Working paper 2002-47, Federal Reserve Board.

Avery, Robert B., Raphael W. Bostic, Paul S. Calem, and Glenn B. Canner. 1999. Consolidation and Bank Branching Patterns, *Journal of Banking and Finance* 23(2–4), 497–532.

Berger, Allen N. 1998. The Efficiency Effects of Bank Mergers and Acquisitions: A Preliminary Look at the 1990s Data, in Yakov Amihud and Geoffrey Miller (eds.), *Bank Mergers and Acquisitions*. Kluwer Academic, Dordrecht, pp. 79–111.

Berger, Allen N. 2003. The Economic Effects of Technological Progress: Evidence from the Banking Industry, *Journal of Money, Credit, and Banking* 35(2), 141–176.

Berger, Allen N., Rebecca S. Demsetz, and Philip E. Strahan. 1999. The Consolidation of the Financial Services Industry: Causes, Consequences, and Implications for the Future, *Journal of Banking and Finance* 23(2–4), 123–194.

Berger, Allen N., and Robert DeYoung. 2001. The Effects of Geographic Expansion on Bank Efficiency. Finance and Economics Discussion Series. Working paper 2001-03. Federal Reserve Board.

Berger, Allen N., and Robert DeYoung. 2002. Technological Progress and the Geographic Expansion of the Banking Industry. Working paper 2002-07, Federal Reserve Bank of Chicago.

Berger, Allen N., and Timothy H. Hannan. 1997. Using Measures of Firm Efficiency to Distinguish among Alternative Explanations of the Structure–Conduct–Performance Relationship, *Managerial Finance* 23(2), 6–31.

Berger, Allen N., David B. Humphrey, and Lawrence B. Pulley. 1996. Do Consumers Pay for One-Stop Banking? Evidence from an Alternative Revenue Function, *Journal of Banking and Finance* 20(9), 1601–1621.

Berger, Allen N., Anil K. Kashyap, and Joseph M. Scalise. 1995. The Transformation of the U.S. Banking Industry: What a Long, Strange Trip It's Been, *Brookings Papers on Economic Activity* 2, 54–219.

Bliss, Richard T., and Richard J. Rosen. 2001. CEO Compensation and Bank Mergers, *Journal of Financial Economics* 61(1), 107–138.

Box, G., and G. Jenkins. 1976. *Time Series Analysis: Forecasting and Control*. Holden-Day, San Francisco.

Box, George E. P., Gwilym M. Jenkins, and Gregory C. Reinsel. 2000. *Time Series Analysis: Forecasting and Control*, 3rd ed. Prentice Hall, New York.

Boyd, John H., and Stanley L. Graham. 1998. Consolidation in U.S. Banking: Implications for Efficiency and Risk, in Yakov Amihud and Geoffrey Miller (eds.), *Bank Mergers and Acquisitions*. Kluwer Academic, Dordrecht, pp. 113–135.

Calomiris, C. W., and J. Karceski. 1998. *Is the Bank Merger Wave of the 1990s Efficient? Lessons from Nine Case Studies*. AEI Press, Washington, DC.

Cole, Rebel A., Lawrence G. Goldberg, and Lawrence J. White. 2004. Cookie Cutter vs. Character: The Micro Structure of Small Business Lending by Large and Small Banks, *Journal of Financial and Quantitative Analysis* 39(2), 227–251.

Cornett, Marcia Millon, Gayane Hovakimian, Darius Palia, and Hassan Tehranian. 2003. The Impact of the Manager–Shareholder Conflict on Acquiring Bank Returns, *Journal of Banking and Finance* 27(1), 103–131.

Critchfield, Tim, Tyler Davis, Lee Davison, Heather Gratton, George Hanc, and Katherine Samolyk. 2004. Community Banks: Their Recent Past, Current Performance, and Future Prospects. *FDIC Banking Review* 16(3–4), 41–56.

DeLong, Gayle L. 2001. Stockholder Gains from Focusing versus Diversifying Bank Mergers, *Journal of Financial Economics* 59(2), 221–252.

Demsetz, Rebecca S., and Philip E. Strahan. 1997. Diversification, Size, and Risk at Bank Holding Companies, *Journal of Money, Credit, and Banking* 29(3), 300–313.

De Nicola, Gianni, and Myron L. Kwast. 2002. Systemic Risk and Financial Consolidation: Are They Related? Working paper WP/02/55, International Monetary Fund.

DeYoung, R., I. Hasan, and B. Kirchhoff. 1998. The Impact of Out-of-State Entry on the Cost Efficiency of Local Banks, *Journal of Economics and Business* 50(2), 191–203.

Emmons, William R., and Stuart I. Greenbaum. 1998. Twin Information Revolutions and the Future of Financial Intermediation, in Yakov Amihud and Geoffrey Miller, (eds.), *Bank Mergers and Acquisitions*, Kluwer Academic, Dordrecht, pp. 37–56.

Gorton, Gary, and Richard Rosen. 1995. Corporate Control, Portfolio Choice, and the Decline of Banking, *Journal of Finance* 50(5), 1377–1420.

Greene, William H. 2000. *Econometric Analysis*, 4th ed. Prentice Hall, New York.

Group of Ten (G10). 2001. Consolidation in the Financial Sector. Working Group Report to the Governors of the Group of Ten, G10.

Hadlock, Charles, Joel Houston, and Michael Ryngaert. 1999. The Role of Managerial Incentives in Bank Acquisitions, *Journal of Banking and Finance* 23(2–4), 221–249.

Hancock, D., D. B. Humphrey, and J. A. Wilcox. 1999. Cost Reductions in Electronic Payments: The Roles of Consolidation, Economies of Scale, and Technical Change, *Journal of Banking and Finance* 23(2–4), 391–421.

Hannan, Timothy H., and Stephen A. Rhoades. 1992. Future U.S. Banking Structure: 1990 to 2010, *Antitrust Bulletin* 37(3), 737–798.

Houston, Joel F., Christopher M. James, and Michael D. Ryngaert. 2000. Where Do Merger Gains Come From? Bank Mergers from the Perspective of Insiders and Outsiders, *Journal of Financial Economics* 60(2–3), 285–331.

Hughes, J. P., and L. J. Mester. 1998. Bank Capitalization and Cost: Evidence of Scale Economies in Risk Management and Signaling, *Review of Economics and Statistics* 80(2), 314–325.

Hughes, J. P., L. J. Mester, and C. G. Moon. 2001. Are Scale Economies in Banking Elusive or Illusive? Incorporating Capital Structure and Risk-Taking into Models of Bank Production, *Journal of Banking and Finance* 25(12), 2169–2208.

Hughes, J. P., W. Lang, L. J. Mester, and C. G. Moon. 1996. Efficient Banking under Interstate Branching, *Journal of Money, Credit, and Banking* 28(4, Pt. 2), 1045–1071.

Hughes, J. P., W. Lang, L. J. Mester, and C. G. Moon. 1999. The Dollars and Sense of Bank Consolidation, *Journal of Banking and Finance* 23(2–4), 291–324.

Hughes, J. P., W. Lang, L. J. Mester, C. G. Moon, and M. S. Pagano. 2003. Do Bankers Sacrifice Value to Build Empires? Managerial Incentives, Industry Consolidation, and Financial Performance, *Journal of Banking and Finance* 27(3), 417–447.

Hunter, William C. 2001. The Internet and the Commercial Banking Industry: Strategic Implications from a U.S. Perspective, in Zuhayr Mikdashi (ed.), *Financial Intermediation in the Twenty-first Century*. Palgrave, New York, pp. 17–28.

Jayaratne, Jith, and John Wolken. 1999. How Important Are Small Banks to Small Business Lending? New Evidence from a Survey of Small Firms, *Journal of Banking and Finance* 23(2–4), 427–458.

Judge, George G., R. Carter Hill, William E. Griffiths, Helmut Lütkepohl, and Tsoun-Chao Lee. 1988. *Introduction to the Theory and Practice of Econometrics*, 2nd ed. John Wiley & Sons, New York.

Kahn, Charles M., George G. Pennachi, and Ben J. Sopranzetti. 2000. Bank Consolidation and Consumer Loan Interest Rates, in *The Changing Financial Industry Structure and Regulation: Bridging States, Countries, and Industries, Proceedings of the 36th Annual Conference on Bank Structure and Competition*. Federal Reserve Bank of Chicago, pp. 563–593.

Kane, Edward J. 2000. Incentives for Banking Megamergers: What Motives Might Regulators Infer from Event-Study Evidence? *Journal of Money, Credit, and Banking* 32(3), 671–701.

Kroszner, Randall, and Philip E. Strahan. 2000. Obstacles to Optimal Policy: The Interplay of Politics and Economics in Shaping Bank Supervision and Regulation Reforms. Working paper 75-82, National Bureau of Economic Research.

Kwan, S. H. 1998. Securities Activities by Commercial Banking Firms' Section 20 Subsidiaries: Risk, Return, and Diversification Benefits. Working paper 98-10, Federal Reserve Bank of San Francisco.

Kwan, Simon H., and James A. Wilcox. 1999. Hidden Cost Reductions in Bank Mergers: Accounting for More Productive Banks. Working paper 99-10, Federal Reserve Bank of San Francisco.

Lown, Cara S., Carol L. Osler, Philip E. Strahan, and Amir Sufi. 2000. The Changing Landscape of the Financial Services Industry: What Lies Ahead? *Federal Reserve Bank of New York Economic Policy Review* 6(4), 39–55.

Milbourn, Todd T., W. A. Boot, and Anjan V. Thakor. 1999. Megamergers and Expanded Scope: Theories of Bank Size and Activity Diversity, *Journal of Banking and Finance* 23(2–4), 195–214.

Mishkin, Frederic S., and Philip E. Strahan. 1999. What Will Technology Do to Financial Structure? in Robert E. Litan and Anthony M. Santomero (eds.), *Brookings–Wharton Papers on Financial Services*. Brookings Institution Press, Washington, DC, pp. 249–287.

Montgomery, Lynne. 2003. Recent Developments Affecting Depository Institutions, *FDIC Banking Review* 15(3), 33–38.

Moore, Robert R., and Thomas F. Siems. 1998. Bank Mergers: Creating Value or Destroying Competition? *Federal Reserve Bank of Dallas Financial Industry Studies* (3rd Quarter).

Nolle, Daniel E. 1995. Banking Industry Consolidation: Past Changes and Implications for the Future. Economic and policy analysis working paper 95-1, Office of the Comptroller of the Currency.

Peek, Joe, and Eric S. Rosengren. 1996. Small Business Credit Availability: How Important Is the Size of the Lender? in A. Saunders and I. Walter (eds.), *Financial System Design: The Case for Universal Banking*. Irwin, pp. 628–655.

Peek, Joe, and Eric S. Rosengren. 1998. Bank Consolidation and Small Business Lending: It's Not Just Bank Size That Matters, *Journal of Banking and Finance* 22(6–8), 799–819.

Penas, María Fabiana, and Haluk Unal. 2004. Gains in Bank Mergers: Evidence from the Bond Markets, *Journal of Financial Economics* 74(1), 149–179.

Peristiani, Stavros. 1997. Do Mergers Improve the X-Efficiency and Scale Economies of U.S. Banks? Evidence from the 1980s, *Journal of Money, Credit, and Banking* 29(3), 326–337.

Pilloff, Steven. 1999. Multimarket Contact in Banking, *Review of Industrial Organization* 14(2), 163–182.

Pilloff, S. J., and A. M. Santomero. 1998. The Value Effects of Bank Mergers and Acquisitions, in Yakov Amihud and Geoffrey Miller (eds.), *Bank Mergers and Acquisitions*. Kluwer Academic, Dordrecht, pp. 59–78.

Prager, R. A., and T. H. Hannan. 1998. Do Substantial Horizontal Mergers Generate Significant Price Effects? Evidence from the Banking Industry, *Journal of Industrial Economics* 46(4), 433–452.

Rhoades, Stephen A. 2000. Bank Mergers and Banking Structure in the United States, 1980–1998. Staff study 174, Federal Reserve Board.

Robertson, Douglas D. 2001. A Markov View of Bank Consolidation: 1960–2000. Economic and policy analysis working paper 2001-4, Office of the Comptroller of the Currency.

Ryan, Sean J. 1999. Finding Value in Bank Mergers, in *Global Financial Crises: Implications for Banking and Regulation, Proceedings of the 35th Annual Conference on Bank Structure and Competition*, 548-52, Federal Reserve Bank of Chicago.

Saunders, Anthony, and Berry Wilson. 1999. The Impact of Consolidation and Safety-Net Support on Canadian, U.S., and U.K. Banks: 1893–1992, *Journal of Banking and Finance* 23(2–4), 537–571.

Shull, Bernard, and Gerald Hanweck. 2001. *Bank Mergers in a Deregulated Environment.* Quorum Books, Westport, CT.

Simons, Katarina, and Joanna Stavins. 1998. Has Antitrust Policy in Banking Become Obsolete? *Federal Reserve Bank of New England Economic Review* (March–April), 13–26.

Stiroh, Kevin J. 2000. How Did Bank Holding Companies Prosper in the 1990s? *Journal of Banking and Finance* 24(11), 1703–1745.

Stiroh, Kevin J. 2004. Diversification in Banking: Is Noninterest Income the Answer? *Journal of Money, Credit, and Banking* 36(5), 853–882.

Strahan, Philip E., and J. P. Weston. 1996. Small Business Lending and Bank Consolidation: Is There a Cause for Concern? *Federal Reserve Bank of New York Current Issues in Economics and Finance* 2, 1–6.

Strahan, Philip E., and J. P. Weston. 1998. Small Business Lending and the Changing Structure of the Banking Industry, *Journal of Banking and Finance* 22(6–8), 821–845.

CHAPTER 11

Safety, Soundness, and the Evolution of the U.S. Banking Industry

Robert DeYoung
University of Kansas

The author thanks Mark Flannery, Ed Kane, Myron Kwast, and Loretta Mester for their helpful comments.

1. INTRODUCTION

Bank failures are the most obvious manifestation of an unsafe and unsound banking system. From the early 1980s through the early 1990s, approximately 10 percent of U.S. commercial banks failed, resounding evidence that the banking system was at the time neither safe nor sound. As Figure 1 shows, this wave of bank failures was an abrupt and substantial departure from normal conditions. The 40 years leading up to this banking recession were nearly failure free: Only 237 banks failed between 1940 and 1980, a rate of fewer than four insolvencies per 10,000 banks per year. But the appearance of safety and soundness during those earlier years is deceptive, because the financial regulations and industry structure during those years were themselves the root causes of the wave of bank insolvencies that occurred later. Hence, the observation that the banking industry has been nearly failure free since the mid-1990s is not, by itself, a good indication of the safety and soundness of today's banking system.

Dramatic changes in financial markets, information technology, risk management, regulatory conditions, and competitive pressures have altered the fabric of the banking industry substantially over the past two decades. Collectively, these changes have dampened some types of risk, amplified other types of risk, and created some new types of risk. On balance, the banking system appears to be safer and sounder today than two decades ago, but it faces new risk challenges that could not have been anticipated in the 1980s.

This chapter documents the evolution of the U.S. commercial banking industry over the past 20 years. We begin with a chronology of the technological, financial, and regulatory changes mentioned earlier. A strategic analysis follows, with special focus given to the "transactions banking" business model, the large financial companies that practice this relatively new approach to banking, and how it compares to the more traditional relationship-based business model. Close attention is paid to the different production

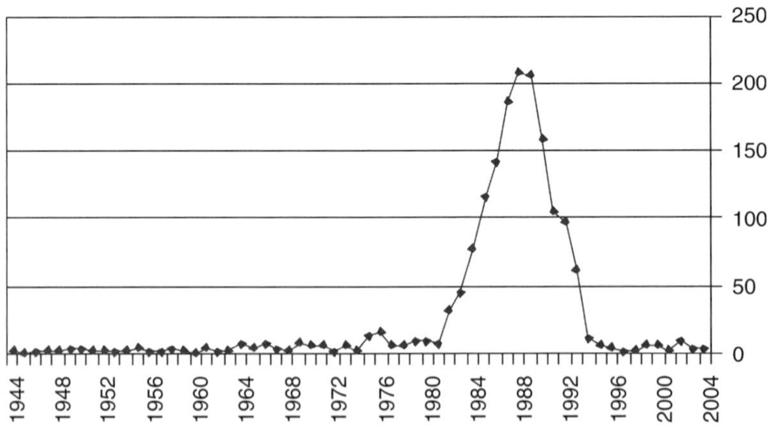

FIGURE 1 Number of commercial bank failures in the United States in the postwar period.
Source: Federal Deposit Insurance Corporation.

technologies, product mixes, strategic behaviors, and risk–return tradeoffs that characterize these two diametrically opposed approaches to commercial banking. The chapter closes with a discussion of what these new developments mean for the ongoing safety and soundness of the banking industry.

2. THE EVOLUTION OF THE U.S. BANKING INDUSTRY[1]

During the 1970s, and indeed during all of the postwar period leading up to the 1970s, U.S. commercial banking was a protected industry. Government regulations shielded banks from geographic competition, from product competition, and to a great extent from price competition. The McFadden Act of 1927 protected banks from out-of-state competitors by prohibiting interstate branch banking; although the act technically permitted interstate banking through multibank holding companies, these organizational structures required state approval, and during the 1970s none of the states approved. In addition to these interstate restrictions, most states imposed partial or blanket restrictions on intrastate branching. The Glass-Steagall Act of 1933 effectively isolated commercial banking as a separate and highly regulated financial sector, insulating banks from competition with investment banks, insurance companies, and brokerage firms. Moreover, depository institutions such as savings and loans and credit unions were not permitted to compete with banks for commercial loans. Regulation Q imposed interest-rate ceilings on all deposits except for large negotiable CDs, effectively prohibiting price competition between banks for deposit accounts.

By the end of the 1970s, there were over 14,000 chartered commercial banks in the United States. About 97 percent of these commercial banks were so-called "community banks" that held less than $1 billion of assets (2001 dollars); these small banks accounted for about one-third of the industry's total assets. The banking industry was the largest category of financial intermediary in the United States, with more than 35 percent of the nation's intermediated assets (Federal Reserve flow of funds accounts). The industry's deposit franchise made it the dominant provider of transactions services through checkable deposit accounts, and commercial banks were an extremely important investment vehicle for consumers through savings accounts and time deposit accounts. For example, consumers allocated approximately 23 percent of their assets to depository institutions in 1983 (the first year these data were available from the Federal Reserve's Survey of Consumer Finance). An important feature of banks' deposit franchise was their access to the payment system, which at the time was predominantly paper based and thus was dependent on physical, brick-and-mortar locations. Thus, community banks enjoyed an especially strong competitive advantage in local markets where regulation prohibited brick-and-mortar entry by out-of-market banks and because automated teller machines (ATMs) were still in their infancy.

[1] This section is based largely on material from Section 3 in DeYoung, Hunter, and Udell (2004).

Loan markets were generally segmented during the 1970s. Banks and thrifts dominated the residential mortgage market. Mortgage holdings by insurance companies and finance companies were relatively small, and the mortgage securitization market was limited mostly to Ginnie Mae pass-throughs. With regard to consumer loans, consumer finance companies tended to attract the higher-risk and subprime borrowers, while banks, thrifts, and captive auto finance companies (for example, GMAC, Ford Motor Credit) tended to attract the prime consumer borrower. Again, because of the extensive limitations on branch banking, community banks' power in local markets afforded them a competitive advantage in consumer lending over larger banks. Data from the Survey of Consumer Finance show that households obtained approximately 60 percent of their mortgage and consumer debt from depository institutions in 1983.

Commercial lending in the 1970s was segmented both across different types of financial institutions and within the commercial banking industry. Large commercial banks made loans to business firms of all sizes and were the major source of short-term financing to large businesses. Small businesses were generally unable to get long-term credit, aside from loans to finance the purchase of specific fixed assets such as equipment and real estate (see Carey et al. 1993). Community banks, constrained by legal lending limits, focused on lending to smaller businesses. Community banks allocated between 20 and 30 percent of their loan portfolio to commercial loans, on average, during the 1970s and early 1980s. Life insurance companies were also active in business finance, but their activities were confined to longer-term loans to medium-sized businesses.

2.1. Financial Innovation and Technological Change

In the late 1960s and early 1970s money market interest rates regularly exceeded the Regulation Q ceiling on deposit interest rates. This gap became huge after the Federal Reserve changed its approach to monetary policy in 1979, with the 90-day Treasury bill rate at one point, exceeding the passbook savings account ceiling by more than 1,000 basis points. As a result, deposits flowed out of low-yielding bank deposits and into higher-yielding investments offered by nonbank institutions. The impact of this disintermediation was felt most acutely by smaller banks and thrifts, which depended on the small retail deposits covered by Regulation Q, and was felt less acutely by large banks that relied more on large-denomination CDs with interest rates that were set in competitive markets.

The threat from disintermediation was especially serious because retail banking customers were gaining access to investment alternatives other than bank deposit products. The most salient change was the introduction of money market mutual funds (MMMFs) in 1971. Unlike existing large-denomination money market instruments, such as negotiable CDs and commercial paper, MMMFs came in denominations affordable to households and small businesses. Moreover, MMMFs had a big competitive advantage over Regulation Q-constrained bank deposits because they paid higher money market investment returns and still allowed consumers (limited) check-writing privileges. As a result, MMMFs grew dramatically beginning in the late 1970s. Later in the decade,

Merrill Lynch took this innovation one step further with its Cash Management Account that included a third dimension, a brokerage account. Innovations elsewhere in the financial services sector, such as universal life insurance, which combined term life insurance with a money market-linked savings component, created additional alternatives to retail bank deposits.

Other innovations had an equally powerful impact on retail banking. One of the most important was the ATM, which reduced the cost of producing transactions services and made them more convenient for retail customers. Banks had initially hoped that the ATM would be, as its name implies, a substitute for human tellers and perhaps even a partial substitute for bank branches. To the contrary, as the number of ATMs has increased, so has the number of bank branches; these unexpected trends imply that bank delivery systems have a variety of complex strategic characteristics: geographic locations that provide customer convenience, revenue centers that generate fee income (for example, third-party ATM fees), and physical brick-and-mortar platforms for person-to-person contact and relationship building. In addition to the ATM, other alternatives to brick-and-mortar banking began to appear in the 1970s and 1980s. Although fully transactional Internet banking did not appear until later, some banks began offering limited forms of computer banking in the 1980s. Customers with a computer and modem could pay bills and transfer money between accounts over telephone lines. Credit cards and debit cards expanded rapidly in the 1970s and 1980s; and although they are not generally thought of this way, these payment vehicles represented yet another alternative to the traditional bank delivery system.

Some of the most fundamental changes in the banking industry are a direct result of loan securitization. But unlike the deregulatory changes just discussed, in which government basically just got out of the way, securitization is a story about government intervention right from the beginning. Securitization began in the 1960s with the creation of the Ginnie Mae pass-through and exploded in the 1980s with the development of the collateralized mortgage obligation. Two government-sponsored enterprises (GSEs), the Federal National Mortgage Association (Fannie Mae) and the Federal Home Loan Mortgage Corporation (Freddie Mac), are dominant forces in the residential mortgage market.[2] As of 2003, investors held approximately $2 trillion in mortgage-backed securities issued by Fannie Mae (about $1,300 billion) and Freddie Mac (about $770 billion), and Fannie and Freddie held an additional $1.5 trillion of mortgages and mortgage-backed securities directly in their own portfolios. Together, mortgages securitized by, or held in the portfolios of, these two GSEs accounted for about 47 percent of total residential mortgage debt in the United States (White 2003).

Securitization combined financial innovation with technological innovation. The financial innovation is the synthetic creation of liquid, traded securities from a pool of

[2]Fannie Mae and Freddie Mac receive an implicit government subsidy because investors treat their debt as if it were backed by a guarantee of the U.S. government. The competitive advantage embodied in this subsidy, and the incentives that it creates for Fannie and Freddie, is the subject of substantial public policy debate (for example, Hendershott and Shilling 1989, ICF 1990, Cotterman and Pearce 1996, Passmore, Sparks, and Ingpen 2001, White 2003).

illiquid, nontraded assets—for example, individual residential mortgages or credit card receivables—where often the payoff characteristics of the traded securities are altered significantly from those of the underlying assets. The technological innovation is the efficient compilation, computation, and dissemination of information related to the performance and operation of the underlying asset pools. Both of these innovations favored large and geographically diverse lenders: The creation of liquid securities that have the risk–return characteristics desired by investors requires that the underlying pool contain large numbers of loans and that the production processes associated with the loan underwriting, marketing, originating, servicing, and securitizing of these loans exhibit substantial scale economies. Hence, large banking companies wanting to access these additional scale efficiencies pressured Congress to relax the extant regulations that (a) restricted their geographic growth and (b) limited their investment banking powers. Loan securitization provided a benefit for small community banks as well, allowing them to geographically diversify their otherwise locally concentrated loan portfolios by investing in securities backed by mortgages originated in other regions of the country.

One of the key inputs for large-scale loan securitization is credit-scoring technology, which transforms quantitative information about individual borrowers (such as income, employment, and payment history) into a single numerical credit score—which lenders can use when screening and approving loan applications, securitizers can use to group loans of similar risk into pools, and investors can use (together with other information) to evaluate the risk of the resulting asset-backed securities. First introduced in the 1950s, credit scoring has become widely used in consumer, mortgage, and micro-small business lending over the past 30 years (Mester 1997). Although the largest banks have developed their own credit-scoring formulas, most lenders rely on third-party credit bureau scores to solicit and prescreen applicants.[3] Research on credit scoring is still relatively new, so it remains difficult to quantify the economic impact of credit scoring on the consumer, real estate, and small business lending markets. For example, it is still an open question as to whether risk is assessed more accurately using automated credit-scoring approaches or the more traditional, case-by-case credit analysis performed by loan officers.[4] It does seem safe to assert, however, that credit scoring has significantly reduced the unit cost of underwriting an individual loan, and as a result it has (a) increased the minimum efficient scale of consumer loan underwriting operations and in the process (b) expanded lenders' incentives to make credit available (Frame, Srinivasan, and Woosley 2001, Berger, Frame, and Miller 2005, DeYoung, Glennon, and Nigro 2008).

[3]Bureau scores are based solely on the credit history of individuals as reflected in credit bureau reports, as opposed to application scores that weigh other factors collected on the loan application (for example, income and employment) in addition to credit bureau information (Avery et al. 1999).

[4]Only one published study has analyzed whether human intervention can improve decision making on applicants rejected on the basis of credit scoring. This study used data from one bank with a historically high "override" rate and found that overrides of applicants who would have been rejected on the basis of the credit score did no better on average than their credit score alone predicted (Mayes 2003, Chap. 12).

2.2. Regulatory Reaction to Financial Innovation and Technological Change

During the 1980s it became increasingly difficult for regulators to protect commercial banks from product competition, interregional competition, and interest rate competition while at the same time ensuring that the industry remained vibrant and healthy. Market conditions, financial innovation, and technological advances simply conspired against preserving the old regime. Regulatory change became inevitable and necessary.

In some ways this change came quickly. A period of high interest rates that began in 1979 led to the rapid dismantling of Regulation Q, culminating with the passage of the Garn–St. Germain Depository Institutions Act in 1982. Among other things, this act allowed thrifts to make commercial loans and thus compete more directly with community banks. The demise of the McFadden Act took longer. At the intrastate level, 32 states liberalized their in-state geographic restrictions on banking between 1980 and 1994. At the interstate level, states began to exploit the multibank holding company loophole in the McFadden Act in the early 1980s, entering into reciprocity agreements with each other that allowed interstate bank ownership through multibank holding companies. By the end of the decade, all but six states allowed some sort of interstate banking, with most being part of large regional compacts.

Expansion of banking powers occurred at a somewhat more incremental and deliberate pace. On the retail side, the first major change came with the Garn–St. Germain Act, which authorized banks and thrifts to offer money market deposit accounts (MMDAs), which are transaction accounts without interest-rate ceilings that could compete directly with MMMFs. Most of the other changes (prior to the late 1990s) were facilitated by Federal Reserve Board rulings. Under the 1956 Bank Holding Company Act and its 1970 amendments, the Federal Reserve had the authority to determine which activities were permissible for banking organizations, subject to the condition that these activities be "closely related to banking." In 1987 the Federal Reserve allowed banks to form investment banking (Section 20) subsidiaries, and in 1989 it granted limited corporate securities underwriting privileges to a select group of banks, gradually relaxing the limitations during the years that followed.

Banking industry deregulation reached its zenith during the 1990s. In 1994 Congress rationalized the patchwork of state-by-state geographic rules by passing the Riegle-Neal Interstate Banking and Branching Efficiency Act, which effectively repealed the McFadden Act at the national level. In 1999 Congress, its hand forced by the announced merger of CitiBank (the largest U.S. bank) and Travelers (one of the largest U.S. insurance companies), passed the Graham-Leach-Bliley (GLB) Act. GLB effectively repealed the Glass-Steagall Act and granted broad-based securities and insurance powers to commercial banking companies.

2.3. Widespread Technology Adoption and Industry Transformation

These congressional acts ratified the decades-long deregulation movement, and as such they marked the culmination of story lines that began in the 1970s and 1980s. By removing long-standing limitations on banks' geographic scope and product mix, the Riegle-Neal and Gramm-Leach-Bliley acts paved the way for nationwide banking franchises and helped accelerate the adoption of new financial processes and information technologies by commercial banks of all sizes.

The immediate response to the Riegle-Neal Act was the highest-ever five-year run of bank mergers in U.S. history, in terms of both the number and the value of the banks acquired (Berger, Buch et al. 2004). Although the "mega-mergers" that combined two large banking companies received the most attention, the vast majority of these mergers involved at least one community bank (DeYoung and Hunter 2003). In general, larger banks have been quicker to adopt new technology than have smaller banks, including electronic payments technologies, transactional Web sites, small business credit-scoring models (Berger 2003), ATMs and ATM networks (Hannan and McDowell 1984), loan securitization, and various off-balance-sheet activities (Berger and Udell 1993). However, the more scalable among these technologies disseminated quite rapidly to smaller banks, courtesy of a highly competitive sector of third-party technology vendors and declining costs of delivering these technologies.[5]

In the 1990s, large banks began to use credit-scoring models to evaluate applications for "micro-small business loans," with principle amounts below $100,000 to $250,000 (depending on the bank). Some banks use their own proprietary models, while other banks have purchased credit-scoring models from outside venders. In general these models rely on information about the entrepreneur (for example, credit bureau reports), mercantile credit information from third-party information exchanges (for example, Dun and Bradstreet), as well as financial information about the small business itself. Recent research suggests that small business credit scoring has enabled banks to extend credit to marginally less creditworthy loan applicants, and by doing so it has increased the overall amount of credit available to small businesses.

Financial technology has also had a significant effect on how banks manage risk. After the run-up in interest rates in the 1970s caught many banks with asset–liability mismatches, the banking industry (a) adopted techniques that more accurately measured exposure to interest-rate risk (for example, duration-based programs) and (b) exploited advances in financial engineering and the development of new and wider derivatives markets to implement strategies to mitigate these exposures. Following some highly visible financial fiascos, including Barings PLC, Orange County, and Metallgesellshaft, banks began to implement market risk management tools to measure and manage their trading risk in the mid-1990s. In the latter half of the 1990s, banks began to adopt similar value at risk-based tools for managing credit risk. The proposed new Basel Capital Accord (Basel II) goes one step further, using these new credit tools to link capital requirements to credit risk.

New technology has improved the efficiency of the payments system, with electronic payments and funds transfer rapidly replacing paper-based payments (cash and checks) and paper record keeping. Gerdes and Walton (2002) found a 3 percent per year decline in the number of checks paid in the United States during the late 1990s, while payments made with credit cards and debit cards were increasing by 7.3 percent and 35.6 percent

[5]Frame and White (2004) survey the literature on technology adoption in the banking industry.

per year, respectively. Humphrey (2002) estimated that checks' market share of total payments fell from 87.8 percent to 72.3 percent during the 1990s, although he found that the number of checks written each year was still rising modestly. The technology-driven switch from paper-based payments to electronic-based payments is also reflected in the steep increase in automated clearinghouse (ACH) transactions, such as monthly mortgage payments and direct payroll deposits. ACH volume handled by the Federal Reserve increased at a 14.2 percent annual rate from 1990 to 2000, and this pace resulted in an 83 percent reduction in the costs of producing these transactions, from $0.959 to $0.158 in 1994 dollars (Berger 2003). However, technology-driven cost reductions in the processing of paper checks and cash payments have been more modest (Bauer and Ferrier 1996, Bohn, Hancock, and Bauer 2001, Gilbert, Wheelock, and Wilson 2002). Recognizing that improvements in information technology could be used to increase the efficiency of check payments, the Check Clearing for the 21st Century Act of 2003 (Check 21) removed the requirement that banks return physical paper checks to the banks against which they were written. Instead, banks could simply transmit electronic check images, saving substantial transportation and handling expenses and potentially easing the competitive disadvantages of check transactions relative to credit and debit card transactions.

Internet banking has further changed the landscape of the financial services industry by reducing the importance of geographic location and dramatically cutting the cost of producing a banking transaction. In its most extreme form, practiced by only a small number of banks, financial services are offered exclusively over the Internet, without any brick-and-mortar branch locations. As of July 2002, just 20 Internet-only banks were in operation; approximately another two dozen Internet-only institutions had failed, been acquired, or liquidated voluntarily or were integrated back into their parent holding companies due to poor financial performance.[6] The more widespread Internet banking approach is the "click-and-mortar" model, which combines a transactional Internet site with traditional brick-and-mortar offices and ATM networks (Furst, Lang, and Nolle 2001, 2002, Sullivan 2001, Berger 2003). Although Internet banking transactions exhibit economies of scale (DeYoung 2005), small banks are able to offer this technology by outsourcing the development and the maintenance of their Internet sites to Web site vendors. Indeed, there is some evidence that offering Internet banking services enhances small-bank profitability (DeYoung, Lang, and Nolle 2007).

Because the shift toward electronic payments allows depositors to know exactly when funds are dispersed and received, households and small businesses have been able to hold lower balances in their transactions accounts. The fraction of household financial assets allocated to transactions accounts declined by a third, from 7.3 percent in 1983 to 4.6 percent in 2001 (Federal Reserve Survey of Consumer Finance). Moreover, the shift from full-service banking offices to more specialized delivery channels (branches, ATMs, Internet sites) has reduced the amount of inputs that banks require to produce a given amount of banking services. Although the number of offices (bank branches plus the head office) per bank has nearly quadrupled since 1970, assets per

[6]Based on internal records compiled by the Federal Financial Institutions Examination Council (FFIEC).

office, deposits per office, and transactions per office have all steadily increased, while the number of full-time employees per office has declined (DeYoung, Hunter, and Udell 2004).

3. A STYLIZED VIEW OF BANKING STRATEGIES

The previous section described myriad ways that deregulation, technological change, and financial innovations have changed the competitive environment for commercial banks. At the risk of oversimplification, this section describes the strategic impact of these phenomena using just four basic parameters: bank size, unit costs, lending technologies, and product differentiation. This approach is derived from a series of studies by DeYoung (2000), DeYoung and Hunter (2003), and DeYoung, Hunter, and Udell (2004) and is illustrated here by the strategic maps in Figures 2 and 3.

The vertical dimension in these maps measures bank size, with large banks located near the bottom of the map and small banks located near the top. Because the production of banking services tends to exhibit scale economies, the vertical dimension also measures unit costs, with low unit costs at the bottom of the map and high unit costs at the top. Research on bank scale economies has evolved over the years, and the literature contains a fair number of inconsistencies; however, some important points of agreement have emerged over time. One point of general agreement is that "traditional" banks—that is, banks that earn interest income by originating and holding loans that are financed by transactions deposits—can capture a substantial portion of available scale economies while still remaining relatively small, with additional unit-cost reductions accumulating at a declining rate with increased bank size (Evanoff and Israilevich 1991). But banks can gain access to a much larger source of scale economies if they

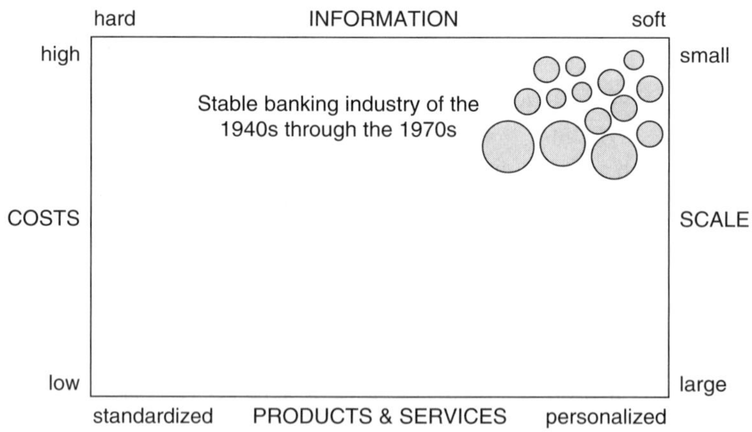

FIGURE 2 Strategic map of commercial banking industry, prederegulation.

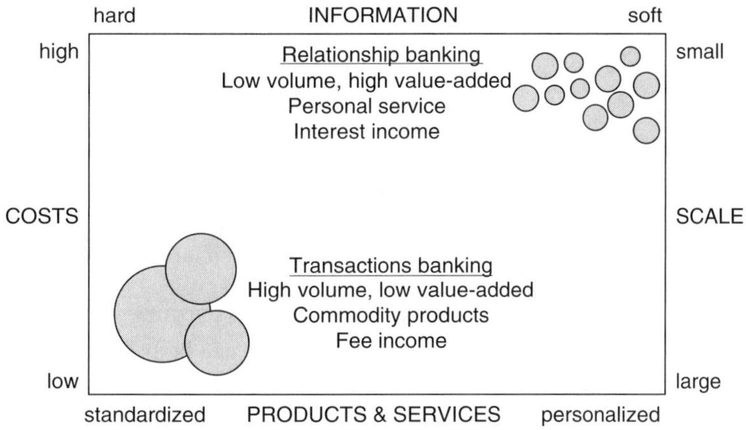

FIGURE 3 Strategic map of commercial banking industry, postderegulation.

change the manner in which they produce financial services. For example, Rossi (1998) shows that financial institutions that use a transactions banking model—for example, banks that earn fee income by originating high volumes of mortgage or consumer loans and selling them to other investors—continue to access unit-cost reductions even at very large scale. Thus, small banks that use traditional lending approaches operate with a unit-cost disadvantage as compared to these banks.

The horizontal dimension in Figures 2 and 3 measures the degree to which banks differentiate their products and services from those of their closest competitors. Banks that offer differentiated products and services (such as customized loan contracts or personalized private banking) are located on the right-hand side, while banks that offer nondifferentiated products and services (such as standardized mortgage loans or discount online brokerage) are located on the left-hand side. Note that not all product differentiation is tangible—it can often be a perception in the mind of the customer. For example, community banks attempt differentiation by knowing the names of their customers on sight, while large banks attempt to differentiate via marketing campaigns to create brand images for otherwise-undifferentiated products. If successfully deployed, both of these strategies can support higher prices for retail banking services.

The horizontal distinction between standardization and customization is also consistent with the distinction researchers have recently made between hard and soft information (Stein 2002, Berger, Miller et al. 2005, Scott 2004). Banks on the left side of this information spectrum use automated lending technologies to originate and securitize standardized mortgage or credit card loans and to deliver credit-scored micro-business loans. Moving to the right, banks emphasize more traditional lending technologies such as asset-based lending and financial statement lending. Finally, at the far right, banks specialize in relationship lending, where loan officers acquire soft information about the borrower over time via financial interactions with the borrower and through interaction with the local community.

3.1. Prederegulation

Figure 2 illustrates the commercial banking industry prior to the deregulation, technological advance, and financial innovation of the 1980s and 1990s. The positions of the circles indicate the business strategies selected by banks, and the circle sizes indicate relative bank size. All banks were clustered near the northeast corner of the strategy space. Geographic regulation restricted the size of banks and prevented most (and perhaps all) of them from fully exploiting available scale economies. The available technology for producing and delivering banking services required interpersonal contact between loan officers and borrowers to collect soft information, paper-based transactions for payments, and visits to the bank to receive cash and deposit checks—all of which required brick-and-mortar bank and branch locations staffed by bank employees. The level of price competition on the deposit side was restricted on the one hand by Regulation Q and on the other hand by the lack of substitute liquidity and transactions providers. Retail deposit competition was nonprice, for example, person-to-person service, the convenience of having a branch nearby, and, of course, free toasters for opening accounts. The price competition that is a hallmark of commodity-based financial services was largely absent. Banks faced relatively little competition from nonbanks or securities markets for supplying credit to businesses.

Before deregulation, banks that specialized in retail banking, small business banking, and corporate banking shared many of the same characteristics, regardless of their size. Small banks tended to offer a somewhat higher degree of person-to-person interaction with retail customers, and large commercial accounts by necessity went to large banks, but small banks and large banks had more commonalities with each other than differences from each other. For the most part, there was a single retail banking strategy (with some variants) and very little strategic difference among most banks' approaches to commercial lending.

3.2. Postderegulation

Deregulation, technological advance, and financial innovation created new strategic opportunities for banks, and, as competition heated up, banks had incentives to pursue those opportunities. As already discussed, the average size of commercial banks began to increase—at first because of modest within-market mergers and then more rapidly because of geographic extension mergers and mega-mergers—and this led to an increasing disparity in bank size within the industry.[7] Although increased size yielded scale economies for banks of all sizes, the largest banks gained access to the lowest unit-cost structures.

Large banks also became less like traditional banks because the size of their operations allowed them to apply more efficiently the new production technologies for which the "hardening" of borrower information is crucial (for example, automated underwriting, securitization, widespread ATM networks, electronic payments). This shift had two effects. First, it reduced large banks' unit costs even further. Second, it changed

[7] See DeYoung (1999, 2000) for a summary of the causes and consequences of U.S. bank mergers.

their retail banking strategy to a high-volume, low-cost, "financial commodity" strategy. Home mortgages, credit cards, and online brokerage are three examples of financial services that have become dominated by large and very large financial institutions, which use hard information and automated production and distribution processes to deliver these services at low unit costs. Because price competition is strong for nondifferentiated products, pricing pressure keeps margins low, despite these banks' low unit costs. High volumes, constant vigilance to keep expenses in line, and continuous innovation are essential for this strategy to earn satisfactory returns for shareholders.

The incentives created by industry deregulation (which increased the potential size and scope of commercial banks) and innovations in information technology and financial markets (which gave large banks access to an entirely new business model) drove a strategic wedge between the large and growing banks on the one hand and the smaller and more slowly growing community banks on the other hand. The result is shown in Figure 3. Large banks have moved in a southwest direction on the map, sacrificing personalized service for large scale and gaining low unit costs by shifting to automated production techniques. Although many community banks have also grown larger via mergers, they have remained relatively small and have continued to occupy the same strategic ground. By virtue of their small size, local economic focus, and person-to-person ethos, community banks are well suited to gathering the soft information necessary to deliver highly differentiated small business credit products and high-end consumer banking services. This more traditional strategy has allowed well-managed community banks to charge prices high enough to earn satisfactory rates of return despite their higher cost structures. In this view of the banking industry, community banks are differentiated from large banks by their "high-value-added" strategy.

Four additional points complete the strategic analysis in Figures 2 and 3. First, the corners of the strategy space represent the only potentially viable strategic choices for banks; being "stuck in the middle" of such a map indicates the lack of a strategy and leads to mediocre financial performance (Porter 1980). Second, the northwest corner of the strategy space (high cost, low value-added) is not a viable strategy, for obvious reasons. Third, the southeast corner of the strategy space (low cost, high value-added) is the most preferred location, but it is unlikely to be a viable long-run strategy. Without some kind of entry barrier (such as patents or monopoly rights), the excess profits generated at this location will invite entry, and the resulting competition will compress margins back to a normal rate of return. Strategy-specific barriers also stand in the way. Large banks may attempt to differentiate their products and services from those of their competitors by creating brand images and other perceived differences, but offering true person-to-person service (as well as other high-value-added retail and small business services) is difficult at a large scale. Small banks may attempt to achieve lower unit costs via growth, but they run the risk of getting stuck in the middle because of the strategic dissonance between large size and personal service. Nonetheless, the mere existence of this strategic ground in the southeast corner of the map, and the excess profits that banks can earn in the short run or moderate run by occupying it, creates an incentive for both large and small banks to innovate. Banks that do not strive via innovation to reach this strategic ground are likely to leave the industry in the long run.

Finally, the dichotomy illustrated in Figure 3 obviously oversimplifies the array of strategic choices available to commercial banks. Some large banks offer customized services to certain sets of clients with idiosyncratic financial needs, such as corporate investment banking clients and high-net-worth "private banking" customers. And some small banks provide extremely standardized retail banking services, such as Internet-only banks (DeYoung 2005). But the simplifications in this framework allow us to isolate the main characteristics of community banks (small size, local focus, and more traditional banking technology) and large banks (large size, broad appeal, and highly automated banking technology), which in turn leads to the realization that community-bank strategies and large-bank strategies rely on different profit drivers. DeYoung, Hunter, and Udell (2004) argue that both small banks and large banks have access to financially viable business models; in particular, they argue that financial success for community banks operating in competitive local markets depends primarily on (a) being large enough to capture some modicum of scale economies and (b) bank managers' ability to effectively and efficiently implement this business model.

4. EVIDENCE CONSISTENT WITH THE STRATEGIC MAP

There is considerable empirical evidence consistent with the strategic dichotomy illustrated in Figure 3. Table 1 presents the average values of selected financial ratios for five different groups of U.S. commercial banks in 2004.[8] To be included in the analysis banks had to meet the following criteria: They held a state or federal commercial bank charter, were located in one of the 50 states or the District of Columbia, were at least 10 full years old,[9] and had reasonably traditional bank balance sheets that included loans, transactions deposits, and insured deposits (mono-line banks and other special-purpose banks were excluded). Banks were also excluded if they did not fall into one of the five asset-size classes represented in Table 1: large banks, with more than \$10 billion in assets; community banks, with either less than \$100 million in assets, \$100 million to \$500 million in assets, or \$500 million to \$2 billion in assets; or rural community banks, with less than \$2 billion in assets. Rural banks are included as a separate category because of their special role in providing agricultural credit and because they tend to face less competition in the rural towns in which they are located; however, rural banks use a business model very similar to that of other community banks and for most purposes can be considered community banks. Finally, the community banks and the rural banks had to meet the following additional conditions: They were domestically owned, derived at least half their deposits from branches located in a single county, and were either freestanding firms, the sole bank in a one-bank holding company, or an affiliate in a multibank holding company composed solely of other community banks.

[8]The author has found results very similar to those in Table 1 using cross sections of data from years other than 2004. For examples, see DeYoung, Hunter, and Udell (2004) and DeYoung (2008).

[9]DeYoung and Hasan (1998) found that the average newly chartered bank in the United States in the 1980s and early 1990s did not become fully financially mature until it was at least nine years old.

TABLE 1 Mean Values of Selected Financial Ratios for Five Different-Sized Groups of U.S. Commercial Banks in 2004

	Large bank	Large community bank	Medium community bank	Small community bank	Rural community bank
Asset size	More than $10 billion	$500 million to $2 billion	$100 to $500 million	Less than $100 million	Less than $2 billion
Credit card loans/total loans	0.076	0.004	0.003	0.002	0.003
Percent of loans sold or securitized	0.262	0.031	0.017	0.006	0.010
Small business loans/total loans	0.044	0.089	0.115	0.143	0.128
Fed funds purchased/assets	0.086	0.039	0.020	0.009	0.011
Percent deposits core	0.287	0.382	0.527	0.618	0.622
Net interest margin	0.032	0.036	0.038	0.039	0.038
Advertising/noninterest expense	0.027	0.020	0.016	0.013	0.015

Source: Federal Deposit Insurance Corporation and author's calculations.

The five size classes in Table 1 correspond to the dichotomy suggested by the strategic map analysis: Banks in the "large bank" group have more than $10 billion of assets, a size that far exceeds most definitions of a community bank. Banks in the other four groups are clearly too small to be producing financial commodity products as their main strategy. Comparing the financial ratios across the columns of Table 1 offers clear support for the hypothesized "strategic wedge" between larger and smaller banks—although along some dimensions size-based differences are more of a continuum than a chasm.

The data for credit card loans, loan sales and securitizations, and small business loans offer clear evidence of a strategic wedge between large and small banks. On average, about 8 percent of loans at the large banks were credit card loans—a classic financial commodity product—compared to less than half of 1 percent for the smaller banks. The production of credit card loans (even after excluding mono-line credit card banks from the data) has clearly gravitated toward large banks because of the scale economies present in this business line. Credit card receivables are often securitized and—consistent with this, the average large bank securitized about 26 percent of its loans during 2004 compared to a mere 3 percent or less at the smaller banks. This finding indicates that most of the loans made by small banks are either nonstandardized (for example, business loans, commercial real estate loans) and hence cannot be securitized or are part of a multiple-product bank–borrower relationship that is enhanced by holding these credits on balance sheet.

Small business loans are the other side of this lending coin. The small business loan is the classic relationship loan, underwritten based on soft information. On average, the large banks had only 4 percent of their loan portfolio invested in small business loans versus between 9 percent and 14 percent for the smaller banks. Moreover, these data likely understate the small business lending gap between large and small banks, because large banks often make "micro-small business loans," which are underwritten based on the personal credit score of the proprietor and hence can be more like credit card loans than relationship loans.

The comparative data for fed funds purchased and core deposits are also consistent with the strategic map. On average, the large banks funded more than 8 percent of their assets with funds purchased overnight from other banks, compared with between 1 percent and 4 percent for the smaller banks. Similarly, only about 29 percent of total deposits at the average large bank were "core" funding (that is, transactions deposits, savings deposits, and certificates of deposit less than $100,000), compared with between 38 percent and 62 percent for the smaller banks. Both of these findings illustrate the difference between the traditional banking approach, in which long-term deposits are used to fund on-balance-sheet portfolios of nonstandardized loans based on close customer relationships, versus the transactional banking approach, in which standardized loans are securitized and sold, funding is short run, and the depositors and borrowers represent two relatively separate sets of customers. However, note that the decline in core deposit funding as banks get larger is relatively gradual rather than a discrete regime shift between small and large banks. This pattern might indicate that the rapid asset growth of the largest community banks requires a less traditional funding mix (it is well known that core deposits cannot be grown as fast as loan accounts), or it might indicate that the largest community banks are growing at the expense of their relationship-based business strategies and are risking getting stuck in the middle of the strategic map.

The differences in net interest margin across the various groups of banks flow directly from the comparative differences in funding and lending just noted. The average net interest margin for the large banks was 3.2 percent, compared to 3.6 percent to 3.9 percent for the smaller banks. Small banks have pricing advantages at both ends of the interest margin. Consumer transactions loans are nondifferentiated credit products sold in highly competitive markets, and these conditions limit the interest rates that large banks can charge—in comparison, small banks can charge relatively high interest rates by making relationship-based loans to informationally opaque borrowers in less competitive local markets. And while the small banks fund their loans with low-cost core deposits, large banks use a more expensive mix of fed funds and other noncore deposits to fund their loans.

Finally, the intensity of advertising expenditures differs substantially by bank size. On average, advertising expenditures account for only 1.3 percent to 2.0 percent of noninterest expenses at the small banks, compared to about 2.7 percent at the large banks. This doubling of advertising intensity from the smallest banks to the large banks is consistent with the strategic map analysis in several ways. First, most large banks are still in the process of growing and entering new geographic markets, and advertising support is essential for establishing presence in a new market. Second, small banks can spend less on advertising because their strategy is locally focused (so word of mouth is relatively more effective) and is based on multiproduct relationships that keep the customer coming back to bank branches and Web sites (where it is inexpensive to communicate with customers). The implications of these advertising patterns will be discussed at greater length later.

TABLE 2 Mean Values of Selected Financial Ratios for Two Different-Sized Groups of U.S. Commercial Banks in 2004

	Large bank	Large community bank
Asset size	More than $10 billion	$500 million to $2 billion
Noninterest income/operating income	0.394	0.219
Composition of noninterest income:		
Depositor services	0.279	0.418
Investment banking	0.059	0.029
Loan servicing	0.046	0.018
Loan securitization	0.041	0.001
Insurance sales and underwriting	0.034	0.020
Other	0.541	0.514

Source: Federal Deposit Insurance Corporation and author's calculations.

Although large banks generate thinner interest margins than small banks, they augment their interest income with large amounts of noninterest (or fee) income. Table 2 shows that noninterest income accounts for nearly 40 percent of operating income (net interest income plus noninterest income) on average in the large bank group, roughly twice as much as the average bank in the large community bank group (about 22 percent). Securitized lending generates relatively little interest income because loans are not retained, but it generates a disproportionate amount of noninterest income through loan origination fees, loan securitization fees, and loan servicing fees. Also note that the composition of noninterest income at large banks includes substantially more fee income from investment banking and insurance activities than at smaller banks; these nontraditional banking activities were made possible by deregulation, and the fact that smaller banks have not taken greater advantage of these powers is due in part to the scale of operations needed to produce these services efficiently.

5. FURTHER IMPLICATIONS OF STRATEGIC CHANGE

While the data offer clear support for the strategic map analysis in Figures 2 and 3, a more complete appreciation of this strategic shift requires analysis outside of this simple and highly stylized framework. This section draws on existing research in banking and finance to examine more closely how the dichotomy of transactions banking versus relationship banking has shaped competitive rivalry and financial performance in the U.S. banking industry.

5.1. Industry Structure

Geographic deregulation released a binding constraint on the size of banking companies wishing to grow larger, and advances in financial and information technologies provided a potentially attractive business model (transactions banking) that could be exploited by large banks. The fastest way for commercial banks to take advantage of these opportunities was to acquire other existing banks. On average, 500 commercial banks were acquired each year between 1990 and 2000, a substantial number in an industry that began the decade with a little over 12,000 banks.

This wave of bank mergers and acquisitions had two effects on the number and size distribution of U.S. banks. First, the number of banks (measured by the number of active federal and state bank charters) has declined dramatically, from around 14,000 banks—a number that had remained remarkably stable since the 1950s—to fewer than 8,000 banks today. Note that this decline in total numbers is a net figure that understates the impact of mergers and acquisitions. The overall number of banks is bolstered by the more than 3,000 new banking charters issued by state and federal banking authorities during the 1980s, 1990s, and 2000s. Strong anecdotal evidence, as well as systematic empirical evidence, indicates that these new, or "de novo," banks tended to start up in the same local markets in which established banks had been acquired (Berger, Bonime et al. 2004, Keeton 2000). On the one hand, the overall number of banks is depressed by the 2,000-plus bank failures displayed in Figure 1.

Second, as illustrated in Figure 4, the size distribution of banks has changed. The population of medium-sized and larger banks has remained relatively stable since 1980, each varying between 300 and 500 banks. The reduction in the number of banks has occurred exclusively among banks with assets of less than $500 million. Three phenomena account for the decline: The vast majority of failed banks since 1980 have been

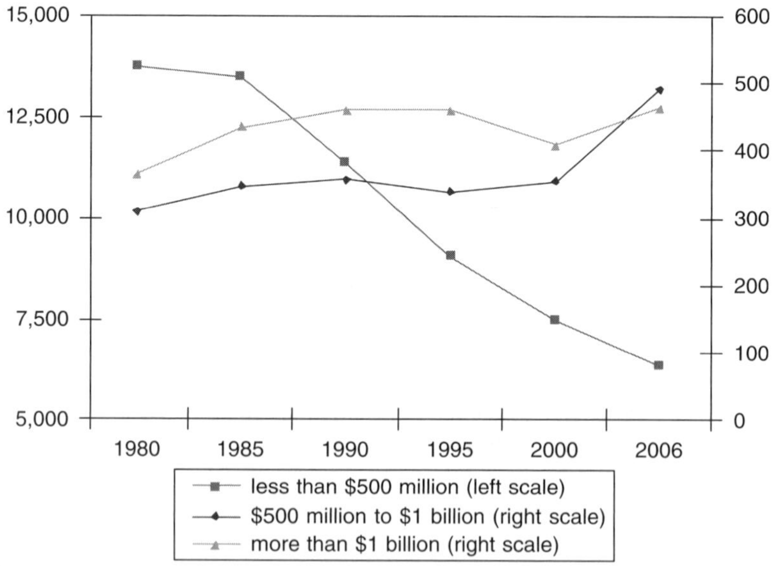

FIGURE 4 Size distribution of U.S. commercial banks, 1980–2006.
Source: Federal Deposit Insurance Corporation.

small banks; most of the acquisition targets since 1980 have been small banks; and some small banks grew up and out of this size group by merging with other small banks.

Figure 4 is a crude version of a survival analysis (Stigler 1958). The figure suggests that economically meaningful scale savings can be captured by growing up to \$500 million in assets but that growing beyond \$500 million—at least for community banks—yields far less substantial gains. The literature on bank scale economies is large and has produced differing estimates of minimum efficient scale over the years.[10] The earliest studies concluded that scale economies were fully exhausted by relatively small banks; most of these studies estimated minimum efficient scale for banks to be less than \$1 billion of assets (2001 dollars). More recent studies have yielded somewhat different insights; many of these studies conclude that scale economies are available for large regional and even superregional banks. The stark differences between these two sets of results may be due to the inferior (though state-of-the-art at that time) methodologies used by the earlier studies, but the more likely explanation is the implementation of high-volume bank production technologies that were not available in past decades.

Efficient scale is likely to be quite different for transactions banks as well as banks that employ other nontraditional banking business models. As noted earlier, Rossi (1998) shows that even very large mortgage banks (which use a classic transactions banking approach) face increasing returns to scale. Hughes et al. (1996) conclude that even the largest commercial bank holding companies (in which product volume is often dominated by transactions banking activities) also exhibit increasing returns to scale. And DeYoung (2005) argues that Internet-only banks (again, banks that use a pure transactions banking strategy) exhibit larger scale economies than similar-sized banks that have branches.

Geographic expansion by merger has eliminated thousands of banking charters and has created very large banking companies. For example, just before the passage of the Riegle-Neal Interstate Banking Act in 1994, only four banks had more than \$100 billion in assets; a decade later 10 banks were that large, with two of these banks approaching \$1 trillion in assets. This industrywide consolidation has had little effect on the structure of local markets—by definition, a geographic expansion merger leaves the target market shares unchanged—but the nature of the competitive rivalry in the target market can change. Studies have shown improved cost efficiency at small local banks following market entry by large out-of-market banks, presumably because of competitive pressure (DeYoung, Hasan, and Kirchhoff 1998; Evanoff and Ors forthcoming). Other studies have shown that outside entrants with stronger "brand images" are able to expand their local market shares more quickly (Berger and Dick, forthcoming), consistent with the idea that perceived differentiation can be an effective tool for large banks that sell financial commodity products.

Geographic expansion mergers have also increased the distances within banking organizations and may have created internal management problems. Berger and DeYoung (2001, 2006) find that banking affiliates located farther away from the headquarters

[10]See Mester (1987), Clark (1988), Evanoff and Israilevich (1991), and Berger and Mester (1997) for reviews of the bank scale economy at various points in time.

bank were less operationally efficient. While improvements in communications and information technologies have proved helpful in reducing these long-distance management problems, such organizational inefficiencies are one reason that small, locally focused banks may continue to be financially viable in competition with large banks. Distances between banks and their loan clientele have also increased over time. This phenomenon is mainly technology driven: automated, credit–scored lending models allow banks to make consumer, mortgage, credit card, and even some small business loans to borrowers they have never met in person, and asset securitization and credit derivatives allow banks to manage the risk associated with this type of lending (Petersen and Rajan 2002, DeYoung, Glennon, and Nigro 2006).

It is important to understand that the reduction in banking companies over the past two decades has not necessarily increased the distances between borrowers and lenders, because banks have simultaneously increased the size of their branching networks. There are about 70,000 commercial bank branches in the United States today, compared to only about 40,000 in 1990. This explosion in bank branches has been largely strategic in nature. For example, in some markets (such as Chicago), large banking companies are "packing the map" with branches in order to establish market presence and to limit entry by competitors. By increasing the size and scope of its branch network, a bank can position itself closer to both its current clients and its rivals' customers. This strategy can be especially important for large, transactions banks; although it is difficult for these banks to offer personalized banking services, they can offer high levels of customer convenience by locating close by. This higher level of convenience may explain why retail customers appear willing to pay higher deposit-related fees at large banks. Finally, physical branches located in prominent places also serve as an important advertising vehicle, especially in markets into which a bank has just expanded.

5.2. Noninterest Income

After these dramatic changes in industry structure, perhaps the next biggest change in the U.S. banking system has been the shift from interest income to noninterest income. As shown in Figure 5, the percentage of total industry income derived from noninterest income doubled between 1980 and 2000.

The increased importance of noninterest income at U.S. banks can be traced to three primary sources. First, product market deregulation (that is, the expansion of Section 20 securities subsidiaries during the 1990s, insurance powers granted to national banks during the late 1990s by the Office of the Comptroller of the Currency, and the Gramm-Leach-Bliley Act of 1999) granted banking companies the power to produce or sell nontraditional banking services, such as equity and debt underwriting, securities brokerage, and insurance products. These lines of business generate primarily fee income and negligible interest income. Second, some traditional lines of banking business now generate fee income instead of or in addition to interest income. For example, while in the past a bank would earn interest income by lending money to a business client, today that bank might now earn a fee by providing a backup line of credit for a

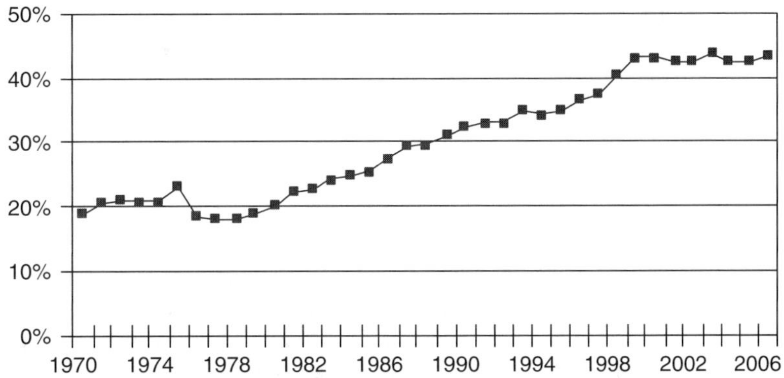

FIGURE 5 U.S. commercial banking industry, aggregate noninterest income as a percent of operating income, 1970–2006.
Source: Federal Deposit Insurance Corporation.

business client that issues its own debt securities. Similarly, the securitization of home mortgages and consumer loans has transformed an interest-based line of business into a fee-based line of business. Third, after the Federal Reserve relaxed Regulation Q, banks began to charge explicit fees for depositor services (teller services, check charges, certified checks, bounced checks, etc.) rather than providing them free of charge in lieu of interest on deposit balances.

DeYoung and Roland (2001) argue that the expansion of noninterest income may have reduced the risk-adjusted returns of banks, contrary to the expectations of many in the industry who expected fee income to be more stable than interest income and/or that fee-based products would diversify bank earnings. First, they point out that the stream of fees generated by some financial services is likely to be more volatile than stream of interest income from loans. For example, compare the fee income from mortgage loans that are originated and securitized to the interest income from a small business loan that is held in portfolio—the former is a nonrepeat business with revenues that are sensitive to volatility in the housing market and mortgage interest rates, while the latter is based on a long-term relationship that both the borrower and the lender have an interest in continuing. Similarly, the fees charged for brokerage activities are based on the value of the assets traded or under management, so this income contains systematic (nondiversifiable) risk associated with the business cycle. Second, the authors point out that the production of fee-based services usually requires high fixed costs (personnel expenses), while producing credit requires high variable costs (interest expenses). The high fixed-to-variable cost ratio for fee-based activities results in a high degree of operating leverage, which of course amplifies revenue volatility into even greater earnings volatility.

Several empirical studies have investigated the riskiness of noninterest income at U.S. commercial banks. DeYoung and Roland (2001) show that (non-deposit-related) fee income is associated with both higher revenue volatility and higher earnings volatility. DeYoung and Rice (2004b) find that marginal increases in noninterest income are associated with a worsening of banks' risk–return tradeoff. Stiroh (2004a, 2004b) finds no evidence of diversification gains at banks that combine interest and noninterest income.

5.3. Financial Performance

Porter (1980) would refer to the two broad strategies illustrated in Figure 3 as "generic strategies." Within any generic strategy there can be many strategic variations having similar though not identical characteristics. DeYoung and Rice (2004a) defined 11 such strategic groups within the U.S. commercial banking industry, with the objective of determining whether these different banking business models generated similar or different financial returns. Banks were assigned to one or more of these strategic groups based on the financial services in which they concentrated, the input mixes and production technologies they used to generate those services, their growth strategies, and the customer segments they targeted. Banks with less than $500 million in assets were excluded from the exercise because, as discussed earlier, these banks are likely operating below minimum efficient banking scale. For the remaining banks, the mean ROE (a measure of expected return) and standard deviation of ROE (a measure of risk) were calculated using data from 1993 through 2003. Finally, the average risk and average return were calculated across the banks in each strategic group.

The results of this exercise are displayed in Figure 6, where the points on the graph represent the risk-expected return combination for each of the 11 strategic groups. The attributes of the "nontraditional" group (large size, substantial loan securitization activity, high noninterest income, low core deposit funding) are closest to the generic "transactions banking" strategy in the southwest corner of Figure 3, while the attributes

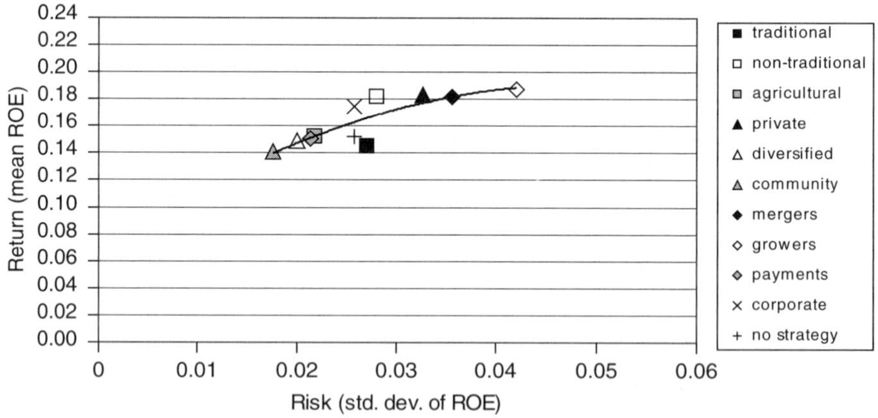

FIGURE 6 Estimated risk and return associated with 11 different commercial banking strategies, 1993–2003.

Excludes assets less than $500 million.

Source: DeYoung and Rice (2004a).

of the "community bank" group (small size, local focus, portfolio lending, low noninterest income, high core deposit funding) are closest to the generic "relationship banking" strategy in the northeast corner of Figure 3. The community banking group generated a very low expected return and very low risk, while the nontraditional group generated relatively higher expected return and relatively higher risk. In other words, transactions (nontraditional) banking is riskier than relationship (community) banking, but the owners of transactions banks receive higher expected returns in order to put up with this riskiness—that is, there is a positive tradeoff between risk and expected return across banking strategies. The regression line running through the 11 points represents the average risk–return tradeoff in the industry, moving from strategic group to strategic group.[11]

The high level of risk for the nontraditional strategic group and the low level of risk for the community banking group are both consistent with the research findings discussed in the prior section: Noninterest income is relatively volatile, while relationship lending income is relatively stable. Similarly, the risk–return positions of the other strategic groups make economic sense. The high expected returns for banks that were growing quickly during the sample period ("growers" and "mergers") reflect the profitable investment opportunities that make firms grow quickly, and the high risk for these banks reflects the transitory expenses associated with rapid growth (for example, one-time merger-related charges and short-run excess capacity at newly established branches). "Diversified" banks that produce a balanced set of different loan and fee-based outputs operated with relatively low risk. "Private" banks that manage the investment portfolios of wealthy clientele had relatively high levels of risk, reflecting the sensitivity of their fee income to systematic or market risk. "Traditional" banks that have not availed themselves of recent financial innovations (banks with no income from asset securitization or banks with a heavy dependence on interest income) and banks with "no strategy" (those that did not fall into any of the other 10 strategic groups) have poor risk-expected return tradeoffs; the former result illustrates the peril of nonprogressive, stagnant management practices, while the latter result illustrates the dangers of being "stuck in the middle."

6. IS THE INDUSTRY SAFE AND SOUND TODAY?

The commercial banking industry has grown far more diverse over a very short amount of time. Today's largest banks dwarf those of just 20 years ago, while small community banks still exist in large numbers. Some banks practice strategies that rely almost completely on noninterest income, while more traditional banks still exist that rely primarily on interest income. Some banks use asset securitization and derivative securities to manage credit and interest-rate risk, while other banks continue to rely primarily on careful loan underwriting, monitoring, and asset–liability management practices. Some banks create brand images with advertising campaigns, while others continue to let word of

[11] The regression was estimated using an intercept term and a simple quadratic specification of risk.

mouth carry their reputations to local customers. Most banks continue to count on core deposit funding, while many of the largest banks purchase a large portion of their funds in financial markets.

Given this increased diversity, one would expect substantial variation in financial performance across banking companies—and perhaps a greater chance that, at any given time, at least some banking companies would be suffering financial distress. Is the banking industry safer and sounder today than 20 years ago? The answer is almost certainly yes. Figure 7 shows the aggregate equity-to-assets ratios for U.S. commercial banks (book values) each year during the postwar period. Note the continuous improvement in the aggregate capital level that started in the early 1990s, increasing from 6 percent then to a historically high level of 10 percent today. This large reservoir of capital provides a substantial margin of safety and soundness against the (perhaps) increased opportunities for risk taking in today's deregulated banking industry.

This large capital cushion is the result of three developments. First and foremost is the stricter supervisory and regulatory framework mandated by the Federal Deposit Insurance Corporation Improvement Act, the centerpiece of which is the doctrine "prompt corrective action" that imposes costly operating restrictions on banks with low and diminishing levels of capital. In addition, the increased competitive pressure facing banking companies—predominantly a result of deregulation and financial innovation—requires banks to operate efficiently or else to exit the industry via acquisition. Efficient operations yield higher earnings, and higher earnings generate increased capital via retained earnings (Berger, DeYoung, and Flannery 2008). And finally, fortunate macroeconomic circumstances over the past 20 years, together with the elimination of so many regulatory constraints, have allowed banks to achieve record earnings levels. Figure 7 illustrates how truly impressive are these earnings increases: Industry return on equity has remained at historically high levels since the early 1990s despite the fact that industry equity levels have nearly doubled.

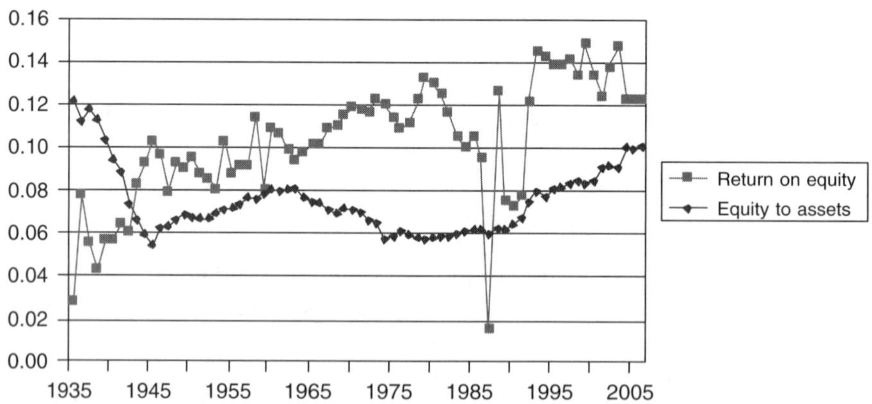

FIGURE 7 U.S. commercial banking industry, aggregate return-on-equity and equity-to-assets ratios, 1935–2006.

Source: Federal Deposit Insurance Corporation.

One should not conclude from this performance that today's banking industry is invulnerable to a banking crisis—unfortunately, history likes to repeat itself, as the current exposures of large banks to poorly performing subprime mortgages reminds us. In the coming years, it is likely that financial markets will continue to evolve, technology will continue to advance, and competition will continue to increase, bringing with them new profitable opportunities as well as new episodes of risk. So long as new regulation does not arise to halt or disrupt these processes, the U.S. commercial banking industry should weather those storms far more safely and soundly than would have been possible 20 years ago.

References

Avery, Robert B., Raphael W. Bostic, Paul S. Calem, and Glenn B. Canner. 1999. Credit Scoring: Statistical Issues and Evidence from Credit Bureau Files. Working paper, Board of Governors of the Federal Reserve System.

Bauer, Paul W., and Gary D. Ferrier. 1996. Scale Economies, Cost Efficiencies, and Technological Change in Federal Reserve Payments Processing, *Journal of Money, Credit, and Banking* 28(4, pt. 2), 1004–1039.

Berger, Allen N. 2003. The Economic Effects of Technological Progress: Evidence from the Banking Industry, *Journal of Money, Credit, and Banking* 35(2), 141–176.

Berger, Allen N., and Robert DeYoung. 2001. The Effects of Geographic Expansion on Bank Efficiency, *Journal of Financial Services Research* 19(2–3), 163–184.

Berger, Allen N., and Robert DeYoung. 2006. Technological Progress and the Geographic Expansion of the Banking Industry, *Journal of Money, Credit, and Banking* 38(6), 1483–1513.

Berger, Allen N., Robert DeYoung, and Mark J. Flannery. 2008. Why Do Large Banking Organizations Hold So Much Capital? *Journal of Financial Services Research*, forthcoming.

Berger, Allen N., and Astrid Dick. Forthcoming. Entry into Banking Markets and the First-Mover Advantage, *Journal of Money, Credit, and Banking*.

Berger, Allen N., W. Scott Frame, and Nathan H. Miller. 2005. Credit Scoring and the Availability, Price, and Risk of Small Business Credit, *Journal of Money, Credit, and Banking* 37(2), 191–222.

Berger, Allen N., and Loretta J. Mester. 1997. Inside the Black Box: What Explains Differences in the Efficiencies of Financial Institutions? *Journal of Banking and Finance* 21(7), 895–947.

Berger, Allen N., and Gregory F. Udell. 1993. Securitization, Risk, and the Liquidity Problem in Banking, in Michael Klausner and Lawrence J. White (eds.), *Structural Change in Banking*. Business One Irwin, Homewood, IL.

Berger, Allen N., Seth D. Bonime, Lawrence G. Goldberg, and Lawrence J. White. 2004. The Dynamics of Market Entry: The Effects of Mergers and Acquisitions on de Novo Entry and Small Business Lending in the Banking Industry, *Journal of Business* 77(4), 797–834.

Berger, Allen N., Claudia M. Buch, Gayle DeLong, and Robert DeYoung. 2004. Exporting Financial Institutions Management via Foreign Direct Investment Mergers and Acquisitions, *Journal of International Money and Finance* 23(3), 333–366.

Berger, Allen N., Nathan H. Miller, Mitchell A. Petersen, Raghuram G. Rajan, and Jeremy C. Stein. 2005. Does Function Follow Organizational Form? Evidence from the Lending Practices of Large and Small Banks, *Journal of Financial Economics* 76(2), 237–269.

Bohn, James, Diana Hancock, and Paul Bauer. 2001. Estimates of Scale and Cost Efficiency for Federal Reserve Currency Operations, *Federal Reserve Bank of Cleveland Economic Review* 37(4), 2–26.

Carey, Mark, Stephen Prowse, John Rea, and Gregory Udell. 1993. The Economics of Private Placements: A New Look, *Financial Markets, Institutions, and Instruments* 2, 1–66.

Clark, Jeffrey A. 1988. Economies of Scale and Scope at Depository Financial Institutions: A Review of the Literature, *Federal Reserve Bank of Kansas City Economic Review*, 16–33.

Cotterman, Robert F., and James E. Pearce. 1996. The Effects of the Federal National Mortgage Association and the Federal Home Loan Mortgage Corporation on Conventional Fixed-Rate Mortgage Yields, in U.S. Department of Housing and Urban Development, *Studies on privatizing Fannie Mae and Freddie Mac, U.S. Department of Housing and Urban Development*, U.S. Department of Housing and Urban Development, Washington, DC.

DeYoung, Robert. 1999. Mergers and the Changing Landscape of Commercial Banking (Part I), *Federal Reserve Bank of Chicago, Chicago Fed Letter* 145.

DeYoung, Robert. 2000. Mergers and the Changing Landscape of Commercial Banking (Part II), *Federal Reserve Bank of Chicago, Chicago Fed Letter* 150.

DeYoung, Robert. 2005. The Performance of Internet-Based Business Models: Evidence from the Banking Industry, *Journal of Business* 78(3), 893–947.

DeYoung, Robert. 2008. Banking in the United States, in *Oxford Handbook of Banking*. Oxford University Press, Oxford.

DeYoung, Robert, Dennis Glennon, and Peter Nigro. 2008. Borrower-Lender Distance, Credit Scoring, and Loan Performance: Evidence from Informationally Opaque Small Business Borrowers, *Journal of Financial Intermediation* 17, 113–143.

DeYoung, Robert, and Iftekhar Hasan. 1998. The Performance of de Novo Commercial Banks: A Profit Efficiency Approach, *Journal of Banking and Finance* 22(5), 565–587.

DeYoung, Robert, Iftekhar Hasan, and Bruce Kirchhoff. 1998. The Impact of Out-of-State Entry on the Efficiency of Local Commercial Banks, *Journal of Economics and Business* 50(2), 191–203.

DeYoung, Robert, and William C. Hunter. 2003. Deregulation, the Internet, and the Competitive Viability of Large Banks and Community Banks, in Benton Gup (ed.), *The Future of Banking*. Quorom Books, Westport, CT.

DeYoung, Robert, William C. Hunter, and Gregory F. Udell. 2004. The Past, Present, and Probable Future for Community Banks, *Journal of Financial Services Research* 25(2), 85–133.

DeYoung, Robert, William W. Lang, and Daniel L. Nolle, 2007. How the Internet Affects Output and Performance at Community Banks, *Journal of Banking and Finance* 31, 1033–1060.

DeYoung, Robert, and Tara Rice. 2004a. How Do Banks Make Money? A Variety of Business Strategies, *Federal Reserve Bank of Chicago Economic Perspectives* 28(4), 52–67.

DeYoung, Robert, and Tara Rice. 2004b. Noninterest Income and Financial Performance at U.S. Commercial Banks, *Financial Review* 39(1), 101–127.

DeYoung, Robert, and Karin P. Roland. 2001. Product Mix and Earnings Volatility at Commercial Banks: Evidence from a Degree of Total Leverage Model, *Journal of Financial Intermediation* 10(1), 54–84.

Evanoff, Douglas, and Philip Israilevich. 1991. Productive Efficiency in Banking, *Federal Reserve Bank of Chicago Economic Perspectives* (July), 11–32.

Evanoff, Douglas D., and Evren Ors. Forthcoming. Local Market Consolidation and Bank Productive Efficiency. Federal Reserve Bank of Chicago manuscript.

Frame, W. Scott, Aruna Srinivasan, and Lynn Woosley. 2001. The Effect of Credit Scoring on Small Business Lending, *Journal of Money, Credit, and Banking* 33(3), 813–825.

Frame, W. Scott, and Lawrence J. White. 2004. Empirical Studies of Financial Innovation: Lots of Talk, Little Action? *Journal of Economic Literature* 42(1), 116–144.

Furst, Karen, William W. Lang, and Daniel E. Nolle. 2001. Internet Banking in the U.S.: Landscape, Prospects, Industry Implications, *Journal of Financial Transformation* 2 (August), 45–52.

Furst, Karen, William W. Lang, and Daniel E. Nolle. 2002. Internet Banking. *Journal of Financial Services Research* 22(1–2), 95–117.

Gerdes, Geoffrey R., and Jack K. Walton II. 2002. The Use of Checks and Other Retail Noncash Payments in the United States, *Federal Reserve Bulletin* (August), 360–374.

Gilbert, R. Alton, David C. Wheelock, and Paul W. Wilson. 2002. New Evidence on the Fed's Productivity in Providing Payments Services. Working paper #2002-020A, Federal Reserve Bank of St. Louis.

Hannan, Timothy H., and John M. McDowell. 1984. The Determinants of Technology Adoption: The Case of the Banking Firm, *RAND Journal of Economics* 15(3), 328–335.

Hendershott, Patrick H., and James D. Shilling. 1989. The Impact of the Agencies on Conventional Fixed-Rate Mortgage Yields, *Journal of Real Estate Finance and Economics* 2(2), 101–115.

Hughes, Joseph P., William W. Lang, Loretta J. Mester, and Choon-Geol Moon. 1996. Efficient Banking Under Interstate Branching, *Journal of Money, Credit, and Banking* 28(4, pt. 2), 1045–1071.

Humphrey, David. 2002. U.S. Cash and Card Payments Over 25 Years. Working paper, Florida State University.

ICF Inc. 1990. Effects of the Conforming Loan Limit on Mortgage Markets. Final Report Prepared for the U.S. Department of Urban Development, Office of Policy Development and Research. Fairfax: ICF, Inc.

Keeton, William R. 2000. Are Mergers Responsible for the Surge in New Bank Charters? *Federal Reserve Bank of Kansas City Economic Review* (First Quarter), 21–41.

Mayes, Elizabeth. 2003. *Credit Scoring for Risk Managers: The Handbook for Lenders*. Elizabeth Mays (ed.), South-Western.

Mester, Loretta J. 1987. Efficient Production of Financial Services: Scale and Scope Economies, *Federal Reserve Bank of Philadelphia Business Review* (January), 15–25.

Mester, Loretta J. 1997. What's the Point of Credit Scoring? *Federal Reserve Bank of Philadelphia Business Review* (September/October), 3–16.

Passmore, Wayne, Roger Sparks, and Jamie Ingpen. 2001. GSEs, mortgage rates, and the long-run effects of mortgage securitization. Finance and Economics Discussion Series. Working paper 2001-26, Federal Reserve Board.

Petersen, Mitchell A., and Raghuram G. Rajan. 2002. Does Distance Still Matter? The Information Revolution and Small Business Lending, *Journal of Finance* 57(6), 2533–2570.

Porter, Michael E. 1980. *Competitive Strategy: Techniques for Analyzing Industries and Competitors*. Free Press, New York.

Rossi, Clifford V. 1998. Mortgage Banking Cost Structure: Resolving an Enigma, *Journal of Economics and Business* 50(2), 219–234.

Scott, Jonathan A. 2004. Small Business and the Value of Community Financial Institutions, *Journal of Financial Services Research* 25(2–3), 207–230.

Stein, Jeremy C. 2002. Information Production and Capital Allocation: Decentralized Versus Hierarchical Firms, *Journal of Finance* 57(5), 1891–1921.

Stigler, George J. 1958. The Economies of Scale, *Journal of Law and Economics* 1 (October), 54–71.

Stiroh, Kevin J. 2004a. Diversification in Banking: Is Noninterest Income the Answer? *Journal of Money, Credit, and Banking* 36(5), 853–882.

Stiroh, Kevin J. 2004b. Do Community Banks Benefit from Diversification? *Journal of Financial Services Research* 25(2–3), 135–160.

Sullivan, Richard J. 2001. Performance and Operation of Commercial Bank Web Sites, *Federal Reserve Bank of Kansas City Financial Industry Perspectives* (December), 23–33.

White, Lawrence J. 2003. Focusing on Fannie and Freddie: The Dilemmas of Reforming Housing Finance, *Journal of Financial Services Research* 23(1), 43–58.

CHAPTER 12

What Caused the Bank Capital Buildup of the 1990s?

Mark J. Flannery
University of Florida

Kasturi P. Rangan
Booz Allen Hamilton

Abstract

Large U.S. banks dramatically increased their capitalization during the 1990s, to the highest levels in more than 50 years. We document this buildup of capital and evaluate several potential motivations. Our results support the hypothesis that regulatory innovations in the early 1990s weakened conjectural government guarantees and enhanced the bank counterparties' incentive to monitor and price default risk. We find no evidence that a bank holding company's market capitalization increases with its asset volatility prior to 1994. Thereafter, the data display a strong cross-sectional relation between capitalization and asset risk. Our estimates indicate that most of the bank capital buildup over the sample period can be explained by greater bank risk exposures and the market's increased demand that large banks' default risk be priced.

1. INTRODUCTION

The data on large U.S. banks' equity ratios in Figure 1 indicate wide variations in the mean capital ratio during the course of the twentieth century. Figure 1 also indicates that the U.S. banking industry has undertaken a dramatic capital buildup over the last decade and a half. Large bank holding companies (BHCs) have more than doubled their equity ratios (measured using equity market values) between 1986 and 2001. Starting from the end of the 1990–91 recession, the expansion has been even more dramatic: The mean market equity ratio in our sample of large BHCs nearly tripled from 5.8 percent in 1990 to 17.5 percent in 2001. These equity ratios currently stand at their highest levels in 70 years. Book-valued capital ratios also rose quite sharply during the 1990s, to the point that virtually *no* large BHCs were operating below or close to the minimum capital levels required by regulators. Indeed, our mean sample BHC holds 75 percent more book capital than the regulatory minimum by the end of our sample period.

In this study we document this buildup of bank capital and investigate its genesis. Several factors might explain the capital buildup, and for expositional ease we classify them into three sets of explanations. First, the observed increase in capitalization might simply reflect an unusual period of bank profitability and share price appreciation during the 1990s. BHC capital ratios might thus have risen "passively," simply because bank managers failed to raise dividends or repurchase shares. Second, regulators may

We thank two anonymous referees and Joel Houston, Mike Ryngaert, M. Nimalendran, Ed Ettin, George Kaufman, Joe Mason, Manju Puri, Jean-Charles Rochet, James Thomson, Larry Wall, and seminar participants at Stanford University, the Federal Reserve Banks of Cleveland, New York, and San Francisco, the University of Kentucky, Tilburg University, Catholic University, the Federal Reserve Bank of Chicago Bank Structure Conference, the 2003 AFA annual meetings, the 2002 WFA meetings, and the 2002 EFA meetings for helpful comments on an earlier draft. Tony Saunders and Berry Wilson graciously provided us their data from Saunders and Wilson (1999) for the first 93 years of Figure 1. A previous version of this chapter was circulated under the title "Market Forces at Work in the Banking Industry: Evidence from the Capital Buildup of the 1990s."

Reprinted from *Review of Finance Advance Access* published online on March 22, 2007 (see *Review of Finance*, doi:10.1093/rof/rfm007) by permission of Oxford University Press.

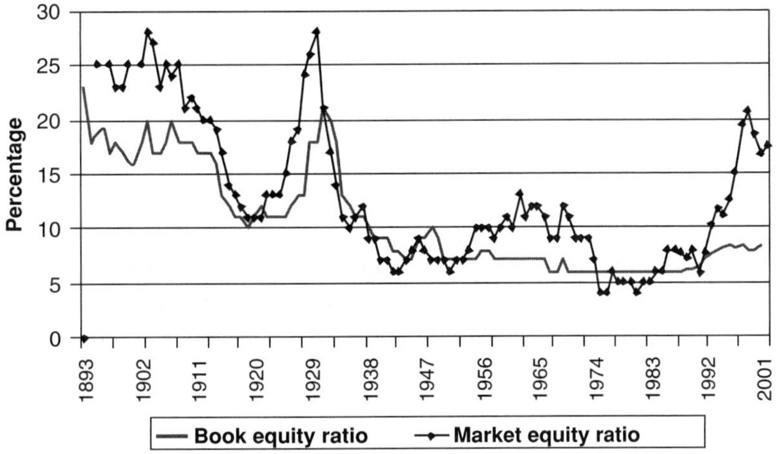

FIGURE 1 Market and book equity ratios for U.S. banks, 1893–2001.

have raised de jure or de facto capital requirements. A new set of risk-based (Basel) capital standards were introduced between year-ends 1990 and 1992, and the FDIC Improvement Act (FDICIA) (1991) sought to impose greater credit risk on uninsured bank liability holders. FDICIA also introduced a mandatory set of prompt corrective actions that increased the cost of violating the capital standard. Hence, direct supervisory pressure may have contributed to the capital buildup. Finally, the observed capital buildup might have been a rational response by market participants to changes in the banking environment, particularly to the withdrawal of implicit government guarantees. Through the late 1980s, creditors often escaped a large bank's failure without serious losses. Regulatory and legislative changes in the early 1990s may have reduced the market's perceived probability that a failed bank's counterparties would enjoy a government bailout. Banks therefore came under greater pressure to control their default probabilities. Rather than paying large default risk premia on uninsured obligations, banks chose to align their capital ratios more closely with their portfolio risk exposures.

Although each of these three explanations contributed to the capital buildup, our results strongly indicate that the majority of the capital buildup can be attributed to market forces. During the first half of our 1986–2001 sample period we find little correlation between portfolio risk and a bank's capitalization. After about 1993, however, bank capital ratios are reliably positively related to portfolio risk exposures, consistent with the hypothesis that counterparties began to price default risk when their conjectural guarantees were weakened by FDICIA and nationwide depositor preference. Bank risk exposures also increased during the 1990s, as banks were permitted to enter new, riskier lines of business (Stiroh 2004). We estimate that the combination of increased risk aversion and increased risk exposure explains the majority of the observed buildup. The passive effects of earning growth accounted for less than 3 percent of the buildup, and the stock market boom affected bank capital ratios only temporarily.

Our findings have several important implications. First, many supervisors and academics have assumed that a federal safety net distorts bank incentives to limit leverage, implying that supervisory capital standards will always constrain bank leverage. While this may have been true in the 1980s, our results clearly show that it is no longer accurate. Large U.S. BHCs hold capital beyond their regulatory requirements, and future theoretical models should recognize this possibility. Second, we demonstrate that market investors can *influence* bank behavior, in the sense of Bliss and Flannery (2002). Prior studies have documented the impact of bank condition on the pricing of its (debt) obligations but have been unable to demonstrate that the banks respond to this price sensitivity. We establish here a connection between investor preferences and bank default risk. Our results indicate that markets can recognize *and* influence bank default risk. Market discipline can thus play an important role in bank supervision, as envisioned by the Third Pillar of Basel II. Third, it has been widely conjectured that the anticipated treatment of failed institutions importantly affects market participants' incentives to discipline bank risk taking. We show that the market's influence on bank leverage became more prominent only after regulatory innovations (FDICIA and national depositor preference) had placed bank counterparties more explicitly at risk.

The remainder of this chapter is organized as follows. Section 2 discusses the determinants of bank leverage and the relationship between a banking firm's book value of equity (the object of supervisory concern) and its market value of equity (the presumed object of market concern). Section 3 documents that bank capital ratios and risks both increased *and* became more dispersed during the 1986–2001 period, and it identifies several hypotheses to explain these developments. Section 4 describes our empirical model; Section 5 reports the main results. In Section 6 we test the hypothesis that higher bank capital ratios reflect increased supervisory pressure. Section 7 provides robustness results, and the final section discusses implications for banking theory and regulation.

2. DETERMINING A BANK'S OPTIMAL LEVERAGE

In an unregulated market, a firm's fixed claimants (*bondholders*) are repaid only if the firm's asset market value exceeds the present value of promised payments (Merton 1974). Bondholders therefore demand a promised interest rate that reflects the amount by which a firm's assets exceed its liabilities, that is, the firm's equity capital ratio. Although capital structure is irrelevant under extreme financial market conditions (Modigliani and Miller 1958), theory implies an optimal leverage due to corporate taxation, bankruptcy costs, and various agency problems. Firms seek to maximize their market value by jointly selecting operating risk and financial (leverage) risk. If conditions change (e.g., through a change in perceived bank risk or a change in creditors' aversion to bank risk), firms should change their preferred level of equity capital.

Banking firms' unique access to a (formal and informal) federal safety net may prominently affect their capital decisions. For example, Merton (1977) concludes that bank shareholders wish to maximize both leverage and portfolio risk when all bank liabilities are guaranteed by federal insurance at a fixed premium. Marcus (1984) shows that this single-period result does not generalize to multiperiod models when the bank expects to earn economic quasi-rents. In a multiperiod model with valuable banking charters, Merton (1978) shows that the value-maximizing choice for equity holders balances two effects: maximizing risk to take advantage of the immediate deposit-insurance subsidy vs. constraining risk to increase the expected duration of the anticipated quasi-rents.[1] Keeley (1990), Berger (1995), and Demsetz, Saidenberg, and Strahan (1996) demonstrate empirically that these rents do affect capital decisions.

Investors have sometimes viewed U.S. regulators as de facto insuring all liabilities, especially at the largest banks (O'Hara and Shaw 1990). However, supervisory and political reactions to the 1980s' thrift debacle almost surely weakened bank creditors' de facto protection during the 1990s.[2] In 1991, FDICIA limited the insurer's ability to engineer "purchase and assumption" transactions that protected uninsured bank claimants from default losses. The Omnibus Budget Reconciliation Act of 1993 subordinated all nondeposit financial claims to a failed bank's deposits. In states without prior depositor preference laws, unsecured nondeposit investors thereby became much more exposed to default losses. Market disciplinary forces became more prominent as conjectured government guarantees abated. In reaction to their increased risk exposure, large liability holders would demand higher returns on their claims, reducing bank equity values. In an effort to mitigate this increase in funding costs, bank owners would likely raise their equity and/or lower risk. Such a response might be particularly important for the largest banks, whose creditworthiness affects their ability to trade in OTC derivatives markets and to provide credit enhancements for commercial paper issuers.

While most nonfinancial firms choose their optimal capital ratios primarily in response to market constraints, regulated financial institutions must also heed their supervisors' capital adequacy requirements. Banking firms must therefore satisfy two equity constraints: Uninsured market counterparties price their claims on the basis of equity's *market* value, while supervisors impose *book* value restrictions.[3] Although

[1] These rents or quasi-rents could derive from several sources. First, banks may have monopoly protection (Keeley 1990). Second, durable bank–borrower relationships may reduce the cost of loan origination and hence make repeat lending more profitable (Berger and Udell 1995, Petersen and Rajan 1995). Third, productive efficiency tends to bestow quasi-rents in a competitive market. Morgan and Stiroh (1999) provide evidence that bank holding companies in the 1990s have had higher productivity and better scale economies, which has translated into improved performance.

[2] Evidence of this change in perceived policy can be seen in banks' subordinated debenture spreads. Avery, Belton, and Goldberg (1988) and Gorton and Santomero (1990) find no evidence that subordinated debenture rates reflect bank risks in 1983–84. Flannery and Sorescu (1996) show that this situation had changed by about 1989, after a regulatory transition toward letting market participants share the losses when a banking firm fails. See also Jagtiani, Kaufman, and Lemieux (2002) or Morgan and Stiroh (1999).

[3] Despite the known faults with book value measures of bank equity, supervisors have chosen to use book values for two main reasons. First, many U.S. banks have no publicly traded equity. An initial effort to treat all regulated banks similarly therefore mandated use of book values. Second, supervisors in the United States and (especially) abroad suspect that market values are excessively volatile and potentially inaccurate. Kane and Ünal (1990) model the deviations of market from book values and show that these differences vary systematically with market conditions.

these two capital ratios reflect similar features of the firm, they are not perfectly correlated.[4] GAAP accounting conventions provide managerial options to raise book capital ratios independent of the market's valuation. For example, many BHCs sold their headquarters building in the late 1980s, booked a capital gain, and then leased it back from the purchaser. A bank can also "cherry-pick" its securities portfolio, realizing the gains on appreciated securities while postponing the sale of assets with unrealized losses. Loan provisioning provides another (notorious) avenue for troubled banking firms to boost their book capital. This reserving system is designed to approximately mark the loan book to market (Flannery 1989), but managers have substantial latitude about how much inside information to reflect in their reported loan loss allowance.[5]

Finance theory indicates that the creditors of any large corporation should assess their default risk exposure on the basis of equity market valuations instead of book valuations. Book values are inherently backward looking, while default probabilities depend on future developments, which investors strive to impound into the firm's stock prices. Equity's *market* value determines the probability of credit loss because it measures the amount that existing shareholders will pay to avoid default. For the case of depository institutions in particular, Saunders (2000) comments that:

> The concept of [a financial institution's] economic net worth is really a *market value accounting* concept. . . . Because it can actually distort the true solvency position of an FI, the book value of capital concept can be misleading to managers, owners, liability holders, and regulators alike. (pp. 444–445)

The ready availability of book value measures from bank call reports and bank holding company Y-9C reports has led some researchers to rely on book values when studying bank leverage (e.g., Berger 1995, Osterberg and Thomson 1996). However, Marcus (1983) and Keeley (1990) have previously used market equity values to measure large banks' capitalization, and KMV successfully markets company default estimates ("EDF™ Credit Measure") derived from the firm's market share price. We use market equity ratios as our primary variable of analysis.

Despite our theoretical and empirical preference for market equity values as the relevant determinant of BHC default risk, we cannot ignore book capital regulations, which may limit a bank's ability to return unwanted capital to shareholders. For example, dividends and share repurchases reduce book and market capital by (roughly) the same dollar amount. Unless a bank can freely exercise GAAP options to increase stated book equity, its ability to reduce market capital ratios may be limited by supervisory constraints on book capital. Since we are interested in the impact of supervisors and market forces on bank equity ratios, our empirical specification must control for possible book equity constraints on market value equity ratios.

[4]For our sample BHCs, the simple correlation between book and market capital ratios is 0.68 across the full time period. Cross-sectional correlations within a year range from 0.49 to 0.71, with a mean of 0.59.

[5]Note that each of these three strategies for raising book capital simultaneously increases the present value of the firm's tax obligations.

3. RISING U.S. BANK CAPITALIZATION, 1986–2001

We begin by establishing that BHC equity ratios rose, in terms of both book and market values, during our sample period for the 100 largest BHCs; then we discuss the possible causes for this capital increase.[6]

3.1. The Supervisors' Focus: Book Capital Ratios

Supervisors' minimum capital requirements are multifaceted. Before the Basel Accord came into effect at the end of 1990, U.S. regulators employed a simple leverage ratio to assess capital adequacy: "Primary" capital (the sum of equity plus loan loss reserves) had to exceed 5.5 percent of assets, while the total amount of primary plus "secondary" (primarily qualifying subordinated debentures) capital had to exceed 6 percent of assets. The Basel Accord sought to relate equity capital more closely to portfolio credit risks by introducing the concept of risk-weighted assets (RWA), which weights on-book assets and off-balance-sheet commitments in proportion to their presumed credit risks. The Basel Accord also established two components of regulatory "capital" (Saunders 2000, p. 457):

Tier 1: Includes common equity, noncumulative preferred stock and minority interests in consolidated subsidiaries.

Tier 2: Includes the loan loss allowance (up to a maximum of 1.25 percent of RWA), cumulative and limited-life preferred stock, subordinated debentures, and certain hybrid securities (such as mandatory convertible debt).

Under the Basel Accord, U.S. regulators set the minimum acceptable level of Tier 1 capital at 4 percent of RWA, while the sum of Tier 1 plus Tier 2 capital must exceed 8 percent of RWA.[7] Well-managed banks' capital levels were intended to exceed these minima, and in 1991 FDICIA specified that an institution with at least 5 percent Tier 1 and 10 percent Tier 2 ratios would be considered "well capitalized" and therefore freed from selected regulatory constraints.

The solid line in Figure 2 illustrates that the 100 largest banks' median ratio of book equity to total assets rose from 5.98 percent in 1986 to 8.19 percent in 2001. U.S. book capital ratios are currently higher than they have been in more than half a century.[8] Figure 3 plots the mean Tier 1 and total (Tier 1 plus Tier 2) capital ratios

[6]We find very similar patterns in the equity ratios of smaller BHCs (asset ranks 101–1,000), but we focus our attention on the largest 100 BHCs, which held more than 71 percent of all (FDIC-insured) banking assets during our sample period.

[7]U.S. supervisors implemented the Basel capital standards in two steps. At year-end 1990, banks and BHCs were required to hold Tier 1 capital of at least 3.625 percent of RWA and total capital (Tier 1 plus Tier 2) of at least 7.25 percent. At year-end 1992, the minimum acceptable ratios became 4 and 8 percent of RWA. In the United States, a "leverage" requirement further mandated that Tier 1 capital exceed 3 percent of total (unweighted) assets. This constraint has not been a major factor for our sample banks, so we omit it from our analysis.

[8]Using means in place of medians reveals very similar patterns in the equity ratios (see Figure 1).

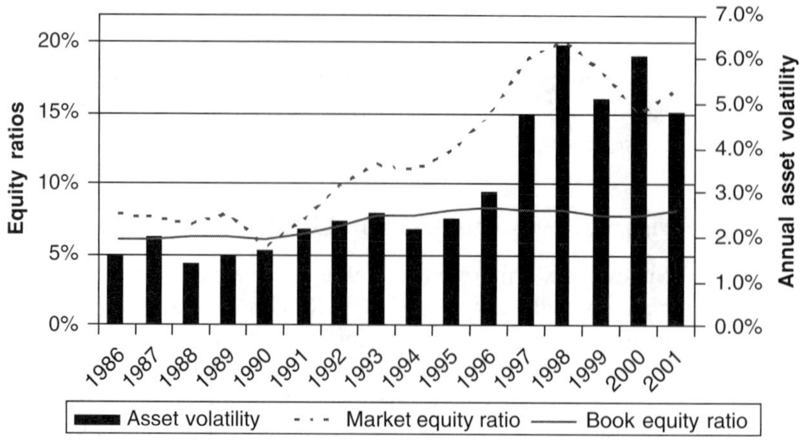

FIGURE 2 Median market and book equity ratios, and asset volatility for the 100 largest U.S. BHCs.

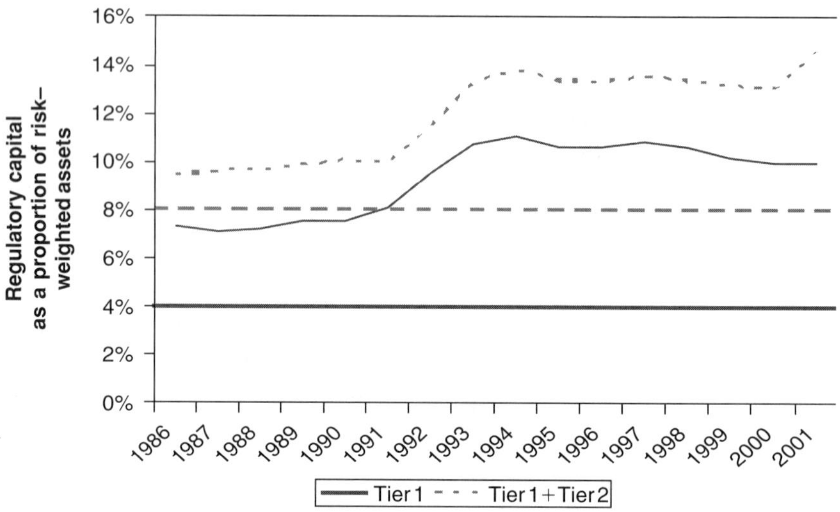

FIGURE 3 Compliance with Basel standards, 100 largest BHCs.

relative to their required minimum values of 4 percent and 8 percent, respectively.[9] The average bank has exceeded the minimum required capital ratio by a comfortable margin throughout our sample period, and this margin expanded considerably early in the 1990s. The sample BHCs' mean Tier 1 (total) capital stood at 7.26 percent (9.44 percent) of RWA in 1986 but reached 11.1 percent (13.8 percent) by 1994 and remained relatively stable thereafter.[10]

[9]The Appendix explains how we compute these ratios from data reported in the Y-9C forms.

[10]Starting in about 1998, the Tier 2 capital ratio rises and the Tier 1 ratio falls. As we discuss in connection with upcoming Figure 8, BHCs were substituting subordinated (Tier 2) debt for equity capital over this period.

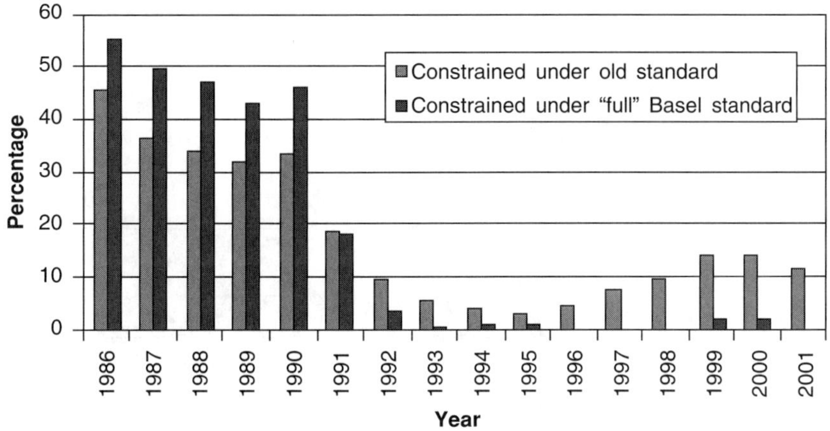

FIGURE 4 Percentage of 100 largest BHCs constrained by supervisory capital standards.

As average capital ratios have risen, the number of individual banks constrained by capital adequacy regulations has fallen sharply. Figure 4 plots the proportion of the 100 largest BHC constrained by de jure capital standards, where we define a firm as *constrained* if its book capital ratio exceeds the regulatory minimum by less than 1.5 percent. The percentage of constrained BHC trended down from the start of the sample period and dropped sharply after the Basel standards were implemented at year-end 1990. Overall, it appears that supervisory capital restrictions have been effectively irrelevant to the 100 largest U.S. BHCs since about 1992. Most of the BHCs with "excess" market-valued capital ratios could have paid out at least some of that excess capital without violating regulatory constraints.

To summarize, the evidence indicates that book capital ratios at the largest U.S. BHCs have risen well above statutory minima. Section 6 evaluates whether this means that supervisory capital standards no longer affect the banks' capital decisions.

3.2. Investors' Focus: Market Capital Ratios

The dashed line in Figure 2 plots the median ratio of common equity's market value to the market value of total assets (defined as the sum of equity's market value plus liabilities' book value).[11] This equity ratio stood at 7.9 percent in 1986, declined until about 1990, and then began a rapid increase. The median market capital ratio peaked in 1998 at 20.1 percent, before ending the sample period at 16.7 percent. At the end of our sample period, bank equity ratios were almost three times their 1990 value (5.8 percent) and more than double their 1986 value. Figure 5 plots histograms showing the distribution of capital ratios during 1986–88 and 1998–2001. The sample's central

[11] For each calendar year, we plot the median quarter-end value.

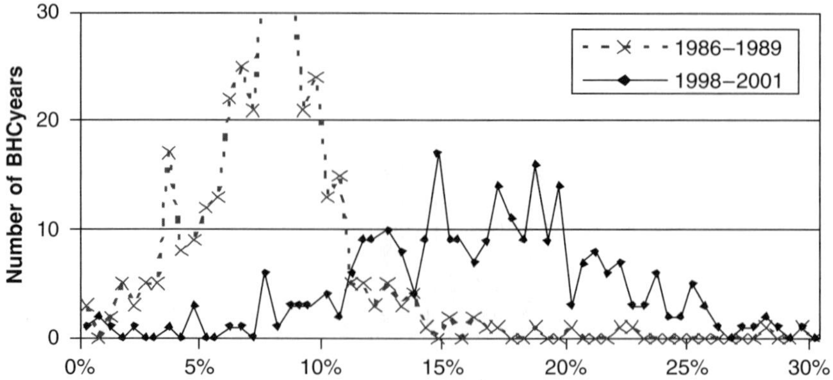

FIGURE 5 Histogram of market equity ratio.

tendency clearly shifts rightward. Equally striking is the *near doubling* of the capital ratios' cross-sectional standard deviation, from 3.53 percent to 6.71 percent.[12]

3.3. BHC Portfolio Volatility and Default Risks

A firm's equity capital protects fixed claimants from default losses in the event of moderate declines in the firm's total market value. Because equity is the junior claim on firm cash flows, its return reflects asset value changes, liability value changes, and other developments. We estimate each BHC's total risk exposure by delevering its equity volatility:

$$\sigma_A = \left(\frac{E}{A}\right)\sigma_E \tag{1}$$

where σ_E is the standard deviation of the BHC's daily equity returns over a calendar quarter, E is the market value of the BHC's equity at the end of the quarter, and A is the quasi-market value of assets (E plus the book value of debt) at the end of the quarter. We annualize the resulting measure of σ_A by multiplying the quarter's daily standard deviation by the square root of 250 (the approximate number of trading days in a year). The variable σ_A incorporates all BHC risks, including asset returns, liability returns, changes in the off-balance-sheet book, and operating efficiencies.

Figure 2 indicates that large BHCs' median asset volatilities rose slowly from 1986 to 1996, then jumped to what appears to be a new, higher level in 1997. Recall that these were not placid times for large BHCs. The Asia crisis of 1997 raised the specter of large default losses for banks with overseas loan portfolios, while the Russian–LTCM disorders in August–September 1998 cast doubt on the stability of the international financial

[12]A similar, although less dramatic, pattern occurred for book equity ratios, which rose from a mean 6.12 percent in 1986–88 to 8.19 percent in 1998–2000, while the cross-sectional standard deviation of this ratio rose from 1.32 percent to 1.81 percent.

system. A general measure of equity market volatility (the CBOE's VXO) was much higher after 1995. The late 1990s also witnessed the implementation of previous deregulatory decisions, which allowed banks to expand their offerings across geographical and product markets. Recent evidence suggests that these changes actually provided few diversification benefits but, rather, increased bank revenue variances (Stiroh 2004, DeYoung and Ronald 2001, and Schuermann 2004).

How can we reconcile Figure 2's sharp increase in portfolio risk with a general view that the U.S. banking sector had low default risk in the 1998–2001 period (including the recession of March–November 2001)? One must simply note that equity ratios rose along with estimated asset volatilities. Figure 6 shows the median BHC's approximate "distance to default," as measured by the ratio of equity capitalization to asset volatility. Assuming that BHC value is distributed normally, the mean 1998–2001 distance to default of 3.08 implies a BHC default probability of roughly 0.2 percent. Had BHC portfolio risk increased with no corresponding change in capitalization, the sector would surely have had numerous BHC failures. However, capitalization did rise over time, and our empirical tests will demonstrate that the *association* between a bank's risk and its capital ratio became closer and more significant later in the sample period.

Figure 7 plots histograms showing the distribution of σ_A during 1986–99 and 1998–2001. The sample BHCs' mean risk rose from 1.76 percent during 1986–89 to 6.09 percent in 1998–2001. At the same time, the cross-sectional standard deviation of asset volatilities more than tripled, from 0.93 percent to 3.49 percent. The concurrent increases in mean capitalization and mean risk illustrated in Figures 5 and 7 suggest that the changes may be related to one another. The fact that both capital ratios and asset volatilities became more dispersed over the period should permit strong statistical tests of the hypothesis that riskier banks have added more to their capital ratios, presumably in response to external pressures.

At very high leverage levels, equity's market value may include the value of safety net subsidies. With nontrivial safety net subsidies, (E/A) in Eq. (1) would be biased

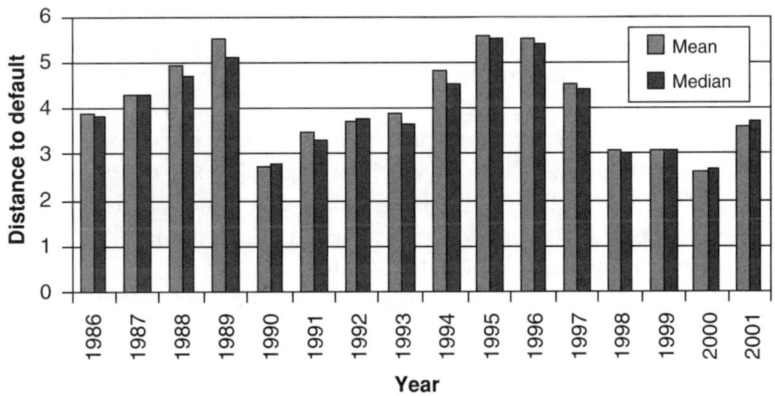

FIGURE 6 Annual estimates of "distance to default."

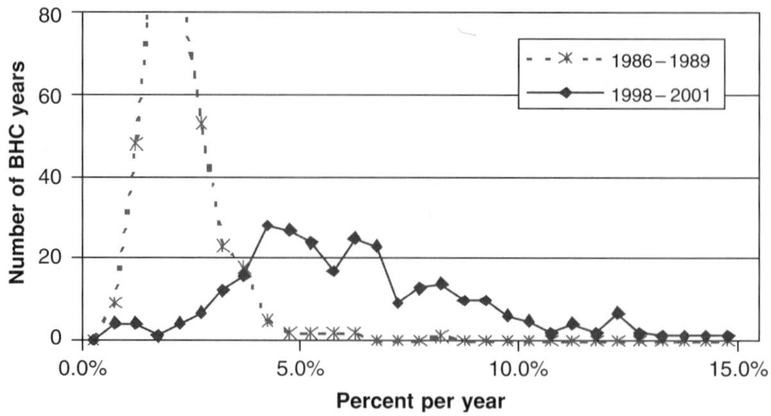

FIGURE 7 Histogram of asset volatility.

upward, and so too would be our measure of σ_A. The resulting positive correlation between leverage and asset risk would bias our regression results toward finding a significant relation between leverage and risk. To address this potential problem, we construct an instrumental variable for σ_A. We also used the method of Ronn and Verma (1986) to adjust measured equity value for safety net subsidies. (Although most of our reported results utilize the asset risk measured defined in Eq. (1), upcoming Table 6 shows that our main conclusions are unaffected if Ronn–Verma estimates of leverage and asset risk are used instead.)

3.4. Possible Causes of the Increased Capitalization

Why have large BHCs increased their capital ratios, and what is responsible for the greater cross-sectional variation in capital? One clear possibility is that the observed increases were not a result of deliberate actions on the part of banks but were an artifact of the sample period under study. The 1990s were exceptionally profitable for the banking industry, and Berger (1995) reports that commercial bank "dividends do not fully respond to changes in earnings, so part of earnings changes accumulate into future changes in the level of capital" (p. 454). Our BHCs clearly exhibit this type of behavior: Their mean earnings rose from 8.1 percent of book equity during 1986–91 to 14.6 percent during 1992–2001, while dividends rose only from 3.4 percent of book equity to 4.1 percent. Hence part of the observed increase in capital could be attributed to the "passive" retention of earnings, although an active decision to build capital through retained earnings would look the same.

Share prices also rose very sharply during the 1990s. Perhaps banks simply rode this boom, accepting whatever level of market capitalization was associated with its share prices. Indeed, if banks felt that the market overvalued their shares, they may have *issued* new shares to take advantage of investors' optimism. Either the stock price effect alone or endogenous share issues would tend to raise bank capital ratios temporarily,

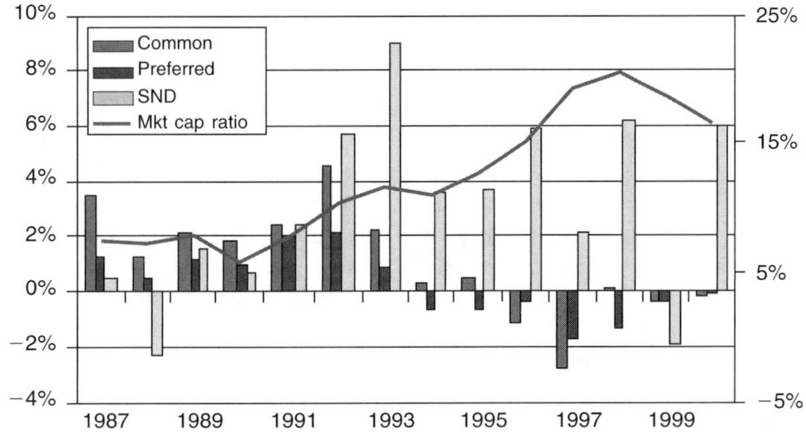

FIGURE 8 Changes in outstanding capital instruments; Top 100 BHCs (% of prior year-end common + preferred equity).

even if bankers were not trying to provide capital protection consistent with their risk exposures. However, the large banks' securities issuance suggests that they were trying to limit the impact of share price increases on their market capital ratios. The line graph in Figure 8 plots the mean market equity ratio of the top 100 BHCs. The bars in Figure 8 plot the net issuance of three security types by the top 100 BHCs, for each year of our sample period. While the dominant security issued before 1992 was common or preferred equity, this situation changed sharply after 1992. In the years 1994 through 2001, the 100 largest U.S. BHCs retired \$331 million of equity while issuing \$1,731 million of net new subordinated debentures. Put another way, each year between 1994 and 2001, the sample BHC retired shares equal to 1.23 percent of their prior year-end's equity value (common plus preferred) while issuing net new debentures equal to 5.76 percent of prior year-end equity. Ceteris paribus, these transactions increased book leverage while share price gains were reducing market leverage, consistent with the hypothesis that managers were trying to "undo" the leverage effects of share price appreciation.[13] Figure 3 shows that beginning in 1998, the mean Tier 1 capital ratio was actually falling in book value terms.

Why might the large banks have chosen to raise their equity ratios? Perhaps tougher capital regulation forced them to do so. This possibility seems particularly relevant for the early 1990s, when U.S. supervisors were implementing Basel capital rules. Figure 3 shows that book equity ratios rose quite sharply between 1991 and 1994. Perhaps the "excess" capital in Figure 3 reflects a rational margin of safety, protecting the banks

[13] At least some of this substitution was probably elicited by an important regulatory change. On October 21, 1996, the Federal Reserve Board decided that deeply subordinated debentures issued to a trust financed by preferred stock ("trust preferred shares") would count as up to 25 percent of Tier 1 regulatory capital (Benston et al. 2003). BHCs thereby acquired an incentive to replace some of their Tier 1 capital (e.g., common and preferred shares) with the new debentures. Even with this caveat, the evidence in Figure 8 suggests managerial decisions actively increased leverage in 1993–95 and perhaps 1996.

from heavy supervisory penalties if they violate the de jure capital standard. Another plausible hypothesis is that higher capitalization was a rational response to regulatory innovations that reduced the extent of the federal safety net. Evidence from the bank debenture market shows that conjectural government guarantees weakened around 1990 (Flannery and Sorescu 1996, Morgan and Stiroh 1999). FIRREA (1989) and FDICIA (1991) legislated less generous government "bailouts," and nationwide depositor preference in 1993 reduced the seniority of many banks' nondeposit claims. As a result of these supervisory changes, bank counterparties should have become more sensitive to default risk. BHCs' asset volatilities were also rising over this period.[14] (See Figure 7 and the right-hand scale in Figure 2.) In response to both of these developments, banks would rationally increase capital ratios to reduce their default risk and hence their funding costs.

We test these alternative explanations via panel regressions for bank capital ratios. The model differentiates between short-run and long-run adjustments and explicitly identifies the impact of unanticipated share price changes on BHC capital ratios. We focus on the determinants of equity's market value while recognizing that supervisory restrictions on book capital may prevent a bank's complete adjustment to its desired market ratio.

4. REGRESSION MODEL

A bank's supervisors and counterparties care primarily about its risk of default, which is jointly determined by its leverage and risk exposures. We are therefore interested in estimating a model of the general form

$$\text{MKTRAT}_{it} = \alpha + \beta\sigma_{Ait} + \gamma Z + \widetilde{\varepsilon}_{it} \tag{2a}$$

$$\sigma_{Ait} = \eta + \kappa\,\text{MKTRAT}_{it} + \lambda Y + \nu_{it}, \tag{2b}$$

where MKTRAT_{it} is the ith bank's target capital ratio, defined as the market value of common equity at time t divided by the market value of its total assets, σ_{Ait} is the bank's risk, Z, Y are sets of predetermined variables (specified later), and $\alpha, \beta, \eta, \kappa$ and the vectors γ and λ are coefficients to be estimated. Identifying both equations in a simultaneous-equation system for the equity ratio and risk is very difficult, and a misspecification in one of the equations can bias the coefficient estimates in both. As we are primarily interested in the determinants of MKTRAT, we use two-stage least squares (2SLS) to estimate Eq. (2a) alone (details in Section 4.2).

The estimated β in Eq. (2a) measures the response of the typical bank's capital ratio to a unit increase in bank risk. Corporate finance theory predicts $\beta > 0$ for a firm subject to normal market forces: Counterparties (e.g., uninsured liability holders) demand more equity protection from firms with greater risk. Our main interest lies in determining

[14]Identifying the source of this increased bank risk lies beyond the scope of this chapter. It could reflect changes in the economy's basic uncertainties, or an endogenous decision to hold riskier assets.

whether supervisory changes in the early 1990s induced banks to hold more equity per unit of risk. If BHCs became more subject to market forces during our sample period, β should have a larger value later in the period. If we knew exactly when market assessments changed, we could add a single "shift" variable to Eq. (2a) and estimate

$$\text{MKTRAT}_{it} = \alpha + (\beta_0 + \beta_1 D)\widehat{\sigma}_{Ait} + \gamma Z + \widetilde{\varepsilon}_{it}, \tag{3}$$

where D equals zero early in the 1986–2001 time period and unity later in the period. A positive coefficient β_1 is consistent with banks reducing their default probabilities by increasing capital per unit of risk. (See the discussion of Table 6 in Hovakimian and Kane 2000.)

Because it is unclear when the risk parameter actually shifted—or how many shifts there may have been—we divided the sample period into four 4-year segments and let the data indicate when the sensitivity of MKTRAT to risk changed. That is, we specify that a bank's target capital ratio take the form

$$\text{MKTRAT}^*_{it} = \alpha_{0i} + \left(\beta_0 + \sum_{k=1}^{3} \beta_k D_k\right)\widehat{\sigma}_{Ait} + \lambda Z_{i,t-1} + \widetilde{\varepsilon}_{it}, \tag{4}$$

where

MKTRAT^*_{it} = bank i's target capital ratio in period t,

$\widehat{\sigma}_{Ait}$ = the fitted value for observed asset volatility (σ_{Ait}) from an instrumental variables regression,

D_1 = 1 during 1990–93 and zero otherwise,

D_2 = 1 during 1994–97 and zero otherwise, and

D_3 = 1 during 1998–2001 and zero otherwise.

The omitted time period is 1986–89, for which the risk sensitivity of MKTRAT* is included in β_0. If BHCs provided greater equity protection to their counterparties after 1989, Eq. (4) should include one or more significantly positive β_k coefficients.[15]

The subperiods defined in Eq. (4) correspond to several logical "break points" in institutional conditions. Flannery and Sorescu (1996) detect increased risk sensitivity in subordinated debt pricing by year-end 1989, so the 1986–89 period can be characterized as substantially prereform. The 1990–93 period includes important changes to capital regulation and the safety net. The last two periods exhibit different stock market trends: predominantly upward during 1994–97, followed by a peak and reversal in 1998–2001.

In addition to σ_A the other determinants ($Z_{i,t-1}$) of the target capital ratio are charter value, regulatory restrictions, firm size, and earnings.

[15]Researchers frequently observe that high risk could enhance a bank's equity value simply because the value of the safety-net subsidy increases with risk. Because equity and asset market values enter the computation for σ, our risk measures may also be biased. When we applied the method of Ronn and Verma (1986) to estimate adjusted market values and bank risks, the results are similar to those for the unadjusted measures. See upcoming Table 6.

HMB(−1)
Banks will protect a valuable charter by lowering their risk and/or leverage (Marcus 1984, Keeley 1990, Demsetz, Saidenberg, and Strahan 1996). Researchers frequently proxy for a bank's charter value with Tobin's q, but the dependent variable in Eq. (4) (MKTRAT*) is likely to be correlated with q by construction because both variables include the market value of equity in their numerator. We mitigate this induced correlation by constructing a dummy variable HMB ("high market-to-book"), which takes the value of 1 if a BHC's market-to-book ratio is in the top 25 percent of sample BHCs in that year. The coefficient on HMB should be positive in Eq. (4).

REGP(−1)
Banks with relatively low book equity ratios may be subject to REGulatory Pressure, which limits their ability to reduce MKTRAT. The dummy variable REGP identifies constrained banks: REGP = 1 if a bank's capital ratio does *not* exceed the regulatory capital minimum by at least 1.5 percent. Otherwise REGP = 0. The sign of REGP's coefficient is theoretically ambiguous: Regulatory pressure might raise MKTRAT by forcing a BHC to hold more capital than is justified by its risk, or it might lower MKTRAT if the constraint depresses the bank's equity value.

LNTA(−1)
Larger banks may be more widely followed by market investors and may therefore have better access to wholesale liabilities, loan sale markets, and so forth. With better access to these liquidity sources, larger banks may therefore require less capital. Alternatively, larger banks have more complex balance sheets, which are optimally financed with a larger proportion of equity capital. We include the natural logarithm of total assets (LNTA) in the MKTRAT equation to control for size-related effects.

ROA(−1)
Market capital ratios may be higher for BHCs with higher returns on assets if sticky dividends cause managers to retain more equity.[16]

Finally, we include firm fixed effects to control for omitted factors that vary across institutions but are relatively constant over time.

4.1. Lags in Adjusting Toward Target Capitalization

In a frictionless world, firms would always maintain their target leverage. However, transaction costs may prevent immediate adjustment to a firm's target, as the firm trades off adjustment costs against the costs of operating with a suboptimal debt ratio. We therefore revise the model in Eq. (4) to permit incomplete (partial) adjustment of the

[16]Banks with high earnings may also hold equity to protect their charter value. However, if HMB adequately controls for this effect, we are left with Berger's (1995) hypothesis about the effect of earnings on capitalization. Section 7 demonstrates that our results are not affected by excluding HMB from the specification.

firm's initial capital ratio toward its target within each time period. The data can then indicate a typical adjustment speed.

Begin by rewriting a BHC's long-run, desired capital ratio in Eq. (4) as

$$\text{MKTRAT}^*_{it} = \delta X_{it}, \tag{5}$$

where X_{it} is a vector of risk and other capital determinants discussed earlier and δ is a vector of coefficients.

A standard partial adjustment model is written:

$$\text{MKTRAT}_{i,t} - \text{MKTRAT}_{i,t-1} = \lambda_1(\text{MKTRAT}^*_{i,t} - \text{MKTRAT}_{i,t-1}) + \mu_{i,t}. \tag{6}$$

Substitute (5) into (6) to give an estimable model:

$$\text{MKTRAT}_{i,t} - \text{MKTRAT}_{i,t-1} = \lambda_1 \beta X_{i,t} - \lambda_1 \text{ MKTRAT}_{i,t-1} + \mu_{i,t} \tag{7}$$

Equation (7) says that managers take actions to close the gap between where they are ($\text{MKTRAT}_{i,t-1}$) and where they wish to be ($\delta X_{i,t}$). The typical firm closes a proportion λ_1 of the gap each year.[17] The assumed smooth-adjustment path may only approximate an individual firm's actual adjustments, particularly if there are fixed costs of changing a firm's capital structure (Fischer, Heinkel, and Zechner 1989, Mauer and Triantis 1994). However, unreported simulation results indicate that this smooth-adjustment specification readily incorporates discrete capital adjustments caused by fixed adjustment costs. The coefficient λ_1 thus reflects the average adjustment speed for a typical firm in the sample.

Share price movements will also affect MKTRAT: An increase (decrease) in a firm's stock price mechanically tends to decrease (increase) its leverage. Hence, our model should allow for the possibility that managers may take actions to offset some share price effects. We augment our basic partial adjustment model in Eq. (7) to recognize the potential effects of share price changes on leverage:

$$\begin{aligned}\text{MKTRAT}_{i,t} - \text{MKTRAT}_{i,t-1} &= \lambda_1(\beta X_{i,tt} - \text{MKTRAT}_{i,t-1}) \\ &\quad + (1 - \lambda_2)\text{ (Share price effect)}_{t-1,t} + \mu_{i,t},\end{aligned} \tag{8}$$

where λ_2 is the adjustment speed to share price effects. Equation (8) says that the observed change in equity ratio is the sum of the partial movement to the target leverage $[\lambda_1(\beta X_{i,tt} - \text{MKTRAT}_{t-1})]$ and the residual portion of the share price effect that has not been offset $[(1 - \lambda_2)\text{ (Share price effect)}_{t-1,t}]$. Because managers cannot anticipate stock price shocks at the beginning of the period, we expect $\lambda_2 < \lambda_1$.

[17]Specification (7) assumes that the firm acts to close any deviation from the desired target ratio, no matter how small. An alternative model would permit small deviations from the target to persist because adjustment costs outweigh the gains from removing small deviations between actual and target leverage. (See Leary and Roberts' (2005) hazard model.) Unreported simulation results indicate that this smooth-adjustment specification readily incorporates discrete capital adjustments caused by fixed adjustment costs.

We estimate the "share price effect" as the impact of the ith firm's stock return on its capital ratio:

$$\mathrm{SPE}_{i,t} = \left(\frac{E_{t-1}(1+\widetilde{R}_{t-1,t})}{D_{t-1}+E_{t-1}(1+\widetilde{R}_{t-1,t})} \right) - \mathrm{MKTRAT}_{t-1}, \tag{9}$$

where

$\widetilde{R}_{t-1,t}$ = the realized return the ith bank's stock between $t-1$ and t,
E_{t-1} = market value of common equity at the end of period $t-1$,
D_{t-1} = book value of BHC outstanding debt at the end of period $t-1$.

SPE measures the change in MKTRAT that will occur if managers leave E and D unchanged during the period. Substituting (9) into (8) gives

$$\mathrm{MKTRAT}_{i,t} = \lambda_1 \beta X_{i,tt} + (1-\lambda_1)\,\mathrm{MKTRAT}_{i,t-1} + (1-\lambda_2)\,\mathrm{SPE}_{i,t} + \mu_{i,t}. \tag{10}$$

In the long run, (10) implies that

1. The firm's actual debt ratio converges to its target debt ratio, $\beta X_{i,t}$.
2. The long-run impact of $X_{i,t}$ on the capital ratio is given by its estimated coefficient, divided by λ_1.

Inserting the two partial adjustments into Eq. (4) gives our main regression specification:

$$\begin{aligned}\mathrm{MKTRAT}_{it} = {} & \alpha_0 + \left(1-\lambda_0-\sum_{k=1}^{3}\lambda_k D_k\right)\mathrm{MKTRAT}_{i,t-1} + \left(\delta_0+\sum_{k=1}^{3}\delta_k D_k\right)\mathrm{SPE}_{i,t} \\ & + \left(\beta_0 \sum_{k=1}^{3}\beta_k D_k\right)\widehat{\sigma}_{it} + \alpha_1 \mathrm{HMB}_{it-1} + \alpha_2 \mathrm{REGP}_{it-1} + \alpha_3 \mathrm{ROA}_{it-1} \\ & + \alpha_4 \mathrm{LNTA}_{i,t-1} + \text{Firm fixed effects} + \widetilde{\mu}_{it}. \end{aligned} \tag{11}$$

4.2. Econometric Issues

We estimate Eq. (11) is a fixed-effects panel regression, in which three of the explanatory variables are likely to be correlated with the residual, σ_A, SPE_{it}, and the lagged dependent variable ($\mathrm{MKTRAT}_{i,t-1}$). OLS coefficient estimates would therefore be biased, and we employ the method of 2SLS to estimate Eq. (11). This procedure requires additional exogenous variables that are correlated with the endogenous regressors but not with the error term in Eq. (2a).

First, we require an instrument for σ_A. Theory suggests that a BHC jointly selects its portfolio risk and its MKTRAT, as in Eqs. (2a) and (2b). In addition, our volatility measure is derived from MKTRAT in Eq. (1), so positive (negative) random errors in MKTRAT will generate over-(under-) estimates of σ_A. We use three exogenous variables to help predict the expected value of σ_A:

VOL–SP_t = the next 30 days' expected stock market volatility, measured by the VXO index published by the CBOE. (See description of VXO at http://www.cboe.com/micro/vix/index.asp.)

VOL–I_t = the standard deviation of the daily yield to maturity on a 1-year, constant-maturity Treasury bond, computed over the preceding quarter.

CRED–SPR_t = the average daily spread between Moody's index of BAA corporate bonds and AAA corporate bonds during the last month of the quarter.

These exogenous variables should capture the external components of financial uncertainty confronted by a BHC in choosing its σ_A and MKTRAT.

Second, SPE_{it} will be correlated with the error term because both SPE_{it} and the dependent variable contain the BHC's realized stock return ($\widetilde{R}_{t-1,t}$). We therefore replace SPE with its fitted value from an instrumental variables regression that includes the exogenous variable

$$\text{SPE}^O_{it} = \left(\frac{E_{t-1}(1+\widetilde{R}^O_{t-1,t})}{D_{t-1}+E_{t-1}(1+\widetilde{R}^O_{t-1,t})}\right) - \text{MKTRAT}_{t-1}, \qquad (12)$$

where $\widetilde{R}^O_{t-1,t}$ = the mean realized return on all the *other* sample BHC's stocks during the period ending at t. SPE^O_{it} will be correlated with the ith firm's share-price effect but does not include the realized value of i's stock return.[18]

Third, dynamic panel regressions generally produce biased estimated coefficients because of the correlation between a panel's lagged dependent variable and the error term (Greene 1993). In addition, serially correlated residuals in Eq. (11) can bias the estimated coefficient on the lagged dependent variable. Both of these problems are addressed by constructing an instrumental variable for MKTRAT_{t-1}, with the fitted values from a first-stage regression that includes the firm's lagged *book* value equity ratio (called $\text{BOOKRAT}_{i,t-1}$) as the identifying exogenous variable. To prevent biases caused by serially correlated residuals, we allow for an AR(1) error structure in Eq. (11).

4.3. Data

Each BHC's stock-price series was obtained from CRSP. We gathered daily interest rates from the Federal Reserve's H.15 report and daily VXO (equity volatility) values from the CBOE Web site. Balance-sheet and income-statement data were taken from the quarterly Consolidated Financial Statements for Bank Holding Companies (FR Y-9C). The sample period begins on June 30, 1986, when the Y-9C reports were substantially revised. We estimate annual regressions using the September Y-9 data. The sample firms

[18] Table 6 demonstrates that substituting the S&P 500 return for $\widetilde{R}^O_{t-1,t}$ leaves our main conclusions unchanged.

comprise the 100 largest U.S. bank holding companies, as measured by book value of total assets. We reselect the 100 largest BHCs at the end of each year's third quarter. We estimate our regression model for the subset of these 100 BHCs with end-of-quarter stock prices available on CRSP and at least 30 days of reported stock returns within the quarter.

The final data set included 1,231 BHC-year observations with which to estimate an annual version of the pooled regression Eq. (11). The total number of banks represented in the sample was 153, and the mean (median) number of banks in each cross section was 77. Although the sample includes a relatively small *number* of BHCs, those firms held a majority of all U.S. banking assets (between 61 percent and 88 percent) during the sample period. In order to limit the influence of extreme outliers, we average σ_A measures over the preceding four quarters and winsorize the resulting variable at the 5 percent and 95 percent levels each year. Table 1 provides summary statistics for the variables used in estimating regression in Eq. (11).

TABLE 1 Summary Statistics

	Mean	Median	Min.	Max.	Std. Dev.
MKTRAT	12.14%	11.05%	0.10%	52.00%	6.58%
σ_A	3.20%	2.54%	0.70%	15.24%	2.12%
HMB	0.25	0	0	1	0.43
REGP	0.12	0	0	1	0.32
TA ($ bill)	37.30	13.10	3.64	1070.00	75.20
ROA	0.95%	−1.06%	−10.74%	3.62%	0.78%
SPE	0.43%	−0.84%	−14.86%	16.73%	3.44%

MKTRAT = the ratio of the common stock's market value to the quasi-market value of assets (book value of liabilities + market value of equity).

σ_A = unlevered standard deviation of asset returns, annualized and computed from the preceding quarter's daily equity returns. We limit the influence of outliers by averaging σ_A measures over the preceding four quarters and winsorizing the resulting variable at the 5 percent and 95 percent levels each year.

HMB = dummy variable equal to 1 if the BHC's ratio of market-to-book asset values is in the highest quartile that period and zero otherwise.

TA = book value of total assets, in billion dollars.

REGP = a dummy variable measuring regulatory pressure to keep capitalization high. REGP equals 1 if a BHC's book equity capital lies within 1.5 percent of mandated minimum value and zero otherwise.

ROA = ratio of net operating income to book value of total assets (TA).

$$\text{SPE}_{i,t} = \left(\frac{E_{t-1}(1 + \widetilde{R}_{t-1,t})}{D_{t-1} + E_{t-1}(1 + \widetilde{R}_{t-1,t})} \right) - \text{MKTRAT}_{t-1} \tag{9}$$

where $\widetilde{R}_{t-1,t}$ = the realized return the ith bank's stock between $t-1$ and t; E_{t-1} = market value of common equity at the end of period $t-1$; D_{t-1} = book value of BHC outstanding debt at the end of period $t-1$.

5. ESTIMATION RESULTS

Table 2 reports the first-stage regressions used to construct our three instrumental variables. Weak instruments generally result in large standard errors for the coefficients of interest and can also yield 2SLS estimates that are strongly biased toward their (inconsistent) OLS values (e.g., Nelson and Startz 1990). Our first-stage regressions indicate that weak instruments are not a problem in the present context: the exogenous

TABLE 2 First-Stage Regressions for 2SLS Procedure, 1986–2001

	$\widehat{\sigma}$	MKTRAT(−1)	SPE
VOL–SP$_t$	0.001	0.002	−0.001
	(14.70)	(15.92)	(−5.36)
VOL–I$_t$	−0.012	−0.015	0.018
	(−2.87)	(−1.71)	(1.73)
CRED–SPR$_t$	−0.008	−0.046	0.032
	(−2.58)	(−7.18)	(4.26)
BOOKRAT(−1)	0.225	1.501	−0.091
	(5.26)	(17.24)	(−0.88)
$\widetilde{R}^{O}_{t-1,t}$	0.082	−0.186	0.780
	(4.50)	(−5.05)	(17.94)
HMB(−1)	0.009	0.019	0.004
	(7.75)	(8.02)	(1.29)
REGP(−1)	−0.002	0.010	−0.004
	(−1.61)	(3.14)	(−1.05)
ROA(−1)	0.227	1.064	0.361
	(3.32)	(7.63)	(2.20)
LNTA(−1)	0.011	0.025	0.001
	(10.21)	(11.73)	(0.49)
Firm fixed effects?	Yes	Yes	Yes
N	1,231	1,231	1,231
R^2 (within)	0.698	0.862	0.344

We use the following first-stage regressions to construct instruments for three endogenous variables in Eq. (11). MKTRAT is the ratio of common equity's market value to the market value of total assets. $\widehat{\sigma}$ is annualized asset volatility, computed from Eq. (1) for the preceding four quarters. HMB is a dummy variable equal to 1 when the BHC's market-to-book ratio is in the sample's highest quartile. REGP is a dummy variable equal to 1 when the BHC's capital ratio is less than 1.5 percent above the required minimum. LNTA is the log of total book assets. ROA is net current operating income divided by total book assets. SPE measures the impact of stock price movements on the BHC's start-of-year MKTRAT. VOL–SP is the implied volatility of the S&P 100 index and VOL–I$_t$ is the volatility of the 1-yr Treasury bond. CRED–SPR$_t$ is the basis point spread between Moody's BAA and AAA corporate bond indices. BOOKRAT is the BHC's ratio of equity's book value to book total assets. $\widetilde{R}^{O}_{t-1,t}$ is the mean realized stock return to all the other banks in our sample for the period ending at t. We also include dummy variables identifying all sample BHCs, although these estimated coefficients are not reported. t-statistics are reported in parentheses below the coefficient estimates.

variables' coefficients are highly significant and the regressions' overall explanatory power is high—"within" R^2 statistics between 0.34 and 0.86. We therefore proceed with confidence that our instruments will perform well in 2SLS estimation.

Table 3 reports the results from estimating three versions of the regression in Eq. (11) for our sample of large BHCs. Panel A of Table 3 reports the full model, which permits partial adjustment toward the target capital ratio and recognizes the contemporaneous effect of stock-price changes on MKTRAT. The impact of risk on capitalization during our four subperiods is shown in the first four rows. During the two periods before 1994, the estimated effect of risk on MKTRAT was insignificantly different from zero. (These two coefficients even have the wrong sign.) For the last two subperiods, however, we find significant positive coefficients on risk, consistent with the hypothesis that bank counterparties demanded greater protection against default following the institutional reforms discussed earlier. During the last subperiod, the target MKTRAT was 2.52 percent higher for each 1 percent increase in risk. In other words, increasing risk by 1 standard deviation raised MKTRAT by 1.3 standard deviations. Another way to assess the economic importance of this effect is to observe that large BHCs were operating with a marginal default probability of approximately 0.6 percent (the cumulative standardized density of −2.52, assuming normally distributed asset returns).

The nonrisk determinants of MKTRAT* generally carry appropriately signed, significant coefficients in Table 3 (Panel A). A relatively high charter value (HMB(−1)) or profitability (ROA(−1)) significantly raises the target capital ratio, while larger banks (LNTA(−1)) tend to hold less equity. The effect of a binding regulatory constraint on book equity (REGP(−1)) is positive but differs insignificantly from zero.

The coefficients on the lagged dependent variable indicate that bankers adjust toward their target capital ratios rather quickly. The estimated adjustment speeds vary across the subperiods between 49 percent and 71 percent per year, although these speeds do not differ significantly from one another across time. The average adjustment speed is about 53 percent per year, which is faster than similar estimates for nonfinancial firms (Flannery and Rangan 2004).

None of the estimated coefficients on SPE differs significantly from unity, implying that managers do not offset stock-price effects on MKTRAT in the year they occur. However, a small (zero) value for λ_2 does not mean that managers never adjust MKTRAT to share price changes. The residual effect of a price change during the period $[t-1, t)$ is impounded in the next period's lagged MKTRAT and hence gets offset at an annual rate of about 53 percent in the years following the initial price shock.

Although we believe that Eq. (11) is the most appropriate specification for large BHCs' capital adjustment process, the stock-price effect and the lag structures on the dependent variable are somewhat new to the literature. We therefore provide two further estimates based on constrained specifications, for the sake of comparison. Panel B of Table 3 removes the effect of contemporaneous stock-price changes on a BHC's observed capital ratio. The resulting coefficients for risk display roughly the same pattern as in Panel A—negative early in the period and positive later, although the effect no longer rises monotonically. The estimated adjustment speeds vary widely over time and average about 31 percent per year.

TABLE 3 Estimation Results, Equity Market Value Capitalization

	Panel A			Panel B			Panel C	
	Coeff. (t-stat)	Implied absolute coeff. (t-stat)	Long-run coeff. (t-stat)	Coeff. (t-stat)	Implied absolute coeff. (t-stat)	Long-run coeff. (t-stat)	Coeff. (t-stat)	Implied absolute coeff. (t-stat)
$\widehat{\sigma}$	−0.380		−0.595	−2.285		−18.578		0.345
	(−0.74)		(−0.66)	(−3.64)		(−0.61)		(1.15)
$\widehat{\sigma} * D_{1990-93}$	−0.215	−0.595	−1.213	−0.937	−3.222	26.472	−0.262	0.083
	(−0.49)	(−1.34)	(−1.04)	(−1.69)	(−6.29)	(0.91)	(−1.56)	(0.40)
$\widehat{\sigma} * D_{1994-97}$	1.604	1.224	1.724	3.564	1.279	1.710	1.159	1.504
	(3.38)	(3.08)	(4.64)	(6.05)	(2.43)	(4.47)	(5.86)	(8.15)
$\widehat{\sigma} * D_{1998-2001}$	1.820	1.441	2.519	2.637	0.352	0.697	1.004	1.348
	(3.92)	(3.92)	(7.86)	(4.48)	(0.70)	(0.87)	(4.58)	(8.60)
HMB(−1)	0.009			0.018			0.015	
	(3.03)			(5.16)			(4.30)	
REGP(−1)	0.001			−0.018			−0.012	
	(0.36)			(−4.25)			(−3.07)	
ROA(−1)	0.390			0.744			0.929	
	(2.44)			(4.23)			(5.40)	
LNTA(−1)	−0.023			0.000			0.009	
	(−6.01)			(0.04)			(2.20)	
MKTRAT(−1)	0.362			0.877				
	(2.84)			(5.09)				
MKTRAT(−1) $* D_{1990-93}$	0.148	0.510		0.245	1.122			
	(1.35)	(4.40)		(1.73)	(7.38)			
MKTRAT(−1) $* D_{1994-97}$	−0.072	0.290		−0.625	0.252			
	(−0.62)	(2.78)		(−4.14)	(1.61)			
MKTRAT(−1) $* D_{1998-2001}$	0.066	0.428		−0.383	0.494			
	(0.56)	(3.97)		(−2.46)	(3.18)			
SPE	1.040							
	(5.23)							
SPE $* D_{1990-93}$	0.003	1.043						
	(0.01)	(17.18)						

Continued

TABLE 3 *Continued*

	Panel A			Panel B			Panel C	
	Coeff. (t-stat)	Implied absolute coeff. (t-stat)	Long-run coeff. (t-stat)	Coeff. (t-stat)	Implied absolute coeff. (t-stat)	Long-run coeff. (t-stat)	Coeff. (t-stat)	Implied absolute coeff. (t-stat)
SPE $* D_{1994-97}$	0.400	1.440						
	(1.61)	(8.12)						
SPE $* D_{1998-2001}$	−0.352	0.688						
	(−1.42)	(4.55)						
Num. obs.		1,079			1,079			1,079
$\overline{R}^2$ (within)		0.77			0.62			0.47
ρ		−0.01			0.08**			0.28***

$$\text{MKTRAT}_{it} = \alpha_0 + \left(1 - \lambda_0 - \sum_{k=1}^{3} \lambda_k D_k\right) \text{MKTRAT}_{i,t-1} + \left(\delta_0 + \sum_{k=1}^{3} \delta_k D_k\right) \text{SPE}_{i,t} + \left(\beta_0 + \sum_{k=1}^{3} \beta_k D_k\right) \widehat{\sigma}_{it}$$
$$+ \alpha_1 \text{HMB}_{it-1} + \alpha_2 \text{REGP}_{it-1} + \alpha_3 \text{ROA}_{it-1} + \alpha_4 \text{LNTA}_{i,t-1} + \text{Firm fixed effects} + [\widetilde{\varepsilon}_{it} - \rho_i \widetilde{\varepsilon}_{i,t-1}] \quad (11)$$

Estimated as a 2SLS regression with AR(1) correction using annual data from 1986–2001. MKTRAT is the ratio of common equity's market value to the market value of total assets. $\widehat{\sigma}_{it}$ is the annualized asset volatility, computed by delevering the standard deviation of daily equity returns over a quarter and averaged over the preceding four quarters. D_k are dummies marking three successive four-year periods, identified by the subscripts on the "D" variables in the table. HMB is a dummy variable equal to 1 when the BHC's market-to-book ratio is in the sample's highest quartile. REGP is a dummy variable equal to 1 when the BHC's capital ratio is less than 1.5 percent above the required minimum. LNTA is the log of total book assets. ROA is net current operating income divided by total book assets. SPE is a proxy for the unanticipated effect that stock price movements have on the BHC's equity ratio. Coefficients for $\widehat{\sigma}_{Ait}$, SPE, and $\text{MKTRAT}_{i,t-1}$ are estimated using fitted values from the first-stage regressions reported in Table 2. For the explanatory variables in Eq. (11) associated with shift dummies, we report both the coefficients themselves (λ_0, $\lambda_1, \ldots, \delta_0, \delta_1, \ldots, \beta_0, \beta_1, \ldots$) and the "Implied absolute coefficients" ($\lambda_0 + \lambda_1$, $\lambda_0 + \lambda_2 \ldots$). We also include dummy variables identifying all sample BHCs, although these estimated coefficients are not reported. t-Statistics are reported in parentheses below the coefficient estimates.

Panel C of Table 3 reports a severely constrained version of regression in Eq. (11), which specifies that BHCs attain their target MKTRAT at all times, at least on average across the sample. The same qualitative result holds: The estimated coefficients on asset risk remain consistent with the hypothesis that BHC provided more capital protection later in the sample period. (Note that omitting the lagged dependent variable means that the model's "short-run" and "long-run" coefficient estimates are identical.)

5.1. Decomposing the Change in BHC Capitalization

The mean BHC market capital ratio increased between 1986 and 2001, and we can use the results in Table 3 to decompose this increase into several component parts. Figure 9 illustrates that an intertemporal change in leverage can be attributed to two broad factors, "market" effects and "passive bank" effects. Begin by considering the lowest dotted line, which represents the banks' initial (1986–89) tradeoff between risk and capitalization. Market discipline should make this line slope up to the right (as shown), but recall

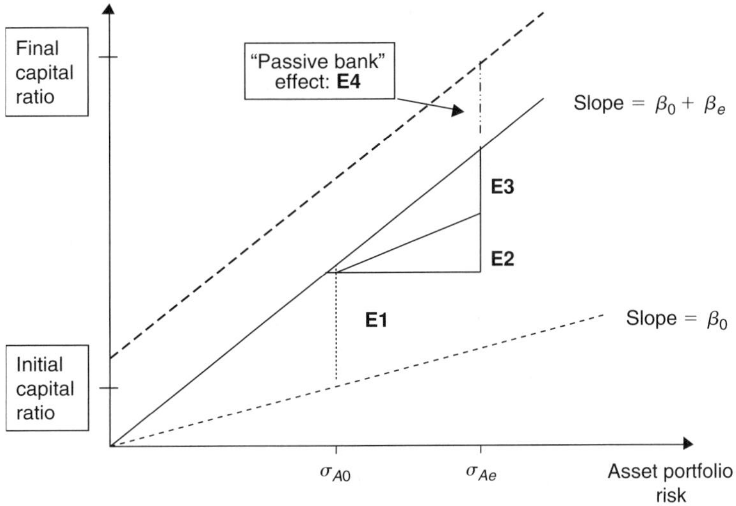

FIGURE 9 "Market" effect = E1 + E2 + E3; "Passive bank" effects occur as a shift in the original schedule, independent of risk exposure.

that the actual slope in Panel A of Table 3 is insignificantly negative. The estimated regression model has a slope of 2.52 for the 1998–2001 time period, corresponding to a leftward rotation of the equilibrium line in Figure 9. Ceteris paribus, this effect would make bank shareholders want to hold higher capital, in the amount, **E1**. Bank portfolios also became riskier during our sample period, meaning that the initial σ_{A0} shifted right to σ_{A3}. The resulting increase in optimal equity can be divided into two parts. **E2** in Figure 9 is the extra capital associated with the change in risk alone (i.e., holding the slope constant at its initial value β_0). **E3** measures the impact of combined changes in bank risk and market sensitivity. Finally, the solid line in Figure 9 will shift up in a roughly *parallel* fashion (**E4**) if managers enhance capital passively and if earnings or stock-price increases are independent of σ_A.

Our estimated regression coefficients from Panel A in Table 3 can be used to estimate the contribution of effects **E1–E4** to the observed change in mean (median) MKTRAT values between 1986–89 and 1998–2001. Table 4 reports the long-run change in MKTRAT associated with each of these effects:

E1. The long-run impact of a change in market risk aversion:

$$\left[\frac{\beta_0 + \beta_3}{1 - \lambda_0 - \lambda_3} - \frac{\beta_0}{1 - \lambda_0}\right] \sigma_{A0}$$

E2. The long-run impact of a change in the asset portfolio risk, independent of the market's changed risk aversion:

$$\left[\frac{\beta_0}{1 - \lambda_0}(\Delta\sigma_A)\right].$$

E3. The interaction between E1 and E2:

$$\left[\frac{\beta_0+\beta_3}{1-\lambda_0-\lambda_3}-\frac{\beta_0}{1-\lambda_0}\right][\Delta\sigma_A].$$

E4. The "passive bank" effect of retained earnings on bank capital, given by

$$\left[\frac{\alpha_3}{1-\lambda_0-\lambda_3}(\Delta \mathrm{ROA}_{t-1})\right].$$

Our empirical model includes three additional adjustments, which we identify as "other (technical) effects" in Table 4. First, we adjust the predicted MKTRAT values in 1998–2001 for the transitory impact of changes in regulatory pressure (REGP). Second, we incorporate the negative impact of asset growth on target capitalization. Third, we recognize that the BHC sample changes between 1986–89 and 1998–2001, so we must recognize differences in the included firms' fixed-effect values.

Table 4 reports each calculated effect as a proportion of the observed change in the typical bank's MKTRAT between 1986–89 and 1998–2001. If sample BHCs were close to their long-run equilibria in each period, these effects should sum to approximately 100 percent. The sample BHCs' mean market capital ratio rose by 9.70 percent between 1986–89 and 1998–2001, from 8.02 percent to 17.72 percent. About 53 percent of the observed change reflects increased market risk aversion (effect **E1**), and this proportion

TABLE 4 Percentage Contributions to the Observed Mean Change in Market Equity Ratios, between 1986–89 and 1998–2001

Contributions	Computed at the means, as a percentage of the observed change in mean MKTRAT = 9.70%	Computed at the medians, as a percentage of the observed change in median MKTRAT = 9.46%
E1: Impact of a change in market risk aversion (β_4)	52.51%***	48.06%***
E2: The impact of higher asset portfolio risk, $\beta_0(\Delta\sigma)$.	−27.42%	−25.54%
E3: The interaction between E1 and E2: $\beta_4(\Delta\sigma)$	143.52%***	133.68%***
The "market discipline" effect (E1 + E2 + E3)	168.61%***	156.20%***
E4: Change in earnings: $\alpha_4(\Delta \mathrm{ROA})$ **(The "passive bank" effect)**	2.94%***	1.49%***
Other (technical) effects	−66.24%***	−49.68%***
Mean predicted change in MKTRAT implied by regression Eq. (11), as a proportion of the actual change in MKTRAT	105.30%	108.00%

Coefficient names refer to Eq. (11). Reported numbers represent the proportion of observed change in the mean market value of equity ratio (MKTRAT) from the 1986–89 period to the 1998–2001 period. The four "effects" are illustrated in Figure 9.

***Significant at the 1 percent level; significant at the 5 percent level; significant at the 10 percent level.

differs from zero at the 1 percent confidence level. The measured increase in risk (**E2**) has a surprising effect of *reducing* desired MKTRAT by 27.42 percent of the observed change. This effect is statistically indistinguishable from zero and results from the negative, but insignificant, coefficient on σ_A in Eq. (11) for the 1986–89 time period. The combined effect of greater risk aversion and riskier assets (**E3**) raises MKTRAT by 143.5 percent of the ratio's actual change. Taken together, the three "active" effects (**E1** + **E2** + **E3**) account for 168.6 percent of the mean change in sample BHCs' capitalization. By contrast, the "passive bank" effect from retained earnings (**E4**) is statistically significant but accounts for less than 3 percent of the observed change. Finally, "other (technical) effects" reduce the predicted equity ratio by 66.24 percent, leaving our model's predicted change in MKTRAT equal to 105 percent of the mean observed change between 1986–89 and 1998–2001. The second column in Table 4 shows the same decomposition in terms of sample medians, with similar results.

The results in Table 4 indicate that most of the large BHCs' MKTRAT increase resulted from active managerial decisions to increase MKTRAT in conjunction with higher risks. An important remaining question is whether this increased risk sensitivity derived from supervisory pressure or market forces.

6. DO HIGHER MARKET RATIOS REFLECT STRICTER REGULATORY CONSTRAINTS?

Perhaps the results in Table 3 reflect, at least in part, supervisory efforts to raise book capital ratios.[19] Supervisors had been explicitly seeking higher minimum capital standards during our sample period, and they were empowered to deal quickly with capital standard violations. FDICIA specifies a series of "prompt corrective actions" that supervisors must take if a bank's book capital falls below 8 percent of risk-weighted assets (Jones and King 1995, p. 492), and bank mergers were likely to gain regulatory approval only if the surviving entity would be "well capitalized" (i.e., more than 10 percent of RWA). Higher capital standards might contribute to the results in Table 3 in either of two ways.

First, we know that the book capital ratios (BOOKRAT) are correlated ($\rho = 0.68$) with the dependent variable in regression in Eq. (11), MKTRAT. Perhaps the "true" linkage is between BOOKRAT and asset risk and the impact of risk on MKTRAT in Table 3 is at least partly spurious. We test whether market risk measures affect book capital ratios by estimating

$$\text{BOOKRAT}_{it} = \alpha_0 + \left(1 - \lambda_0 - \sum_{k=1}^{3} \lambda_k D_k\right) \text{BOOKRAT}_{i,t-1} + \left(\beta_0 + \sum_{k=1}^{3} \beta_k D_k\right) \widehat{\sigma}_{Ait} + \alpha_1 \text{HMB}_{it-1} + \alpha_3 \text{ROA}_{it-1} + \alpha_4 \text{LNTA}_{i,t-1} + \text{Firm fixed effects} + \widetilde{\varepsilon}_{it} \tag{13}$$

[19]Wall and Peterson (1995) discuss this possibility for their 1989–92 sample period.

Compared to regression in Eq. (11), this specification replaces MKTRAT with BOOKRAT as the dependent variable and removes SPE (because share price does not directly affect BOOKRAT).

Panel A of Table 5 reports the results of this regression. Portfolio risk significantly *negatively* affects BOOKRAT in the first two subperiods, as it did in Table 3. However, unlike the results for MKTRAT, the risk coefficient in Table 5 remains negative ($t = -1.76$) during the 1994–97 subperiod and becomes insignificantly positive

TABLE 5 Estimation Results for Book Value Capitalization and Excess Regulatory Capital

	Panel A: Book capital ratio			Panel B: Book capital cushion		
	Coeff. (t-stat)	Implied absolute coeff. (t-stat)	Long-run coeff. (t-stat)	Coeff. (t-stat)	Implied absolute coeff. (t-stat)	Long-run coeff. (t-stat)
$\hat{\sigma}$	−0.388		−0.714	−0.204		−0.142
	(−3.35)		(−2.79)	(−1.43)		(−1.36)
$\hat{\sigma} * D_{1990-93}$	0.208	−0.180	−0.345	0.133	−0.071	−0.133
	(1.87)	(−2.22)	(−2.04)	(1.43)	(−0.72)	(−0.69)
$\hat{\sigma} * D_{1994-97}$	0.265	−0.123	−0.252	0.214	0.010	0.038
	(2.42)	(−1.95)	(−1.76)	(1.88)	(0.12)	(0.14)
$\hat{\sigma} * D_{1998-2001}$	0.491	0.103	0.166	0.158	−0.046	−0.100
	(4.28)	(1.47)	(−1.56)	(1.21)	(−0.53)	(−0.47)
HMB(−1)	0.000					
	(0.33)					
ROA(−1)	0.546					
	(9.07)					
LNTA(−1)	0.001					
	(0.55)					
BOOKRAT(−1)	0.457					
	(5.71)					
BOOKRAT(−1) * $D_{1990-93}$	0.022	0.479				
	(0.57)	(6.32)				
BOOKRAT(−1) * $D_{1994-97}$	0.057	0.514				
	(1.48)	(7.06)				
BOOKRAT(−1) * $D_{1998-2001}$	−0.077	0.380				
	(−1.54)	(5.05)				
CUSHION(−1)				−0.433		
				(−2.56)		
CUSHION(−1) * $D_{1990-93}$				0.901	0.467	
				(6.80)	(3.31)	

Continued

TABLE 5 *Continued*

	Panel A: Book capital ratio			Panel B: Book capital cushion		
	Coeff. (*t*-stat)	Implied absolute coeff. (*t*-stat)	Long-run coeff. (*t*-stat)	Coeff. (*t*-stat)	Implied absolute coeff. (*t*-stat)	Long-run coeff. (*t*-stat)
CUSHION(−1) $* D_{1994-97}$				1.164 (8.33)	0.731 (4.90)	
CUSHION(−1) $* D_{1998-2001}$				0.973 (6.55)	0.540 (3.64)	
Num. obs.		1,079			1,018	
$\overline{R}^2$ (within)		0.41			0.22	
ρ		0.05			0.12**	

$$\text{BOOKRAT}_{it} = \alpha_0 + \left(1 - \lambda_0 - \sum_{k=1}^{3} \lambda_k D_k\right) \text{BOOKRAT}_{i,t-1} + \left(\beta_0 + \sum_{k=1}^{3} \beta_k D_k\right) \widehat{\sigma}_{it} + \alpha_1 \text{HMB}_{it-1} + \alpha_3 \text{ROA}_{it-1} + \alpha_4 \text{LNTA}_{i,t-1} + \text{Firm fixed effects} + [\widetilde{\varepsilon}_{it} - \rho_i \widetilde{\varepsilon}_{i,t-1}] \quad (13)$$

$$\text{CUSHION}_{it} = \delta_0 + \left(1 - \lambda_0 - \sum_{k=1}^{3} \lambda_k D_k\right) \text{CUSHION}_{i,t-1} + \left(\beta_0 + \sum_{k=1}^{3} \beta_k D_k\right) \widehat{\sigma}_{it} + \text{Firm fixed effects} + [\widetilde{\omega}_{it} - \rho_i \widetilde{\omega}_{iit-1}] \quad (14)$$

Estimated as a 2SLS regression with AR(1) correction using annual data from 1986–2001. BOOKRAT is the ratio of common equity's book value to the book value of total assets. CUSHION_{it} is excess regulatory capital: total regulatory capital (equity plus qualifying debt) less the required supervisory minimum, as a proportion of total assets (before 1991) or risk-weighted assets (after 1990). $\widehat{\sigma}_{A\,it}$ is the annualized asset volatility, computed by delevering the standard deviation of daily equity returns over a quarter and averaged over the preceding four quarters. D_k are dummies marking three successive four-year periods, identified by the subscripts on the "*D*" variables in the table. HMB is a dummy variable equal to 1 when the BHC's market-to-book ratio is in the sample's highest quartile. REGP is a dummy variable equal to 1 when the BHC's capital ratio is less than 1.5 percent above the required minimum. LNTA is the log of total book assets. ROA is net current operating income divided by total book assets. Coefficients for $\widehat{\sigma}_{A\,it}$, $\text{CUSHION}_{i,t-1}$ and $\text{BOOKRAT}_{i,t-1}$ are estimated using fitted values from first-stage regressions. For the explanatory variables in Eqs. (13) and (14) associated with shift dummies, we report both the coefficients themselves ($\lambda_0, \lambda_1, \ldots, \delta_0, \delta_1, \ldots, \beta_0, \beta_1, \ldots$) and the "implied absolute coefficients" ($\lambda_0 + \lambda_1, \lambda_0 + \lambda_2 \ldots$). We also include dummy variables identifying all sample BHCs, although these estimated coefficients are not reported. *t*-Statistics are reported in parentheses below the coefficient estimates.

($t = 1.56$) during 1998–2001. The estimated risk coefficients for BOOKRAT rise over time, but their pattern is quite different from the corresponding results in Table 3. Even if supervisory pressure on BOOKRAT might partially explain our results, it cannot fully account for them.

Supervisory capital requirements may affect observed MKTRAT because bankers hold "excess" capital to protect themselves against violating book capital restrictions. Under this view, the "excess" book capital in Figure 3 cannot actually be distributed back to shareholders because it serves to protect against potential supervisory interventions.[20] Lindquist (2004) observes that a protective equity cushion would likely vary directly with the firm's risk exposure. For a protective equity cushion to cause the results in Table 3, the cushion would have to increase over time *and* vary across BHCs in proportion to their σ_A. We test for this relationship by regressing "excess" book capital on BHC risk. Recognizing the potential for costly adjustment suggests the specification

$$\text{CUSHION}_{it} = \delta_0 + \left(1 - \lambda_0 - \sum_{k=1}^{3} \lambda_k D_k\right) \text{CUSHION}_{i,t-1} + \left(\beta_0 + \sum_{k=1}^{3} \beta_k D_k\right) \widehat{\sigma}_{Ait} + \text{Firm fixed effects} + \widetilde{\varpi}_{it} \quad (14)$$

where CUSHION_{it} = the difference between observed *book* capital (equity plus qualifying debt) and the operative minimum requirement:[21]

- 6 percent of total assets during the period 1986–1990-III
- 7.25 percent of risk-weighted assets during the period 1990-IV through 1992-III
- 8 percent of risk-weighted assets starting in 1992-IV.

σ_A = the instrument for observed asset volatility.[22] If capital standards became more strictly applied between 1987 and 2001, the coefficients on σ_A should rise later in the period.

Panel B of Table 5 reports the estimation results for Eq. (14).[23] Throughout the sample period, a BHC's risk exposure has no significant effect on CUSHION. Perhaps the cost of violating de jure capital standards did not really rise over time, or perhaps σ_A imperfectly measures the relevant uncertainty for a capital cushion. Regardless, the increasing effect of σ_A on MKTRAT in Table 3 does not seem to result from bankers' desire to hold a protective cushion of equity above the required minimum level.

7. ROBUSTNESS

To summarize our results thus far, we find that the largest 100 U.S. BHCs held more equity capital per unit of risk exposure by the latter half of the 1990s. We assess the

[20] Osterberg and Thomson (1996) study publicly traded BHCs' leverage decisions in 1986–87 and conclude that "even if a bank meets or exceeds the capital guidelines, the guidelines influence movements of bank leverage" (p. 327).

[21] Note that the de facto capital standard could be above these minima—e.g., 10 percent of RWA under Basel. Any uniform change in measuring CUSHION would induce an offsetting change in the regression's constant term, without affecting the slope coefficients.

[22] The relevant risk is that some losses will make book equity inadequate. A measure of credit risk alone (e.g., the ratio of risk-weighted assets to total on-book assets) is incomplete because it ignores other reasons for changes in book capital ratios. Although σ_A includes some risks that do not affect book equity (e.g., unrealized losses on loans or bonds), we feel that this risk measure most closely approximates the type of risk that should affect an equity cushion.

[23] Including the other variables from Eq. (12)—HMB(−1), ROA(−1), and LNTA(−1)—on the right-hand side of Eq. (14) results in an identical pattern among the β_k.

robustness of these results by modifying several features of regression in Eq. (11). In order to save space, we report only the estimated (short-run and long-run) impact of σ_A on MKTRAT for each specification in Table 6. The revised results always correspond closely to the results in the first column of Table 3. BHC risk became a significant influence on capitalization after 1993, following several years of supervisory reform.

7.1. Adjust for Possible Safety Net Subsidies in MKTRAT

The positive coefficients on risk in Table 3 may reflect the tendency of the safety net subsidy to increase with risk. If MKTRAT includes this type of subsidy, a positive coefficient on risk could reflect either market discipline or a risk-sensitive government subsidy. Ronn and Verma (1986) employ a method for estimating asset values and return volatilities that takes this phenomenon into account. We used their method to compute alternative values for each bank's capital ratio and risk. The first column of Table 6 reports the results of estimating Eq. (11) with these adjusted (and winsorized) MKTRAT and σ_A values.[24] We again find that risk had a significantly perverse effect on MKTRAT through 1993, after which its effect became positive and statistically significant.

7.2. Alternative Instrument for BHCs' Realized Stock Return

Thus far, we have used an equal-weighted index of our sample BHCs to instrument for the impact of exogenous price changes on a bank's capital ratio. If all BHCs were simultaneously moving to align their MKTRAT with their risk, this variable may be correlated with each bank's MKTRAT. We therefore reestimated our main regression model using the S&P 500 index return to instrument for a firm's SPE. The estimated risk coefficients' magnitudes increased somewhat, but their time pattern remains the same as in Table 3.

7.3. Estimates for the 20 Largest Banks

The top 100 BHCs are not homogeneous in terms of their activities or in terms of their claim on possible safety net guarantees. We therefore wished to compare the "mega" banks against those that are merely "large." In order to preserve a reasonable number of data points for the mega subsample, we assigned the 20 largest banks (by asset book value) to the mega group each year. The third column in Table 6 shows a familiar pattern, with risk becoming a more important influence on MKTRAT later in the sample period. Unlike the general case in Table 3, mega banks exhibit significantly positive risk sensitivity only in the last (1998–2001) subperiod, perhaps because market participants were slower to accept that the mega banks' conjectural guarantees had been reduced.

[24] We also estimated Eq. (10) for a dependent variable that entirely removes the insurance value from equity's market value. (Ronn and Verma 1986 point out that an extreme assumption underlies this adjustment: that competition forces none of the insurance value to be passed through to bank customers.)

TABLE 6 Robustness Results

	(1) Asset values and return volatilities adjusted for safety net subsidies			(2) SP500 return as alternative instrument for BHC's realized stock return			(3) "Mega" BHC: asset ranks 1–20			(4) "Large" BHC: asset ranks 21–100			(5) Exclude HMB		
	Coeff.	SR	LR	Coeff.	SR	LR	Coeff.	SR	LR	Coeff.	SR	LR	Coeff.	SR	LR
δ_0 (1986–89)	−0.917		−1.473	−0.438		−1.018	−3.386		10.486	−0.093		−0.133	−1.154		−2.191
	(−2.24)		(−1.74)	(−0.86)		(0.70)	(−1.91)		(1.01)	(−0.15)		(0.14)	(−2.07)		(1.39)
δ_1 (1990–93)	−0.949	−1.865	−6.538	−0.483	−0.921	−3.338	−0.015	−3.371	9.803	0.424	−0.517	−0.984	−0.264	−1.417	−4.255
	(−2.25)	(−5.69)	(−2.23)	(−1.00)	(−2.10)	(1.15)	(−0.01)	(−2.53)	(1.24)	(0.78)	(−1.06)	(0.87)	(−0.56)	(−3.03)	(1.48)
δ_2 (1994–97)	1.883	0.966	1.298	3.349	2.911	3.026	3.108	0.278	−0.887	1.397	−1.304	1.697	2.476	1.323	1.663
	(4.15)	(4.13)	(5.52)	(6.50)	(9.25)	(19.08)	(1.87)	(0.25)	(0.20)	(2.32)	(−3.16)	(4.51)	(4.66)	(3.13)	(4.72)
δ (1998–2001)	1.316	0.399	1.001	2.003	1.565	2.522	4.511	1.125	2.984	1.586	1.494	2.172	2.464	1.311	2.209
	(3.06)	(2.35)	(3.20)	(3.88)	(4.65)	(10.71)	(2.69)	(0.93)	(3.59)	(2.68)	(3.84)	(6.62)	(4.72)	(3.32)	(6.42)
N		1,079			1,079			266			791			1,079	
R^2 (within)		0.74			0.70			0.76			0.73			0.73	

Variations on the regression specification:

$$\text{MKTRAT}_{i,t} = \alpha_0 + \left(1 - \lambda_0 - \sum_{k=1}^{3} \lambda_k D_k\right)\text{MKTRAT}_{i,t-1} + \left(\delta_0 + \sum_{k=1}^{3} \delta_k D_k\right)\text{SPE}_{i,t-1} + \left(\beta_0 + \sum_{k=1}^{3} \beta_k D_k\right)\widehat{\sigma}_{Ait}$$
$$+ \alpha_1 \text{HMB}_{i,t-1} + \alpha_2 \text{REGP}_{i,t-1} + \alpha_3 \text{ROA}_{i,t-1} + \alpha_4 \text{LNTA}_{i,t-1} + \text{Firm fixed effects} + [\widetilde{\varepsilon}_{it} - \rho_i \widetilde{\varepsilon}_{i,t-1}] \quad (11)$$

Estimated as a 2SLS regression with AR(1) correction using annual data from 1986–2001. MKTRAT is the ratio of common equity's market value to the market value of total assets. $\widehat{\sigma}_{A\,it}$ is the annualized asset volatility, computed by delevering the standard deviation of daily equity returns over a quarter and averaged over the preceding four quarters. D_k are dummies marking three successive four-year periods, identified by the subscripts on the "D" variables in the table. HMB is a dummy variable equal to 1 when the BHC's market-to-book ratio is in the sample's highest quartile. REGP is a dummy variable equal to 1 when the BHC's capital ratio is less than 1.5 percent above the required minimum. LNTA is the log of total book assets. ROA is net current operating income divided by total book assets. MTKRAT is a proxy for the unanticipated effect that stock-price movements have on the BHC's equity ratio. Coefficients for $\widehat{\sigma}_{A\,it}$, SPE, and $\text{MKTRAT}_{i,t-1}$ are estimated using fitted values from first-stage regressions. The first column of coefficients reports the individual δ_k for $k = 0, 3$. The second column of coefficients is the sum of $\delta_0 + \delta_k$ for $k = 1, 3$, and the third column presents the long-run coefficients. t-Statistics are reported in parentheses below the coefficient estimates.

7.4. Estimate for 80 "Next Largest" Banks

Banks that did not qualify as "mega" institutions were assigned to the "large" category, and estimation results for these firms are presented in the fourth column of Table 6. The results are very similar to those in Table 3: Large banks' capital ratios show no sensitivity to risk before 1994, but the short-run and long-run coefficients on risk become significantly positive (and larger) in the subsequent two periods.

7.5. Excluding the Charter Value Proxy

We used the proxy HMB ("high market-to-book") for charter value to reduce the possible effect of charter value's endogeneity on estimated coefficients. However, HMB could still be correlated with the residual in Eq. (11). To check whether this effect materially influences our coefficients of interest, we excluded HMB from the regression specification and obtained very similar estimates.

8. SUMMARY AND IMPLICATIONS

This chapter has evaluated the capitalization decisions of large bank holding companies over the period 1986–2001, when financial supervisors were trying to reverse the market's conjecture that large banks' default risks were borne mostly by the government. Toward this end, bank supervisors and the U.S. Congress revised their methods for resolving failed institutions (late 1980s), mandated prompt corrective actions vis-à-vis poorly capitalized institutions (1991), and introduced nationwide depositor preference (1993). The large banks' counterparties (depositors, guarantee beneficiaries, FX and derivatives traders) thus became more exposed to banks' true default risks. At the same time, supervisors became more resolved to raise book capital ratios. During the 1990s, U.S. bank equity ratios attained their highest levels in more than 50 years, with virtually all large BHCs' equity ratios comfortably exceeding supervisory standards.

Over the same period, restrictions on permissible bank activities were removed, allowing BHCs to select from a broader array of potential risk exposures. The typical BHC's risk exposure increased over our sample period, as the diversification effects of new business activities were (apparently) outweighed by the higher risks associated with those new lines of business. The cross-sectional variation in risk exposures also increased dramatically, as did the cross-sectional variation in capital ratios. Our regression model estimates that the cross-sectional correlation between risk and capitalization also rose, consistent with the hypothesis that uninsured bank counterparties demanded greater protection as government conjectural guarantees receded. Although capitalization did not reflect a bank's portfolio risk before about 1994, U.S. BHCs with greater risks were holding significantly more equity capital during the second half of our sample period. It appears that supervisory changes made uninsured bank counterparties feel more exposed to default risks, and the counterparties pressured bankers to provide equity protection to replace the waning government (implicit) guarantees. United States supervisors and legislators deserve plaudits for initiating the process that made market discipline more relevant to large banks and their customers.

Regulatory influence may also have continued via pressure to raise de jure (book) capital ratios. We cannot rule this out. However, we conclude that supervisory pressure on book capital ratios alone cannot completely account for our empirical results. Market-related bank responses to counterparty risk exposures contributed substantially to our sample banks' increased capital ratios between 1986–89 and 1998–2001. Since the late 1990s, it appears that large U.S. banking firms have chosen their own (market-valued) capital ratios in response to market pressures.

Two implications follow from our analysis. First, academic and industry models of banking firms should not assume that supervisory capital standards always constrain a bank. Such an assumption is simply inconsistent with the existing facts, at least for the largest (and hence most important) U.S. banking firms. During the 1990s, sharply higher capital levels accompanied increased risk taking within the banking sector, and banks with the riskiest portfolios ended up holding the most equity. Second, the market's ability to induce higher capitalization at riskier banks provides further support for the role of market forces in supervising large financial firms. Supervisory capital standards might again become binding if banks suffer large losses that drive their capital ratios closer to statutory minima, but now market disciplinary forces appear to have a larger impact on BHC capital ratios than regulatory standards do.

References

Avery, R., T. Belton, and M. Goldberg. 1988. Market Discipline in Regulating Bank Risk: New Evidence from the Capital Markets, *Journal of Money, Credit and Banking* 20, 597–610.

Benston, George, Paul Irvine, Jim Rosenfeld, and Joseph F. Sinkey Jr. 2003. Bank Capital Structure, Regulatory Capital, and Securities Innovations, *Journal of Money, Credit and Banking* 35(3),

Berger, A. N. 1995. The Relationship Between Capital and Earnings in Banking, *Journal of Money, Credit and Banking* 27(2), 432–456.

Berger, Allen N., and Gregory F. Udell. 1995. Relationship Lending and Lines of Credit in Small Firm Finance, *Journal of Business*.

Bliss, Robert R., and Mark J. Flannery. 2002. Market Discipline in the Governance of U.S. Bank Holding Companies: Monitoring versus Influencing, *European Finance Review* 6(3), 361–395.

Demsetz, R. S., M. R. Saidenberg, and P. E. Strahan. 1996. Banks with Something to Lose: The Disciplinary Role of Franchise Value, *Economic Policy Review*, Federal Reserve Bank of New York.

DeYoung, Robert, and Karin P. Roland. 2001. Product Mix and Earnings Volatility at Commercial Banks: Evidence from a Degree of Total Leverage Model, *Journal of Financial Intermediation* 10, 54–84.

Fischer, E. O., R. Heinkel, and J. Zechner. 1989. Dynamic Capital Structure Choice: Theory and Tests, *Journal of Finance* 44(1), 19–40.

Flannery, Mark J. 1989. Capital Regulation and Insured Banks' Choice of Individual Loan Default Risk, *Journal of Monetary Economics* 235–258.

Flannery, Mark J., and Kasturi P. Rangan. 2004. Partial Adjustment Toward Target Capital Structures. Working paper, University of Florida.

Flannery, Mark J., and Kasturi P. Rangan. What Caused the Bank Capital Buildup of the 1990s? Review of Finance Advance Access published on March 22, 2007, doi:10.1093/rof/rfm007. Reprinted by permission of Oxford University Press.

Flannery, M. J., and S. Sorescu. 1996. Evidence of Bank Market Discipline on Subordinated Debenture Yields: 1983–1991, *Journal of Finance* 51(4), 1347–1377.

Gorton, Gary, and Anthony M. Santomero. 1990. Market Discipline and Bank Subordinated Debt, *Journal of Money, Credit and Banking* 22, 119–128.

Greene, William H. 1993. *Econometric Analysis*. Macmillan, New York.

Hovakimian, Armen, and Edward J. Kane. 2000. Effectiveness of Capital Regulation at U.S. Commercial Banks, 1985 to 1994, *Journal of Finance* 55(1), 451–468.

Hovakimian, Armen, Tim Opler, and Sheridan Titman. 2001. The Debt-Equity Choice, *Journal of Financial and Quantitative Analysis* 36(1),

Jagtiani, J., G. Kaufman, and C. Lemieux. 2002. The Effect of Credit Risk on Bank and Bank Holding Company Bond Yields: Evidence from the Post-FDICIA Period. *Journal of Financial Research* 25(4), 559–575.

Jones, D. S., and K. K. King. 1995. The Implementation of Prompt Corrective Action: An Assessment, *Journal of Banking and Finance* 19(3–4), 491–510.

Kane, Edward J., and Halük Ünal. 1990. Modeling Structural and Temporal Variation in the Market's Valuation of Banking Firms, *Journal of Finance* 45(1), 113–136.

Keeley, M. C. 1990. Deposit Insurance, Risk and Market Power in Banking, *American Economic Review* 80(5), 1183–1200.

Leary, Mark, and Michael Roberts. 2005. Do Firms Rebalance their Capital Structure? *Journal of Finance* 60(6), 2575–2619.

Lindquist, Kjersti-Gro. 2004. Banks' Buffer Capital: How Important Is Risk? *Journal of International Money and Finance* 23, 493–513.

Marcus, Alan J. 1983. The Bank Capital Decision: A Time Series–Cross Section Analysis, *Journal of Finance* 38(4), 1217–1232.

Marcus, Alan J. 1984. Deregulation of Bank Financial Policy, *Journal of Banking and Finance*, 8, 557–565.

Mauer, David C., and Alexander J. Triantis. 1994. Interactions of Corporate Financing and Investment Decisions: A Dynamic Framework, *Journal of Finance* 49(4), 1253–1277.

Merton, R. C. 1974. On the Pricing of Corporate Debt: The Risk Structure of Interest Rates, *Journal of Finance* 29, 449–470.

Merton, R. C. 1977. An Analytic Derivation of the Cost of Deposit Insurance Loan Guarantees, *Journal of Banking and Finance* 2(1), 3–11.

Merton, R. C. 1978. On the Costs of Deposit Insurance When There Are Surveillance Costs, *Journal of Business* 51, 439–452.

Modigliani, Franco, and Merton H. Miller. 1958. The Cost of Capital, Corporation Finance and the Theory of Investment, *American Economic Review* 48(3), 261–297.

Morgan, D. P., and K. J. Stiroh. 1999. Bond Market Discipline of Banks: Is the Market Tough Enough? Working paper, Federal Reserve Bank of New York.

Nelson, Charles R., and Richart Startz. 1990. The Distribution of the Instrumental Variables Estimator and Its *t*-Ratio When the Instrument Is a Poor One, *Journal of Business* 63(1), S125–S140.

O'Hara, M., and W. Shaw. 1990. Deposit Insurance and Wealth Effects: The Value of Being "Too Big to Fail," *Journal of Finance* 45(5), 1587–1600.

Osterberg, William P., and James B. Thomson. 1996. Optimal Financial Structure and Bank Capital Requirements: An Empirical Investigation, *Journal of Financial Services* 10(4), 315–332.

Petersen, M. A., and R. G. Rajan. 1995. The Effect of Credit Market Competition on Lending Relationships, *Quarterly Journal of Economics* 110, 407–443.

Rangan, Kasturi P. 2001. The Changing Face of Bank Capital Structure (1986–1998): Regulators vs. Markets. University of Florida doctoral dissertation.

Ronn, Ehud I., and Avinash K. Verma. 1986. Pricing Risk-Adjusted Deposit Insurance: An Options-Based Model, *Journal of Finance* 41(4), 871–895.

Saunders, A. 2000. *Financial Institutions Management*. McGraw-Hill Higher Education, New York.

Saunders, A., and B. Wilson. 1999. The Impact of Consolidation and Safety-Net Support on Canadian, U.S., and U.K. Banks: 1893–1992, *Journal of Banking and Finance* 23(2–4), 537–571.

Schuermann, Til. 2004. Why Were Banks Better Off in the 2001 Recession? *Federal Reserve Bank of New York Current Issues in Economics and Finance* 10(1), 1–7.

Stiroh, K. J. 2004. Diversification in Banking: Is Noninterest Income the Answer? *Journal of Money, Credit and Banking* 36(5), 853–882.

Wall, L. D., and D. R. Peterson. 1995. Bank Holding Company Targets in the Early 1990s: The Regulators versus the Markets, *Journal of Banking and Finance* 19(3–4), 563–574.

APPENDIX

Estimating BHC Risk-Weighted Assets (RWA) in the 1986–91 Period

The Basel Accord established risk weights of 0, 20, 50, or 100 percent for each asset category on and off a BHC's balance sheet. The risk-weighted sum of the asset categories was termed *risk-weighted assets* (RWA), and capital standards (Tier 1 and Tier 2) were set as proportions of RWA. BHCs were required to report their RWA explicitly on the Y-9C forms from 1996, and there is sufficient information reported from 1992–96 that we can construct RWA accurately. However, prior to 1992 the Y-9C does not provide enough detail to construct RWA or (therefore) the Tier 1 and Tier 2 capital ratios. For the data reported in Figures 3 and 4, we estimate these capital ratios using a methodology developed by Rangan (2001).

The basic idea is that we can use empirical regularities from the 1992–2001 period to estimate a BHC's RWA in an earlier year. First, we run a pooled regression of the following specification:

$$\mathrm{RWA}_{jt} = a_0 + \sum_i b_i A_{ijt} + cO_{ijt} + \varepsilon_{jt}. \tag{A-1}$$

A_{ijt} is the dollar value of asset category i in BHC j's balance sheet at time t.
O_{jt} is the notional value of all off-balance sheet assets of BHC j at time t.

The balance-sheet asset categories (A_{ijt}) correspond to those reported on the Y-9C form: securities, federal funds sold, trading account securities, premises and fixed assets, acceptances outstanding, loans secured by real estate, commercial and industrial loans, agricultural loans, "other" loans, intangible assets, bad loans (past due and nonaccruing), other real estate owned, and miscellaneous other assets. Because asset composition varies greatly among BHCs of different sizes, we partition our sample into three size categories (asset ranks 1–20, 21–50, and 51–100) and estimate $(A - 1)$ separately for each size category. The regression R^2 statistics range from 0.92 to 0.98.

The estimated coefficients in $(A - 1)$ measure the risk-weight contribution of each balance sheet category to RWA over the estimation time period. If the risk-weight contributions (coefficients) estimated from $(A - 1)$ are the same in the pre-Basel period, we can estimate each BHC's RWA in the pre-Basel period (1986Q3–1991Q4) by applying the estimated coefficients to the observed asset categories and off-balance-sheet assets.

CHAPTER 13

Basel II: A Case for Recalibration

Paul H. Kupiec
FDIC

The views expressed are those of the author and do not reflect the views of the FDIC. I am grateful to Rosalind Bennett, Steve Burton, Sanjiv Das, Lee Davidson, Mark Flannery, Bob Jarrow, and Ed Kane for useful discussions and comments on an earlier draft of this chapter.

Abstract

Objectives for Basel II include the promulgation of a sound standard for risk measurement and risk-based minimum capital regulation. The AIRB approach, which may be mandatory for large U.S. banks, will give rise to large reductions in regulatory capital. This chapter assesses whether the reductions in minimum capital are justified by improvements in the accuracy of risk measurement under Basel II. Review of credit loss data and analysis of the economics of capital allocation methods identify important shortcomings in the AIRB framework that lead to undercapitalization of bank credit risks.

1. INTRODUCTION

Under the June 2004 Basel II agreements, national supervisory authorities may choose among three alternative frameworks to set minimum regulatory capital for their internationally active banks. The standardized approach links minimum capital requirements to third-party credit ratings. The Foundation and Advanced Internal Ratings Based (AIRB) approaches assign minimum capital using a regulatory model that uses bank estimates of an individual credit's probability of default (PD), loss given default (LGD), and expected exposure at default (EAD). The U.S. implementation of Basel II will include a modified version of the AIRB framework that will be mandatory for the largest internationally active banks.[1]

In the June 2006 discussion of the Basel II framework, the Basel Committee on Banking Supervision (BCBS) outlines its objectives for the revised Capital Accord. These include (BCBS 2006b, pp. 2–4):

- Strengthen the soundness and stability of the international banking system.
- Promote the adoption of stronger risk management practices.
- Institute more risk-sensitive capital requirements that are conceptually sound.
- Provide a detailed set of minimum requirements designed to ensure the integrity of bank internal risk assessments.
- Broadly maintain the aggregate level of capital requirements.
- Prevent capital adequacy regulation from becoming a significant source of competitive inequality among internationally active banks.
- Create incentives for the adoption of the more advanced framework approaches.

[1]See U.S. Basel II NPR (2006). In the United States, Basel II implementation will require only the largest banks, the so-called core banks, to adopt the AIRB approach, while other banks may petition supervisors for AIRB capital treatment (so-called opt-in banks). Core banks are defined as institutions with total consolidated assets (excluding insurance subsidiary assets) in excess of $250 billion or total on-balance-sheet foreign exposure of $10 billion or more. A revised version of the 1988 Basel Accord, so-called Basel 1A, has been proposed as an alternative regulatory standard for non-AIRB banks, but has yet to be finalized.

This chapter will review the available evidence and assess the degree to which the U.S. implementation of Basel II promises to meet the ambitious goals articulated by the international bank supervisory community. The assessment will focus on the goals of improving financial stability and promoting sound risk measurement practices. We begin with a discussion of the AIRB approach, including the logic used to set minimum capital requirements, the mathematical foundations of the AIRB rule, and the calibrations that have been selected in the U.S. implementation. Following this discussion, we review the existing evidence on the likely capital implications of Basel II and contrast these results with the goal of financial stability. Section 3 analyzes the AIRB as a risk measurement standard. We consider the benefits the AIRB approach may engender as it functions as the minimum risk measurement standard for bank internal capital allocation systems. A final section concludes the paper.

2. A REVIEW OF THE AIRB CAPITAL FRAMEWORK

The introductory section of the US Basel II NPR explains the logic that underlies the Basel II AIRB minimum capital rules. To set minimum capital needs, the AIRB focuses on the probability distribution of *potential credit losses*. The Basel II "soundness standard" for participating institutions is defined as the percentage of potential losses that must be covered by bank capital. The soundness standard determines the minimum probability that a bank will remain solvent over the coming year (e.g., 99.9 percent) (US Basel II NPR 2006, pp. 55832–55833).

To restate the logic of the Basel II AIRB minimum capital rule in statistical terms, let $\widetilde{L}$ represent a credit portfolio's random potential loss and $\Psi(L),\ L \in [0, L]$ represent the cumulative distribution function for potential credit losses. The AIRB capital rule sets minimum capital equal to $\Psi^{-1}(0.999)$, or the inverse of the cumulative portfolio credit loss distribution evaluated at the 99.9 percentile.

The AIRB framework uses a regulatory model to approximate a bank's credit loss distribution and estimate $\Psi^{-1}(0.999)$. The framework is a modified version of the single-factor Gaussian credit loss model first proposed by Vasieck (1991). Using a restrictive set of assumptions, this model creates a synthetic probability distribution for the default rate on a perfectly diversified portfolio of credits. AIRB capital requirements are set using a tail value of this synthetic distribution.

The single-factor Gaussian model of portfolio credit losses uses a latent random factor to model whether an individual credit defaults within an unspecified time frame called the *capital allocation horizon*. There is a unique latent factor for each credit, with the properties

$$
\begin{aligned}
\widetilde{V}_i &= \sqrt{\rho}\,\widetilde{e}_M + \sqrt{1-\rho}\,\widetilde{e}_i \\
\widetilde{e}_M &\sim \phi(e_M) \\
e_i &\sim \phi(e_i), \\
E(\widetilde{e}_i\widetilde{e}_j) &= E(\widetilde{e}_M\widetilde{e}_j) = 0\,\forall\, i, j.
\end{aligned}
\tag{1}
$$

$\widetilde{V}_i$ is normally distributed with $E(\widetilde{V}_i) = 0$ and $E(\widetilde{V}_i^2) = 1$. $\widetilde{e}_M$ is a factor common to all credits' individual latent factors, and the correlation between individual latent factors is ρ.

Firm i is assumed to default when $\widetilde{V}_i < D_i$, implying an unconditional probability that firm i will default, $PD_i = \Phi(D_i)$. The loss incurred should firm i default, LGD, is exogenous to the model and not specific to an individual credit. Time does not play an independent role in this model but is implicitly recognized through the calibration of input values; PD_i, for example, will differ according to the capital allocation horizon.

The model calculates the portfolio default rate distribution for a portfolio of N credits, where N is a very large number and each credit is identical regarding its default threshold, $D_i = D$, and its latent factor correlation, ρ. For such a portfolio, credit losses depend only on the default rate experienced by the portfolio. The capitalization rate required for a single credit added to this so-called "asymptotic" portfolio is identical to the capitalization rate for the entire portfolio because idiosyncratic risks have been fully diversified. The model calculates capital for a perfectly diversified portfolio and ignores capital needs generated by risk concentrations.

The probability distribution for the portfolio default rate is defined using an indicator function,

$$\widetilde{I}_i = \begin{cases} 1 & \text{if } \widetilde{V}_i < D \\ 0 & \text{otherwise} \end{cases} \tag{2}$$

$\widetilde{I}_i$ is binomially distributed with an expected value of $\Phi(D)$. Conditional on a specific value for e_M, default indicators are independent and identically distributed binomial random variables. The default rate on a portfolio of N credits is

$$\widetilde{X} = \frac{\sum_{j=1}^{N} \widetilde{I}_j}{N}.$$

If $\widetilde{I}_j \mid e_M$ is used to represent the distribution of $\widetilde{I}_i$ conditioned on a realized value $\widetilde{e}_M = e_M$, then as $N \to \infty$, the Strong Law of Large Number requires,

$$\lim_{n\to\infty}\left(\widetilde{X} \mid e_M\right) = \lim_{n\to\infty}\left(\frac{\sum_{i=1}^{n}\left(\widetilde{I}_i \mid e_M\right)}{n}\right) \xrightarrow[a.s.]{} E\left(\widetilde{I}_i \mid e_M\right) = \Phi\left(\frac{D - \sqrt{\rho}\, e_M}{\sqrt{1-\rho}}\right). \tag{3}$$

Recall that under Basel II, minimum capital requirements are set using the inverse of this unconditional portfolio loss distribution function, $\Psi^{-1}(\alpha)$, $\alpha \in [0, 1]$. Equation (3) defines the inverse of the cumulative distribution for the portfolio's default rate. The portfolio default rate determines the unconditional portfolio loss distribution under the single-factor Gaussian assumptions. Substituting for the default barrier, $D = \Phi^{-1}(\text{PD})$, and the identity, $\Phi^{-1}(\alpha) = -\Phi^{-1}(1-\alpha)$, the inverse of the unconditional cumulative distribution for the portfolio default rate is given by

$$\Phi\left(\frac{\Phi^{-1}(\mathrm{PD}) + \sqrt{\rho}\,\Phi^{-1}(\alpha)}{\sqrt{1-\rho}}\right), \quad \alpha \in [0, 1]. \tag{4}$$

Assuming an identical exposure (EAD) for each credit in the portfolio and an exogenous identical LGD per dollar of EAD for all portfolio credits, the inverse of the portfolio unconditional credit loss distribution is

$$\Psi^{-1}(\alpha) = \mathrm{LGD} \cdot \mathrm{EAD} \cdot \Phi\left(\frac{\Phi^{-1}(\mathrm{PD}) + \sqrt{\rho}\,\Phi^{-1}(\alpha)}{\sqrt{1-\rho}}\right), \quad \alpha \in [0, 1]. \tag{5}$$

Basel II sets minimum capital equal to the 99.9th percentile level of this loss distribution. Adding the requirement that bank loan loss reserves (which count as regulatory capital) must be equal to (or greater than) expected portfolio loss, the bank minimum capital requirement in excess of loan loss reserves is

$$K = \mathrm{EAD}\left[\mathrm{LGD} \cdot \Phi\left(\frac{\Phi^{-1}(\mathrm{PD}) + \sqrt{\rho}\,\Phi^{-1}(0.999)}{\sqrt{1-\rho}}\right) - \mathrm{PD} \cdot \mathrm{LGD}\right] \tag{6}$$

The Basel II AIRB capital rule appears in Eq. (6) with two additional modifications. Basel II assigns the correlation using a regulatory function that differs among regulatory exposure classes (wholesale, revolving retail, mortgages, and other retail). For wholesale exposures, Eq. (6) is also multiplied by a regulatory maturity adjustment function.

The maturity factor for wholesale exposures (corporate, bank, and sovereign credits) is plotted in Figure 1. There is no theoretical basis for the maturity correction factor as it was calibrated to make the AIRB rule mimic the capital allocation behavior of capital

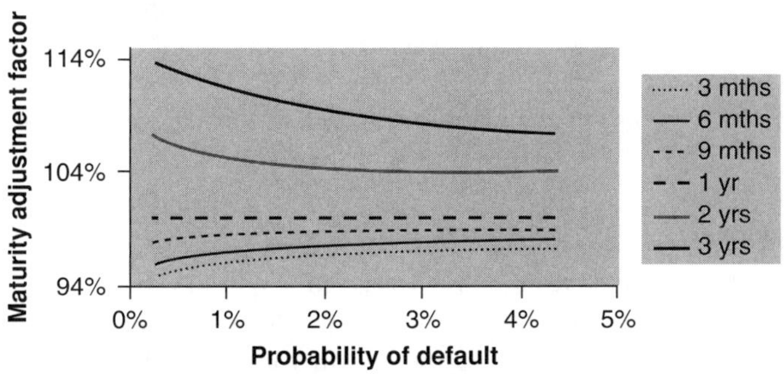

FIGURE 1 Maturity adjustment factors for corporate, bank, and sovereign credits.
Source: Author's calculations using June 2006 AIRB maturity adjustments.

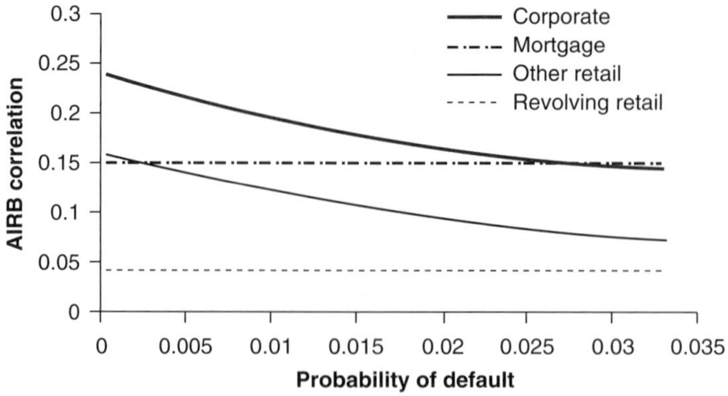

FIGURE 2 Basel II US AIRB correlation assumptions.
Source: Author's calculations using June 2006 AIRB correlation assignment rules.

estimates calculated using KMV Portfolio Manager for different maturity and wholesale credit risk profiles (BCBS 2005, p. 9). The maturity adjustment factor is 1 for 1-year credits; it lowers capital for shorter-term credit and raises capital for longer-term credits.

A regulatory function is used to specify the AIRB correlation parameter ρ. The correlation assignment depends on the type of credit (wholesale, residential mortgage, other retail, or qualifying revolving retail) and PD. The regulatory correlation is a constant for mortgages and revolving retail credits and a declining function of PD for wholesale and other retail credits. AIRB correlation assumptions are plotted in Figure 2.

The AIRB correlation functions were calibrated using datasets made available by G10 bank supervisors (see BCBS 2005). The BCBS interpretation of these data reportedly guided the calibration of the wholesale correlation curve. The data characteristics the BCBS reproduced include (1) default correlation increases with firm size and (2) default correlations decrease as PD increases. Correlations mimic these features within a bound of 24 percent correlation for the lowest PDs and 12 percent correlation for the highest PD wholesale exposures.

AIRB retail correlation assignments reportedly were "reverse engineered" from bank internal model data. Correlations were chosen so that, when used in conjunction with Eq. (6), they produced an AIRB capital requirement that was approximately equivalent to the capital requirement that was assigned by the internal capital allocation models of a group of large internationally active banks (see BCBS 2005, p. 14).

2.1. Discussion

The AIRB is based on a very simple (and restrictive) model of portfolio credit risk in which potential credit losses are driven by the distribution of the proportion of portfolio credits that may default in a large and perfectly diversified portfolio. The model focuses entirely on a portfolio's default rate and does not include other factors that may generate capital needs. The model, moreover, excludes interest earnings and thereby fails to measure the diversification benefits that arise from income that is generated when credits fully perform.

Among the more important risk factors that are omitted from the AIRB framework are systematic credit risks that are driven by random LGDs and, on portfolios of undrawn credit commitments, random EADs. Depending on the characteristics of the LGD and EAD distributions, uncertainty in these factors may generate sources of risk that require additional capital. Appropriately measured, required capitalization rates may far exceed those calculated using the simple Vasicek approximation for a portfolio loss distribution.

Empirical evidence concerning LGDs finds significant time variability in realized LGDs. Default losses clearly increase in periods when default rates are elevated. Studies by Frye (2000), Schuermann (2004), Araten, Jacobs, and Varshney (2004), Altman et al. (2004), Hamilton et al. (2004), Carey and Gordy (2004), Emery, Cantor, and Arnet (2004), and others show pronounced decreases in the recovery rates during recessions and periods of heightened defaults.

There is relatively little published evidence that characterizes the empirical characteristics of EADs for revolving exposures. The evidence that is available, including studies by Allen and Saunders (2003), Asarnow and Marker (1995), Araten and Jacobs (2001), and Jiménez, Lopez, and Saurina (2006) suggests that obligors draw on their lines of credit as their credit quality deteriorates. In other words, EADs and PDs are positively correlated, suggesting that there is at least one common factor that simultaneously determines EAD and default realizations.

Basel II documents indicate that the BCBS is aware that the stochastic nature of LGD and EAD may affect minimum capital needs. The committee nonetheless did not decide to generalize the Vasicek model to account for these effects and instead focused on including guidance that seeks to bolster the magnitude of bank LGD estimates.

The Basel II discussion defines ELGD as the simple average of historical LGD observations and requires that the LGD input into the AIRB capital rule equal expected loss given default (ELGD) plus an adjustment for the potential that losses might be elevated from ELGD should default occur during a recession. The framework excludes any formal method of adjustment or a technical standard to guide the estimation of so-called "downturn LGD." For revolving credits, Basel II requires that EAD estimates include recognition that obligors may draw on their credit lines, but again Basel II excludes any formal method, process, or standard for modeling EAD.

The calibration of the regulatory default correlation function raises a number of issues. For wholesale credits (corporate, bank, and foreign sovereign exposures) and other retail credits (auto loans, boat loans, personal loans, etc.), the BCBS specifies a correlation parameter that declines as a credit's PD increases. Low-PD credits may have up to twice the default correlation of high-PD exposures. Independent empirical evidence does not support this calibration.

In contrast to the BCBS characterization of the stylized facts (BCBS 2005, p. 12), studies including Allen, DeLong, and Saunders (2004), Cowan and Cowan (2004), Dietsch and Petey (2004), and Das, Duffie, Kapadia, and Saita (2004) find that default correlation increases as the credit quality of a portfolio declines (PD increases). The choice of the shape of the Basel II correlation curve is not consistent with empirical evidence, but likely was selected to attenuate fears that the AIRB might create "procyclicality," or capital requirements that systematically vary with the business cycle.

Concerns about "procyclicality" are based on the idea that, during recessions, any given set of bank credits is more likely to be reclassified into lower-rated buckets.[2] In boom periods, the reverse will likely occur. If a portfolio of given credits migrates through various PD grades in response to changing economic conditions, AIRB minimum capital will rise during recessions and decline during booms. Such a cycle in minimum capital has the potential to discourage the extension of new bank credit during recessions and overly stimulate bank lending during boom periods and thereby unintentionally reinforce the bank lending cycle. It is seems likely that the BCBS intends to dampen the inherent procyclicality of the AIRB capital rule by specifying a correlation function that declines as PD increases. This calibration will reduce the minimum capital fluctuations that a credit may generate as it moves through an upgrade/downgrade cycle.

3. THE AIRB AND FINANCIAL STABILITY

Basel II will enhance financial stability if it improves upon the 1988 Basel Accord's ability to ensure that systemically important institutions retain adequate minimum capital to achieve social policy objectives. In a variety of published papers and public addresses, members of the BCBS have explained that the complexity of the AIRB is needed to ensure risk and minimum capital are properly aligned given the complexity of large international banking organizations and the need to foreclose opportunities for regulatory arbitrage that exist under the 1988 Basel Accord.[3] Capital savings that arise under the AIRB are intended to offset costs associated with developing and operating AIRB systems. Reductions in capital also reflect a presumption that the AIRB approach will improve the accuracy of bank credit risk measures and thereby improve the assignment of minimum capital allocations within banks.

The BCBS has conducted two quantitative impact studies (QISs) following the June 2004 publication of the Basel II framework. QIS 4 included banks in the United States, Germany, and South Africa. QIS 5 included banks in adopting countries in other nations. Both studies reported substantial declines in minimum capital requirements for AIRB banks relative to capital required under the 1988 Basel Accord. Figure 3 plots a histogram of estimates of the effective change in the levels of minimum capital that would be required under the AIRB approach for banks participating in the QIS 4 exercise, relative to capital levels required under the U.S. implementation of the 1988 Basel Accord.

[2]See, for example, Turner (2000), Lowe (2002), Allen and Saunders (2003), Kashyap and Stein (2004), or Gordy and Howells (2004).
[3]See, for example, Greenspan (1998), BCBS (1999), Mingo (2000), D. Jones (2000), or Meyer (2001) or, more recently, Bies (2005).

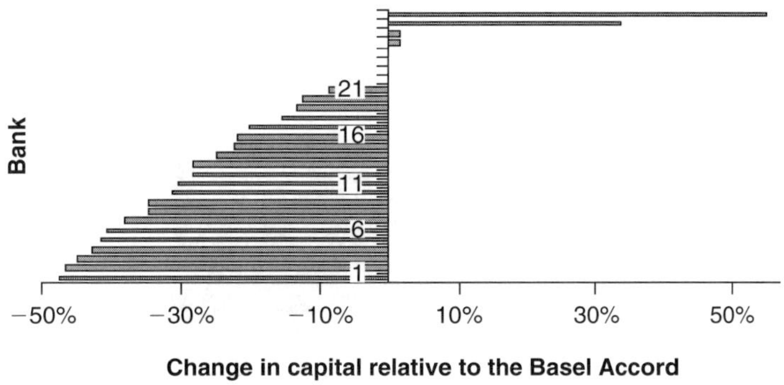

FIGURE 3 Estimates of effective AIRB changes in minimum required capital of QIS 4 banks.
Source: QIS 4 Interagency Analysis.

The QIS 4 study included 26 U.S. institutions, all of which reported using the AIRB approach.[4] The results show that, in aggregate, minimum regulatory capital for these institutions fell by 15.5 percent relative to existing capital requirements. Among these banks, the median reduction in capital was 26 percent and the median reduction in Tier I capital requirements was 31 percent. Of the few banks that experienced increases in minimum capital requirements under the AIRB, the increases were driven primarily by increases in capital for consumer retail portfolios and to a lesser extent by equity exposures.

In addition to large declines in capital, QIS 4 results show a high degree of dispersion in reported estimates of minimum capital requirements. Banks reported widely divergent capital estimates for their constituent portfolios (corporate, mortgages, etc.). Although these differences could owe to differences in bank risk profiles that reflect differentiation among customer bases and business strategies, additional analysis conducted by the U.S. regulatory agencies using shared national credit data and a hypothetical mortgage portfolio indicated that banks reported widely divergent capital estimates for positions with substantially similar risk characteristics. The analysis suggested that a significant share of the variation in QIS 4 results may be attributed to differences in bank estimates of PDs and LGDs among credits with approximately equivalent risk characteristics. For the wholesale portfolio, for example, QIS 4 LGD estimates on nondefaulted credits varied from about 15 to 55 percent across banking institutions.

The minimum regulatory capital treatment of securitization exposures provides one indicator of the degree to which the AIRB approach meets Basel II objectives. Bank securitization activities have been specifically identified as the means through which Basel Accord minimum capital standards have been eroded (e.g., D. Jones 2000, Mingo 2000). The Basel AIRB approach includes a complex set of capital rules for measuring capital requirements on exposures related to securitized positions. Figure 4 plots the

[4]See the Federal Reserve Board Press release "Summary Findings of the Fourth Quantitative Impact Study," available at www.federalreserve.gov.

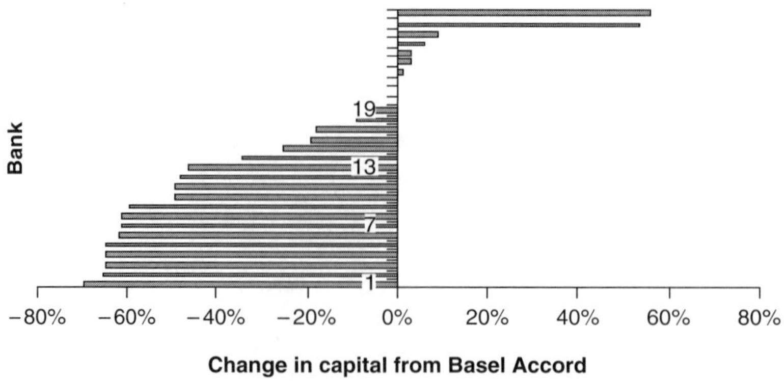

FIGURE 4 QIS 4 estimates of AIRB change in captial for securitization exposures.
Source: Author's calculations using QIS 4 Interagency data.

histogram of the changes in effective minimum capital required by the AIRB approach for QIS 4 participating banks. Changes are calculated relative to existing minimum capital requirements. In these estimates, AIRB rules that require deductions from capital are treated as a capital requirement of 100 percent. Figure 4 shows, for most banks, the AIRB will result in substantial reductions in required capital for exposures related to securitizations. Although a full analysis is not possible using QIS 4 data, a large part of the reductions likely owe to reductions in AIRB capital requirements for the assets that are included in these securitization structures.[5]

The QIS 5 study includes 382 banks in 32 countries outside of the United States.[6] Of the banks that participated, the largest internationally active banks, so-called Group 1 banks, posted capital declines of 7.1 percent on average under the AIRB approach. Smaller banks, so-called Group 2 banks that are primarily nationally focused institutions, experienced much larger declines in minimum regulatory capital (BCBS 2006a). Within Europe,[7] Group 1 banks posted average capital declines of 8.3 percent under the AIRB. For European Group 2 banks, capital declines averaged 26.6 percent under the AIRB. The QIS 5 analysis attributed the large declines in minimum regulatory capital requirements to bank concentrations in retail lending, especially residential mortgages.

The BCBS discussion of QIS 5 results does not provide detailed analysis of the dispersion of bank minimum capital estimates. The study does, however, report significant variation in AIRB input values. LGD estimates for wholesale credits, for example, range from 10.8 to 67.6 percent across reporting banks.

[5]The Basel II capital rules for securitization exposures have a "look through" property, meaning that the minimum capital requirements that apply to the collateral in these structures in part determines the capital requirements for a bank's securitization position.

[6]See, BCBS (2006a). QIS 5 AIRB capital rules include a 1.06 scaling factor that was not included in the June 2004 calibration or the instructions that guided QIS 4. The inclusion of this scaling factor means the reported capital declines will appear less severe than those reported in the United States.

[7]So-called CEBS (Committee of European Bank Supervisors) banks.

The results of the QIS 4 and QIS 5 studies show that, under the AIRB approach, most banks will face large reductions in their minimum required capital levels on their current portfolio positions. In practice, the AIRB will result in further capital reductions as banks optimize and adjust their positions to maximize the benefits available through new (unanticipated) regulatory arbitrage opportunities available under the AIRB approach.

Given the potential for large reductions in minimum bank capital that may materialize under the AIRB approach, it is important to assess whether or not these reductions are justified by improvements in risk measurement standards. There is a strong presumption in many Basel II–related documents and policy discussions that the AIRB approach represents a rigorous scientifically supported standard for measuring bank minimum capital needs. Unfortunately, this confidence is misplaced. A large body of evidence shows that the AIRB framework will undercapitalize credit risks.

There are many sources of bias in the AIRB capital rule. One source of undercapitalization arises because the AIRB underestimates the 99.9 percent loss value for banks' portfolio credit loss distributions. The AIRB approach synthesizes an estimate of a bank's 99.9 percent credit loss critical value using a model that ignores systematic risks in LGDs and the draw rates on revolving lines of credit. In addition, AIRB minimum capital requirements must be fortified to account for exposure concentrations that are assumed-away in the AIRB framework. A second source of bias is a flaw in the logic used to set AIRB minimum capital requirements. The AIRB capital rule ignores the need for a bank to pay interest on its own liabilities.

Some may argue that the weaknesses in the AIRB rule are known and market discipline and national supervisory discretion that may be exercised under pillar 2 will bolster bank capital and attenuate these weaknesses. Such claims are, however, untested. The Basel II prescription for pillar 2 powers does not ensure that national supervisors have the legal powers prescribed or that discretionary powers will be utilized. Claims of the veracity of market discipline or the ability to use pillar 2 supervisory powers to correct for AIRB shortcomings should not be a basis for codifying into regulation a seriously flawed risk measurement standard. The following sections discuss these issues in more detail.

4. ESTABLISHING A SOUND BENCHMARK FOR RISK MEASUREMENT PRACTICES

4.1. The Need for Capital for Bank Interest Expenses

Although the U.S. Basel II NPR discussion mirrors a textbook description of a credit value-at-risk (VaR) calculation, the procedure described will not set minimum capital requirements to ensure the 99.9 percent targeted soundness standard. An important flaw in the credit VaR capital allocation method is its failure to recognize a bank's need to pay interest on its own liabilities. This oversight creates little bias when VaR measures are used to set capital over short horizons, as they are, for example, in the 1-day and 10-day horizons used in the market risk rule. Over longer horizons like the 1-year horizon used for Basel II, ignoring the need to pay interest will cause a substantial divergence between the intended and actual AIRB soundness standard. The magnitude of the deterioration in the intended safety margin will, moreover, depend on the level of interest rates. The omitted interest-rate effect will magnify the procyclical nature of the AIRB capital rules.

Consider the problem of setting capital for a single credit. To avoid any questions about the magnitudes of the capital variations involved, we frame the example in terms of an exact pricing model for credit risk. We will use the Black and Scholes (1973) and Merton (1974) model (hereafter BSM) to frame the analysis, but the qualitative result is true for any equilibrium asset pricing model.

Under simplifying assumptions, the BSM model establishes equilibrium pricing relationships that must hold for risky discount debt instruments. When the default-free term structure is not stochastic and flat at a rate r_f and a firms' assets have an initial value of A_0 and evolve in value following geometric Brownian motion with an instantaneous volatility of σ, the BSM model has shown that the equilibrium price, B_0, of a one-year risky discount bond with a promised maturity value of Par is

$$B_0 = e^{-r_f}\,\Phi\left(\frac{\ln(A_0) - \ln(\text{Par}) + \left(r_f - \frac{\sigma^2}{2}\right)}{\sigma}\right) - A_0\,\Phi\left(\frac{\ln(\text{Par}) - \ln(A_0) - \left(r_f + \frac{\sigma^2}{2}\right)}{\sigma}\right). \tag{7}$$

The value-at-risk measure for this bond is calculated using the physical probability distribution for the value of this bond at the end of one year, $\widetilde{B}_1$. Under the BSM model assumptions, $\widetilde{B}_1$, the physical probability distribution for the bond's value after one year, is

$$\widetilde{B}_1 = \text{Min}\left[A_0 e^{\left(\mu - \frac{\sigma^2}{2}\right)T + \sigma\sqrt{T}\,\widetilde{z}},\ \text{Par}\right], \tag{8}$$

where $\widetilde{z}$ is a standard normal variable, $\mu = r_f + \lambda\sigma$, and λ is the market price of risk.

The critical value of this distribution used to set a VaR(α) measure is

$$\text{Min}\left[A_0\, e^{\left(\mu - \frac{\sigma^2}{2}\right)T + \sigma\sqrt{T}\,\Phi^{-1}(1-\alpha)},\ \text{Par}\right],$$

which simplifies to

$$A_0\, e^{\left(\mu - \frac{\sigma^2}{2}\right)T + \sigma\sqrt{T}\,\Phi^{-1}(1-\alpha)}$$

when the probability of default on the bond exceeds $(1 - \alpha)$.

To determine the capital needed to fund this bond, note that any debt issue with a par value greater than

$$A_0\, e^{\left(\mu-\frac{\sigma^2}{2}\right)T+\sigma\sqrt{T}\,\Phi^{-1}(1-\alpha)}$$

will default with a probability greater than $(1-\alpha)$ if $\widetilde{B}_1$ is the only source of funds available to repay the funding debt. Thus

$$\mathrm{Par}_F\ (\alpha) = A_0\, e^{\left(\mu-\frac{\sigma^2}{2}\right)T+\sigma\sqrt{T}\,\Phi^{-1}(1-\alpha)}$$

is the maximum permissible par value for the funding debt. The cash flows from $\widetilde{B}_1$ "pass through" the firm to pay off the funding debt issue, and so the BSM model can be used to price the bond issued by the bank. The difference between B_0 and the market value of the funding debt issue is the minimum equity capital needed to fund the risky bond. The minimum amount of capital needed to achieve a soundness standard of α is

$$B_0 - \mathrm{Par}_F\ (\alpha)e^{-r_f}[1-\Phi(d(\alpha))] - A_0\Phi(d(\alpha)+\sigma), \tag{9}$$

where $d(\alpha)=\Phi^{-1}(1-\alpha)+(\mu-r_f)/\sigma$.

The potential importance of the omission of bank funding costs from the Basel II AIRB capital calculations is illustrated in Figure 5 for a risky 1-year BSM discount bond. The bond has a par value of 70 and, for the rights to this claim, the bank lends \$66.14. The underlying assets of the borrower have an initial value of 100, and these assets evolve in value following geometric Brownian motion with an instantaneous drift rate of $\mu=0.10$, and an instantaneous volatility $\sigma=0.25$. One-year Treasury bonds pay a 5 percent rate.

The probability distribution of $\widetilde{B}_1$ is plotted in Figure 5(a). In this example we consider a soundness standard of 99 percent, which dictates that the bank's equity must be large enough to absorb 99 percent of all potential losses. The 99 percent critical value of the loss distribution is equivalent to the 1 percent critical value of the bond's future value distribution, or \$59.82 in this example. Under the AIRB approach for setting capital, this bond requires \$7.32 in capital (\$66.14 – \$59.82) to cover both expected and unexpected losses. To fund the bond, the bank must sell debt that has an initial market value of \$59.82.

Figure 5(b) illustrates the potential outcome one year after the bond is purchased and funded according to an AIRB approach for setting minimum capital. If the bank raises \$59.82 in debt finance to fund the bond, it owes bank debt holders \$63.04 at the end of the year.[8] After accounting for the interest payments that are due on the bank debt, the true probability that the bank defaults on its debt is 1.7 percent.[9] The actual default rate is 70 percent higher than the minimum regulatory soundness standard.

[8]This value is calculated by inverting the BSM pricing model to find the par value of debt that would raise \$59.82 when it is sold to investors. The bank's debt is risky, so it must pay a rate higher than the one-year risk-free rate.

[9]The probability distribution for $\widetilde{B}_1$ includes the interest that is paid to the bank on the purchased risky bond.

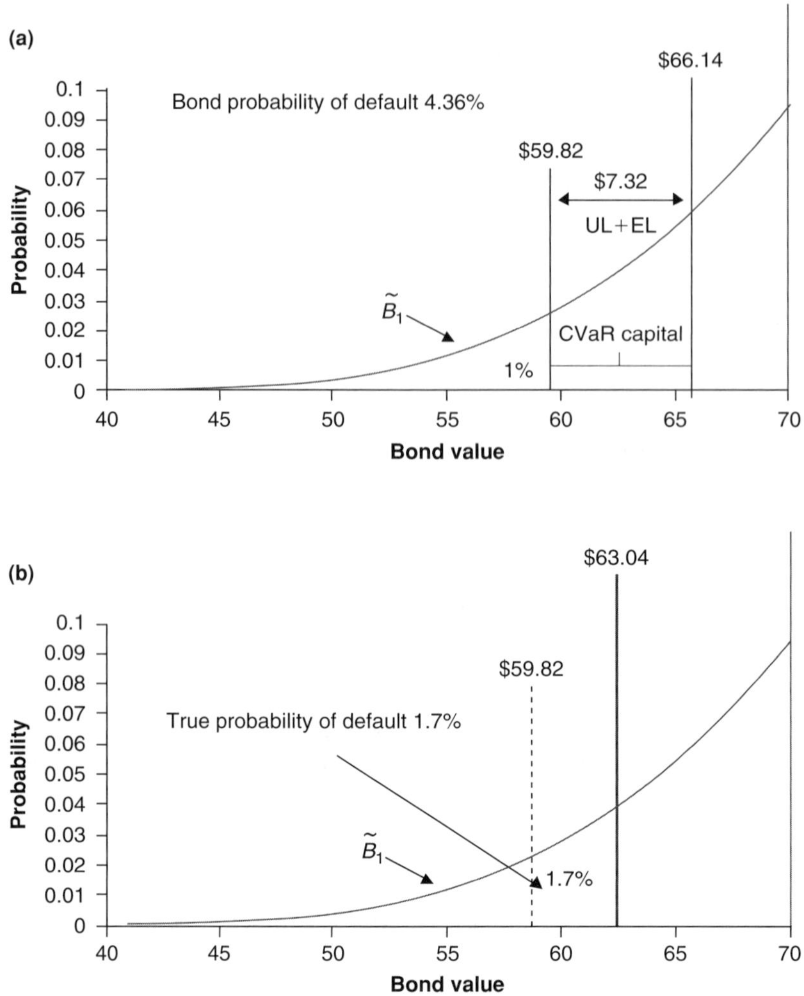

FIGURE 5 **(a)** Credit VaR calculation. **(b)** Financial position after 1 year.
Source: Author's calculations.

There is nothing "staged" about this example. The AIRB approach for setting minimum regulatory capital requirements excludes any consideration of the need to compensate bank debt holders for the time value of money and credit risk. As a consequence the credit VaR–based AIRB rule will always understate capital requirements. This is true in a portfolio context also, as long as the bank earns and pays competitive rates of return on its loans and liabilities. Kupiec (2007b) provides additional discussion, including the portfolio generalization of this result.

4.2. Procyclicality of the AIRB Soundness Standard

The omission of bank interest expense in the AIRB capital rule engenders a soundness standard that varies over the business cycle. The soundness standard set by AIRB minimum capital requirements will decline (i.e., the probability of default will increase) when interest rates are high and the central bank is attempting to dampen economic activity and bank lending. Conversely, AIRB capital standards engender the strictest solvency standard when interest rates are low and the central bank is attempting to stimulate bank lending and economic activity. As a consequence, the potential safety net benefits to the banking system are increased during the boom phase of the economic cycle, when banks compete on underwriting standards and stock up on the "bad loans" that default when a subsequent downturn materializes.

The procyclicality of the soundness standard is illustrated in Figure 6. Figure 6(a) illustrates the credit VaR capital calculation for a bond identical to that analyzed in

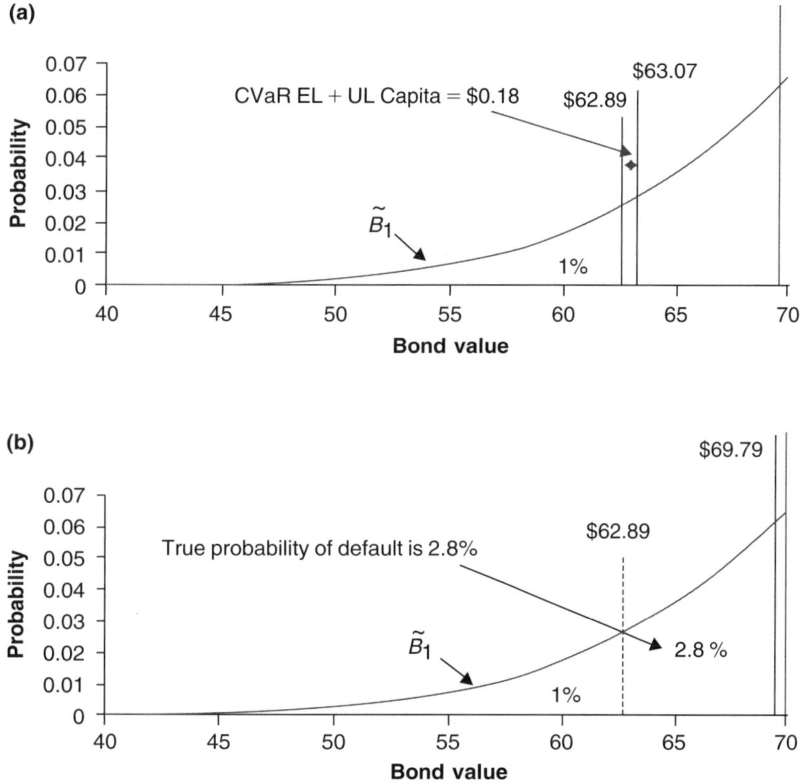

FIGURE 6 (**a**) Credit VaR calculation with 10% risk-free rate. (**b**) Financial position after 1 year.
Source: Author's calculations.

Figure 5(a) with a one-year Treasury rate of 10 percent instead of 5 percent. Since this new bond must satisfy equilibrium conditions, the higher default-free rate requires an increase in the instantaneous drift rate ($\mu = 15$ percent) on the value of the underlying assets. Under these new equilibrium conditions, the credit VaR approach requires only $.18 for its minimum capital requirement, so the bond can be purchased for $63.07 and funded with $62.89 in debt.

Figure 6(b) shows the possible outcomes one year later. After one year, the bank must pay its debt holders $69.79 to avoid default and retire its debt with accrued interest. The probability that the value $\widetilde{B}_1$ is less than $69.79 is 2.8 percent. Thus the actual soundness standard set by the AIRB minimum capital rule is 97.20 percent and not the targeted 99.9 percent. The actual soundness standard set by the AIRB rule declined from 1.7 percent to 2.8 percent as risk-free interest rates rose by 5 percentage points.[10]

The omission of bank interest costs will induce procyclicality in the AIRB regulatory soundness standard. To the extent that minimum regulatory capital requirements impose binding constraints on bank capital positions, this procyclicality may work to magnify the bank lending cycle. During the initial upturn phase of the business cycle, the demand for credit is strong and banks may expand lending and grow without relaxing their underwriting standards or offering concessionary spreads.

As the recovery phase matures toward the peak of the business cycle, growth opportunities wane, and banks compete aggressively to continue to grow. In this portion of the cycle, banks' risk of booking marginal quality credits increases. Concurrently, at this stage of the cycle, the central bank typically begins to increase interest rates in order to attenuate aggregate demand imbalances. Under the AIRB approach to setting capital, the increase in risk-free interest rates will automatically reduce banks' minimum regulatory solvency standard.

When governments provide implicit or underpriced explicit guarantees on bank liabilities, bank debt is priced to reflect this guarantee. Because bank shareholders do not pay (or pay a fair price) for this guarantee, they profit from a government safety net subsidy. A reduction in a bank's soundness standard is equivalent to expanding the safety net subsidy enjoyed by banks. Banks may utilize the increased subsidy and continue to grow by adding marginal loans that otherwise might have been rejected under a stricter solvency standard. Reverse incentives will arise in a recession, as decreases in interest rates strengthen the regulatory solvency standard and discourage bank lending.

4.3. Incorporating Portfolio Interest Income

Quite apart from the need to recognize that bank capital requirements must be set to ensure that a bank can meet its interest expenses, well-formulated capital allocation estimates should also recognize the interest income received by a bank on fully performing credits. The AIRB framework calculates capital requirements using an approximation for the distribution of the default rate on a well-diversified portfolio. The model does

[10]Notice that this increase in capital is for credit risk and not for interest-rate risk as the one-year default free rate was changed ceteris peribis and not converted into a random variable.

not include any recognition of the loss diversification benefits that arise from the interest payments that are received on fully performing credits. Portfolio interest income can be recognized by formulating the model using an asymptotic approximation for the portfolio return distribution instead of the portfolio loss distribution (Kupiec 2007a).

Consider the portfolio of identical credits analyzed in Section 2. Let YTM represent the yield to maturity, calculated using the initial market value of an individual credit, and let LGD represent the loss from initial loan value should a loan default. All loans in a portfolio are assumed to have identical values for YTM, PD, and LGD.

Let $\widetilde{R}_p$ represent the return on the portfolio of credits. The end-of-horizon conditional portfolio return is given by

$$\widetilde{R}_p = \text{YTM} - (\text{YTM} + \text{LGD})\widetilde{X}, \tag{10}$$

where the distribution for $\widetilde{X}$ follows from Eq. (3). Applying the same logic used in Section 2 to derive the Vasicek approximation for the portfolio's loss distribution, the unconditional cumulative return distribution for the portfolio, $\widetilde{R}_P$, can be derived from the distribution for the portfolio default rate [Eq. (3)].[11] The critical value of the portfolio return distribution that is consistent with a regulatory soundness standard of 99.9 percent is

$$\left(1 + \text{YTM} - (\text{YTM} + \text{LGD})\Phi\left(\frac{\Phi^{-1}(\text{PD}) + \sqrt{\rho}\,\Phi^{-1}(0.999)}{\sqrt{1-\rho}}\right)\right). \tag{11}$$

Assuming the bank earns and pays competitive rates on its assets and liabilities, YTM is a conservative estimate of the equilibrium required rate of return on the bank's funding debt when it is issued. Using this approximation, the minimum required portfolio (and individual credit) capitalization rate to ensure a 99.9 percent solvency standard is

$$K(\alpha) \approx \frac{\text{YTM} + \text{LGD}}{1 + \text{YTM}}\Phi\left(\frac{\Phi^{-1}(\text{PD}) + \sqrt{\rho}\,\Phi^{-1}(0.999)}{\sqrt{1-\rho}}\right). \tag{12}$$

Equation (12) is an approximation for the capital needed in a single-common-factor framework. It includes capital for both expected and unexpected loss as well as capital to cover bank interest expenses. Unlike the Basel II AIRB capital rule, it fully recognizes the capital-reducing benefits of competitive rates of interest income earned by the fully performing credits in a portfolio. Capital requirements set according to Eq. (12) are uniformly larger than the capital requirements set by the Basel AIRB formula even when including capital for expected loss [Eq. (5)]. The relationship between the capital recommended by Eqs. (5) and (12) is illustrated in Figure 7.

Figure 7 compares minimum capital requirements for a 99.9 percent soundness standard as set by the Basel AIRB rule for expected and unexpected loss [Eqs. (5) and (12)]. The minimum capital estimates are for hypothetical credit portfolios that are composed

[11] Kupiec (2007a) provides a full derivation.

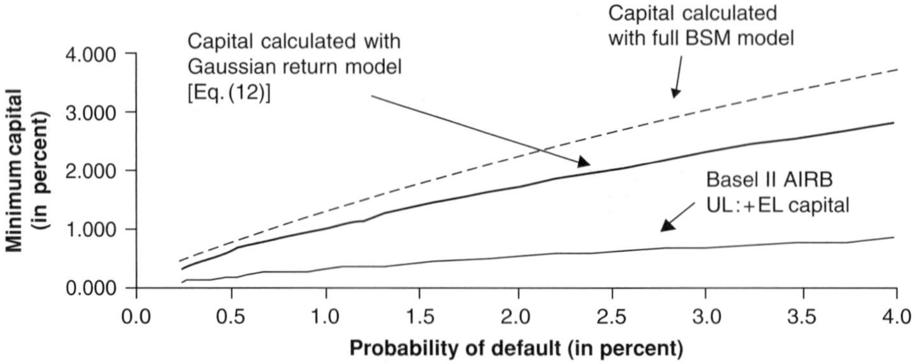

FIGURE 7 Capital requirements recognizing bank interest income and expense.
Source: Author's calculations.

of credits that are priced to satisfy BSM equilibrium conditions (Kupiec 2007b includes additional details).

It is important to remember that the Basel AIRB rule and Eq. (12) are approximations for the true capital needed to satisfy a regulatory soundness standard. Both of these models are developed under a set of restrictive assumptions that allow the models to be parameterized in terms of PD and LGD and admit a closed-form expression for capital. For reference, Figure 7 also includes the exact capital that is required to ensure the 99.9 percent soundness standard. These exact capital requirements are calculated using a full BSM capital allocation model developed in Kupiec (2007a). The full BSM model expression for capital is significantly more complex than Eqs. (5) or (12), and it is not directly parameterized using common measures of credit risk (PD, LGD, default correlation) but instead is calibrated using a deeper set of model parameters (volatilities, drift rates, initial asset values, etc.).

4.4. Capital for Systematic Risk in PD and LGD

Many studies have recognized that credit loss rate realizations may be tied to the business cycle. Recovery values tend to be depressed for defaults that occur when default rates are elevated. The Basel II AIRB model framework takes LGD as an exogenous parameter. Correlation between PD and LGD is not modeled, but must be accounted for through some ad hoc adjustment to Eq. (5). In the Basel II framework, this adjustment is made through requirements on how the LGD parameter must be estimated.

The U.S. Basel II NPR makes a distinction between two loss-given-default parameters. One parameter, expected loss given default, or ELGD, is the default-frequency weighted average default experience for an LGD grade. The second measure of loss given default, LGD, is the parameter that is to be used as the AIRB input. LGD is the greater of a bank's ELGD estimate for the exposure or the loss per dollar of EAD that the bank would likely incur should the exposure default within a one-year horizon during an economic downturn (U.S. Basel II NPR 2006, pp. 55847–55848). This regulatory definition of downturn LGD is not restrictive as to how LGD may be estimated. It is possible to formally incorporate random LGD into the AIRB model and to derive a rigorous statistical characterization of LGD.

4.5. Random Loss Given Default and "Downturn" LGD

Assume that a generic credit has a potential loss given default, $\widetilde{\text{LGD}}_i$, that is random. LGD uncertainty is driven by a latent Gaussian factor, $\widetilde{Y}_i$, with the following properties:

$$\begin{aligned} \widetilde{Y}_i &= \sqrt{\rho_Y}\,\widetilde{e}_M + \sqrt{1-\rho_Y}\,\widetilde{e}_{iY}, \\ \widetilde{e}_M &\sim \phi(e_M), \\ e_{iY} &\sim \phi(e_{iY}), \\ E(\widetilde{e}_{iY}\,\widetilde{e}_{jY}) &= E(\widetilde{e}_M\,\widetilde{e}_{jY}) = E(\widetilde{e}_{iY}\,\widetilde{e}_j) = 0\,\forall\, i, j. \end{aligned} \tag{13}$$

The common Gaussian factor, $\widetilde{e}_M$, in the latent factor $\widetilde{Y}_i$ is identical to the common Gaussian factor in Eq. (1), and so the latent default factor $\widetilde{V}_i$ and loss given default factor, $\widetilde{Y}_i$, are positively correlated, provided $\sqrt{\rho_Y} > 0$.

The unconditional distribution for $\widetilde{\text{LGD}}_i$ can be approximated to any desired level of precision using a step function that is driven using the realized value of $\widetilde{Y}_i$. Without loss of generality, we assume that higher LGD realizations are associated with smaller realized values for $\widetilde{Y}_i$. For expositional simplicity, consider the following simple approximation:

$$\widetilde{\text{LGD}}_i = \begin{bmatrix} \text{LGD}_0 & \text{for } \widetilde{Y}_i > B_{i1} \\ \text{LGD}_0 + \Delta\text{LGD} & \text{for } B_{i2} < \widetilde{Y}_i < B_{i1} \\ \text{LGD}_0 + 2\,\Delta\text{LGD} & \text{for } B_{i3} < \widetilde{Y}_i < B_{i2} \\ \text{LGD}_0 + 3\,\Delta\text{LGD} & \text{for } \widetilde{Y}_i \le B_{i3}, \end{bmatrix} \tag{14}$$

where $B_{i3} < B_{i2} < B_{i1}$. Let $\Omega(\text{LGD}_i)$ represent the cumulative distribution function for $\widetilde{\text{LGD}}_i$. Each level of the LGD step function approximation has an associated cumulative probability. This cumulative probability in turn defines the cumulative probability of the latent variable $\widetilde{Y}_i$ crossing the threshold. This association is described in Table 1.

TABLE 1 Probability Distribution Approximation for LGD

Loss step function increment	LGD level	Cumulative probability of LGD level	Cumulative probability for latent variable $\widetilde{Y}_i$
0	LGD_{i0}	$\Omega(\text{LGD}_{i0})$	$1-\Phi(B_{i1})$
ΔLGD	$\text{LGD}_{i0} + \Delta\text{LGD}$	$\Omega(\text{LGD}_{i0} + \Delta\text{LGD})$	$1-\Phi(B_{i2})$
$2\,\Delta$LGD	$\text{LGD}_{i0} + 2\,\Delta\text{LGD}$	$\Omega(\text{LGD}_{i0} + 2\,\Delta\text{LGD})$	$1-\Phi(B_{i3})$
$3\,\Delta$LGD	$\text{LGD}_{i0} + 3\,\Delta\text{LGD}$	$\Omega(\text{LGD}_{i0} + 3\,\Delta\text{LGD})$	$\Phi(B_{i3})$

In this example, the loss distribution for an individual account can be defined using four indicator functions, one for default status and three to represent the realized LGD:

$$\widetilde{I}_i = \begin{cases} 1 & \text{if } \widetilde{V}_i < D_i \\ 0 & \text{otherwise} \end{cases}, \quad \widetilde{H}_{ij} = \begin{cases} 1 & \text{if } \widetilde{Y}_i < B_{ij} \\ 0 & \text{otherwise} \end{cases} \quad \text{for } j = 1,\ 2,\ 3. \tag{15}$$

Each indicator variable has a binomial distribution with a mean equal to the cumulative standard normal distribution evaluated at the indicator function's threshold value. For example, $\widetilde{I}_i$ has a binomial distribution with an expected value of $\Phi(D_i)$; similarly, $\widetilde{H}_{i1}$ is binomial with an expected value of $\Phi(B_{i1})$, and so on for the remaining indicators.

The loss rate (LR) for account i measured relative to EAD_i can be written

$$\text{L}\widetilde{\text{R}}_i = \widetilde{I}_i \left(\text{LGD}_{i0} + \Delta\text{LGD} \sum_{k=1}^{3} \widetilde{H}_{k1} \right). \tag{16}$$

Define $\widetilde{I}_i \,|\, e_M$ and $\widetilde{H}_{ik} \,|\, e_M$ as the distributions of the default indicator functions conditional on a realized value for e_M for $(k = 1, 2, 3)$. The conditional indicator functions are independent binomial random variables with the properties

$$E(\widetilde{I}_i \,|\, e_M) = \Phi\left(\frac{D - \sqrt{\rho_d}\, e_M}{\sqrt{1-\rho_d}} \right), \quad E\left(\widetilde{H}_{il} \,|\, e_M\right) = \Phi\left(\frac{B_{il} - \sqrt{\rho_Y}\, e_M}{\sqrt{1-\rho_Y}} \right). \tag{17}$$

Using the conditional indicator function notation, the conditional loss rate for an individual credit can be written

$$L\widetilde{R}_i \,|\, e_M = (\widetilde{I}_i \,|\, e_M) \left(\text{LGD}_{i0} + \Delta\text{LGD} \sum_{k=1}^{3} \left(\widetilde{H}_{k1} \,|\, e_M \right) \right). \tag{18}$$

4.6. Asymptotic Portfolio Loss Distribution

Consider a portfolio composed of N accounts with identical latent-factor correlations $\{\rho, \rho_Y\}$, default thresholds $D_i = D$, and unconditional loss given default distributions $\text{LG}\widetilde{\text{D}}_i = \text{LG}\widetilde{\text{D}}$. Individual credit LGDs are drawn from a common distribution defined by Eq. (14) with parameters $B_{i1} = B_1$, $B_{i2} = B_2$, and $B_{i3} = B_3$. Under these assumptions, $\widetilde{I}_i \,|\, e_M$ and $\widetilde{H}_{ik} \,|\, e_M$ are independent and identically distributed across individual credits i in the portfolio, $\widetilde{I}_i \,|\, e_M \sim \widetilde{I}_j \,|\, e_M, \forall i, j$, and $\widetilde{H}_{ik} \,|\, e_M \sim \widetilde{H}_{jk} \,|\, e_M, \forall i, j, k$.

Define $\text{L}\widetilde{\text{R}}_P \,|\, e_M$ as the loss rate on the portfolio of accounts conditional on a realization of e_M,

$$\text{L}\widetilde{\text{R}}_P \,|\, e_M = \left(\frac{\sum_{i=1}^{N} \left(\text{L}\widetilde{\text{R}}_i \,|\, e_M \right)}{N} \right).$$

Because $(\widetilde{\mathrm{LR}}_i \,|\, e_M)$ is independent of $(\widetilde{\mathrm{LR}}_j \,|\, e_M)$ for all $i \neq j$ and these conditional losses are identically distributed, the Strong Law of Large Numbers requires, for all e_M,

$$\lim_{N\to\infty}\left(\widetilde{\mathrm{LR}}_P \,|\, e_M\right) = \lim_{N\to\infty}\left(\frac{\sum_{i=1}^{N}\left(\widetilde{\mathrm{LR}}_i \,|\, e_M\right)}{N}\right) \xrightarrow[a.s.]{} E\left(\widetilde{\mathrm{LR}}_i \,|\, e_M\right). \tag{19}$$

Independence of the conditional indicator functions for a single credit implies

$$E\left(\widetilde{I}_i \,|\, e_M \cdot \widetilde{H}_{ik} \,|\, e_M\right) = E\left(\widetilde{I}_i \,|\, e_M\right) \cdot E\left(\widetilde{H}_{ik} \,|\, e_M\right) \quad \forall\, k, i. \tag{20}$$

And so the asymptotic portfolio return distribution converges almost surely to

$$\lim_{N\to\infty}\left(\widetilde{\mathrm{LR}}_P \,|\, e_M\right) = \lim_{N\to\infty}\left(\frac{\sum_{i=1}^{N}\left(\widetilde{\mathrm{LR}}_i \,|\, e_M\right)}{N}\right) \xrightarrow[a.s.]{} E\left(\widetilde{I} \,|\, e_M\right) \cdot \left(\mathrm{LGD}_0 + \Delta\mathrm{LGD}\sum_{k=1}^{3} E\left(H_k \,|\, e_M\right)\right). \tag{21}$$

The i subscript has been dropped on the indicator functions in the final term of Eq. (21) as they are no longer necessary.

The number of steps that may be included in the approximations for the LGD unconditional density functions is not restricted. If the number of steps in the approximations is M, after substituting the binomial expressions for the conditional indicators' expected values, the conditional portfolio loss distribution converges almost surely to

$$\lim_{N\to\infty}\left(\widetilde{\mathrm{LR}}_P \,|\, e_M\right) \xrightarrow[a.s.]{} \Phi\left(\frac{D - \sqrt{\rho_d}\, e_M}{\sqrt{1-\rho_d}}\right) \cdot \left(\mathrm{LGD}_0 + \Delta\mathrm{LGD}\sum_{k=1}^{M} \Phi\left(\frac{B_k - \sqrt{\rho_Y}\, e_M}{\sqrt{1-\rho_Y}}\right)\right). \tag{22}$$

The inverse of the unconditional distribution function for the portfolio loss rate can be derived using Eq. (22) and the density function for $\widetilde{e}_M$. For a soundness standard (α), the critical value of $\widetilde{e}_M$ is $\Phi^{-1}(1-\alpha)$. Latent factor threshold values can be defined using the characteristics of the individual account's unconditional PDs and their unconditional LGD probability distribution. These threshold values are defined in Table 2.

TABLE 2 Latent Factor Model Parameters

Default process	LGD Process
$D = \Phi^{-1}(\text{PD})$	$B_1 = \Phi^{-1}(1 - \Omega(\text{LGD}_0))$
	$B_2 = \Phi^{-1}(1 - \Omega(\text{LGD}_0 + \Delta\text{LGD}))$
	$\vdots$
	$B_M = \Phi^{-1}(\text{LGD}_0 + (M-1)\Delta\text{LGD})$

Making use of the identity $\Phi^{-1}(1-\alpha) = -\Phi^{-1}(\alpha)$, the inverse of the unconditional cumulative distribution function for the asymptotic portfolio loss rate can be written

$$\text{LR}_p(\alpha) = \Phi\left(\frac{\Phi^{-1}(\text{PD}) + \sqrt{\rho_d}\,\Phi^{-1}(\alpha)}{\sqrt{1-\rho_d}}\right) \cdot (\text{LGD}_0 + \Delta\text{LGD}\; B(\alpha)), \quad \text{for } \alpha \in [0,1], \tag{23}$$

where

$$B(\alpha) = \sum_{j=1}^{M} \Phi\left(\frac{\Phi^{-1}(1 - \Omega(\text{LGD}_0 + (j-1)\Delta\text{LGD})) + \sqrt{\rho_Y}\,\Phi^{-1}(\alpha)}{\sqrt{1-\rho_Y}}\right). \tag{24}$$

The first term in Eq. (23) is the inverse of the cumulative distribution function of the Vasicek portfolio loss rate model, the standard Gaussian model in which LGD is an exogenous constant. The second term in the Equation adjusts the distribution to account for random LGD.

When $\rho_Y \to 0$, it is straightforward to show

$$(\text{LGD}_0 + \Delta\text{LGD}\; B(\alpha)) \to E(\widetilde{\text{LGD}}).$$

So when LGD is random but uncertainty is completely idiosyncratic, Eq. (23) becomes

$$\text{LR}_p(\alpha) = \Phi\left(\frac{\Phi^{-1}(\text{PD}) + \sqrt{\rho_d}\,\Phi^{-1}(\alpha)}{\sqrt{1-\rho_d}}\right) \cdot E(\widetilde{\text{LGD}}). \tag{25}$$

When $\rho_Y \neq 0$, the function $B(\alpha)$ can be interpreted as a function that shifts the probability distribution for $\widetilde{\text{LGD}}$. When $\rho_Y > 0$, the $B(\alpha)$ function shifts probability mass into the right tail of the unconditional LGD distribution and, in effect, forms a new "stress LGD" distribution.[12] A numerical example that follows will help to clarify the transformation.

As an example, we consider the capital calculation for a portfolio of credits that have unconditional LGD distributions consistent with the distribution in Table 3. In this distribution, one-third of all loss rates are 33.3 percent, one-third are 66.7 percent, and the

[12]Should $\rho_Y < 0$, $B(\alpha)$ would shift weight toward the left tail of the LGD distribution.

TABLE 3 Step Function Approximation for the Corporate LGD Distribution

LGD rate threshold	Cumulative probability of LGD level	Cumulative probability of LGD increment	Threshold for $\widetilde{Y}$
33%	33%	33.3%	0.432
67%	67%	33.3%	−0.432
100%	100%	33.3%	
Mean	66.70%		

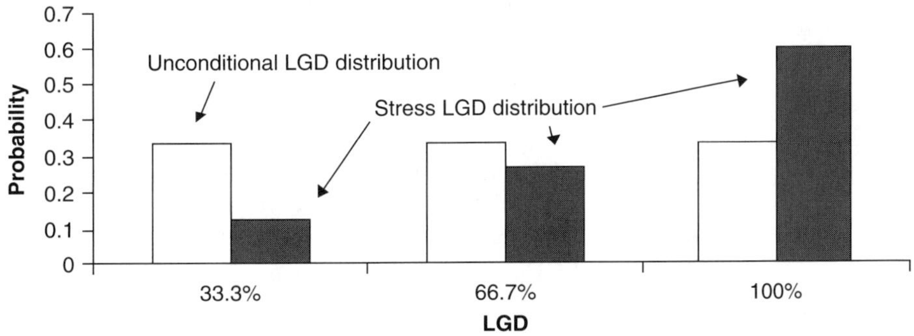

FIGURE 8 Unconditional and stress LGD distributions.
Source: Author's calculations.

final one-third are 100 percent. In step function form, the distribution can be parameterized with $\text{LGD}_0 = .333$ and $\Delta\,\text{LGD} = .333$. The cumulative probability associated with the first threshold value is .333; the second threshold has a cumulative probability of .667. The expected value of the unconditional LGD distribution is 66.70 percent.

In this example, we assume the correlation among LGDs is positive and take $\rho_Y = .05$. The threshold values for the latent variable $\widetilde{Y}_i$ are set as

$$B_1 = \Phi^{-1}(1 - \Omega(\text{LGD}_0)) = 0.431644 \quad \text{and}$$
$$B_2 = \Phi^{-1}(1 - \Omega(\text{LGD}_0 + \Delta\text{LGD})) = -0.431644.$$

Using these thresholds in the $B(\alpha)$ function, the loss-given-default term in Eq. (23) is

$$\text{LGD}_0 + \Delta\text{LGD}\, B(\alpha) = .333 + .333(.8753 + .6049) = 0.827.$$

The final value for the loss-given-default term, 0.827, is equivalent to the expected value of a new shifted LGD distribution, where probability mass in the unconditional LGD distribution has been shifted to higher LGD realizations. We call this new, modified LGD distribution the stress LGD distribution.

Figure 8 plots the unconditional and stress LGD distributions for $\alpha = 99.9$ percent and $\rho_Y = .05$. The amount of probability mass that is shifted under the stress measure

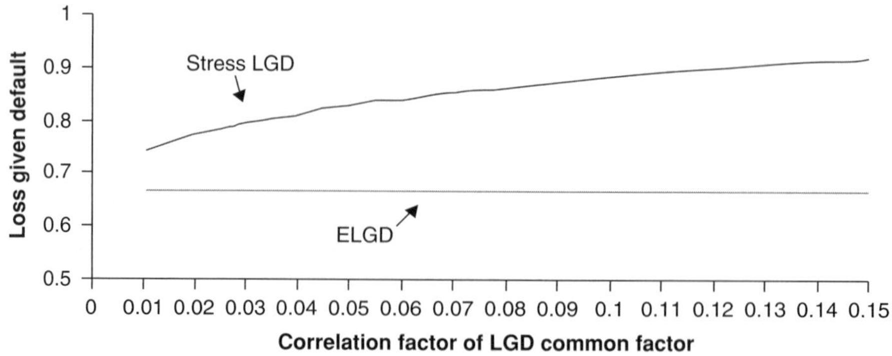

FIGURE 9 Correlation and stress LGD.
Source: Author's calculations.

depends on α, the cumulative probability at which the portfolio loss rate is being evaluated, and on the latent LGD factor correlation ρ_Y.

If stress LGD is defined to be the expected value of the stress LGD distribution, $E(\widetilde{\text{LGD}}^S) = (\text{LGD}_0 + \Delta\text{LGD}\, B(\alpha))$, upon substitution using the Equation for capital that recognizes interest payments and expense (Eq. (12)), the approximate minimum capital requirement necessary to ensure a soundness standard of 99.9 percent can be written as

$$K(\alpha) \approx \frac{\text{YTM} + E(\widetilde{\text{LGD}}^S)}{1+\text{YTM}} \Phi\left(\frac{\Phi^{-1}(\text{PD}) + \sqrt{\rho}\,\Phi^{-1}(.999)}{\sqrt{1-\rho}}\right). \tag{26}$$

To provide a sense of the potential importance of a positive correlation between PD and LGD, consider an example in which credits' unconditional LGD is consistent with the unconditional LGD distribution in Table 3. Figure 9 plots the expected value of the unconditional LGD distribution and the corresponding stressed LGD measure that is appropriate for use in setting capital for an asymptotic portfolio of credits. Small increases in the correlations between exposures' potential LGDs can lead to large changes in minimum capital requirements. For example, an increase in ρ_Y from 0 to 10 percent will increase required capital by 28.2 percent when capital is calculated using Eq. (26) using the unconditional LGD distribution in Table 3.[13]

4.7. Random Exposures at Default (EADs)

The AIRB framework treats EAD as an exogenous parameter. For revolving exposures, banks using the AIRB are required to estimate EAD, but Basel II rules give very little guidance as to how EAD should be estimated. For example, the guidance suggests that banks must have methods for estimating EAD, but the only quantitative standard

[13]If one uses the AIRB rule for setting capital [Eq. (5)], the increase in capital necessary to account for random LGD is nearly 33 percent.

imposed is that an EAD estimate must be at least as large as an obligor's current exposure. As discussed in Section 2, there is a growing body of evidence that suggests that credit facility draw rates are higher for low-quality credits and credits nearing default, implying a positive correlation between PD and EAD.

Similar to the case of random LGD, if the random exposure realizations of the credits in a portfolio are positively correlated, then the ability to reduce credit risk using portfolio diversification is limited. Kupiec (2008) includes a random EAD into the Vasicek framework and shows that, similar to the case of correlated LGDs, an expression for minimum capital can be defined in terms of "stressed EAD." Correlation among EADs will lead to the need for substantially higher minimum capital requirements.

The Basel II AIRB capital rule will underestimate capital needs for revolving credit portfolios unless banks somehow compensate and input EAD rates that are significantly elevated relative to their average facility EADs. The Basel AIRB standard is underdeveloped relative to the treatment of revolving credit exposures. Further model development and recalibration can deliver substantial improvements in accuracy even in the context of the simple single-factor Gaussian approximation for measuring portfolio credit risks.

5. CONCLUSION

Basel II objectives include the enhancement of financial stability and the promotion of sound risk measurement standards. Unless Basel II fortifies the minimum bank capital requirements for any given set of exposures, it is unclear how it will lead to enhanced stability in the banking sector. Quantitative impact studies (QISs) show that large internationally active banks will benefit from large capital reductions under Basel II, especially under the AIRB approach. Once banks are allowed to optimize under the AIRB approach, capital levels will be further eroded.

The results of the QIS studies call into question whether the Basel AIRB approach in its current form should even be considered a minimum regulatory capital standard. The idea of a standard implies that positions with identical risks are subject to identical minimum capital requirements. QIS studies show that AIRB estimates of minimum capital requirements for positions with similar risks vary by wide margins across banks. These results suggest that the AIRB rule and its associated guidance for implementation standards have been vaguely formulated and allow substantial capital differences or subjective interpretations. It is difficult to envision that supervisors around the globe will use pillar 2 powers and impose national implementation standards that ensure equal capital for equal risk. With wide latitude to interpret the input values for the AIRB capital rule, the AIRB approach cannot be viewed as a well-formulated standard.

Concerns about reductions in required capital under the AIRB approach are amplified when the economic foundations of the AIRB rule are examined. The current AIRB capital rule cannot accurately measure the credit risks taken in large, complex banking institutions. The AIRB framework does not formally model capital needs that arise because EAD and LGD are themselves random factors with systematic components. The stochastic properties of EAD and LGD create potentially large unexpected credit losses that are not modeled in the AIRB framework. The current framework, moreover, is without a sound economic foundation. It ignores the capital needed to satisfy bank interest expenses. This oversight leads to a large understatement in AIRB capital requirements. The AIRB also omits any measure of the capital benefits that are generated by bank interest earnings on its credit portfolio. The adequacy of banks' pricing of credit risk is a primary factor of importance in measuring portfolio credits risk and assigning minimum capital needs.

The analysis in this chapter suggests that it is improbable that the AIRB approach will either enhance financial stability or serve as a sound standard against which bank credit risk measurement processes are evaluated. Although the list of apparent weaknesses in the AIRB approach discussed here may seem long, there are still other serious shortcomings that have not been discussed. This chapter's analysis has not addressed issues attendant on the AIRB approach's not setting capital surcharges for credit risk concentrations, which undoubtedly are an important source of risk in many banking institutions. The analysis has also been silent on issues regarding the accuracy of an AIRB operational risk measurement standard. Analysis of these and other issues are left for future research.

References

Allen, Linda, Gayle DeLong, and Anthony Saunders. 2004. Issues in the Credit Risk Modeling of Retail Markets, *Journal of Banking and Finance* 28, 727–752.

Allen, Linda, and Anthony Saunders. 2003. A Survey of Cyclical Effects of Credit Risk Measurement Models. BIS working paper no. 126.

Altman, Edward, Brooks Brady, Andrea Resti, and Andrea Sironi. 2004. The Link Between Default and Recovery Rates: Theory Empirical Evidence and Implications, *Journal of Business* 78(6), 2203–2228.

Araten, Michel, Michael Jacobs Jr., and Peeyush Varshney. 2004. Measuring LGD on Commercial Loans: An 18-Year Internal Study, *Journal of Risk Management Association* (May), 28–35.

Asarnow, Elliot, and James Marker. 1995. Historical Performance of the U.S. Corporate Loan Market, *Commercial Lending Review* 10(2), 13–32.

Basel Committee on Banking Supervision. 1999. *Capital Requirements and Bank Behavior: The Impact of the Basel Accord*. BCBS working paper No. 1, Bank for International Settlements. Available at www.bis.org.

Basel Committee on Banking Supervision. 2001. *The Internal Ratings-Based Approach Consultative Document*. Bank for International Settlements, May. Available at www.bis.org.

Basel Committee on Banking Supervision. 2002. *Overview Paper for the Impact Study*. Bank for International Settlements, October. Available at www.bis.org.

Basel Committee on Banking Supervision. 2004. *Basel II: International Convergence of Capital Measurement and Capital Standards: A Revised Framework*. Bank for International Settlements, June. Available at www.bis.org.

Basel Committee on Banking Supervision. 2005. *An Explanatory Note on the Basel II IRB Risk Weight Functions*. Bank for International Settlements, July. Available at www.bis.org.

Basel Committee on Banking Supervision. 2006a. *Results of the Fifth Quantitative Impact Study (QIS 5)*. Bank for International Settlements, June 16. Available at www.bis.org.

Basel Committee on Banking Supervision. 2006b. *International Convergence of Capital Measurement and Capital Standards: A Revised Framework Comprehensive Version*. Bank for International Settlements, June 16. Available at www.bis.org.

Bies, Susan. 2005. Remarks by Governor Susan Bies at the Standard and Poor's North American Finanical Institutions Conference, www.federalreserve.gov.

Black, F., and J. C. Cox. 1976. Valuing Corporate Securities: Some Effects of Bond Indenture Provisions, *Journal of Finance* 31, 351–367.

Black, F., and M. Scholes. 1973. The Pricing of Options and Corporate Liabilities, *The Journal of Political Economy* 81, 637–654.

Carey, Mark, and Michael Gordy. 2004. Measuring Systematic Risk in Recoveries on Defaulted Debt I: Firm-Level Ultimate LGDs. Memo, available of the FDIC CFR Web site at www.fdic.gov/bank/analytical/cfr/2005/MCarey–MGordy.pdf.

Cowan, Adrian, and Charles Cowan. 2004. Default Correlation: An Empirical Investigation of a Subprime Lended, *Journal of Banking and Finance* 28, 753–771.

Cartarineu-Rabell, Eva, Patricia Jackson, and Dimitrios Tsomocos. 2003. Procyclicality and the New Basel Accord Banks' Choice of a Loan Rating System. Working paper no. 181, Bank of England.

Das, Sanjiv. 2006. Basel II Technical Issues: A Comment. Memo, Santa Clara University.

Das, Sanjiv, Darrell Duffie, Nikunj Kapadia and Leandro Saita. 2004. Common Failings: How Corporate Defaults are Correlated. *Journal of Finance*, Vol. 62, No. 1, pp. 93–117.

Dietsch, Michel, and Jöel Petey. 2004. Should SME Exposures Be Treated as Retail or Corporate Exposures? A Comparative Analysis of Default Probabilities and Asset Correlations in French and German SMEs, *Journal of Banking and Finance* 28, 773–788.

Emery, Kenneth, Richard Cantor, and Robert Avner. 2004. Recovery Rates on North American Syndicated Bank Loans, 1989–2003, Moody's Investor Service, March.

Eom, Young, Jean Helwege, and Jing-zhi Huang. 2004. Structural Models of Corporate Bond Pricing: An Empirical Analysis, *Review of Financial Studies* 17, 499–544.

Finger, Chris. 1999. Conditional Approaches for CreditMetrics Portfolio Distributions, *CreditMetrics Monitor*, 14–33.

Frye, Jon. 2000. Depressing Recoveries, *Risk* 11, 108–111.

Gordy, Michael. 2003. A Risk-Factor Model Foundation for Ratings-Based Bank Capital Rules, *Journal of Financial Intermediation* 12, 199–232.

Gordy, Michael, and Bradley Howells. 2004. Procyclicality in Basel II: Can We Treat the Disease without Killing the Patient? Memo, Federal Reserve Board.

Greenspan, Alan. 1998. Remarks by Chairman Greenspan Before the Conference on Capital Regulation in the 21st Century, Federal Reserve Bank of New York, February 26, 1998.

Hamilton, David, Praveen Varma, Sharon Ou, and Richard Cantor. 2004. Default and Recovery Rates of Corporate Bond Issuers: A Statistical Review of Moody's Ratings Performance, 1920–2003. Special Comment, Moody's Investor Service, January.

History of the Eighties—Lessons for the Future. Volume I: An Examination of the Banking Crisis of the 1980s and Early 1990s. Washington, DC: Federal Deposit Insurance Corporation, 1997.

Jackson P., W. Perraudin, and V. Saporta. 2002. Regulatory and "Economic" Solvency Standards for International Active Banks, *Journal of Banking and Finance* 26, 953–973.

Jiménez, Gabreil, Jose Lopez, and Jesús Saurina. 2006. What Do One Million Credit Line Observations Tell Us About Exposure at Default? A Study of Credit Line Usage by Spanish Firms. Draft working paper, Banco de España.

Jones, David. 2000. Emerging Problems with the Basel Capital Accord: Regulatory Capital Arbitrage and Related Issues, *Journal of Banking and Finance* 24(1–2), 35–58.

Jones, E. P., S. Mason, and E. Rosenfeld. 1984. Contingent Claims Analysis of Corporate Capital Structures: An Empirical Investigation, *Journal of Finance* 39, 611–625.

Kashyap, Anil, and Jeremy Stein. 2004. Cyclical Implications of the Basel II Capital Standards, *Economic Perspectives* 28, 18–31.

Kupiec, Paul. 2004a. Estimating Economic Capital Allocations for Market and Credit Risks, *Journal of Risk* 6(4), 11–29.

Kupiec, Paul. 2004b. Capital Adequacy and Basel II. Working paper No. 2004-02, FDIC CFR, www.fdic.gov.

Kupiec, Paul. 2007a. Capital Allocations for Portfolio Credit Risk. *Journal of Financial Services Research* 32(1–2), 103–122.

Kupiec, Paul. 2007b. Financial Stability and Basel II, *Annals of Finance* 3, 107–130.

Kupiec, Paul. 2008. A Generalized Single-Factor Model of Portfolio Credit Risk. *Journal of Derivates*, forthcoming.

Lowe, Philip. 2002. Credit Risk Measurement and Procyclicality. Working paper No. 116, BIS.

Merton, Robert. 1974. On the Pricing of Corporate Debt: The Risk Structure of Interest Rates, *Journal of Finance* 29, 449–470.

Meyer, Laurence. 2001. Remarks by Governor Laurence H. Myer at the Risk Management Association's Conference on Capital Management, Washington, DC, May 17.

Mingo, John J. 2000. Policy Implications of the Federal Reserve Study of Credit Risk Models at Major U.S. Banking Institutions, *Journal of Banking and Finance* 24, 15–33.

Ogden, J. 1987. Determinants of the Ratings and Yields on Corporate Bonds: Tests of the Contingent Claims Model, *Journal of Financial Research* 10, 329–339.

Schönbucher, P. 2000. Factor Models for Portfolio Credit Risk. Memo, Department of Statistics, Bonn University.

Schuermann, Til. 2004. What Do We Know About Loss-Given-Default? in D. Shimko (ed.), *Credit Risk Models and Management*, 2nd ed. Risk Books, London.

Turner, Philip. 2000. Procyclicality of Regulatory Ratios? Working paper No. 13, CEPA Working Paper Series III.

U.S Basel II NPR. 2006. Risk-Based Capital Standards: Advanced Capital Adequacy Framework and Market Risk; Proposed Rules and Notices, *Federal Register* 71(185), 55830–55958, September 26.

Vasicek, O. A. 1991. Limiting Loan Loss Probability Distribution. Working paper, KMV Corporation.

SECTION 6

Competition and Regulation in Banking

Overview by Xavier Vives
IESE Business School

1. INTRODUCTION

Banking has evolved from a tightly regulated to a mostly liberalized industry subject to competition. The move has been contentious, since it has been claimed that stability has suffered. This section takes stock of what we know about the relationship of competition, regulation, and stability in banking from the perspective of theory, in Chapter 14, by Elena Carletti, and empirics, in Chapter 15, by Hans Degryse and Steven Ongena. The picture that arises is somewhat complex but illuminating.

The relations between competition, regulation, and stability in banking have been subject to intense debate. A somewhat simplistic idea has been that banking is fragile, competition exacerbates this fragility, and regulation has to come to the rescue. In fact, the banking sector was tightly regulated until the liberalization process started in the 1970s. The general benefits of competition impinged on the liberalization of the industry, and a question now is whether the pendulum has not swung too far with too much competitive intensity. In order to whet the appetite for the chapters in this section, let us provide some introductory insights on why banking is fragile, the relation between competition and stability, and the role and the optimal design of regulation.

This overview draws from my joint work with Douglas Gale, Carmen Matutes, and Jean-Charles Rochet and from the overviews in Vives (2001, 2006). Financial support from the Spanish Ministry of Education and Science (project SEJ2005-08263) and from the Abertis Chair on Regulation, Competition, and Public Policy is gratefully acknowledged.

2. FRAGILITY IN BANKING

Banks provide transaction services and risk sharing. They also finance and monitor entrepreneurial projects, which are illiquid and opaque because of asymmetric-information problems, such as adverse selection and moral hazard. Altogether banks perform a central function in overcoming asymmetric-information problems in an economy. We could say that banks protect entrepreneurs that need finance from the liquidity needs of investors. The standard deposit contract, redeemable at par, and loan provision to opaque entrepreneurial projects are complementary to the function of a bank.[1] However, their liquidity creation role leaves banks vulnerable to runs. A deposit redeemable at par leaves banks exposed to failure when returns are low. This possibility has desirable incentive properties[2] but may lead to failures, panic, and systemic crises, with potentially a major impact on the economy given the central role played by financial intermediation.

The coordination problem of depositors, who may decide to call back their short-term deposits, can make a sound bank fail. Two views of crises have been advanced: the multiple equilibrium panic view[3] and the information-based view.[4] According to the former, runs are triggered by events unrelated to the fundamentals ("sunspots"), while according to the latter runs are triggered by bad news on the assets of the bank. Those views have been reconciled by introducing asymmetric information and linking the probability of a run to the strength of fundamentals.[5] To this should be added the danger of systemic risk owing to contagion from the failure of an entity.[6]

In summary, banking is fragile and institutions face an important probability of failure and a potentially severe moral-hazard problem, and failure has associated with it a large social cost, which may be of a systemic nature.

3. THE NATURE OF COMPETITION IN BANKING AND STABILITY

The standard model of perfect competition is not appropriate for the banking sector. Financial intermediation arises in fact in response to the incompleteness of markets. The main sources of frictions in banking that lead to imperfect competition are switching costs and networks, particularly in retail banking, and asymmetric information,

[1]For different versions of the story, see Diamond and Dybvig (1983) and Holmström and Tirole (1997, 1998).

[2]In Diamond and Rajan (2001) the demand deposit contract creates a coordination problem for investors that prevents the banker from extorting rents on his abilities to collect illiquid loans. In Calomiris and Kahn (1991) or Gale and Vives (2002) it disciplines bank managers subject to a moral hazard problem.

[3]Diamond and Dybvig (1983).

[4]Gorton (1985, 1988), Jacklin and Battacharya (1988).

[5]See Rochet and Vives (2004) and Goldstein and Pauzner (2005). Postlewaite and Vives (1987) provided an early model with a unique equilibrium where the probability of a crisis is determined by the realization of the liquidity needs of depositors, which is private information.

[6]See, e.g., Allen and Gale (2001).

particularly in corporate banking. These frictions raise entry barriers and explain the importance of reputation in the sector. The exercise of market power is therefore a natural phenomenon in banking.[7]

The specificities of the banking industry do affect the desirability of competition in the sector. Competition is not the culprit for the fragile character of banking. A monopoly bank can be subject to a run. Fragility comes from the coordination problem faced by investors that generates multiple equilibria, some of which may imply the collapse of institutions or the whole system.[8] However, more competition, by raising deposit rates, may exacerbate the coordination problem of depositors.[9] Another matter is that the intensity of competition can be excessive in banking. On the one hand, competition erodes rents that provide banks with a charter value and incentives to monitor projects.[10] Furthermore, an increase in the number of banks that face an adverse-selection problem in the loan market lowers the average creditworthiness of successful loan applicants (who pass a screening test).[11] On the other hand, competition tends to lower the rates that firms have to pay for loans and therefore may improve the average quality of loan applicants and/or lower the need to ration credit. For example, better terms for entrepreneurs means that they make more profits and become more cautious, affecting in turn the probability of failure of the bank. When both banks and firms have to monitor their investments there is a potential ambiguous relationship between market structure and risk taking.[12]

Indeed, a bank faces both adverse-selection and moral-hazard problems when lending to firms. A higher rate set by the bank will tend to draw riskier applicants—adverse selection—and/or induce the borrower firms, which have also limited liability, to choose riskier projects—moral hazard. Banks may find it optimal, then, to ration credit instead of raising the interest rate. A bank with market power has more incentive to alleviate this asymmetric-information problem by investing in monitoring the projects of firms and establishing long-term relationships with customers.[13] This effect tends to increase the availability of credit to firms. Market power also has the usual effect of increasing the lending rate and therefore increasing the tendency toward credit rationing to avoid the increase of the average riskiness of the pool of applicants. Even abstracting from the possibility of banking failure, market power presents a welfare tradeoff, since more bank market clout diminishes the moral-hazard problem faced by the bank but aggravates the problem for the entrepreneur. The result is that some market power tends to be good, unless monitoring is very costly.[14] If to this we add the possibility of banking failure, the analysis becomes more complex. In principle, a first effect of higher lending rates due to market power is to depress investment and, under plausible assumptions,

[7] Vives (1991).
[8] Matutes and Vives (1996).
[9] Rochet and Vives (2004) and Goldstein and Pauzner (2005).
[10] Keeley (1990).
[11] See Broecker (1990), Riordan (1993), and Marquez (2002) for theories of excessive competition in the credit market due to a winner's-curse problem.
[12] Caminal and Matutes (2002), Boyd and de Nicolo (2005).
[13] Besanko and Thakor (1993), Petersen and Rajan (1994, 1995).
[14] Caminal and Matutes (1997).

to decrease the overall portfolio risk of the bank. More rivalry, then, should increase the probability of failure of the bank and have adverse welfare consequences. However, more competition may also destroy incentives to monitor and therefore reduce lending. If the latter effect is strong enough, a monopolistic bank may be more exposed to aggregate uncertainty (because it tends to ration credit less) and be more likely to fail.[15]

All in all it seems plausible to expect that, once a certain threshold is reached, an increase in the level of competition will tend to increase risk-taking incentives and the probability of failure of banks. This tendency may be checked by reputational concerns,[16] by the presence of private costs of failure of managers, or by regulation.

4. THE ROLE OF REGULATION

Fragility and potential excessive risk taking in banking have led to the establishment of facilities to stabilize the system and prudential measures to check risk taking. The lender of last resort (LOLR) facility, typically at the central bank, and deposit insurance are two of the basic policy instruments to stabilize the system.

A potential problem is that the policy of a well-intentioned LOLR may be time inconsistent. Ex post, once an institution is in trouble, it is typically optimal to help whenever this salvages the value of projects monitored by a bank. However, if bankers anticipate the help, they will tend to exert a suboptimal level of (unobservable) effort. For example, ex ante the central bank may want to commit to closing the bank if the returns are low enough (pointing to a solvency problem), while helping the bank if the returns are only moderately low (pointing to a liquidity problem). Such a commitment provides incentives for bank managers to monitor the projects they finance. In this way the central bank may implement the second-best solution in a competitive banking system. Building a central bank with a "tough" reputation can alleviate the time-inconsistency problem.[17]

The LOLR facility and the deposit insurance system may introduce distortions into the decisions of financial entities. Indeed, they reduce the incentive of depositors to monitor the bank, and, coupled with the bank's limited liability, they may give rise to excessive risk taking. Competition for deposits may be excessive, and the situation may be made worse with flat premium deposit insurance, since the latter increases the elasticity of the residual supply of deposits faced by a bank.[18] Risk-based deposit insurance moderates risk-taking incentives, but banks still may take too much risk in the presence of a social cost of failure. On the asset side, limited liability will induce banks to take excessive risk, except if the risk position of the bank can be assessed by investors (e.g., with enough disclosure) and investors are not protected.

[15] Caminal and Matutes (2002).

[16] Because a better reputation lowers the cost of outside finance to the bank (see Boot and Greenbaum 1993).

[17] See Gale and Vives (2002).

[18] Matutes and Vives (1996, 2000).

TABLE 1 Banking Regimes, the Incentives to Take Risk on the Liability and Asset Sides, and Regulatory Instruments When Charter Values Are Low and the Social Cost of Failure Is High

	Risk-taking incentives		
Banking regimes	Liability (rates)	Asset (investment)	Regulation
Free banking (observable risk/high disclosure)	Medium-low	Absent	Capital requirements
Free banking (unobservable risk/low disclosure)	Medium-high	Maximal	Capital requirements and asset restrictions
Risk-insensitive insurance	High	Maximal	Capital requirements and asset restrictions
Risk-based insurance	Low	Absent	Capital requirements

Source: Taken from Vives (2006) and based on Matutes and Vives (2000) as well as Cordella and Yeyati (2002) and Hellmann, Murdock, and Stiglitz (2000).

The need for regulation is particularly acute when charter values are low, such that incentives to take risks are high, and the social cost of failure is high—making it so that banking failure has a large impact. With either very high disclosure requirements or risk-based insurance, banks pay if they take more risk, and capital requirements may be a sufficient instrument to control risk taking. Otherwise, capital requirements may need to be complemented with restrictions on the bank portfolio. Both risk-based (deposit) insurance and disclosure requirements have been proposed to limit risk-taking behavior in a move toward the top and the bottom rows of Table 1. This movement has been accompanied by a reform of the 1988 Basel Accord on capital requirements to adjust them better for risk (so-called Basel II). The three pillars on which modern regulatory reform is based are capital requirements, supervision, and market discipline.

5. WHAT NEXT?

The issues discussed in this overview are dealt with at length in the survey of the theoretical literature in Chapter 14, by Elena Carletti. Chapter 15, by Hans Degryse and Steven Ongena, reviews the empirical evidence on the source of bank rents. Those authors analyze the implications of market structure and frictions on banking performance. It is found that average market concentration results in significant spreads in both deposit and loan markets. Increases in competition are met by institutions trying to obtain fee income from stable relationships with customers. Switching costs are found to be an important source of rents. However, the evidence so far on the link between the duration of relationships and spreads is ambiguous. There are also some intriguing differences between banks in the United States and those in Europe. Indeed, only banks in Europe seem to extract rents with higher loan rates from their relationship borrowers. As far as location goes, it is found that close borrowers tend to pay a higher loan rate but that distance has a small effect on credit availability. Finally, regulation continues to be a very relevant source of bank rents. In Europe, competition policy authorities have an important role to play to ensure that cross-border mergers are not unduly prevented.

The picture that follows from the two chapters is complex, and a host of issues is left open and in need of further research. The very model of banking competition would gain with a better integration of competition on both sides of the balance sheet of the bank as well as a careful consideration of both depositors and borrowers. We also need to understand better the relationship between competition and fragility. A better understanding of the relationship would yield insights on how to design more effective regulation. For example, our knowledge of the impact of capital requirements is still somewhat fragmentary. An improved theory of bank capital would help here. On the empirical side, we need more work targeted at checking the impact of electronic banking and the interplay with traditional banking, to ascertain the impact of competition on risk-taking incentives and failure probabilities, and to analyze the incentives and consequences of mergers. New knowledge would also be welcome to design an appropriate competition policy for banking that is consistent with the regulatory frame.[19] Finally, it is necessary to study more deeply the role of banks, competition, and the appropriate regulation for emerging economies.

References

Allen, F., and D. Gale. 2001. Financial Contagion, in *Journal of Political Economy* 108(1), 1–33.

Besanko, D., and A. Thakor. 1993. Relationship Banking, Deposit Insurance and Bank Porfolio, in C. Mayer and X. Vives (eds.), *Capital Markets and Financial Intermediation.* Cambridge University Press, Cambridge.

Boot, A., and S. Greenbaum. 1993. Bank Regulation, Reputation and Rents: Theory and Policy Implications, in C. Mayer and X. Vives (eds.), *Capital Markets and Financial Intermediation.* Cambridge University Press, Cambridge.

Boyd, J., and G. De Nicolò. 2005. The Theory of Bank Risk Taking and Competition Revisited, *Journal of Finance* 60(3), 1329–1343.

Broecker, T. 1990. Credit-Worthiness Tests and Interbank Competition, *Econometrica* 58(2), 429.

Calomiris, Ch., and C. Khan. 1991. The Role of Demandable Debt in Structuring Optimal Banking Arrangements, *American Economic Review* 81(3), 497–513.

Caminal, R., and C. Matutes. 1997. Can Competition in the Credit Market Be Excessive? London, CEPR discussion paper No. 1665.

Caminal, R., and C. Matutes. 2002. Market Power and Banking Failures, *International Journal of Industrial Organization* 20(9), 1341–1361.

Cordella, T., and E. L. Yeyati. 2002. Financial Opening; Deposit Insurance, and Risk in a Model of Banking Competition, *European Economic Review* 46(3), 471–485.

Diamond, D., and P. Dybvig. 1983. Bank Runs, Deposit Insurance and Liquidity, *Journal of Political Economy* 91, 401–419.

Diamond, D., and R. Rajan. 2001. Liquidity Risk, Liquidity Creation and Financial Fragility: A Theory of Banking, *Journal of Political Economy* 109(2), 287–327.

Gale, D., and X. Vives. 2002. Dollarization, Bailouts, and the Stability of the Banking System, *Quarterly Journal of Economics* 117(2), 467–502.

[19]Some headway is made by Perotti and Suárez (2002).

Goldstein, I., and A. Pauzner. 2005. Demand Deposit Contracts and the Probability of Bank Runs, *Journal of Finance* 60(3), 1293–1327.

Gorton, G. 1985. Bank Suspension of Convertibility, *Journal of Monetary Economics* 15(2), 177–193.

Gorton, G. 1988. Banking Panics and Busines Cycles, *Oxford Economic Papers* 40(4), 751–781.

Hellmann, T. F., Murdock, K., and J. E. Stiglitz. 2000. Liberalization, Moral Hazard in Banking, and Prudential Regulation: Are Capital Requirements Enough? *American Economic Review* 90(1), 147–165.

Holmström, B., and J. Tirole. 1997. Financial Intermediation, Loanable Funds and the Real Sector, *Quarterly Journal of Economics* 112(3), 663–691.

Holmström, B., and J. Tirole. 1998. Private and Public Supply of Liquidity, *Journal of Political Economy* 106(1), 1–40.

Jacklin, C., and S. Battacharya. 1988. Distinguishing Panics and Information-Based Bank Runs: Welfare and Policy Implications, *Journal of Political Economy* 96(3), 568–592.

Keeley, M. 1990. Deposit Insurance, Risk, and Market Power in Banking, *American Economic Review* 80(5), 1183–1200.

Marquez, R. 2002. Competition, Adverse Selection, and Information Dispersion in the Banking Industry, *Review of Financial Studies* 15(3), 901–926.

Matutes, C., and X. Vives. 1996. Competition for Deposits, Fragility, and Insurance, *Journal of Financial Intermediation* 5(2), 184–216.

Matutes, C., and X. Vives. 2000. Imperfect Competition, Risk Taking and Regulation in Banking, *European Economic Review* 44(1), 1–34.

Perotti, E., and J. Suarez. 2002. Last Bank Standing: What Do I Gain If You Fail? *European Economic Review* 46(9), 1599–1622.

Petersen, M., and R. Rajan. 1994. The Benefits of Lending Relationships: Evidence from Small Business Data, *Journal of Finance* 49(1), 3–37.

Petersen, M., and R. Rajan. 1995. The Effect of Credit Market Competition on Lending Relationships, *Quarterly Journal of Economics* 110(2), 407–443.

Postlewaite, A., and X. Vives. 1987. Bank Runs as an Equilibrium Phenomenon, *Journal of Political Economy* 95(3), 485–491.

Riordan, M. 1993. Competition and Bank Performance: A Theoretical Perspective, in C. Mayer and X. Vives (eds.), *Capital Markets and Financial Intermediation*. Cambridge University Press, Cambridge.

Rochet, J.-C., and X. Vives. 2004. Coordination Failures and the Lender of Last Resort: Was Bagehot Right After All? *Journal of the European Economic Association* 2(6), 1116–1147.

Vives, X. 1991. Banking Competition and European Integration, in A. Giovanni and C. Mayer (eds.), *European Financial Integration*. Cambridge University Press, Cambridge.

Vives, X. 2001. Restructuring Financial Regulation in the European Monetary Union, *Journal of Financial Services Research* 19(1), 57–82.

Vives, X. 2006. Banking and Regulation in Emerging Markets, *World Bank Research Observer* 21(2), 179–206.

CHAPTER 14

Competition and Regulation in Banking

Elena Carletti
University of Frankfurt

I would like to thank Franklin Allen, Hans Degryse, Martin Hellwig, Steven Ongena, and Xavier Vives for valuable comments and discussions.

1. INTRODUCTION

It is well known that banks are special in that they are vulnerable to instability. As the numerous episodes of crises show, banks are fragile and are prone to take excessive risks. Their function as intermediaries between firms and borrowers and the maturity transformation they operate in their asset-liability management make banks play an important role as providers of liquidity to depositors but also exposes them to runs and systemic crises. The great reliance on deposits as source of funds creates a severe agency problem between banks and depositors, in that, being subject to limited liability, banks do not bear the downside risk and have strong incentives to choose risks that are excessive from the viewpoint of depositors. The need of a stable banking sector, together with that of protecting consumers, provides the motivation for the introduction of deposit insurance schemes and lender-of-last-resort facilities. These safety arrangements are effective in pursuing a stable system, but they introduce several distortions and call for further regulatory measures, such as capital requirements.

Whereas the speciality of the banking system and the need of regulation have attracted much attention in both academic and policy debates, the issue of how competition affects the stability of the system and the effectiveness of regulation is not well understood yet. The desirability of competition in the banking sector has been questioned for a long time. Following the crises of the 1930s, competition was kept limited in an attempt to preserve stability. The process of deregulation in recent decades lifted many of the restrictions on competition and opened up the possibility for banks to expand their investments in riskier activities and new locations. A new wave of failures followed in the 1980s and 1990s. The increase in competition following the deregulation wave was regarded as the main reason behind this new instability. As found by Keeley (1990), the decline of banks' margins and charter values magnified the agency problem between banks and depositors (or deposit insurance funds), thus inducing banks to take excessive risks and increasing dramatically their failure probabilities.

The idea of a negative relationship between competition and stability has been pervasive in the literature since the 1990s, but more recent contributions indicate that the relationship is much more complex. What are the tradeoffs between competition and stability? How does competition affect the vulnerability of banks to runs and systemic crises and their incentives to take risk? How does competition influence the effectiveness of the regulatory tools aiming at preserving stability? Can regulation "correct" the potential negative effects of competition on stability? This chapter aims at providing insights to these questions by reviewing the literature on competition, stability, and regulation in banking.

We start by looking at these issues separately. First, we briefly describe the reasons behind the risk of instability in the banking sector and the need of regulation. Following what was already mentioned, we distinguish between sources of instability on the liability side (runs and systemic crises) and on the asset side (excessive risk taking) and discuss how regulation can help achieve a stable system. Then we analyze how competition operates in this sector. The main conclusion is that, as often argued, the standard competitive paradigm is not appropriate for the banking industry. The presence of important market failures changes dramatically the nature of competition and its outcome. Asymmetric information, switching costs, and network externalities create entry barriers and allow banks to retain some market power in the form of informational rents or enhanced differentiation. Interestingly, this literature proceeds by taking the behavior of agents as exogenous. There is no concern for banks' incentives to take risk or depositors' desire to run prematurely. The only focus is on how the competitive mechanism operates in the presence of market failures. This is a very different approach from the stability literature, which instead focuses exclusively on the behavior of agents within the context of agency theory.

To understand better the link between competition and stability, we then review the literature addressing how competition affects the fragility and the risk-taking problem as well as the need of regulating the sector. Surprisingly, the issues have not been studied as extensively as one might expect. Despite a growing interest, the literature is still rather limited and inconclusive on many aspects of the tradeoff between competition and stability. What emerges is that, whereas the literature on stability is centered on banks' vulnerability to bank runs and systemic crises, most of the contributions analyzing the impact of competition on stability have instead addressed the impact of competition on banks' incentives to take risks and the possibility of correcting its perverse impact through appropriate regulatory measures. In addition to the limited focus, the literature is still inconclusive. Whereas the prevailing view is that competition worsens the risk-taking problem because lower margins and charter values increase the attractiveness of risky investments, some recent contributions have shown that competition may actually lead to the opposite result—improving the risk of banks' portfolios once specific features of the banking system, such as the relationship with borrowers or banks' monitoring function, are explicitly taken into account.

Regulation may help mitigate the tradeoff between competition and stability, as long as such tradeoff exists. But how to design regulation appropriately? Again, the literature is inconclusive. Although there seems to be consensus on the negative effect of flat deposit insurance premia, the results are split on the effectiveness of capital regulation. While this seems effective in some contexts, it needs to be complemented by direct restrictions on competition, such as interest rate ceilings, among others. Overall, what emerges is again the need of further attention and research on the impact of competition on stability as well as on the appropriate design of regulation.

The rest of the chapter proceeds as follows. Section 2 introduces the issue of bank stability, distinguishing between vulnerability to runs and systemic crises and excessive risk taking. Section 3 reviews the contributions on the functioning of competition in the presence of asymmetric information, switching costs, and network externalities. Section 4 analyzes more deeply the link between competition and stability, in particular the link between market structure and financial fragility and between market structure and excessive risk taking. Section 5 looks at the impact of regulatory tools on the tradeoff between competition and stability. Section 6 concludes the chapter.

2. BANK INSTABILITY AND THE NEED OF REGULATION

It is well known that banks are special because they are more vulnerable to instability than firms in other sectors and also because less wealthy people may hold some nonnegligible share of their wealth in various forms of bank deposits. The potential instability of the banking system and the need of consumer protection are the fundamental rationales behind the introduction and development of regulation.

The course of events, and in particular the U.S. experience, suggest two possible connotations of the term *instability*: The crises that occurred in the 1930s show that the banking system is fragile, since it is vulnerable to runs and panics; the massive distress which came to light in the 1980s and 1990s demonstrates that intermediaries may have strong incentives to assume excessive risk and that, as a result, the system has a high probability of failure.

2.1. Bank Fragility: Individual Runs and Systemic Crises[1]

Intermediaries emerge as a response to the imperfection and incompleteness of financial markets. In an economy characterized by asymmetric information and uncertainty, intermediaries are valuable because they have economies of scale in producing information and provide insurance to depositors who are uncertain in their timing of consumption. Information production and insurance provision are the two main characteristics of bank specificity, but they are also the sources of their fragility. The informational asymmetries existing between banks, borrowers, and depositors and the maturity transformation that banks operate by investing short-term deposits in long-term assets expose banks to the possibility of runs. Banks offer depositors demandable contracts that allow depositors to withdraw a fixed amount on demand. If the total value of the early withdrawals exceeds the amount available from short-term investments, a run originates and the bank has to sell its illiquid assets. This illiquidity problem may turn into insolvency and force the premature liquidation of the bank if no assets are left after satisfying the early withdrawals.

To illustrate the basic mechanism triggering a run, consider a three-date economy, with one bank operating under perfect competition and raising funds from a continuum of depositors of measure one. The bank invests a fraction M in a short-term asset and a fraction $1 - M$ in a long-term asset. The former simply transfers the unit invested from date 0 to date 1, while the latter yields $R > 1$ at date 2 and $\ell < R$ if interrupted prematurely at date 1. Depositors are all ex ante identical, but they face a preference shock at date 1. A fraction t of them becomes of type 1 (early type) and wishes to consume at date 1, while the remaining fraction, $1 - t$, turns to be of type 2 (late type) and prefers consuming at date 2. Depending on the specific assumptions on the return of the long-term investment and on the structure of the preference shocks, the rationale behind depositors' withdrawal differs, and runs can be either irrational or information-induced events.

[1]The literature on invidual runs and systemic crises is vast. We describe here only a few contributions. Excellent broader reviews are contained in Gorton and Winton (2003) and De Bandt and Hartmann (2002).

Following D. Diamond and Dybvig (1983), suppose initially that the return R and the fraction t of early depositors are deterministic and that the liquidation value of the long-term investment is $\ell = 1$. Then, the bank offers a deposit contract to depositors so as to maximize

$$U^* = \max_{\{c_{ij}\}} tU^1(c_{11}) + (1-t)U^2(c_{22}), \tag{1}$$

subject to:

$$tc_{11} \leq M \tag{2}$$

$$(1-t)c_{22} \leq R(1-M) \tag{3}$$

$$U^1(c_{11}) \geq U^1(c_{22}) \tag{4}$$

$$U^2(c_{22}) \geq U^2(c_{11}), \tag{5}$$

where expression (1) is depositors' expected utility, with c_{ij} being the consumption of type j at date i; constraints (2) and (3) represent the resource balance constraints at dates 1 and 2, respectively; and conditions (4) and (5) are the incentive compatibility constraints stating that the deposit contract should be designed so that each type of depositors prefers its own withdrawal profile. If depositors are risk averse, with RRA > 1, that is, $-u''(c)/u'(c) > 1$, then the optimal deposit contract satisfies

$$1 < c_{11}^* < c_{22}^* < R.$$

This result shows that the deposit contract offers insurance to depositors and is Pareto improving relative to the autarkic situation, where individuals invest directly. The insurance provision, however, makes the bank vulnerable to runs. There is a good equilibrium that realizes optimal risk sharing when depositors choose the withdrawal decisions embedded in the deposit contract; but there is also a bad equilibrium in which all depositors withdraw their funds prematurely and the bank collapses. The condition $c_{11}^* > 1$ implies that depositors find it optimal to withdraw if they simply fear that others will withdraw first. There is no rational motivation behind such a panic run other than a coordination failure due to sunspots. The possibility of a run is intrinsic in the provision of insurance. If $c_{11}^* \leq 1$, no run would occur.

An alternative explanation for the occurrence of bank runs is that they are linked to changes in fundamental variables and are therefore information based (or fundamental based). If the return on the long-term investment is stochastic, the perspective of a negative shock increases the probability that the bank is unable to meet its future commitments. If depositors anticipate this, they withdraw their funds and force the premature closure of the bank. Jacklin and Bhattacharya (1988) formalize this mechanism in a context where the assumptions of an illiquid and risky long-term asset and depositors with RRA < 1 lead to an optimal contract satisfying

$$c_{11}^* < 1 < c_{22}^*.$$

Whereas this solution excludes the possibility of irrational runs, it still leaves room for information-based runs. After the contract is signed, some type 2 depositors receive a partial signal s describing the posterior distribution of the success probability of the long-term asset. Thus, they update their priors p and choose to withdraw prematurely whenever

$$\widehat{E}\left[U^2(c_{11})\right] > \widehat{E}\left[U^2(c_{22})\right],$$

that is, whenever the expected utility from withdrawing prematurely calculated using the posterior beliefs on the success probability p, $\widehat{E}\left[U^2(c_{11})\right]$, exceeds the expected utility from waiting and receiving the consumption profile initially designed for them, $\widehat{E}\left[U^2(c_{22})\right]$. This triggers a run. Given the total illiquidity of the long-term asset, the bank does not have enough funds to satisfy the withdrawal demands at date 1 and has to close down. The origin of the run is now the rational response of depositors to the arrival of sufficiently negative information on the future solvency of the bank. Therefore, the run is information based and is efficient, as long as it leads to the liquidation of an impending insolvent bank.

Panic and information-based runs can also be related, as shown by Chari and Jagannathan (1988). The analysis focuses on the signal-extraction problem faced by uninformed depositors in their withdrawal decisions in a framework characterized by shocks to asset returns and to the proportions of early depositors and informed depositors. Late-type depositors who remain uninformed know that other depositors may be informed on the future return of bank assets and try to infer such information from the size of the withdrawal queue at date 1. However, since the proportion of early depositors is stochastic and unobservable, uninformed depositors may not be able to infer the bank's future performance correctly. In particular, they may not be able to distinguish whether a long queue is formed by the informed depositors receiving a negative signal or simply by a large proportion of early depositors wishing to consume early. A pure panic run generates from uninformed depositors' confusion between insolvency and high liquidity shocks. It occurs when uninformed depositors withdraw prematurely for *fear* that some depositors have received a bad signal on the bank's future performance in cases where no one is informed about it.

A common feature in this strand of literature is the presence of multiple equilibria, in one of which a bank run occurs. A potential problem with this approach is that individuals may not want to deposit in the first place, since they cannot calculate the probability that a run will occur. Consequently, runs should not be observed in equilibrium because no one would deposit anticipating a run. This leaves open the important question of whether the emergence of banks as liquidity providers is desirable from an ex ante perspective. One way around the multiplicity of equilibria, as suggested by Postlewaite and Vives (1987), is to associate a bank with a sort of Prisoner's Dilemma–type situation, in which agents withdraw their deposits for self-interest reasons rather than for consumption reasons. In this context, agents do not condition their behavior on any exogenous event, and there is only a unique equilibrium involving a positive probability of a bank run. A bank run may occur because depositors have incomplete information about the liquidity shocks they face.

Another way around the multiplicity of equilibria is suggested by Rochet and Vives (2004) and Goldstein and Pauzner (2005). They analyze a modification of the Diamond and Dybvig model, in which the fundamentals of the economy uniquely determine whether a bank run occurs. The key features of the analysis are the assumptions that fundamentals are stochastic and investors obtain noisy private signals on the realization of the fundamentals. This leads to a unique equilibrium in which a bank run occurs when the fundamentals are below some critical level. Importantly, despite being determined by fundamentals, runs can be also driven by bad expectations. Depositors tend to withdraw prematurely for fear that others will do so. Thus a run may occur even when the economic environment is sufficiently good that a run would not occur if depositors had not had bad expectations on other depositors' actions. In this respect the model reconciles the view of bank runs as panics due to coordination failure and the view of runs as being linked to fundamentals. The uniqueness of the equilibrium also allows the determination of the ex ante probability of a bank run. This is increasing in the short-term payment the bank offers and therefore in the risk sharing embodied in the banking contract. When the short-term asset is set at the autarkic level, only efficient runs occur. Depositors withdraw prematurely only if the long-term return of the bank's asset is lower than its liquidation value. In contrast, when the short-term asset is above the autarkic level, inefficient runs occur when a bank is forced to liquidate the long-term asset even though it has a high expected return. Given this inefficiency, having banks offering short-term payments above the autarkic level is viable and desirable, provided that maintaining the long-term investments till maturity is generally efficient.

To sum up, bank runs result from either (both) a coordination failure among depositors or (and) an expectation of poor performance of the bank. Runs may be costly, because they force the interruption of a production process and the premature liquidation of assets. Moreover, runs may trigger a systemic crisis if they propagate through the economy. A systemic crisis has a narrow and a broad interpretation (De Bandt and Hartmann, 2002). A crisis in the narrow sense refers to a situation in which the failure of one bank or even only the release of bad news about its state of solvency leads in a sequential fashion to the failure of numerous other banks or of the system as a whole. A crisis in the broad sense also includes the simultaneous failure of many banks or of the whole system as result of a generalized adverse shock. The sequential spreading out of failures in a narrow crisis implies a strong spillover effect, defined as contagion, which can take place through contagious runs or domino effects (Schoenmaker 1996). The former refers to the propagation of a run from a single bank to other banks. As for individual runs, such propagation can be due to sunspots or be information based. The domino effect refers to the mechanism through which difficulties faced by a single bank spread to others through the payment system and/or the interbank market. If relationships among banks are neither collateralized nor insured against, the distress of one bank may trigger a chain of subsequent failures. Other banks may incur a liquidity or an insolvency problem, depending on the intensity of the linkages with the distressed bank and on the correlation of shocks in the system. The channels of contagious runs and domino effects can work in conjunction as well as independently. In most cases, however, a systemic crisis is the result of the propagation of an individual failure through both of them.

Most of the interrelations among banks occur through the payment system. Their internal arrangement determines how individual shocks propagate and thus the severity of the contagion risk. Depending on the timing and the methodology of settlement, payment systems can be classified as net settlement systems (only net balances are settled and at a certain point in time), pure gross systems (payments between members are settled without netting and a certain point in time), real-time gross systems (payments between members are settled without netting and immediately after every transaction), and correspondent banking (payments are settled bilaterally between a correspondent bank and members of a group of small or foreign banks). Net systems economize on liquidity but expose banks to contagion because they involve the transfer of asset claims from one location to another. By contrast, gross systems entail high liquidity costs but do not face any risk of contagion (Freixas and Parigi 1998).

Surprisingly, the academic literature has devoted attention to the issue of contagion and systemic risk only very recently. The former models of individual runs can be read in terms of generalized systemic crises, but they are not suited to the analysis of the propagation mechanism of individual failures. The analysis of such mechanism requires models with multiple banks.

Rochet and Tirole (1996) examine the domino effect in a model of interbank lending with heterogeneous banks. Some banks are good at collecting deposits but have poor investment opportunities; others have plenty of investment opportunities but need funds. This leaves room for interbank lending, although it exposes banks to the risk of contagion. If a borrowing bank is hit by a liquidity shock, the lending bank may be negatively affected and be forced to shut down. The survival of the lending bank depends on the severity of the shock affecting the borrowing bank and on the revenues (or losses) of the interbank loan. Clearly, the greater the liquidity shock faced by the borrowing bank, the more likely is the closure of the lending bank.

The occurrence of contagious runs and domino effects is analyzed by Allen and Gale (2000a) in an economy where banks hold interregional deposits on other banks to insure against liquidity preference shocks. The economy works well and achieves optimal risk sharing when there is no aggregate uncertainty; but it may lead to a systemic crisis when there is excess aggregate demand for liquidity. In such a case, each bank starts to withdraw deposits from banks in other regions in an attempt to satisfy depositors' withdrawal demands and to avoid liquidating the long-term assets. This mutual liquidation denies liquidity to the troubled bank, which then experiences a run. Depending on the structure of the interbank market, the individual run propagates to other banks and leads to a systemic crisis. If regions are well connected (complete interbank market), contagion is avoided. If connections among regions are limited (incomplete interbank market) and liquidity shocks are strong enough, contagion arises.

In a similar spirit, Freixas, Parigi, and Rochet (2000) analyze the risk of contagious runs through the payment system when banks are located in different regions and face both liquidity and solvency shocks. The former originate from depositors' geographical consumption preferences, the latter from shocks to the return of bank assets. Depositors have two ways to satisfy their wish to consume in a different location from where they have deposited initially. They can withdraw their funds and transfer cash to the other region, or they can transfer deposits from one bank to another through the payment system. When banks are subject only to liquidity shocks, the economy shows multiple equilibria. Either depositors do not run and the payment system is efficient in reducing the opportunity costs of holding liquid assets, or depositors run and banks have to liquidate the long-term assets (speculative gridlock equilibrium). This latter equilibrium resembles the sunspot equilibrium in Diamond and Dybvig. When banks also face (idiosyncratic) solvency shocks, the stability of the system depends on the architecture of the payment system. As in Allen and Gale (2000a), the closure of an insolvent institution is less likely to generate contagious runs when payment systems are well diversified.

2.2. Excessive Risk Taking

A second source of instability of the banking system relates to risk taking on the asset side. As is well known from agency theory, in a principal–agency relationship the objectives of the involved parties are not perfectly aligned, so the agent does not always act in the best interest of the principal. The problem can be limited by designing appropriate incentive schemes for the agent or by controlling his decisions through costly monitoring. In general, though, the divergence of interests will not be completely resolved, at least not at zero cost. Applying these arguments to corporate finance, it is easy to see that there is a misalignment in the objectives of debt holders and firm managers. Even if all parties are utility maximizers, their attitude toward risks diverges. Whereas debt holders bear the downside risk, the manager pursuing shareholders' interests benefit from upside potential. Thus, the manager has strong incentives to engage in activities that have very high payoffs but very low success probabilities (Jensen and Meckling 1976).

While this agency problem is present in all leveraged firms, two features of the banking system make it more severe among banks. First, the opacity and the long maturity of banks' assets make it easier to cover any misallocation of resources, at least in the short run. Second, the wide dispersion of bank debt among small, uninformed (and often fully insured) investors prevents any effective discipline on banks. Thus, because banks can behave less prudently without being easily detected or paying additional funding costs, they have stronger incentives to take risk than firms in other industries.

To illustrate the agency problem between banks and depositors, we use a simple model adapted from Holmstrom and Tirole (1997), Cerasi and Daltung (2000), and Carletti (2004). Consider a two-date economy ($T = 0, 1$), in which at date 0 a bank invests in a project, which yields a return R if successful and 0 if unsuccessful. The success probability of the project depends on the monitoring effort $m \in [0, 1]$ that the bank exerts. It is p_H if the bank monitors and p_L if it does not, with $p_H > p_L$, $\Delta p = p_H - p_L$, and $p_H R > 1 > p_L R$. Monitoring is costly; an effort m entails a private cost $C(m) = \frac{c}{2}m^2$. The choice of the monitoring effort depends crucially on the financing structure of the bank. If it is self-financed, it chooses m so as to maximize its expected profit.

$$\Pi = mp_H R + (1 - m)p_L R - y - \frac{c}{2}m^2,$$

where y represents the return on an alternative safe investment. In this case the first-order condition gives

$$m = \frac{\Delta p\, R}{c}.$$

By contrast, if the bank raises external funds in the form of debt with promised (gross) return r_D, it chooses m so as to maximize

$$\Pi = mp_H(R - r_D) + (1 - m)p_L(R - r_D) - \frac{c}{2}m^2.$$

The first-order condition is then given by

$$m = \frac{\Delta p(R - r_D)}{c}.$$

Clearly, raising deposits reduces the equilibrium monitoring effort. The reason is that the bank now has to share the benefit of greater monitoring with depositors. If the deposit rate is set before m is chosen, increasing monitoring simply raises the probability of repaying depositors without reducing the funding costs. This worsens the bank's incentive and leads to a lower equilibrium effort.

2.3. The Need of Regulation

The vulnerability of banks to runs and systemic crises and the consequent concern for consumers' wealth are the main factors justifying the need of regulation and safety net arrangements in the form of deposit insurance and lender of last resort. For example, as shown by D. Diamond and Dybvig (1983), deposit insurance prevents the occurrence of panic (sunspot) runs without reducing banks' ability to transform short-term liabilities into long-term assets. A demand deposit contract with government deposit insurance achieves optimal risk sharing among depositors as unique Nash equilibrium. Government's ability to levy nondistortionary taxes and deposit insurance guarantees induce depositors not to withdraw prematurely. Consequently, bank liquidation policy is independent of the volume of withdrawals, no strategic issues of confidence arise, and no bank runs take place.

The underlying idea behind the introduction of regulation and safety net arrangements is that runs and systemic crises are inefficient and therefore have to be prevented. Whereas this is always true for panic runs, it may not be the case for information-based runs. These are efficient whenever the liquidation value of the long-term asset is higher than its long-term expected return. Given this distinction, it is important to understand why bank runs occur and eventually how to deal with them. Allen and Gale (1998) analyze the potential costs of bank runs and the need for central bank intervention. In their model, bank runs are information-based events that play the important role of sharing risk among depositors. Their welfare properties depend on the potential costs of early withdrawal. When withdrawing early involves no costs, runs are efficient, since they occur only when banks' long-term asset returns are low. The optimal deposit contract reaches the first-best solution in terms of both risk sharing and portfolio choice, and regulation is not needed. In contrast, when there are real costs associated with early withdrawals (e.g., because the return of the safe asset is higher within the banking system than outside), bank runs reduce the consumption available to depositors. Then laissez-faire does not achieve the first-best allocation any longer, and there is scope for central bank intervention in the form of money injection. If the central bank grants an interest-free loan to banks when runs occur, banks can avoid liquidating the safe assets prematurely and depositors receive higher consumption levels. The first-best allocation can then be achieved again by a combination of standard deposit contracts, runs, and policy intervention. In a similar spirit, central bank intervention is needed when the long-term asset can be liquidated and traded on market. Bank runs are again costly, and the premature liquidation of long-term assets forces down the price in the market and makes crises worse. The intervention of the central bank is needed to prevent the collapse of asset prices.

The issue of the optimal form of central bank intervention have long been debated in the academic literature. According to the "classical" view of Bagehot (1873), central banks should lend freely at a penalty rate and against good collateral. This should prevent banks from using central bank lending to fund current operations and should guarantee that emergency liquidity loans are extended only to illiquid but solvent banks. This view has been criticized in various ways. First, according to Goodhart (1987), it is virtually impossible, even for central banks, to distinguish illiquidity from insolvency at the time the lender of last resort (LOLR) should act. Banks demanding such assistance are under a suspicion of insolvency since they could otherwise raise funds from the market. Second, it has been argued, for example, by Goodfriend and King (1988), that there is no need for central bank's loans to individual banks since open market operations are sufficient to deal with systemic liquidity crises. In other words, LOLR should intervene at the macroeconomic level but not at the microeconomic level.

This debate is also relevant with respect to the possible consequences that the safety net arrangements can create. If on the one hand both deposit insurance and LOLR may suffice to prevent runs and systemic crises, on the other hand they have side effects and bring in new inefficiencies. For example, they worsen the problem of excessive risk taking and call for further regulatory measures. Both deposit insurance and a systematic use of the lender of last resort induce banks to undertake greater risks, since depositors do not have incentives to monitor their banks' asset values and can rely on future bailouts in case of distress (e.g., Merton 1977, Boot and Greenbaum 1993).

Some of these issues have recently been addressed in formal theoretical models. Rochet and Vives (2004) provide a possible theoretical foundation of Bagehot's view using the "global game" approach. Their analysis builds on a model of banks' liquidity crises with a unique Bayesian equilibrium. At this equilibrium there is an intermediate range of values of the bank's asset in which, due to a coordination failure, depositors may run despite the bank's being solvent. Thus, as argued by Bagehot, a solvent bank may face a liquidity problem and be in need of assistance. The likelihood that this will happen decreases with the ex ante strength of the fundamentals. The optimal policy consists of prudential measures and ex post emergency loans. Liquidity and solvency regulation can solve depositors' coordination problem and avoid the failure of solvent banks but may be too costly in terms of foregone returns. Thus they need to be complemented by emergency discount-window lending. The optimal policy is richer when bank managers can exert an effort and influence the risk of asset returns, since it has to account for the effect it has on bank managers' incentives. Depending on the value of the fundamentals, the optimal policy may comprise early closure of solvent banks to prevent moral hazard and emergency liquidity assistance.

The relationship between banks' moral hazard and optimal central bank intervention is also analyzed by Freixas, Parigi, and Rochet (2004) in a model in which banks are subject to both liquidity and solvency shocks and can operate under moral hazard either in screening loan applicants or in monitoring borrowers. Given the difficulty to discern banks' solvency state, insolvent banks may be able to borrow from the interbank market or from the central bank and "gamble for resurrection" (i.e., invest in projects with negative net present value). The optimal policy depends on the nature of the banks' incentive problem. If banks face moral hazard in monitoring borrowers, there is no need for central bank intervention. A secured interbank market suffices to implement the first-best allocation. In contrast, if banks face moral hazard mainly in screening loan applicants, the central bank should provide emergency liquidity assistance but at a penalty rate to discourage insolvent banks from borrowing.

Gale and Vives (2002) build on the time inconsistency embodied in central bank bailout policy to characterize the optimality of dollarization as a way of devaluing depositors' claims and avoiding bank failure. The idea is that competitive banking systems lead to excessive liquidation when banks face moral-hazard problems. By using dollarization as a credible commitment not to bail out banks, the central bank can then implement the incentive-efficient solution and avoid failures.

To sum up, the debate around the optimal central bank intervention centers on the tradeoff between the benefits (prevention of crises) and the costs (distortion of incentives and moral-hazard problem) of bailing out distressed banks. This tradeoff may call for other regulatory measures, such as capital regulation, rate regulation, and entry restrictions. These too, though, have been heavily criticized as not being effective or as inducing other negative distortions, such as a reduction in competition. The side effects of regulation are therefore crucial for understanding the role and the importance of competition in the banking sector.

3. COMPETITION IN BANKING

Analyzing how competition works in the banking sector and whether it is beneficial is a difficult task. On the one hand, the general argument in favor of competition in terms of cost minimization and allocative efficiency apply to the banking industry. On the other hand, however, the presence of various market failures distorts the functioning of competition and makes the standard competitive paradigms inappropriate for the banking sector. The presence of asymmetric information in corporate relationships and of switching costs and networks in retail banking alters the market mechanism. This creates significant entry barriers, which affect the industry structure and lead to an ambiguous relation between the number of banks and the competitive outcome. We analyze these effects in more detail later.

It is worth noting, though, that other aspects of the role and specificity of banks also affect the working of competition in this sector. For example, the simple fact that banks compete on both sides of the balance sheet may lead to departures from the competitive outcome. Stahl (1988) and Yannelle (1989, 1997) show that when banks compete for both loans and deposits, they may want to corner one market in an attempt to achieve a monopoly on the other. Furthermore, the role of banks as financiers of industrial loans may create endogenous entry barriers in both the banking sector and the borrowing industries, thus leading to a natural monopoly in both sectors (González-Maestre and Granero 2003).

3.1. Competition Under Asymmetric Information

As already mentioned, banks emerge as intermediaries between depositors and borrowers. Thus, their two main functions are to provide insurance to depositors and to screen and monitor investment projects. The former creates the risk of instability; the latter creates important informational asymmetries among banks and potential borrowers and among banks themselves, which may distort the competitive mechanism significantly.

Broecker (1990) analyzes how competition in the credit market affects the screening problem banks face in the choice of granting loans. The setup is such that firms applying for credit differ in their ability to repay loans, that is, in their creditworthiness, and banks perform independent and imperfect screening tests to discern firms' quality and decide whether to grant loans. Conditional on their own test results, banks compete with each other by setting a loan rate. Given, however, that screening tests are imperfect, the competitive market mechanism does not work properly, in that it leads to a negative externality among banks. Increasing the loan rate above that of the competitor has two (opposite) effects on the profit of the deviating bank. On the one hand, it increases its profit through the usual price effect. On the other hand, it worsens the quality of firms accepting the loan, thus reducing its profit. A firm will indeed accept the least favorable loan rate only after being rejected by all other banks setting more favorable rates; but this implies that the firm has a low creditworthiness on average. Because of this "winner's curse" problem, increasing the number of banks performing screening tests decreases the average creditworthiness of firms and increases the probability that a bank does not grant any loan. In the limit, the number of active banks is positive and the equilibrium maintains some degree of oligopolistic competition.

Similar conclusions are reached by Riordan (1993). Using the theory of common value auctions, he shows that a higher number of competing banks worsens the informativeness of the signal that banks receive on firms' loan quality and makes them more conservative in granting loans. Both of these two effects are detrimental for social welfare, since they reduce the quality of banks' portfolios and lead to the financing of less efficient investment projects.

The relationship between the degree of market competition (or integration) and banks' screening incentives is also analyzed by Gehrig (1998). In a context where banks use imperfect creditworthiness tests to discriminate between good and bad projects, he shows that screening incentives increase with the profitability of loans. Thus, more intense competition due to the entry of outside banks worsens the quality of banks' portfolios, since it reduces the investment that banks make to improve the precision of their screening tests.

Besides acquiring information on borrowers through screening, banks monitor them in the course of the relationship, thus obtaining further information on their quality. This creates an informational asymmetry among banks. If a borrower needs a renewal of the loan, the incumbent bank has better information about his quality relative to outside banks. This gives the incumbent bank an informational monopoly over its borrowers, which reduces competition from outside banks and allows the incumbent bank to "hold up" its borrowers and extract monopoly rents. Such expropriation disincentivizes the borrower from exerting more effort, thus reducing the expected return of investment projects (Rajan 1992) and leading to an inefficient allocation of capital toward lower-quality firms (Sharpe 1990).

The heterogeneity of borrowers and the consequent informational advantages of incumbent banks affect the competitive market mechanism in several ways. As already mentioned, an increase in the number of competing banks reduces the screening ability of each of them. Consequently, more low-quality borrowers obtain financing, and banks may have to increase loan rates to compensate for the higher portfolio risk, thus leading to an inverse relationship between competition and level of loan rates (Marquez 2002). This result may not obtain any longer, however, when information acquisition is endogenous. In such a context, competition lowers loan rates, in the usual way. Hauswald and Marquez (2005) show that when banks acquire information to soften competition and increase market shares, a higher number of banks reduces the winner's-curse problem originating from competitors' superior information, thus leading to lower loan rates. In other words, an increase in the number of competing banks reduces the degree of product differentiation among banks and thus loan rates.

The presence of adverse selection affects also the structure of the industry. The informational advantage of the incumbent banks allows them to reject the riskier borrowers in need of refinancing. Because outside banks cannot distinguish between new borrowers and old, riskier borrowers rejected by their previous incumbent banks, they face an adverse selection problem that may keep them out of the market. An equilibrium of blockaded entry may then emerge, where only two banks are active and make positive profits, even under pure Bertrand price competition (Dell'Ariccia, Friedman, and Marquez 1999); or, more generally, the equilibrium is characterized by a finite number of banks, even in the absence of exogenous fixed costs (Dell'Ariccia 2001). The general idea is that the heterogeneity of borrowers and the acquisition of information gathered through lending generate endogenous fixed costs, which limit the number of active competitors.

To sum up, focusing mostly on an adverse-selection problem (i.e., heterogeneity of borrowers), the literature on competition with asymmetric information discusses the possibility for lenders to exercise market power, the imperfect functioning of competitive markets, and the endogenous entry barriers that the informational advantage of incumbent banks can generate. Despite not addressing directly the consequences for stability, this literature provides some intuitions about the effect that competition may have on banks' solvency. Because banks' screening abilities worsen with the number of competing banks, tougher competition leads to riskier bank portfolios and high failure probabilities. The mechanism behind the negative relationship between competition and stability derives exclusively from the heterogeneity of borrowers. This contrasts sharply with the mechanism in the literature on competition and stability, where the focus is on how competition modifies the behavior of either borrowers or banks. We come back to this issue in Section 4.

3.2. Competition and Switching Costs

Switching costs are an important source of market power in retail banking (e.g., P. Diamond 1971). In moving from one bank to another, consumers may incur costs associated with the physical change of accounts, bill payments, or lack of information (Vives 2001). Switching costs produce in general two opposing effects on the degree of competition. On the one hand, they may lead to collusive behavior once banks have established a customer base that remains locked in. On the other hand, they induce fierce competition to enlarge the customer base. Thus, switching costs may lead banks to offer high rates initially to attract customers and then to reduce them subsequently, when consumers are locked in.

A different result may be obtained when switching costs are combined with asymmetric information about borrowers' creditworthiness. Bouckaert and Degryse (2004) analyze a two-period model where heterogenous borrowers face switching costs of changing banks and banks face an adverse-selection problem. In such a context, banks find it convenient to disclose their private information about borrowers' creditworthiness and to induce them to switch banks in order to soften overall competition. Disclosure of borrowers' quality removes the information disadvantage of rival banks in the interim period, thus allowing them to poach only good borrowers and have positive second-period profits. This relaxes the initial competition for enlarging the customer base, and it increases banks' overall profits. Thus, the removal of future informational entry barriers may emerge for strategic reasons as it softens overall competition.

The presence of switching costs can also affect significantly the link between the number of banks and the degree of market competition. Allen and Gale (2000b, 2004) show that a small fixed cost of switching banks may imply higher rates in a system with many small independent banks (unitary system) than in a system with two large banks having extensive nationwide branching networks (branching system). This result is obtained in a model characterized by fixed costs of switching banks, customers' initial limited information about the future offer of banks' services and prices, and product diversity in the services that banks provide at different locations. Consumers are allocated randomly at each location every period and have to choose which bank to patronize. In a unitary system, each bank consists of one branch in one location. Thus, each bank can raise its initial rate by a small amount without losing its customers, because of the fixed cost of switching. The only equilibrium is when all banks charge the monopoly rate. In a branch system, there are only two banks, with one branch in each of the locations. Although consumers change location in each period, they can stay with the same bank if they wish. This possibility increases the costs for each bank of deviating from the equilibrium strategy and losing customers. As a result, branch banking supports more efficient equilibria, where the two banks may charge a rate close to the perfectly competitive level.

3.3. Competition and Networks

A final important element affecting the nature of competition in retail banking is the presence of networks. This introduces elements of nonprice competition in the interaction between banks, thus affecting the pricing of banking products and the structure of the industry.

The possibility for banks to share automatic teller machine (ATM) networks can be used as a strategic variable to affect price competition. Matutes and Padilla (1994) analyze this issue in a two-period model, where banks choose first whether to build compatible ATM networks and then compete imperfectly on the deposit market. A large ATM network has two opposite effects. On the one hand, it allows banks to offer lower deposit rates, because depositors benefit from easier access to their deposits when they need cash unexpectedly (network effect). On the other hand, a large ATM network increases price rivalry, because it makes banks more substitutable. Depositors benefit from the location of a bank ATM and the high rates offered by a rival bank sharing the same network (substitution effect). Banks choose to share ATM networks when the network effect dominates, that is, when depositors do only a small number of transactions through ATMs. The equilibrium is characterized by either partial sharing of ATM networks or no sharing. The former emerges when the network effect dominates, the latter when the substitution effect prevails. Full sharing does not occur in equilibrium, since banks prefer to maintain some differentiation and face softer competition in the deposit market. However, if future entry is possible, banks can use sharing agreements to exclude rivals from the market when the network effect is sufficiently high. Then, the threat of entry may lead all incumbent banks to share their network, since this allows them to credibly commit to fierce postentry competition and foreclose any potential entrant.

Sharing of networks is also used to limit competition in McAndrews and Rob (1996) in a two-period model where banks choose whether to own jointly the switches in ATM networks and then to compete on the pricing of ATM services. Given the presence of fixed costs in operating a switch and network effects in the demand of ATM services, banks prefer to join switches as a way to achieve a more concentrated structure in the switches industry and monopoly prices in the sale of ATM services to consumers. The implications in terms of welfare are ambiguous. Whereas the joint ownership is inefficient because it leads to the extraction of monopoly rents from final consumers, it is beneficial in that it saves the fixed costs of setting up a switch and gives consumers the possibility of benefiting from a larger network.

Similar results are obtained in a context where banks have to decide first whether to offer remote access to their customers, such as postal or telephone services, and then to compete for deposits (Degryse 1996). Depositors differ in terms of taste over location and quality (remote access). Thus, as in Matutes and Padilla (1994), the decision of a bank to offer remote access has the double effect of introducing vertical differentiation between banks and reducing the degree of horizontal differentiation. Consumers with a higher taste for remote access have lower transportation costs if this access is available. Thus, introducing remote access produces two opposite effects. It steals depositors from the rival bank (stealing effect), but it also increases the substitutability between banks (substitution effect). The equilibrium depends on which of these two effects prevails. For low and high values of the ratio of quality difference to transportation cost, only one bank offers remote access and offers lower deposit rates.

The impact of networks on the structure of the industry and the possibility of entry is analyzed by Gehrig (1996) in a model that also applies to the banking sector, despite being developed for the brokerage industry. Intermediaries reduce search frictions by facilitating the matching between buyers. Similar to the models described earlier, they first choose the size of their network and then compete in prices. Setting up a large network involves costs, but it also increases the probability with which an intermediary is able to match buyers. Thus, the size of the network differentiates the quality of matching services, and intermediaries may relax price competition by choosing networks of different sizes and offering products of different quality. Intermediaries with large networks gain market power and can command higher prices than rivals with smaller networks. Vertical differentiation and fixed costs of establishing a network imply that the industry converges to an oligopolistic structure, with a few large intermediaries having large networks and a number of smaller competitive intermediaries active in "niche" markets. The different size of intermediaries allows them to differentiate and relax price competition. Still, as the size of the market grows relative to the cost of establishing a network, the importance of smaller intermediaries vanishes because many more can enter the market and the degree of vertical differentiation among the large intermediaries disappears. Competition becomes tighter and equilibrium prices approximate perfectly competitive levels. As in McAndrews and Rob (1996), there is a tradeoff between competition and fixed costs of setting up a network. An increase in the number of active players leads to more competitive outcomes but also to higher fixed costs, thus having an ambiguous effect on welfare.

One important final note is that competition in networks can also be analyzed in two-sided markets. Rochet and Tirole (2002) analyze this issue using the context of credit card associations. They develop a model in which customers' banks and merchants have market power, and consumers and merchants decide rationally whether to buy or accept credit cards. The focus is on the factors affecting merchants' resistance to accept credit cards and on the collusive determination of interchange fees, that is, the fees that merchants' banks (the acquirers) pay to consumers' banks (the issuers). Merchants' decisions depend on their technological benefit of accepting cards but also on the effects that card acceptance has on consumers and price competition. As in the ATM literature, merchants can then use card acceptance to increase their customer base and relax price competition. Different from the ATM literature, however, the system has to attract two sides of the market, that is, issuers and acquirers, merchants, and consumers. Thus, changes in interchange fees and prices affect the relative price structure of the two sides, with important consequences on the equilibrium outcomes.

4. COMPETITION AND STABILITY: A POSITIVE OR A NEGATIVE LINK?

In the previous sections we described the specificity of banks and the potential sources of their instability. We then discussed how the presence of market imperfections, such as asymmetric information, switching costs, and network externalities, affect the competitive mechanism in the banking sector and its outcome. Interestingly, these two strands of literature do not have much in common. In other words, the literature on competition in the presence of market failures does not say much on how competition affects the stability of the sector, in the sense of either fragility or excessive risk taking. The one implication that can be drawn is that when borrowers are heterogeneous and banks perform screening tests to sort out borrowers, an increase in the number of competing banks worsens the quality of the tests. This aggravates the information problem that banks face, thus increasing the riskiness of their portfolios. But this result depends entirely on the adverse-selection problem that banks face vis-à-vis borrowers, a problem that the stability literature does not address directly.

We now turn more directly to the relationship between competition and stability. We structure the analysis according to the effects that competition, either in the deposit market or in the loan market, has on the two sources of bank instability we outlined in Section 2. We start by discussing the effects of competition on banks' vulnerability to individual runs and systemic risk; we then move on to the effects that competition has on excessive risk taking. It is worth pointing out, though, that only few of the papers we discuss endogenize aspects of industrial organization in their analysis. The majority of them just compare the equilibria achievable in different market settings without taking into account any strategic interaction among intermediaries.

4.1. Market Structure and Financial Fragility

The relationship between competition and financial fragility has largely been ignored in the banking literature. Most of the contributions on bank runs and systemic risk reviewed in Section 2 pay very little attention to the strategic interaction between banks, simply assuming that they operate in a perfectly competitive environment. Runs and systemic crises occur either as a consequence of a coordination failure among depositors or as their rational response to the impending banks' solvency problems. These models do not provide any insights concerning which market structure is more fragile.

A few models address directly the relationship between competition and liability risk. Smith (1984) analyzes this issue in a framework à la Diamond and Dybvig (1983), where banks compete to attract depositors who have different probability distributions over the dates of withdrawal. In the case when an adverse-selection problem is present, that is, when depositors only know their own probability of withdrawals, there may not exist any Nash equilibrium. The equilibrium contract, either pooling or separating, is destroyed by the possibility for banks to offer positive profit contracts to a specific segment of depositors. The banking system is then not viable, or is "unstable." The problem can be resolved by appropriate regulatory measures, such as ceilings on deposit rates.

A similar positive relationship between competition and fragility also emerges from the works of Rochet and Vives (2004) and Goldstein and Pauzner (2005), where higher deposit rates lead to more coordination failures and bank runs.[2]

Allen and Gale (2004) analyze the link between competition and stability in the interbank market. Banks have no incentives to provide liquidity to a troubled bank when the interbank market is perfectly competitive, because each of them acts as price taker and assumes that its action does not affect the equilibrium. In contrast, when the interbank market is imperfectly competitive, banks may want to help a troubled bank in order to prevent contagion. Since the provision of liquidity resembles the provision of a public good, when the number of banks is not too large each bank may have an incentive to coordinate with the others and provide liquidity, as long as avoiding contagion makes everybody better off. However, a coordination failure may still arise, in that each bank may find it optimal not to provide any liquidity if it thinks the others will not contribute anything.[3]

Importantly, this coordination failure may occur independent of the degree of competition in the market and thus occur in any market structure. This is formally shown by Matutes and Vives (1996) in a model à la D. Diamond (1984) enriched with elements of product differentiation, network externalities, and the possibility of

[2] The question of whether competition increases bank fragility can be posed in terms of whether cooperatives distributing profits to their members are less or more fragile than profit-maximizing institutions. Rey and Tirole (2000) suggest that cooperatives are more fragile than institutions making positive profits, because the lack of a buffer and the sharing of fixed costs among members create a network externality, which exposes cooperatives to runs. Differently, institutions making positive profits are less prone to runs because they can use their buffer to bear the risk of members' exit and avoid the consequent negative externality on the remaining members.

[3] See also Sáez and Shi (2004).

bank failures. Consider two banks, $i = a, b$, each located at the opposite extremes of a unit segment [0, 1] and competing for depositors with a reservation value of v and linear transportation costs $c \geq 0$. Banks offer depositors a standard debt contract with a (gross) return r_i^D and nonpecuniary bankruptcy penalties, and they obtain a deposit market share of d_i. Then they invest in risky projects, which require a minimum initial investment I and yield a (random) return $\widetilde{R}_i$. The distribution function of $\widetilde{R}_i$ depends on the market share d_i each bank obtains in the deposit market. In particular, the larger a bank, the more it can diversify away risk and decrease the probability of going bankrupt. Depositors do not observe the returns of banks' investments but are endowed with homogeneous prior beliefs (p_a, p_b) about their success probabilities. Given these beliefs, banks set r_i^D and depositors choose which bank to patronize. The market share and the aggressiveness of each bank i depend crucially on depositors' perceptions of its success probability and in particular on whether the difference $p_i r_i - p_j r_j$ is in the interval $[-c, c]$ and $p_i r_i - cd_i$ is above v. Both banks are active and have market share

$$d_i = \frac{1}{2} + \frac{(p_i r_i - p_j r_j)}{2c}$$

if both $p_i r_i - p_j r_j \in [-c, c]$ and $p_i r_i - cd_i \geq v$; banks enjoy local monopolies if $p_i r_i - cd_i < v$; and only the bank with higher expected return is active if $p_i r_i - p_j r_j$ is not in the interval $[-c, c]$. Depositors' perceptions of p_a and p_b differentiate the model from the standard Hotelling game and introduce vertical product differentiation into banking competition. In equilibrium, the success probabilities p_a and p_b are endogenously determined by depositors' expectations, which are self-fulfilling given the use of standard deposit contracts and the presence of economies of scale. A bank perceived to be safer commands a higher margin and a larger market share, which in turn makes it safer because of better diversification.

The self-fulfilling character of depositors' expectations implies multiple equilibria. Possible equilibria include corner solutions, where only one bank is active, and even equilibria where no banks are active. These are due to a coordination problem among depositors, which arises for reasons similar to those encountered in the network literature. A bank is a large network that requires a minimum size to be viable and in which each customer benefits from a larger number of members. In this view, the nonbanking equilibrium is reminiscent of the bad equilibrium in D. Diamond and Dybvig (1983) and can be interpreted as a "systemic confidence crisis." The coordination problem among depositors occurs irrespective of the degree of competition in the deposit market. A monopoly bank can suffer from fragility in the same way as can a competitive bank. Deposit insurance can prevent depositors' coordination failure and thus bank failures. Since depositors are repaid with certainty, they view $p_i = 1, i = A, B$, and the model converges to a Hotelling game with no vertical product differentiation and no more multiple equilibria. As in D. Diamond and Dybvig (1983), deposit insurance eliminates the nonbanking equilibrium and stabilizes the system, but it is not always welfare enhancing. On the one hand, by ensuring that all banks remain active, deposit insurance may preclude the realization of desirable diversification economies. Also, deposit insurance induces fiercer competition for deposits, which in turn increases the deadweight loss in case of failure and decreases the success probability of banks. On the other hand, deposit insurance has the positive effect of extending the market. This could transform a market where banks have local monopoly power to one where banks compete. Thus, the net welfare effects of deposit insurance are ambiguous and cannot be assessed independent of the market structure, even in the absence of moral-hazard considerations.

An ambiguous relationship between competition and stability is also found by Carletti, Hartmann, and Spagnolo (2003) in a model analyzing the effects of bank mergers on loan competition, reserve management, and banking system liquidity. Banks compete for loans and engage in interbank lending in order to deal with stochastic liquidity shocks à la D. Diamond and Dybvig (1983). A merger creates an internal money market where the merged banks can reshuffle liquidity. This affects their reserve management, pushing toward higher reserves when borrowing on the interbank market is not so costly relative to raising deposits and keeping more reserves initially, and toward lower reserves otherwise. The merger also modifies loan rates and banks' market shares. The overall effect on loan rates depends on how strong is the increase in market power relative to potential efficiency gains. More importantly, the change in banks' size affects aggregate liquidity. Greater heterogeneity among banks increases the variance of the aggregate liquidity demand and leads, ceteris paribus, to higher aggregate liquidity needs. This asymmetry channel, together with the change in reserve holdings, determines the effect of bank consolidation on the aggregate liquidity. Thus, the model suggests that imperfect loan market competition increases the volatility of the aggregate demand in the interbank market and may negatively affect the working of the interbank market. This would not occur if banks were perfectly competitive.

The relationship between crises and market structure is also analyzed by Boyd, De Nicoló, and Smith (2004) in a monetary, general equilibrium economy in which banks provide intertemporal insurance to risk-averse depositors and a monetary authority controls the rate of inflation. The model generates two different types of crises. In the first one (*banking crisis*), banks exhaust their reserve assets but do not liquidate the long-term asset. In the second one (*costly banking crisis*), banks liquidate the long-term asset, thus creating a real cost for the economy. The level of the inflation rate determines the relationship between crises and the market structure of the banking system. A monopolistic banking system faces a higher probability of banking crises when the inflation rate is below some threshold, while a competitive system is more fragile otherwise. This result is driven by a tradeoff implicit in banks' behavior. A monopolistic bank limits reserve holdings and offers lower deposit rates relative to a competitive bank. When the inflation rate is low, the first effect dominates, thus increasing the probability of banking crises in monopolistic banking systems. Concerning resource losses, costly banking crises are always more likely to occur under competition than under monopoly because the latter provides poorer intertemporal insurance to depositors. Thus, despite being more stable, a monopolistic banking system is not necessarily welfare enhancing.

4.2. Market Structure and Risk Taking

Most of the literature on the relationship between competition and stability analyzes the impact that competition has on banks' incentives to take risks. This focus originates from some empirical studies finding a negative effect of higher charter values on risk taking. For example, Keeley (1990) finds that the surge of bank failures in the United States during the 1980s derived mostly from various deregulation measures and market factors that reduced banks' monopoly rents and increased the value of their put option on the deposit insurance fund. Similarly, Edwards and Mishkin (1995) argue that the excessive risk taking observed in the 1980s in the United States was the banks' obvious response to the erosion of profits due to competition from financial markets. This decreased the banks' cost advantages in the acquisition of funds and undermined their position in the loan market.

Following these empirical findings, the theoretical literature has initially stressed how competition worsens banks' incentives to take risk (e.g., Besanko and Thakor 1993, Boot and Greenbaum 1993, Allen and Gale 2000b, 2004) and how regulation can help in mitigating this perverse link (e.g., Hellmann, Murdock, and Stiglitz 2000, Perotti and Suarez 2002, Repullo 2004). Despite this still being the prevailing view, more recent studies have suggested that the detrimental relationship between competition and bank risk taking is not robust. In particular, a higher degree of competition may induce banks to become more prudent once particular aspects of bank–firm relationships (e.g., entrepreneurs' effort) or important bank functions (e.g., monitoring) are taken into account. In the following we describe the most important contributions on the link between competition and risk taking, postponing to the next section the discussion of the importance and role of bank regulation in mitigating the negative effects that competition may have on stability.

The perverse link between competition and bank risk taking has been shown in several different frameworks. The general idea is that greater competition reduces banks' charter values (or rents available to shareholders and/or managers). This increases the attractiveness of the gains from taking risks and therefore the incentives to exploit the nonconvexity in banks' payoff functions. Besanko and Thakor (1993) use this idea in a framework of relationship banking, where banks acquire private information on their borrowers. This gives banks an informational monopoly and generates informational rents. As long as banks appropriate at least part of these rents, they have an incentive to limit their risk exposure and enjoy the value of the relationship. However, as soon as the banking industry becomes more competitive, relationship banking decreases in value and banks take more risks, particularly when deposits are backed by a risk-insensitive insurance scheme. Boot and Greenbaum (1993) obtain similar results in a two-period model in which banks can acquire funding-related reputational benefits and improve their rents through costly monitoring.

To see how competition may exacerbate the bank risk–shifting problem, we consider the simple model by Allen and Gale (2000b, 2004). Consider n banks choosing a portfolio consisting of perfectly correlated risks and competing à la Cournot on the deposit market. Each bank i receives a per-unit return $R_i \in [0, \overline{R}]$ with probability $p(R_i)$ and 0 with probability $(1 - p(R_i))$, with $p(R_i)$ satisfying

$p(0) = 1, p(\overline{R}) = 0,\ p'(R_i) < 0$, and $p''(R_i) < 0$. Each bank raises an amount d_i of deposits and faces an upward-sloping supply of funds. Given a total demand for deposits equal to $D = \sum_i d_i$, the opportunity costs of funds is $r_D(D)$, which satisfies $r'_D(D) > 0,\ r''_D(D) > 0,\ r_D(0) = 0$, and $r_D(\infty) = \infty$. Depositors are insured and the supply of funds is independent of the banks' portfolio risk. The payoff to the bank i is then given by

$$\Pi_i(R, d) = p(R_i)[R_i - r_D(D)]d_i,$$

where $R = (R_1, \ldots, R_n)$ and $d = (d_1, \ldots, d_n)$. A Nash–Cournot equilibrium, where each bank i chooses a strictly positive pair (R_i, d_i), has then to satisfy

$$p(R_i)[R_i - r_D(D) - r'_D(D)d_i] = 0$$

$$p'(R_i)[R_i - r_D(D)]d_i + p(R_i)d_i = 0.$$

In a symmetric equilibrium these conditions reduce to

$$R - r_D(nd) - r'_D(nd)d = 0$$

$$p'(R)[R - r(nd)] + p(R) = 0,$$

which imply

$$-\frac{p(R)}{p'(R)} = R - r_D(nd) = r'_D(nd)d.$$

This condition characterizes a symmetric equilibrium where each bank chooses the riskiness and size of the portfolio equal to (R^*, d^*). The equilibrium depends on the number of banks n. As $n \to \infty$, $d = \frac{D}{n} \to 0$, since D must be bounded above when n increases if $r_D(\infty) \to \infty$. This implies $r_D(nd)d \to 0$, and thus $R - r_D(nd) \to 0$ and $p(R) = 0$. An increase in competition then has a negative effect on bank riskiness. As $n \to \infty$, banks choose the maximum level of risk, that is, $R \to \overline{R}$. The reason is that banks become smaller and behave more like perfect competitors, thus increasing their size as long as profits are positive. In equilibrium, they make zero profits and have extreme incentives for taking risks.

The result of a positive perverse relationship between competition and the risk-taking problem extends to richer frameworks. Banks have an incentive to engage in risk shifting as long as their objective function is convex. The problem is particularly acute when banks are close to bankrupt, and it is worsened by competition. The property of a convex objective function holds, for example, in the presence of increasing returns to scale and in dynamic stationary environments in which banks compete for market share and play the short-run strategy at each date (Allen and Gale 2000b, 2004).

One crucial element is how banks operate on the asset side. A common assumption of the models showing a positive relationship between competition and risk taking is that banks have complete control over the risk of their portfolios. Each bank invests in assets with given risk characteristics and determines the riskiness of its portfolio.

As competition for deposits becomes tougher, profits decline and banks' preference for risk increases. However, the assumption that banks determine exclusively their portfolio risk covers an important risk-incentive mechanism on the asset side because it ignores the bank–borrower relationship. Once this is taken into account, the result can change dramatically. When banks as well as entrepreneurs can influence the risk of investment projects, the relationship between competition and risk taking becomes ambiguous. This is formally shown by Caminal and Matutes (2002) in a model in which banks compete for loans and can use monitoring or credit rationing to deal with an entrepreneurial moral-hazard problem. Given limited liability and nonverifiable actions, entrepreneurs have distorted incentives to allocate funds among alternative projects, which have different levels of risk and are subject to multiplicative aggregate shocks. Monitoring and credit rationing help in reducing entrepreneurial moral hazard, but they are imperfect substitute tools for the bank. The former requires the use of costly resources, while the latter reduces the potential gain from trade. If the bank does not monitor, credit has to be restricted in order to increase the marginal return of the funds invested and induce entrepreneurs to choose appropriate projects. The choice between monitoring and credit rationing depends on the banks' profits and hence on the degree of competition. A monopoly bank uses more monitoring and less credit rationing. This may induce a monopoly bank to grant larger loans and thus to have a higher failure probability than a competitive bank, since projects are subject to multiplicative shocks. As a consequence, the relationship between market power and failure probability is ambiguous.[4]

Our discussion also suggests that when entrepreneurs choose exclusively the risk of the investment projects, banks may become riskier as competition decreases. Greater competition in the loan market reduces the loan rates that entrepreneurs pay, thus increasing their profits and reducing their incentives to take risks. To show this mechanism, Boyd and De Nicoló (2005) extend the model of Allen and Gale (2000b, 2004) described earlier. In particular, they introduce many entrepreneurs who borrow from banks at a rate r_L and invest in investment projects yielding a per-unit return $R \in [0, \overline{R}]$ with probability $p(R)$ and 0 with probability $(1 - p(R))$. Given a total amount of deposits and thus of loans equal to D in the economy, the loan rate is $r_L(D)$ and satisfies $r_L(0) > 0$, $r'_L < 0$, $r''_L \leq 0$, and $r_L(0) > r_D(0)$. The return R is still a measure of project risk, but it is now chosen by the entrepreneurs to maximize $p(R)[R - r_L]$. Thus, R satisfies

$$r_L = R + \frac{p(R)}{p'(R)}, \tag{6}$$

and it increases with r_L. Each bank chooses the amount of deposits d_i to maximize

$$p(R)[r_L(D) - r_D(D)]d_i,$$

[4]Koskela and Stenbacka (2000) find an unambiguous positive relationship between competition and stability, but their framework is somewhat different. Banks compete in the loan market, but, absent any moral-hazard problem, stability refers to entrepreneurs' bankruptcy risk. Under the assumption of a mean-shifting investment technology, a monopoly bank charges higher lending rates than competitive banks, which leads to lower investments and thus to a higher probability of bankruptcy.

where r_L satisfies Eq. (6). The equilibrium depends again on the number of banks n. Different from Allen and Gale, though, the level of R is now strictly decreasing in n and prices converge to the competitive outcome; that is, $r_L(D) - r_D(D) = 0$ as $n \to \infty$. This occurs because banks take into account the risk-incentive mechanism of the entrepreneurs when setting loan rates, thus anticipating that the risk of their portfolio increases with loan rates.

5. COMPETITION AND REGULATION

As discussed earlier, market power is often thought to be associated with a lower probability of bank failure, in both static and dynamic contexts. High margins act as buffers against expected losses; high future expected profits increase the opportunity cost of going bankrupt, thus reducing banks' incentives to take excessive risk. The implication of this (still prevailing) view is that the banking system needs to be regulated to limit the adverse consequences of intense competition and achieve stability. But how is regulation to be designed appropriately? One possibility is to limit competition directly. Ceilings on interest rates or limited entry are examples of how to reduce competition and induce banks to behave more prudently. Another possibility is to design regulation in a way to "correct" the negative effects of competition. For example, risk-adjusted deposit insurance premia or appropriate capital requirements may be effective ways to control risk taking, even in the presence of intense competition. What is important is that the design of regulation has to take account of the effects that different market structures have on banks' incentives to take risk. As argued by Boyd and Gertler (1993), the poor performance of the U.S. banking system in the 1980s resulted from enhanced competition and an inadequate regulatory policy that encouraged excessive risk taking. The main source of problems was in fact the great risks taken by large banks, which faced more intense competition while being implicitly insured through the "too-big-to-fail" policy. Similarly, Edwards and Mishkin (1993) argue that the decline of bank profitability induced by enhanced competition entails a risk to the financial system only if regulators fail to adapt their policies to the changing financial environment.

A growing literature analyzes how regulation affects the relationship between competition and stability, in particular, risk taking. Starting from the standard paradigm that competition leads to higher risk, most contributions focus on the effectiveness of regulation in reducing the negative consequences of competition. Results are ambiguous and sensitive to the specific framework of analysis. Regulation such as risk-adjusted deposit insurance or capital requirement is sufficient to eliminate the negative impact of competition on risk taking in some cases; but specific restrictions on competition such as interest rate ceilings or entry restrictions are needed in other cases.

Following the mainstream, we will describe how regulation can remove the perverse effects of competition on risk taking. It is worth pointing out, though, that besides removing such effects, regulation may directly influence the "sign" of the relationship between competition and stability. For example, the effect of high charter values on banks' incentives may depend crucially on how they are generated. Nagarajan and Sealey (1995) show that high margins may not be effective in improving banks' incentives when they result from a forbearance policy extending the expiration date of equity holders' call options. More precisely, high charter values induce banks to choose high asset quality only if they are generated by an optimal forbearance policy, which takes into account the performance of both individual banks and the overall market.

Matutes and Vives (2000) examine the impact of deposit insurance on bank competition and risk-taking incentives in a context where banks are subject to limited liability and their failure implies social costs. In line with the charter value literature, banks choose the risk level of their portfolios $\gamma_i \in [\underline{\gamma}, \overline{\gamma}]$ and have a per-unit return $\widetilde{R}_i \in [\underline{R}, \overline{R}]$ with density function $g_i = (R_i, \gamma_i)$ and distribution function $G_i(\cdot)$. The choice of γ_i is not observable,[5] and higher levels of risk (higher γ_i) are associated with mean preserving spreads over G_i, so $E(R_i)$ is the same for all G_i but the variance increases with γ_i. Banks raise funds from investors in the form of standard deposit contracts promising a (gross) return equal to r_i^D. This implies that depositors are repaid fully only when the bank does not go bankrupt, and they get whatever is left otherwise. The supply of deposits is elastic and equal to

$$d_i = a + b\Phi_i^e(r_i^D) - c\Phi_j^e(r_j^D),$$

where $\Phi_i^e(r_i) = \Phi_i^e(r_i^D, \gamma_i^e)$ is the depositors' assessment of the expected return of one unit invested in bank i and γ_i^e is their assessment of bank risk. Given depositors' priors $\Phi_i^e(r_i)$, banks set r_i^D and depositors choose how much to supply. Banks retain some market power and have positive profits only if $R_i > r_i^D$. Otherwise, they fail and impose a social cost K on the economy. Then banks choose γ_i to maximize their expected profits:

$$\Pi_i = d_i \int_{r_i^D}^{\overline{R}} (R_i - r_i^D) g_i(R_i, \gamma_i) dR_i.$$

The nonobservability of γ_i together with the limited liability imply that banks always choose the maximum level of risk; that is, $\gamma_i = \overline{\gamma}$. This is the only credible level consistent with depositors' priors γ_i^e as banks' expected profits are increasing in γ_i. As a consequence, banks behave aggressively on the deposit market to increase their deposit base. The equilibrium is inefficient because it involves a high risk of bank failure and high social failure costs. The inefficiency may be ameliorated with the introduction of a deposit insurance scheme, but its effectiveness crucially depends on how the scheme is designed. When deposits are insured through a flat-rate scheme, banks still have the incentive to take the maximum level of risk, and both deposit rate regulation and asset restrictions are necessary to improve welfare. In contrast, when deposit insurance premia are risk based, deposit insurance may be sufficient to improve welfare. If the

[5] Matutes and Vives (2000) also analyze the case with disclosure requirements when γ_i is observable. In this case regulation is a sufficient instrument to increase welfare.

regulator observes γ_i, banks pay a premium contingent on their asset risk and deposit rates equal to

$$\tau_i(r_i^D, \gamma_i) = 1 - \frac{(E(R_i) - r_i^D)}{\int_{r_i^D}^{\overline{R}} (R_i - r_i^D) g_i(R_i, \gamma_i) dR_i}$$

and have expected profits equal to

$$\Pi_i = (1 - \tau_i) d_i \int_{r_i^D}^{\overline{R}} (R_i - r_i^D) g_i(R_i, \gamma_i) dR_i$$
$$= (E(R_i) - r_i^D) d_i.$$

Banks' expected profits are independent of the level of risk because the positive effect of higher risk on expected margins is offset by an increase in the premium banks have to pay. Thus, banks behave less aggressively on the deposit market because expanding their deposit base is no longer profitable. Concerning the choice of risk, any level of risk is consistent with the equilibrium when the deposit insurance premia are set simultaneously to the choice of γ_i, whereas the maximal risk is still chosen when the premia are set before γ_i is determined. In this case, restrictions on deposit rate ceilings and assets are again necessary to improve welfare.

Similar results are obtained by Cordella and Yeyati (2002) in a framework that extends Matutes and Vives (2000) to explicitly endogenize competition for deposits. As before, banks have limited liability and choose privately the level of risk of their portfolios. Each bank chooses a monitoring effort m_i, which determines the success probability of its portfolio at a cost m_i^2. Banks compete à la Salop (1979) on the deposit market and incur a fixed entry cost F. The deposit supply function is

$$d_i(r_i^D, r^D, m_i, m_i^e, n) = \frac{1}{n} + \frac{[a + (1-a)m_i^e] r_i^D - [a + (1-a)m^e] r^D}{c},$$

where n is the number of banks, $a \in [0, 1]$ is the fraction of insured deposits, r_i^D and r^D are the deposit rates set by bank i and by all other banks, respectively, m_i^e and m^e are depositors' assessments of the success probability of bank i and of all other banks, and c is depositors' transportation cost. Banks' expected profits are $\Pi_i - F$, where

$$\Pi_i = d_i[m_i(R_i - r_i^D) - m_i^2 - m_i \tau r_i],$$

with $\tau = \frac{a(1-m^e)}{m^e}$ representing the premium that each bank pays on the liabilities $d_i r_i$. Since both deposit rates and insurance premia are set as functions of expected rather than actual risk and deposits, banks have incentives to choose lower monitoring efforts. The equilibrium of the benchmark case can be improved by disclosing the level of monitoring m_i either to depositors (scenario D) or to a deposit insurance agency, which can then charge risk-based premia (scenario R). In both cases, banks choose higher monitoring efforts than under the benchmark scenario. The economy converges to the same equilibrium in terms of risk and expected returns on deposits in the limiting cases when there is no insurance ($a = 0$) in scenario D and full insurance ($a = 0$) in scenario R. The reason is that the disciplining effect in each scenario depends on the fraction of deposits that are priced correctly, namely, $(1 - a)$ in scenario D and a in scenario R. Thus, the two systems converge at the opposite extremes of the deposit insurance coverage, and welfare is always higher than in the benchmark case.

An alternative way to restore prudent behavior is to introduce capital requirements. Hellmann, Murdock, and Stiglitz (2000) analyze the relationship between competition for deposits, risk taking, and capital regulation in a dynamic framework where banks choose privately their asset risk and compete for deposits. Banks operate for T periods and can invest in either a prudent or a risky asset each period. The former yields a safe return S, while the latter yields $\overline{R}$ with probability p and $\underline{R}$ with probability $(1 - p)$. The risky asset has a higher return in case of success ($\overline{R} > S$) but a lower one in expectation ($S > p\overline{R} + (1 - p)\underline{R}$). Each bank i competes for insured deposits by offering a deposit rate r_i^D and raises an amount $d_i(r_i^D, r_{-i}^D)$, where r_{-i}^D is the rate offered by the other banks. Each bank also raises an amount of capital k, even if costly ($\rho > S$), and it invests a total amount of $(1 + k)d_i(r_i^D, r_{-i}^D)$. Prudential regulation requires that at the end of each period a regulator inspects the amount of capital each bank has and closes it down if such an amount is negative. The per-period profit of the bank is

$$\Pi_P(r_i^D, r_{-i}^D, k) = (S(1 + k) - r_i^D - \rho k)d_i(r_i^D, r_{-i}^D)$$

when it invests in the prudent asset and

$$\Pi_R(r_i^D, r_{-i}^D, k) = [p(\overline{R}(1 + k) - r_i^D) - \rho k]d_i(r_i^D, r_{-i}^D)$$

when it gambles and invests in the risky asset. In this case, the bank has a positive return if the asset succeeds, while it is closed down if it fails. After raising capital and attracting depositors, banks choose the asset portfolio to maximize their expected discounted profits $V = \sum_{t=0}^{T} \delta^t \Pi_t$. As $T \to \infty$, banks play an infinitely repeated static Nash equilibrium, so the game has a static structure within each time period. Banks choose to gamble and invest in the risky asset whenever

$$V_R(r_i^D, r_{-i}^D, k) = \frac{\Pi_R(r_i^D, r_{-i}^D, k)}{(1 - \delta p)} > V_P(r_i^D, r_{-i}^D, k) = \frac{\Pi_P(r_i^D, r_{-i}^D, k)}{(1 - \delta)},$$

that is, whenever

$$\Pi_R(r_i^D, r_{-i}^D, k) - \Pi_P(r_i^D, r_{-i}^D, k)V_R(r_i^D, r_{-i}^D, k) > (1 - p)\delta V_P(r_i^D, r_{-i}^D, k). \quad (7)$$

Equation (7) defines a critical level of the deposit rate, $\hat{r}^D$, such that banks gamble when $r^D(k) > \hat{r}^D(k)$ and behave prudently otherwise. This implies that banks choose to gamble for sufficiently competitive deposit markets (i.e., when the supply of deposit is sufficiently elastic), since their per-period gains from this strategy ($\Pi_R - \Pi_P$) then exceed the franchise value (δV_p) that banks lose when the risky asset fails (with probability $(1-p)$). The critical level of deposit rates, $\hat{r}^D(k)$, increases with the level of capital k; but in an unregulated equilibrium banks prefer not to raise any capital, since it is costly and decreases their franchise value (franchise-value effect).

A possible way to restore prudent bank behavior is to introduce capital requirements. If banks hold sufficient capital, they internalize the negative consequences of gambling and choose to behave prudently (capital-at-risk effect). Capital regulation, however, is a Pareto-inefficient policy in a dynamic framework. When all competitors set a deposit rate consistent with prudent behavior, for a given amount of deposits a bank is indifferent between the prudent and the risky asset. The bank must then earn a higher expected margin from the risky asset than from the gambling asset, since it loses the franchise value if the risky asset fails. This implies that the bank has an incentive to offer a slightly higher deposit rate than its competitors, so as to "steal" depositors, and invests in the risky asset (market-stealing effect). Because each bank has an incentive to do so, capital requirements coupled with freely determined deposit rates do not achieve Pareto-efficient equilibria. Capital requirements become effective only when they raise banks' costs to the level that banks are no longer willing to pay out higher deposit rates. But then other forms of regulation, such a deposit-rate controls, may achieve Pareto efficiency. By preventing the market-stealing effects, deposit-rate controls increase banks' per-period profits and franchise values and induce prudent behavior.

A different result on the effectiveness of capital regulation is obtained by Repullo (2004) in a similar dynamic model, where, as before, banks can invest in either a prudent or a risky asset, but compete à la Salop (1979) on the deposit market. Depositors are insured and face a unit traveling cost of c. Thus, each of the n banks raises an amount $\frac{1}{n}$ of deposits every period and raises an amount of capital k at a cost of c. As in Hellmann, Murdock, and Stiglitz (2000), the equilibrium reached in an unregulated economy depends on the level of intermediation margins (equal to $\frac{c}{n}$) and thus on the degree of deposit competition. All banks choose the risky asset for low margins (i.e., when competition is intense), the prudent assets for high margins (i.e., when competition is not intense), and both types of assets in the intermediate cases. When banks choose to gamble in an unregulated economy, capital requirements are an efficient regulatory measure because they reduce deposit rates without affecting banks' franchise value. Hence, only the capital-at-risk effect is at work, and capital regulation is effective in ensuring the existence of the prudent equilibrium. The different results relative to Hellmann, Murdock, and Stiglitz (2000) depend on the more explicit analysis of deposit market competition and on the use of internal capital instead of outside capital. This particular assumption modifies the way in which capital regulation enters into banks' profit functions and affects franchise values. Given constant intermediation margins, the franchise values are equal to

$$V_P = \frac{c}{\rho n^2}$$

when banks behave prudently and to

$$V_R = \frac{pc}{[\rho + (1-p)]n^2}$$

when they gamble. In both cases the franchise values do not depend on the capital requirement k because the negative effect of a higher level of capital is passed onto depositors in the form of lower deposit rates. Hence, capital requirements are effective in implementing prudent behavior, although they make depositors worse off. Deposit-rate ceilings do not do any better. Only risk-based capital requirements improve welfare, since they implement prudent behavior without reducing deposit rates.

Risk-based capital requirements are also effective in reducing banks' portfolio risk in Bolt and Tieman (2004) in a dynamic duopoly, where banks compete for borrowers by setting acceptance criteria. In particular, banks offer differentiated loans and face a linear demand equal to

$$L_i(\alpha_i, \alpha_j) = L + a\alpha_i - b\alpha_j,$$

where higher α_i and α_j represent lower acceptance criteria and the parameter b is a measure of the degree of substitution between loans of banks i and j (with $i \neq j$). Easing the acceptance criteria increases the demand for loans and thus the banks' per-period profits, but it also worsens the quality of their portfolios, since riskier borrowers obtain financing. Thus, banks face a tradeoff between increasing market shares in the short run and securing continuation in the long run. As standard in the charter value literature, competition (here intended as lower b) increases the attractiveness of larger market shares, thus inducing banks to ease acceptance criteria and increase risk. Prudential regulation can help in removing the negative effects of competition. Capital requirements (in particular if risk based) lead to less risk taking because they improve banks' incentives to set tight acceptance criteria and reduce their failure probabilities.

An alternative regulatory instrument to create charter values and solve the tradeoff between competition and stability is analyzed by Perotti and Suarez (2002) in a dynamic model where two banks compete on the deposit market and invest in either a prudent or a speculative asset. As in Hellmann, Murdock, and Stiglitz (2000) and Repullo (2004), the choice of lending must tradeoff the short-term gains from risk taking against the risk of losing charter value. Intense competition increases risk taking by enlarging short-term gains and reducing future charters. Different from previous works, however, the degree of competition is endogenous and is driven by banks' failures and regulatory policies on mergers and entry. When a bank fails as a result of unsuccessful speculative lending, the regulator has to decide whether to merge it with the incumbent surviving bank (merger policy) and/or whether to allow entry (entry policy). A merger with the incumbent bank modifies the market structure to a monopoly until the entry of a new bank brings it back to a duopoly. The possibility of obtaining monopoly rents (albeit temporarily) gives banks an additional incentive, beside the increase of charter value, to behave prudently and remain solvent. Said differently, banks' speculative lending decisions become strategic substitutes, in that the incentive of a bank to take risks decreases with the risk position of the competing bank. As a consequence, merger and entry policies imply a tradeoff between competition and stability. Allowing a merger when a bank is insolvent involves prudent behavior but also monopoly inefficiencies. The optimal policy instrument is a combination of mergers following a failure and subsequent entry. This creates ex ante incentives for banks to remain solvent to acquire failing institutions while limiting the ex post market power that surviving banks get through the rescue.

6. CONCLUSION

This chapter reviewed the main literature on stability and competition in the banking industry. Each of these two issues has received a large amount of attention in recent decades, but the two strands of literature remain somewhat disconnected. The stability literature proceeds typically under the assumption that banks operate in a perfect competitive system, thus disregarding the implications of different banking structures for the safety of the sector. In contrast, the competition literature analyzes the operation of the competitive mechanism in the presence of market failures, disregarding the effects on depositors' and agents' behavior. Thus, whether greater competition enhances or worsens the stability of the system remains unclear.

Only very recently has the literature addressed more directly how competition affects stability. The general argument is that competition worsens stability. Higher deposit rates increase the probability of bank runs; lower margins worsen the problem of excessive risk taking. However, this view has been challenged by recent contributions that consider imperfect competition and endogenize important aspects of industrial organization. For example, it has been shown that coordination problems among depositors can emerge independent of competition and that banks operating in monopolistic settings may face higher failure probabilities than those operating in competitive industries. Furthermore, the (few) contributions addressing the optimal regulation in models of imperfect competition suggest that, even if competition hurts stability, its negative effects can be ameliorated by designing financial regulation appropriately.

Despite the growing attention to the issue of competition and stability, additional research seems warranted in several directions. First, the link between market structure and bank fragility is worth further study. Models of runs and panics should be extended to situations of imperfect competition. Second, the effects of imperfect competition on bank risk taking should be examined in richer frameworks, which consider competition on both loan and deposit markets. Third, on the normative side, more research is needed for a better understanding of the effectiveness of regulation.

References

Allen, F., and D. Gale. 1998. Optimal Financial Crises, *Journal of Finance* 53, 1245–1284.
Allen, F., and D. Gale. 2000a. Financial Contagion, *Journal of Political Economy* 108(1), 1–29.
Allen, F., and D. Gale. 2000b. *Comparing Financial Systems*. MIT Press, Cambridge, MA.

Allen, F., and D. Gale. 2004. Competition and Stability, *Journal of Money, Credit and Banking* 36(3), 453–480.

Allen, F., H. Gersbach, J. P. Krahnen, and A. M. Santomero. 2001. Competition Among Banks: Introduction and Conference Overview, *European Finance Review* 5, 1–11.

Bagehot, G. 1873. *London Street: A Description of the Money Market*. H. S. King, London.

Besanko, D., and A. V. Thakor. 1993. Relationship Banking, Deposit Insurance and Bank Portfolio, in C. Mayer and X. Vives (eds.), *Capital Markets and Financial Intermediation*. Cambridge University Press, Cambridge, UK, pp. 292–318.

Bolt, W., and A. F. Tieman. 2004. Banking Competition, Risk, and Regulation, *Scandinavian Journal of Economics* 106(4), 783–804.

Boot, A. W., and S. Greenbaum. 1993. Bank Regulation, Reputation and Rents: Theory and Policy Implications, in C. Mayer and X. Vives (eds.), *Capital Markets and Financial Intermediation*. Cambridge University Press, Cambridge, UK, pp. 262–285.

Bouckaert, J., and H. Degryse. 2004. Softening Competition by Inducing Switching in Credit Markets, *Journal of Industrial Economics* 52, 27–52.

Boyd, J. H., and G. De Nicoló. 2005. The Theory of Bank Risk Taking and Competition Revisited, *Journal of Finance*, forthcoming.

Boyd, J. H., G. De Nicoló, and B. D. Smith. 2004. Crises in Competitive Versus Monopolistic Banking Systems, *Journal of Money, Credit and Banking* 36(3), 487–506.

Boyd, J. H., and M. Gertler. 1993. U.S. Commercial Banking: Trends, Cycles and Policy, NBER macro annual.

Broecker, T. 1990. Creditworthiness Tests and Interbank Competition, *Econometrica* 58, 429–452.

Caminal, R., and C. Matutes. 2002. Market Power and Banking Failures, *International Journal of Industrial Organization* 20(9), 1341–1361.

Canoy, M., M. van Dijk, J. Lemmen, R. de Mooij, and J. Weigand. 2001. Competition and Stability in Banking. CBP document, no. 015, Netherlands Bureau for Economic Policy Analysis, December.

Carletti, E. 1998. Competition, Stability and Regulation, Traduzione Italiana, in M. Polo (ed.), *Industria Bancaria e Concorrenza*. Il Mulino, Bologna, pp. 67–136.

Carletti, E. 2004. The Structure of Bank Relationships, Endogenous Monitoring, and Loan Rates, *Journal of Financial Intermediation* 13, 58–86.

Carletti, E., and P. Hartmann. 2002. Competition and Stability: What's Special About Banking? in P. Mizen (ed.), *Monetary History, Exchange Rates and Financial Markets: Essays in Honour of Charles Goodhart*, vol. 2. Edward Elgar. Cheltenham, UK, pp. 202–229.

Carletti, E., P. Hartmann, and G. Spagnolo. 2003. Bank Mergers, Competition and Liquidity. ECB working paper 292, Frankfurt, Germany.

Cerasi, V., and S. Daltung. 2000. The Optimal Size of a Bank: Costs and Benefits of Diversification, *European Economic Review* 44(9), 1701–1726.

Chari, V. V., and R. Jagannathan. 1988. Banking Panics, Information and Rational Expectations Equilibrium, *Journal of Finance* 43, 749–763.

Cordella, T., and L. Yeyati. 2002. Financial Opening, Deposit Insurance and Risk in a Model of Banking Competition, *European Economic Review* 46, 471–485.

De Bandt, O., and P. Hartmann. 2002. Systemic Risk in Banking: A Survey, in C. A. E. Goodhart and G. Illing (eds.), *Financial Crises, Contagion and the Lender of Last Resort—A Reader*. Oxford University Press, London, pp. 249–298.

Degryse, H. 1996. On the Interaction Between Vertical and Horizontal Product Differentiation: An Application to Banking, *Journal of Industrial Economics* 44(2), 169–182.

Dell'Ariccia, G. 2001. Asymmetric Information and the Structure of the Banking Industry, *European Economic Review* 45, 1957–1980.

Dell'Ariccia, G., E. Friedman, and R. Marquez. 1999. Adverse Selection as Barrier to Entry in the Banking Industry, *RAND Journal of Economics* 30, 515–534.

Diamond, D. W. 1984. Financial Intermediation and Delegated Monitoring, *Review of Economic Studies* 51, 393–414.

Diamond, D. W., and P. H. Dybvig. 1983. Bank Runs, Deposit Insurance and Liquidity, *Journal of Political Economy* 91, 401–419.

Diamond, P. 1971. A Model of Price Adjustment, *Journal of Economic Theory* 3, 156–168.

Edwards, F., and F. Mishkin. 1995. The Decline of Traditional Banking: Implications for Financial Stability and Regulatory Policy, *Federal Reserve Bank of New York Economic Policy Review* 1, 27–45.

Freixas, X., and B. Parigi. 1998. Contagion and Efficiency in Gross and Net Interbank Payment Systems, *Journal of Financial Intermediation* 7, 3–31.

Freixas, X., B. Parigi, and J. C. Rochet. 2000. Systemic Risk, Interbank Relations and Liquidity Provision by the Central Bank, *Journal of Money, Credit and Banking* 32(3), 611–638.

Freixas, X., B. Parigi, and J. C. Rochet. 2004. The Lender of Last Resort: A 21st Century Approach, *Journal of the European Economic Association* 2(6), 1085–1115.

Gale, D., and X. Vives. 2002. Dollarization, Bailouts and the Stability of the Banking System, *Quarterly Journal of Economics* 117(2), 467–502.

Gehrig, T. 1996. Natural Oligopoly and Customer Networks in Intermediated Markets, *International Journal of Industrial Organization* 14(1), 101–118.

Gehrig, T. 1998. Screening, Cross-Border Banking and the Allocation of Credit, *Research in Economics* 52(4), 387–407.

Goldstein, I., and A. Pauzner. 2005. Demand Deposit Contracts and the Probability of Bank Runs, *Journal of Finance* 60, 1293–1328.

González-Maestre, M., and L. M. Granero. 2003. Industrial Loans and Market Structure, *European Economic Review* 47, 841–855.

Goodfriend, M., and R. King. 1988. Financial Deregulation, Monetary Policy and Central Banking, *Federal Reserve Bank of Richmond Economic Review* 74, 3–22.

Goodhart, C. A. E. 1987. Why Do Banks Need a Central Bank? *Oxford Economic Papers* 39, 75–89.

Gorton, G., and A. Winton. 2003. Financial Intermediation, in G. M. Constantinides, M. Harris, and R. Stulz (eds.), *Handbook of Economics and Finance*. North Holland, Amsterdam.

Hauswald, R., and R. Marquez. 2005. Competition and Strategic Information Acquisition in Credit Markets, *Review of Financial Studies*, forthcoming.

Hellmann, T. F., K. Murdock, and J. Stiglitz. 2000. Liberalization, Moral Hazard in Banking and Prudential Regulation: Are Capital Requirements Enough? *American Economic Review* 90(1), 147–165.

Holmstrom, B., and J. Tirole. 1997. Financial Intermediation, Loanable Funds and the Real Sector, *Quarterly Journal of Economics* 112, 663–691.

Jacklin, C. J., and S. Bhattacharya. 1988. Distinguishing Panics and Information-Based Bank Runs: Welfare and Policy, *Journal of Political Economy* 96, 568–592.

Jensen, M., and W. Meckling. 1976. Theory of the Firm: Managerial Behavior, Agency Costs and Ownership Structure, *Journal of Financial Economics* 3, 305–360.

Keeley, M. 1990. Deposit Insurance, Risk and Market Power in Banking, *American Economic Review* 80, 1183–1200.

Koskela, E., and R. Stenbacka. 2000. Is There a Tradeoff Between Bank Competition and Financial Fragility? *Journal of Banking and Finance* 24(12), 1853–1874.

Marquez, R. 2002. Competition, Adverse Selection and Information Dispersion in the Banking Industry, *Review of Financial Studies* 15(3), 901–926.

Matutes, C., and A. J. Padilla. 1994. Shared ATM Networks and Banking Competition, *European Economic Review* 38, 1057–1069.

Matutes, C., and X. Vives. 1996. Competition for Deposits, Fragility and Insurance, *Journal of Financial Intermediation* 5(2), 184–216.

Matutes, C., and X. Vives. 2000. Imperfect Competition, Risk Taking and Regulation in Banking, *European Economic Review* 44(1), 1–34.

McAndrews, J. J., and R. Rob. 1996. Shared Ownership and Pricing of a Network Switch, *International Journal of Industrial Organization* 14(6), 727–745.

Merton, R. 1977. An Analytical Derivation of the Cost of Deposit Insurance and Loan Guarantees, *Journal of Banking and Finance* 1, 3–11.

Nagarajan, S., and C. W. Sealey. 1995. Forbearance, Deposit Insurance Pricing and Incentive Compatible Bank Regulation, *Journal of Banking and Finance* 19(6), 1109–1130.

Parigi, B. 1998. Competition in Banking: A Survey of the Literature, Traduzione Italiana, in M. Polo (ed.), *Industria Bancaria e Concorrenza*. Il Mulino, Bologna, pp. 19–66.

Perotti, E., and J. Suarez. 2002. Last Bank Standing: What Do I Gain If You Fail? *European Economic Review* 46(9), 1599–1622.

Postleweite, A., and X. Vives. 1987. Bank Runs as an Equilibrium Phenomenon, *Journal of Political Economy* 95, 485–491.

Rajan, R. 1992. Insiders and Outsiders: The Choice Between Informed and Arm's-Length Debt, *Journal of Finance* 47, 1367–1400.

Repullo, R. 2004. Capital Requirements, Market Power and Risk Taking in Banking, *Journal of Financial Intermediation* 13, 156–182.

Rey, P., and J. Tirole. 2000. Loyalty and Investment in Cooperatives. Mimeo, University of Toulouse, Toulouse, France.

Riordan, M. 1993. Competition and Bank Performance: A Theoretical Perspective, in C. Mayer and X. Vives (eds.), *Capital Markets and Financial Intermediation*. Cambridge University Press, Cambridge, UK.

Rochet, J. C., and J. Tirole. 1996. Interbank Lending and Systemic Risk, *Journal of Money, Credit and Banking* 28, 733–762.

Rochet, J. C., and J. Tirole. 2002. Cooperation Among Competitors: The Economics of Credit Card Associations, *RAND Journal of Economics* 33(4), 1–22.

Rochet, J. C., and X. Vives. 2004. Coordination Failures and the Lender of Last Resort: Was Bagehot Right After All? *Journal of European Economic Association* 2–6, 1116–1147.

Sáez, L., and X. Shi. 2004. Liquidity Pools, Risk Sharing and Financial Contagion, *Journal of Financial Services Research* 25(1), 5–23.

Salop, S. 1979. Monopolistic Competition with Outside Goods, *Bell Journal of Economics* 10, 141–156.

Schoenmaker, D. 1996. Contagion Risk in Banking. LSE Financial Market Group discussion paper, no. 204, London.

Sharpe, S. 1990. Asymmetric Information, Bank Lending, and Implicit Contracts: A Stylized Model of Customer Relationships, *Journal of Finance* 45, 1069–1087.

Shy, O., and R. Stenbacka. 2004. Market Structure and Risk Taking in the Banking Industry, *Journal of Economics* 82, 249–280.

Smith, B. D. 1984. Private Information, Deposit Interest Rates and the "Stability" of the Banking System, *Journal of Monetary Economics* 14, 293–317.

Stahl, D. O. 1988. Bertrand Competition for Inputs and Walrasian Outcomes, *American Economic Review* 78, 189–201.

Vives, X. 1991. Banking Competition and European Integration, in A. Giovannini and C. Mayer (eds.), *European Financial Intermediation*. Cambridge University Press, Cambridge, pp. 9–31.

Vives, X. 2001. Competition in the Changing World of Banking, *Oxford Review of Economic Policy* 17, 535–554.

Vives, X. 2002. External Discipline and Financial Stability, *European Economic Review* 46, 821–828.

Yanelle, M. O. 1989. The Strategic Analysis of Intermediation, *European Economic Review* 33, 294–301.

Yanelle, M. O. 1997. Banking Competition and Market Efficiency, *Review of Economic Studies* 64, 215–239.

CHAPTER 15

Competition and Regulation in the Banking Sector: A Review of the Empirical Evidence on the Sources of Bank Rents

Hans Degryse
Hogenheuvel College

Steven Ongena
CentER, Tilburg University

We received valuable comments from Jan Bouckaert, Elena Carletti, Michel Dietsch, Frank Verboven, Xavier Vives (the section editor), and participants at the workshop on Relationship Banking in Lille. Degryse holds the TILEC-AFM Chair on Financial regulation, and gratefully acknowledges financial support from FWO-Flanders and the Research Council of the University of Leuven.

Abstract

We combine recent findings from the empirical banking literature with established insights from studies of banking competition and regulation. Motivated by modern theory of financial intermediation, we center our review on the various sources of bank rents. We start with a concise overview and assessment of the different *methodological approaches* taken to address banking competition. We then structure our discussion of the *empirical findings* based on a framework that finds its roots in the different theories of financial intermediation. We categorize and assess the many empirical findings in the literature on competition in banking. We focus on *market structure*, *switching costs*, *location*, and *regulation*.

Our review highlights that more concentrated markets are associated with significant spreads in both deposit markets and loan markets. Fiercer competition lowers spreads but may also spur banks to tie customers in relationships that possibly encompass more fee-related products and cross-selling. Relationships shield rents, providing an explanation for the steep growth in fee income sought by the banks. Relationship duration does not seem uniformly linked to higher loan spreads, though loan fees and the pricing of other products may be important and missing in those studies finding a negative correspondence. The few studies that focus on location as a source for bank rents find that close borrowers pay a higher loan rate. The effects of distance on credit availability, on the other hand, seem small. Though distance effects on branch efficiency seem minimal, distance constrains lending to informationally difficult but sound firms. To cross national borders to engage new customers or to merge with another bank continues to be an adventurous endeavor. Finally, regulation continues to be a fine source of rents for banks in many countries.

1. INTRODUCTION

This review combines recent findings from the empirical banking literature with established insights from studies of banking competition and regulation. Motivated by modern theory of financial intermediation, we center our review on the different sources of bank rents. "Sailing this tack" ensures that we don't replicate the many excellent reviews on financial intermediation that also feature discussions of the various aspects of competition in the banking sector.[1]

We start with a concise overview of the different *methodological approaches* taken to address competition in general and banking in particular. Our review of the traditional and new empirical methods employed in industrial organization (IO) is brief, specifically applied to banking, and mostly illustrative.[2] We first discuss the traditional studies of structure–conduct–performance, bank efficiency, and economies of scale and scope. Then we turn to the new empirical IO approaches taken by Panzar and Rosse (1987), the conjectural variations, structural demand, and other structural models (sunk costs and entry). We highlight the strengths and weaknesses of these different approaches and are naturally drawn to focus on the differences in data requirements and treatment of endogeneity in each method.

Figure 1 shows how research on banking competition has evolved over time. The figure highlights that since the early 1990s, a sea change took place in modeling competition, measuring concentration and conduct, and arriving at fruitful applications. The literature basically abandoned the traditional structure–conduct–performance paradigm stating that banks in less concentrated markets behave less competitively and capture more profits.

The literature has pushed in two directions since. One strand of the literature embarked on modeling market structure as endogenous. We review this part of the literature in Section 2. A second push in the literature intended to capture the "special nature of banking competition" by also looking at nonprice dimensions of banking products. Theoretical work tackled, for example, the availability of credit and the role bank–firm relationships play in overcoming asymmetric-information problems. Consequently, in Sections 3–6 we structure our discussion of the *empirical findings* in the literature based on a framework that finds its roots within the different theories of financial intermediation (see the companion chapter in this volume, Chapter 14, by Carletti, reviewing the theoretical banking competition literature). We categorize and assess the many empirical findings in the literature on competition in banking by distinguishing

[1]See Berger and Udell (1998, 2002), Berger (2003), Bernanke (1993), Bhattacharya and Thakor (1993), Buch (2002), Carletti and Hartmann (2003), Danthine (2001), Danthine et al. (1999), Danthine, Giavazzi, and von Thadden (2001), Davis (1996), Degryse and Ongena (2004), Dermine (2003), Freixas and Rochet (1997), Gertler (1988), Giannetti et al. (2002), Gorton and Winton (2003), Greenbaum (1996), Hellwig (1991), Mayer (1996), Nakamura (1993), Neuberger (1998), Pagano (2002), Scholtens (1993), Swank (1996), Thakor (1995, 1996), Van Damme (1994), and Vives (2001b, 2002), among others.

[2]For general overviews, also see Berger et al. (2004a) and Shaffer (2004). We mention more specific reviews later in the text.

	Early 1990s	Now also
Models	SCP hypothesis	Various models of competition
Measures of concentration	HHI or CRn	Bank size and type (foreign, state) Broader measures of competition
Measures of conduct	Bank prices Bank profitability	Bank efficiency, service quality, risk Firms' access to credit Banking system stability
Empirical models	Static cross section Short-run	Dynamic effects over time of bank consolidation
Data	U.S. MSAs or non-MSA counties	Differently defined U.S. markets Other countries

FIGURE 1 Evolution of research on the impact of bank concentration and competition on bank performance.
The figure displays the changes that took place in the literature investigating the impact of bank concentration and competition on bank performance. The figure contrasts the models, the measures of concentration, the measures of conduct, the empirical models, and the data sources that were used in the early 1990s with those that are used today.
Source: Berger et al. (2004a).

between four possible sources of bank rents: *market structure*, *switching costs* (includes *informational rents*), *location*, and *regulation*.

Market structure consists, for example, of the number of players in the market but may also refer to the existence of alternative providers of finance. *Switching costs* can be the fixed technical costs of switching banks existing in retail deposit markets but can also be the costs of engaging a new bank rooted in pervasive informational asymmetries in business loan markets. *Location* stands for both *distance* and *borders* (see also Degryse and Ongena 2004). We think of distance as pertaining to physical proximity that can be bridged by spending distance-related costs. For a given location of bank and borrower, distance per se is exogenous and bridging it (i.e., the lender visiting the borrower and/or the borrower visiting the lender) may be adequate to reduce informational problems for the lender concerning its decision about granting and pricing the loan. *Borders* introduce a "discontinuity": borders arise endogenously through the actions of the competing lenders or result as an artifact of differences in legal practice and exogenous regulation (Buch 2002).

In addition to differentiating between the sources of rents, we further frame our discussion by distinguishing between *conduct* and *strategy*. Conduct comprises the offering, pricing, and availability of loans and/or deposits, while strategy concerns market presence and structure and deals with the entry, location, composition, and heterogeneity in bank (branches) present in the market.

Four sources of rents and two levels of decision making yield the eight-celled matrix depicted in Figure 2. We assign the relevant empirical findings in the banking literature to one of these eight cells. Within each cell, we group current empirical work by market, that is, *loan*, *deposit*, and *interbank* market, and also discuss findings on the *interplay* between any of these three markets.

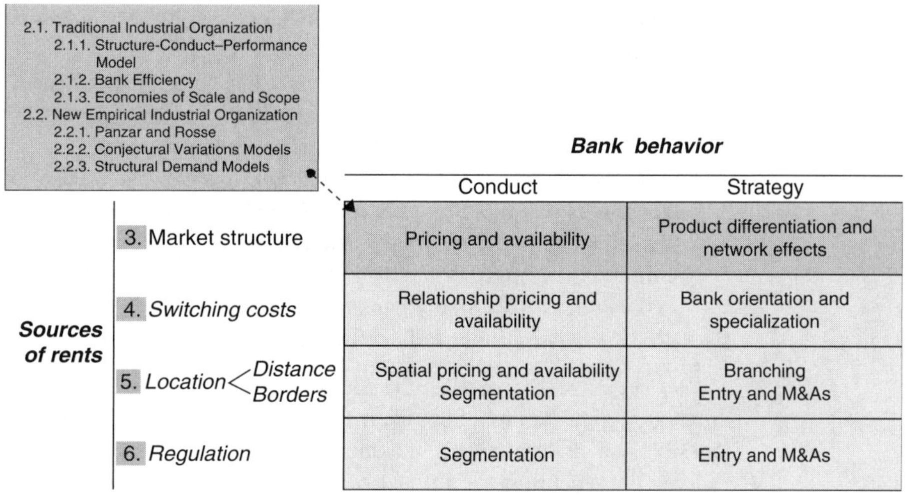

FIGURE 2 Road map of this chapter.
The figure displays the structure of the chapter. Section 2 reviews the six groups of standard methodologies displayed in the box in the upper left corner. Section 3 discusses research employing these standard methodologies on the effects of market structure on bank conduct and strategy. Sections 4–6 discuss findings employing other methodologies on the effects of switching costs, location, and regulation on bank conduct and strategy.

Are these rents large and persistent, hence central to individual bank decision making? Our review demonstrates they may well be. In addition, the special nature of banking and the recurring and ubiquitous fretting by regulators and market participants about banking sector stability and competitiveness indicate why the sources of rents, their magnitude, persistence, and interdependence may well be key in understanding the dynamics in banking sectors around the world.

Economic theory offers conflicting predictions about the relationship between bank rents and fragility. Chapter 14 in this volume, by Carletti, provides a comprehensive overview of this substantial literature, so we will be rather brief here. One side of the literature, the concentration-stability view, argues that there is a positive link between concentration and stability. A more concentrated market structure enhances profits and hence increases the franchise values of the banks. Higher franchise values reduce the banks' incentives to take excessive risk, resulting in lower fragility (in Hellmann, Murdock, and Stiglitz 2000, among many others, for example). On the other hand, the proponents of the concentration-fragility view argue that if more concentration leads to greater market power, then the higher interest rates charged by banks may induce the firms to assume greater risk, resulting in more risky bank portfolios and fragility (in Boyd and De Nicolo 2005, for example).

Many papers ultimately bear on the issue of whether bank rents are important and persistent (we tabulate and evaluate the plethora of findings in Tables 1 to 6 and Figure 3, as shown later in this chapter). By way of preview, we hold the empirical literature dealing with competition in banking to suggest the following (also see Figure 4).

- *Market concentration* results in significant spreads in deposit markets and loan markets. Fiercer competition lowers spreads but may also spur banks to tie customers in rent-shielding relationships that possibly encompass more fee-related products and cross-selling.

- Bank–borrower *relationship duration* does not seem uniformly linked to increasing loan spreads, though loan fees and pricing of other products may be important and missing in those studies finding a negative correspondence.
- The few studies that focus on *location* as a source for bank rents find that close borrowers pay a higher loan rate. The effects of distance on credit availability, on the other hand, seem small. Though distance effects on branch efficiency seem minimal, to cross borders to enter or merge with another bank continues to be a risky endeavor for many banks.
- *Regulation* continues to be a fine source of rents for banks in many countries.

We organize the rest of the chapter as follows. Section 2 reviews the different methodological approaches taken to address banking competition, including, where possible, an assessment of the methods. Section 3 summarizes the many empirical studies documenting the impact of competition on loan conditions and market presence. Section 4 discusses switching costs, Section 5 assesses location as a source of bank rents, and Section 6 deals with the current state of banking regulation and its relation to competition. Section 7 concludes the chapter.

2. MEASURING BANKING COMPETITION

We start with a review of the different methodological approaches that have been employed to investigate banking competition. This empirical research can be subdivided into the more *traditional IO* and the *new empirical IO* (NEIO) approaches. Within the traditional methods, we distinguish between the *structure–conduct–performance* (SCP) analyses, studies of *efficiency*, and studies of *scale and scope economies*. The new empirical IO methods aim to measure the degree of competition directly. We differentiate between the approaches taken by Panzar and Rosse (1987), the *conjectural variations* models, *structural demand* models, and *other structural* models (sunk costs and entry) (see Bresnahan 1989 for a review). The usefulness of the different approaches hinges on data availability and the questions being addressed. The special nature of banking markets prompted the introduction of alternative and complementary approaches. For brevity's sake we do not introduce these approaches in this methodology section (but we will come back to some of these developments in later sections).

2.1. Traditional Industrial Organization

2.1.1. Structure–Conduct–Performance Model

The structure–conduct–performance (SCP) model is originally due to Bain (1956). SCP research was quite popular until the beginning of the 1990s. Figure 1 summarizes the characteristics of SCP research. The SCP hypothesis argues that higher concentration in the banking market causes less competitive bank conduct and leads to higher bank profitability (but lower performance from a social point of view). To test the SCP hypothesis, researchers typically regress a measure of bank performance, such as bank profitability, on a proxy for market concentration, that is, an n-bank concentration ratio or a Herfindahl–Hirschman index (HHI). A representative regression specification is

$$\Pi_{ijt} = \alpha_0 + \alpha_1 CR_{jt} + \sum_k \gamma_k X_{k,ijt} + \varepsilon_{ijt},$$

where Π_{ijt} is a measure of bank i's profitability in banking market j at time t, CR_{jt} is the measure of concentration in market j at time t, and $X_{k,ijt}$ stands for a k-vector of control variables that may affect bank profits (e.g., variables that control for the profitability implications of risk taking). Banks operating in more concentrated markets are able (within the SCP paradigm) to set higher loan rates or lower deposit rates as a result of noncompetitive behavior or collusion. Hence, the SCP hypothesis implies that $\alpha_1 > 0$, that is, that higher market concentration implies more market power and higher bank profits. The market structure itself, however, is assumed to be exogenous.

Numerous studies document, for example, a positive statistical relationship between measures of market concentration and bank profitability. Because Gilbert (1984) and, recently, Berger et al. (2004) have written excellent critical reviews of this early approach, there is no need to make another attempt in this setting (but we will discuss some of the results later in this chapter). However, to illustrate SCP research in general, we briefly discuss Berger and Hannan (1989). While many studies focus on *profitability*-concentration, Berger and Hannan (1989) actually study the *deposit rate*–concentration link. Nevertheless their study is representative of the SCP approach, given their measurement of concentration, reduced-form estimation, and interpretation.

Berger and Hannan (1989) study U.S. retail deposit markets. Their analysis covers 470 banks operating in 195 local banking markets offering six different deposit products. Using quarterly data from 1983:III to 1985:IV, they estimate the following specification:

$$r_{ijt} = \alpha_0 + \alpha_1 CR_{jt} + \sum_k \gamma_k X_{k,ijt} + \varepsilon_{ijt},$$

where r_{ijt} is the interest rate paid on the retail deposit by bank i in banking market j at time t. The SCP hypothesis implies that $\alpha_1 < 0$, that is, that higher market concentration implies more market power and lower deposit rates.[3]

Researchers have employed many different concentration measures to capture noncompetitive behavior. Berger and Hannan use both a three-bank concentration ratio (CR3) and the HHI.[4] Their results overall show a negative impact of market concentration on deposit rates, independent of the concentration measure being used. For

[3]In the *relative* market power hypothesis in Shepherd (1982), only banks with large market shares and well-differentiated products enjoy market power in pricing.

[4]As control variables they include time dummies, the one-year growth in market deposits, the proportion of bank branches in total number of branches of financial institutions (including S&L branches), a wage rate, per capita income, and a Metropolitan Statistical Area dummy variable.

example, moving from the least concentrated market toward the most concentrated market in their sample yields a reduction of about 47–52 basis points on money market deposit accounts.

While the early SCP approach was successful in documenting the importance of market structure for various bank interest rates, Berger et al. (2004) surely present the consensus view when they write, "The [empirical banking] literature has now advanced well past this simple approach." We summarize the notable differences between the SCP and more recent studies both within an SCP framework and beyond in Figure 1.

2.1.2. Studies of Bank Efficiency

The efficiency hypothesis provides an alternative explanation for the positive link between bank profitability and concentration or market share. The efficiency hypothesis (see Demsetz 1973 or Peltzmann 1977) entails that more efficient banks will gain market share. Hence market concentration is driven (endogenously) by bank efficiency. Two types of efficiency can be distinguished (Berger 1995). In an *X-efficiency* narrative, banks with superior management and/or production technologies enjoy higher profits and as a result grow larger market shares. Alternatively, some banks may produce at more *efficient scales* than others, again leading to higher per-unit profits, larger market shares, and higher market concentration.

The positive relationship between structure and performance reported in the SCP literature is spurious in the two versions of the efficiency hypothesis, for both structure and performance are determined by efficiency. Initially, the empirical literature aimed to disentangle the SCP and efficiency hypotheses through the following regression specification:

$$\Pi_{ijt} = \alpha_0 + \alpha_1 CR_{jt} + \alpha_2 \mathrm{MS}_{ijt} + \sum_k \gamma_k X_{k,ijt} + \varepsilon_{ijt},$$

with MS_{ijt} the market share of bank i in market j for period t (the notation for the other variables remains the same as earlier).

SCP implies that $\alpha_1 > 0$, whereas both efficiency hypotheses imply that $\alpha_2 > 0$. Most studies find a positive and statistically significant α_2 but an α_1 close to zero and insignificant. These findings support both efficiency hypotheses; that is, larger market shares go together with higher profitability.

Berger (1995) goes one step further than the standard bank efficiency study and aims to differentiate further between the SCP and efficiency hypotheses by including direct measures of both X-efficiency and scale efficiency into the regression specification (as additional variables in the $X_{k,ijt}$-vector). He argues that after controlling for efficiency, MS_{ijt} captures the relative market power of banks. Berger derives both efficiency measures from the estimation of a translog cost function. X-efficiency is separated from random noise by assuming that X-efficiency differences will persist over time and that random noise does not. The X-efficiency measure for bank i then equals the ratio of the predicted costs for the most efficient bank in the sample to the predicted costs for bank i

for any given vector of outputs and inputs. Berger also computes scale efficiencies on the basis of the translog cost function by taking the ratio of the minimum predicted average costs for bank i to the actual predicted average costs for bank i, given output mix and input prices. By construction both measures range between 0 and 1.

Berger (1995) estimates a cost function using data from 4,800 U.S. banks during the 1980s. Mean scale inefficiencies amount to over 15 percent. Including both computed efficiency measures in the performance equation, which also contains market share and concentration, Berger finds that in 40 of 60 regressions, market share actually retains its positive sign. However, the economic significance of market share seems very small: a 1 percent increase in market share boosts return on assets with less than one-tenth of a percent. Nevertheless, Berger interprets these findings as evidence in favor of the relative market power hypothesis: Market share does represent the market power of larger banks, and their market power may be grounded in advertising, local networks, or business relationships. Results further show that X-efficiency also contributes positively to explaining profits, whereas the results on scale efficiency, on the other hand, are mixed and never economically important.

Studies of operational efficiency of financial institutions are also related to the efficiency hypotheses. Operational efficiency requires (1) optimization of the input mix to avoid excessive input usage (technical X-inefficiency) or suboptimal input allocation (allocative X-inefficiency), and (2) production at an optimal scale and in an optimal mix to achieve economies of scale and scope. For more on X-efficiency studies analyzing financial institutions we refer the reader to surveys by L. Allen and Rai (1996), Molyneux, Altunbas, and Gardener (1996), and Berger and Humphrey (1997) or to recent work by Turati (2001). We turn to economies of scale and scope in the next subsection.

2.1.3. Studies of Economies of Scale and Scope

Studies of economies of scale and scope in banking address the question of whether financial institutions produce the optimal output mix in terms of both size and composition. L. Allen and Rai (1996), for example, estimate economies of scale and scope while controlling for X-efficiency. In particular, they estimate the following equation:

$$\ln(\mathrm{TC}_{it}) = f(y_{it}, p_{it}) + \varepsilon_{it},$$

where TC_{it}, y_{it}, and p_{it} are total costs, outputs, and input prices of bank i at time t, respectively. They consider only one market (hence j is dropped as a subscript). ε_{it} is a composite error term that can be decomposed into statistical noise and X-inefficiency. Allen and Rai pursue two identification strategies. First, they follow the so-called *stochastic cost frontier* approach (see also, for example, Mester 1993), whereby the error term is assumed to consist of random noise and a one-sided inefficiency measure. Second, they estimate a *distribution-free model*, whereby X-efficiency differences are assumed to persist over time while random noise is not.

Allen and Rai estimate a translog cost function with total costs due to labor, capital, and borrowed funds, employing data from 24 countries for the period 1988–1992. They obtain the price of labor by dividing staff expenses by the total number of employees; the price of fixed capital by dividing capital equipment and occupancy expenses by fixed assets; and interest costs by taking total interest expenses over total interest-bearing liabilities.

They distinguish between countries with and without universal banking (i.e., so-called *separated* banking occurs in countries that prohibit the functional integration of commercial and investment banking) and between small and large banks (smaller or larger in asset size than the median bank in each country).

Allen and Rai find evidence of significant scale economies for *small banks* in all countries. Large banks in separated markets, on the other hand, show significant diseconomies of scale amounting to 5 percent of optimal output levels. They do not find any evidence of significant economies of scope.[5] Many other papers present comparable results on economies of scale and scope. Detailed reviews are provided by Berger and Humphrey (1997) and Cavallo and Rossi (2001).

2.2. New Empirical Industrial Organization

A fundamental criticism leveled against the SCP and the efficiency hypotheses relates to the embedded one-way causality from market structure to performance. In other words, most SCP studies do *not* take into account the conduct of the banks in the market and the impact of the performance of the banks on market structure.

New empirical industrial organization (NEIO) circumvents this problem and does not try to infer the degree of competition from "indirect proxies" such as market structure and market shares. Indeed, NEIO aims to infer firms' conduct directly—without even taking into account market structure—employing a variety of alternative methodologies with sometimes substantially different data requirements. We highlight a number of approaches.

2.2.1. Panzar and Rosse

Panzar and Rosse (1987) present a reduced-form approach using industry- or bank-level data to discriminate between perfect competition, monopolistic competition, and monopoly. The Panzar and Rosse methodology investigates the extent to which changes in factor input prices are reflected in equilibrium industry or bank-specific revenues.

[5]Recent work by Vander Vennet (2002) revisits the issue employing a large European dataset. He distinguishes between universal banks, financial conglomerates (institutions that offer the entire range of financial services), and specialized banks. In contrast to previous studies, he nicely allows for heterogeneity in bank types within each country. In line with L. Allen and Rai (1996) he finds large unexploited *scale* economies for the small-specialized banks. But in addition Vander Vennet (2002) also reports unexploited *scope* economies for the smallest specialized banks and for the largest financial conglomerates and universal banks.

In particular, the empirical Panzar and Rosse methodology can be applied to banking by the following revenue equation:

$$\ln(\mathrm{INTR}_{it}) = \alpha + \sum_f \beta_f \ln\left(P_{f,it}\right) + \sum_k \gamma_k X_{k,it} + \varepsilon_{it},$$

where INTR_{it} is the ratio of total interest revenue to total assets of bank i at time t. $P_{f,it}$ and $X_{k,it}$ denote the (price of) factor input f and control variable k, respectively, of bank i at time t. The application may consider one market only or many markets (in which case j should be added as subscript). Moreover, some authors use variables that are not scaled and/or total revenues (including noninterest rate revenues) as left-hand-side variables. The Panzar and Rosse (1987) H-statistic can be computed as follows:

$$H = \sum_f \beta_f.$$

Hence H is the sum of the elasticities of the (scaled) total interest revenue of the banks with respect to their factor input prices. In most studies three different input prices are considered: (1) the *deposit rate*, measured by the ratio of annual interest expenses to total assets; (2) *wages*, measured by the ratio of personnel expenses to total assets; and (3) *price of equipment, or fixed capital*, measured by the ratio of capital expenditures and other expenses to total assets.

A monopoly situation yields an H-statistic that can be negative or zero. What will happen to a monopolist's revenues when all factor prices increase 1 percent? For a monopolist such an increase in factor prices leads to lower revenues (since the price elasticity of demand exceeds 1). In other words, the sum of the elasticities should be negative. Perfect competition implies an H-statistic equal to 1. Indeed, an increase in input prices augments both marginal costs and total revenues to the same extent as the original increase in input prices. Monopolistic competition yields values of H in between zero and 1. Banks will produce more, but less would be optimal in each individual case, leading to an H-statistic in between 0 and 1. It is worth stressing though that the interpretation of competition based on the H-statistic requires that the banking sector be in a long-run equilibrium (Nathan and Neave 1989).

Many studies bring the Panzar and Rosse (1987) methodology to banking. Bikker and Haaf (2002) offer a broad review of the results of many other studies (their Table 4). By far the most comprehensive application to date of the Panzar and Rosse (1987) methodology is a recent paper by Claessens and Laeven (2004). They compute the Panzar and Rosse H-statistic for 50 countries for the period 1994–2001. They exclude countries with less than 20 banks or 50 bank-year observations but still end up with 35,834 bank-year observations in total.

The empirical results by Claessens and Laeven (2004) show that most banking markets are actually characterized by monopolistic competition, with H-statistics ranging between 0.6 and 0.8. In addition, Claessens and Laeven aim to identify factors that determine banking competition across countries by regressing the estimated country H-statistics on a number of country characteristics. They find no evidence of a negative relationship between bank system concentration and H, but they do find that fewer entry and activity restrictions result in higher H-statistics and hence more competition.

The Panzar and Rosse methodology seems well designed to compare competition across banking markets. Data requirements are quite low, and the necessary data are readily available in many countries. And as already discussed, Claessens and Laeven (2004) nicely exploit this attractive feature of the methodology and document that entry barriers, not market structure, determine competition in most banking markets.

2.2.2. Conjectural-Variations Method

Another methodology to infer the degree of competition was introduced by Iwata (1974), Bresnahan (1982), and Lau (1982). This methodology is often referred to as the conjectural-variations approach. It is based on the idea that a bank when choosing its output takes into account the "reaction" of rival banks. The equilibrium oligopoly price is then characterized by the following first-order condition:

$$P(Q,Y;\alpha) + \lambda Q P'(Q,Y;\alpha) = C'(Q,Z;\beta),$$

where P is the market's equilibrium price, $P(Q,Y,\alpha)$ is the market inverse demand function, Q is the market level quantity, and $C'(Q,Z,\beta)$ is the market marginal cost. α and β are vectors of unknown parameters associated with demand and costs, respectively. Y and Z are vectors of variables that affect demand and costs, respectively. λ is the conjectural elasticity of total bank industry output to variation of bank i output; that is,

$$\lambda = \frac{\partial Q}{\partial Q_i}\frac{Q_i}{Q}.$$

In other words, λ is the perceived response of industry output to a change in quantity by bank i (see Vives 1999 for more on this methodology).

One can also compute the conjectural elasticity or conduct parameter:

$$\lambda = \eta(P)\left[\frac{P - \mathrm{MC}}{P}\right],$$

where $\eta(P)$ is the price elasticity of demand and $\mathrm{MC}(= C'(Q,Z;\beta))$ the marginal cost. This implies that λ is the elasticity-adjusted Lerner index. A nice feature of the conjectural-variations model is the possibility of writing different types of competition compactly. It nests the joint profit maximization ($\lambda = 1$), perfect competition ($\lambda = 0$), and the Cournot equilibrium, or zero-conjectural-variations, model ($\lambda = 1/I$, with I the number of firms in the market; that is, the perceived variation of other participants in the industry to changes in bank i's output is zero).[6]

[6]The conjectural variations approach has been subject to a number of important criticisms. Corts (1999), for example, argues that the conduct parameter λ may hinge not only on the firm's static first-order condition, but also on the dynamics, i.e., the incentive compatibility constraints associated with collusion. In the dynamic case, the estimated λ may be biased when the incentive compatibility constraints are a function of demand shocks.

Shaffer (1993) applies this methodology to banking (see also Spiller and Favaro 1984 for an earlier application and Berg and Kim 1994). He approximates the demand function as

$$Q = a_0 + a_1 P + a_2 Y + a_3 PZ + a_4 Z + a_5 PY + a_6 YZ + e,$$

where Z is an additional exogenous variable, such as the price of a substitute for banking services, and e is an error term.[7] He derives the unobserved marginal cost from estimating a translog cost function:

$$\begin{aligned}\ln \mathrm{TC} = {} & \beta_0 + \beta_1 \ln Q + \beta_2 (\ln Q)^2 + \beta_3 \ln W_1 + \beta_4 \ln W_2 + \beta_5 (\ln W_1)^2/2 \\ & + \beta_6 (\ln W_2)^2/2 + \beta_7 \ln W_1 \ln W_2 + \beta_8 \ln Q \ln W_1 + \beta_9 \ln Q \ln W_2,\end{aligned}$$

where TC is total cost, Q is output, and W_1, W_2 are input prices. Assuming that banks are input price takers, the supply relation becomes

$$P = \left[\frac{-\lambda Q}{a_1 + a_3 Z + a_5 Y}\right] + \mathrm{MC}.$$

An important issue is whether banks can be viewed as price takers in the input market. The "price taking" assumption is especially problematic in deposit markets, where banks may enjoy market power. If this is indeed the case, then the estimated degree of market power λ will be overestimated, because some of the "input market power" will wrongly be attributed to market power on the asset side.

Shaffer (1993) applied this specific conjectural-variations method to the Canadian banking sector, using annual data from 1965–1989. The application is attractive because "Canada ... had but 12 chartered banks in 1980 [and] six of these banks have dominated the Canadian financial sector since the 1930s" (p. 50). The low number of players for a long time raised concerns about competition in the Canadian financial sector. And that was (is) also increasingly the case in other parts of the world where bank consolidation gathered momentum.

In his study, Shaffer (1993) follows the so-called intermediation approach of banking. According to this view, banks use labor and deposits to originate loans. The quantity of output Q is the dollar value of assets, and the price P is the interest rate earned on assets. Input prices are the annual wage rate and the deposit rate.[8] The exogenous variables are output and the 3-month Treasury bill rate. The regression results show that λ is not significantly different from zero, implying that the estimates are consistent with perfect competition. Shaffer (1989) actually shows that U.S. banking markets are even more competitive than Cournot competition (λ is again close to zero and not statistically significant).

[7]Shaffer introduces interaction terms between the price P and the exogenous variables Y and Z as well as between these exogenous variables, in order to capture the rotation of the demand curve to identify λ.
[8]In certain specifications, researchers also include the price of capital, since this price may vary over time.

Shaffer's paper focuses on one "aggregate" market; to implement his approach it suffices to have aggregate data. In this aggregate setting λ captures the "average industry" market power. Shaffer's methodology has been extended to allow for heterogeneity within and between different sectors and countries and to include bank heterogeneity. The potential to include bank heterogeneity and to estimate specific λ_{ij} is an attractive feature of the conjectural-variations methodology.

2.2.3. Structural Demand Models

Another strand of the new empirical industrial organization uses characteristics-based demand systems. Dick (2002), for example, estimates a demand model for deposit services following a methodology prevalent in the discrete-choice literature. Consumers choose a particular bank based on prices and bank characteristics. In particular, she starts from a consumer's utility function to derive a demand model and introduces product differentiation through bank heterogeneity. Dick adds a model of firm conduct in order to define the price–cost margin. She defines the relevant banking market as geographically local, be it either a Metropolitan Statistical Area (MSA) or a non-MSA rural county. Her study considers only commercial banks, but it incorporates other financial institutions as providing the outside good in the demand model. Market shares are computed on the basis of dollar deposits at each bank branch in the United States.

Consumers c and banks i populate markets j. The utility a consumer c derives from depositing at bank i stems from both individual and product characteristics. Formally, consumer c derives indirect utility from choosing bank i's services in market j. The consumer utility includes both the mean utility from buying at bank i in market j, δ_{ij}, and a mean zero random disturbance, ε_{cij}:

$$u_{cij} \equiv \delta_{ij} + \varepsilon_{cij} \equiv p^d_{ij}\alpha^d - p^s_{ij}\alpha^s + X_{k,ij}\beta + \xi_i + \varepsilon_{cij}.$$

p^d_{ij} represents the deposit rate paid by bank i in market j; p^s_{ij} are the service charges on deposits by bank i in market j; $X_{k,ij}$ is a vector capturing k observed product characteristics for the (singular) product offered by bank i in market j; ξ_i are the unobserved bank product characteristics. The taste parameters to be estimated are α^d, α^s, and β.

A consumer c chooses a bank i in market j if and only if $u_{cij} \geq u_{crj}$, for $r = 0$ to I_j, with 0 the outside good and I_j the number of banks in market j. Making assumptions on the distribution of ε_{ci} then allows one to obtain a closed-form solution for the market share of bank i. A multinomial logit specification is obtained when assuming that ε_{ci} is an independent and identically distributed (iid) extreme value, yielding bank i's market share s_i in market j:

$$s_i = \frac{\exp(\delta_i)}{\sum_{r=0}^{I_j} \exp(\delta_r)}.$$

Other assumptions may yield a nested logit model.[9]

Dick (2002) estimates this discrete choice model on U.S. data for the period 1993–1999. Her results indicate that consumers respond significantly to changes in deposit rates but to a lesser extent to changes in account fees. Bank characteristics such as geographic diversification, density of the local branch network, and bank age and size increase the attractiveness of a bank to consumers. The computed price elasticities in the logit model are around 6 for the deposit rate but below 1 for the account fees. The implied price–cost margin is 10 percent for the deposit rate and 25 percent for the service fees.

2.2.4. Other Structural Models

Sunk-Cost Models

Sutton (1991) finds that some product markets remain concentrated even when growing in size. Vives (2000) introduces endogenous sunk-costs models to banking. He argues that investments in information technology become more important when markets grow. When the level of these "quality investments" can be chosen by individual banks and a bank's market share is sufficiently responsive to these investments, then a new global marketplace with only a few global players may arise. The outcome of this "competition through endogenous sunk costs" is that the number of "dominant" banks in the market remains approximately the same and that only the number of "fringe" banks will increase in market size.

Dick (2005) investigates a cross-sectional sample of U.S. MSAs. As endogenous sunk costs Dick takes bank branch and automatic teller machine (ATM) networks, advertising, and branding expenses. She defines banks that hold jointly more than 50 percent of market deposits as the dominant banks. All other banks are her fringe banks. She finds there is a lower bound to concentration and that markets remain concentrated across all market sizes. She also reports, in line with Sutton (1991), that the number of dominant banks remains unchanged in market size and is independent of the total number of banks in the MSA. Finally, she finds that the level of bank quality investments increases in market size and that dominant banks offer higher quality than fringe banks.

A further illustration can be found in Dick (2006). In this paper she explores the impact of the Riegle-Neal Interstate Banking and Branching Efficiency Act of 1994 on various aspects of banking markets. In particular, she examines the effects of the act on bank market concentration, structure, and service quality, by comparing markets in 1993 and 1999. She finds that market concentration at the regional level increased dramatically but that market structure at the MSA level, that is, the presence of a few dominant banks, remained unchanged. However, nationwide branching did lead to increases in product quality because consumers can now enjoy expanded branch and ATM network coverage.

[9]The idea in the nested logit model is that consumer tastes are correlated across bank products i. Making a priori groups G, a product i belonging to one of the groups then provides a utility to consumer c equal to $u_{cij} \equiv \delta_{ij} + \varsigma_{cg} + [1-\sigma]\,\varepsilon_{cij}$, where ς_{cg} denotes the group-specific component for individual c.

Structural Models of Entry

A number of recent papers aim to infer competitive behavior from observed industry structure that produces insights about unobserved firm profitability. The underlying idea in these so-called "structural models of entry" is that the entry decisions of potential competitors and the continuation decisions of the incumbent firms occur only when these decisions are actually profitable. The entry decision hinges on the level of fixed costs, the nature of postentry competition, and the (future) entry or continuation decisions of other firms. A crucial advantage of the structural entry models is that detailed data on prices and volumes are not necessary for the analysis. We refer the interested reader to Bresnahan and Reiss (1991, 1994) for more on this methodology. Important starting assumptions are that (1) markets are nonoverlapping, that is, consumers do not buy from banks outside the geographically defined market, and (2) all banks are competing with each other.

Cohen and Mazzeo (2003) bring this structural methodology to banking data. More formally, they let $\Pi_i\,(I; X_k)$ be the expected long-run profits for bank i (or branch i) that chooses to be active in a certain market j. I is the number of banks active in market j (where, for brevity, subscript j is dropped) and X_k captures a k-vector of demand and cost shifters. Not operating in a market yields zero profits. The equilibrium condition then requires that

$$\Pi_i\,(I) \geq 0 > \Pi_i\,(I+1).$$

Entry of one additional bank in the market where I banks are already active implies that competition would become too intense given the market characteristics to generate positive profits. Cohen and Mazzeo (2003), following Bresnahan and Reiss (1991), take the following profit function to capture bank behavior in a symmetric equilibrium in market j:

$$\Pi_j = (\text{Variable profits}_j * \text{Market size}_j) - \text{Entry cost}_j.$$

In this setup, variable profits hinge on the number of banks in the market:

$$\Pi_{I,j} = X_k\beta - \mu_I + \varepsilon_j,$$

with X_k exogenous market factors, μ_I the effect of I competitors on per-bank profits, and ε_j a market-level error term assumed to follow a normal distribution. Given that banks will not enter when having negative profits, the probability of observing I banks becomes

$$P(\Pi_I \geq 0 \text{ and } \Pi_{I+1} < 0) = \Phi\left(\overline{\Pi}_I\right) - \Phi\left(\overline{\Pi}_{I+1}\right),$$

with Φ the cumulative normal density function and $\overline{\Pi}_I = X_k\beta - \mu_I$. The parameters β and μ_I are estimated with an ordered probit model.

Cohen and Mazzeo (2004) extend this basic framework to accommodate for differentiation among different types of competitors: multimarket bank, single-market bank, and thrifts. They do this by allowing for a separate profit function for competitors of each type in each market. Suppose there are two types of banks, A and B. An additional market participant of type A will always decrease profits in the market, but this decrease is assumed to be larger for type A than for type B banks. They exploit data from 1,884 non-MSA areas as of June 2000. Population, per capita income, and the number of farms and nonfarms capture market size. Cohen and Mazzeo focus on the cross-type effects, measuring how banks of one type affect the profits of other-type banks. They find that the effects of same-type banks on these banks' profits are greater than the impact of the other-type institutions. This result suggests that differentiation between bank types is an important feature of banking markets. Moreover, multimarket banks and single-market banks affect each other more than thrifts do.

3. COMPETITION: CONDUCT AND STRATEGY

Section 2 showed that the competition literature has made substantial progress by modeling market structure as endogenous. Furthermore, methodologies have been developed to exploit the rich heterogeneity and different dimensions of the available datasets. However, "it can be argued that the standard competitive paradigm is not appropriate for the banking industry" (Vives 1991, 2001a, F. Allen et al. 2001, and Chapter 14 in this volume, by Carletti). Hence to capture the "special nature of banking competition," we review the available empirical evidence and structure our discussion within a framework that finds its roots within the different theories explaining the existence of financial intermediation.

To categorize and assess the many empirical findings in the literature on competition in banking, we focus (as already indicated) on four possible sources of rents for banks: *market structure*, *switching costs*, *location*, and *regulation*. And for each of these sources we frame our discussion by distinguishing between *conduct* and *strategy*, yielding the eight-celled matrix already introduced in Figure 2. We strive to assign the relevant empirical findings in the banking literature to one of these eight cells. Within each cell, we discuss (where applicable) empirical work on *loan*, *deposit*, and *interbank* markets and also discuss findings on the *interplay* between any of these three markets.

In this section we start discussing the impact of market structure on loan and deposit conditions and then turn to the question of whether market structure determines market presence.

3.1. Market Structure and Conduct

3.1.1. Loan Markets

Local Markets

There is ample empirical work starting from the SCP paradigm investigating the impact of bank market concentration on bank loan rates (see, for example, Gilbert and Zaretsky 2003 for a recent review). Table 1 displays the results of selected studies that regress

TABLE 1 Empirical Work Investigating the Impact of Market Concentration on Loan Rates and Credit Availability

Papers	Data source and years No. observations in regressions Observation type	Concentration in bank markets Geo span: Avg. pop./area Average HHI	Loan rate or credit measure Impact of concentration **Impact of ΔHHI = 0.1, in basis points**
Hannan (1991)	STB ±8,250 U.S. firms	Bank deposits 4,725 HHI: 0.14	Loan rate Mostly positive **−6 to 61*****
Petersen and Rajan (1995)	NSSBF 1987 ±1,400 U.S. small firms	Bank deposits ±2,250,000[a] HHI: 0.17[a]	Most recent loan rate (prime rate on RHS) Mostly negative, especially for young firms 0 yrs: **−170**,** 10 yr: **−3,** 20 yr: **46**[a]
Hannan (1997)	FRB Survey 1993 1,994/7,078 U.S. banks	Bank deposits ±2,500,000[a] HHI: 0.14	Small business floating loan rate Positive **31***** (unsecured), **12***** (secured)
Cavalluzzo, Cavalluzzo, and Wolken (2002)	NSSBF 1993 ±2,600 U.S. small firms	Bank deposits ±2,500,000[a] HHI: 0.14	Most recent interest rate on line of credit No effect, but positive for Hispanics All: **−8**, Hispanic: **124****
Cyrnak and Hannan (1999)	FRB Survey 1996 511/2,059 U.S. banks	Bank deposits ±2,750,000[a] HHI: 0.16	Small business floating loan rate Positive **55***** (unsecured), **21***** (secured)
Sapienza (2002)	Credit register 107,501 Italian firms	Bank loans 600,000[a] HHI: 0.06	Loan rate – Prime rate Positive **59*****
Degryse and Ongena (2005)	One bank 15,044 Belgian small firms	Bank branches 8,632 HHI: 0.17	Loan rate Mostly positive **−4 to 5*****
Kim, Kristiansen, and Vale (2005)	Central Bank of Norway 1,241 Norwegian firms	Bank business credit 250,000[a] HHI: 0.19	Credit line rate −3-month money market rate Insignificantly positive **3**[b]

Fischer and Pfeil (2004)	Survey 1992–1995[s] 5,500 German banks	Bank branches n/a HHI: ±0.20 (West)/±0.30 (East)	Bank interest margins Positive **20***
Claeys and Vander Vennet (2005)	Bankscope 1994–2001 2,279 Banks 36 European countries	Bank loans 30,000,000[a] HHI: 0.10	Bank net interest margin Positive (West)/often negative (East) West: **14***** to **23*****; East: **−110***** to **190*****
Corvoisier and Gropp (2001, 2002)	ECB 2001 ±240 EU countries—years	Bank loans 30,000,000[a] HHI: 0.13	Country-specific loan rate margin Positive **10** to **20****[c] and **50*****[d]
Petersen and Rajan (1994)	NSSBF 1987 ±1,400 U.S. small firms	Bank deposits ±2,250,000[a] HHI: 0.17[a]	% Total debt/assets Positive **36*****
Petersen and Rajan (1995)	NSSBF 1987 ±1,400 U.S. small firms	Bank deposits ±2,250,000[a] HHI: 0.17[a]	% Trade credit paid before due date Positive, especially for young firms **140***** to **280*****,[p] ≤10 yr: **175**** to **740**,[r] >10 yr: **150*** to **0**[r]
Cavalluzzo, Cavalluzzo, and Wolken (2002)	NSSBF 1993 ±2,600 U.S. small firms	Bank deposits ±2,500,000[a] HHI: 0.14	Various credit availability measures No effect overall but significant positive effects for African Americans and females
Zarutskie (2004)	SICTF 1987–1998 ±250,000 U.S. firms—years	Bank deposits ±2,250,000[a] HHI: 0.19	% Outside debt/assets Positive **19** to **77*****
Scott and Dunkelberg (2001), Scott (2003)	CBSB 1995 ±2,000 U.S. small firms	Bank deposits ±2,500,000[a] HHI: 0.19	No credit denial Positive **+** to **+++**[e]

Continued

TABLE 1 *Continued*

Papers	Data source and years No. observations in regressions Observation type	Concentration in bank markets Geo span: Avg. pop./area Average HHI	Loan rate or credit measure Impact of concentration **Impact of ΔHHI = 0.1, in basis points**
Angelini, Di Salvo, and Ferri (1998)	Survey 1995 2,232 Italian small firms	Bank loan Median: <10,000 HHI: 0.42	Perceived access to credit No effect **0**
Shikimi (2005)	JADE 2000–2002 28,622 Japanese small firms	Credit N/a CR3: 0.44	% debt/assets No effect **0**

The table lists the main findings of selected empirical work investigating the impact of bank market concentration on bank loan rates and measures of bank credit availability. The measure of concentration in all studies is either the three-bank concentration ratio (CR3) or the Herfindahl–Hirschman index (HHI), which can be calculated by squaring the market share of each bank competing in the market and then summing the resulting numbers ($0 < HHI < 1$).

[a]Authors' calculations or estimates.

[b]For HHI increasing from 0.09 to 0.19.

[c]Their models 2 and 5.

CBSB: Credit, Banks and Small Business Survey collected by the National Federation of Independent Business.

[d]Coefficients in regressions for short-term loans in their models 3, 5, and 6.

[e]Based on the COMPETITION variable, not on the HHICTY.

JADE: Japanese accounts and data on enterprises. NSSBF: National Survey of Small Business Finance.

[p]Linear approximation using their Table IV coefficients and assuming that the mean HHI below 0.1 equals 0.05 and above 0.18 equals 0.59.

[r]Linear approximation assuming that the mean HHI below 0.1 equals 0.05 and above 0.18 equals 0.59, based on means and medians in their Table V.

SBIF: Chilean Supervisory Agency of Banks and Financial Institutions. SICTF: Statistics of Income Corporate Tax Files. STB: Federal Reserve's Survey of the Terms of Bank lending to business. yr: years.

0: Included in the specifications but not significant.

*** Significant at 1%, ** at 5%, * at 10%.

Source: Degryse and Ongena (2003).

bank loan rates on a Herfindahl–Hirschman index (HHI) of market concentration (we do not report any studies that employ *number of competitors* as a measure; these studies typically find no impact on the loan rate). Studies employ both U.S. and international data.

Though mostly positive, the magnitude of the impact of the concentration index on loan rates varies widely. To benchmark the results, we calculate the impact of a change in the HHI of 0.10, which according to widely accepted cutoffs could mark the transition from a competitive market (HHI < 0.10) to a concentrated market (HHI > 0.18). Illustrating the wide range of results, we note that recent studies, for example, indicate that a ΔHHI = 0.1 increases the loan rate by between 21*** and 55*** basis points (bp) in the United States (Cyrnak and Hannan 1999) and 59*** bp in Italy (Sapienza 2002),[10] but only 3 bp in Norway (Kim, Kristiansen, and Vale 2005) and –4 to 5*** bp in Belgium (Degryse and Ongena 2005). However, it remains difficult to compare results across specifications, banking markets, periods, and HHI measures that are alternatively based on loans, deposits, or branches and that vary widely (across studies) in geographical span (Morgan 2002). Indeed a serious related problem of interpretation is that local market concentration is often negatively correlated with market size.

In their seminal paper, Petersen and Rajan (1995) investigate the effects of competition between banks not only on the loan rate but also on the availability of bank credit to firms. Petersen and Rajan model how especially firms with uncertain future cash flows are negatively affected by competition between banks. Banks may be unwilling to invest in relationships by incurring initial loan losses that may never be recouped in the future (as firms can later on obtain a low loan rate in a competitive banking or financial market).

Petersen and Rajan provide evidence on the impact of concentration on both loan rates and availability of credit. They document that young firms—having uncertain future cash flows—in more concentrated banking markets obtain substantially lower loan rates than firms in more competitive banking markets. The loan rates decreases by more than 150** basis points for de novo firms if the HHI increases by 0.10. They also document somewhat easier access to bank credit in more concentrated markets (see the second row in our Table 1), but even for young firms the effects seem modest economically speaking and statistically not always significant. An increase of 0.1 in the HHI roughly augments the percentage trade credit paid before the due date by between 1.5*** and 3*** percent across all firms and by around 2* to 8 percent for young firms.

The effects of banking competition on the firms' capital structure decisions seem even more subdued. For example, Petersen and Rajan (1994) document that a ΔHHI = 0.1 increases firm percent total debt/assets by only 0.36 percent, while a recent paper by Zarutskie (2004) shows an increase in percent outside debt/assets by only between 0.19 and 0.77*** percent. Similarly, Cavalluzzo, Cavalluzzo, and Wolken (2002) find no significant aggregate effect of an increase in HHI on a variety of credit availability measures (though they do find significant positive effects for small firms owned by

[10] As in the tables, we star the coefficients to indicate their significance levels: *** significant at 1%, ** significant at 5%, and * significant at 10%.

African Americans or females), while Angelini, Di Salvo, and Ferri (1998) record no economically significant effect on perceived access to credit for a sample of small Italian firms.

Multimarket

The presence of banks operating in several geographical areas or several industries—multimarket banks—may impact local loan rate conditions. The influence on the local loan rates depends on whether the multimarket banks apply uniform or discriminatory pricing across local markets and on the structure of each local banking market (including the importance of the multimarket banks present in that market).

Radecki (1998), for example, reports that most banks set uniform rates on auto loans and home equity loans *within* a U.S. state. Loan rates, however, can differ *across* states. Berger, Rosen, and Udell (2002) address the issue of whether in the United States large regional or nationwide banks compete in different ways than small, local institutions. Their study is motivated by the observation that U.S. banking consolidation over the period 1984–1998 had only a minor impact on "local" HHI but a major effect on bank size because many "market-extension" M&As, that is, mergers between banks operating in different local markets, took place. Berger, Rosen, and Udell (2002) document that loan rates to small and medium enterprises (SMEs) are lower in markets with a large-bank presence. They find that interest rate spreads charged in markets with a large-bank presence are 35* bp lower than in other markets.

A key paper by Sapienza (2002) investigates the impact of Italian bank M&As on interest rates to continuing borrowers. She can actually compare the impact of "in-market" versus "out-of-market" bank mergers on loan rates. Interestingly enough she finds that "in-market" mergers decrease loan rates but only if the acquired bank has a sufficiently low local market share. The decrease in loan rates is much less important for "out-of-market" mergers.

Panetta, Schivardi, and Shum (2004) study the link between firm risk, measured by bank credit ratings, and interest rates. They find that the risk–rate schedule becomes steeper after bank mergers (i.e., the merged bank prices risk sharper) and attribute this result to the informational benefits arising from bank mergers. Important in this context is their finding that the risk–rate schedules are even steeper for "out-of-market" than for "in-market" mergers, suggesting that "out-of-market" mergers yield even more informational benefits to the banks than "in-market" mergers. Finally, a recent paper by Berger, Hasan, and Klapper (2004) reports cross-country evidence on the importance of small, domestic, community banks for local economic activity in general. They find that higher shares of community banks in local bank markets are associated with more overall bank lending, faster GDP growth, and higher SME employment.

3.1.2. Deposit Markets

Local Markets

There is also a long line of research, at least going back to Berger and Hannan (1989), investigating the impact of bank market concentration on bank deposit rates. Table 2

TABLE 2 Empirical Work Investigating the Impact of Market Concentration on Deposit Rates

Papers	Data source and years No. observations in regressions Observation type	Concentration in markets Geo span: avg. pop./area Average CR3 or HHI	Deposit rate measure Impact of concentration on deposit rate **Impact of ΔCR3 = 0.3 or ΔHHI = 0.1[b] in BP**
Berger and Hannan (1989)	FRB Survey 1985 4,047 U.S. banks	Bank deposits 2,000,000[a] CR3: n/a	Bank rates **−18*****(demand), **−12***** to **−1** (time), **−19***** (savings)
Calem and Carlino (1991)	FRB Survey 1985 444/466 U.S. banks	Bank deposits 2,000,000[a] CR3: 0.45	Bank rates **−17***** (time), **−5** (savings)
Neumark and Sharpe (1992)	FRB Survey 1983–1987 49 months, 255 banks U.S. banks—years	Bank deposits 2,000,000[a] HHI: 0.08	Bank deposit rates **−26***** (time), **−27***** (savings)
Sharpe (1997)	FRB Survey 1983–1987 49 months, 222 banks U.S. banks—years	Bank deposits 2,000,000[a] HHI: 0.08	Bank deposit rates Restricted market: **−19***** (time), **−20***** (savings) Liberalized market: **−7***** (time), **−4** (savings)
Neuberger and Zimmerman (1990)	California 1984–87 3,415 Californian NOW accounts	Bank deposits n/a CR3: 0.63	NOW account rate **−5*****
Hannan (1997)	FRB Survey 1993 ±330 U.S. Banks	Bank deposits 2,500,000[a] HHI: 0.14	Bank rates **−5** (demand), **−5** (time), **−6*** (savings)[1]
Radecki (1998)	FRB Survey 1996 197 U.S. Banks	Bank deposits MSA = 2,650,000; state = 10,240,000 HHI: MSA = 0.17; State = 0.11	Bank rates MSA = mixed; state = negative MSA[2] = **10*** (demand), **3** (time), **5** (savings) State[3] = **−4** (demand), **−6** (time), **−33***** (savings)
Hannan and Prager (2004)	Reports of C&I 1996/1999 6,141/5,209 U.S. banks—years	Bank deposits 96 = 1,034,000; 99 = 1,092,000 HHI: 1996 = 0.23; 1999 = 0.22	Bank rates 96[1] = **−4***** (demand), **−3***** (time), **−1** (savings) 99[1] = **−4*** (demand), **−7***** (time), **−4***** (savings)

Continued

TABLE 2 *Continued*

Papers	Data source and years No. observations in regressions Observation type	Concentration in markets Geo span: avg. pop./area Average CR3 or HHI	Deposit rate measure Impact of concentration on deposit rate **Impact of ΔCR3 = 0.3 or ΔHHI = 0.1[b] in BP**
Heitfield and Prager (2004)	Reports C&I 1988, 92, 96, 99 ±11,500/10,250/8,250/7,250 U.S. banks—years	Bank deposits ±1,000,000 HHI: ±0.22	Bank rates 1999 Local = **−1***** (demand), **−0** (savings) 1999 State = **−23*** (demand), **−8***** (savings)
Rosen (2003)	Reports C&I 1988–2000 89,166 U.S. banks—years	Bank deposits ±1,000,000 HHI: 0.35	Bank rates Urban: **−8***** (demand), **−7***** (savings) Rural: **−1** (demand), **1** (savings)
Fischer and Pfeil (2004)	Survey 1992–1995[5] 5,943/5,873 German banks	Bank branches n/a HHI: ±0.20 (west)/±0.30 (east)	Bank interest margins **9** (time), **−2**** (savings)
Corvoisier and Gropp (2002)	ECB 2001 246 EU country—years	Bank deposits 30,000,000[a] HHI: 0.13	Country-specific deposit rate margins[c] **−70***** (demand), **50***** (time), **140***** (savings)[6]

The table lists the main findings of empirical work investigating the impact of bank market concentration on bank deposit rates. The measure of concentration in all studies is either the three-bank concentration ratio (CR3) or the Herfindahl–Hirschman index (HHI), which can be calculated by squaring the market share of each bank competing in the market and then summing the resulting numbers ($0 < HHI < 1$).

[a]Authors' calculations.

[b]Assuming equal market shares for the three largest banks and market shares of the other atomistic banks that can be disregarded, an increase in the CR3 from 0.1 to 0.4 increases the HHI from 0.003 to 0.053, while an increase in the CR3 from 0.3 to 0.6 increases the HHI from 0.03 to 0.12. BP: basis points.

[c]The margin in their paper is the money market rate minus the deposit rate. For consistency, we multiply all results by −1.

C&I: Condition and income; MSA: Metropolitan Statistical Area.

[1236] Their models 1, 2, 3, or 6.

***Significant at 1%, **at 5%, *at 10%.

Source: Fischer (2001).

summarizes the findings of this literature. Studies employ both the three-bank concentration ratio (CR3) and the HHI as concentration measures. Overall most papers find a negative impact of an increase in concentration on time and savings deposit rates, but, as with the loan rate studies, the effects vary across samples and specifications. We take a change in CR3 by 0.3 to be approximately comparable to a change in HHI by 0.1. The effect of the changes in either the CR3 or the HHI on U.S. time and savings deposits rates ranges then from –26*** to –1 and from –27*** to +5 basis points, respectively. Rates on demand deposits seem less affected by market concentration, with estimates varying from –18*** to +10* bp. But there is evidence of more downward price rigidity and upward price flexibility in demand deposit rates than in time deposit rates, especially in more concentrated markets (Neumark and Sharpe 1992).

More recent studies typically find smaller negative effects for all deposit products, possibly reflecting the widening geographical scope of banking competition (Radecki 1998) and the ensuing difficulties delineating the relevant local market (Heitfield 1999, Biehl 2002). Geographical markets in the United States for demand deposits may be currently "smaller than statewide" but not necessarily "local" (Heitfield and Prager 2004), suggesting that both local and statewide measures of concentration and multimarket contact variables should be included in the analysis. Heitfield and Prager (2004) finds that the coefficients on "state" concentration measures became larger in absolute value over time than the coefficients on the "local" measures, in particular for demand deposits. In 1999, for example, a 0.1 change in the local HHI affected the NOW deposit rate by only –1* bp, while a similar change in the state HHI decreased the rate by 23*** bp.

A recent paper by Corvoisier and Gropp (2002) studies European national banking markets, in geographical and economic span often comparable to U.S. states. They find a substantial effect of –70*** bp on demand deposit rates (corresponding to an increase in HHI of 0.1) but a surprising increase of +50*** and +140*** bp for time and savings deposits rates, respectively. Corvoisier and Gropp argue that local markets are more relevant for demand deposits, whereas customers may shop around for time and savings deposits. Shopping around would imply an increase in contestability, breaking the expected link between HHI and this deposit rate. Demand deposit rates are often posted within a national market after being determined at the banks' headquarters, where competition (or lack thereof) may be perceived to be nationwide. On the other hand, for the time and savings deposit markets, the coefficient on HHI may actually pick up bank efficiency (even though various bank cost measures are included) or the effect of bank mergers caused by an unobservable increase in contestability. In any case, this study again underlines the methodological difficulties in interpreting the reduced-form coefficients in interest rate–market concentration studies.

Multimarket

A number of papers explore the impact of multimarket banks on deposit pricing. Radecki (1998) provides evidence of uniform pricing across branches of banks operating throughout an entire U.S. state or large regions of a state. He interprets this finding as evidence in favor of an increase of the geographic reach of deposit markets over time.

Heitfield (1999) shows, however, that uniform pricing is only practiced by multimarket banks that operate statewide but not by single-market banks that operate in one MSA only. Hence "charging the same deposit rate" may result from a deliberate decision of uniform pricing and not mechanically from a geographical expansion of market boundaries. Heitfield and Prager (2004) further fine-tune the previous findings by exploring heterogeneity in the pricing of several deposit products. They report that the geographic scope of the markets for NOW accounts remains local but that the scope of money market deposit accounts and savings accounts markets has broadened over time.

Hannan and Prager (2004) explore the competitive impact of multimarket banks on local deposit conditions, using U.S. data for 1996 and 1999. They document that multimarket banks offer lower deposit rates than single-market banks operating in the same market. Moreover, a greater presence of multimarket banks relaxes competition because single-market banks offer lower deposit rates. On the other hand, Calem and Nakamura (1998) argue that multimarket banks mitigate localized market power in rural areas[11] but that multimarket branching reduces competition in already-competitive (urban) markets. Recent work by Barros (1999) reasons that the presence of banks across markets may lead to local interest-rate dispersion, without implying different conduct of banks. Collusive behavior among banks could impact the degree of price dispersion. His empirical findings for Portugal provide strong support for Nash behavior, but, given the small sample size, collusion cannot be rejected. Using a similar setup, collusive behavior among Spanish banks in the loan market in the early 1990s can also not be rejected (Jaumandreu and Lorences 2002).

What about the impact of M&As? Focarelli and Panetta (2003) document that "in-market" mergers hurt depositors in the short run due to lower deposit rates—a drop of 17*** bp. The short-run impact of "out-of-market" mergers, however, is negligible. In the long run, depositors gain from both "in-market" and "out-of-market" mergers because deposit rates increase by 14*** and 12*** bp, respectively, compared to the premerger level. Hence, in the long run, efficiency gains seem to dominate over the market power effect of bank mergers, leading to more favorable deposit rates for consumers.

3.1.3. Interplay Between Markets

The links between the different banking markets also have been recently empirically investigated.[12] Park and Pennacchi (2003), for example, discuss the impact of the entry by large multimarket banks on competition in *both* loan and deposit markets. Park and Pennacchi (2003) posit that multimarket banks may enjoy a funding advantage in the wholesale market. As a result they establish that a higher presence of the multimarket banks promotes competition in loan markets but harms competition in deposit markets

[11] Rosen (2003) finds that having more large banks in a market generally increases deposit rates at all banks but also increases their sensitivity to changes in the concentration ratio.

[12] Kashyap, Rajan, and Stein (2002), for example, link lending and deposit taking at the bank level, while Berg and Kim (1998) connect behavior in retail and corporate banking markets.

if these multimarket banks have funding advantages. Hence, their paper nicely shows that the impact of "size–structure" could be asymmetric across markets.

3.2. Market Structure and Strategy: Product Differentiation and Network Effects

Empirical work measuring product differentiation and network effects in banking is still rather limited, despite the fact that theoretical models are already highly developed and rich in testable hypotheses (see Chapter 14 in this volume, by Carletti). Within the area of product differentiation, we can distinguish between studies dealing with *vertical* and *horizontal* differentiation.

Kim, Kristiansen, and Vale (2005), for example, study whether banks can pursue strategies in order to vertically differentiate their products and services. If customers are willing to pay for banks enjoying a higher reputation, then banks may invest in variables increasing their reputation. They consider a bank's capital ratio, its ability to avoid loan losses, bank size, and branch networks as possible strategies. The empirical question addressed is whether borrowers are actually willing to pay for "quality" characteristics. If so, a strategy of vertical differentiation would allow banks to charge higher loan rates and to soften competition.

Using panel data of Norwegian banks over the period 1993–1998, Kim, Kristiansen, and Vale (2005) find empirical support only for the ability to avoid loan losses, measured by the ratio of loss provisions. A doubling of the loss provisions relative to the mean implies a reduction in the interest rate spread of about 56*** bp. Other evidence for willingness to pay for bank reputation is provided in Billett, Flannery, and Garfinkel (1995). They find that announcements of banks loans granted by lenders with higher credit ratings are associated with larger abnormal returns on the borrowing firm shares.

Another element leading to vertical differentiation stems from network effects (see Chapter 14 in this volume, by Carletti). For example, depositors exhibit a higher willingness to pay for banks with a larger ATM network. The size of this network also hinges on the degree to which depositors can use rivals' ATMs. The ATM market has exhibited a varying degree of compatibility between networks. Over time, networks in several countries moved from incompatibility toward compatibility. However, as documented in Knittel and Stango (2004), new ATM charges to rivals' clients reintroduces some incompatibility. We expect that such rival charges have a larger impact on depositors of banks owning few ATMs.

Knittel and Stango (2004) evaluate the effect of the introduction of such surcharge fees on deposit account prices, measured as the ratio of annual income associated with deposit accounts over deposit account balances. Indeed they find that (1) a doubling of the number of ATMs in the local market increases banks' deposit account prices by 5–10 percent and that (2) incompatibility strengthens the link between banks'own ATMs and deposit account prices and weakens the link between rivals' ATMs and deposit account prices.

ATMs also have aspects of horizontal differentiation, for customers prefer banks with conveniently located ATMs. Banks also compete for clients by establishing branches and locating them optimally. Optimal location allows the banks to increase market share and to avoid perfect competition because clients may have preferences over locations. In other words, branching provides local market power.

Some papers start from an equilibrium situation, taking branching decisions as exogenously given, and address whether there is evidence for localized competition. Barros (1999), for example, documents for Portugal that the volume of deposits banks attract hinges on the network of branches. He also finds indirect evidence for the importance of transportation costs: Urban markets have higher transportation costs than rural markets. In Degryse and Ongena (2005) we find evidence of spatial price discrimination in Belgium: Borrowers located close to the loan-granting branch and far from competing branches pay significantly higher loan rates.

Other papers also endogenize bank branching decisions. When deciding on the location of their branches, banks take into account all existing networks and their expectations of rivals' future location and network choices. The papers endogenizing branching decisions incorporate features of both horizontal and vertical product differentiation, because *all* consumers may have a preference for larger networks but clients may disagree on the optimal location of specific branches. Using panel data from Norwegian banks, Kim and Vale (2001) report that a bank-specific branch network positively affects market shares in loan markets but does not affect the total size of loan markets. On the other hand, Kim, Kristiansen, and Vale (2005) find no evidence for the size of a bank branch network as a quality variable for borrowers in the Norwegian banking market.

Product differentiation also dictates just how far different types of financial institutions are perceived as substitutes. As indicated in the methodology section, Cohen and Mazzeo (2004) present results for thrifts, multimarket banks, and single-market banks operating in the United States. They find that competition is more intense between financial institutions of the same type than between institutions of differing types. This suggests that there is substantial differentiation between types of financial institutions.

4. SWITCHING COSTS

Switching costs for bank customers are a source of considerable rents for banks. There are fixed technical costs of switching banks (Klemperer 1995) that may be relevant in all deposit markets. Think about the shoe leather and other search costs a depositor incurs when looking for another bank branch, the opportunity costs of her time for opening the new account, transferring the funds, and closing the old account. Such costs are mostly exogenous to both the depositor's and the banks' behavior, but they allow the incumbent bank to lower deposit rates to captured customers. Switching costs are endogenous when banks charge leaving customers for closing accounts.

In loan markets it is often conjectured that, in addition to these fixed technical costs of changing banks, there are informational switching costs. Borrowers will face these costs when considering a switch, because the current "inside" financier is more informed about borrower quality and recent repayment behavior. Such switching costs

TABLE 3 Event Studies on the Impact of Loan, Distress, and Merger Announcements on Borrowing Firm Stock Prices.

Paper	Country Period	Avg. (Med.) Size, in mil. $	Announcement (events) Affected borrowers	**2-Day mean AR, in %** Cross-sectional results (difference?)
Mikkelson and Partch (1986)	United States 1972–82	n/a	Credit agreement (155)	**0.89*** **
James (1987)	United States 1974–83	L: 675 (212)	Bank loan agreement (80)	**1.93*** **
Lummer and McConnell (1989)	United States 1976–86	n/a	Bank credit agreement (728) Renewals (357)/new (371)	**0.61*** ** 1.24***/–0.01 (n/a)
Slovin, Johnson, and Glascock (1992)	United States 1980–86	E: 281 (68) For initiations	Loan agreement (273) Renewals (124)/initiations (149) Small firms (156)/large firms (117)	**1.30*** ** 1.55***/1.09*** (n/a) 1.92***/0.48 (n/a)
Best and Zhang (1993)	United States 1977–89	n/a	Bank credit agreement (491) Renewals (304)/new (187) Noisy renewals[a] (156)/accurate new[a] (187)	**0.32** ** 1.97**/0.26 (no) 0.60**/–0.05 (*)
Billett, Flannery, and Garfinkel (1995)	United States 1980–89	E: 316 (79)	Loan (626) Renewals (187)/new banks (51) Banks' rating: AAA (78)/<BAA (29)	**0.68*** ** 1.09***/0.64* (no) 0.63***/–0.57 (no)
Fields et al. (2006)	United States 1980–2003	E: 738 (136) BA: 1,216 (212)	Bank loan renewal (594) 1980–1989 (160)/1990–1999 (291)	**0.48* ** 0.93**/0.50 (n/a)
Aintablian and Roberts (2000)	Canada 1988–95	n/a	Corporate loan (137) Renewals (35)/new (69)	**1.22*** ** 1.26***/0.62 *** (*)[a]
Andre, Mathieu, and Zhang (2001)	Canada 1982–95	n/a	Bank credit agreement (122) Lines of credit <1988 (13)/>1988 (33) Term loans <1988 (22)/>1988 (54)	**2.27*** ** 4.82/0.32 1.14/3.30***
Boscaljon and Ho (2005)	Asia 1991–2002	n/a	Commercial bank loans (128) Renewals (72)/new (56) Before crisis (57)/after crisis (71) HK (44)/SK (39)/Taiwan (25)/ Thai (20)	**1.25*** ** 1.23 ***/1.27*** (no) 0.13/2.14*** 1.63***/2.61***/0.21/–0.94
Fery et al. (2003)	Australia 1983–99	n/a	Signed credit agreements (196) Published: single (18)/multiple (22) Nonpublished: single (56)/multiple (89)	**0.38* ** 1.62**/0.89 0.02/0.25
Slovin, Sushka, and Polonchek (1993)	United States 1984	E: 1,085 (692)	Continental Illinois distress (1) 29 firms (direct lender/lead manager)	**–4.16*** ** Firms with low leverage and other banks
Ongena, Smith, and Michalsen (2003)	Norway 1988–91	S: 400	Bank distress (6) 217 main bank firms	**–1.7** ** Equity-issuing firms with undrawn credit (no)

may provide the informed-relationship bank with extra potential to extract rents.[13] Of course, the existence of switching costs may fan competition to draw customers, so some of these rents will be competed away ex ante.

Given their elusive character, we first review the evidence on *existence*, *magnitude*, and *determinants* of switching costs in loan, deposit, and interbank markets. We highlight loan renewal and bank distress event studies suggesting their existence and review studies assessing the magnitudes and determinants involved. In a second and a third step, we discuss the impact of switching costs on bank *conduct* and *strategy* in the different markets.

4.1. Evidence on the Existence, Magnitude, and Determinants of Switching Costs

4.1.1. Loan Markets

Evidence on the existence, the magnitude, and the determinants of switching costs in credit markets comes from a variety of studies. Analyses of firm value following bank loan, distress, and merger announcements provide indirect evidence on the existence and magnitude of the informational problem and resulting switching costs facing credit market participants. Studies of the duration of bank–firm relationships probe for the determinants of the switching costs.

Existence of Switching Costs

Loan Renewal Announcements Motivated by Fama's (1985) conjectures regarding the uniqueness of bank loans and following work by Mikkelson and Partch (1986), James (1987) studies the average stock-price reaction of firms that publicly announce a bank loan agreement or renewal.[14] The results in the seminal paper by James (1987) are key in our current thinking of the role banks play in credit markets. The second row of Table 3 summarizes his findings. James finds that bank loan announcements are associated with *positive* and statistically significant stock-price reactions that equal 193*** bp in a two-day window, while announcements of privately placed and public issues of debt experience zero or negative stock-price reactions. This result holds independent of the type of loan, the default risk, and the size of the borrower. The positive stock-price reaction supports the Fama (1985) argument that a bank loan provides accreditation for a firm's ability to generate a certain level of cash flows in the future.

Results in James (1987) spawned numerous other event studies. The upper part of Table 3 exhibits key results. To concentrate on the possible existence of switching costs, we highlight Lummer and McConnell (1989). They divide bank loan announcements into first-time loan initiations and follow-up loan renewals. Because loan initiations are loans to new customers while renewals are loans to established customers, the

[13] See Berger and Udell (2002), Boot (2000), and Ongena and Smith (2000a). Other reviews on various aspects of bank relationships include Berlin (1996), Bornheim and Herbeck (1998), Degryse and Ongena (2002), Eber (1996), Elyasiani and Goldberg (2004), Holland (1994), Ongena (1999), Rivaud-Danset (1996), and Samolyk (1997).

[14] Our discussion is partly based on Ongena and Smith (2000a).

Karceski, Ongena, and Smith (2005)	Norway 1983–2000	S: ±500	Completed bank mergers (22) 342 acquirers, 78 targets, 1,515 rivals	**0.29, −0.76**, 0.06** Firms with relationship with acquiring banks
Chiou (1999)	Japan 1997–98	A: 3,913 (1110)	Daiwa Bank scandal (1) 32 Main bank firms	**−0.98***** Large firms and with no main bank
Brewer et al. (2003)	Japan 1997–98	A: 1,450	Three bank failures (3) 327	**0.17; −1.32***; −0.49**** Firms with alternative financing (no)
Miyajima and Yafeh (2003)	Japan 1995–2001	A: 2,293[a]	Actions (11), downgrading (5), mergers (3) 9,250 + 4,016 + 2,606	**n/a; −3.1[n/a]; 0** Large, profitable, tech, low debt, bonds (no)
Hwan Shin, Fraser, and Kolari (2003)	Japan	S: 790 (716)[a]	3-Way alliance (1) 570	**−0.31***** Main bank, high debt, profitable
Bae, Kang, and Lim (2002)	S. Korea 1997–98	BA: 404	Negative bank news (113) 486	**−1.26***** Healthy, unconstrained firms
Sohn (2002)	S. Korea 1998	A: 324[a]	Closure/transfer of five banks (1) 118	**−4.85***** Firms with no prior relationship
Djankov, Jindra, and Klapper (2005)	Indonesia, Thailand, S. Korea 1997–99	n/a	Closures (52) Foreign sales (209) Domestic mergers (92) Nationalizations (94)	**−3.94***** **−1.05*** **−1.27** **3.14***** Large firms (no)

The table lists the main findings of event studies tracing the impact of bank loan, bank distress, or bank merger announcements on the stock prices of borrowing firms. The first column provides the paper citation. The second column reports the country affiliation of the affected firms and the period during which the announcements were made. The average (median) *firm size* column lists both the size measure and the average (median) size of the firms in millions of US$. The fourth column reports on the first row the type of announcement and the number of events and on the second row the number of affected borrowers. The final column provides on the first row a two-day mean abnormal return, in most cases over either [−1, 0] or [0, 1] interval, in percent. If two-day CARs are not reported over either interval, the shortest reported interval including either one of these two-day periods is used. The second row provides a breakdown of the announcements in key categories reported in the paper (in parentheses we report whether the differences in mean abnormal returns between reported groups of announcements are significantly different from zero) or key results from any cross-sectional exercises reported in the paper as an answer to the question "Which firms suffer the least?" Between brackets we report if abnormal returns differ between affected and unaffected firms (i.e., firms not borrowing from the affected bank at the time of the announcement).

A: assets.

[a]Authors' calculations.

Avg.: average.

[b]Their Table 1b does not specify which firm-size measure is used (the use of market equity is possibly implied in the text).

BA: book assets. E: market equity. HK: Hong Kong. L: total liabilities. Med.: median. Mil: million. n/a: not available. S: sales. Thai: Thailand.

*** Significant at 1%, ** significant at 5%, * significant at 10%.

Source: Ongena and Smith (2000a).

difference in stock-price reactions between the two categories should act as a measure of the value of an established relationship. Consistent with this argument, Lummer and McConnell (1989) find that stock-price reactions to bank loan announcements are driven by renewals. The abnormal returns in the event period associated with announcements of initiations are not statistically different from zero, while renewals are positive and statistically significant.

The results in Lummer and McConnell (1989), however, have been difficult to duplicate.[15] Slovin, Johnson, and Glascock (1992), Best and Zhang (1993), and Billett, Flannery, and Garfinkel (1995), for example, document positive and significant price reactions to both initiation and renewal announcements, but they find little difference in price reactions between the two categories. Best and Zhang (1993) do find that price reactions to renewal announcements are significantly larger than initiations when analyst uncertainty about the loan customer is high. In their study, Billett, Flannery, and Garfinkel (1995) argue that the Lummer and McConnell (1989) results may be driven by their system for classifying loans into initiation and renewal categories. Overall, the evidence on the differential wealth effects of loan renewals versus loan initiations is inconclusive.

In addition, the entire literature on loan announcements has come under increasing scrutiny. First, the literature may be suffused with insidious reporting issues (James and Smith 2000) because both firms and newspaper editors may push only "positive news" stories; Australian evidence by Fery et al. (2003) is suggestive in this regard. Second, it is not clear that initiations or renewals in the United States still resulted in excessive returns during the 1990s (Fields et al. 2006, Andre, Mathieu, and Zhang 2001), raising some doubt about the robustness of the initial findings. Finally, there may be substantial differences across countries in loan announcement returns (Boscaljon and Ho 2005).

Bank Distress and Merger Announcements Another important event study containing evidence on the value of bank relationships and hence the existence of switching costs is an innovative paper by Slovin, Sushka, and Polonchek (1993). They examine the influence of the 1984 impending insolvency of Continental Illinois on the stock price of firms with an ongoing lending relationship with that bank. Slovin, Sushka, and Polonchek (1993) report an average abnormal two-day return of −420*** bp around the insolvency announcement and an abnormal increase of 200** bp on the announcement of the FDIC rescue. They argue that such large price changes are estimates of the potential value tied directly to this specific firm–bank relationship. The existence of these quasi-rents implies that borrowers are bank stakeholders.

Many event studies have sought to replicate and extend the initial results by Slovin, Sushka, and Polonchek (1993). We summarize the results in the lower part of Table 3. All studies focus on countries other than the United States, and many trace the impact on the borrowers' stock prices of bank events other than distress, such as scandals, transfers, and bank mergers, that could also be unsettling to the borrower–bank relationship.

[15] With the exception of Aintablian and Roberts (2000): They use Canadian bank loan announcements. Their reported statistics imply that mean excess returns on new loans and renewals differ at a 10% level of significance.

Most studies find smaller and seemingly more temporary effects than the initial −4.2*** percent documented by Slovin, Sushka, and Polonchek (1993). In addition, the three studies that actually check whether returns differ between firms related to the affected banks and all other firms find that the differences are not significant (Ongena, Smith and Michalsen 2003, Brewer et al. 2003, Miyajima and Yafeh 2003). Of course, the different results across the various studies may stem from heterogeneity in the value of the specific bank relationships that are being considered.

Magnitude of Switching Costs

Kim, Kliger, and Vale (2003) provide the first estimates of switching costs faced by the average bank borrower. Kim, Kliger, and Vale (2003) develop a novel structural estimation technique to extract switching cost estimates. They employ Norwegian loan market share data for the period 1988–1996. Their findings imply average annualized bank rents of roughly 4 percent of the banks' marginal cost of funding. Switching costs drop to almost zero for customers of large banks. In Degryse and Ongena (2005) we study borrowers of a large Belgian bank in 1997. The increase of the loan rate for the average bank–firm relationship points to annual "information rents" of less than 2 percent of the bank's marginal cost of funding. This estimate may actually constitute a lower bound in case the resolution of uncertainty for the inside bank results in actuarially better setting of loan rates over time. However, at this point it should also be noted that empirical results in the literature on relationship duration and loan rates yields rather mixed results. We return extensively to this issue in Section 4.2. Finally, and in a very different setting, Yasuda (2005) finds that preexisting relationships with firms issuing corporate bonds in the United States allow the underwriting banks to charge 1–4 percent (of the issue size) extra.

Research has recently started to focus on the magnitude and determinants of borrower switching rates, a natural corollary to the contours of borrowers' switching costs (Karceski, Ongena, and Smith 2005). Table 4 lists estimates of the length of bank–firm relationships culled from a variety of studies. Comparisons of estimates present a challenge because (1) relationship definitions may differ across studies and (2) censoring issues are often left unrecognized, since in numerous cases the end of the sample period or firm age prevents researchers from observing the entire relationship spell.

Nevertheless, two broad patterns seem to emerge. First, there is substantial variation in duration of relationships across countries. For example, small U.S. and Belgian firms report relationships to last between 5 and 10 years on average, while small Italian and French firms report duration of 15 years or more. Second, there are also substantial differences between firms within the same country, often related to firm size. As an illustration, consider small and large firms in Germany. Small firms report durations between 5 and 12 years; large firms report more than 22 years' duration.

The pattern in relationship duration across countries is reminiscent of the cross-border variation in the number of relationships recently documented by Ongena and Smith (2000b). They find that, roughly speaking, the number of relationships increases "going south," from 1 in northern Europe to 15 in southern Europe. While theoretical work is continuing to explore this surprising cross-border variation in the

TABLE 4 Duration of Bank Relationships

Paper	Country	Year(s)	Sample size	Firm size	Duration, in years
Bodenhorn (2003)	United States	1855	2,616	Small firms	4.1
Petersen and Rajan (1995)	United States	1987	3,404	Employees: 26 (5)	10.8
Blackwell and Winters (1997)	United States	1988	174	Book assets: 13.5	9.01
Cole (1998)	United States	1993	5,356	Book assets: 1.63	7.03
Brick and Palia (2006)	United States	1993	766	Sales: 11.1 (5)	8.5 (6)
Scott (2004)	United States	2001	1,380	Employees: 16.6 (6)	4.5 (4.5)
Angelini, Di Salvo, and Ferri (1998)	Italy	1995	1,858	Employees: 10.3	14.0
Guiso (2003), Herrera and Minetti (2007)	Italy	1997	4,267	Employees: 67.7	16.1
Castelli, Dwyer Jr., and Hasan (2006)	Italy	1998–2000	10,764	Employees: 80 (30)[a]	17.6 (15)
Hernandez-Canovas and Martinez-Solano (2006)	Spain	1999	153	Sales: 10.0 (4.1)	16.8 (15)
Farinha and Santos (2002)	Portugal	1980–1996	1,471	Employees: 46.0	(4.7)
Ziane (2003)	France	2001	244	Employees: 32 (22)	14.4 (10)
Degryse and Van Cayseele (2000)	Belgium	1997	17,776 loans	Employees: (1)	7.82
De Bodt, Lobez, and Statnik (2005)	Belgium (F)	2001	296	Total assets: 0.03	11.7 (15)[a]
Elsas and Krahnen (1998)	Germany	1992–1996	125/year	Sales: (30–150)	22.2
Harhoff and Körting (1998)	Germany	1997	994	Employees: ±40 (10)	±12
Lehmann and Neuberger (2001), Lehmann, Neuberger, and Rathke (2004)	Germany	1997	357	SMEs	4.8[ac]
Thomsen (1999)	Denmark	1900–1995	948	Assets: 125	15.5
Ongena and Smith (2001)	Norway	1979–1995	111/year	Market equity: 150	(15.8–18.1)

Sjögren (1994)	Sweden	1916–1947	50	Largest firms	>20 (5–29)
Zineldin (1995)	Sweden	1994	179	Employees: (<49)	(>5)
Horiuchi, Packer, and Fukuda (1988)	Japan	1962–1972	479	Largest firms	(21)
Gan (2003)	Japan	1984–1993	11,393	All publicly listed	6.85 (7)
Uchida, Udell, and Watanabe (2006)	Japan	2002	1,863	SMEs	31.9
Menkhoff and Suwanaporn (2003), Menkhoff, Neuberger, and Suwanaporn (2006)	Thailand	1992–1996	555	Assets: 880 (10)	7.96
Alem (2003)	Argentina	1998–1999	4,158	80% corporations	8
Bebczuk (2004)	Argentina	1999	143	Sales: 3.9	19.6

The table lists the reported duration of bank relationships. The first column provides the *paper* citation. The second column reports the *country* affiliation of the related firms and the third column the sample *year(s)*. *Sample size* is the number of firms (unless indicated otherwise). The *average (median) firm size* column lists both the size measure and the average (median) size of the firms in millions of US$ or number of employees. The final column provides the average (median) *duration* of firm–bank relationships, in years.

[a] Authors' calculation.

number of relationships (for example, Carletti 2004, Carletti, Cerasi, and Daltung 2004, Detragiache, Garella, and Guiso 2000, von Rheinbaben and Ruckes 2004, Volpin 2001), there is hardly any theoretical or empirical work linking cross-border variation in the number of bank relationships with duration.

Determinants of Switching Costs

Recent papers, however, started to explore the impact of *relationship*, *firm*, *bank*, and *market*-specific characteristics on the duration of bank–firm relationships within a country. Table 5 summarizes the findings. Take duration itself. Both Ongena and Smith (2001) and Farinha and Santos (2002) find that the estimated hazard functions display positive duration dependence, indicating that the likelihood a firm replaces a relationship increases in duration or, alternatively and as symbolized in the table, that the continuation of a relationship is negatively affected by duration itself. The number of bank relationships the firm maintains also negatively influences the length of a relationship. Hence both duration and the number of (other) bank relationships decrease borrowers' reticence to drop a relationship. An increase in duration may result in fiercer holdup, making switching more attractive. Alternatively, relationship continuation and/or multiplicity may impart a good repayment record to competing banks, thereby lowering borrowers' switching costs.

Most studies find that young, small, high-growth, intangible, constrained, or highly leveraged firms switch banks faster ceteris paribus. But there are some notable exceptions. Interestingly enough, the direction in which particular firm variables affect switching rates changes sign going "north to south" in Europe, not unlike the increase that is observed in the number and duration of relationships. For example, small firms exhibit severe relationships more easily than large firms in Norway, Denmark, and Belgium, at the same rate in the UK and Germany, but at a slower rate in Portugal and Italy. Hence in Norway small firms may churn bilateral relationships, while in Italy small firms cherish their multiple relationships. On the other hand, in Norway large firms nurture a few steady relationships; while in Italy large firms continue to juggle, and drop, (too) many relationships.

A few studies also include bank and market characteristics. Larger and to a lesser extent more liquid and efficient banks seem to retain borrowers longer. Berger et al. (2005) show it is the number of branches that matters for borrower retention, not bank asset size. The latter variable is actually negatively related to duration. Borrowers of target banks in a merger are often dropped. Market characteristics seem mostly to have no effect on the drop rate.

4.1.2. Deposit Markets

There are only a few studies on the magnitude and determinants of customer switching cost in bank deposit markets. Shy (2002), for example, illustrates the application of a methodology similar to Kim, that of Kliger, and Vale (2003) by estimating depositor switching costs for four banks in Finland in 1997. He finds that costs are approximately

TABLE 5 Determinants of the Duration of Bank Relationships

	Paper	BMPRS	SCS	BDSS	S	HM	FS	DMM	HK	HPW	T	OS	KOS	UUW
	Country	US	US	US	IT	IT	PT	BE	DE	UK	DK	NO	NO	JP
	Years	1993	1993	86–01	89–95	2001	80–96	97–03	1997	1996	00–95	79–95	79–00	2002
	Obs	1,131	935	401,699	50,000	3,494	1,471	600,000	1,228	±120	948	383	598	1,863
	Model	IV	Logit	Logit	Probit	OLS	TVD	Logit	Logit	Logit	Logit	D	TVD	IV
	Dependent	Length	Drop	Choose^s	Drop	Length	Hazard	Drop	Drop	Drop	Drop	Hazard	Hazard	Length
Relation	Duration		0				↔↔↔				+/↔↔↔	↔↔↔	↔↔↔	
	Switches						↔↔↔							
	Number							↔↔↔				↔↔↔	↔	
	Scope		+++	+++										
	Trust		+++											
Firm	Age	+++			0	+++/↔↔	0	+++	0	↔	++	+		+++/↔↔
	Size	+	0	+++	↔↔↔	0	↔↔↔	+++	0	0	++	+++	+++	+++
	Growth		0				↔↔↔			0		↔		
	Cash flow					+++	++							+++
	Intangibles						0		↔	↔				
	Profitability			+++	+++		0	+++		0		↔↔	0	+++
	Fixed assets					+++								
	Constrained								↔	↔↔↔				
	Leverage	0			↔↔↔		0	+++		++		↔↔↔		↔↔↔
	Bank debt						↔↔↔							
	Urban								0					
	Audit/certified					↔↔↔								0
	Major Owner					↔↔↔								

Continued

TABLE 5 *Continued*

	Paper	BMPRS	SCS	BDSS	S	HM	FS	DMM	HK	HPW	T	OS	KOS	UUW
Bank	Age	+++					0							
	Size	↔↔↔	0				0	+++	0		++	++		0
	No. branches	+++				↔↔								0
	Growth						0							
	Liquidity						0	+++						
	Profitability		↔↔↔		T: +++	0	0	↔↔↔						
	Efficiency				T: ↔↔↔			+++		++				
	Risk				T: ↔↔↔			↔↔↔				0		
	Merged				T: ↔↔↔			T: ↔↔↔				0	T: ↔↔↔	
	State												+	
Market	Local banks			+++			0							
	Concentration	+	0			++	0		0					0

The table summarizes the results from studies on the determinants of the duration of bank relationships. Positive signs indicate that an increase in the indicated variable corresponds to a significantly longer duration of the bank relationships.
The first column lists the variable names. The other columns contain the results from the respective papers.
The *paper* citations on the first row are abbreviated to conserve space: BMPRS: Berger et al. (2005), SCS: Saparito, Chen, and Sapienza (2004), BDSS: Bharath et al. (2006), S: Sapienza (2002), HM: Herrera and Minetti (2007), FS: Farinha and Santos (2002), DMM: Degryse, Masschelein, and Mitchell (2006), HK: Harhoff and Körting (1998), HPW: Howorth, Peel, and Wilson (2003), T: Thomsen (1999), OS: Ongena and Smith (2001), KOS: Karceski, Ongena, and Smith (2005), and UUW: Uchida, Udell, and Watanabe (2006).
The second row lists *Country* codes: US: United States, IT: Italy, PT: Portugal, BE: Belgium, DE: Germany, DK Denmark, NO: Norway, JP: Japan.
The third row lists the sample *years*.
The fourth row reports the number of *observations* (Obs).
The next row lists whether the employed empirical *model* is an instrumental variable (IV), logit, probit, duration (D), or time-varying duration (TVD) model.
The sixth row indicates the specific *dependent* variable used in the paper.
Other rows list the sign and significance levels of the coefficients on the independent variables as reported in the paper. Significance levels are based on all reported exercises and the authors' assessment.
A: acquiring banks. [s] the signs of the independent variables are reversed to facilitate comparisons. T: target banks. 0: Included in the specifications but not significant.
+++ Positive and significant at 1%, ++ at 5%, + at 10%.
↔↔↔ Negative and significant at 1%, ↔↔ at 5%, ↔ at 10%.

0, 10, and 11 percent of the value of deposits for the smallest to largest commercial bank and up to 20 percent for a large Finnish bank providing many government services.

Kiser (2002) focuses on the length of household deposit relationships with their banks and on the determinants of their switching costs. She uses U.S. Survey data for 1999. Median U.S. household tenure at banks equals 10 years. The geographical stability of the household and the quality of the customer service offered at the bank are key factors in determining whether or not customers stay with the bank. Switching costs seem nonmonotonic in income: Higher income as well as more educated households and lower income as well as minority households switch less often. Hence, the opportunity cost of time for the first group and the information available to households in the other group may play a role in determining household switching.

4.1.3. Interbank Market

While the existence and importance of relationships between borrowers/depositors and banks have been widely documented and discussed by bankers and academics alike, recent preliminary evidence by Cocco, Gomes, and Martins (2003) shows that even in the anonymous and highly liquid interbank market, relationships between banks may play a role in overcoming informational problems and in the provision of insurance. Especially smaller, less profitable, risky banks that are subject to frequent liquidity shocks seem to rely on relationships.

4.1.4. Interplay Between Markets

Interesting questions arise about how switching costs in one market may be linked to behavior in another market. *Switching costs in deposit markets* may have consequences for *behavior in loan markets*. Berlin and Mester (1999), for example, tie bank funding to orientation (relationship versus transactional banking). In particular, Berlin and Mester show that banks with better access to rate-inelastic core deposits engage in more loan rate smoothing (relationship lending) than banks that lack such access. In other words, banks enjoying market power in core deposits can insulate their borrowers from adverse credit shocks by loan rate smoothing.

4.2. Switching Costs and Conditions: Relationships as a Source of Bank Rents?

Are relationships a source of bank rents? If so, how do banks extract rents? Do relationship banks simply charge higher loan rates or also impose more stringent loan conditions? Are banks applying the "bargain, then ripoff" strategy? That is, are they first competing fiercely for new customers and then charging above marginal cost prices (e.g., Sharpe 1990)? To commence answering these questions, many studies have run reduced-form regressions of the cost of credit for the borrowing firms on *duration* and/or *number* of bank–firm relationships (studies typically control for a variety of firm, bank, and market characteristics). Some studies also include proxies for the *scope* of the relationship, such as the number of other bank products the borrower obtains from the relationship bank.

Panel A in Table 6 lays out the many findings.[16] The results seem rather mixed. Most U.S. studies document that loan rates actually decrease by around 3** to 9** bp per relationship year, while many European studies find that loan rates are either unaffected or increase by around 1*** to 10*** bp per year (though there may even be regional variation within countries in this respect). The impact of the number of relationships on the loan rate seems equally mixed. Most U.S. studies find loan rates increase by 10*** to 30*** bp per additional bank, while many European studies (again with a few exceptions) report that loan rates are either unaffected or decrease by around 1*** to 10*** bp per extra bank. A few U.S. studies find no or a small negative effect of scope, and the same seems true in Europe, with a few exceptions (that document large positive or negative coefficients).

Overall it seems that only European banks extract rents from their relationship borrowers (i.e., those with long relationships and few banks) through higher loan rates, while U.S. banks actually charge lower rates. What could account for these remarkably divergent results? We offer a number of tentative explanations. First, the set and definition of control variables that are included differ from study to study. However, the overlap seems large enough to make results comparable. Second, the definition of what constitutes a bank–firm relationship diverges across studies. For example, in some cases frequent past borrowing defines a relationship; in other cases firms or banks assess and report whether or not a relationship existed.

Third, the cost of credit, the dependent variable, differs across studies. Often spreads are used, in some cases reference interest rates are included on the right-hand side. Following Berger and Udell (1995), some studies consider only lines of credit, while others include all types of corporate loans. However, a priori it may seem unclear why banks would extract rents from relationship customers through only one class of loans. Loan fees, on the other hand, are potentially a thornier problem. Fees are not relevant in most European studies. For example, there are no fees on lines of credit in Italy or small loans in Belgium. But fees may play a role in the United States, though most studies do not adjust for it (Hao 2003).

Fourth, the composition of the pool of borrowers may change over (relationship) time as banks get to know their customers better and favor certain types. Controls in cross-sectional studies may fail to capture these dynamic effects and differences in the average (median) duration across studies and therefore may complicate comparisons.

Finally, most studies implicitly assume the loan collateral decision to be taken either independently or sequentially after the loan-granting decision but before the determination of the loan rate. Under these assumptions, most studies find that relationship borrowers pledge less collateral; that is, an increase in the duration of the relationship increases the probability that no collateral is pledged, while the number of

[16]There is only indirect evidence of the impact of relationship duration on the deposit rate. Sharpe (1997), for example, shows that the amount of household migration, in most cases probably resulting in the severance of a deposit relationship, has a positive effect on the level of deposit interest rates. The magnitude of this effect in some cases depends on the degree of market concentration.

TABLE 6 Duration, Number, and Scope of Bank Relationships and the Cost/Availability of Credit and Collateral

Panel A	Paper	Source Year	Observations/ firm size	Cost of credit, in basis points	Duration $\Delta = 1$ year	Number $\Delta = 1$ bank	Scope $\Delta = 1$
United States	Bodenhorn (2003)	1 Bank 1855	2,616/s	Loan rate—A1 commercial paper	−2.9**		
	Petersen and Rajan (1994)	NSSBF 1987	1,389/s	Most recent loan rate (prime on RHS)	3.7	32.1***	0.8^{che}
	Berger and Udell (1995)	NSSBF 1987	371/s	Line of credit—prime rate	−9.2**		
	Uzzi (1999)	NSSBF 1987	2,226/s	Most recent loan rate (prime on RHS)	−1.3**		−4.2**
	Blackwell and Winters (1997)	6 Banks 1988	174/s	Revolver—prime rate	−0.9		0.0
	Berger, Rosen, and Udell (2002)	NSSBF 1993	520/s	Line of credit—prime rate	−5.3**		
	Brick and Palia (2006)	NSSBF 1993	766/s	Line of credit—prime rate	−2.4**	−18.8	
	Hao (2003)	LPC 1988–99	948/l	Facility coupon + fees—LIBOR		8.0^{***lf}	
	Bharath et al. (2006)	LPC 1986–01	9,709/l	Facility coupon + fees—LIBOR			-6.6^{***a}
Canada	Mallett and Sen (2001)	CFIB 1997	2,409/s	Loan interest rate	0		0
Italy	Conigliani, Ferri, and Generale (1997)	CCR 1992	33,808/m	Loan interest rate	-14.1^{***cl}	−2***	
	Ferri and Messori (2000)	CCR 1992	33,808/m	Loan interest rate	nw: −19.1* ne: $-13.5^{n/a}$ so: $9.6^{n/a}$	nw: −0.3 ne: $0.7^{n/a}$ so: -13.6^{*a}	
	D' Auria, Foglia, and Reedtz (1999)	CCR 1987–94	120,000/l	Loan interest rate—Treasury bill rate	2.5***	−1.3***	
	Angelini Di Salvo, and Ferri (1998)	Survey 1995	2,232/s	Line of credit	ccb: −1.8 oth: 6.4***	−10.0***	
	Cosci and Meliciani (2002)	1 Bank 1997	393/s	Interest payments—total debt		−0.2	
	Pozzolo (2004)	CCR 1992–96	52,359	Loan interest rate	43***		
Spain	Hernandez-Canovas and Martinez-Solano (2006)	Survey 99–00	184/s	Avg. cost of bank finance—interbank	5*	60*	8.5
France	Ziane (2003)	Survey 2001	244/s	Credit interest rate	−20.2	51.4	20.1*
Belgium	Degryse and Van Cayseele (2000)	1 Bank 1997	17,429/s	Loan yield till next revision	7.5***		−39.3***
	Degryse and Ongena (2005)	1 Bank 1997	15,044/s	Loan yield till next revision	11.0***		−40.7***

Continued

TABLE 6 *Continued*

Panel A	Paper	Source Year	Observations/ firm size	Cost of credit, in basis points	Duration Δ = 1 year	Number Δ = 1 bank	Scope Δ = 1
Germany	Harhoff and Körting (1998)	Survey 1997	994/s	Line of credit	1.7	−0.2	
	Elsas and Krahnen (1998)	5 banks 1996	353/ml	Line of credit—FIBOR	0.3		−4.8
	Machauer and Weber (1998)	5 banks 1996	353/ml	Line of credit—interbank overnight	−0.3	0.0	1.3
	Ewert, Schenk, and Szczesny (2000)	5 banks 1996	682/ml	Line of credit—FIBOR	0.7***	0.6	−22.1
	Lehmann and Neuberger (2001)	Survey 1997	318/sm	Loan rate—refinancing rate	1.8[a]		−5.6
	Lehmann, Neuberger, and Rathke (2004)	Survey 1997	W: 267/sm	Loan rate—refinancing rate	w: 1.6		w: −2.0
			E: 67/sm		e: −0.5		e: 20.3
Finland	Peltoniemi (2004)	1 bank 95–01	279/s	Effective loan rate	−12***		6.6[al]
		1 Nonbank	576/s		−2*		
Japan	Weinstein and Yafeh (1998)	JDB 1977–86	6,836/l	Nonbond interest expenses—debt			53***
	Miarka (1999)	1985–1998	1,288/sm	Interest rate on borrowing			−22.2***
	Shikimi (2005)	JADA 00–02	78,695	Loan rate–prime rate		18***	
	Kano et al. (2006)	SFE 2002	1,960	Maximum loan rate < 1 yr	No / −3.5***[s]		No / 4**[as]
Thailand	Menkhoff and Suwanaporn (2003)	9 banks 92–96	416/l	Loan rate—min. overdraft rate	−0.9	−6.5**	−22.0**
Argentina	Streb et al. (2002)	CDSF 1999	8,548	Highest overdraft interest rate		6.9***	−69.0***
Chile	Repetto, Rodriguez, and Valdes (2002)	SBIF 1990–98	20,000	Interest rate paid	−65.1**[cl]	−47.0**	−26.5
57 countries	Qian (2005)	LPC 1980–04	3,608–l	Drawn all-in spread		−28.7***[a]	

Panel B	Paper	Source Year	Observations/ firm size	No Collateral, in %	Duration Δ = 1 year	Number Δ = 1 bank	Scope Δ = 1
United States	Bodenhorn (2003)	1 bank 1855	2,616/s	No guarantors	2.6**		
	Berger and Udell (1995)	NSSBF 1987	371/s	No collateral	12.1**		
	Chakraborty and Hu (2006)	NSSBF 1993	983/s	No collateral L/C	2*[a]	−1.2[a]	−7.4[al]
			649/s	No collateral non L/C	−1[a]	−1.4[a]	3**[al]
	Hao (2003)	LPC 1988–99	948/l	Not secured		1[lf]	
	Roberts and Siddiqi (2004)	LPC 1988–03?	218/l	No collateral		−0.0[a]	

Italy	Pozzolo (2004)	CCR 1992–96	52,359	No real guarantees	−17***	5***	
				No personal guarantees	14***	1***	
France	Ziane (2003)	Survey 2001	244/s	No collateral	8.3	−2.3**	−2.8*
Belgium	Degryse and Van Cayseele (2000)	1 bank 1997	17,429/s	No collateral	4.2*		−64.5***
Germany	Harhoff and Körting (1998)	Survey 1997	994/s	No collateral	7.0**	−10.0**	
	Machauer and Weber (1998)	5 banks 1996	353/ml	Unsecured % of credit line	−0.1*	0.6**	−9.4***
	Elsas and Krahnen (2002)	5 banks 1996	472/ml	No collateral			−17.6**
	Lehmann and Neuberger (2001)	Survey 1997	318/sm	No collateral	−0.8[a]		−4.1***
	Lehmann, Neuberger, and Rathke (2004)	Survey 1997	W: 267/sm	No collateral	w: − 1.6***		w: − 15***
			E: 67/sm		e:5.2**		e:−12.9**
Finland	Peltoniemi (2004)	1 bank 95–01	562/s	No collateral	−2[a]		50***[a1]
Japan	Kano et al. (2006)	SFE 2002	1,960	No collateral	–*		–**
Thailand	Menkhoff, Neuberger, and Suwanaporn (2006)	9 banks 92–96	4161	No collateral	1	23**	−33**

Panel C	Paper	Source Year	Observations/ firm size	Availability of credit, in %	Duration $\Delta = 1$ year	Number $\Delta = 1$ bank	Scope $\Delta = 1$
United States	Petersen and Rajan (1994)	NSSBF 1987	1,389/s	% Trade credit paid on time	2.3**	−1.9**	
	Uzzi (1999)	NSSBF 1987	2,226/s	Credit accessed	−0.1		0.5
	Cole (1998)	NSSBF 1993	2,007/s	Extension of credit	5.0***	−12.0***	−22.0[che]
	Cole, Goldberg, and White (2004)	NSSBF 1993	585/s	Extension of credit by small banks	−0.0	−1.1	5.9**[che]
	Scott and Dunkelberg (2003)	CBSB 1995	520/s	Single credit search	21.5***	−25.7***	
Italy	Angelini, Di Salvo, and Ferri (1998)	Survey 1995	2,232/s	No rationing	7.0**	−6.4**	
	Cosci and Meliciani (2002)	1 bank 1997	393/s	1 – [Credit used/credit offered]		23.3**	
	Guiso (2003)	SMF 1997	3,236/s	No loan denial	0.8	0.0	−0.1
France	Dietsch (2003)	1993–2000	2,530,353	Loans/turnover	2.7**[a]	1.5**[a]	10.1**

Continued

TABLE 6 *Continued*

Panel C	Paper	Source Year	Observations/ firm size	Availability of credit, in %	Duration $\Delta = 1$ year	Number $\Delta = 1$ bank	Scope $\Delta = 1$
Belgium	De Bodt, Lopez, and Statnik (2005)	Survey[f] 2001	296/s	No rationing	20.0**[a]	−22.0**	
Germany	Lehmann and Neuberger (2001)	Survey 1997	318/sm	Credit approval	0.1***[a]		0.9***
Japan	Shikimi (2005)	JADA 00–02	78,695	Debt/assets		18***	
	Kano et al. (2006)	SFE 2002	1,960	No loan denial	0.0		0.0/++**[s]
Thailand	Menkhoff and Suwanaporn (2003)	9 banks 92–96	416/1	Ratio L/C/(liabilities + L/C)	0.3	0.0	9.6***
Argentina	Streb et al. (2002)	CDSF 1999	8,548	Unused credit line ratio		−2.7***	21.4
	Bebczuk (2004)	UIA 1999	139	Probability of obtaining credit	no		
Chile	Repetto, Rodriguez, and Valdes (2002)	SBIF 1990–98	20,000	Debt/capital	1.7**	11.9**	−45.4**

The table reports the coefficients from studies on the impact of the duration, scope, and number of bank relationships on the cost of credit.
The first column lists the *country* affiliation of the related firms.
The second column provides the *paper* citation.
The third column reports the data *source* and *year(s)*.
The fourth column lists the number of *observations* and an indication *firm size* (small, medium, and/or large).
The fifth column gives a precise definition of the *dependent variable*.
The next three columns indicate the impact on the dependent variable of an increase in *duration* (by one year), *number* (by one relationship), and *scope* (from 0 to 1) of bank relationships. Coefficients and significance levels are based on the reported base specification. All coefficients for logged duration or number measures are averaged over the [1, 4] interval.
[a]Authors' calculations.
[a1]for a doubling from 10 to 20 bank services taken.
CBSB: credit, banks and small business survey collected by the National Federation of Independent Business. ccb: credit granted by chartered community banks to CCB members. CCR: Central Credit Register. CDSF: Center of Debtors of the Financial System at the Central Bank of Argentina. CFIB: Canadian Federation of Independent Business.
[che]Checking account at the bank.
[cl]based on contract length.
[dv] based on a dummy.
[f] French-speaking part.
JADE: Japanese accounts and data on enterprises. JDB: Japan Development Bank. l: large. L/C: line of credit. LPC: Loan pricing Corporation Dealscan database.
[lf]number of lenders in facility.
m: medium. NSSBF: National Survey of Small Business Finances. ne: Northeast. nw: Northwest. oth: all other credit. RHS: right-hand side. s: small. so: South. SBIC: small business investment companies. SBIF: Chilean Supervisory Agency of Banks and Financial Institutions. SFE: Survey of the Financial Environment. SMF: Survey of Manufacturing Firms.
[s]Result only for small banks/firms without audits and low banking market competition.
*** Significant at 1%, ** at 5%, * at 10%.

relationships decreases that probability (Table 6, Panel B). Not surprisingly, increasing the scope of the relationship increases collateral pledging, presumably to cover the increase in products and bank exposure. Similarly most studies find that relationship borrowers (longer duration, fewer banks) have better access to credit (Table 6, Panel C).

A recent paper by Brick and Palia (2006) revisits the U.S. NSSBF data but relaxes the independence assumption and examines the joint impact of duration and number of relationships on loan rate, fees, and collateral (again Panel A). They find that endogenizing collateral and fees does not necessarily weaken any significant negative impact of duration on loan rate though the effect does not survive in any of their robustness exercises (an earlier version of the paper that included the 1998 SSBF in the sample showed that the effect of duration on loan rates was actually eliminated because of joint estimation) and introduces a negative (though not always statistically significant) impact of the number of banks on the rate. Hence, joint estimation makes the U.S. results somewhat more comparable to the European findings estimated under the independence assumption. However, not only fees but also collateral may play a smaller role in a few European samples, making the modeling of fee and collateral decisions potentially less influential. For example, in Degryse and Van Cayseele (2000) only 26 percent of loans are collateralized, while in Berger and Udell (1995) 53 percent is.

However, the point raised by Brick and Palia (2006) is more general, we think, once the cross-selling of loans and other commercial bank products are also considered (see also Jiangli, Unal, and Yom 2004). Indeed, a number of recent papers find evidence of relationship tie-in pricing between investment and commercial bank services (Drucker and Puri 2005, Bharath et al. 2006) and document the importance of cross-selling efforts toward larger firms at the level of the relationship manager (Liberti 2004).

To conclude, estimating the impact of relationship characteristics on the loan rate fielding a single equation could be problematic, in particular when loan fees, collateral requirements, and cross-selling opportunities are important.

4.3. Market Structure and Market Presence: Bank Orientation and Specialization

4.3.1. Local Markets: Indirect and Direct Evidence

Switching costs may play a further key role in how market structure determines bank strategy and market presence. Theory offers conflicting views on the relation between interbank competition and bank orientation (relationship versus transactional banking) and specialization (see also Degryse and Ongena 2006). A first set of theories argues that competition and relationships are incompatible. Mayer (1988) and Petersen and Rajan (1995) hypothesize that long-term relationships, allowing firms to share risks with their banks intertemporally, only arise if banks enjoy the possibility of extracting profits later on in the relationship, that is, when the flexibility of the borrowing firms to switch banks is limited.

On the other hand, Boot and Thakor (2000) argue that more interbank competition leads to more relationship lending. A bank offering a relationship loan augments a borrower's success probability in their model. Relationship lending then allows extracting higher rents from the borrower. Fiercer interbank competition pushes banks into offering more relationship lending, because this activity permits banks to shield their rents better.[17]

Most empirical work so far has investigated the effects of interbank competition on indirect measures of bank orientation. Figure 3 summarizes the main empirical findings. In their seminal paper, Petersen and Rajan (1995) find that young firms in more concentrated banking markets (HHI > 0.18) obtain lower loan rates and take more early (trade credit) payment discounts (i.e., have easier access to bank credit) than firms in more competitive banking markets. Banks seemingly smooth loan rates in concentrated markets and as a result provide more financing, in line with the predictions of their theoretical model.[18]

Black and Strahan (2002) revisit the local competition–bank orientation issue, exploring an alternative measure of local credit availability. In particular, they investigate the rate of new business incorporations across United States. They find that deregulation of bank branching restrictions positively affects new incorporations and, more importantly, that, in contrast to Petersen and Rajan (1995), deregulation reduces the *negative* effect of banking market concentration on new incorporations. They also find that the widespread presence of small banks decreases business formation.[19]

Recent papers by Fischer (2000) and Elsas (2005) investigate the local competition–bank orientation correspondence using German data. Fischer (2000) focuses on the transfer of information and the availability of credit and finds that both are higher in more concentrated markets. Elsas (2005) studies the determinants of relationship lending as measured by the Hausbank status. He finds that the incidence of Hausbank status is actually lowest for an intermediate range of market concentration with an HHI of around 0.2, though he notes that most observations of the HHI are also in that low range. Nevertheless his findings broadly suggest the presence of more relationship banking in more competitive markets.

[17] See also Freixas (2005) and Gehrig (1998). Further, relationship lending is nonmonotonically related to the degree of concentration in banking markets in Dinç (2000) and Yafeh and Yosha (2001).

[18] Recent work by Zarutskie (2006), Bergstresser (2001a, 2001b), and Scott and Dunkelberg (2001) analyzing other U.S. datasets broadly confirm these findings. Closest in spirit to Petersen and Rajan's study is the paper by Zarutskie (2005). She employs a dataset containing almost 200,000 small firm-year observations. She finds that the probability of small firms utilizing bank debt increases when the concentration (in local deposit markets) is high, though the effects seem economically small. Similarly, Bergstresser (2001a) finds that in more concentrated markets there are fewer constrained consumer-borrowers, while Bergstresser (2001b) documents that in more concentrated markets banks raise the average share of assets lent. Scott and Dunkelberg (2001) find that more competition not only increases the availability of credit but also decreases the loan rate and improves service performance (including knowledge of business, industry, provision of advice, etc.) by banks.

[19] Cetorelli (2001, 2003a, 2003b) and Cetorelli and Strahan (2005) also find that banking market power may represent a financial barrier to entry in product markets. However, Bonaccorsi di Patti and Dell'Ariccia (2004) find opposite results for Italy, while Ergungor (2005) finds no evidence that market concentration has any impact on the value of small business loans in the United States.

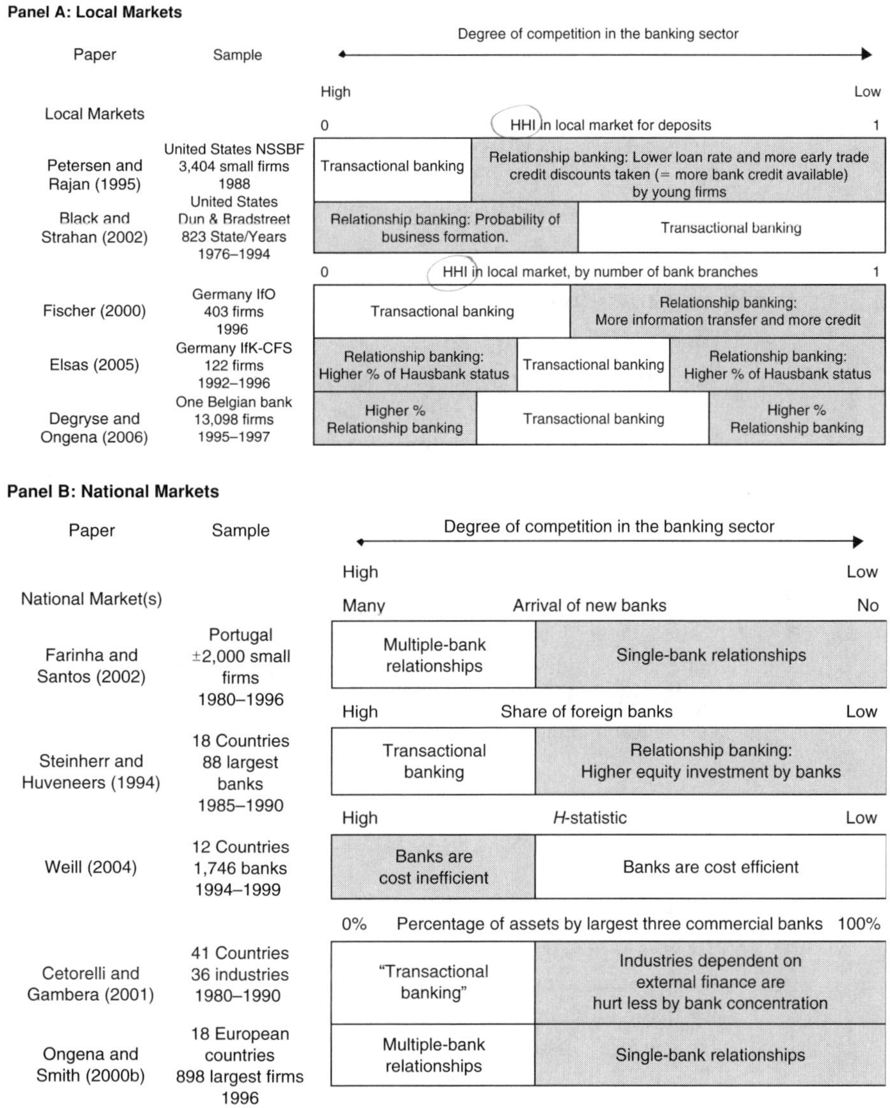

FIGURE 3 Empirical findings on competition and bank orientation.

The figure displays the empirical results of research on the impact of competition on direct and indirect measures of bank orientation. It lists the paper and the sample being used and graphically represents the findings of each paper. Panel A reports findings for local markets, Panel B for national markets.

Source: Degryse and Ongena (2006).

In Degryse and Ongena (2006) we employ detailed information on bank–firm relationships and industry classification of more than 13,000 Belgian firms to study the effect of market structure on bank orientation and specialization. We find that bank branches facing stiff local competition engage considerably more in relationship-based lending (the effect is convex in HHI but decreases for most observed values of HHI) and specialize somewhat less in a particular industry. Our results may illustrate that competition and relationships are not necessarily inimical.

4.3.2. National and Cross-Border Studies

Other papers study the effect of *nationwide* competition on commitment and relationship banking. Farinha and Santos (2002), for example, study the switching from single- to multiple-bank relationships by new Portuguese firms. They find that the arrival of new banks, potentially leading to less concentrated and more competitive banking markets, increases switching rates. There are also *cross-border* studies. Steinherr and Huveneers (1994), for example, document a negative correspondence between the share of foreign banks and equity investment by banks in 18 countries, Cetorelli and Gambera (2001) find that industries that rely heavily on external finance grow faster in countries with more concentrated banking systems (than those in countries with competitive systems), while Ongena and Smith (2000b) highlight the positive effect of concentration of the national banking markets on the incidence of single-bank relationships. The latter two studies measure concentration by calculating the percentage assets of the largest three commercial banks.

5. LOCATION

5.1. Distance Versus Borders

To structure our discussion, we distinguish between distance and borders (see also Degryse and Ongena 2004). We think of *distance* as pertaining to physical proximity that can be bridged by traditional modes of transportation, say, car or train travel. By spending distance-related costs, banks or their clients can communicate across the distance and engage in transactions with one another. For given locations of banks and borrowers, distance per se is exogenous and bridging it (i.e., the lender visiting the borrower and/or the borrower visiting the lender) may be adequate to reduce informational problems for the lender concerning its decision about granting and pricing the loan. Competing banks, therefore, play no (or a rather mechanical) role in theoretical competition models featuring only distance.

Borders, on the other hand, are not merely bridgable by car or train travel or even more modern technological ways of interacting. Borders introduce a “discontinuity”: They endogenously arise through the actions of the competing lenders or result as an artifact of differences in legal practice and exogenous regulation (Buch 2002). In this section we discuss only the effects of informational borders that arise because of adverse selection, relationship formation, or (lack of) information sharing between banks. The next section, on "Regulation," deals with the *exogenous* borders, which can consist of differences in legal, supervisory, and corporate governance practices and political, language, or cultural barriers but can also be "regulatory borders" that may simply prohibit "foreign" banks from engaging borrowers, setting up branches, and/or acquiring local banks.

5.2. Distance and Conditions: Spatial Pricing

Recent theory highlights the importance of distance for the pricing and the availability of bank loans. Lending conditions may depend on both the distance between the borrower and the lender and the distance between the borrower and the closest competing bank. We discuss *spatial pricing* in this section and return to *spatial rationing* in Section 5.3.

Distance may determine the pricing of loans because either the *transportation costs* incurred by the borrower (Lederer and Hurter 1986, Thisse and Vives 1988), the *monitoring costs* incurred by the lender (Sussman and Zeira 1995), or the *quality of information* obtained by the lender (Hauswald and Marquez 2006) are *distance related* (see also Degryse and Ongena 2005). Most theories featuring distance-related costs or informational quality generate spatial pricing: Loan rates decrease in the distance between the borrower and the lender but increase in the distance between the borrower and the closest competing bank (these loan rate schedules hold for a given number of banks). The availability of information to the borrowers, experience, and other product characteristics may abate the strength of this distance–loan rate correspondence.

Petersen and Rajan (2002) are among the first to provide evidence of spatial loan pricing. They find, for example, that a small business located one mile from the lending bank ceteris paribus pays on average 38*** basis points less than a borrower located around the corner from the lending bank. In Degryse and Ongena (2005) we also include the distance to the closest competitors. We find a somewhat smaller impact of physical distance on the loan rates than Petersen and Rajan (2002), but the impact we measure is still highly statistically significant and economically relevant. The impact on the loan rate of both distance to the lender and distance to the closest competitor is actually similar in absolute magnitude, but of an appropriate opposite sign, which in itself is also evidence suggestive of spatial price discrimination. For small loans, for example, loan rates decrease 7*** basis points per mile to the lender and similarly increase 7*** basis points per mile to the closest (quartile) competitor. We further deduce that, given current transportation costs and opportunity costs of travel, the average first-time borrower in our sample needs to visit the lender between two and three times to obtain a bank loan.

Spatial price discrimination caused by either (borrower) transportation costs, (lender) monitoring costs, or asymmetric information may explain the results in both Petersen and Rajan (2002) and Degryse and Ongena (2005). Transportation cost may provide the most consistent and comprehensive interpretation of all the results documented in Degryse and Ongena (2005). Inferred changes in lending technology may make an interpretation of the results in Petersen and Rajan (2002) more difficult.

In Degryse and Ongena (2005) we also run through a number of straightforward exercises but cannot find any trace of adverse selection's increasing in the (admittedly short) distances to the uninformed lenders. In either case, our results suggest that the distance to the closest competitors is important for competitive conditions and that the actual location of the bank branches may be relevant when assessing the intensity of competition. Our estimates also indicate that spatial price discrimination targeting borrowers located near the lending bank branch yields average bank rents of around 4 percent (with a maximum of 9 percent) of the bank's marginal cost of funding. Taken at face value, our findings substantiate an important additional source of rents accruing to financial intermediaries, based on location.

5.3. Distance and Conditions: Availability

Distance also affects the availability of credit. Stein (2002), for example, models the organizational impact of the ease and speed at which different types of information can "travel" within an organization. "Hard" information (for example, accounting numbers, financial ratios) can be passed on easily within the organization, while "soft" information (for example, a character assessment, the degree of trust) is much harder to relay. Hence, if the organization employs mostly soft information, a simple and flat structure and local decision making may be optimal. Recent empirical evidence by Liberti (2004) indeed confirms that bank centralization and the intensity of usage of hard information go hand in hand.

The type of information, hard or soft, that is needed and available to arrive at optimal lending decisions also translates into a correspondence between distance and credit rationing. For example, lines embedded in credit cards are extended solely on the basis of a quantitative analysis of hard and easily verifiable information (for example, age, profession, and address of the applicant). As a result, credit cards are offered by mail and across large distances in the United States (Ausubel 1991).

A lot of small business lending, on the other hand, is still "character" lending. To screen successfully, loan officers need to interact with the borrower, establish trust, and be present in the local community. This "soft" information is difficult to convey to others within the organization.[20] As a result, small (opaque) firms borrow from close, small banks (Petersen and Rajan 2002, Saunders and Allen 2002), while large banks lend mainly to distant, large firms, employing predominantly hard information in the loan decision (Berger et al. 2005, Cole, Goldberg, and White 2004, Uchida, Udell, and Watanabe 2006; see also Chapter 4 in this volume, by Strahan. Small firms, then, may be subject to credit rationing when seeking financing across larger distances.

However, from an empirical point of view, the severity of credit rationing's affect on small firms is not entirely clear. For example, the results in Petersen and Rajan (2002) indicate that the effect may be economically rather small in the United States, while findings by Carling and Lundberg (2005) and Uchida, Udell, and Watanabe (2006)

[20] Although Uchida, Udell, and Yamori (2006) fail to find evidence on this account using recent Japanese surveydata.

seemingly indicate the absence of distance-related credit rationing in the Swedish and Japanese banking sectors. Alternatively, results in Degryse and Ongena (2005) suggest that transportation costs that are fixed per loan (i.e., do not vary by loan size) may explain why larger loans are obtained across larger distances (mainly by larger firms).

5.4. Distance and Strategy: Branching

Only a very few papers study the importance of distance in determining the strategy of banks, that is, in determining their market presence via branching or servicing within certain areas (the cell "Location/Strategy" in Figure 2). A recent paper by De Juan (2003) is an exception. She studies how distance between banks' own branches influences bank branching decisions in Spain. She finds that the number of a bank's own branches in a particular (sub)market has a positive (but small) effect on the further entry decision of the bank in that market. Hence, her results suggest that branch expansion is partly affected by the proximity of other branches of the same bank (see also Felici and Pagnini 2005, Cerasi, Chizzolini, and Ivaldi 2002).

Results by Berger and DeYoung (2001) may provide a partial explanation for these findings. Berger and DeYoung document how the efficiency of bank branches slips somewhat as the distance between branch and headquarters of the bank increases (see also Bos and Kolari 2006). Hence, in order to guarantee consistency in servicing across bank branches, banks may decide to branch out methodically across certain areas rather than to build isolated outposts.

5.5. Borders and Conduct: Segmentation

Next we turn to the impact of borders on conduct and strategy. Recent literature investigates how different types of borders shape lending conditions and result in segmentation of credit markets. National borders, which often coincide with many of the exogenous economic borders discussed earlier, continue to play an important role across the world. Buch, Driscoll, and Ostergaard (2003), for example, suggest that national borders in Europe still hold back cross-border bank investments. As a result, European banks "over" invest domestically, and it is in particular country-specific credit risk that does not seem fully reflected in the interbank rates.

But other types of borders also result in segmented credit markets. Empirical evidence suggests that "outside" lenders often face difficulties (or hesitate) in extending credit to mainly small local firms (Shaffer 1998, Berger, Klapper, and Udell 2001, Harm 2001, Guiso, Sapienza, and Zingales 2004). This happens in particular when existing relationships between incumbent banks and borrowers are strong (Bergström, Engwall, and Wallerstedt 1994) or when the local judicial enforcement of creditor rights is poor (Fabbri and Padula 2004, Bianco, Jappelli, and Pagano 2005). In all these cases borders will lead to market segmentation and difficulties for cross-border outside banks to engage any local borrowers. In effect this market segmentation highlights the importance for the outside banks to strive to build an actual physical presence in the targeted market.

5.6. Borders and Strategy: Entry and M&As

5.6.1. Entry

Indeed, academics and bankers alike have long recognized borders as important factors in impelling bank entry and cross-border bank mergers and acquisitions. A literature going back to Goldberg and Saunders (1981) and Kindleberger (1983) asserts that banks often pursue a "follow-the-customer" strategy when deciding on cross-border market entry (see also Grosse and Goldberg 1991, Ter Wengel 1995, Brealey and Kaplanis 1996, Buch 2000, Buch and Golder 2002, Boldt-Christmas, Jacobsen, and Tschoegl 2001). Recent evidence, however, casts some doubt on the "follow-the-customer" strategy as the only game in town (Pozzolo and Focarelli 2006). In particular, banks entering the U.S. market do not have primarily a follow-the-home-country-customer motive but apparently engage many local borrowers (Seth, Nolle, and Mohanty 1998, Stanley, Roger, and McManis 1993, Buch and Golder 2001).

However, banks encounter many difficulties (in other countries than the United States) in successfully pursuing a strategy of engaging local firms by cross-border entry through local branches. DeYoung and Nolle (1996) and Berger et al. (2000), for example, document how most foreign bank affiliates are less efficient than domestic banks, the exceptions being the foreign affiliates of U.S. banks in other countries and most foreign bank affiliates in, for example, Eastern Europe and South America. The latter affiliates are often financially sounder than the domestic banks (Crystal, Dages, and Goldberg 2002). Why are most foreign bank affiliates less efficient than the local crowd? A paper by Buch (2003a) documents that the inefficiencies by foreign bank affiliates are due mostly to the presence of economic borders (language, culture, etc.) and do not seem driven by physical distance.[21] Similarly, Gobbi and Lotti (2004) find that outside banks enter new markets only when the provision of financial services that do not require the intensive use of proprietary information seems profitable in these markets.

But there may be a second reason why banks shy away from following the customer, apart from the fear of getting stuck with inefficient branch outposts. Findings by Berger et al. (2003) suggest customers are not that interested in being followed![22] Indeed, they find that foreign affiliates of multinational companies choose host nation banks for cash management services more often than home-nation or third-nation banks. This result is consistent with so-called "concierge" benefits dominating "home cookin" benefits. This is a surprising finding given that these large multinationals might be expected to be prime targets for preferential treatment by their home nation banks. On the other hand, the opening of a foreign affiliate may be a good occasion for a firm to escape a

[21] Magri, Mori, and Rossi (2005) find that physical distance negatively affected foreign bank entry in Italy during the period 1983–1998. However, they interpret distance as proxy for geographical and cultural *differences* between countries and in addition find that risk differentials between countries positively affected entry.

[22] In addition, large banks in particular may face competition for their customers from other large home-nation banks (Buch and Lipponer 2005), in which case banks may not enter to avoid one another (for example, Merrett and Tschoegl 2004).

holdup problem at "home." In this way, the establishment of new plants or subsidiaries in foreign countries is an opportunity to add a new (foreign) bank relationship.

Berger et al. (2003) also find that bank reach (global versus local) is strongly associated with bank nationality. For example, if a host-nation bank is the choice of nationality, then the firm is much less likely to choose a global bank. Finally, they also find that bank nationality and bank reach both vary significantly with the legal and financial development of the host nation. For example, firms appear to be much less likely to choose a host-nation bank and more likely to choose a global bank when operating in the former socialist nations of Eastern Europe.

Berger et al. (2003) conclude on the basis of this evidence that the extent of future bank globalization may be significantly limited because many corporations continue to prefer local or regional banks for at least some of their services (see also Berger and Smith 2003). Of course this conclusion is reached within a particular financial architecture and hence is predicated on the continuing (and endogenous) absence of foreign direct investment and possibly more importantly cross-border mergers taking place (Dermine 2003). The point being that if more foreign direct investment (FDI) and mergers in particular take place, firm preferences may change.

5.6.2. M&As

Cross-border bank mergers and acquisitions (M&As) are still a rare species in many parts of the world. Focarelli and Pozzolo (2001), for example, demonstrate that cross-border bank M&As occur relative to within-border M&As less frequently than cross-border M&As in other industries, ceteris paribus, while Berger, Demsetz, and Strahan (1999) show that cross-border bank M&As occur less frequently than domestic bank M&As (see also Danthine et al. 1999). And it is again economic borders,[23] not distance, that make cross-border bank M&As less likely (Buch and DeLong 2004).

Hence, taken together, these studies suggest that not only exogenous economic borders (which also affect other industries) but also endogenous economic borders specific to the banking industry (information asymmetries in assessing target-bank portfolios) may make it hard to pull off a successful cross-border bank M&A.

Bank managers are apparently aware of the difficulties awaiting them when engaging in a cross-border M&A and seem to refrain from undertaking many. But investors also recognize the dangers. A recent study by Beitel, Schiereck, and Wahrenburg (2004), for example, documents that the combined cumulative abnormal returns for stocks of bidder- and target-bank in cross-border bank M&As in Europe over the last few decades is actually zero or negative! This finding stands in stark contrast with other industries, where the combined CARs of cross-border M&As are typically found to be

[23]Regulatory restrictions explicitly prohibiting bank M&As have been removed in Europe. However, national and political interests frequently result in the mobilization of the national antitrust or banking-safety apparatus to block cross-border bank M&As. We acknowledge these actions resort somewhere in the gray area between explicit prohibition of cross-border bank M&As (regulatory restrictions) and inherent political and cultural differences creating difficulties in making a cross-border bank M&A possible and successful (economic borders).

positive. Hence investors seemingly evaluate cross-border bank M&As as destroying value. Beitel, Schiereck, and Wahrenburg's (2004) results are quite similar to findings in DeLong (2001). She reports that in the United States only the combined CARs of geographically focused bank M&As are positive, although it is not entirely clear what factors are driving this empirical finding.

The evidence presented so far does not make clear whether it is exogenous or endogenous (informational) economic borders that create most problems in making a cross-border bank M&A possible and successful. A recent paper by Campa and Hernando (2004) suggests exogenous borders may play a role. Their study shows that the combined CARs of M&As are typically lower in industries, such as banking, that until recently were under government control or are still (or were) most heavily regulated. CARs of cross-border M&As in these industries are actually negative, evidence in line with Beitel, Schiereck, and Wahrenburg (2004). One possible interpretation is that the (lingering) effects of regulation make for harder economic borders.

Bank industry observers sometimes note, for example, that bank organization and corporate governance may be an area shaped in ways that may hinder merger activity. The mutual structure of dominant banks in France and Germany in particular (for example, Credit Agricole, Landesbanken) is often passed off as a major hurdle for these banks to initiate and pursue a successful M&A (Wrighton 2003). But exogenous economic borders may also make cross-border bank M&As result in complex holding structures (Dermine 2003), possibly further complicating future M&A activity (see also Barros et al. 2005).

The impact of endogenous (informational) economic borders on cross-border bank M&A activity is less researched. It is possible that the domestic merger activity we have observed until now in Europe, creating so-called "national champions," is partly made possible by the existence of informational borders. Outside banks seeking to acquire a local bank find it more difficult than incumbent banks to assess the value of the loan portfolio of the possible target banks. As a result outside banks refrain from stepping in, and most M&A activity, driven, for example, by (revenue and cost) scale and scope considerations, occurs between domestic banks. However, as the domestic banks increase in size and possibly partly refocus their lending toward larger firms, they become easier-to-value targets. Moreover, concerns about national competition policy may hinder further domestic consolidation. Hence one could argue that informational borders may have a tendency partly and endogenously to self-destruct and that "national champions" will almost inevitably metamorphose into "European champions." Consequently, national-competition authorities may have a key role to play in preventing further domestic consolidation (see Vives 2005) and also enhancing the transparency of the process of decision making on bank M&As (recent work by Carletti, Hartmann, and Ongena 2006, for example).

A natural question, then, is how borrowers will be affected by cross-border bank M&As. It is possible that "in the first round," small local firms serviced by domestic target banks suffer somewhat, as with domestic mergers (Sapienza 2002, Bonaccorsi Di Patti and Gobbi 2007, Karceski, Ongena, and Smith 2005). Eventually niche banks may arise that take over part of the lending activities ceased by the merged bank (Berger et al. 1998).

6. REGULATION

6.1. Regulation and Market Structure

Banking is an industry that in most countries is subject to a tight set of regulations (Vives 1991 and Fischer and Pfeil 2004 provide reviews). Some of the regulations tend to *soften competition*. Examples include restrictions on the entry of new banks or limitations on the free deployment of competitive tools by banks. Other regulations *restrict banking activities* in space and scope, putting limitations on the bank's potential to diversify and exploit scale/scope economies. Finally there is *prudential* regulation that alters the competitive position of banks vis-à-vis other nonbank institutions (see, for example, Dewatripont and Tirole 1994). In the last two decades, several countries, including the European Union countries and the United States, have implemented a series of deregulatory changes, with the objective of stimulating competition and enhancing financial integration.

A number of papers investigate whether specific deregulatory initiatives have changed competition. Angelini and Cetorelli (2003), for example, consider the impact of the Second European Banking Directive on competition within the Italian banking industry, by analyzing data over the period 1983–1997. Using a conjectural-variations model they compute a Lerner index L for bank i:

$$L \equiv \frac{p_i - MC_i}{p_i} = \frac{-\frac{\theta_i}{\tilde{\varepsilon}}}{p_i},$$

with θ_i being the conjectural elasticity of total industry output with respect to the output of bank i and $\tilde{\varepsilon} = \frac{\partial Q/\partial p}{Q}$ being the market demand semielasticity to the price. The computed Lerner index remained constant during the 1983–1992 period but steadily decreased thereafter, suggesting a substantial increase in the degree of competition after 1993.

Angelini and Cetorelli (2003) further explore whether the changes in the Lerner index after 1993 can be attributed to the Second Banking Directive. After controlling for changes in market structure (HHI, number of banks operating in each regional market, number of branches per capita) and some other exogenous variables, they find that a dummy variable equal to 1 for years in the period 1993–1997 explains a considerable fraction of the drop in the Lerner index. The Lerner index drops from about 14 percent before 1992 to about 6 percent after 1992. The deregulation dummy can explain about 5 percentage points of this drop.

Gual (1999) studies the impact of European banking deregulation over the period 1981–1995 on the European banking market structure. He computes the elasticity of concentration to competition (which is measured directly by deregulation): Evaluated at the sample means, an increase in deregulation of 10 percent leads to an increase in the CR5 ratio of 0.86 percent.

Finally, in a widely cited study, Spiller and Favaro (1984) look at the effects of entry regulation on oligopolistic interaction in the Uruguayan banking sector. Before June 1978 entry was totally barred. They find, unexpectedly, that following the relaxation of the legal entry barriers, the degree of oligopolistic interaction among the leading banks actually reduced, pointing to less competition.

6.2. Regulation and Conduct

How does banking regulation contribute to bank interest margins? Jayaratne and Strahan (1998) find that permitting statewide branching and interstate banking in the United States decreased operating costs and loan losses, reductions that were ultimately passed on to borrowers in lower loan rates. And using data from banks covering 72 countries, a recent paper by Demirguc-Kunt, Laeven, and Levine (2004) examines the impact of banking regulation on bank net interest margins. The information on commercial banking regulation is taken from Barth, Caprio, and Levine (2001). Regulatory variables include the fraction of entry that is denied, a proxy for the degree to which banks face regulatory restrictions on their activities in, for example, securities markets and investment banking, and a measure of reserve requirements. They also employ an indicator of "banking freedom," taken from the Heritage Foundation, which provides an overall index of the openness of the banking industry and the extent to which banks are free to operate their business. The different regulatory variables are entered one at a time in a regression that also features bank-specific and macroeconomic controls.

The results in Demirguc-Kunt, Laeven, and Levine (2004) indicate that restrictive banking regulation substantially hikes net interest margins. For example, an increase of one standard deviation in entry or activity restrictions, reserve requirements, or banking freedom results, respectively, in 50***, 100***, 51*, and 70*** basis points extra for the incumbent banks. However, when including, in addition to the bank-specific and macroeconomic controls, an index of property rights, the regulatory restrictions turn insignificant and do not provide any additional explanatory power. Demirguc-Kunt, Laeven, and Levine interpret this result as indicating that banking regulation reflects something broader about the competitive environment. Their interpretation fits with findings in Kroszner and Strahan (1999) and, more recently, Garrett, Wagner, and Wheelock (2004), who investigate the political and economic drivers of bank branching deregulation across U.S. states, and with results in Jayaratne and Strahan (1996) showing that loan rates decrease by 30** bp on average following deregulation.

6.3. Regulation and Strategy

How does the presence of foreign banks influence competition? Foreign-owned banks not only may compete in different ways than domestically owned institutions, but could also be affected differently by domestic regulation. Levine (2003) distinguishes between entry restrictions for foreign versus domestic banks (he thus further refines the analysis by Demirguc-Kunt, Laeven, and Levine (2004). Levine substantiates that restrictions on foreign bank entry determine interest rate margins,[24] while restrictions on domestic bank entry do not. In contrast to the contribution of foreign ownership of domestic banks on banking efficiency in developing nations, the fraction of the domestic banking industry held by foreign banks does not determine bank interest margins.

State-owned banks may also compete in different ways than privately owned institutions. Government ownership of banks remains pervasive around the world, in particular in developing countries (La Porta, Lopez-de-Silanes, and Shleifer 2002). Cross-border exercises indicate that more state ownership of the banking sector leads to less competition (Barth, Caprio, and Levine 2004) and slower subsequent financial development (La Porta, Lopez-de-Silanes, and Shleifer 2002). However, firms that actually borrow from state-owned banks pay less than the firms that borrow from the privately owned banks (Sapienza 2004).

6.4. Regulation and Financial Stability and Development

Do regulatory restrictions offer benefits in other dimensions? Beck, Demirguc-Kunt, and Levine (2004) examine the link with financial stability. They study the impact of bank concentration, bank regulation, and national institutions fostering, for example, competition or property rights on the likelihood of experiencing a banking crisis. They find that fewer regulatory restrictions—lower barriers to bank entry and fewer restrictions on bank activities—lead to less banking fragility, suggesting that regulatory restrictions are not beneficial in the stability dimension. Black and Strahan (2002) find that the deregulation of restrictions on branching and interstate banking stimulated rates of incorporation in the United States, suggesting that access to finance increases following deregulation.

Deregulation also generates interesting dynamic effects. When deregulation induces a more competitive outcome, then we can expect that "good banks" should survive and grow faster whereas "weak banks" should shrink and eventually exit. Stiroh and Strahan (2003), for example, assess the competitive dynamics in terms of market share and industry exits after the deregulation in the U.S. banking industry. Banks that are performing well are more likely to gain market share after deregulation. Moreover they find an interesting heterogeneity in line with deregulatory forces: The strengthening in the performance-market share link is strongest in unit-banking states and in more concentrated markets. Branching deregulation had the largest impact for small banks, whereas interstate deregulation had its greatest impact for large banks. They also find that the poorest-performing banks were shrinking after deregulation, that the exit rate increased by 3.6 percent after a state removed its interstate banking restrictions, and that the relative profitability of banks exiting increased after deregulation. Finally, Buch (2003b) explores the impact of deregulation on gross financial assets of banks. She finds

[24]Magri, Mori, and Rossi (2005), for example, document that foreign banks successfully entered the Italian banking market following the lowering of the regulatory barriers under the Second Directive, enacted in 1992.

that the EU–single market program and the Basel Capital Accord have a positive impact on intra-EU asset holdings and lending to OECD countries, respectively.

7. CONCLUSION

Trying to summarize in a few paragraphs the many results this vast empirical literature on competition in banking has generated is reckless and bound to ignore the many subtleties involved. Figure 4 nevertheless aims to offer a very crude and simple meta-analysis of the many studies we canvassed, by providing averages of the spreads banks are estimated to collect. A few broad results seem to emerge.

1. Market definition is key, but studies continue to find that average market concentration, compared to a situation with a zero HHI, results in significant spreads in

Sources of Rents		Loan conditions *First row: spreads in basis points* *Second row: credit availability*	Loan market presence *First row: at the branch level* *Second row: at the bank level*
	HHI [0 to sample average]	**40***** → **−7**^{1} N/a	Loan loss avoidance Location, branching, type
	Duration [0 to sample average]	^{NO}**188**^{***2}, ^{EU}**34**^{3}, ^{US}**−23**^{***3} Less collateral and rationing	% Relationship banking: ^{BE}**−6%**, ^{DE}**−40%**^{8} No effect on specialization
	Distance [0 to sample median]	^{US}**126**^{***4}, ^{BE}**14**^{***5} Small to no effect	No effect on branch efficiency Cross-border entry/M&As difficult
	Regulation [After to before deregulation]	^{WO}**50 − 100**^{***6}, ^{US}**30**^{**7} N/a	Branching/entry now allowed M&As still often blocked in EU

FIGURE 4 Broad summary of documented bank behavior in loan markets.
The figure broadly summarizes representative findings on bank behavior in loan markets. For each source of rents, the figure reports the impact on loan conditions (spreads/credit availability) and the impact on loan market presence (branch/bank level). Numerical values are the averages of estimates from earlier tabulated papers for relevant proxies and ranges. For *market structure* we report the effects when increasing HHI from 0 to the sample average, for *switching costs* when increasing relationship duration from 0 to the sample average, for *location* when increasing distance from 0 to the sample median, and for *regulation* when going from after to before deregulation.
N/a: as far as we are aware no studies document results. ^{BE}: Belgium. ^{EU}: European Union countries. ^{NO}: Norway. ^{US}: United States.^{DE}: Germany. ^{WO}: World.
[1]For each study in Table 1 we set insignificant coefficients equal to zero and multiply the resulting minimum and maximum coefficients by the average HHI. We average and determine significance levels across all U.S. and west European data studies.
[2]We multiply the marginal value of lock-in (0.16) in Table 4 in Kim, Kliger, and Vale (2003) by an approximate mean loan rate (0.118).
[3]For each study in Table 6/Panel Awe set insignificant coefficients equal to zero, where applicable average, and multiply the resulting coefficients by the average duration in Table 4. We average and determine significance levels across studies.
[4]We multiply the coefficient on the predicted distance variable (0.546) in Table VIII Model I in Petersen and Rajan (2002) by the log of 1 plus the median actual distance (9 miles).
[5]We multiply the coefficient on the distance variables (8.3) in Table V/Model V in Degryse and Ongena (2005) by the log of 1 plus the median distance (6.9 minutes).
[6]The effect of a one standard deviation change in regulatory variables in Demirguc-Kunt, Laeven, and Levine (2004).
[7]The effect of state branching deregulation in Jayaratne and Strahan (1996).
[8]Approximate estimates of percentage relationship orientation from Degryse and Ongena (2007) and Elsas (2005), respectively.
***Significant at 1%, **at 5%, *at 10%.

both deposit and loan markets of up to 50 basis points. Decreases in bank market concentration could lower spreads. However, lower concentration may also lead to more bank efforts to shield rents by tying customers in purposely built relationships in which fees and cross-selling achieve renewed primacy. While theory has explored the conditions under which these relationships may arise and be sustainable, empirical work has only recently started to investigate the competition–bank orientation nexus.

2. Switching costs are an important source of bank rents, for depositors as well as borrowers. The few studies that try to gauge the importance of switching costs find magnitudes of 10–20% of the checking account deposit volume and roughly 4% of banks' marginal cost of lending. Future work, however, should further quantify the magnitude of switching costs and address the impact of electronic banking on entry barriers and switching costs (see Claessens, Glaessner, and Klingebiel 2002, for example). Bank–borrower relationships are important to overcome asymmetric-information problems but may also lead to informational-holdup problems. Current studies do not uniformly link relationship duration to positive spreads. Spreads at average duration range from almost +200 in Norway to –23 basis points in the United States. However, methodological issues have been raised recently that could explain or even overturn the negative-impact results. On the other hand, in the few studies addressing the issue mostly indirectly, relationship borrowers seem to enjoy lower collateral requirements and less credit rationing. Recent work has started to focus on the dynamic patterns in loan conditions during a relationship.
3. Few studies have looked at location as a source for bank rents. The few that have find that close borrowers pay a higher loan rate. Borrowers at an average distance seem to pay between 10 and 130 basis points more as a result. Effects of distance on credit availability, however, seem small. Though distance effects on branch efficiency seem minimal, to cross borders to enter or merge with another bank continues to be an adventurous endeavor.
4. Finally, regulation continues to be a fine source of rents for banks in many countries. Estimates range from 30 to 100 basis points on average. Though branching and entry is mostly permitted now on both sides of the Atlantic, M&As are still often blocked in Europe by regulators, under the pretext of the safe and sound management doctrine. Other agencies, such as competition authorities, may end up playing a key role in limiting this regulatory discretion.

To conclude, more empirical research estimating bank rents seems warranted. Setting out directions in this regard for future research often results in not much more than myopic and highly individual lists of current interests and never-finished projects, lists that are bound to be either ill-directed from the start or outdated the moment they are in print. Nevertheless, our "wish list" would definitely include the following issues:

- The development of loan conditions throughout the life cycle of the bank–firm relationship and the differences in these relationships across countries and time

- Bank organization and its impact on competition, in both deposit and loan markets, both domestically and internationally
- The geography of bank financing: "Is distance dead?" Or "Will it die another day?" (but hopefully not before we can analyze its effects)
- The impact of technology on bank organization (and incentives for loan officers, for example), banking geography, and banking activities, in particular the supply of relationship versus transactional banking products
- The role banks (may or may fail to) play in the development of emerging economies, such as China and India, and the provision of different financial solutions there
- The effects of monetary policy on bank behavior, risk taking, in particular (Rajan 2006)
- And finally, the impact of the development of the regulatory and wider institutional framework (such as competition policy) on competition and bank rents

Given the speed at which evidence in this area is currently being collected, we suspect that the authors of the next comparable review may face an even more insurmountable task than we already had. We wish them good luck.

References

Aintablian, S., and G. S. Roberts. 2000. A Note on Market Response to Corporate Loan Announcements in Canada. *Journal of Banking and Finance* 24, 381–393.

Alem, M. 2003. Insurance Motives in Lending Relationships: Evidence from Argentina. Mimeo, University of Chicago.

Allen, F., H. Gersbach, J. P. Krahnen, and A. M. Santomero. 2001. Competition Among Banks: Introduction and Conference Overview, *European Finance Review* 5, 1–11.

Allen, L., and A. Rai. 1996. Operational Efficiency in Banking: An International Comparison, *Journal of Banking and Finance* 20, 655–672.

Andre, P., R. Mathieu, and P. Zhang. 2001. A Note on: Capital Adequacy and the Information Content of Term Loans and Lines of Credit, *Journal of Banking and Finance* 25, 431–444.

Angelini, P., and N. Cetorelli. 2003. Bank Competition and Regulatory Reform: The Case of the Italian Banking Industry, *Journal of Money, Credit, and Banking* 35, 663–684.

Angelini, P., R. Di Salvo, and G. Ferri. 1998. Availability and Cost of Credit for Small Businesses: Customer Relationships and Credit Cooperatives, *Journal of Banking and Finance* 22, 925–954.

Ausubel, L. M. 1991. The Failure of Competition in the Credit Card Market, *American Economic Review* 81, 50–76.

Bae, K. H., J. K. Kang, and C. W. Lim. 2002. The Value of Durable Bank Relationships: Evidence from Korean Banking Shocks, *Journal of Financial Economics* 64, 181–214.

Bain, J. 1956. *Barriers to New Competition.* Harvard University Press, Cambridge, MA.

Barros, P. P. 1999. Multimarket Competition in Banking, with an Example from the Portuguese Market, *International Journal of Industrial Organization* 17, 335–352.

Barros, P. P., E. Berglof, P. Fulghieri, J. Gual, C. Mayer, and X. Vives. 2005. *Integration of European Banks: The Way Forward.* Centre for Economic Policy Research, London.

Barth, J. R., G. Caprio, and R. Levine. 2001. The Regulations and Supervision of Banks Around the World: A New Database, Mimeo, World Bank.

Barth, J. R., G. Caprio, and R. Levine. 2004. Bank Regulation and Supervision: What Works Best? *Journal of Financial Intermediation* 13, 205–248.

Bebczuk, R. N. 2004. What Determines the Access to Credit by SMEs in Argentina? Working paper, Universidad Nacional de la Plata.

Beck, T., A. Demirguc-Kunt, and R. Levine. 2004. Bank Concentration and Crises. Mimeo, World Bank.

Beitel, P., D. Schiereck, and M. Wahrenburg. 2004. Explaining M&A Success in European Banks, *European Financial Management* 10, 109–140.

Berg, S. A., and M. Kim. 1994. Oligopolistic Interdependence and the Structure of Production in Banking: An Empirical Evaluation, *Journal of Money, Credit, and Banking* 26, 309–322.

Berg, S. A., and M. Kim. 1998. Banks as Multioutput Oligopolies: An Empirical Evaluation of the Retail and Corporate Banking Markets. *Journal of Money, Credit, and Banking* 30, 135–153.

Berger, A. N. 1995. The Profit–Structure Relationship in Banking. Tests of Market-Power and Efficient-Structure Hypotheses, *Journal of Money, Credit, and Banking* 27, 404–431.

Berger, A. N. 2003. The Economic Effects of Technological Progress: Evidence from the Banking Industry, *Journal of Money, Credit, and Banking* 35, 141–176.

Berger, A. N., R. Demsetz, and P. Strahan. 1999. The Consolidation of the Financial Services Industry: Causes, Consequences, and Implications for the Future, *Journal of Banking and Finance* 23, 135–194.

Berger, A. N., and R. Deyoung. 2001. The Effects of Geographic Expansion on Bank Efficiency, *Journal of Financial Services Research* 19, 163–184.

Berger, A. N., and T. H. Hannan. 1989. The Price-Concentration Relationship in Banking, *Review of Economics and Statistics* 71, 291–299.

Berger, A. N., I. Hasan, and L. F. Klapper. 2004. Further Evidence on the Link Between Finance and Growth: An International Analysis of Community Banking and Economic Performance, *Journal of Financial Services Research* 25, 169–202.

Berger, A. N., and D. B. Humphrey. 1997. Efficiency of Financial Institutions: International Survey and Directions for Future Research, *European Journal of Operational Research* 98, 175–212.

Berger, A. N., L. F. Klapper, and G. F. Udell. 2001. The Ability of Banks to Lend to Informationally Opaque Small Businesses, *Journal of Banking and Finance* 25, 2127–2167.

Berger, A. N., R. J. Rosen, and G. F. Udell. 2002. Does Market Size Structure Affect Competition? The Case of Small Business Lending. Mimeo, Board of Governors of the Federal Reserve System.

Berger, A. N., and D. C. Smith. 2003. Global Integration in the Banking Industry, *Federal Reserve Bulletin* 90, 451–460.

Berger, A. N., and G. F. Udell. 1995. Relationship Lending and Lines of Credit in Small Firm Finance, *Journal of Business* 68, 351–381.

Berger, A. N., and G. F. Udell. 1998. The Economics of Small Business Finance: The Roles of Private Equity and Debt Markets in the Financial Growth Cycle, *Journal of Banking and Finance* 22, 613–673.

Berger, A. N., and G. F. Udell. 2002. Small Business Credit Availability and Relationship Lending: The Importance of Bank Organisational Structure, *Economic Journal* 112, 32–53.

Berger, A. N., A. Saunders, J. M. Scalise, and G. F. Udell. 1998. The Effects of Bank Mergers and Acquisitions on Small Business Lending, *Journal of Financial Economics* 50, 187–230.

Berger, A. N., R. Deyoung, H. Genay, and G. Udell. 2000. Globalization of Financial Institutions: Evidence from Cross-Border Banking Performance, *Brookings-Wharton Papers on Financial Services* 3, 23–120.

Berger, A. N., Q. Dai, S. Ongena, and D. C. Smith. 2003. To What Extent Will the Banking Industry be Globalized? A Study of Bank Nationality and Reach in 20 European Nations, *Journal of Banking and Finance* 27, 383–415.

Berger, A. N., A. Demirguc-Kunt, R. Levine, and J. G. Haubrich. 2004. Bank Concentration and Competition: An Evolution in the Making, *Journal of Money, Credit, and Banking* 36, 433–451.

Berger, A. N., N. M. Miller, M. A. Petersen, R. G. Rajan, and J. C. Stein. 2005. Does Function Follow Organizational Form? Evidence from the Lending Practices of Large and Small Banks, *Journal of Financial Economics* 76, 237–269.

Bergstresser, D. 2001a. Banking Market Concentration and Consumer Credit Constraints: Evidence from the Survey of Consumer Finances. Mimeo, MIT.

Bergstresser, D. 2001b. Market Concentration and Loan Portfolios in Commercial Banking. Mimeo, MIT.

Bergström, R., L. Engwall, and E. Wallerstedt. 1994. Organizational Foundations and Closures in a Regulated Environment: Swedish Commercial Banks 1831–1990, *Scandinavian Journal of Management* 10, 29–48.

Berlin, M. 1996. For Better and for Worse: Three Lending Relationships, *Federal Reserve Bank of Philadelphia Business Review* November, 3–12.

Berlin, M., and L. J. Mester. 1999. Deposits and Relationship Lending, *Review of Financial Studies* 12, 579–607.

Bernanke, B. S. 1993. Credit in the Macroeconomy, *Federal Reserve Bank of New York Quarterly Review* 18, 50–70.

Best, R., and H. Zhang. 1993. Alternative Information Sources and the Information Content of Bank Loans, *Journal of Finance* 48, 1507–1522.

Bharath, S., S. Dahiya, A. Saunders, and A. Srinivasan. 2006. So What Do I Get? The Bank's View of Lending Relationships, *Journal of Financial Economics*, Forthcoming.

Bhattacharya, S., and A. V. Thakor. 1993. Contemporary Banking Theory, *Journal of Financial Intermediation* 3, 2–50.

Bianco, M., T. Jappelli, and M. Pagano. 2005. Courts and Banks: Effects of Judicial Enforcement on Credit Markets, *Journal of Money, Credit, and Banking* 37, 223–244.

Biehl, A. R. 2002. The Extent of the Market for Retail Banking Deposits, *Antitrust Bulletin* 47, 91–106.

Bikker, J. A., and K. Haaf. 2002. Competition, Concentration and Their Relationship: An Empirical Analysis of the Banking Industry, *Journal of Banking and Finance* 26, 2191–2214.

Billett, M. T., M. J. Flannery, and J. A. Garfinkel. 1995. The Effect of Lender Identity on a Borrowing Firm's Equity Return, *Journal of Finance* 50, 699–718.

Black, S. E., and P. E. Strahan. 2002. Entrepreneurship and Bank Credit Availability, *Journal of Finance* 57, 2807–2834.

Blackwell, D. W., and D. B. Winters. 1997. Banking Relationships and the Effect of Monitoring on Loan Pricing, *Journal of Financial Research* 20, 275–289.

Bodenhorn, H. 2003. Short-Term Loans and Long-Term Relationships: Relationship Lending in Early America, *Journal of Money, Credit, and Banking* 35, 485–505.

Boldt-Christmas, M., F. S. Jacobsen, and A. E. Tschoegl. 2001. The International Expansion of the Norwegian Banks, *Business History* 43, 79–104.

Bonaccorsi Di Patti, E., and G. Dell'ariccia. 2004. Bank Competition and Firm Creation, *Journal of Money, Credit, and Banking* 36, 225–252.

Bonaccorsi Di Patti, E., and G. Gobbi. 2007. Winners or Losers? The Effects of Banking Consolidation on Corporate Borrowers, *Journal of Finance*, Forthcoming.

Boot, A. W. A. 2000. Relationship Banking: What Do We Know? *Journal of Financial Intermediation* 9, 3–25.

Boot, A. W. A., and A. V. Thakor. 2000. Can Relationship Banking Survive Competition? *Journal of Finance* 55, 679–713.

Bornheim, S. P., and T. H. Herbeck. 1998. A Research Note on the Theory of SME–Bank Relationships, *Small Business Economics* 10, 327–331.

Bos, J. W. B., and J. W. Kolari. 2006. Large Bank Efficiency in Europe and the United States: Are There Economic Motivations for Geographic Expansion in Financial Services? *Journal of Business*, Forthcoming.

Boscaljon, B., and C. C. Ho. 2005. Information Content of Bank Loan Announcements to Asian Corporations during Periods of Economic Uncertainty, *Journal of Banking and Finance* 29, 369–389.

Boyd, J. H., and G. De Nicolo. 2005. The Theory of Bank Risk Taking and Competition Revisited, *Journal of Finance* 60, 1329–1343.

Brealey, R. A., and E. C. Kaplanis. 1996. The Determination of Foreign Banking Location, *Journal of International Money and Finance* 15, 577–597.

Bresnahan, T. 1982. The Oligopoly Solution Is Identified, *Economics Letters* 10, 87–92.

Bresnahan, T. 1989. Empirical Studies of Industries with Market Power, in R. Schmalensee and R. D. Willig (eds.), *Handbook of Industrial Organization*. Elsevier Science, Amsterdam, pp. 1011–1057.

Bresnahan, T. F., and P. C. Reiss. 1991. Entry and Competition in Concentrated Markets, *Journal of Political Economy* 99, 977–1009.

Bresnahan, T., and P. Reiss. 1994. Measuring the Importance of Sunk Costs, *Annales d'Economie et de Statistique* 34, 181–217.

Brewer, E., H. Genay, W. C. Hunter, and G. G. Kaufman. 2003. The Value of Banking Relationships During a Financial Crisis: Evidence from Failures of Japanese Banks, *Journal of Japanese and International Economies* 17, 233–262.

Brick, I. E., and D. Palia. 2006. Evidence of Jointness in the Terms of Relationship Lending. Mimeo, Rutgers Business School.

Buch, C. M. 2000. Why Do Banks Go Abroad? Evidence from German Data. *Financial Markets, Institutions and Instruments* 9, 33–67.

Buch, C. M. 2002. Financial Market Integration in the U.S.: Lessons for Europe, *Comparative Economic Studies* 44, 46–71.

Buch, C. M. 2003a. Information or Regulation: What Is Driving the International Activities of Commercial Banks? *Journal of Money, Credit, and Banking* 35, 851–869.

Buch, C. M. 2003b. What Determines Maturity? An Analysis of German Commercial Banks' Foreign Assets, *Applied Financial Economics* 13, 337–351.

Buch, C. M., and G. L. Delong. 2004. Cross-Border Bank Mergers: What Lures the Rare Animal? *Journal of Banking and Finance* 28, 2077–2102.

Buch, C. M., J. C. Driscoll, and C. Ostergaard. 2003. International Diversification in Bank Asset Portfolios. Mimeo, Kiel Institute of World Economics.

Buch, C. M., and S. M. Golder. 2001. Foreign versus Domestic Banks in Germany and the U.S.: A Tale of Two Markets? *Journal of Multinational Financial Management* 11, 341–361.

Buch, C. M., and S. M. Golder. 2002. Domestic and Foreign Banks in Germany: Do They Differ? *Kredit und Kapital*, 19–53.

Buch, C. M., and A. Lipponer. 2005. Clustering or Competition? The Foreign Investment Behavior of German Banks. Mimeo, University of Tubingen.

Calem, P. S., and G. A. Carlino. 1991. The Concentration/Conduct Relationship in Bank Deposit Markets, *Review of Economics and Statistics* 73, 268–276.

Calem, P. S., and L. I. Nakamura. 1998. Branch Banking and the Geography of Bank Pricing, *Review of Economics and Statistics* 80, 600–610.

Campa, J. M., and I. Hernando. 2004. Shareholder Value Creation in European M&As, *European Financial Management* 10, 47–81.

Carletti, E. 2004. The Structure of Bank Relationships, Endogenous Monitoring, and Loan Rates, *Journal of Financial Intermediation* 13, 58–86.

Carletti, E. 2008. Competition and Regulation in Banking, in A. V. Thakor, and A. W. A. Boot (eds.), *Handbook of Financial Intermediation and Banking*. North-Holland, Amsterdam, This volume Chapter 14.

Carletti, E., V. Cerasi, and S. Daltung. 2004. Multiple-Bank Lending: Diversification and Free-Riding in Monitoring. Mimeo, Center for Financial Studies.

Carletti, E., and P. Hartmann. 2003. Competition and Stability: What's Special About Banking? in P. Mizen (ed.), *Monetary History, Exchange Rates and Financial Markets: Essays in Honour of Charles Goodhart*. Edward Elgar, Cheltenham, UK, pp. 202–229.

Carletti, E., P. Hartmann, and S. Ongena. 2006. The Economic Impact of Merger Control: What Is Special About Banking? Mimeo, Tilburg University.

Carling, K., and S. Lundberg. 2005. Asymmetric Information and Distance: An Empirical Assessment of Geographical Credit Rationing, *Journal of Economics and Business* 57, 39–59.

Castelli, A., G. P. Dwyer Jr., and I. Hasan. 2006. Bank Relationships and Small Firms, Financial Performance. Working paper, Federal Reserve Bank of Atlanta.

Cavallo, L., and S. Rossi. 2001. Scale and Scope Economies in the European banking systems, *Journal of Multinational Financial Management* 11, 515–531.

Cavalluzzo, K. S., L. C. Cavalluzzo, and J. D. Wolken. 2002. Competition, Small Business Financing, and Discrimination: Evidence from a New Survey, *Journal of Business* 75, 641–680.

Cerasi, V., B. Chizzolini, and M. Ivaldi. 2002. Branching and Competition in the European Banking Industry, *Applied Economics* 34, 2213–2225.

Cetorelli, N. 2001. Does Bank Concentration Lead to Concentration in Industrial Sectors? Working paper, Federal Reserve Bank of Chicago.

Cetorelli, N. 2003a. Bank Concentration and Competition in Europe. Mimeo, Federal Reserve Bank of Chicago.

Cetorelli, N. 2003b. Life-Cycle Dynamics in Industrial Sectors: The Role of Banking Market Structure, *Review of the Federal Reserve Bank of St. Louis* 85, 135–147.

Cetorelli, N., and M. Gambera. 2001. Banking Market Structure, Financial Dependence and Growth: International Evidence from Industry Data, *Journal of Finance* 56, 617–648.

Cetorelli, N., and P. Strahan. 2005. Finance as a Barrier to Entry: Bank Competition and Industry Structure in Local U.S. Markets, *Journal of Finance*, Forthcoming.

Chakraborty, A., and C. X. Hu. 2006. Lending Relationships in Line-of-Credit and Nonline-of-Credit Loans: Evidence from Collateral Use in Small Business, *Journal of Financial Intermediation* 15, 86–107.

Chiou, I. 1999. Daiwa Bank's Reputational Crisis: Valuation Effects on Bank–Firm Relationships. Mimeo, New York University Stern School of Business.

Claessens, S., T. Glaessner, and D. Klingebiel. 2002. Electronic Finance: Reshaping the Financial Landscape Around the World, *Journal of Financial Services Research* 22, 29–61.

Claessens, S., and L. Laeven. 2004. What Drives Bank Competition? Some International Evidence, *Journal of Money, Credit, and Banking* 36, 563–583.

Claeys, S., and R. Vander Vennet. 2005. Determinants of Bank Interest Margins in Central and Eastern Europe: A Comparison with the West. Mimeo, Ghent University.

Cocco, J. F., F. J. Gomes, and N. C. Martins. 2003. Lending Relationships in the Interbank Market. Mimeo, London Business School.

Cohen, A., and M. Mazzeo. 2003. Market Structure and Competition Among Retail Depository Institutions. Mimeo, Northwestern University.

Cohen, A., and M. Mazzeo. 2004. Competition, Product Differentiation and Quality Provision: An Empirical Equilibrium Analysis of Bank Branching Decisions. Mimeo, Northwestern University.

Cole, R. 1998. The Importance of Relationships to the Availability of Credit, *Journal of Banking and Finance* 22, 959–977.

Cole, R. A., L. G. Goldberg, and L. J. White. 2004. Cookie-Cutter versus Character: The Micro Structure of Small Business Lending by Large and Small Banks, *Journal of Financial and Quantitative Analysis* 39, 227–252.

Conigliani, C., G. Ferri, and A. Generale. 1997. The Impact of Bank–Firm Relations on the Propagation of Monetary Policy Squeezes: An Empirical Assessment for Italy, *Banca Nazionale del Lavoro* 202, 271–299.

Corts, K. S. 1999. Conduct Parameters and the Measurement of Market Power, *Journal of Econometrics* 88, 227–250.

Corvoisier, S., and R. Gropp. 2001. Contestability, Technology, and Banking. Mimeo, European Central Bank.

Corvoisier, S., and R. Gropp. 2002. Bank Concentration and Retail Interest Rates, *Journal of Banking and Finance* 26, 2155–2189.

Cosci, S., and V. Meliciani. 2002. Multiple Banking Relationships: Evidence from the Italian Experience, *Manchester School Supplement* 37–54.

Crystal, J. S., B. G. Dages, and L. S. Goldberg. 2002. Has Foreign Bank Entry Led to Sounder Banks in Latin America? *Current Issues in Economics and Finance* 8, 1–6.

Cyrnak, A. W., and T. H. Hannan. 1999. Is the Cluster Still Valid in Defining Banking Markets? Evidence from a New Data Source. *Antitrust Bulletin* 44, 313–331.

Danthine, J.-P. 2001. Banking: Is Bigger Really Better? in Z. Mikdashi (ed.), *Financial Intermediation in the 21st Century*. Palgrave, London.

Danthine, J.-P. F. Giavazzi, and E.-L. Von Thadden. 2001. European Financial Markets After EMU: A First Assessement, in C. Wyplosz (ed.), *EMU: Its Impact on Europe and the World*. Oxford University Press, Oxford, UK.

Danthine, J.-P., F. Giavazzi, X. Vives, and E.-L. Von Thadden. 1999. *The Future of European Banking*. Centre for Economic Policy Research, London.

D' Auria, C., A. Foglia, and P. M. Reedtz. 1999. Bank Interest Rates and Credit Relationships in Italy, *Journal of Banking and Finance* 23, 1067–1093.

Davis, E. P. 1996. Banking, Corporate Finance, and Monetary Policy: An Empirical Perspective, *Oxford Review of Economic Policy* 10, 49–67.

De Bodt, E., F. Lobez, and J. C. Statnik. 2005. Credit Rationing, Customer Relationship, and the Number of Banks: An Empirical Analysis, *European Financial Management* 11, 195–228.

Degryse, H., N. Masschelein, and J. Mitchell. 2006. SMEs and Bank Lending Relationships: The Impact of Mergers. Discussion paper, TILEC—Tilburg University.

Degryse, H., and S. Ongena. 2002. Bank Relationships and International Banking Markets, *International Journal of the Economics of Business* 9, 401–417.

Degryse, H., and S. Ongena. 2003. Distance, Lending Relationships, and Competition. Discussion paper, Center for Economic Studies—KU Leuven & CentER—Tilburg University.

Degryse, H., and S. Ongena. 2004. The Impact of Technology and Regulation on the Geographical Scope of Banking, *Oxford Review of Economic Policy* 20, 571–590.

Degryse, H., and S. Ongena. 2005. Distance, Lending Relationships, and Competition, *Journal of Finance* 60, 231–266.

Degryse, H., and S. Ongena. 2006. The Impact of Competition on Bank Orientation. Mimeo, Tilburg University.

Degryse, H., and P. Van Cayseele. 2000. Relationship Lending Within a Bank-Based System: Evidence from European Small Business Data, *Journal of Financial Intermediation* 9, 90–109.

De Juan, R. 2003. The Independent Submarkets Model: An Application to the Spanish Retail Banking Market, *International Journal of Industrial Organization* 21, 1461–1487.

Delong, G. L. 2001. Stockholder Gains from Focusing versus Diversifying Mergers, *Journal of Financial Economics* 59, 221–252.

Demirguc-Kunt, A., L. Laeven, and R. Levine. 2004. Regulations, Market Structure, Institutions, and the Cost of Financial Intermediation, *Journal of Money, Credit, and Banking* 36, 563–583.

Demsetz, H. 1973. Industry Structure, Market Rivalry, and Public Policy, *Journal of Law and Economics* 16, 1–9.

Dermine, J. 2003. European Banking: Past, Present, and Future, in V. Gaspar, P. Hartmann, and O. Sleijpen (eds.), *The Transformation of the European Financial System*. ECB, Frankfurt, pp. 31–95.

Detragiache, E., P. G. Garella, and L. Guiso. 2000. Multiple versus Single Banking Relationships: Theory and Evidence, *Journal of Finance* 55, 1133–1161.

Dewatripont, M., and J. Tirole. 1994. *The Prudential Regulation of Banks*. MIT Press, Cambridge, MA.

Deyoung, R., and D. E. Nolle. 1996. Foreign-Owned Banks in the United States: Earning Market Share or Buying It? *Journal of Money, Credit, and Banking* 28, 622–636.

Dick, A. 2002. Demand Estimation and Consumer Welfare in the Banking Industry. Discussion series paper, Board of Governors of the Federal Reserve System, Finance and Economics.

Dick, A. 2005. Market Size, Service Quality and Competition in Banking, *Journal of Money, Credit, and Banking*, Forthcoming.

Dick, A. 2006. Nationwide Branching and Its Impact on Market Structure, Quality and Bank Performance, *Journal of Business* 79, Forthcoming.

Dietsch, M. 2003. Financing Small Businesses in France, *European Investment Bank Papers* 8, 93–119.

Dinç, I. 2000. Bank Reputation, Bank Commitment, and the Effects of Competition in Credit Markets, *Review of Financial Studies* 13, 781–812.

Djankov, S. D., J. Jindra, and L. Klapper. 2005. Corporate Valuation and the Resolution of Bank Insolvency in East Asia, *Journal of Banking and Finance* 29, 2095–2118.

Drucker, S., and M. Puri. 2005. On the Benefits of Concurrent Lending and Underwriting, *Journal of Finance*, Forthcoming.

Eber, N. 1996. Relations de Credit de Long Terme et Structure des Marches Bancaires Locaux, *Revue Economique* 3, 755–764.

Elsas, R. 2005. Empirical Determinants of Relationship Lending, *Journal of Financial Intermediation* 14, 32–57.

Elsas, R., and J. P. Krahnen. 1998. Is Relationship Lending Special? Evidence from Credit-File Data in Germany, *Journal of Banking and Finance* 22, 1283–1316.

Elsas, R., and J. P. Krahnen. 2002. Collateral, Relationship Lending, and Financial Distress: An Empirical Study on Financial Contracting. Mimeo, Center for Financial Studies.

Elyasiani, E., and L. G. Goldberg. 2004. Relationship Lending: A Survey of the Literature, *Journal of Economics and Business* 56, 315–330.

Ergungor, O. E. 2005. The Profitability of Bank–Borrower Relationships, *Journal of Financial Intermediation* 14, 485–512.

Ewert, R., G. Schenk, and A. Szczesny. 2000. Determinants of Bank Lending Performance in Germany, *Schmalenbach Business Review* 52, 344–362.

Fabbri, D., and M. Padula. 2004. Does Poor Legal Enforcement Make Households Credit Constrained? *Journal of Banking and Finance* 28, 2369–2397.

Fama, E. F. 1985. What's Different about Banks? *Journal of Monetary Economics* 15, 5–29.

Farinha, L. A., and J. A. C. Santos. 2002. Switching from Single to Multiple Bank Lending Relationships: Determinants and Implications, *Journal of Financial Intermediation* 11, 124–151.

Felici, R., and M. Pagnini. 2005. Distance, Bank Heterogeneity, and Entry in Local Banking Markets. Working paper, Bank of Italy.

Ferri, G., and M. Messori. 2000. Bank–Firm Relationships and Allocative Efficiency in Northeastern and Central Italy and in the South, *Journal of Banking and Finance* 24, 1067–1095.

Fery, J., D. Gasborro, D. R. Woodliff, and J. K. Zumwalt. 2003. Market Reaction to Published and Non-published Corporate Loan Announcements, *Quarterly Review of Economics and Finance* 43, 1–10.

Fields, L. P., D. R. Fraser, T. L. Berry, and S. Byers. 2006. Do Bank Loan Relationships Still Matter? *Journal of Money, Credit, and Banking* 38, 1195–1209.

Fischer, K. H. 2000. Acquisition of Information in Loan Markets and Bank Market Power: An Empirical Investigation. Mimeo, Johann Wolfgang Goethe University, Frankfurt.

Fischer, K. H. 2001. Banken und unvollkommener Wettbewerb. Empirische Beitrage zu einer Industrieokonomik der Finanzmarkte. PhD dissertation, Goethe University, Frankfurt.

Fischer, K. H., and C. Pfeil. 2004. Regulation and Competition in German Banking, in J. P. Krahnen, and R. H. Schmidt (eds.), *The German Financial System*. Oxford University Press, Frankfurt, pp. 291–349.

Focarelli, D., and F. Panetta. 2003. Are Mergers Beneficial to Consumers? Evidence from the Market for Bank Deposits, *American Economic Review* 93, 1152–1171.

Focarelli, D., and A. F. Pozzolo. 2001. The Patterns of Cross-Border Bank Mergers and Shareholdings in OECD Countries, *Journal of Banking and Finance* 25, 2305–2337.

Freixas, X. 2005. Deconstructing Relationship Banking, *Investigaciones Economicas* 29, 3–31.

Freixas, X. and J. C. Rochet. 1997. *Microeconomics of Banking*. MIT Press, Cambridge, MA.

Gan, J. 2003. How Does a Shock to Bank Health Unrelated to Firm Performance Affect Firm Performance? Mimeo, HKUST.

Garrett, T. A., G. A. Wagner, and D. C. Wheelock. 2004. A Spatial Analysis of State Banking Regulation. Working paper, Federal Reserve Bank of St. Louis.

Gehrig, T. 1998. Screening, Cross-Border Banking, and the Allocation of Credit, *Research in Economics* 52, 387–407.

Gertler, M. 1988. Financial Structure and Aggregate Economic Activity, *Journal of Money, Credit and Banking* 20, 559–588.

Giannetti, M., L. Guiso, T. Jappelli, M. Padula, and M. Pagano. 2002. Financial Market Integration, Corporate Financing, and Economic Growth. Economic paper, European Commission.

Gilbert, R. 1984. Bank Market Structure and Competition: A Survey, *Journal of Money, Credit, and Banking* 16, 617–644.

Gilbert, R. A., and A. M. Zaretsky. 2003. Banking Antitrust: Are the Assumptions Still Valid? *Review of the Federal Reserve Bank of St. Louis*, 29–52.

Gobbi, G., and F. Lotti. 2004. Entry Decisions and Adverse Selection: An Empirical Analysis of Local Credit Markets. Mimeo, Bank of Italy.

Goldberg, L. G., and A. Saunders. 1981. The Determinants of Foreign Banking Activity in the United States, *Journal of Banking and Finance* 5, 17–32.

Gorton, G., and A. Winton. 2003. Financial Intermediation, in G. Constantinides, M. Harris, and R. Stulz (eds.), *Handbook of the Economics of Finance*. North Holland, Amsterdam.

Greenbaum, S. I. 1996. Twenty-Five Years of Banking Research, *Financial Management* 25, 86–92.

Grosse, R., and L. G. Goldberg. 1991. Foreign Bank Activity in the United States: An Analysis by Country of Origin, *Journal of Banking and Finance* 15, 1093–1112.

Gual, J. 1999. Deregulation, Integration and Market Structure in European Banking, *Journal of Japanese and International Economies* 12, 372–396.

Guiso, L. 2003. Small Business Finance in Italy, *European Investment Bank Papers* 8, 121–147.

Guiso, L., P. Sapienza, and L. Zingales. 2004. Does Local Financial Development Matter? *Quarterly Journal of Economics* 119, 929–970.

Hannan, T. H. 1991. Bank Commercial Loan Markets and the Role of Market Structure: Evidence from Surveys of Commercial Lending, *Journal of Banking and Finance* 15, 133–149.

Hannan, T. 1997. Market Share Inequality, the Number of Competitors, and the HHI: An Examination of Bank Pricing, *Review of Industrial Organization* 12, 23–35.

Hannan, T. H., and R. A. Prager. 2004. The Competitive Implications of Multimarket Bank Branching, *Journal of Banking and Finance* 28, 1889–1914.

Hao, L. 2003. Bank Effects and the Determinants of Loan Yield Spreads. Mimeo, York University.

Harhoff, D., and T. Körting. 1998. Lending Relationships in Germany—Empirical Evidence from Survey Data, *Journal of Banking and Finance* 22, 1317–1353.

Harm, C. 2001. European Financial Market Integration: The Case of Private Sector Bonds and Syndicate Loans, *Journal of International Financial Markets, Institutions, and Money* 11, 245–263.

Hauswald, R., and R. Marquez. 2006. Competition and Strategic Information Acquisition in Credit Markets, *Review of Financial Studies* 19, 967–1000.

Heitfield, E. A. 1999. What Do Interest Rate Data Say About the Geography of Retail Banking Markets? *Antitrust Bulletin* 44, 333–347.

Heitfield, E. A., and R. A. Prager. 2004. The Geographic Scope of Retail Deposit Markets, *Journal of Financial Services Research* 25, 37–55.

Hellmann, T., K. Murdock, and J. E. Stiglitz. 2000. Liberalization, Moral Hazard in Banking and Prudential Regulation: Are Capital Controls Enough? *American Economic Review* 90(1), 147–165.

Hellwig, M. 1991. Banking, Financial Intermediation and Corporate Finance, in A. Giovannini and C. P. Mayer (eds.), *European Financial Integration*. Cambridge University Press, Cambridge MA, pp. 35–63.

Hernandez-Canovas, G., and P. Martinez-Solano. 2006. Banking Relationships: Effects on the Debt Terms of the Small Spanish Firms, *Journal of Small Business Management* 44, 315–333.

Herrera, A. M., and R. Minetti. 2007. Informed Finance and Technological Change: Evidence from Credit Relationships, *Journal of Financial Economics* 83, 223–269.

Holland, J. 1994. Bank Lending Relationships and the Complex Nature of Bank–Corporate Relations, *Journal of Business Finance and Accounting* 21, 367–391.

Horiuchi, T., F. Packer, and S. Fukuda. 1988. What Role Has the "Main Bank" Played in Japan? *Journal of Japanese and International Economies* 2, 159–180.

Howorth, C., M. J. Peel, and N. Wilson. 2003. An Examination of the Factors Associated with Bank Switching in the UK Small-Firm Sector, *Small Business Economics* 20, 305–317.

Hwan Shin, G., D. R. Fraser, and J. W. Kolari. 2003. How Does Banking Industry Consolidation Affect Bank-Firm Relationships? Evidence from a Large Japanese Bank Merger, *Pacific-Basin Finance Journal* 11, 285–304.

Iwata, G. 1974. Measurement of Conjectural Variations in Oligopoly, *Econometrica* 42, 947–966.

James, C. 1987. Some Evidence on the Uniqueness of Bank Loans, *Journal of Financial Economics* 19, 217–235.

James, C., and D. C. Smith. 2000. Are Banks Still Special? New Evidence on Their Role in the Corporate Capital-Raising Process, *Bank of America—Journal of Applied Corporate Finance* 13, 52–63.

Jaumandreu, J., and J. Lorences. 2002. Modelling Price Competition Across Many Markets: An Application to the Spanish Loans Market, *European Economic Review* 46, 93–115.

Jayaratne, J., and P. E. Strahan. 1996. The Finance-Growth Nexus: Evidence from Bank Branch Deregulation, *Quarterly Journal of Economics* 111, 639–670.

Jayaratne, J., and P. E. Strahan. 1998. Entry Restrictions, Industry Evolution, and Dynamic Efficiency: Evidence from Commercial Banking, *Journal of Law and Economics* 41, 239–274.

Jiangli, W., H. Unal, and C. Yom. 2004. Relationship Lending, Accounting Disclosure, and Credit Availability during Crisis. Mimeo, Federal Deposit Insurance Corporation.

Kano, M., H. Uchida, G. F. Udell, and W. Watanabe. 2006. Information Verifiability, Bank Organization, Bank Competition and Bank-Borrower Relationships. Mimeo, Wakayama University.

Karceski, J., S. Ongena, and D. C. Smith. 2005. The Impact of Bank Consolidation on Commercial Borrower Welfare, *Journal of Finance* 60, 2043–2082.

Kashyap, A., R. Rajan, and J. C. Stein. 2002. Banks as Liquidity Providers: An Explanation for the Co-Existence of Lending and Deposit-Taking, *Journal of Finance* 57, 33–73.

Kim, M., D. Kliger, and B. Vale. 2003. Estimating Switching Costs: The Case of Banking, *Journal of Financial Intermediation* 12, 25–56.

Kim, M., E. G. Kristiansen, and B. Vale. 2005. Endogenous Product Differentiation in Credit Markets: What Do Borrowers Pay For? *Journal of Banking and Finance* 29, 681–699.

Kim, M., and B. Vale. 2001. Non-Price Strategic Behavior: The Case of Bank Branches, *International Journal of Industrial Organization* 19, 1583–1602.

Kindleberger, C. P. 1983. International Banks as Leaders or Followers of International Business, *Journal of Banking and Finance* 7, 583–595.

Kiser, E. K. 2002. Predicting Household Switching Behavior and Switching Costs at Depository Institutions, *Review of Industrial Organization* 20, 349–365.

Klemperer, P. 1995. Competition When Consumers Have Switching Costs: An Overview with Applications to Industrial Organization, Macroeconomics, and International Trade, *Review of Economic Studies* 62, 515–539.

Knittel, C., and V. Stango. 2004. Compatibility and Pricing with Indirect Network Effects: Evidence from ATMs. Discussion paper, National Bureau for Economic Research.

Kroszner, R. S., and P. E. Strahan. 1999. What Drives Deregulation? Economics and Politics of the Relaxation of Bank Branching Restrictions, *Quarterly Journal of Economics* 124, 1437–1467.

La Porta, R., F. Lopez-de-Silanes, and A. Shleifer. 2002. Government Ownership of Banks, *Journal of Finance* 57, 265–301.

Lau, L. J. 1982. On Identifying the Degree of Competitiveness from Industry Price and Output Data, *Economic Letters* 10, 93–99.

Lederer, P., and A. P. Hurter. 1986. Competition of Firms: Discriminatory Pricing and Location, *Econometrica* 54, 623–640.

Lehmann, E., and D. Neuberger. 2001. Do Lending Relationships Matter? Evidence from Bank Survey Data in Germany, *Journal of Economic Behavior and Organization* 45, 339–359.

Lehmann, E., D. Neuberger, and S. Rathke. 2004. Lending to Small and Medium-Sized Firms: Is There An East–West Gap in Germany? *Small Business Economics* 23, 23–39.

Levine, R. 2003. Denying Foreign Bank Entry: Implications for Bank Interest Margins. Mimeo, University of Minnesota.

Liberti, J. M. 2004. Initiative, Incentives and Soft Information: How Does Delegation Impact the Role of Bank Relationship Managers? Mimeo, Kellogg School of Management, Northwestern University.

Lummer, S. L., and J. J. McConnell. 1989. Further Evidence on the Bank Lending Process and the Capital Market Response to Bank Loan Agreements, *Journal of Financial Economics* 25, 99–122.

Machauer, A., and M. Weber. 1998. Bank Behavior Based on Internal Credit Ratings of Borrowers, *Journal of Banking and Finance* 22, 1355–1383.

Magri, S., A. Mori, and P. Rossi. 2005. The Entry and the Activity Level of Foreign Banks in Italy: An Analysis of the Determinants, *Journal of Banking and Finance* 29, 1295–1310.

Mallett, T., and A. Sen. 2001. Does Local Competition Impact Interest Rates Charged on Small Business Loans? Empirical Evidence from Canada, *Review of Industrial Organization* 19, 437–452.

Mayer, C. 1988. New Issues in Corporate Finance, *European Economic Review* 32, 1167–1189.

Mayer, C. 1996. The Assessment: Money and Banking, Theory and Evidence, *Oxford Review of Economic Policy* 10, 1–13.

Menkhoff, L., D. Neuberger, and C. Suwanaporn. 2006. Collateral-Based Lending in Emerging Markets: Evidence from Thailand, *Journal of Banking and Finance* 30, 1–21.

Menkhoff, L., and C. Suwanaporn. 2003. The Rationale of Bank Lending in Pre-Crisis Thailand. Discussion paper on development policy, Center for Development Research ZEF.

Merrett, D. T., and A. E. Tschoegl. 2004. The Geography of Australian Banking 1942. Mimeo, University of Melbourne.

Mester, L. J. 1993. Efficiency in the Savings and Loan Industry, *Journal of Banking and Finance* 17, 267–286.

Miarka, T. 1999. The Recent Economic Role of Bank-Firm Relationships in Japan. Discussion paper, WZB.

Mikkelson, W. H., and M. M. Partch. 1986. Valuation Effects of Security Offerings and the Issuance Process, *Journal of Financial Economics* 15, 31–60.

Miyajima, H., and Y. Yafeh. 2003. Japan's Banking Crisis: Who Has the Most to Lose? Working paper, Center for Economic Institution.

Molyneux, P. Y., Y. Altunbas, and E. P. M. Gardener. 1996. *Efficiency in European Banking*. John Wiley & Sons, London.

Morgan, D. 2002. How Big Are Bank Markets? Evidence Using Branch Sale Premia. Mimeo, Federal Reserve Bank of New York.

Nakamura, L. I. 1993. Commercial Bank Information: Implications for the Structure of Banking, in M. Klausner and L. J. White (eds.), *Structural Change in Banking*. New York University Salomon Center, New York, pp. 131–160.

Nathan, A., and H. Neave. 1989. Competition and Contestability in Canada's Financial System: Empirical Results, *Canadian Journal of Economis* 22, 567–594.

Neuberger, D. 1998. Industrial Organization of Banking: A Review, *International Journal of the Economics of Business* 5, 97–118.

Neuberger, J. A., and G. C. Zimmerman. 1990. Bank Pricing of Retail Deposit Accounts and The California Rate Mystery, *Economic Review Federal Reserve Bank of San Francisco*, 3–16.

Neumark, D., and S. A. Sharpe. 1992. Market Structure and the Nature of Price Rigidity: Evidence from the Market for Consumer Deposits, *Quarterly Journal of Economics* 107, 657–680.

Ongena, S. 1999. Lending Relationships, Bank Default, and Economic Activity, *International Journal of the Economics of Business* 6, 257–280.

Ongena, S., and D. C. Smith. 2000a. Bank Relationships: A Survey, in P. Harker and S. A. Zenios (eds.), *The Performance of Financial Institutions*. Cambridge University Press, London, pp. 221–258.

Ongena, S., and D. C. Smith. 2000b. What Determines the Number of Bank Relationships? Cross-Country Evidence, *Journal of Financial Intermediation* 9, 26–56.

Ongena, S., and D. C. Smith. 2001. The Duration of Bank Relationships, *Journal of Financial Economics* 61, 449–475.

Ongena, S., D. C. Smith, and D. Michalsen. 2003. Firms and Their Distressed Banks: Lessons from the Norwegian Banking Crisis (1988–1991), *Journal of Financial Economics* 67, 81–112.

Pagano, M. 2002. Measuring Financial Integration. Speech, ECB-CFS Research Network.

Panetta, F., F. Schivardi, and M. Shum. 2004. Do Mergers Improve Information? Evidence from the Loan Market. Mimeo, Bank of Italy.

Panzar, J. C., and J. N. Rosse. 1987. Testing for Monopoly Equilibrium, *Journal of Industrial Economics* 35, 443–456.

Park, K., and G. Pennacchi. 2003. Why Does Institution Size Matter for Banking Market Competition? Mimeo, University of Illinois.

Peltoniemi, J. 2004. The Value of Relationship Banking: Empirical Evidence on Small Business Financing in Finnish Credit Markets. Academic dissertation, University of Oulu.

Peltzmann, S. 1977. The Gains and Losses from Industrial Concentration, *Journal of Law and Economics* 20, 229–263.

Petersen, M. A., and R. G. Rajan. 1994. The Benefits of Lending Relationships: Evidence from Small Business Data, *Journal of Finance* 49, 3–37.

Petersen, M. A., and R. G. Rajan. 1995. The Effect of Credit Market Competition on Lending Relationships, *Quarterly Journal of Economics* 110, 406–443.

Petersen, M. A., and R. G. Rajan. 2002. Does Distance Still Matter? The Information Revolution in Small Business Lending, *Journal of Finance* 57, 2533–2570.

Pozzolo, A. F. 2004. The Role of Guarantees in Bank Lending. Mimeo, Ente Luigi Einaudi.

Pozzolo, A. F., and D. Focarelli. 2006. Where Do Banks Expand Abroad? An Empirical Analysis, *Journal of Business* 79, Forthcoming.

Qian, J. 2005. How Law and Institutions Shape Financial Contracts: The Case of Bank Loans. Mimeo, Boston College.

Radecki, L. J. 1998. The Expanding Geographic Reach of Retail Banking Markets, *FRBNY Economic Policy Review* 15–34.

Rajan, G. R. 2006. Has Finance Made the World Riskier? *European Financial Management* 12, 499–533.

Repetto, A., S. Rodriguez, and R. O. Valdes. 2002. Bank Lending and Relationship Banking: Evidence from Chilean Firms. Mimeo, Universidad de Chile.

Rivaud-Danset, D. 1996. Les Contrats de Credit dans une Relation de Long Terme: de la Main Invisible a la Poignee de Main, *Revue Economique* 4, 937–962.

Roberts, G. S., and N. A. Siddiqi. 2004. Collaterilization and the Number of Lenders in Private Debt Contracts: An Empirical Analysis, *Research in Finance* 21, 229–252.

Rosen, R. J. 2003. Banking Market Conditions and Deposit Interest Rates. Working paper, Federal Reserve Bank of Chicago.

Samolyk, K. 1997. Small Business Credit Markets: Why Do We Know So Little About Them? *FDIC Banking Review* 10, 14–32.

Saparito, P. A., C. C. Chen, and H. J. Sapienza. 2004. The Role of Relational Trust in Bank–Small Firm Relationships, *Academy of Management Journal* 47, 400–410.

Sapienza, P. 2002. The Effects of Banking Mergers on Loan Contracts, *Journal of Finance* 329–368.

Sapienza, P. 2004. The Effects of Government Ownership on Bank Lending, *Journal of Financial Economics* 72, 357–384.

Saunders, A., and L. Allen. 2002. *Credit Risk Measurement*. Wiley, New York.

Scholtens, L. J. R. 1993. On the Foundations of Financial Intermediation: A Review of the Literature, *Kredit und Kapital* 26, 112–141.

Scott, J. A. 2003. Soft Information, Loan Officers, and Small Firm Credit Availability. Mimeo, Temple University.

Scott, J. A. 2004. Small Business and the Value of Community Financial Institutions, *Journal of Financial Services Research* 25, 207–230.

Scott, J. A., and W. C. Dunkelberg. 2001. Competition and Credit Market Outcomes: A Small Firm Perspective. Mimeo, Temple University.

Scott, J. A., and W. C. Dunkelberg. 2003. A Note on Loan Search and Banking Relationships. Mimeo, Temple University.

Seth, R., D. E. Nolle, and S. K. Mohanty. 1998. Do Banks Follow Their Customers Abroad? *Financial Markets, Institutions, and Instruments* 7, 1–25.

Shaffer, S. 1989. Competition in the U.S. Banking Industry, *Economics Letters* 29, 321–323.

Shaffer, S. 1993. A Test of Competition in Canadian Banking, *Journal of Money, Credit, and Banking* 25, 49–61.

Shaffer, S. 1998. The Winner's Curse in Banking, *Journal of Financial Intermediation* 7, 359–392.

Shaffer, S. 2004. Patterns of Competition in Banking, *Journal of Economics and Business* 56, 287–313.

Sharpe, S. A. 1990. Asymmetric Information, Bank Lending and Implicit Contracts: A Stylized Model of Customer Relationships, *Journal of Finance* 45, 1069–1087.

Sharpe, S. A. 1997. The Effect of Consumer Switching Costs on Prices: A Theory and Its Applications to the Bank Deposit Market, *Review of Industrial Organization* 12, 79–94.

Shepherd, W. 1982. Causes of Increased Competition in the U.S. Economy 1939–1980, *Review of Economics and Statistics* 64, 613–626.

Shikimi, M. 2005. Do Firms Benefit from Multiple Banking Relationships? Evidence from Small and Medium-Sized Firms in Japan. Discussion paper, Hitotsubashi University.

Shy, O. 2002. A Quick-and-Easy Method for Estimating Switching Costs, *International Journal of Industrial Organization* 20, 71–87.

Sjögren, H. 1994. Long-Term Financial Contracts in the Bank-Orientated Financial System, *Scandinavian Journal of Management* 10, 315–330.

Slovin, M. B., S. A. Johnson, and J. L. Glascock. 1992. Firm Size and the Information Content of Bank Loan Announcements, *Journal of Banking and Finance* 16, 35–49.

Slovin, M. B., M. E. Sushka, and J. A. Polonchek. 1993. The Value of Bank Durability: Borrowers as Bank Stakeholders, *Journal of Finance* 48, 289–302.

Sohn, W. 2002. Banking Relationships and Conflicts of Interest: Market Reactions to Lending Decisions by Korean Banks. Mimeo, Columbia University.

Spiller, P. T., and E. Favaro. 1984. The Effects of Entry Regulation on Oligopolistic Interaction: The Uruguayan Banking Sector, *RAND Journal of Economics* 15, 244–254.

Stanley, T. O., C. Roger, and B. McManis. 1993. The Effects of Foreign Ownership of U.S. Banks on the Availability of Loanable Funds to Small Businesses, *Journal of Small Business Management* 31, 51–66.

Stein, J. 2002. Information Production and Capital Allocation: Decentralized versus Hierarchical Firms, *Journal of Finance* 57, 1891–1922.

Steinherr, A., and C. Huveneers. 1994. On the Performance of Differently Regulated Financial Institutions: Some Empirical Evidence, *Journal of Banking and Finance* 18, 271–306.

Stiroh, K., and P. Strahan. 2003. Competitive Dynamics of Deregulation: Evidence from U.S. Banking, *Journal of Money, Credit, and Banking* 35, 801–828.

Streb, J. M., J. Bolzico, P. Druck, A. Henke, J. Rutman, and W. S. Escudero. 2002. Bank Relationships: Effect on the Availability and Marginal Cost of Credit for Firms in Argentina. Working paper, UCEMA.

Sussman, O., and J. Zeira. 1995. Banking and Development. Discussion paper, CEPR.

Sutton, J. 1991. *Sunk Cost and Market Structure: Price Competition, Advertising, and the Evolution of Concentration*. MIT Press, Cambridge, MA.

Swank, J. 1996. Theories of the Banking Firm: A Review of the Literature, *Bulletin of Economic Research* 48, 173–207.

Ter Wengel, J. 1995. International Trade in Banking Services, *Journal of International Money and Finance* 14, 47–64.

Thakor, A. V. 1995. Financial Intermediation and the Market for Credit, in R. Jarrow (ed.), *Handbooks in OR and MS*. North Holland, Amsterdam, pp. 1069–1087.

Thakor, A. V. 1996. The Design of Financial Systems: An Overview, *Journal of Banking and Finance* 20, 917–948.

Thisse, J. F., and X. Vives. 1988. On the Strategic Choice of Spatial Price Policy, *American Economic Review* 78, 122–137.

Thomsen, S. 1999. The Duration of Business Relationships: Banking Relationships of Danish Manufacturers 1900–1995. Mimeo, Copenhagen Business School.

Turati, G. 2001. Cost Efficiency and Profitability in European Commercial Banking. Mimeo, U.C. del S. Cuore.

Uchida, H., G. F. Udell, and W. Watanabe. 2006. Bank Size and Lending Relationships in Japan. Mimeo, Wakayama University.

Uchida, H., G. F. Udell, and N. Yamori, 2006. Loan Officers and Relationship Lending. Mimeo, Wakayama University.

Uzzi, B. 1999. Embeddedness in the Making of Financial Capital: How Social Relations and Networks Benefit Firms Seeking Financing, *American Sociological Review* 64, 481–505.

Van Damme, E. 1994. Banking: A Survey of Recent Microeconomic Theory, *Oxford Review of Economic Policy* 10, 14–33.

Vander Vennet, R. 2002. Cost and Profit Efficiency of Financial Conglomerates and Universal Banks in Europe, *Journal of Money, Credit, and Banking* 34, 254–282.

Vives, X. 1991. Regulatory Reform in Europe, *European Economic Review* 35, 505–515.

Vives, X. 1999. *Oligopoly Pricing: Old Ideas and New Tools*. MIT Press, Cambridge, MA.

Vives, X. 2000. Lessons from European Banking Liberalization and Integration, in S. Claessens and M. Jansen (eds.), *The Internationalization of Financial Services*. Kluwer Law International, London, pp. 177–198.

Vives, X. 2001a. Competition in the Changing World of Banking, *Oxford Review of Economic Policy* 17, 535–547.

Vives, X. 2001b. Restructuring Financial Regulation in the European Monetary Union, *Journal of Financial Services Research* 19, 57–82.

Vives, X. 2002. Industrial Organization of Banking, Bank Competition and Bank Market Integration, Speech, ECB-CFS Research Network.

Vives, X. 2005. Europe Banks Future on the Urge to Merge, *Wall Street Journal Europe* May 13, A6.

Volpin, P. F. 2001. Ownership Structure, Banks, and Private Benefits of Control. Mimeo, London Business School.

Von Rheinbaben, J., and M. Ruckes. 2004. The Number and the Closeness of Bank Relationships, *Journal of Banking and Finance* 28, 1597–1615.

Weill, L. 2004. On the Relationship Between Competition and Efficiency in the EU Banking Sectors, *Kredit und Kapital* 37, 329–352.

Weinstein, D. E., and Y. Yafeh. 1998. On the Costs of a Bank-Centered Financial System: Evidence from the Changing Main Bank Relations in Japan, *Journal of Finance* 53, 635–672.

Wrighton, J. 2003. Why Unity in Europe Hasn't Yet Extended to the Banking System, *Wall Street Journal Europe* (Paris).

Yafeh, Y., and O. Yosha. 2001. Industrial Organization of Financial Systems and Strategic Use of Relationship Banking, *European Finance Review* 5, 63–78.

Yasuda, A. 2005. Do Bank Relationships Affect the Firm's Underwriter Choice in the Corporate-Bond Underwriting Market? *Journal of Finance* 60, 1259–1292.

Zarutskie, R. 2004. New Evidence on Bank Competition, Firm Borrowing and Firm Performance. Mimeo, Duke University.

Zarutskie, R. 2005. Evidence on the Effects of Bank Competition on Firm Borrowing and Investment, *Journal of Financial Economics*, Forthcoming.

Ziane, Y. 2003. Number of Banks and Credit Relationships: Empirical Results from French Small Business Data, *European Review of Economics and Finance*, 2, 32–48.

Zineldin, M. 1995. Bank–Company Interactions and Relationships: Some Empirical Evidence, *International Journal of Bank Marketing* 13, 30–40.

Index

E

M

Q